eb Warrior Guide to

eb Programming

Xue Bai
Michael Ekedahl
Joyce Farrell
Don Gosselin
Diane Zak
Shashi Kaparthi
Peter MacIntyre
Bill Morrissey

THOMSON
COURSE TECHNOLOGY

Australia • Canada • Mexico • Singapore • Spain • United Kingdom • United States

The Web Warrior Guide to Web Programming

by Xue Bai, Michael Ekedahl, Joyce Farrell, Don Gosseli
Shashi Kaparthi, Peter MacIntyre, and Bill Morrissey

Executive Editor:
Jennifer Locke

Acquisitions Editor:
Bill Larkin

Developmental Editor:
Lisa Ruffolo

Editorial Assistant:
Christy Urban

Associate Product Manager:
Janet Aras

Production Editor:
Kristen Guevara

Cover Designer:
Joseph Lee, Black Fish Design

Composi
Gex Pub

Manufac
Denise Po

Marketing
Angie Laug

Printed in Canada

1 2 3 4 5 6 7 8 9 WC 07 06 05 04 03

For more information, contact Course Technology, 25 Thomson Place, Boston, Massachusetts, 02210.

Or find us on the World Wide Web at:
www.course.com

ISBN 0-619-06458-

BRIEF

Contents

TABLE OF

Contents

CHAPTER FOUR
XML: Part II 4-1

CHAPTER FIVE
Visual Basic .NET: Part I 5-1

Preface

The Web Warrior Guide to Web Programming provides a survey of the programming languages and tools used to develop Web-based applications. If you are a new or beginning programmer, this book introduces you to the basics of programming logic and object-oriented programming, and then explores how to create Web applications using a variety of programming tools, including Extensible Markup Language (XML), Visual Basic .NET, C#, Active Server Pages.NET, CGI/Perl, Java, JavaServer Pages (JSP) technology, Personal Home Page (PHP), and Macromedia ColdFusion. You also examine Structured Query Language (SQL) statements that you can use to manipulate data in a database, such as one created in Microsoft Access.

This book assumes that you are familiar with HTML, though you might have little or no programming experience. Each chapter provides clear, non-technical explanations of the important concepts and techniques of a particular programming language or technology. The focus, however, is on learning by doing as you complete typical Web programming tasks, such as developing dynamic Web pages, which are interactive Web pages that can accept and retrieve information for users. In the tasks, Hands-on Exercises, and Web Programming Projects throughout the book, you create many different Web applications ranging from simple Web pages that link to other Web pages, Web server applications that respond to user requests, and scripts that process data and interact with databases.

The Approach

This book introduces a variety of programming languages, focusing on what you need to know to start creating dynamic Web applications. In each chapter except for the introductory programming chapter, you perform tasks that let you use a particular Web technology to build and create interactive Web pages, such as those that include forms where users can enter data and then retrieve the information they want. In addition to step-by-step tasks, each chapter includes a Chapter Summary, Review Questions, Hands-on Exercises, and Web Programming Projects that highlight major concepts and let you practice the techniques you learn. The Hands-on Exercises are guided activities that reinforce the skills you learn in the chapter and build on your learning experience by providing additional ways to apply your knowledge in new situations. At the end of each chapter are three Web Programming Projects that let you use the skills you learned in the chapter to create a Web application on your own.

Overview of This Book

The examples, steps, exercises, and projects in this book will help you achieve the following objectives:

- Understand Web programming in general and object-oriented programming in particular
- Use Access and SQL to create database tables and manipulate and retrieve data
- Create effective XML documents
- Use VB .NET to create Web applications
- Design and write C# programs that display Web forms
- Build Web forms using ASP.NET
- Use the Perl language to create CGI scripts that process data
- Create applications and applets with Java
- Use JSP to process Web data
- Write PHP scripts that interact with databases
- Design and create an interactive Web application with ColdFusion MX

The Web Warrior Guide to Web Programming presents ten Web-based programming tools that you can use to create Web applications. After providing the fundamentals of programming and working with databases, the book includes nine pairs of chapters. Each pair covers a language or technology in two parts—Part I introduces the basics of using the language, and Part II covers more advanced concepts. **Chapter 1** provides a basic understanding of the nature of computer programming, including the elements and techniques that are common to all languages. In **Chapter 2** you use Microsoft Access and SQL statements to manipulate and process data. You can use these tools in any Web application to acquire and provide data from Web pages. After reading Chapters 1 and 2, you can work through the remaining pairs of chapters in any order.

Chapters 3 and **4** cover XML, a markup language you use to structure data presented on Web pages and to define, organize, and transfer data between Web applications. In **Chapters 5** and **6**, you use VB .NET to create Win forms containing buttons that the user clicks, boxes in which the user enters text, and other visual elements including check boxes and list boxes. You also create VB .NET applications that work with databases to store and retrieve information. In **Chapters 7** and **8**, you create Web forms using C#, an object-oriented and component-oriented language. Unlike many other programming languages, in C# every piece of data can be treated as an object and employ the principles of object-oriented programming. C# is ideal for Web programming, where building small, reusable components is more important than building huge, standalone applications.

In **Chapters 9** and **10**, you build Web forms with ASP.NET, a technology that uses information from a Web server and client (or user) computer to create and send dynamic Web pages to users. You convert existing HTML files into ASP.NET pages, and then use ASP.NET to build Web forms that display data contained in a database. **Chapters 11** and **12** cover CGI/Perl. You use the Perl programming language to create CGI scripts, which are sets of instructions that tell a computer how to perform a task. A dynamic Web page usually requires both an HTML document and a script to process the data submitted by or retrieved for the user. **Chapters 13** and **14** introduce you to the Java programming language, an object-oriented, event-driven language that you can use to build Web-based applications and applets, which are programs run from another application. Users can also run applets on a Web page, making them popular among programmers. In **Chapters 15** and **16**, you explore JavaServer Pages, the Java-based technology for creating dynamic Web pages that run on any Web server, browser, or operating system. **Chapters 17** and **18** cover PHP, an open-source scripting technology supported by a large community of users and developers. You can use PHP on any computer platform to create dynamic Web pages that interact with databases. **Chapters 19** and **20** cover ColdFusion MX, a Web application server that lets you design and deliver e-commerce and other Web-based applications. ColdFusion provides a set of tools that allows you to create dynamic Web sites by using a tag-based, embedded language that is very similar to HTML.

The Web Warrior Guide to Web Programming is a superior textbook because it also includes the following features:

- **Chapter Objectives** Each chapter begins with a list of objectives so you know the topics that will be presented in the chapter. In addition to providing a quick reference to topics covered, this feature provides a useful study aid.
- **Step-by-Step Methodology** As new concepts are presented in each chapter, step-by-step instructions allow you to actively apply the concepts you are learning.
- **Tips** These notes provide additional information—practical advice and proven strategies related to the concept being discussed. Tips also provide suggestions for avoiding or resolving typical problems.
- **Chapter Summaries** Each chapter concludes with a summary that recaps the programming concepts and techniques covered in the section. This feature provides a concise means for you to review your understanding of the main points in each chapter.
- **Review Questions** End-of-chapter assessment begins with a set of multiple choice review questions that reinforce the main ideas introduced in each chapter. These questions ensure you have mastered the concepts and understand the information you have learned.

Hands-on Exercises Each chapter includes five Hands-on Exercises designed to provide you with practical experience. They guide you through the major techniques introduced in each chapter as you create Web components, forms, and applications.

Web Programming Projects Each chapter concludes with three Web Programming Projects designed to help you apply what you have learned to real-world situations. They give you the opportunity to independently synthesize and evaluate information and design potential solutions.

Teaching Tools

The following supplemental materials are available when this book is used in a classroom setting. All of the teaching tools available with this book are provided to the instructor on a single CD-ROM.

Electronic Instructor's Manual. The Instructor's Manual that accompanies this textbook includes:

- Additional instructional material to assist in class preparation, including suggestions for lecture topics.
- Solutions to all end-of-chapter exercises.

ExamView®. This textbook is accompanied by ExamView, a powerful testing software package that allows instructors to create and administer printed, computer (LAN-based), and Internet exams. ExamView includes hundreds of questions that correspond to the topics covered in this text, enabling students to generate detailed study guides that include page references for further review. The computer-based and Internet testing components allow students to take exams at their computers, and also save the instructor time by grading each exam automatically.

PowerPoint Presentations. This book comes with Microsoft PowerPoint presentations for each chapter. These are included as a teaching aid for classroom presentation, to make available to students on a network for chapter review, or to be printed for classroom distribution. Instructors can add their own slides for additional topics they introduce to the class.

Data Files. Data files containing all of the data necessary to perform the steps in the chapters, exercises, and projects are provided through the Course Technology Web site at **www.course.com**, and are also available on the Teaching Tools CD-ROM.

Solution Files. Solutions to steps within a chapter and end-of chapter exercises are provided on the Teaching Tools CD-ROM and may also be found on the Course Technology Web site at **www.course.com**. The solutions are password protected.

Distance Learning. Course Technology is proud to present online courses in WebCT and Blackboard, as well as MyCourse 2.0, Course Technology's own course enhancement tool, to provide the most complete and dynamic learning experience possible. When you add online content to one of your courses, you're adding a lot: self tests, lecture notes, a gradebook, and, most of all, a gateway to the twenty-first century's most important information resource. Instructors are encouraged to make the most of your course, both online and offline. For more information on how to bring distance learning to your course, contact your local Course Technology sales representative.

ACKNOWLEDGMENTS

All of the authors would like to thank the reviewers who provided insights for the chapters and helped to shape this book, including Adeleye Bamkole, Passaic County Community College; Al Beddow, Spokane Falls Community College; Amy Berger, San Diego State University; Ayad Bou Diab, Georgia Perimeter College; Chadi Bou Diab, Georgia Perimeter College; Ali Farahani, Fort Hays State University; Bonnie Gauthier, New Brunswick Community College; Chang T. Hsieh, The University of Southern Mississippi; Brenda Jacobsen, Idaho State University; Brian Johnson, Forest Hills Northern High School; Cliff Kettemborough, The University of California Irvine; Christopher King, Maryland State Department of Education; Bernie Kirkey, University College of the Cariboo; Jeanine Meyer, Purchase College; Amy K. Saenz, Harford Community College; Craig Shaw, Central Community College; J. Rene Tubilleja, DeVry Institute in New York; Jamie Weare, Santa Fe Community College; Carol Welch, University of Maine.

I would like to thank Lisa Ruffolo, Development Editor, who made my chapters more interesting to read and easy to understand. I want to thank the reviewers for their invaluable ideas and comments to improve the chapters. I especially want to thank my daughter, Lynne Yuwei. Bai. Most of the work was done when she went to bed and she made the work more interesting because I could always see her sleeping when I was writing chapters. She gives me so much happiness since she was born. —Xue Bai

I would like to thank the people at Course Technology for making this project a success. —Michael Ekedahl

Particular thanks to Lisa Ruffolo who organized everything as Developmental Editor. Thank you to the Math and Computing Department at University of Wisconsin – Stevens Point for their support of my writing career, and to Geoff Farrell for encouragement every day. —Joyce Farrell

My sincere thanks to my co-authors for their hard work on this project, along with Lisa Ruffolo for giving the book a common voice. My thanks also goes to Bill Larkin for his patience with me during a very busy year. A very special thanks goes to Margarita Leonard for all of the schedules you've adjusted, fires you've put out, and challenges you've faced with me during the years we've worked together. We'll miss you Margarita! —Don Gosselin

I want to thank all of the people who have made this book a reality: Lisa Ruffolo (Development Editor), my co-authors, the great reviewers, and the many wonderful people at Course Technology who worked tirelessly on making this book a success. A special thanks to my sweet husband, Charles, for taking care of the farm and horses while I sat in front of the computer. —Diane Zak

I would like to thank my wife, Rakhee, for her support and love. Your co-authoring the ColdFusion book with me really made writing this one easy. Thanks to Nikitha, my daughter, for her inspiration. —Shashi Karparthi

I would like to thank the entire open source community for putting together such lovely and logical Web development tools, and the fine people at Course Technology who have given me this opportunity to show that PHP/MySQL are tools that can compete on a "level playing field" with any other Web development tools out there. I would also like to dedicate the chapters that I wrote to my lovely wife, Dawn Etta Riley. Without your patience and understanding I would not have been able to finish this project! I know it has been hard sometimes and the nights long, but reward comes with hard work, as you know! I love you very much and appreciate all that you do for me and all that you are to me. —Peter MacIntyre

I would like to dedicate the Access/SQL chapter to my loving family: my wife Nadine and my two sons Ben and Brandon. Their support and patience helped to motivate me throughout the project. Without it, I would never have pulled it off. Also, special thanks to the hard working people at Course Technology that have made this chapter possible for me: Lisa Ruffolo, Margarita Leonard, Bill Larkin, and Janet Aras and the many reviewers that ensured my work was ready for print. Thanks for everything! It was a pleasure working with you. —Bill Morrissey

Read This Before You Begin

The following information will help you as you prepare to use this textbook.

To the User of the Data Files

To complete the steps and projects in this book, you will need data files that have been created specifically for this book. Your instructor will provide the data files to you. You also can obtain the files electronically from the Course Technology Web site by connecting to *www.course.com* and then searching for this book title. Note that you can use a computer in your school lab or your own computer to complete the Hands-on Exercises and Web Programming Projects in this book.

The data files for this book are organized such that the examples and exercises are divided into folders named Chap.*xx*, where *xx* is the chapter number. Many chapters contain a completed program and a partially completed program that you finish by performing the steps appearing throughout each chapter. You can save the student files anywhere on your system unless specifically indicated otherwise in the chapter.

Using Your Own Computer

To use your own computer to complete the steps, exercises, and projects, you will need the following software and hardware:

Hardware. Each of the tools and technologies you will study in this book include different system requirements. Be sure your hardware configuration and operating system meet the minimum system requirements before installing any of the tools discussed in this book. System requirements vary according to hardware configuration and operating system. You can find a listing of the system requirements for Visual Studio .NET by using a Web browser to search for "Visual Studio .NET Requirements" in the MSDN Library at *msdn.microsoft.com.*

Software. You need the following software for most or all of the chapters in this book:

- Microsoft IIS installed and set up to work with Visual Studio .NET. Be sure to install IIS before you install Microsoft .NET Framework.
- Microsoft Visual Studio .NET Professional Edition including the Microsoft .NET Framework.
- Microsoft Internet Explorer 6 or later. You can download the most recent version of Internet Explorer from *microsoft.com/windows/ie.*
- Microsoft Access 2000 or 2002.

The following chapters require additional software. These chapters were tested using the software versions identified in the following list:

- **Chapters 3 and 4 (XML)**: Altova xmlspy 5. You can download a trial copy of xmlspy 5 from *altova.com/download.html*.
- **Chapters 11 and 12 (CGI/Perl)**: ActiveState ActivePerl 5.6.1 Build 633 for Windows. You can download this version from *www.activestate.com*. Download the Windows MSI package, which has a filename of ActivePerl-5.6.1.633-mswin32-x86.msi.
- **Chapters 13 and 14 (Java)**: Java Development Kit (JDK) 1.4, which you can download from *java.sun.com*.
- **Chapters 15 and 16 (JavaServer Pages)**: Java Development Kit (JDK) 1.4, which you can download from *java.sun.com*; and Tomcat 4.03 (ta-tomcat-4.0.3.exe), which you can download from *jakarta.apache.org/tomcat*.
- **Chapters 17 and 18 (PHP)**: Apache Web Server 1.3.26, PHP 4.2.1, and MySQL 3.23.51.
- **Chapters 19 and 20 (ColdFusion MX)**: Macromedia ColdFusion MX Server.

Data Files. You will not be able to complete the chapters, exercises, and projects in this book using your own computer unless you have the data files. You can get the data files from your instructor, or you can obtain the data files electronically from the Course Technology Web site by connecting to *www.course.com* and then searching for this book title.

Web server setup. Some of the technologies in this book require a Web server to test the files that you create using your Web browser. The Web server can be located at your school or Internet Service Provider. If you have appropriate software, such as IIS or Apache, you can also use your personal computer as a Web server. Use the instructions in the following tables as a guide when setting up your computer as a personal Web server.

Installing and Configuring IIS 5.0 in Windows 2000 Professional
Note: IIS 5.0 is not installed on Windows 2000 Professional by default. However, if you *upgraded* to Windows 2000, IIS 5.0 will be installed by default if Personal Web Server (PWS) was installed on your previous version of Windows. ***To install IIS 5.0:*** 1. Log on as Administrator. 2. Click **Start**, point to **Settings**, click **Control Panel** and start the **Add/Remove Programs** application. 3. Select **Add/Remove Windows Components**. 4. Select the **Indexing Service** and **Internet Information Services (IIS)** options. 5. Click **Next**. Insert the Windows CD when prompted, then click **OK**. 6. Click **Finish** when prompted, then click **Exit**. 7. Close the Add/Remove Programs box, then close the Control Panel.

Installing and Configuring IIS 5.0 in Windows XP Professional

To install IIS 5.0:

1. Log on as Administrator.
2. Click **Start**, click **Control Panel**, and then double-click the **Add/Remove Programs** icon.
3. In the left panel of the dialog box, click the **Add/Remove Windows Components** icon.
4. In the Windows Components Wizard dialog box, select **Internet Information Services (IIS)**.
5. Click the **Next** button. Insert the Windows CD when prompted, and then click **OK**.
6. With Internet Information Services (IIS) selected in the Windows Components Wizard dialog box, click the **Details** button.
7. If necessary, select the check boxes for the following options: **World Wide Web Service**, **FrontPage 2000 Server Extensions**, and **Internet Information Services Snap-In**. Click the **OK** button.
8. Click **Next** and then click **Finish** to complete the IIS installation.
9. Close the Add/Remove Programs dialog box, then close the Control Panel.

Preparing to use CGI/Perl

To set the properties of the WebProg folder so that you can run the scripts contained in the folder:

1. Download or copy the data files that come with this book to the WebProg directory.
2. In Explorer, right-click the **WebProg** folder, and then click **Properties**.
3. Click the **Web Sharing** tab on the WebProg Properties dialog box.
4. Click the **Share this Folder** option button. The Edit Alias dialog box opens.
5. Leave WebProg as the alias.
6. Select the **Read** check box, the **Script source access** check box, and the **Scripts** option button.
7. Click **OK** to close the Edit Alias dialog box, and then click OK to close the WebProg Properties dialog box.
8. Close Explorer.

To identify the Perl program as the script engine for .pl files:

1. Click **Start**, point to **Settings**, and then click **Control Panel**. (In Windows XP, click **Start**, and then click **Control Panel**.)
2. Double-click **Administrative Tools**, then double-click **Computer Management**.
3. Expand the **Services and Applications** folder, then expand the **Internet Information Services** folder.
4. Expand the **Default Web Site** folder.
5. Right-click the **WebProg** folder, then click **Properties**.
6. Click the **Virtual Directory** tab if necessary, then click the **Configuration** button.
7. Scroll until you see the .pl extension information.

Preparing to use CGI/Perl (continued)

8. Click the **.pl** extension. Click the **Edit** button. The Add/Edit Application Extension Mapping dialog box opens. Select the **Script engine** option, and then deselect the **Check that file exists** option. Click **OK** to close the Add/Edit Application Extension Mapping dialog box.
9. Click **OK** to close the Application Configuration dialog box.
10. Click **OK** to close the WebProg Properties dialog box. Close the Computer Management and Administrative Tools windows.

Preparing to use JSP technology

To install the Java Software Development Kit:

1. Locate the file named **j2sdk-1_4_1-windows-i586.exe**, which is located in the software folder in your student data files.
2. Double-click **j2sdk-1_4_1-windows-i586.exe** and follow the instructions to install Java JDK to your computer. You can change the installation location, which is C:\j2sdk1.4.1 by default. The book assumes you are using the default location.

To install and configure the Tomcat server:

1. Locate the file named **jakarta-tomcat-4.1.12.exe**, which is located in the software folder in your student data files.
2. Double-click **jakarta-tomcat-4.1.12.exe** and follow the instructions to install the Tomcat server on your computer. By default, tomcat is installed in the directory C:\Program Files\Apache Group, and the default installation location is used in this book.
3. During installation, the Testing Installer Options dialog box requests an administrator password. Enter a password and click the **Next** button to continue the installation. Record your password and store it in a safe place—the administrator account is used to configure Web applications.
4. If necessary, use Windows Explorer to create a working folder for your JSP Web applications. This text uses C:\work folder as the working folder.
5. Click **Start**, point to **All Programs**, point to **Apache Tomcat 4.1**, and then click **Tomcat Administration**. The Tomcat Web Server Administration Tool page opens. Use the user name: admin and the password you provided in Step 3 to log on.
6. In the left pane, click the **expand** icon (+) next to Service, and then click **Host (local host)**. In the right pane, click **Available**. The Create new Context page opens.
7. In the Document Base text box, enter the name of the working folder you created in Step 4; then enter ***/work folder*** in the Path text box, where *work folder* is the name of your working folder. Click the **Save** button to save your changes, and then click the **Commit Changes** button.
8. Log out of the Administration Tool.

To set up system environment variables:

1. On the desktop, right-click the **My Computer** icon, and then click **Properties**. The System Properties dialog box opens.

Preparing to use JSP technology (continued)

2. Click the **Advanced** tab, and then click the **Environment Variables** button. The Environment Variables Setup window opens.
3. The System variables pane lists the existing system variables. Locate and then click **Path Variable**.
4. Click the **Edit** button to open the Edit System Variable dialog box.
5. At the end of the Variable value text box, add the following text:

   ;c:\j2sdk1.4.1\bin;
6. Click the **OK** button to close the Edit System Variable dialog box.
7. Click the **OK** button to close the System Properties dialog box.
8. Restart computer to have the new settings take effect.

To start the Tomcat server:

1. Click **Start**, point to **All Programs**, point to **Apache Tomcat 4.1**, and then click **Start Tomcat**.
2. A Tomcat starting window appears. You can minimize this window, but do not close it.

To stop the Tomcat server:

1. Click **Start**, point to **All Programs**, point to **Apache Tomcat 4.1**, and then click **Stop Tomcat**. The Tomcat window closes.

Preparing to use PHP, Apache, and MySQL

To set up the software:

1. First install Apache, and then install PHP by double-clicking the EXE or ZIP file and following the instructions that appear. Accept the default locations.
2. Navigate to the C:\Program Files\Apache Group\Apache\conf directory. Open the httpd.conf file in a text editor and add these three lines of code to the bottom of the httpd.conf file.

   LoadModule php4_module c:/php/sapi/php4apache.dll
   AddModule mod_php4.c
   AddType application/x-httpd-php .php
3. Save the **httpd.conf** file. Stop and then restart the Apache service.
4. Start Internet Explorer. In the Address text box, type **http://localhost/phpinfo.php**. (This is a sample file provided with the installation). If a Web page opens, your setup is working.

   If a Web page does not open, close the browser, return to the **httpd.conf** file and delete the three lines you added earlier. Replace them with the following three lines:

   ScriptAlias /php/ "c:/php/"
   AddType application/x-httpd-php .php
   Action application/x-httpd-php "/php/php.exe"
5. Save the **httpd.conf** file. Stop and then restart the Apache service again.

Preparing to use PHP, Apache, and MySQL (continued)

6. Start Internet Explorer. In the Address text box, type **http://localhost/phpinfo.php**. If a Web page opens, your setup is working.
7. Open the **php.ini** file in a text editor. Find **register_globals**. If this line appears as register_globals = Off, change Off to **On**.
8. Install MySQL by double-clicking the ZIP file.

Preparing to use ColdFusion MX

To set up the ColdFusion data files:

1. After installing ColdFusion MX to use IIS as a Web server, use Windows Explorer to navigate to C:\InetPub\wwwroot.
2. If necessary, create a folder named **WebProg** in C:\InetPub\wwwroot.
3. Navigate to the Data Disk for this book and copy the **Chap19** and **Chap20** folders to **C:\InetPub\wwwroot\WebProg**.

The URL to browse a file named aFile.cfm in the Chapter subfolder in the Chap19 folder with your Web browser is http://localhost/WebProg/Chapter19/Chapter/aFile.cfm. Your computer is both a server and a client.

Visit Our World Wide Web Site

Additional materials designed especially for this book might be available for your course. Periodically search *www.course.com* for more details.

CHAPTER

1

INTRODUCTION TO PROGRAMMING LOGIC

In this chapter you will:

- Understand the nature of computers and programming
- Explore the programming process
- Use pseudocode statements
- Use and name variables
- Describe data types
- Understand decision-making and loop execution
- Understand modularization and abstraction in procedural programs
- Describe object-oriented programming

When you learn to write computer programs, you gain a powerful tool. Not only does learning to program provide you with the capability to control the world's most powerful devices so you can use them to manage businesses, serve customers, provide information, solve problems, and entertain people, but learning to program also helps you to think clearly, logically, and creatively. Although you can learn to program in many different programming languages, all those languages use common elements and techniques. This chapter provides you with a basic understanding of the nature of computer programming.

UNDERSTANDING THE NATURE OF COMPUTERS AND PROGRAMMING

The two major components of any computer system are its hardware and its software. Hardware is the equipment, or the devices, associated with a computer. For a computer to be useful, however, it needs more than equipment; a computer needs to be given instructions. The instructions that tell the computer what to do are called software, or programs, and are written by programmers.

Together, computer hardware and software accomplish four major operations:

1. Input
2. Processing
3. Output
4. Storage

Hardware devices that perform input include keyboards and mice. Through these devices, **data**, or facts, enter the computer system. Processing data items may involve organizing them, checking them for accuracy, or performing mathematical operations on them. The piece of hardware that performs these sorts of tasks is the **Central Processing Unit**, or **CPU**. After data items have been processed, the resulting information is sent to a printer, monitor, or some other output device. Often, you also want to store the output information on hardware such as magnetic disks or tapes. Computer software consists of all the instructions that control when the data items are input, how they are processed, and the form in which they are output or stored.

Computer hardware by itself is useless without a programmer's instructions or software, just as your stereo equipment doesn't do much until you provide music on a CD or tape. You can enter instructions into a computer system through any of the hardware devices you use for data, such as a keyboard or disk drive.

You write computer instructions in a computer **programming language**. Just as some humans speak English and others speak Japanese, programmers write programs in different languages; some examples are C#, Visual Basic, Pascal, COBOL, RPG, C++, Java, and Fortran. Some programmers work exclusively in one language; others know several and use the one that seems most appropriate to the task at hand.

No matter which programming language a computer programmer uses, the language has rules governing its word usage and punctuation. These rules are called the language's **syntax**. If you ask, "How the get to store do I?" in English, most people can figure out what you probably mean even though you have not used proper English syntax. However, computers are not nearly as smart as most humans; with a computer you might as well have asked, "Xpu mxv ot dodnm cadf B?" Unless the syntax is perfect, the computer cannot interpret the programming language instruction at all. Every computer operates on circuitry that consists of millions of on-off switches. Each programming language uses a piece of software to translate the specific programming language into the computer's on-off circuitry language, or **machine language**. The language translation software is called a **compiler** or **interpreter**, and it tells you whether you have used a programming language incorrectly. Therefore, syntax errors are relatively easy to locate and correct. If you write a computer program using a language such as C++, but spell one of its words incorrectly or reverse the proper order of two words, the translator lets you know it found a mistake as soon as you try to run the program.

Although there are differences in how compilers and interpreters work, their basic function is the same—to translate your programming statements into code the computer can use.

For a program to work properly, you must give the instructions to the computer in a specific sequence, you must not leave any instructions out, and you must not add extraneous instructions. This is called developing the **logic** of the computer program. Suppose you instruct someone to make a cake as follows:

Stir

Add two eggs

Add a gallon of gasoline

Bake at 350 degrees for 45 minutes

Add three cups of flour

Even though you have used the English language syntax correctly, the instructions are out of sequence, some instructions are missing, and some instructions belong to procedures other than baking a cake. If you follow these instructions, you are not going to end up with an edible cake, and you may end up with a disaster. Logical errors are much more difficult to locate than syntax errors; it is easier for you to determine if "eggs" is spelled incorrectly in a recipe than it is for you to tell if there are too many eggs or they are added too soon.

Just as baking directions can be given correctly in French or German or Spanish, the same logic of a program can be expressed in any number of programming languages. This chapter is almost exclusively concerned with this logic development process. Because this chapter is not concerned with any specific language, it could have been written in Japanese or C# or Java. The logic is the same in any language. In the chapters later in this book, you will apply your understanding of logic by using a variety of programming languages.

Once instructions have been input to the computer and translated into machine language, a program can be **run** or **executed**. You can write a program that takes a number (an input step), doubles it (processing), and tells you the answer (output) in a programming language such as Pascal or C++, but if you were to write it in English, it would look like this:

```
Get inputNumber
Compute calculatedAnswer as inputNumber times 2
Print calculatedAnswer
```

The instruction to `Get inputNumber` is an example of an input operation. When the computer interprets this instruction, it knows to look to an input device to obtain a number. Computers often have several input devices, perhaps a keyboard, a mouse, a CD drive, and two or more disk drives. When you learn a specific programming language, you learn how to tell the computer which of those input devices to access for input. For now, however, it doesn't really matter which hardware device is used as long as the computer knows to look for a number. The logic of the input operation—that the computer must obtain a number for input, and that the computer must obtain it before multiplying it by two—remains the same regardless of any specific input hardware device.

Many computer professionals categorize disk drives and CD drives as storage devices rather than input devices. Such devices actually can be used for input, storage, and output.

Processing is the step that occurs when the mathematics is performed to double the `inputNumber`; the statement `Compute calculatedAnswer as inputNumber times 2` represents processing. Mathematical operations are not the only kind of processing, but they are very typical. After you write a program, it can be used on computers of different brand names, sizes, and speeds. Whether you use an IBM, Macintosh, or UNIX system, and whether you use a personal computer that sits on your desk or a mainframe that costs hundreds of thousands of dollars and resides in a special building in a university, multiplying by two is the same process. The hardware is not important; the processing is the same.

In the number-doubling program, the `Print calculatedAnswer` statement represents output. Again, within a particular program this statement could cause the output to appear on the monitor, which might be a flat panel screen or a cathode ray tube, or the output could go to a printer, which might be a laser printer or inkjet. The logic of the process is the same no matter what hardware device you use.

Besides input, processing, and output, the fourth operation in any computer system is storage. Storage comes in two broad categories. All computers have **internal storage**, probably referred to more often as **memory**, **main memory**, or **primary memory**. This storage is inside the machine. Computers also use **external storage**, which is permanent storage outside the main memory of the machine on some device such as a floppy disk, hard disk, magnetic tape, or CD. In other words, external storage is outside the main memory, not necessarily outside the computer. Both programs and data are sometimes stored on each of these kinds of media.

To use computer programs, you must load them into memory first. You might type a program into memory from the keyboard, or you might use a program that has already been written and stored on a disk. Either way, a copy of the instructions must be placed in memory before the program can be run.

A computer system needs both internal memory and external storage. Internal memory is needed to run the programs, but internal memory is **volatile**—that is, its contents are lost every time the computer loses power. Therefore, if you are going to use a program more than once, you must store it, or **save** it, on some nonvolatile medium. Otherwise, the program in main memory is lost forever when the computer is turned off. External storage (usually disks or tape) provides that nonvolatile medium.

Even though a hard disk is located inside your computer, the hard disk is not the main, internal memory. Internal memory is temporary and volatile; a hard disk provides permanent, nonvolatile storage.

Once you have a copy of a program in main memory, you must also place any data that the program needs into memory. For example, after you place the following program:

```
Get inputNumber
Compute calculatedAnswer as inputNumber times 2
Print calculatedAnswer
```

into memory and start to run it, you need to provide an actual `inputNumber`—say, 8—that you also place in main memory. The `inputNumber` is placed in memory in a specific memory location that the program calls `inputNumber`. Then, and only then, can the `calculatedAnswer`, in this case 16, be calculated and printed.

Computer memory consists of millions of numbered locations where data can be stored. The memory location of `inputNumber` has a specific numeric address, for example, 48604. Your program associates `inputNumber` with that address. Every time you refer to `inputNumber` within a program, the computer retrieves the value at the associated memory location.

EXPLORING THE PROGRAMMING PROCESS

A programmer's job involves writing instructions such as the three instructions in the doubling program in the preceding section. A programmer's job can be broken down into six programming steps:

1. Understand the problem.
2. Plan the logic.
3. Code the program.
4. Translate the program into machine language.
5. Test the program.
6. Put the program into production.

Understand the Problem

Professional computer programmers write programs to satisfy the needs of others. Some examples might be a Human Resources Department that needs a printed list of all employees, the Accounting Department that wants a list of clients who are 30 or more days overdue in their payments, and the office manager who would like to be notified when specific supplies reach the reorder point. Because programmers are providing a service to these users, programmers must first understand what the users want. Truly understanding a problem may be one of the most difficult aspects of programming.

Plan the Logic

The heart of the programming process lies in planning the program's logic. During this phase of the programming process, the programmer plans the steps to the program, deciding what steps to include and how to order those steps. There are many ways to plan the solution to a problem. The two most common tools are flowcharts and pseudocode. Both tools involve writing the steps of the program in English, much as you would plan a trip on paper before getting into the car, or plan a party theme before going shopping for food and favors.

You may hear programmers refer to planning a program as "developing an algorithm." An algorithm is the sequence of steps necessary to solve any problem.

The programmer doesn't worry about the syntax of any language at this point, only about figuring out what sequence of events can lead from the available input to the desired output.

Code the Program

Once the programmer has developed the logic of a program, only then can he or she write the program in one of more than 400 programming languages available. Now the programmer can worry about each command being spelled correctly and all of the punctuation getting into the right spots—in other words, using the correct *syntax*.

Some very experienced programmers can successfully combine the logic planning and the actual instruction writing, or **coding** of the program, in one step. This may work for planning and writing very simple programs, just as you can plan and write a postcard to your friend in one step. A good term paper or a Hollywood screenplay, however, needs planning before writing, and so do most programs.

Translate the Program into Machine Language

Even though there are many programming languages, all computers know only one language, their machine language, which consists of many 1s and 0s. Computers understand this machine language because computers themselves are made up of thousands of tiny electrical switches, each of which can be set in either the on or off state, which is represented by a 1 or 0, respectively.

Languages such as Java or Visual Basic are available for programmers to use only because someone has written a translator program (a compiler or interpreter) that changes the English-like **high-level language** in which the programmer writes into the **low-level machine language** that the computer understands. If you write a programming language statement incorrectly (for example by misspelling a word, using a word that doesn't exist in the language, or using illegal grammar) the translator program doesn't know what to do and issues an error message. You receive the same response when you speak nonsense to a human language translator. Imagine trying to look up a list of words in a Spanish-English dictionary if some of the listed words are misspelled—you can't complete the task until the words are spelled correctly. Although making errors is never desirable, syntax errors are not a major concern to programmers because the compiler or translator catches every syntax error, and the computer cannot execute a program that contains syntax errors.

Test the Program

A program that is free of syntax errors is not necessarily free of **logical errors**. The sentence `The girl goes to school`, although syntactically perfect, is not logically correct if the girl is a baby or a dropout.

Once a program is free from syntax errors, the programmer can test it—that is, execute it with some sample data to see whether or not the results are logically correct. Recall the number-doubling program:

```
Get inputNumber
Compute calculatedAnswer as inputNumber times 2
Print calculatedAnswer
```

If you provide the value 2 as input to the program and the answer 4 prints out, you have executed one successful test run of the program.

However, if the answer 40 prints out, maybe it's because the program contains a logical error. Maybe the second line of code was mistyped with an extra zero so the program reads:

```
Get inputNumber
Compute calculatedAnswer as inputNumber times 20
Print calculatedAnswer
```

The error of placing 20 instead of 2 in the multiplication statement caused a logical error. Notice that nothing is syntactically wrong with this second program—it is just as reasonable to multiply a number by 20 as by 2—but if the programmer intends only to double the `inputNumber`, then a logical error has occurred.

Be sure to test a program with many sets of data. For example, if you write the program to double a number and enter 2 and get an output value of 4, it doesn't mean you have a correct program. Perhaps you have typed this program by mistake:

```
Get inputNumber
Compute calculatedAnswer as inputNumber plus 2
Print calculatedAnswer
```

An input of 2 results in an answer of 4, but it doesn't mean your program doubles numbers—it actually only adds 2 to them. If you test your program with additional data—say, a 3—then as soon as you see the answer 5, you know you have a problem.

Selecting test data is somewhat of an art in itself, and it should be done carefully. If the Human Resources Department wants a list of names of five-year employees, it would be a mistake to test the program with a small sample file of only long-term employees. If no new employees are part of the data being used for testing, you don't really know if the program would have eliminated them from the five-year list. Many companies don't know that their software has a problem until an unusual circumstance occurs, for example, the first time an employee has more than nine dependents, the first time a customer orders more than 999 items at a time, or when, in an example that has been well documented in the popular press, a new century begins.

Put the Program into Production

Once the program has been tested adequately, the organization can use it. Putting it into production might mean simply running the program once if the program was written to satisfy a user's request for a special list, or it might be a process that takes months if the program is to run regularly from now on, or if the program is one of a large system of programs being developed. Perhaps data-entry people must be trained to prepare the input for the new program, users must be trained to understand the output, and existing data in the company must be changed to an entirely new format to accommodate this program. **Conversion** to using a new program or set of programs can sometimes take an organization months or years to accomplish.

You might consider maintaining programs as a seventh step in the programming process. After programs are put into production, making required changes is called maintenance. Maintenance is necessary for many reasons. For example, new tax rates are legislated, the format of an input file is altered, or the end user requires additional information not included in the original output specifications.

You might consider retiring the program as the eighth and final step in the programming process. A program is retired when it is no longer needed by an organization—usually when a new program is in the process of being put into production.

USING PSEUDOCODE STATEMENTS

When programmers plan the logic for a solution to a programming problem, they often use one of two tools, **flowcharts** or **pseudocode** (pronounced "sue-dough-code"). A flowchart is a pictorial representation of the logical steps it takes to solve a problem. Pseudocode is an English-like representation of the same thing. *Pseudo* is a prefix that means "false," and to *code* a program means to put it in a programming language; therefore *pseudocode* simply means "false code," or sentences that appear to have been written in a computer programming language but don't necessarily follow all the syntax rules of any specific language.

You have already seen pseudocode, and there is nothing mysterious about it. The following three statements constitute a pseudocode representation of a number-doubling problem:

```
get inputNumber
compute calculatedAnswer as inputNumber times 2
print calculatedAnswer
```

Using pseudocode involves writing down all the steps you will use in a program. Some professional programmers prefer writing pseudocode to drawing flowcharts, because using pseudocode is more similar to writing the final statements in the programming language. Others prefer using flowcharts to represent the logical flow, because they can more easily visualize how the program statements connect.

To be complete, a segment of pseudocode usually includes a **terminal statement** with a start element and stop element at each end. To make the start and stop statements easier to identify, most programmers indent the statements that fall between them. Figure 1-1 shows the pseudocode for the number-doubling program.

```
start
    get inputNumber
    compute calculatedAnswer as inputNumber times 2
    print calculatedAnswer
end
```

Figure 1-1 Pseudocode for number-doubling program

USING AND NAMING VARIABLES

Programmers commonly refer to the locations in memory called `inputNumber` and `calculatedAnswer` as **variables**. Variables are memory locations, the contents of which can vary. Sometimes `inputNumber` holds a 2 and `calculatedAnswer` holds a 4; other times `inputNumber` holds a 6 and `calculatedAnswer` holds a 12. It is the ability of memory variables to change in value that makes computers and programming worthwhile. Because one memory location can be used over and over again with different values, you can write program instructions once and then use them for thousands of separate calculations. *One* set of payroll instructions at your company produces each individual's paycheck, and *one* set of instructions at your electric company produces each household's bill.

The number-doubling example requires two variables, `inputNumber` and `calculatedAnswer`. These can just as well be named `userEntry` and `programSolution`, or `inputValue` and `twiceTheValue`. As a programmer, you choose reasonable names for your variables. The language interpreter then associates the names you choose with specific memory addresses.

Every computer programming language has its own set of rules for naming variables. Most languages allow both letters and digits within variable names. Some languages allow hyphens in variable names, for example `hourly-wage`. Others allow underscores, as in `hourly_wage`. Still others allow neither. Some languages allow dollar signs or other special characters in variable names, for example `hourly$`; others allow foreign alphabet characters such as π or Ω.

Different languages put different limits on the length of variable names, although, in general, newer languages allow longer names. For example, in some very old versions of BASIC, a variable name could consist of only one or two letters and one or two digits. You could have some cryptic variable names like `hw` or `a3` or `re02`. In other languages, variable names can be very long. Many modern languages, such as C++, C#, and Java, allow over 200 characters in a variable name. Variable names in these languages usually consist of lowercase letters, don't allow hyphens, but do allow underscores, so you can use a name like `price_of_item`. These languages are case sensitive, so `HOURLYWAGE`, `hourlywage`, and `hourlyWage` are three separate variable names, although the last example, in which the new word begins with an uppercase letter, is easiest to read.

Most programmers who use the more modern languages employ the format in which multiple-word variable names are run together, and each new word within the variable name begins with an uppercase letter. This format is called **camel casing**, because such variable names, like `hourlyWage`, have a "hump" in the middle. Many variable names in this text are shown using camel casing.

Even though every language has its own rules for naming variables, when designing the logic of a computer program, you should not concern yourself with the particular syntax of any particular computer language. The logic, after all, works with any language. The variable names used throughout this chapter follow only two rules:

- **Variable names must be one word**. That one word can contain letters, digits, hyphens, underscores, or any other characters you choose, with one exception—there can be *no spaces*. Therefore `r` is a legal variable name, as is `rate`, as is `interestRate`. The variable name `interest rate` is not allowed because of the space. No programming language allows spaces within a variable name, and if you see `interest rate` in a flowchart or pseudocode, you should assume that the programmer is discussing two variables, `interest` and `rate`, each of which individually would be a fine variable name.

When you write a program, your compiler may show variable names in a different color from the rest of the program. This visual aid helps your variable names stand out from words that are part of the programming language.

- **Variable names must have some appropriate meaning.** This is not a rule of any programming language. If you really were computing an interest rate in a program, the computer wouldn't care if you called the variable `g` or `u84` or `fred`. As long as the correct numeric result is placed in the variable, its actual name doesn't really matter. However, it's much easier to follow the logic of a program that has a statement in it like `compute finalBalance as equal to initialInvestment times interestRate` than one that has a statement in it like `compute someBanana as equal to j89 times myFriendLinda`. You might think you can remember how you intended to use a cryptic variable name within a program, but six months later when a program requires changes, you and other programmers working with you will appreciate clear, descriptive variable names.

Notice that the pseudocode in Figure 1-1 follows these two rules for variables; both variable names, `inputNumber` and `calculatedAnswer`, are one word, and they have some appropriate meaning. Some programmers have fun with their variable names by naming them after their friends or creating puns with them, but such behavior is unprofessional and marks those programmers as amateurs.

Another general rule in all programming languages is that variable names may not begin with a digit, although usually they may contain digits. Therefore, in most languages `budget2013` is a legal variable name, but `2013Budget` is not.

Assigning Values to Variables

When you create a flowchart or pseudocode for a program that doubles numbers, you can include the statement `compute calculatedAnswer as inputNumber times 2`. This statement incorporates two actions. First, the computer computes the arithmetic value of `inputNumber` times 2. Second, the computed value is stored in the `calculatedAnswer` memory location. A statement that assigns a value to a variable is an **assignment statement**. Most programming languages allow a shorthand expression for assignment statements using an equal sign as the **assignment symbol** or **assignment operator**. For example, you can write `calculatedAnswer = inputNumber * 2`.

In Pascal, the same expression is `calculatedAnswer := inputNumber * 2`. You type a colon followed by an equal sign to create the assignment symbol. Java, C++, C#, Visual Basic, and COBOL all use the equal sign for assignment.

According to the rules of algebra, a statement such as `calculatedAnswer = inputNumber * 2` should be exactly equivalent to the statement `inputNumber * 2 = calculatedAnswer`. To most programmers, however, `calculatedAnswer = inputNumber * 2` means "multiply `inputNumber` by 2 and store the result in the variable called `calculatedAnswer`." Whatever operation is performed to the right of the equal sign results in a value that is placed in the memory location to the left of the equal sign. Therefore the statement `inputNumber * 2 = calculatedAnswer` means to take the value of `calculatedAnswer` and store it in a location called `inputNumber * 2`. There is a location called `inputNumber`, but there can't be a location called `inputNumber * 2`. For one thing, `inputNumber * 2` can't be a variable because it has spaces in it. For another, a location can't be multiplied. Its contents can be multiplied, but the location itself cannot be. The statement `inputNumber * 2 = calculatedAnswer` contains a syntax error, no matter what programming language you use; a program with such a statement cannot execute.

When you create an assignment statement, it may help to imagine the word "let" in front of the statement. Thus you can read the statement `calculatedAnswer = inputNumber * 2` as "Let calculatedAnswer equal inputNumber times two." The BASIC programming language allows you to use the word "let" in such statements.

Computer memory is made up of millions of distinct locations, each of which has an address. Fifty years ago, programmers had to deal with these addresses and had to remember, for instance, that they had stored a salary in location 6428 of their computer. Today we are very fortunate that high-level computer languages allow us to pick a reasonable "English" name for a memory address and let the computer keep track of where it is. Just as it is easier for you to remember that the president lives in the White House than at 1600 Pennsylvania Avenue, Washington, D.C., it is also easier for you to remember that your salary is in a variable called `mySalary` than at memory location 6428.

Similarly, it does not usually make sense to perform mathematical operations on memory addresses, but it does make sense to perform mathematical operations on the *contents* of memory addresses. If you live in `blueSplitLevelOnTheCorner`, you can't add 1 to that, but you certainly can add one person to the number of people already in that house. For our purposes, then, the statement `calculatedAnswer = inputNumber * 2` means exactly the same thing as the statement `move inputNumber * 2 to calculatedAnswer`, which also means exactly the same thing as the statement `multiply inputNumber times 2 resulting in calculatedAnswer`. None of these statements, however, is equivalent to `inputNumber * 2 = calculatedAnswer`, which is an illegal statement.

Many programming languages allow you to create constants. A constant is a named memory location, similar to a variable, except its value never changes during a program. If you are working with a programming language that allows this, you might create a constant for a value such as `pi = 3.14` or `countySalesTaxRate = .06`.

Describing Data Types

Computers deal with two basic types of data—character and numeric. When you use a specific numeric value, such as 43, within a program, you write it using the digits and no quotation marks. A specific numeric value is often called a **numeric constant**, because it does not change—a 43 always has the value 43. When you use a specific character value, or **string** of characters, such as "Chris," you enclose the string or **character constant** within quotation marks.

Some languages require single quotes surrounding character constants, others require double quotes. Many languages, such as C++, C#, Java, and Pascal, reserve single quotes for a single character such as 'C', and double quotes for a character string such as "Chris".

Similarly, most computer languages allow at least two distinct types of variables. One type of variable can hold a number and is often called a **numeric variable**. In the statement `calculatedAnswer = inputNumber * 2`, both `calculatedAnswer` and `inputNumber` are numeric variables; that is, their intended contents are numeric values such as 6 and 3, 150 and 75, or -18 and -9.

Most programming languages have a separate type of variable that can hold letters of the alphabet and other special characters such as punctuation marks. Depending on the language, these variables are called **character**, **text**, or **string variables**. If a working program contains the statement `lastName = "Lincoln"`, then `lastName` is a character or string variable. By convention, and unlike numeric data, string data items usually are enclosed within quotation marks. This helps you distinguish string data from variable names.

Programmers must distinguish between numeric and character variables because computers handle the two types of data differently. Therefore means are provided within the syntax rules of computer programming languages to tell the computer which type of data to expect. How this is done is different in every language; some languages have different rules for naming the variables, but with others you must include a simple statement (called a **declaration**) telling the computer which type of data to expect.

Some languages allow for several types of numeric data. Languages such as Pascal, C++, C#, and Java distinguish between **integer** or whole-number variables and **floating-point** or fractional numeric variables that contain a decimal point. Therefore, in some languages the numbers 4 and 4.3 would have to be stored in different types of variables.

Many programming languages allow for a Boolean data type. **Boolean** data holds only one of two values—true or false. Boolean variables are particularly useful when it comes to making programming decisions. You learn about decision making in the next section of this chapter.

Some programming languages allow even more specific variable types. As you become familiar with the programming languages discussed in this book, you will learn about the specific data types allowed in each language.

Values such as "monitor" and 2.5 are called constants or literal constants because they never change. A variable value *can* change. Thus `inventoryItem` can hold "monitor" at one moment during the execution of a program, and later you can change its value to hold "modem".

UNDERSTANDING DECISION MAKING

The reason people think computers are smart lies in the computer program's ability to make decisions. A medical diagnosis program that can decide if your symptoms fit various disease profiles seems quite intelligent, as does a program that can offer you different potential vacation routes based on your destination.

Figures 1-2 and 1-3 show the two most common forms of the decision or selection structure. You can refer to the structure in Figure 1-2 as a **dual-alternative** or **binary** selection because there are two possible outcomes: depending on the answer to the question, the logical flow proceeds either to one outcome or the other. The choices are mutually exclusive; that is, the logic can flow only to one of the two alternatives, never both. This selection structure also is called an **if-then-else** structure.

```
if the answer to the question is yes, then
    do something
else
    do somethingElse
endif
```

Figure 1-2 Dual-alternative decision structure

```
if the answer to the question is yes, then
    do something
```

Figure 1-3 Single-alternative decision structure

The pseudocode segment in Figure 1-3 represents a **single-alternative** or **unary** selection. Action is required for only one outcome of the question. This form of the if-then-else structure is called simply an **if-then**, because no "else" action is necessary.

You can call a single-alternative decision (or selection) a *single-sided decision*. Similarly, a dual-alternative decision is a *double-sided decision* (or selection).

For example, consider Figure 1-4. It shows the pseudocode for some typical decisions in a business program. Many organizations pay employees time-and-a-half (one and a half times their usual hourly rate) for hours in excess of 40 per week; also, many organizations provide optional insurance coverage for employees. The dual-alternative decision calculates **grossPay** using one of two methods depending on **hoursWorked**. The single-alternative decision in Figure 1-4 deducts $50 from an employee's **grossPay** if the employee has selected the insurance option.

```
if hoursWorked <= 40 then
     grossPay = hoursWorked * hourlyRate
else
     overtimeHours = hoursWorked - 40
     grossPay = hourlyRate * 40 + 1.5 * overtimeHours * hourlyRate
endif
if insuranceOption = "Y" then
     grossPay = grossPay - 50
endif
```

Figure 1-4 Pseudocode for overtime decision and insurance decision

The expressions `hoursWorked <= 40` and `insuranceOption = "Y"` that appear in Figure 1-4 are Boolean expressions. A **Boolean expression** is one that represents only one of two states, usually expressed as true or false. Every decision you make in a computer program involves evaluating a Boolean expression. A true or false evaluation is "natural" from a computer's standpoint because computer circuitry consists of two-state, on-off switches, often represented by 1 or 0; so every computer decision yields a true-or-false, yes-or-no, 1-or-0 result.

George Boole was a mathematician who lived from 1815 to 1864. He approached logic more simply than his predecessors by expressing logical selections with common algebraic symbols. He is considered the founder of symbolic logic, and Boolean—or true/false—expressions are named for him.

Usually, you can compare only values that are of the same type; that is, you can compare numeric values to other numeric values and character values to other characters. You can ask every programming question by using only three types of comparisons (Boolean expressions). For any two values that are the same type, you can decide whether:

- The two values are equal.
- The first value is greater than the second value.
- The first value is less than the second value.

Usually, character variables are not considered to be equal unless they are identical, even including the spacing and whether or not they appear in uppercase or lowercase. For example, "black pen" is *not* equal to "blackpen", "BLACK PEN", or "Black Pen".

Some programming languages allow you to compare a character to a number. If this is the case, then a single character's numeric code value is used in the comparison. For example, most microcomputers use the ASCII coding system in which an uppercase A is represented numerically as a 65, an uppercase B is a 66, and so on.

In any Boolean expression, the two values used can be either variables or constants. For example, the expression `currentTotal = 100?` compares a variable, `currentTotal`, to a constant, 100. Depending on `currentTotal`'s value, the expression is true or false. In the expression `currentTotal = previousTotal?`, both values are variables, and the result is either true or false depending on the values stored in each of the two variables. Although it's legal to do this, you would never use expressions in which you compare two constants, for example `20 = 20?` or `30 = 40?`. Such expressions are considered **trivial** because each always results in the same value: true for the first expression and false for the second.

Each programming language supports its own set of **logical comparison operators**, or comparison symbols, that express these Boolean tests. For example, many languages use the equal sign (=) to express testing for equivalency, so `balanceDue = 0?` compares `balanceDue` to zero. COBOL programmers can use the equal sign, but they also can spell out the expression as in `balanceDue equal to 0?`. C#, C++, and Java programmers use two equal signs to test for equivalency, so they write `balanceDue == 0?` to compare the two values.

The reason some languages use two equal signs for comparisons is to avoid confusion with assignment statements such as `balanceDue = 0`. In C++ or Java, this statement only assigns the value zero to `balanceDue`; it does not compare `balanceDue` to zero.

Whenever you use a comparison operator, you must provide a value on each side of the operator. Comparison operators are sometimes called *binary operators* because of this requirement.

Most languages allow you to use the algebraic signs for greater than (>) and less than (<) to make the corresponding comparisons. Additionally, COBOL, which is very similar to English, allows you to spell out the comparisons in expressions such as `daysPastDue is greater than 30` or `packageWeight is less than maximumWeightAllowed`.

In addition to the three basic comparisons you can make, most programming languages provide three others. For any two values that are the same type, you can decide whether:

- The first is greater than or equal to the second.
- The first is less than or equal to the second.
- The two are not equal.

Most programming languages allow you to express "greater than or equal to" by typing a greater-than sign immediately followed by an equal sign (>=). When you are drawing a flowchart or writing pseudocode, you may prefer a greater-than sign with a line under it (≥) because mathematicians use that symbol to mean "greater than or equal to." However, when you write a program, you type >= as two separate characters because no single key on the keyboard expresses this concept. Similarly, "less than or equal to" is written with two symbols, < followed by =. The symbol for "not equal to" varies among languages, but most often is expressed using two symbols—either an exclamation point followed by an equal sign (!=)or a less-than symbol followed by a greater-than symbol (<>).

The operators >= and <= are always treated as a single unit; no spaces separate the two parts of the operator. Also, the equal sign always appears second. No programming language allows => or =< as comparison operators.

Any logical situation can be expressed using just three types of comparisons: equal, greater than, and less than. You never need the three additional comparisons (greater than or equal, less than or equal, or not equal), but using them often makes decisions more convenient. For example, assume you need to issue a 10% discount to any customer whose age is 65 or greater but charge full price to other customers. You can use the greater-than-or-equal-to symbol to write the logic as follows:

```
if customerAge >= 65 then
     discount = .10
else
     discount = 0
endif
```

As an alternative, if you want to use only the three basic comparisons (=, >, and <) you can express the same logic by writing:

```
if customerAge < 65 then
     discount = 0
else
     discount = .10
endif
```

In any decision for which `a >= b` is true, then `a < b` is false. Conversely, if `a >= b` is false, then `a < b` is true. By rephrasing the question and swapping the actions taken based on the outcome, you can make the same decision in multiple ways. It is often clearest for you to ask a question so the positive or true outcome results in the unusual action. When your company policy is to "provide a discount for those who are 65 and older," the phrase `greater than or equal to` comes to mind, so it is the most natural to use. Conversely, if your policy is to "provide no discount for those under 65," then it is more natural to use the `less than` syntax. Either way, the same people receive a discount.

Table 1-1 summarizes the six comparisons and contrasts trivial (both true and false) and typical examples of their use.

Table 1-1 Logical comparisons

Comparison	Trivial true example	Trivial false example	Typical example
Equal to	7 = 7?	7 = 4?	amtOrdered = 12?
Greater than	12 > 3?	4 > 9?	hoursWorked > 40?
Less than	1 < 8?	13 < 10?	hourlyWage < 5.65?
Greater than or equal to	5 >= 5?	3 >= 9?	customerAge >= 65?
Less than or equal to	4 <= 4?	8 <= 2?	daysOverdue <= 60?
Not equal to	16 <> 3?	18 <> 18?	customerBalance <> 0?

Understanding Loop Execution

If making decisions is what makes computers seem intelligent, it's looping that makes computer programming worthwhile. When you use a loop within a computer program, you can write one set of instructions that operates on multiple, separate sets of data. Consider the following set of tasks required for each employee in a typical payroll program:

- Determine regular pay
- Determine overtime pay, if any
- Determine federal withholding tax based on gross wages and number of dependents
- Determine state tax based on gross wages, number of dependents, and state of residence
- Determine insurance deduction based on insurance code
- Determine Social Security deduction based on gross
- Subtract federal tax, state tax, Social Security, and insurance from gross

In reality, this list is too short—companies deduct stock option plans, charitable contributions, union dues, and other items from checks in addition to the items mentioned in this list. Sometimes they also pay bonuses and commissions. Sick days and vacation days are taken into account and handled appropriately. As you can see, payroll programs are complicated.

The advantage of having a computer perform payroll calculations is that all of the preceding instructions need to be written *only once*. Then the instructions can be repeated over and over again using a **loop**, the structure that repeats actions while some condition continues.

Almost every program has a **main loop**, or a basic set of instructions that are repeated for every record. In addition to this main loop, loops also are used any time you need to perform a task several times and don't want to write identical or similar instructions over and over. Suppose, for example, as part of a much larger program, you want to print a warning message on the computer screen when the user has made a potentially dangerous menu selection, say, "Delete all files". To get the user's attention, you want to print the message four times. You can write this program segment as shown in Figure 1-5, but using a loop as shown in Figure 1-6 is much more efficient.

```
print "Warning!"
print "Warning!"
print "Warning!"
print "Warning!"
```

Figure 1-5 Printing four warning messages in sequence

```
count = 1
while count < 5
     print "Warning!"
count = count + 1
```

Figure 1-6 Using a loop to print four warning messages

The pseudocode segment in Figure 1-6 shows three steps that must occur in every loop:

1. You must initialize a variable that controls the loop. The variable in this case is named `count`.
2. You must compare the variable to some value that stops the loop. In this case you compare `count` to the value 5.
3. Within the loop, you must alter the variable. In this case, you alter `count` by adding 1 to it.

On each pass through the loop, the value in the `count` variable determines whether the loop continues. Therefore variables such as `count` are known as **loop control variables**. Any variable that determines whether a loop continues is a loop control variable. To stop a loop, you compare the loop control value to a **sentinel value** (also known as a limit, or ending value), in this case the value 5. The decision that controls every loop is always based on a Boolean comparison. You can use any of the six comparison operators that you use with decisions to control a loop.

Just as with a selection, the Boolean comparison that controls a loop must compare the same type of values: numeric values are compared to other numeric values and character values to other character values.

The statements that execute within a loop are known as the **loop body**. The body of the loop may contain any number of statements, including decisions, other loops, and calls to modules, a process you will understand after reading the next section of this chapter. Once your program enters the body of a structured loop, the entire loop body must execute. Your program can leave a structured loop only at the comparison that tests the loop control variable.

Every programming language supports arranging instructions one after another, in sequence, and creating selections and loops. Using combinations of sequence, selection and loop structures, you can solve any programming problem, from the most trivial to the most complicated. Solving programming problems using these three structures is known as **structured programming**. Using structured techniques makes programs easier to understand, but long programs benefit from further organization. By using modules, programmers further simplify the programming process.

Understanding Modularization and Abstraction in Procedural Programs

Throughout most of computer programming history, which now totals about 50 years, the majority of programs were written procedurally. A procedural program consists of a series of steps or procedures that take place one after the other. The programmer determines the exact conditions under which a procedure takes place, how often it takes place, and when the program stops. It is possible to write procedural programs as one long series of steps. However, modularization, or breaking programs into reasonable units called modules, subroutines, functions, or methods, provides many benefits:

- Modularization provides **abstraction**; in other words, it allows you to see the big picture more easily.
- Modularization allows multiple programmers to work on a problem, each contributing one or more modules that later can be combined into a whole program.
- Modularization allows you to reuse your work; you can call the same module from multiple locations within a program.

In many programming languages, you usually can create variables within programs that are known to the entire program; a **global variable** is one that is available to every module in a program. That is, every module has access to the variable, can use its value, and can change its value. With many older computer programming languages, all variables are global variables. Newer, more modularized languages allow you to use local variables as well. A **local variable** is one with a name and value known only to its own module. A local variable is declared within a module and ceases to exist when the module ends.

Many languages refer to a local variable "going out of scope" at the end of its module. In other words, the program "loses sight of" the variable.

Declaring variables locally within modules employs a principle known as **encapsulation**, also known as **information hiding** or **data hiding**. These terms all mean the same thing—that the data or variables you use are completely contained within, and accessible only to, the module in which they are declared. In other words, the data and variables are hidden from the other program modules. Using encapsulation provides you with two advantages:

- Because each module needs to use only the variable names declared within the module, multiple programmers can create the individual modules without knowing the data names used by the others.
- Because the variable names in each module are hidden from all other modules, programmers can even use the same variable names as those used in other modules and no conflict arises.

Passing Values to a Module

It may be convenient for a programmer to use local variables without worrying about naming conflicts, but, by definition, a local variable is accessible to one module only. The problem is that sometimes more than one module needs access to the same variable value; when this happens you can pass a local variable from one module to another. **Passing a variable** means that you send a copy of data in one module of a program to another module for use. Exactly how you accomplish this differs slightly among languages, but it usually involves including the variable name within parentheses in the call to the module that needs to receive a copy of the value.

Figure 1-7 shows two modules you can use in an arithmetic drill program. The `getDrill()` module can pass a copy of the `usersChoice` value to the `displayDrill()` module. Then, in the `displayDrill()` module, you declare a name for the passed value within parentheses in the **module header** or introductory title statement. The passed variable named within the module header often is called a **parameter** or an **argument**.

In Figure 1-7, the `displayDrill()` module declares a numeric variable named `option` in its header statement. Declaring a variable within the parentheses of the module header indicates that this variable is not a regular variable that is declared locally within the module, but is a special variable that receives its value from the outside. In Figure 1-7, `option` receives its value when the `getDrill()` module calls the `displayDrill()` module. The `getDrill()` module passes the value of `usersChoice` to `displayDrill()`; then within the `displayDrill()` module, `option` takes on the value of `usersChoice`.

```
getDrill()
   num usersChoice
   print "Enter 1 for addition drill, 2 for subtraction"
   read usersChoice
   displayDrill(usersChoice)
return

displayDrill(num option)
   num usersAnswer
   if option = 1 then
      print "What is 3 + 4?"
   else
      print "What is 8 - 1?"
   endif
   read usersAnswer
   if usersAnswer = 7 then
      print "Very good"
   endif
return
```

Figure 1-7 The `getDrill()` and `displayDrill()` modules

Passing a copy of a value to a module sometimes is called *passing by value*. Some languages allow you to pass the actual memory address of a variable to a module; this is called *passing by reference*. When you pass by reference, you lose some of the advantages of information hiding because the module has access to the address of the passed variable, not just a copy of the value of the passed variable. However, program performance improves because the computer doesn't have to make a copy of the value, thereby saving time.

Within the `displayDrill()` module of the arithmetic drill program, you *could* choose to name the passed local value `usersChoice` instead of `option`. Whether the variable name that holds the choice in `displayDrill()` is the same as the corresponding value in the `getDrill()` module is irrelevant. The `usersChoice` and `option` variables represent two unique memory locations.

Returning a Value from a Module

Suppose you decide to organize the arithmetic drill program so that the `displayDrill()` module does not print the "Very good" message when the user's answer is correct, but passes the user's input value back to the `getDrill()` module. In this case, you pass `usersChoice` to the `displayDrill()` module as before, but the `displayDrill()` module must **return the value** of the user's answer back to the `getDrill()` module. Just as you can pass a value into a module, you can pass back, or return a value to a calling module. Usually, this is accomplished within the return statement of the called module as shown in Figure 1-8.

In Figure 1-8, notice that within the `getDrill()` module, you call the `displayDrill()` module and pass the `usersChoice` value into it. Then you assign the return value of the displayDrill() module to the variable named answer. The value stored in answer can then be compared to the value 7. The answer variable is declared locally within the getDrill() module; its whole life lies within the module, it is declared, assigned a value, tested, and then ceases to exist.

```
getDrill()
   num usersChoice
   num answer
   print "Enter 1 for addition drill, 2 for subtraction"
   read usersChoice
   answer = displayDrill(usersChoice)
   if answer = 7 then
     print "Very good"
   endif
return

displayDrill(num option)
     num usersAnswer
     if option = 1 then
       print "What is 3 + 4?"
         else
           print "What is 8 - 1?"
     endif
         read usersAnswer
return usersAnswer
```

Figure 1-8 The displayDrill() module returns a value to getDrill()

Understanding the Advantages of Encapsulation

When you write a module that receives a variable, you can give the variable any name you like. This feature is especially beneficial if you consider that a well-written module may be used in dozens of programs, each supporting its own unique variable names. To beginning programmers, using only global variables seems like a far simpler option than declaring local variables and being required to pass them from one module to another. If a variable holds a count of correct responses, why not create a single variable, give it one name, and let every module in the program have access to the data stored there?

As an example of why this is a limiting idea, consider that a module might be useful in other programs. If it is well written, a module might be used by other programs in the company or sold to other companies around the world. If the variables that a module uses are not declared to be local, then every programmer working on every application has to know the names of those variables to avoid conflict. Maintaining a list of unusable variable names is nearly impossible, and even if you could provide unique variable names for every program, there are other benefits to using local variables that are passed to modules. Passing values to a module helps facilitate encapsulation. A programmer can write a program (or module) and use procedures developed by others without knowing the details of those procedures. For example, you do not need to understand how a telephone connects you to the person you want; you need only to understand the **interface**, or outside connection, to the procedure; that is, you need to know only what number to enter into a telephone to get a specific result. Using a procedure requires only that you know what information to send to the procedure. You don't need to know—maybe you don't even care—how the procedure uses the data you send, so long as the results are what you want.

When procedures use local variables, the procedures become miniprograms that are relatively autonomous. Routines that contain their own sets of instructions and their own variables are not dependent on the program that calls them. The details within a routine are hidden and contained or encapsulated, which helps to make the routine reusable.

There are many real-world examples of encapsulation. When you build a house, you don't invent plumbing and heating systems. You incorporate systems that have already been designed. You don't need to know all the fine details of how the systems work; they are self-contained units you attach to your house. This certainly reduces the time and effort it takes to build a house. Assuming the plumbing and electrical systems you choose are already in use in other houses, choosing existing systems also improves your house's **reliability**. Not only is it unnecessary to know how your furnace works, but if you replace one model with another, you don't care if its internal operations are different. Whether heat is created from electricity, natural gas, or a hamster on a wheel, only the result—a warm house—is important to you.

Similarly, software that is reusable saves time and money and is more reliable. If a module has been tested previously, you can be confident that it will work correctly when you use it within a different program. If another programmer creates a new and improved version of a module, you don't care how it works so long as it correctly calculates and prints using the data you send to it.

The concept of passing variables to modules allows programmers to create variable names locally in a module without changing the value of similarly named variables in other modules. The ability to pass values to modules makes programming much more flexible because independently created modules can exchange information efficiently. However, there are limitations to the ways procedural programs use modules. Any program that uses a module must not reuse its name for any other module within the same program. You also must know exactly what type of data to pass to a module, and if you have use for a similar module that works on a different type of data or a different number of data items, you must create a new module with a different name. These limitations are eliminated in programs that are object oriented.

An Overview of Object-Oriented Programming

Object-oriented programming is a style of programming that focuses on an application's data and the methods you need to manipulate that data. Object-oriented programming uses all of the concepts you are familiar with from modular procedural programming, such as variables, modules, and passing values to modules. Modules in object-oriented programs continue to use sequence, selection, and looping structures. However, object-oriented programming adds several new concepts to programming and involves a different way of thinking. There's even a considerable amount of new vocabulary involved. You first will read about object-oriented programming concepts in general, then you will learn the specific terminology.

Most object-oriented programming languages use the term *method* in place of module, subroutine, or procedure.

With object-oriented programming:

- You analyze the objects you are working with and the tasks that need to be performed with and on those objects.
- You pass messages to objects, requesting the objects to take action.
- The same message works differently (and appropriately) when applied to different objects.
- A module or procedure can work appropriately with different types of data it receives, without the need to write separate modules.
- Objects can share or inherit traits of objects that have already been created, reducing the time it takes to create new objects.
- Encapsulation and information hiding are more complete than with the modules used in procedural programs.

But what, first of all, is an object? The real world is full of objects. Consider a door. A door needs to be opened and closed. You open a door with an easy-to-use interface known as a doorknob. Object-oriented programmers would say you are "passing a message" to the door when you "tell" it to open by turning its knob. The same message (turning a knob) has a different result when applied to your radio than when applied to a door. The procedure you use to open something—call it the "open" procedure—works differently on a door to a room than it does on a desk drawer, a bank account, a computer file, or your eyes, but you can call all those procedures "open."

With object-oriented programming you focus on the objects that are manipulated by the program—for example, a customer invoice, a loan application, or a menu from which the user selects an option. You define the methods each of the objects use; you also define the information that must be passed to those methods.

With object-oriented programming, you can create multiple methods with the same name, and they act differently and appropriately when used with different types of objects. For example, you can use a method named `print()` to print a customer invoice, loan application, or envelope. Because you use the same method name, `print()`, to describe the different actions needed to print these diverse objects, you can write statements in object-oriented programming languages that are more like English; you can use the same method name to describe the same type of action no matter what type of object is being acted upon. It is convenient to use the method name `print()` instead of remembering `printInvoice()`, `printLoanApplication()`, and so on. Just as people do, object-oriented languages understand verbs in context.

Another important concept in object-oriented programming is **inheritance**, the process of acquiring the traits of one's predecessors. In the real world, a new door with a stained-glass window inherits most of its traits from a standard door. It has the same purpose, it opens and closes in the same way, and it has the same knob and hinges. The door with the stained-glass window simply has one additional trait—its window. Even if you have never seen a door with a stained-glass window, when you encounter one you know what it is and how to use it because you understand the characteristics of all doors. With object-oriented programming, once you have created an object, you can develop new objects that possess all the traits of the original object plus any new traits you desire. If you develop a `customerBill` object, there is no need to develop an `overdueCustomerBill` object from scratch. You can create the new object to contain all the characteristics of the already developed object and simply add necessary new characteristics. This not only reduces the work involved in creating new objects, but also makes them easier to understand because they possess most of the characteristics of previously developed objects.

Real-world objects often employ encapsulation or information hiding. When you use a door, you usually are unconcerned with the latch or hinge construction features, and you don't have access to the interior workings of the knob or what may be written on the inside of the door panel. You care only about the functionality and the interface. Similarly, the detailed workings of objects you create within object-oriented programs can be hidden to outside programs and modules if you want them to be. When the details are hidden, programmers can focus on the functionality and the interface, as people do with real-life objects.

In summary, in order to understand object-oriented programming, you must consider four concepts that are integral components of all object-oriented programming languages:

- Classes
- Objects
- Inheritance
- Polymorphism

Defining Classes

A **class** is a category of things. An **object** is a specific item that belongs to a class; an object is an **instance** of a class. A class defines the characteristics of its objects and the methods that can be applied to its objects.

For example, Dish is a class. When you know an object is a Dish, you know you can hold it in your hand and eat from it. `myDilbertMugWithTheChipInTheHandle` is an object, and it is an instance of the Dish class. This is an **is-a relationship**, because you can say, "My coffee mug **is a** Dish." Each button on the toolbar of a word-processing program is an instance of a Button class. In a program used to manage a hotel, `pentHouse` and `bridalSuite` are instances of `HotelRoom`.

In object-oriented languages such as C++ and Java, most class names are written with the initial letter and each new word in uppercase, such as `Dish` or `HotelRoom`. Names of specific objects usually are written in lowercase or using camel casing.

A class contains three parts:

- Every class has a name.
- Although not required, most classes contain data.
- Although not required, most classes contain methods.

For example, you can create a class named `Employee`. Data members of the `Employee` class include fields such as `idNum`, `lastName`, `hourlyWage`, and `weeklySalary`. The name and data of a class constitute what procedural programming languages call a **record**. When you work with classes, you call the data fields **attributes**.

The methods of a class include all the actions you want to perform with the class; these are what you call modules or subroutines in procedural programming. Appropriate methods for the `Employee` class include `setEmployeeData()`, `calculateWeeklyPay()`, and `showEmployeeData()`. The job of `setEmployeeData()` is to give values to an `Employee`'s data fields; the purpose of `calculateWeeklyPay()` is to multiply the `Employee`'s `hourlyWage` by 40; and the purpose of `showEmployeeData()` is to print the values in the `Employee`'s data fields. In other words, the `Employee` class methods are simply what you would have created as modules in a procedural program that uses employee records. The major difference is that with object-oriented languages, you think of the class name, data, and methods as a single encapsulated unit.

Programmers often use a **class diagram** to illustrate class features. A class diagram contains a rectangle divided into three sections as shown in Figure 1-9. The top section contains the name of the class, the middle section contains the names of the attributes, and the bottom section contains the methods. The generic class diagram shows two attributes and three methods, but for a given class there might be any number of either, including none. Figure 1-10 shows the class diagram for the `Employee` class.

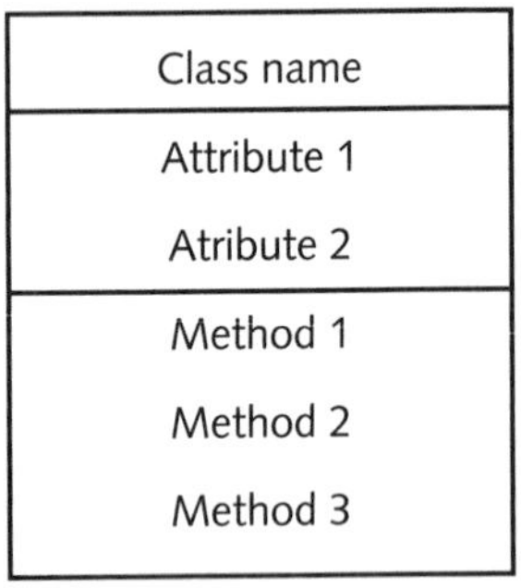

Class name
Attribute 1 Atribute 2
Method 1 Method 2 Method 3

Figure 1-9 Generic class diagram

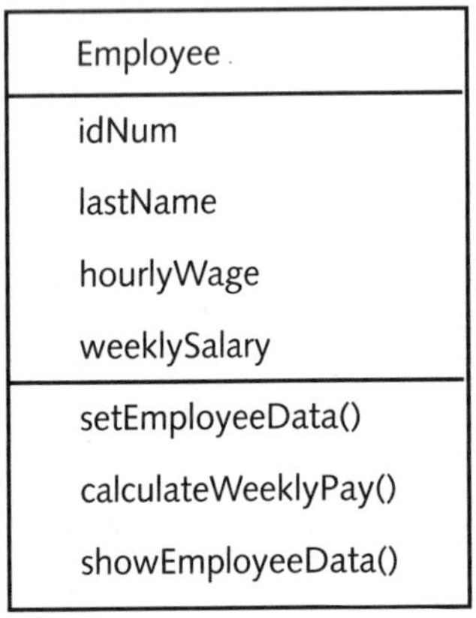

Employee
idNum lastName hourlyWage weeklySalary
setEmployeeData() calculateWeeklyPay() showEmployeeData()

Figure 1-10 `Employee` class diagram

Figures 1-9 and 1-10 show that a class diagram is intended to be only an overview of class attributes and methods. A class diagram shows *what* data and methods the class uses, not the details of the methods nor *when* they are used. It is a design tool that helps you see the big picture in terms of class requirements. Later, when you write the code that actually creates the class, you include data types and method implementation details. For example, Figure 1-11 shows the pseudocode you can use to show the details for the `Employee` class.

```
class Employee
   num idNum
   char lastName
   num hourlyWage
   num weeklySalary
   setEmployeeData(num id, char last, num rate)
      idNum = id
      lastName = last
      if rate <= 25.00 then
        hourlyWage = rate
      else
        hourlyWage = 25.00
      endif
return
calculateWeeklyPay()
   weeklySalary = hourlyWage * 40
return
showEmployeeData()
   print idNum, lastName, weeklySalary
return
```

Figure 1-11 `Employee` class

In addition to the data fields required, Figure 1-11 shows the complete methods for the `Employee` class. Notice that the header for the `setEmployeeData()` method indicates that this method requires three arguments—a numeric ID number, a character name, and a numeric pay rate. These values that are passed in from the outside are then assigned to the field names within the `Employee` class. This is the commonly used method of assigning values to class fields. Usually you do not want any outside programs or methods to alter your class's data fields unless you have control over the process, so you force other programs and methods to use a procedure such as `setEmployeeData()`. For example, if the only way a program can set the fields of the `Employee` class shown in Figure 1-12 is by using the `setEmployeeData()` method, then you guarantee that the `hourlyWage` field never holds a value greater than 25.00. Object-oriented programmers usually specify that their data fields have **private** access—that is, the data cannot be accessed by any method that is not part of the class. The methods themselves, such as `setEmployeeData()`, support **public access**—that is, other programs and methods may use these methods that control access to the private data.

Instantiating and Using Objects

When you write an object-oriented program, you create objects that are members of a class in the same way you create variables in procedural programs. Instead of declaring a numeric variable named `money` with a statement that includes the type and identifying name such as `num money`, you **instantiate**, or create, a class object with a statement that includes the type of object and an identifying name, such as `Employee mySecretary`. When you declare `money` as a numeric variable, you automatically gain many capabilities—for example, you can perform math with the value in the `money` variable and you can compare its value to other numeric variables. Similarly, when you declare **mySecretary** as an **Employee** type object, you also automatically gain many capabilities. You can use any of the **Employee**'s methods such as (**setEmployeeData()**, **calculateWeeklyPay()**, and **showEmployeeData()**) with the **mySecretary** object. The usual syntax is to provide an object name, a dot (period), and a method name. For example, you can write a program such as the one shown in pseudocode in Figure 1-12.

```
start
   declare variables--------------Employee mySecretary
   mySecretary.setEmployeeData(123, "Tyler", 12.50)
   mySecretary.calculateWeeklyPay()
   mySecretary.showEmployeeData()
end
```

Figure 1-12 Program that uses an `Employee` object

In the program in Figure 1-12, the focus is on the object—the **Employee** named **mySecretary**—and the methods you can use with that object. This is the essence of object-oriented programming.

Understanding Inheritance

The concept of class is useful because of its reusability; you can create new classes that are descendants of existing classes. The **descendant classes** (or **child classes**) can inherit all of the attributes of the **original class** (or **parent class**), or the descendant class can override those attributes that are inappropriate. In geometry, a **Cube** is a descendant of a **Square**. A **Cube** has all the attributes of a **Square**, plus one more: depth. A **Cube**, however, has a different method of calculating total area (or volume) than a **Square** has. In programming, if you already have created a **Square** class and you need a **Cube** class, it makes sense to inherit existing features from the **Square** class, adding only the new feature (depth) that a **Cube** requires and modifying the method that calculates volume.

Some programmers call a parent class a *base class* or *superclass*. You can refer to a child class as a *derived class* or *subclass*.

As another example, to accommodate part-time workers in your personnel programs, you might want to create a child class from the **Employee** class. Part-time workers need an ID, name, and hourly wage just as regular employees do, but the regular **Employee** pay calculation assumes a 40-hour work week. You might want to create a **PartTimeEmployee** class that inherits all the data fields contained in the **Employee** class, but adds a new one—**hoursWorked**. In addition, you want to create a modified **setEmployeeData()** method that includes assigning a value to **hoursWorked**, and a new **calculateWeeklyPay()** method that operates correctly for **PartTimeEmployee**s. This new method multiplies hourlyWage by hoursWorked instead of by 40. The showEmployeeData() module that already exists within the Employee class works appropriately for both the Employee and the PartTimeEmployee classes, so there is no need to include a new version of this module within the PartTimeEmployee class; PartTimeEmployee objects can simply use their parent's existing method. When you create a child class, you can show its relationship to the parent with a class diagram such as the one for PartTimeEmployee in Figure 1-13. The complete PartTimeEmployee class appears in Figure 1-14.

class PartTimeEmployee descends from Employee
num hoursWorked
setEmployeeData(num id, char last, num rate, num hours) calculateWeeklyPay()

Figure 1-13 Class diagram for PartTimeEmployee

```
class PartTimeEmployee descends from Employee
    num hoursWorked
    setEmployeeData(num id, char last, num rate, num hours)
      Employee's setEmployeeData (id, last, rate)
      hoursWorked = hours
    return
    calculateWeeklyPay()
      weeklySalary = hourlyWage * hoursWorked
    return
```

Figure 1-14 PartTimeEmployee class

The PartTimeEmployee class shown in Figure 1-14 contains five data fields—all the fields that an Employee contains, plus one new one, hoursWorked. The PartTimeEmployee class also contains three methods. The methods setEmployeeData() and calculateWeeklyPay() have been rewritten for the PartTimeEmployee child class. These methods **override** (take precedence over) the parent class method when a PartTimeEmployee object uses them. Notice that the setEmployeeData() method in the PartTimeEmployee class requires an extra argument that the Employee class version does not. The PartTimeEmployee class uses three of the four arguments it receives to pass on to its parent where the idNum, lastName, and hourlyWage fields can be set.

The PartTimeEmployee class also contains the showEmployeeData() method, which it inherits unchanged from its parent. When you write a program such as the one shown in Figure 1-15, different setEmployeeData() and calculateWeeklyPay() methods containing different statements are called for the two objects, but the same showEmployeeData() method is called in each case.

```
start
   declare variables--------------- Employee mySecretary
                                    PartTimeEmployee myDriver
   mySecretary.setEmployeeData(123, "Tyler", 12.50)
   myDriver.setEmployeeData(345, "Greene", 8.50, 15)
   mySecretary.calculateWeeklyPay()
   myDriver.calculateWeeklyPay()
   mySecretary.showEmployeeData()
   myDriver.showEmployeeData()
end
```

Figure 1-15 Program that uses `Employee` and `PartTimeEmployee` objects

A good way to determine if a class is a parent or a child is to use the "is-a" test. A child "is an" example of its parent. For example, a `PartTimeEmployee` "is an" `Employee`. However, it is not necessarily true that an `Employee` "is a" `PartTimeEmployee`.

When you create a class that is meant only to be a parent class and not to have objects of its own, you create an abstract class. For example, suppose you create an `Employee` class and two child classes, `PartTimeEmployee` and `FullTimeEmployee`. If your intention is that every object belongs to one of the two child classes and that there are no "plain" `Employee` objects, then `Employee` is an abstract class.

Understanding Polymorphism

Methods or functions need to operate differently depending on the context. Object-oriented programs use the feature called **polymorphism** to allow the same operation to be carried out differently depending on the context; this is never allowed in nonobject-oriented languages.

With the `Employee` and `PartTimeEmployee` classes you need a different `calculateWeeklyPay()` method depending on the type of object you use. Without polymorphism, you must write a different module with a unique name for each method, because two methods with the same name cannot coexist in a program. Just as your blender can produce juice whether you insert a fruit or a vegetable, with polymorphism, a `calculateWeeklyPay()` method produces a correct result whether it operates on an `Employee` or a `PartTimeEmployee`. Similarly, you might want a `computeGradePointAverage()` method to operate differently for a pass-fail course than it does for a graded one, or you might want a word-processing program to produce different results when you press Delete with one word in a document highlighted than when you press Delete with a filename highlighted.

When you write a polymorphic method in an object-oriented programming language, you must write each version of the method, and that can entail a lot of work. The benefit of polymorphism does not seem obvious while you are writing the methods, but the benefits are realized when you can use the methods in all sorts of applications. When you can use a single, simple, easy-to-understand method name such as `showData()` with all sorts of objects such as `Employee`s, `PartTimeEmployee`s, `InventoryItem`s, and `BankTransaction`s, then your objects behave more like their real-world counterparts and your programs are easier to understand.

An object-oriented concept closely related to polymorphism is method overloading. **Method overloading** occurs when different methods exist with the same name but different argument lists. Just as your blender can produce juice whether you insert two vegetables or three, overloading a method allows the same method to accept different types and numbers of arguments to manipulate. For example, you can create two `multiply()` methods, one that accepts two arguments and one that accepts three. You must create both versions of the method, but when you use it you remember only one name: `multiply()`. As with polymorphism, the method acts appropriately based on the context.

When two objects of different classes can use the same method name, you are using polymorphism. When you create a child class that contains a method with the same name as a method in the parent class, you are overriding the parent's method. When a single object can use methods with the same name but different argument lists, you are using method overloading.

Figure 1-16 shows an `Inventory` class that contains several versions of a `changeData()` method. When an `Inventory` item uses the `changeData()` method, the computer determines which of the three available methods to call based on the arguments used with the method.

```
class Inventory
   num stockNum
   char itemDescription
   num price
   setInvData(num id, char desc, num pr)
         stockNum = id
         itemDescription = desc
         price = pr
   return
   changeData(char desc)
         itemDescription = desc
   return
   changeData(num pr)
         price = pr
   return
   changeData(char desc, num pr)
         itemDescription = desc
         price = pr
   return
   showInvData()
         print stockNum, itemDescription, price
   return
```

Figure 1-16 `Inventory` class

When you execute the program shown in Figure 1-17, each of the three `changeData()` methods are called one time, depending on the argument used. When you read the program, it should seem clear in each instance whether the programmer intends to change the price or the description or both. The method name `changeData()` is clear, appropriate, and easy to remember, no matter which type of data needs the change. Using `changeData()` with appropriate arguments is superior to being required to remember to use multiple method names such as `changeDescription()`, `changePrice()`, and `changeDescriptionAndPrice()`.

```
start
   declare variables --------------- Inventory wheelCover
   wheelCover.setInvData(3772, "Chrome cover", 49.95)
   wheelCover.changeData(39.95)
   wheelCover.changeData("Deluxe chrome cover")
   wheelCover.changeData(89.95, "Super deluxe chrome cover")
   wheelCover.showInvData()
end
```

Figure 1-17 Program that uses all three versions of `changeData()`

The Advantages of Object-Oriented Programming

Using the features of object-oriented programming languages provides you with many benefits as you develop your programs. When you use objects in your programs, you save development time because each object automatically includes appropriate, reliable methods. When you use inheritance, you can develop new classes more quickly by extending classes that already exist and work; you need to concentrate only on the new features your new class adds. When you use preexisting objects, you need to concentrate only on the interface to those objects, not on the internal instructions that make them work. By using method overloading and polymorphism, you can use reasonable, easy-to-remember names for methods and concentrate on the purpose of the methods rather than on memorizing different method names.

You will more fully appreciate the benefits of objects, classes, and object-oriented programming as you develop GUI applications with features such as clickable buttons and editable text fields. Most programming languages that have been created for designing Web-based applications include a wealth of preexisting classes from which you can create buttons, menus, scroll bars, and other interesting and useful items with which users can interact. For example, when you create a screen that contains a clickable button using a language like C# or Java, you create an instance of a Button class (or one with a similar name) and use the methods included within the class to set and retrieve your button's attributes. Using your understanding of the sequence, selection and looping structures, you write code that provides useful tasks for your button to perform. With your knowledge of the basics of how programming languages work, you are ready to learn the syntax of any number of powerful languages with which you can create exciting Web programs.

Chapter Summary

- Together, computer hardware (equipment) and software (instructions) accomplish four major operations: input, processing, output, and storage. You write computer instructions in a computer programming language that requires specific syntax; the instructions are translated into machine language by a compiler or interpreter. When both the syntax and logic of a program are correct, you can run or execute the program to produce the desired results. A programmer's job involves understanding the problem, planning the logic, coding the program, translating the program into machine language, testing the program, and putting the program into production.
- Variables are named memory locations, the contents of which can vary. As a programmer, you choose reasonable names for your variables. Every computer programming language has its own set of rules for naming variables; however, all variable names must be written as one word without embedded spaces and should have appropriate meaning.
- Programs make selections by testing a value and taking different courses of action. Looping involves repeating instructions. Structured programs contain sequences of statements, selections, and loops.
- A procedural program consists of a series of steps or procedures that take place one after the other. Breaking programs into reasonable units called modules, subroutines, functions, or methods provides abstraction, allows multiple programmers to work on a problem, allows you to reuse your work, and to identify structures more easily.
- When multiple modules need access to the same variable value, you can pass a variable to the module. The passed variable is called a parameter or an argument and usually is named within the module header.
- Object-oriented programming is a style of programming that focuses on an application's data and the methods you need to manipulate that data. With object-oriented programming you create classes and objects. You pass messages to objects; the same message works differently (and appropriately) when applied to different objects. Additionally, objects can share or inherit traits of objects that have already been created, reducing the time it takes to create new objects. Encapsulation and information hiding are more complete than with the modules used in procedural programs.
- A class is a category of items and an object is a specific item that belongs to a class; an object is an instance of a class. You can create classes that are descendants of existing classes. The descendant classes (or child classes) can inherit all of the attributes of the original class (or parent class), or the descendant class can override those attributes that are inappropriate.
- Object-oriented programs use polymorphism to allow the same operation to be carried out differently depending on the context. Method overloading occurs when different methods exist with the same name but different argument lists. When you use objects in your programs, you save development time. When you use preexisting objects, you need to concentrate only on the interface to those objects, not on the internal instructions that make them work.

Review Questions

1. Another name for computer instructions is ______________.
   a. hardware
   b. software
   c. firmware
   d. languages
2. The rules of a programming language are its ______________.
   a. logic
   b. formulas
   c. syntax
   d. hardware
3. Which of the following activities must occur first as a programmer develops a program?
   a. Test the program.
   b. Understand the problem.
   c. Plan the logic.
   d. Code the program.
4. Every variable has a(n) ______________.
   a. unique memory location
   b. name
   c. both of these
   d. none of these
5. Which of the following is a valid way to express the pseudocode that calculates a student's score as a test score plus 5 extra credit points?
   a. `final score = test score + 5`
   b. `totalScore = original score + five`
   c. `examScore + 5 = studentScore`
   d. `finalScore = examScore + 5`
6. The two most basic types of data include ______________.
   a. character and numeric
   b. integer and decimal
   c. floating-point and nonnumeric
   d. character and string

7. A Boolean expression represents ________________.
   a. a calculated numeric answer
   b. one of two alternatives—true or false
   c. one of three alternatives—less than, equal, or greater than
   d. a string of characters enclosed in double quotes
8. If the expression `size > 32` evaluates as `true`, then which of the following must be `true`?
   a. `size >= 32`
   b. `size <= 32`
   c. `size = 32`
   d. `size < 32`
9. Which is not a step that must occur in every loop?
   a. You must initialize a variable that controls the loop.
   b. You must compare a variable to some value that stops the loop.
   c. Within the loop, you must add 1 to a variable.
   d. Within the loop, you must alter the loop control variable.
10. Which of the following is not a benefit of modularization within a program?
    a. Modularization provides abstraction.
    b. Modularization allows multiple programmers to work on a problem.
    c. Modularization allows you to reuse your work.
    d. Modularization prevents syntax errors.
11. Sending data from one module of a program to another is known as ________________.
    a. creating a bridge
    b. passing a value
    c. transferring a commodity
    d. conveying a variable
12. Which is a feature of object-oriented programming?
    a. You pass messages to objects, requesting action.
    b. The same message reliability works the same way with every object.
    c. Each object contains totally unique traits from all others, providing clarity.
    d. Encapsulation is abandoned, providing clearer code.

13. An object is _______________.
    a. a category of classes
    b. an instance of a class
    c. a procedure associated with a class
    d. a definition of a set of characteristics
14. _______________ allows the same operation to be carried out differently depending on the context; this is never allowed in nonobject-oriented languages.
    a. Parsing
    b. Inheritance
    c. Polymorphism
    d. Looping
15. Which pair of words is the best example of the class/object relationship?
    a. Bird/robin
    b. Evergreen/tree
    c. Sister/brother
    d. School/student

HANDS-ON EXERCISES

Exercise 1-1

If `myAge` and `yourRate` are numeric variables, and `departmentCode` is a character variable, which of the following statements are valid assignments? If a statement is not valid, why not?

a. `myAge = 23`
b. `myAge = yourRate`
c. `myAge = departmentCode`
d. `myAge = "departmentCode"`
e. `42 = myAge`
f. `yourRate = 3.5`
g. `yourRate = myAge`
h. `yourRate = departmentCode`
i. `6.91 = yourRate`

j. `departmentCode = Personnel`
k. `departmentCode = "Personnel"`
l. `departmentCode = 413`
m. `departmentCode = "413"`
n. `departmentCode = myAge`
o. `departmentCode = yourRate`
p. `413 = departmentCode`
q. `"413" = departmentCode`

Exercise 1-2

Write pseudocode to represent the logic of a program that allows the user to enter two values. The program prints the sum of the two values.

Exercise 1-3

1. Plan the logic for a program that contains two modules. The first module asks for your employee ID number. Pass the ID number to a second module that prints a message indicating whether the ID number is valid or invalid. A valid employee ID number falls between 100 and 799, inclusive.
2. Plan the logic for a program that contains two modules. The first module asks for your employee ID number. Pass the ID number to a second module that returns a code to the first module that indicates whether the ID number is valid or invalid. A valid employee ID number falls between 100 and 799, inclusive. The first module prints an appropriate message.

Exercise 1-4

1. Plan the logic for an insurance company's premium-determining program that contains three modules. The first module prompts the user for the type of policy needed—health or auto. Pass the user's response to the second module where the premium is set—$250 for a health policy or $175 for auto. Pass the premium amount to the last module for printing.
2. Modify the plan you created in the previous step (Exercise 1-4, Step 1) so that the second module calls one of two additional modules—one that determines the health premium or one that determines the auto premium. The health insurance module asks users whether they smoke; the premium is $250 for smokers and $190 for nonsmokers. The auto insurance module asks users to enter the number of traffic tickets they have received in the last three years. The premium is $175 for those with three or more tickets, $140 for those with one or two tickets, and $95 for those with no tickets. Each of these two modules returns the premium amount to the second module, which sends the premium amount to the printing module.

Exercise 1-5

1. Identify three objects that might belong to each of the following classes:
   - Automobile
   - NovelAuthor
   - CollegeCourse
2. Identify three different classes that might contain each of these objects:
   - Ludwig von Beethoven
   - My pet cat named Socks
   - Apartment 14 at 101 Main Street

WEB PROGRAMMING PROJECT

Design a class named **House** that holds the street address, price, number of bedrooms, and number of baths in a **House**. Include methods to set the values for each data field. In the set methods, do not allow the price, bedrooms, or baths to be negative. Include a method that displays all the values for a **House**. Create the class diagram, then write the pseudocode that defines the class.

CHAPTER

2

ACCESS AND SQL

In this chapter you will:

- Understand key database concepts
- Create an Access database
- Use Access and SQL to create database tables
- Manipulate data using SQL
- Retrieve data using SQL
- Retrieve data using advanced techniques

A relational database such as Microsoft Access lets you organize data for easy storage and retrieval. Whether you are developing for a legacy, client-server, or Web application, a relational database is an essential part of any modern development effort. Throughout this chapter, you learn about the Microsoft Access database program, concentrating mainly on the Structured Query Language (SQL) syntax as a means to manipulate and process your data. To provide a hands-on approach to Access and SQL, this chapter uses the fictional example of the ABC (Advanced Business Computing) College database. This example helps you complete the chapter objectives and cover fundamental Access and SQL principles. The College.mdb database is included with the data files in your course materials.

Understanding Key Database Concepts

Before you explore SQL and Microsoft Access, read through the following brief introduction of database fundamentals, whether this material is review or new for you. As in any development project, proper planning helps to avoid many of the pitfalls that you might encounter during the development stage. This section introduces you to key concepts of a relational database and explains how to model a simple database application.

Using Databases

A database, in simplest terms, is a collection of information that is logically organized to allow easy access to the information. A telephone or address book can be considered a database, even though the data is represented in printed form. A computerized **database** is a collection of data that is organized and stored in electronic format and accessible by a computer. Most current database systems, including Oracle, Sybase, Microsoft SQL Server, and Microsoft Access, are known as relational database management systems (RDBMS). Access supports the relational database model, but is limited in terms of performance and processing capabilities, such as support for large numbers of users, scalability, and advanced features such as triggers and stored procedures. Regardless of these limitations, Access supports the ANSI SQL standard and provides an easy-to-use interface.

A database consists of one or more tables. A table holds data that belongs to an entity in your program. An **entity** is any person, place, or thing for which you collect data. For example, a system used by a college to maintain student information could have entities for students, courses, instructors, and grades. Each entity contains one or more attributes. An **attribute** describes a single piece of information for the entity; in a table, these attributes are represented by columns. A column contains a single value.

A table also can contain one or more records. A record corresponds to one row; in fact, records are often referred to as rows in SQL. For example, information stored in one row in a students table corresponds to a single student, and this record consists of one or more columns. Table 2-1 shows the attributes that belong to the Student entity in the ABC College database. In a database table, the attributes are columns, or fields, and the data type determines the type of information that can appear in that column.

Table 2-1 Attributes for students entity

Attribute	Data type	Size	Example
student_id	Number	Long Integer	20010640
last_name	Text	50 characters	Smith
first_name	Text	35	Albert
middle_initial	Text	1	M
address_line1	Text	75	182 Edward Street
address_line2	Text	75	Apt #5

Table 2-1 Attributes for students entity (continued)

Attribute	Data type	Size	Example
city	Text	30	Boston
state	Text	2	MA
zip_code	Text	5	02101
application_date	Date/Time	n/a	8/24/2005
full_time	Yes/No	n/a	Yes
major	Text	50	Software Engineering
scholarship	Currency	n/a	$0.00

Understanding SQL

SQL is an English-like computer language that you use to access and manipulate data in a relational database management system. It is powerful and in some cases complex; however, it is not as powerful as a programming language. Almost all modern relational databases support SQL and comply with the American National Standards Institute (ANSI) SQL standard in varying degrees. Throughout the chapter, you use most of the common SQL commands to manipulate or retrieve data. When retrieving data, you concentrate on the SELECT statement, the command used to retrieve data from a table in SQL.

Designing a Database

Before you create any database, you should design the entities and relationships your database comprises. For simple databases, you can use pencil and paper. For more complex database applications, design tools such as Oracle Designer 2000 provide more robust features. Whichever method you choose, the basic planning principles are the same. By doing the design work before you develop your application's database, you avoid many problems later.

Lay out your database by creating an entity relationship diagram (ERD). An ERD should contain all entities in your database, and should show the relationships between each entity. For example, the ABC College database consists of four tables. Each table may or may not share a relationship with the other tables. A line connecting two tables indicates that the tables share a relationship. The connecting line also reflects the cardinality of their relationship. **Cardinality** defines the numeric relationships between occurrences of the entities on either end of the relationship line. In Figure 2-1, the Student entity has a one-to-many relationship with the Grade entity, as indicated by the symbol 1:N. In plain English, this means that a student may have one or more grades, depending on the number of courses in which the student is enrolled. By contrast, the Grade entity can have one and only one Student. In other words, a single grade can only belong to one student.

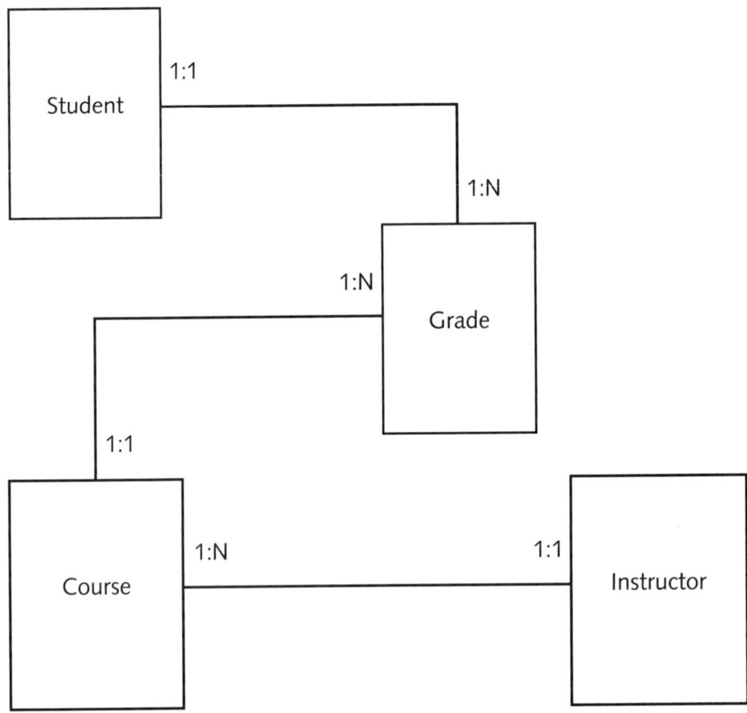

Figure 2-1 Entity relationship diagram

Using NULL Values

A NULL value represents an unknown value or a value that has no meaning. In most programming languages, variables are initialized to an arbitrary value such as zero or an empty string, depending on the data type. In SQL, NULL indicates that a column in a database table is empty, or has not been assigned a value. For instance, in the students table, the scholarship column can contain NULL values. If a student record has a NULL stored in the scholarship column, it could mean that the student does not receive a scholarship. When retrieving data, you must handle NULL values in a special way using a specific operator in SQL; this method is explained later in the "Using the IS NULL/IS NOT NULL Operator" section.

Creating an Access Database

The first step in creating any database in Access is to create the database file. In Access, the database includes all database objects, such as tables and queries, in a single file.

To create the College.mdb database file in Access:

1. Start Microsoft Access 2002.
2. Click **File** on the menu bar, and then click **New**.
3. In the New File task pane, click **Blank Database**. The File New Database dialog box opens.
4. In the File name text box, which is selected by default, type **College.mdb**. Click the **Save in** list arrow, navigate to the **Chap02\Chapter** folder in your work folder, and then click the **Create** button. The College : Database window opens in the Microsoft Access window. See Figure 2-2.

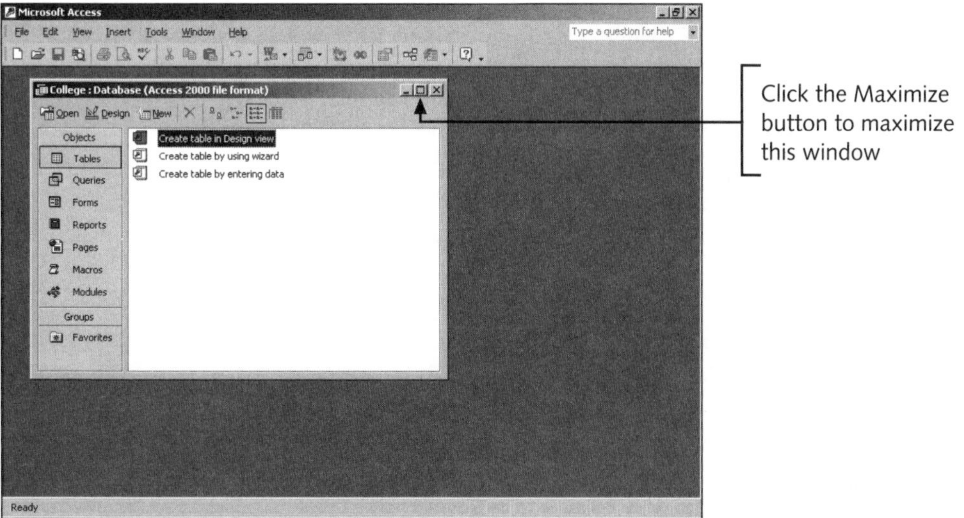

Figure 2-2 Access database window

5. Click the **Maximize** button to maximize the College : Database window. Leave this window open for the next set of steps.

USING ACCESS AND SQL TO CREATE DATABASE TABLES

In a relational database, a table stores application data according to entities. Each entity in your application's data model is a table in the database, and a table can contain one or more columns. Each column is based on a specific data type, which determines the type of data that column can contain. For example, a column based on the Text data type can contain any combination of text and numbers. See Table 2-2 for a list of data types supported in Access.

Table 2-2 Microsoft Access column data types

Data type	Usage	Size
Text	Combinations of text and numbers, such as names, addresses, and postal codes; you can also use Text columns for numeric data that will not be used in calculations, such as phone numbers	Up to 255 characters
Memo	Lengthy text or numbers, such as notes and long descriptions	Up to 64,000 characters
Number	Numeric data used for calculations; the field size defines the length of the number and numeric precision	1, 2, 4, or 8 bytes
Date/Time	Dates and times	8 bytes
Autonumber	Automatically generates a unique sequential number for a column; the Autonumber data type is useful for primary key values that are assigned by your application or system	4 bytes
Yes/No	Fields that contain one of two values, such as Yes/No, True/False, and On/Off	1 bit
OLE Object	Objects such as Microsoft Word documents, Microsoft Excel spreadsheets, images, pictures, sound, video, or other forms of binary formatted data	Up to 1 GB
Hyperlink	Used for storing hyperlinks, such as a URL or UNC path	Up to 64,000 characters
Lookup wizard	Used to create a column or field that allows you to select, or look up, a value from another table or list of values	Usually 4 bytes, depending on the size of the lookup field or column

Using Access to Create a Table

In Access, you can create tables using either the Access Table Design view or the SQL CREATE TABLE statement. In the following steps, you create a table using the Table Design view. You also assign the primary key to the student_id field. The **primary key** is the field that uniquely identifies each record stored in the table. For the students table, the student ID uniquely identifies each student. Access prevents any duplicate or NULL values from being entered in the primary key field.

To create a table in Access:

1. With College.mdb open in the Database window, click **Tables** on the Objects bar, if necessary.
2. Double-click **Create table in Design view**.
3. A new table, named Table1 by default, opens in Table Design view. Create the students table using the table attributes listed in Table 2-1. In the first row of the Field Name column, type **student_id**. Press **Tab** and then type **Number** in the Data Type column.

   On the General tab in the Field Properties area, make sure Long Integer appears in the Field Size text box. If it does not, click the **Field Size** text box, click the **Field Size** list arrow, and then click **Long Integer**. See Figure 2-3.

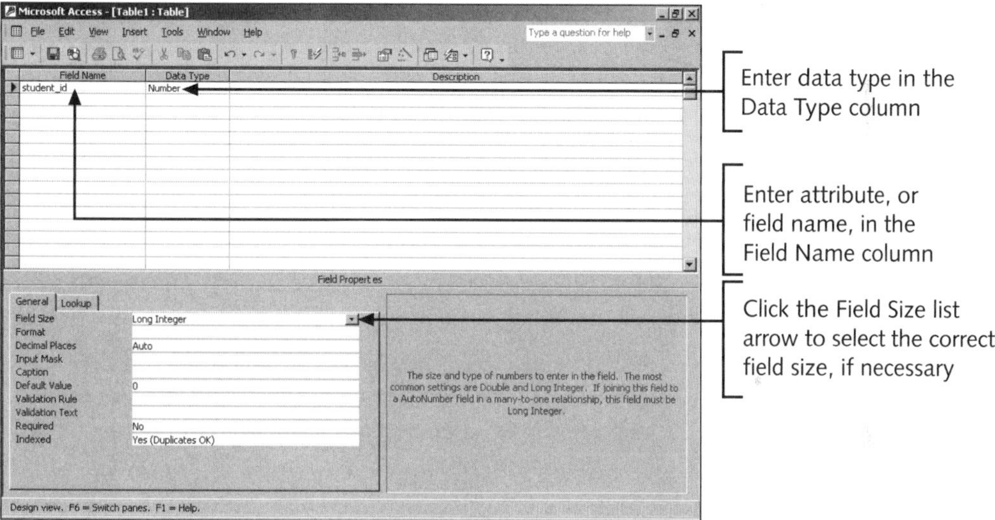

Figure 2-3 Entering the first attribute for the students table

   Repeat this step for the rest of the attributes listed in Table 2-1.

4. To save the table, click **File** on the menu bar, and then click **Save**. In the Save As dialog box, type **students** and then click **OK**. If you see a message indicating that you have not defined a primary key, click the **No** button. You assign a primary key in the next step. The students table in Table Design view is shown in Figure 2-4.

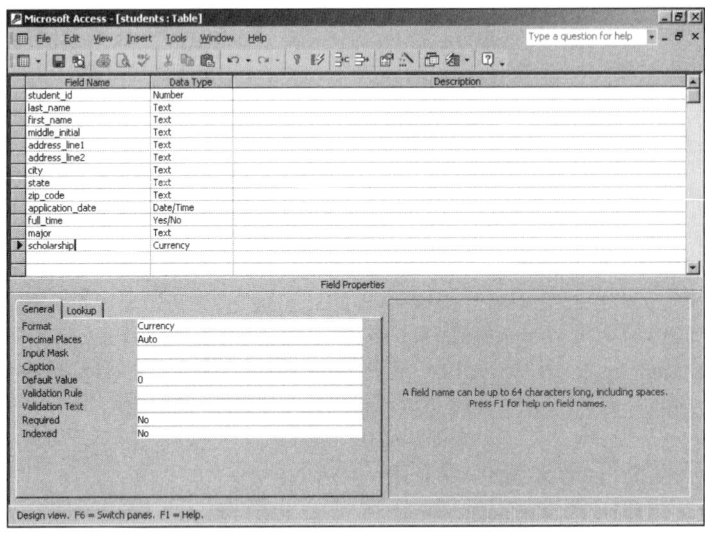

Figure 2-4 Creating the students table using Access

5. To assign the primary key to the student_id attribute, right-click the **student_id** text box, and then click **Primary Key**. A key icon appears to the left of the student_id field.
6. Save the students table, and then click the **Close Window** button to close the table. Leave the Database window open for the next set of steps.

Now that you have created the students table, you are ready to add data to it. To do so, you can import a text file named students.txt from the Chap02\Chapter folder in your work folder. This file contains 25 student records, each containing all the attributes you added to the students table. Each attribute is separated by a comma, making student.txt a comma-delimited text file.

To import data into the students table:

1. With College.mdb open in the Database window, click **File** on the menu bar, point to **Get External Data**, and then click **Import**. The Import dialog box opens.
2. Click the **Files of type** list arrow, and then click **Text Files (*.txt, *.csv, *.tab, *.asc)**. Navigate to the Chap02\Chapter folder in your work folder, click **students.txt**, and then click the **Import** button. The Import Text Wizard starts.
3. In the first Import Text Wizard dialog box, you select the format of the data you are importing. Make sure the Delimited option button is selected, and then click **Next**.

4. In the second Import Text Wizard dialog box, you select the character the import file uses to separate fields. Make sure the Comma option button is selected, and then click **Next**.
5. In the third Import Text Wizard dialog box, click the **In an Existing Table** list arrow, click **students**, and then click **Finish**. A message appears indicating that the data has been successfully imported. Click **OK**.
6. To verify that the students table contains the student data, double-click **students** in the Database window. The students table opens, as shown in Figure 2-5.

Microsoft Access - [students : Table]

student_id	last_name	first_name	middle_initial	address_line1	address_line2	city	state
19980118	Stevenson	Alfred	J	56 Fenway Drive		Boston	MA
19990402	Edwards	Ralph	S	26 North Street		Plymouth	NH
19990501	Howards	Dale	F	77 First Street		Burlington	VT
19990519	Phillips	Denise	S	56 Springfield L		Bangor	ME
20000060	Richards	Susan	A	34 Ivory Lane		Concord	NH
20000234	Hickox	Steven	E	97 Granville Stre		Manchester	NH
20000515	Thompson	Alicia	P	53 Evergreen Te		Springfield	MA
20000719	Iverson	Edward	A	29 Humbolt Driv		Boston	MA
20000875	Alverdson	Jan	G	95 West Street		Boston	MA
20000987	Stevenson	Jack	E	112 Meadowvale		Boston	MA
20010102	Smith	Frank	R	1011 Fifth Aveni		New York	NY
20010123	Gregory	Ann	J	21 Southdale Di		Fitchburg	MA
20010282	Carleson	Jeff	H	27 College Stre		New York	NY
20010341	Ford	Laura	A	35 Spring Stree		Pittsburgh	PA
20010522	Murray	Anita	V	68 Rose Avenue		Fitchburg	MA
20010587	Carson	John	E	88 Wall Street		New York	NY
20010640	Smith	Albert	M	182 Edward Str	Apt #5	Boston	MA
20010642	Bellows	Steven	A	14 Sydney Stre		Trenton	NJ
20010645	Jones	Robert	T	24 Lighthouse F		Portland	ME
20010715	Klein	Kathy	P	71 Main Street	Apt 11A	Bangor	ME
20010757	Gallagher	Tracey	D	10 Burnside Ave		Boston	MA
20010838	Roberts	Karl	G	109 Avery Terra		Springfield	MA
20010929	Jackson	Stewart	J	114 University L		Boston	MA
20020001	Ferguson	Mary	D	44 Carrie Drive		Boston	MA
20020005	Adams	Melissa	P	101 Princeton S	Apt 7C	Rochester	NY

Record: 1 of 25

Datasheet View

Figure 2-5 Verifying the data in the students table

7. Click the **Close Window** button to close the students table. Leave the Database window open for the next set of steps.

Using SQL to Create Tables

Although you will probably create most of your tables using Table Design view in Access, you can also create tables using the SQL CREATE TABLE statement. In Access, you create a SQL statement using SQL view in Query Design view. The SQL syntax for the CREATE TABLE command is as follows. Note that in the following syntax, the text in angle brackets and italics are placeholders that you replace with specific text. Text in square brackets are optional elements.

CREATE TABLE *table*
(<*column name*> [data type] [NULL/NOT NULL] [PRIMARY KEY])

To enter SQL statements in Access:

1. With College.mdb open in the Database window, click **Queries** on the Objects bar.
2. Double-click **Create query in Design view**.
3. The Show Table dialog box opens in the Query Design window. Click the **Close** button to close the Show Table dialog box.
4. Click **View** on the menu bar, then click **SQL View**. The SQL View window opens, and inserts SELECT; as the first statement.
5. Delete the **SELECT;** statement, and then enter the following SQL CREATE TABLE command:

```
CREATE TABLE courses
   (course_no TEXT(5) NOT NULL,
   course_name TEXT(50) NOT NULL,
   faculty TEXT(50) NOT NULL,
   instructor_id NUMBER NOT NULL);
```

This SQL code creates in the current database a table named courses. The courses table has four fields: course_no, course_name, faculty, and instructor_id. The value in parentheses indicates the size of the field, if appropriate. None of the fields can contain a NULL value.

Now that you've entered the SQL statement, you can have Access execute the statement by running a query. Access then creates a table named courses. You can also import a text file named courses.txt to enter data in the new table.

To create a table using SQL:

1. In the SQL View window, click **Query** on the menu bar, and then click **Run** to process your SQL CREATE TABLE statement.
2. Click the **Close Window** button to close the SQL View window, and then click the **No** button when asked if you want to save the query.
3. To verify your results, click **Tables** on the Objects bar, click **courses**, and open it in Design view by clicking the **Design** button. See Figure 2-6.
4. Click the **Close Window** button to close the Table Design View window.
5. To import data into the new table, click **File** on the menu bar, point to **Get External Data**, and then click **Import**. The Import dialog box opens.
6. Make sure the Files of type text box shows Text Files, navigate to the Chap02\Chapter folder in your work folder, if necessary, click **courses.txt**, and then click the **Import** button. The Import Text Wizard starts.

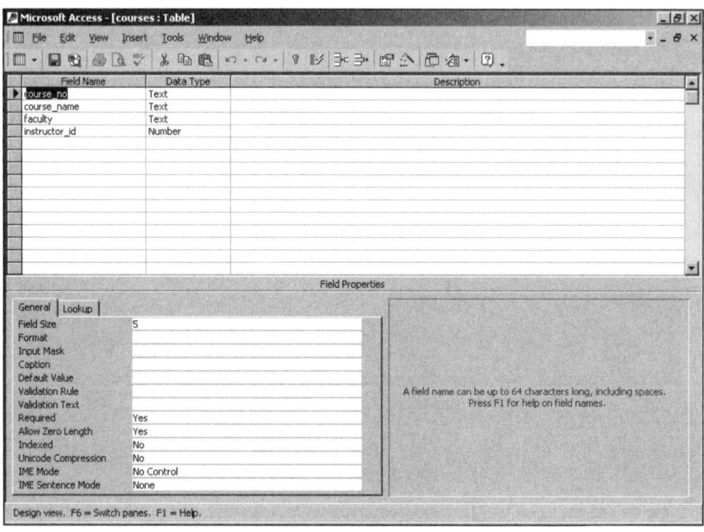

Figure 2-6 Creating the courses table using SQL

7. Click the **Next** button until you open the third Import Text Wizard dialog box, the one that asks, "Where would you like to store your data?" Click the **In an Existing Table** list arrow, and then click **courses**.
8. Click the **Finish** button. A message appears indicating that the data has been successfully imported. Click **OK**.
9. To verify that Access imported the data into the courses table, double-click **courses** to open the table. Save the table, if necessary, then click the **Close Window** button and leave the Database window open for the next set of steps.

To successfully relate students, courses, and grades, the College database needs one more table for the grade data. You can create a table named grades by using a SQL CREATE TABLE statement, and then importing data from a comma-delimited text file named grades.txt.

To create the grades table using SQL:

1. With College.mdb open in the Database window, click **Queries** on the Objects bar.
2. Double-click **Create query in Design view**.
3. Click the **Close** button to close the Show Table dialog box, if necessary.
4. Click **View** on the menu bar, then click **SQL View**. The SQL View window opens, and inserts SELECT; as the first statement.

5. Delete the **SELECT;** statement, and then enter the following SQL CREATE TABLE command:

```
CREATE TABLE grades
   (student_id NUMBER NOT NULL,
   course_no TEXT(5) NOT NULL,
   grade NUMBER NOT NULL);
```

This SQL code creates in the current database a table named grades. The grades table has three fields: student_id, course_no, and grade. The value in parentheses indicates the size of the field, if appropriate. None of the fields can contain a NULL value. Note that the student_id and course_no fields are also included in the students and courses tables, respectively.

Now you can have Access execute this SQL statement by running a query. Access then creates a table named grades. You can also import a text file named grades.txt to enter data in the new table.

To create the grades table and import grade data:

1. In the SQL View window, click **Query** on the menu bar, and then click **Run** to process your SQL CREATE TABLE statement.
2. Click the **Close Window** button to close the SQL View window, and then click the **No** button when asked if you want to save the query.
3. To verify your results, click **Tables** on the Objects bar, click **grades**, and open it in Design view by clicking the **Design** button.
4. Click the **Close Window** button to close the Table Design view window.
5. To import data into the new table, click **File** on the menu bar, point to **Get External Data**, and then click **Import**. The Import dialog box opens.
6. Make sure the Files of type text box shows Text Files, navigate to the Chap02\Chapter folder in your work folder, if necessary, click **grades.txt**, and then click the **Import** button. The Import Text Wizard starts.
7. Click the **Next** button until you open the third Import Text Wizard dialog box, the one that asks, "Where would you like to store your data?" Click the **In an Existing Table** list arrow, and then click **grades**.
8. Click the **Finish** button. A message appears indicating that the data has been successfully imported. Click **OK**.
9. To verify that Access imported the data into the grades table, double-click **grades** to open the table. See Figure 2-7.

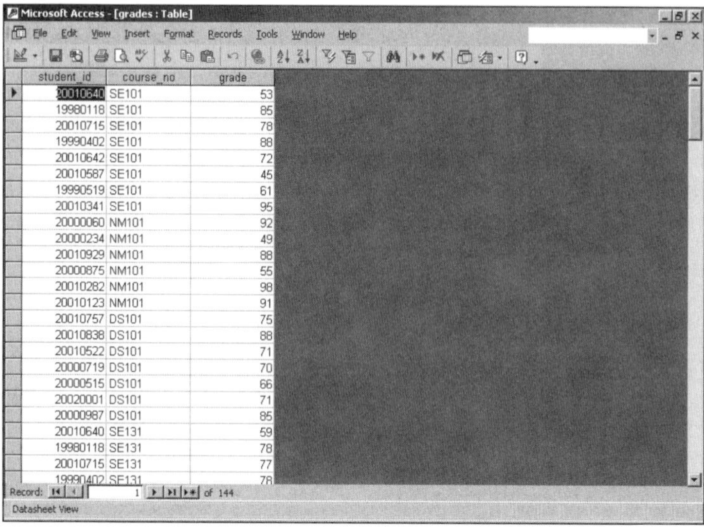

student_id	course_no	grade
20010640	SE101	53
19980118	SE101	85
20010715	SE101	78
19990402	SE101	88
20010642	SE101	72
20010587	SE101	45
19990519	SE101	61
20010341	SE101	95
20000060	NM101	92
20000234	NM101	49
20010929	NM101	88
20000875	NM101	55
20010282	NM101	98
20010123	NM101	91
20010757	DS101	75
20010838	DS101	88
20010522	DS101	71
20000719	DS101	70
20000515	DS101	66
20020001	DS101	71
20000987	DS101	85
20010640	SE131	59
19980118	SE131	78
20010715	SE131	77
19990402	SE131	78

Figure 2-7 Verifying the data in the grades table

10. Click the **Close Window** button and leave the Database window open for the next set of steps.

Using SQL to create tables can result in extra work. However, once you have written SQL to create your table, it is faster to use SQL to revise or re-create the table than to use Access Design view. Using SQL may also be useful when you have to export your table to another database.

Setting the Primary Keys

Recall that a primary key uniquely identifies a field, or attribute, in a table. It is composed of one or more columns that form a unique column value. When multiple columns form the primary key, it is referred to as a composite primary key. For example, because each student is assigned a unique ID number, you assigned the primary key to the student_id field in the students table. No two records can contain the same primary key value; if they do, Access displays an error message.

Just as you added a primary key to the students table, you also need to add a primary key to the courses table.

To modify the courses table to include a primary key:

1. With College.mdb open in the Database window, click **Tables** on the Objects bar, if necessary.
2. Click **courses**, and then click the **Design** button to open the courses table in Table Design view.

3. Right-click the **course_no** text box, and then click **Primary Key**. A primary key icon appears to the left of the course_no field.
4. Save your changes by clicking **File** on the menu bar and then clicking **Save**. Then click the **Close Window** button to close the courses table.

In SQL, you use the ALTER TABLE command to change the structure of a table. However, Access 2002 does not support this SQL command.

Manipulating Data Using SQL

After you create tables and enter the initial data, you can insert, change, and delete data in Access by opening a table in Datasheet view and manipulating the data. However, if you want users to be able to manipulate data whether they are working on the Web, a client-server network, or other environment, you can use SQL statements to insert, change, and delete data. SQL provides a common means by which your users can manipulate the data in your database. You use three SQL commands to manipulate data: INSERT, UPDATE, and DELETE.

Inserting New Data

In SQL, you use the INSERT statement to add new data to your database tables. The basic INSERT statement allows you to insert one record per statement. You must also specify the table name and the columns where you want to insert the data, along with the specific values to be inserted. If you are inserting data in all columns, you do not have to explicitly state the column names. When inserting data, you must consider all table constraints, meaning that any columns that do not allow NULL values must have a non-NULL value.

The SQL syntax for the INSERT statement is as follows:

INSERT INTO *table* [(*column1*, *column2* ...)]
VALUES (*value1*, *value2*, ...)

Suppose ABC College decides to add a new course to the curriculum named Introduction to Access 2002. You can use the INSERT statement to create the required entry in the courses table.

To add a record to the courses table:

1. With College.mdb open in the Database window, click **Queries** on the Objects bar.
2. Double-click **Create query in Design view**.
3. Close the Show Table dialog box, if necessary.
4. Click **View** on the menu bar, then click **SQL View**. Delete the **SELECT;** statement.

5. In the SQL View window, enter the following SQL INSERT statement:

```
INSERT INTO courses
VALUES ("SE201","Introduction to Access 2002","Software
Engineering",1);
```

   This SQL code inserts values into the courses table. It inserts SE201 in the first field (the course_no field), Introduction to Access 2002 in the second field (the course_name field), Software Engineering in the third field (the faculty field), and then inserts 1 in the fourth field (the instructor_id field).

6. Click **Query** on the menu bar, then click **Run** to process your INSERT statement.
7. A dialog box informs you that you are about to append one row to a table. Click the **Yes** button.
8. Click the **Close Window** button to close the SQL View window, and then click the **No** button when asked if you want to save the query.
9. To verify your results, click **Tables** on the Objects bar, and then double-click **courses**. The new record in the table should be for course number SE201, Introduction to Access 2002. Click the **Close Window** button to close the table, but leave the Database window open for the next set of steps.

A variation of the INSERT statement allows you to insert multiple records into a table at the same time. The format is similar to the INSERT statement you just entered, except for the VALUES clause, in which you use a SELECT statement to provide the values to be inserted into the table, and specify column constraints such as primary key values and NOT NULL. For example, suppose you want to copy the students table in the College.mdb database. You could use the multiple-row INSERT format to copy each row from the students table to your second table (students2) using the following syntax:

```
INSERT INTO students2 SELECT * FROM students;
```

This format is useful when you need to copy certain values from one table to another. But in most cases, you use the single-record INSERT format.

Updating Data

When you need to update existing data in a table, use the SQL UPDATE statement. You can only use the UPDATE statement on one table at a time. When updating data, you usually specify a WHERE clause to update one or more specific records in the table. If you exclude the WHERE clause, the update applies to every record in the table. The syntax for the UPDATE statement is as follows:

UPDATE *table*
SET *column* = *value* | *column* | *expression*, *column2* = *value* | *column* | *expression*, ...
WHERE *condition*

For example, suppose ABC College wants to increase its student scholarships by five percent. You could use the UPDATE statement to apply increases to any student who is receiving a scholarship (*Hint*: Use Scholarship > 0 in the WHERE statement).

To increase student scholarships by five percent:

1. Start by identifying a scholarship amount so you can verify that your SQL statements increase it by five percent. With College.mdb open in the Database window, click **Tables** on the Objects bar, if necessary, and then double-click **students**. Scroll to the scholarship column for the fourth record, the one for Denise Phillips. Her scholarship amount should be $1250. Click the **Close Window** button to close the students table.
2. In the Database window, click **Queries** on the Objects bar, and then double-click **Create query in Design view**.
3. Close the Show Table dialog box, if necessary.
4. Click **View** on the menu bar, and then click **SQL View**. Delete the **SELECT;** statement.
5. Enter the following SQL UPDATE statement:

```
UPDATE students
SET scholarship = scholarship * 1.05
WHERE scholarship > 0;
```

6. After entering the SQL command, click **Query** on the menu bar, and then click **Run** to process your UPDATE statement.
7. A dialog box informs you that you are about to update nine rows to a table. Click the **Yes** button.
8. Click the **Close Window** button to close the SQL View window, and then click the **No** button when asked if you want to save the query.
9. To verify your results, click **Tables** on the Objects bar, and then double-click **students**. Scroll to the scholarship column for the fourth record, the one for Denise Phillips. Her scholarship amount should now be $1312.50, an increase of five percent. Click the **Close Window** button to close the table, but leave the Database window open for the next set of steps.

When specifying criteria to use in the WHERE clause of the UPDATE statement, you can include one or more conditions using the logical operators AND and OR. More details on these operators are included later in this chapter.

Deleting Data

In some circumstances, you need to remove data from your database. You might need to perform routine database maintenance or delete real-time transactions by application users. Whatever the reason, you use the DELETE statement to delete data from a database. In almost every DELETE statement you write, you use a WHERE clause to specify what records to delete. Removing the wrong data can be disastrous, so use caution when you write SQL to delete data. Once the data has been removed, you cannot recover it without using the INSERT statement to reinsert the data or restoring it from a backup (provided you've made one). The syntax for the DELETE statement is as follows:

DELETE FROM *table*
WHERE *condition*

For example, suppose that ABC College did not reach the minimum quota for enrollment in the Introduction to Access 2002 course and therefore cancelled the course. Because the course is not offered this semester, it is probably a good idea to remove it from your database and prevent users from inadvertently entering data related to this course. To remove this course from the courses table, prepare and execute the following DELETE statement.

To delete SE201 from the courses table:

1. With College.mdb open in the Database window, click **Queries** on the Objects bar.
2. Double-click **Create query in Design view**.
3. Close the Show Table dialog box, if necessary.
4. Click **View** on the menu bar, then click **SQL View**. Delete the **SELECT;** statement.
5. Enter the following SQL DELETE statement:

```
DELETE FROM courses
WHERE course_no = "SE201";
```

6. Click **Query** on the menu bar, then click **Run** to process your DELETE statement.
7. A dialog box informs you that you are about to delete one row from a table. Click the **Yes** button.
8. Click the **Close Window** button to close the SQL View window, and then click the **No** button when asked if you want to save the query.
9. To verify your results, click **Tables** on the Objects bar, and then double-click **courses**. The record for the Introduction to Access 2002 course has been removed. Click the **Close Window** button to close the table, but leave the Database window open for the next set of steps.

RETRIEVING DATA USING SQL

You've now seen how to create a database and database tables, and how to manipulate data stored in a database. In this section you learn how to retrieve information from a relational database using the SQL SELECT statement. The SELECT statement is a very powerful SQL command and lets you retrieve data in many ways. For example, you can use a simple SELECT statement to retrieve all data from one table, or you can use more complex queries and statements that involve multiple tables and several criteria.

The syntax of the SELECT statement is as follows:

SELECT *column1, column2, column3, ...*
FROM *table1, table2, ...*
WHERE *condition*

When you need to retrieve all columns from a table, you can use the wildcard symbol (*) instead of listing each column separately in your SELECT statement. The wildcard symbol indicates that all columns are returned in the result set.

Because there are many variations of the SELECT statement, the following sections cover only the more common usages.

Retrieving All Data

In some cases, you may want to retrieve all records from a single table. This is generally not the most common usage of the SELECT statement, but it is the easiest variation to explain first. For example, assume that you want a complete listing of all students at ABC College. In the following steps, you only retrieve the students' ID number, last name, and first name.

To retrieve a list of all students using the SELECT statement:

1. With College.mdb open in the Database window, click **Queries** on the Objects bar.
2. Double-click **Create query in Design view**.
3. Close the Show Table dialog box, if necessary.
4. Click **View** on the menu bar, then click **SQL View**.
5. Begin entering SQL code after the SELECT statement. The complete code should match the following SELECT statement:

```
SELECT student_id, last_name, first_name
FROM students;
```

6. Click **Query** on the menu bar, then click **Run** to process your SELECT statement. The query results show a table containing student_id, last_name, and first_name columns. See Figure 2-8.

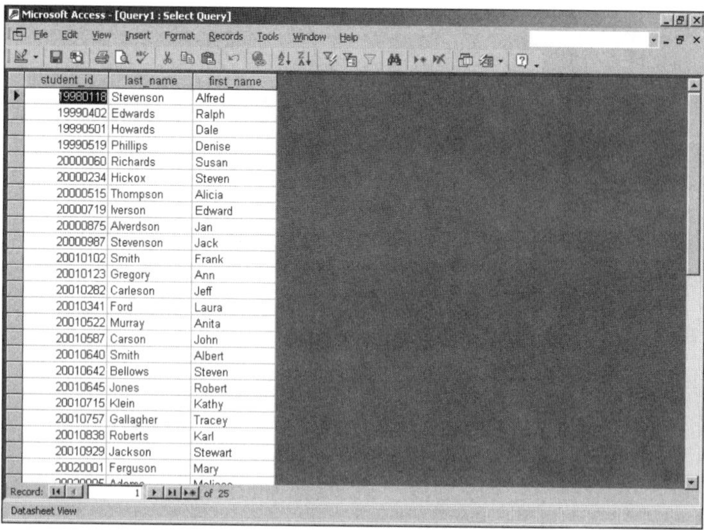

student_id	last_name	first_name
19980118	Stevenson	Alfred
19990402	Edwards	Ralph
19990501	Howards	Dale
19990519	Phillips	Denise
20000060	Richards	Susan
20000234	Hickox	Steven
20000515	Thompson	Alicia
20000719	Iverson	Edward
20000875	Alverdson	Jan
20000987	Stevenson	Jack
20010102	Smith	Frank
20010123	Gregory	Ann
20010282	Carleson	Jeff
20010341	Ford	Laura
20010522	Murray	Anita
20010587	Carson	John
20010640	Smith	Albert
20010642	Bellows	Steven
20010645	Jones	Robert
20010715	Klein	Kathy
20010757	Gallagher	Tracey
20010838	Roberts	Karl
20010929	Jackson	Stewart
20020001	Ferguson	Mary

Figure 2-8 Results from SELECT statement to retrieve all students

7. Click the **Close Window** button to close the window, and then click the **No** button when asked if you want to save the query. Leave the Database window open for the next set of steps.

Retrieving Specific Data Using the WHERE Clause

In most cases, you do not want to retrieve all the data from a table, but a subset of records that meet a specific set of criteria. In these cases, you include a WHERE clause with the SELECT statement to explicitly define the retrieval criteria. The WHERE clause in a SELECT statement is used exactly like an UPDATE or DELETE statement, in which you define one or more conditions that determine which records are returned in the result set.

The retrieval criteria you specify are composed of one or more conditions, which are made up of logical expressions using one or more operators. Table 2-3 lists the most common logical operators used for single-value comparisons.

Table 2-3 Logical operators used in SQL

Operator	Description	Example
=	Equal to	student_id = 1234567
>	Greater than	scholarship > 1000
<	Less than	scholarship < 3000
>=	Greater than or equal to	Grade >= 50
<=	Less than or equal to	Grade <= 49
<>	Not equal to	state <> "MA"

These operators are the most common in SQL. However, a few others are covered in the rest of this section.

Using the IS NULL/IS NOT NULL Operator

Use the IS NULL operator to test whether data exists in a column. If the column is empty, or in SQL terms is said to be NULL, then the condition is satisfied. Conversely, if you want to test a column to make sure it is not empty, you use the IS NOT NULL operator. The syntax for IS NULL/IS NOT NULL is as follows:

WHERE *column* IS NULL {IS NOT NULL}

For example, you could prepare the following query to determine which student addresses do not contain a second address line. See Figure 2-9.

```
SELECT * FROM students
WHERE address_line2 IS NULL
```

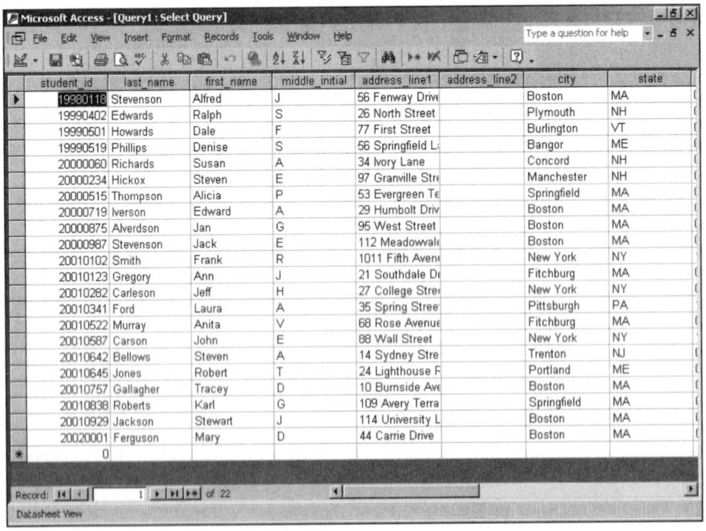

Microsoft Access - [Query1 : Select Query]

student_id	last_name	first_name	middle_initial	address_line1	address_line2	city	state
19980118	Stevenson	Alfred	J	56 Fenway Drive		Boston	MA
19990402	Edwards	Ralph	S	26 North Street		Plymouth	NH
19990501	Howards	Dale	F	77 First Street		Burlington	VT
19990519	Phillips	Denise	S	56 Springfield L:		Bangor	ME
20000060	Richards	Susan	A	34 Ivory Lane		Concord	NH
20000234	Hickox	Steven	E	97 Granville Stre		Manchester	NH
20000515	Thompson	Alicia	P	53 Evergreen Te		Springfield	MA
20000719	Iverson	Edward	A	29 Humbolt Driv		Boston	MA
20000875	Alverdson	Jan	G	95 West Street		Boston	MA
20000987	Stevenson	Jack	E	112 Meadowvale		Boston	MA
20010102	Smith	Frank	R	1011 Fifth Aveni		New York	NY
20010123	Gregory	Ann	J	21 Southdale Di		Fitchburg	MA
20010282	Carleson	Jeff	H	27 College Stre		New York	NY
20010341	Ford	Laura	A	35 Spring Stree		Pittsburgh	PA
20010522	Murray	Anita	V	68 Rose Avenue		Fitchburg	MA
20010587	Carson	John	E	88 Wall Street		New York	NY
20010642	Bellows	Steven	A	14 Sydney Stre		Trenton	NJ
20010645	Jones	Robert	T	24 Lighthouse F		Portland	ME
20010757	Gallagher	Tracey	D	10 Burnside Ave		Boston	MA
20010838	Roberts	Karl	G	109 Avery Terra		Springfield	MA
20010929	Jackson	Stewart	J	114 University L		Boston	MA
20020001	Ferguson	Mary	D	44 Carrie Drive		Boston	MA
0							

Record: 1 of 22

Datasheet View

Figure 2-9 Results from SELECT statement using IS NULL operator

Using the LIKE Operator

Use the LIKE operator when you need to retrieve records where a text column or field partially matches a string value or expression. The string value usually contains one or more wildcard symbols (*), which represent multiple unknown characters and allow you to compare partial character strings. Unlike the equal to (=) operator, the LIKE operator does not require an exact match in order for a record or row to be returned. The LIKE operator is only used for string comparisons on Text or Memo fields. For example, suppose that you wanted a listing of all students whose last name begins with S. You could retrieve this information using the following query. See Figure 2-10.

```
SELECT * FROM students
WHERE last_name LIKE "S*";
```

Microsoft Access - [Query1 : Select Query]

student_id	last_name	first_name	middle_initial	address_line1	address_line2	city	state
19980118	Stevenson	Alfred	J	56 Fenway Drive		Boston	MA
20000987	Stevenson	Jack	E	112 Meadowvale		Boston	MA
20010102	Smith	Frank	R	1011 Fifth Aveni		New York	NY
20010640	Smith	Albert	M	182 Edward Str	Apt #5	Boston	MA
0							

Figure 2-10 Results from SELECT statement using LIKE operator

The LIKE operator is useful when you need to search for partial substrings in Text columns.

In other relational database management programs such as Oracle, Sybase, or SQL Server, the percent (%) symbol is used to indicate the wildcard.

Using the BETWEEN Operator

The BETWEEN operator is useful for comparing a column to a range of values. You can use it for text, numeric, and date data types. Although numeric values can be tested using two expressions combined with the AND operator, the BETWEEN simplifies your SQL into one expression. For example, suppose you wanted to know which students at ABC College have scholarships of more than $1000 but less than $3000. You could determine which students fall within this range by executing the following query. See Figure 2-11.

```
SELECT *
FROM students
WHERE scholarship BETWEEN 1000 AND 3000;
```

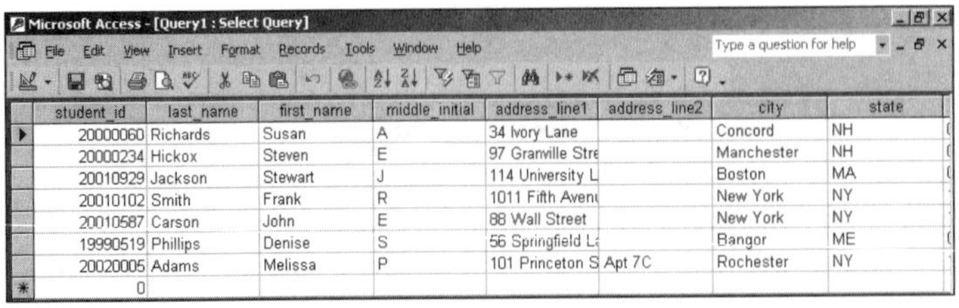

Microsoft Access - [Query1 : Select Query]

student_id	last_name	first_name	middle_initial	address_line1	address_line2	city	state
20000060	Richards	Susan	A	34 Ivory Lane		Concord	NH
20000234	Hickox	Steven	E	97 Granville Stre		Manchester	NH
20010929	Jackson	Stewart	J	114 University L		Boston	MA
20010102	Smith	Frank	R	1011 Fifth Avenu		New York	NY
20010587	Carson	John	E	88 Wall Street		New York	NY
19990519	Phillips	Denise	S	56 Springfield La		Bangor	ME
20020005	Adams	Melissa	P	101 Princeton S	Apt 7C	Rochester	NY
0							

Figure 2-11 Results from SELECT statement using BETWEEN operator

Using the IN Operator

Use the IN operator when you want to compare a column to a list (subset) of values. You can use this operator with numeric or text columns; it offers a more simplified option than using several OR statements. The syntax of the IN operator is as follows:

IN (*value1, value2, ...*)

For example, if you wanted a list of all students that reside in the states of Maine, Massachusetts, or New Hampshire, you could prepare the following query using the IN operator. See Figure 2-12.

```
SELECT last_name, first_name, state
FROM students
WHERE state IN ("ME", "MA", "NH");
```

Microsoft Access - [Query1 : Select Query]

last_name	first_name	state
Jones	Robert	ME
Smith	Albert	MA
Gallagher	Tracey	MA
Richards	Susan	NH
Stevenson	Alfred	MA
Hickox	Steven	NH
Roberts	Karl	MA
Klein	Kathy	ME
Murray	Anita	MA
Edwards	Ralph	NH
Jackson	Stewart	MA
Iverson	Edward	MA
Thompson	Alicia	MA
Alverdson	Jan	MA
Phillips	Denise	ME
Ferguson	Mary	MA
Stevenson	Jack	MA
Gregory	Ann	MA

Figure 2-12 Results from SELECT statement using IN operator

As mentioned, the IN operator prevents you from having to code multiple OR statements to achieve the same result. You also could rewrite the previous example as follows:


```
SELECT last_name, first_name, state
FROM students
WHERE state = "ME"
     OR state =  "MA"
     OR state =  "NH";
```

In a later section, you learn how to use the IN operator in conjunction with nested queries to create dynamic lists.

Sorting Data

Often, it is useful to sort your data by a particular field or column, in ascending or descending order. In SQL, you use the ORDER BY clause to sort the data in your result set. The format of the ORDER BY clause is as follows:

ORDER BY {*column1* [, *column2*] ...}{ASC/DESC}

The following SELECT statement returns a result set containing the last_name and first_name columns from the students, ordered by the student_id column. See Figure 2-13.

```
SELECT student_id, last_name, first_name
FROM students
ORDER BY student_id;
```

Microsoft Access - [Query1 : Select Query]

File Edit View Insert Format Records Tools

student_id	last_name	first_name
19980118	Stevenson	Alfred
19990402	Edwards	Ralph
19990501	Howards	Dale
19990519	Phillips	Denise
20000060	Richards	Susan
20000234	Hickox	Steven
20000515	Thompson	Alicia
20000719	Iverson	Edward
20000875	Alverdson	Jan
20000987	Stevenson	Jack
20010102	Smith	Frank
20010123	Gregory	Ann
20010282	Carleson	Jeff
20010341	Ford	Laura
20010522	Murray	Anita
20010587	Carson	John
20010640	Smith	Albert
20010642	Bellows	Steven
20010645	Jones	Robert
20010715	Klein	Kathy
20010757	Gallagher	Tracey
20010838	Roberts	Karl
20010929	Jackson	Stewart
20020001	Ferguson	Mary

Record: 1 of 25

Datasheet View

Figure 2-13 Results from SELECT statement using ORDER BY clause in ascending order

You can sort the result set by more than one column, and you can change the default sorting order from ascending (ASC) to descending (DESC). The following example returns a result set that lists student information ordered by the amount of scholarship money received, in descending order from highest to lowest. See Figure 2-14.

```
SELECT student_id, last_name, first_name, scholarship
FROM students
ORDER BY scholarship DESC;
```

Microsoft Access - [Query1 : Select Query]

student_id	last_name	first_name	scholarship
20020005	Adams	Melissa	$2,940.00
20010587	Carson	John	$2,310.00
20000234	Hickox	Steven	$2,100.00
20010102	Smith	Frank	$1,890.00
20000060	Richards	Susan	$1,575.00
19990519	Phillips	Denise	$1,312.50
20010929	Jackson	Stewart	$1,076.25
20010522	Murray	Anita	$892.50
20010642	Bellows	Steven	$603.75
20010341	Ford	Laura	$0.00
19990402	Edwards	Ralph	$0.00
19990501	Howards	Dale	$0.00
20000515	Thompson	Alicia	$0.00
20000719	Iverson	Edward	$0.00
20000875	Alverdson	Jan	$0.00
20000987	Stevenson	Jack	$0.00
19980118	Stevenson	Alfred	$0.00
20010282	Carleson	Jeff	$0.00
20010640	Smith	Albert	$0.00
20010645	Jones	Robert	$0.00
20010715	Klein	Kathy	$0.00
20010757	Gallagher	Tracey	$0.00
20010838	Roberts	Karl	$0.00
20020001	Ferguson	Mary	$0.00

Record: 1 of 25

Datasheet View

Figure 2-14 Results from SELECT statement using ORDER BY clause in descending order

Grouping Data

When working with large amounts of data, it is often useful to group data to provide summary information. In SQL, you use the GROUP BY clause to group data by one or more columns. The SQL syntax for the GROUP BY clause is as follows:

GROUP BY {*column1* [,*column2*]...}

When using the GROUP BY clause, only those columns that are referenced in the GROUP BY clause can appear in the column list of the SELECT statement.

The GROUP BY clause is often used with aggregate SQL functions, as discussed in the next section.

For example, to return the total number of students for each major, you would use the following SQL statement. You will learn more about COUNT later. See Figure 2-15.

```
SELECT major, COUNT(*)
FROM students
GROUP BY major;
```

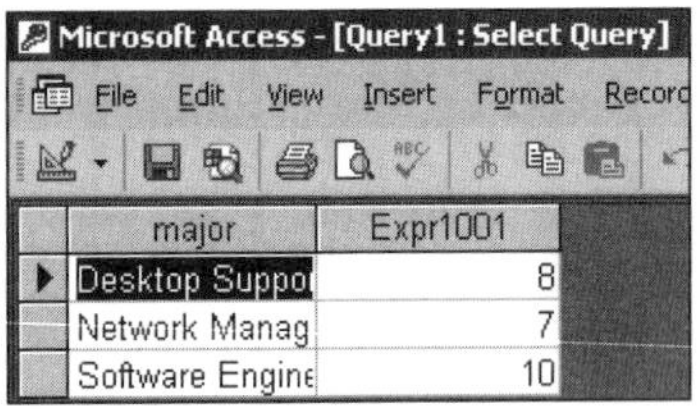

major	Expr1001
Desktop Suppo	8
Network Manag	7
Software Engine	10

Figure 2-15 Results from SELECT statement using GROUP BY clause

In some cases, you may need to restrict the rows that are returned by the GROUP BY clause. To do this, you must use the HAVING clause. The HAVING clause contains an expression that is evaluated after the data is grouped, and only the rows that meet the criteria of the expression are returned in the final result set. The format of the HAVING clause is as follows:

HAVING <*expression*>

For example, to obtain a list of the total amount of all awarded scholarships grouped by major, you would use the following SQL statement. You will learn more about the SUM function later. See Figure 2-16.

```
SELECT major, SUM(scholarship)
FROM students
GROUP BY major
HAVING SUM(scholarship) > 0;
```

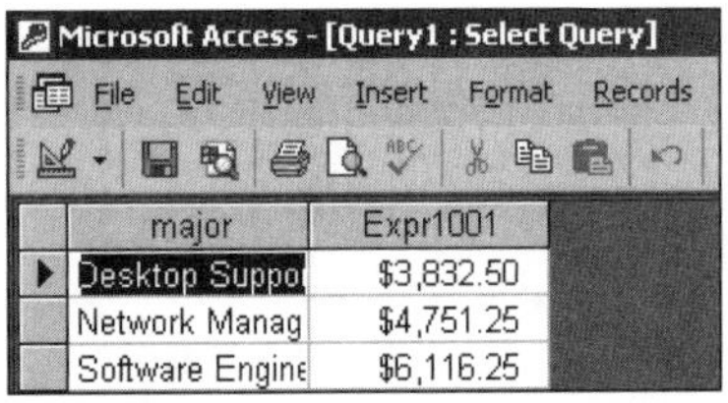

major	Expr1001
Desktop Suppo	$3,832.50
Network Manag	$4,751.25
Software Engine	$6,116.25

Figure 2-16 Results from SELECT statement using HAVING clause

Aggregate Functions in SQL

Aggregate functions are often used in SQL for reporting purposes, where you require information that is summarized. SQL has five main aggregate functions you can use. Although several other functions are available, the following sections cover the main ones.

COUNT()

The COUNT function is used to compute the total number of rows returned in the result set of a SELECT statement. You often use this function when you want to determine how many records are in a given table. For example, if you wanted to see how many students are currently on file at ABC College, you could use the following SELECT statement. See Figure 2-17.

```
SELECT COUNT(*) FROM students;
```

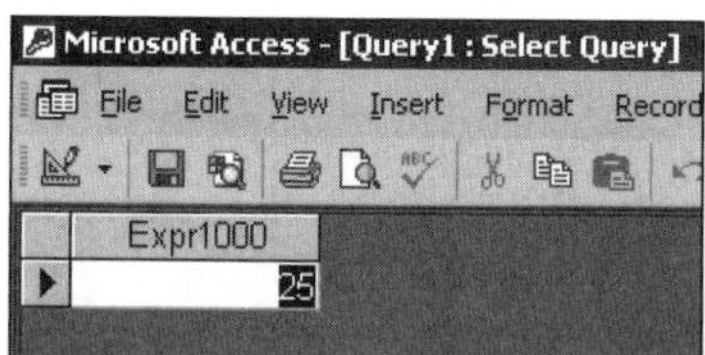

Figure 2-17 Results from SELECT statement using COUNT() function

SUM()

Use the SUM function to compute the sum of a numeric column from the result set of a SELECT statement. You often use this function with the GROUP BY clause, which was covered in the previous section. To see a straightforward example of the SUM function, you could determine the total value of scholarships awarded for all students enrolled at ABC College. The following query would provide this information. See Figure 2-18.

```
SELECT SUM(scholarship) FROM students;
```

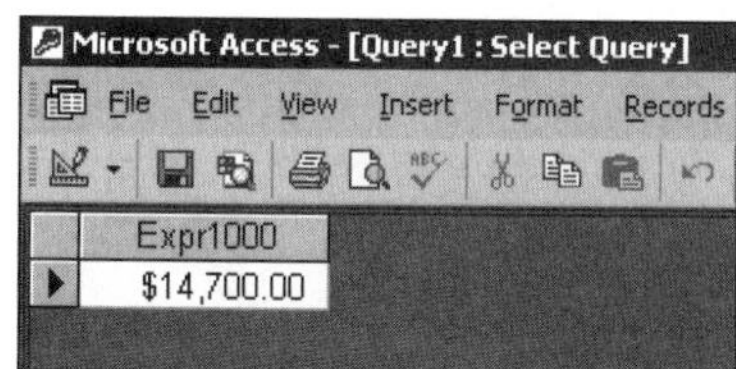

Figure 2-18 Results from SELECT statement using SUM() function

AVG()

Use the AVG function to compute the average value of a numeric column from the result set of a SELECT statement. For example, you would use the following query to determine the average scholarship amount for all the students enrolled at ABC College. See Figure 2-19.

```
SELECT AVG(scholarship) FROM students
WHERE scholarship > 0;
```

In the previous SELECT statement, you added the WHERE clause to include only students who have scholarships. If you did not include this WHERE clause, the calculations would be skewed because students without scholarships automatically default to the value $0.00, and the AVG() function would include these zero values in its calculation. The WHERE clause excludes students without scholarships and ensures that the correct group of students is averaged.

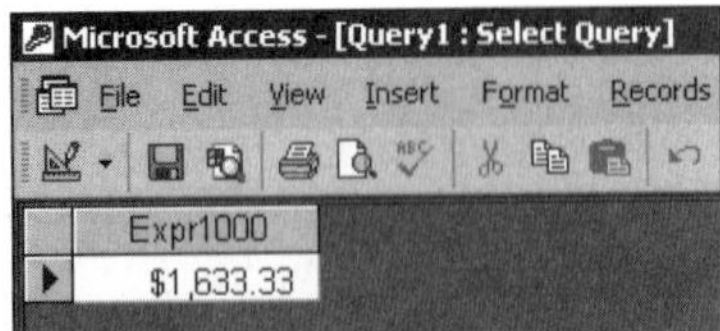

Figure 2-19 Results from SELECT statement using AVG() function

MAX()

Use the MAX function to compute the maximum value for a numeric column from the result set of a SELECT statement. You often use this function when creating a record in which you manually generate a value for a column designated as the primary key for the table. In the ABC College example, you can use the following query to determine the maximum scholarship amount from the students that are currently on file. See Figure 2-20.

```
SELECT MAX(scholarship) FROM students;
```

Figure 2-20 Results from SELECT statement using MAX() function

MIN()

Use the MIN function to compute the minimum value for a numeric column from the result set of a SELECT statement. Continuing from the previous example, you can use the following query to determine the minimum scholarship amount from the students currently on file. See Figure 2-21.

```
SELECT MIN(scholarship) FROM students
WHERE scholarship > 0;
```

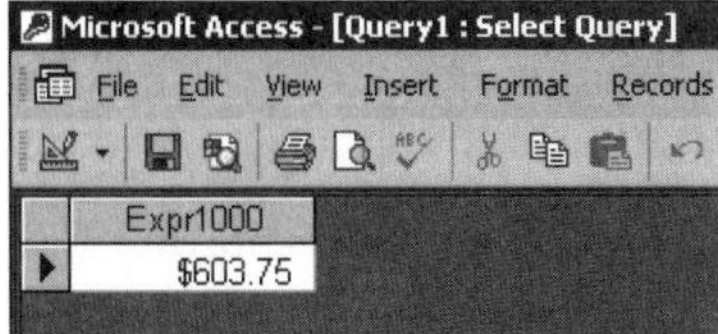

Figure 2-21 Results from SELECT statement using MIN() function

Retrieving Data Using Advanced Techniques

The previous section covered the basics of the SQL SELECT statement, focusing on retrievals involving a single table. In this section, you examine more complex queries that retrieve data from multiple tables, as well as nested SELECT statements.

Retrieving Data from More Than One Table

When retrieving data from a relational database such as Access, the data often comes from multiple tables. In order to retrieve data from more than one table, you need to join tables based on a relationship, which is usually done using a foreign key. A foreign key is a table column that is a primary key column from another table. For example, in the ABC College database, the student_id column is the primary key column that identifies a unique student. In the grades table, the student_id column is used to join the grades table to the students table. The student_id column becomes a foreign key column, which maintains what is called a primary–foreign key relationship. A student can have one or more grades depending on how many courses the student has enrolled in. Recall the entity relationship diagram (refer back to Figure 2-1), which shows that the Student entity maintains a one-to-many relationship with the Grade entity.

To see how to create a query that joins the students table to the grades table, execute the following SQL in Access.

To retrieve a list of grades for each student:

1. With College.mdb open in the Database window, click **Queries** on the Objects bar.
2. Double-click **Create query in Design view**.
3. Close the Show Table dialog box, if necessary.
4. Click **View** on the menu bar, then click **SQL View**.
5. Enter the following SQL SELECT statement:

```
SELECT last_name, first_name, grade
FROM students, grades
WHERE students.student_id = grades.student_id
```

6. Click **Query** on the menu bar, then click **Run** to process your SELECT statement. The query results show a table containing the names of students and their grades.
7. Click the **Close Window** button to close the window, and then click the **No** button when asked if you want to save the query. Leave the Database window open for the next set of steps.

If two tables in the FROM clause share the same column name, you must indicate in both the SELECT and WHERE clauses the table to which the column belongs. You do this by prefixing the column with the table name to which the column belongs. For example, in the previous query you needed to reference the student_id column in the WHERE clause by joining the students table to the grades table. Assume that you also want to include the student_id as part of the result set returned. You therefore need to include the student_id column in the SELECT clause, and specify the table to which the column belongs. You can include this column by modifying the original SELECT statement as follows:

```
SELECT students.student_id, last_name, first_name, grade
FROM students, grades
WHERE students.student_id = grades.student_id
```

Rather than including the full table name when referencing which table a column belongs to, you can use a table alias. A table alias provides a short form of reference to a table. You create an alias by including it in the FROM clause immediately following the table name.

You can incorporate table aliases into the previous example by modifying the SELECT statement as follows:

```
SELECT s.student_id, last_name, first_name, grade
FROM students s, grades g
WHERE s.student_id = g.student_id
```

When choosing alias names, try to maintain some consistency and do not use names that are more than a few characters; this negates any benefit of using an alias. One popular standard is to use the first character of the table name or the beginning character of each unique word of the table name.

Subqueries

Using the IN operator discussed earlier in this chapter, you can use nested queries (subqueries) to dynamically create lists or subsets. This is useful when you need to create a query where the list is not known at development time. To elaborate, suppose you want to produces the list of all students that have failed at least one course at ABC College. You could retrieve this information from the College database by using the IN operator along with a nested query that produces the list of student_id values you want.

To retrieve a list of students who have failed at least one course:

1. With College.mdb open in the Database window, click **Queries** on the Objects bar.
2. Double-click **Create query in Design view**.
3. Close the Show Table dialog box, if necessary.
4. Click **View** on the menu bar, then click **SQL View**.
5. Enter the following SQL SELECT statement:

```
SELECT student_id, last_name, first_name
FROM students
WHERE student_id IN (SELECT DISTINCT(student_id)
                FROM grades WHERE grade < 50);
```

6. Click **Query** on the menu bar, then click **Run** to process your SELECT statement. The query results show a table containing names of students who have failed at least one course.
7. Click the **Close Window** button to close the window, and then click the **No** button when asked if you want to save the query. Leave the Database window open for the next set of steps.

In the previous example, you included the DISTINCT function in the nested SELECT statement. The DISTINCT function returns rows where the student_id is unique. This prevents duplicate student_id values from appearing if the same student has failed more than one course. The query returns the same result if the DISTINCT function is omitted; however, the list contains duplicates that might increase the processing time for an SQL statement.

Correlated Subqueries

When using subqueries, you sometimes need to maintain a link between the records retrieved from the primary SELECT statement and the records retrieved by the nested or subquery SELECT statement. You use a correlated subquery when you need to reference one or more columns of the main SELECT statement from the inner subquery.

The syntax of the correlated subquery is the same as that of a normal subquery, except that the correlated subquery references one or more columns from tables referenced in the main SELECT statement.

For example, suppose you want to know the highest grade achieved by each student at ABC college. You can retrieve this information by using a correlated subquery.

To retrieve the highest grade achieved for each student:

1. With College.mdb open in the Database window, click **Queries** on the Objects bar.

2. Double-click **Create query in Design view**.
3. Close the Show Table dialog box, if necessary.
4. Click **View** on the menu bar, then click **SQL View**.
5. Enter the following SQL SELECT statement:

```
SELECT s.student_id, s.last_name, s.first_name, g.grade
FROM students s, grades g
WHERE s.student_id = g.student_id
   AND g.grade = (SELECT MAX(grade) FROM grades g2
                 WHERE g2.student_id = s.student_id);
```

6. Click **Query** on the menu bar, then click **Run** to process your SELECT statement. The query results show a table showing the students who have achieved the highest grades at the college.
7. Click the **Close Window** button to close the window, and then click the **No** button when asked if you want to save the query. Leave the Database window open for the next set of steps.

The previous example made reference to the grades table in both the parent SELECT statement and the subquery SELECT statement. To distinguish which table is being referenced in both SELECT statements, two different table aliases were used. Although not required, it removes some ambiguity and clearly indicates which table you are referencing.

Using EXISTS

The EXISTS operator is used to test for the existence of rows returned by a nested or subquery SELECT statement. In other words, it returns TRUE in a WHERE clause of the main SELECT statement if the nested query returns at least one record or row. It does not attempt to match a column or columns, and is typically used with correlated subqueries. The syntax for the EXISTS operator is as follows:

WHERE EXISTS (*SELECT* ...)

To work through an example using the EXISTS operator, you prepare a query to determine which students are enrolled in at least one course at ABC College.

To retrieve a list of students who are enrolled in at least one course:

1. With College.mdb open in the Database window, click **Queries** on the Objects bar.
2. Double-click **Create query in Design view**.
3. Close the Show Table dialog box, if necessary.
4. Click **View** on the menu bar, then click **SQL View**.

5. Enter the following SQL SELECT statement:

```
SELECT student_id, last_name, first_name
FROM students
WHERE EXISTS (SELECT * FROM grades
              WHERE grades.student_id = students.
              student_id);
```

6. Click **Query** on the menu bar, then click **Run** to process your SELECT statement. The query results show a table containing the students enrolled in at least one course.

7. Click the **Close Window** button to close the window, and then click the **No** button when asked if you want to save the query. Exit from Access.

When using the EXISTS operator, you do not have to specify a column (or columns) in the SELECT clause of the subquery. The EXISTS operator only checks to see if any records are retrieved by the subquery, and doesn't care if a column is specified or not. In the previous example, you could substitute a constant value of 1 instead of the wildcard symbol (*). In some databases, this change would yield better response time because the database wouldn't have to return any records from the table.

Chapter Summary

- A database is central to many applications and systems. The most common type of database used today is a relational database management system, such as Microsoft Access. A database contains one or more tables.
- Structured Query Language is an English-like computer language used to manipulate and retrieve data from a relational database management system. Access provides support for SQL.
- Tables are modeled after entities in a database model (known as an entity relationship diagram). Tables are composed of one or more columns. Each column has a specific data type as defined when the table is created.
- A primary key value is made up of one or more columns in a table that are used to identify a unique record. When a primary key value is specified on a table, no two records can contain the same value in the primary key.
- Use the SQL CREATE TABLE statement to create a table in a database, the INSERT statement adds a new record to a table, and the UPDATE statement updates one or more records in a table. When updating data, a WHERE clause is usually specified to indicate what records are to be updated.
- The DELETE statement in SQL is used to permanently remove one or more records from a table. A WHERE clause is almost always specified to indicate what records are to be deleted. When the WHERE clause is omitted, all data is deleted from a table. Caution should be exercised when using the DELETE statement.

- The SELECT statement is used in SQL for retrieving records from one or more tables. It forms the basis for most of the SQL you write.
- A WHERE clause is used to specifically restrict what rows are returned by a SELECT statement. A WHERE clause can contain one or more conditions joined by one or more logical operators (AND, OR, NOT).
- The ORDER BY clause is used to sort data returned by a SQL SELECT statement. When the sort order is not explicitly specified, the default sort order is descending.
- The GROUP BY clause is used to group the data returned by a SELECT statement by one or more columns. In conjunction with the GROUP BY clause, a HAVING clause can be used to restrict the grouped data.
- Aggregate functions are used for providing summarized numerical data in SQL. The most common SQL aggregate functions used are COUNT(), SUM(), MIN(), MAX(), and AVG().
- Subqueries provide a way to create dynamic conditions at run time (i.e., lists of values tested by the IN operator). Correlated subqueries are a form of subquery in which the inner query is dependent on the results returned by the outer query.
- The EXISTS operator is used for testing existence in an inner subquery.

REVIEW QUESTIONS

1. What type of database is Access?
   a. modern
   b. relational database management system
   c. flat file
   d. ASCII
2. Tables in a database are composed of ______________.
   a. properties
   b. identities
   c. features
   d. columns
3. To create a table in SQL, use the ______________ statement.
   a. NEW TABLE
   b. INSERT TABLE
   c. CREATE TABLE
   d. ALTER TABLE

4. Use a(n) ________________ to ensure that each record in a table contains a unique column value.
   a. primary key
   b. identity value
   c. foreign key
   d. unique value
5. You use the ________________ data type to store the value $199.99.
   a. NUMERIC
   b. DOLLAR
   c. CURRENCY
   d. DOUBLE
6. Which one of the following data types would you use in Access to store both numeric and character data in a column?
   a. CURRENCY
   b. TEXT
   c. DATE/TIME
   d. AUTONUMBER
7. You use the ________________ clause to sort data returned by a SELECT statement.
   a. ORDER BY
   b. SORT DATA
   c. GROUP BY
   d. HAVING
8. Use the ________________ function to determine the total number of records in a table.
   a. SUM()
   b. MAX()
   c. RECORDCOUNT()
   d. COUNT()
9. When appending new data to a table in SQL, you would use the ________________ statement.
   a. APPEND
   b. INSERT
   c. UPDATE
   d. CREATE

10. Use the ______________ SQL statement when you need to remove one or more records from a single table.
    a. REMOVE
    b. ERASE
    c. UPDATE
    d. DELETE
11. When a primary key of one table appears in another table, this column is referred to as a ______________.
    a. foreign key
    b. domestic key
    c. duplicate key
    d. unique key
12. Use the ______________ operator when you need to check for a possible range of values in a WHERE clause.
    a. RANGE
    b. EXISTS
    c. BETWEEN
    d. SUBSET
13. To compare a column to a list of possible values in the WHERE clause of a SELECT statement, you use the ______________ operator.
    a. =
    b. <>
    c. IS NULL
    d. IN
14. In a ______________ subquery, the inner query depends on the rows of the outer query.
    a. dependent
    b. grouped
    c. synchronized
    d. correlated
15. To prevent duplicate column values from being displayed in a SELECT statement, you use the ______________ function.
    a. UNIQUE
    b. DUPLICATE
    c. DISTINCT
    d. ALL

HANDS-ON EXERCISES

Exercise 2-1

The first step in developing an Access database system is to create the database file. To do this, you create a Guestbook database for the home page on your Web site using Access. You also create a single table using the Design view in Access.

To create a database and table in Access:

1. Start Access 2002.
2. Click File on the menu bar, then click New.
3. In the New File task pane, click Blank Database.
4. In the File name text box, type Guestbook.mdb. Click the Save in list arrow, navigate to the Chap02 folder in your work folder, and then click the Create New Folder button. Type Ex01 as the name of the new folder, click OK, and then click the Create button. The Database window opens in the Microsoft Access window.
5. To create a single table, click Tables on the Objects bar.
6. Double-click Create table in Design view.
7. Enter the following table attributes and columns:

Field name	Data type	Size	Properties	Description
email_address	Text	100	Primary key	The e-mail address of the person signing your guestbook
name	Text	75	NOT NULL	The person's full name
website	Text	100	NULL	The person's homepage or Web site
Comments	Memo	n/a	NULL	Comments left by the person signing your guestbook

8. Save your table as **guest**, and then close the Guestbook.mdb file.

Exercise 2-2

In some cases, it is useful to create your tables in Access using SQL. If written correctly, SQL is compatible with other database platforms. In this project, you extend the ABC College database from the chapter exercises to include the instructors table. This table contains information that is useful for registering students and tracking enrollment.

To use SQL to extend the ABC College database:

1. In Access 2002, open the ABC College database file, **College.mdb**, from the Chap02\Chapter folder in your work folder.
2. Click Queries on the Objects bar, and then click Create query in Design view. Close the Show Table dialog box. Change to SQL View.

3. Enter the following SQL statement:

```
CREATE TABLE instructors
 (instructor_id NUMERIC PRIMARY KEY,
 last_name TEXT(50) NOT NULL,
 first_name TEXT(35) NOT NULL,
 m_initial TEXT(1) NULL,
 faculty TEXT(50) NULL)
```

4. Use the Run command to execute this statement, and then verify your results by opening the table in the Design view. Check to make sure the properties are set correctly.
5. Click File on the menu bar, point to Get External Data, and then click Import.
6. Import the data in the **instructors.txt** data file from the Chap02\Exercises folder to a new instructors table.
7. Click the Next button until you are asked where to store the data. Click the In an Existing Table list arrow, and then click the instructors table you just created.
8. Click the Finish button. When you receive a message indicating that the data has been successfully imported, click OK. Leave the database open for the next exercise.

Exercise 2-3

The SELECT statement allows you to retrieve data from your database in your applications. Using the SELECT statement, retrieve data from the College.mdb database. You use a WHERE clause to restrict the SELECT statement to only retrieve data that matches the criteria you specify.

To use the SELECT statement to retrieve data:

1. With the College database open in Access, click Queries on the Objects bar, if necessary, and then double-click Create query in Design view. Close the Show Table dialog box, and then change to SQL View.
2. To determine which students have earned a passing grade in the Principles of Network Management course (NM101), enter the following SQL statement:

```
SELECT student_id
FROM grades
WHERE grade >= 50
AND course_no = "NM101";
```

3. Execute this statement and verify your results.
4. Enter a new SQL statement to change the course_no to produce a listing for other courses (SE101, DS101, and so on). You can retrieve a complete listing of courses by querying the Courses table:

```
SELECT DISTINCT course_no, course_name
FROM courses;
```

5. Execute this statement, and then verify your results.
6. Close the SQL Design View window, leaving the College database open in Access for the next exercise.

Exercise 2-4

SQL provides useful functions for processing aggregate data. It is very common to use these functions in most of the applications you develop. Using the College.mdb database, provide statistical data that can be used for enrollment purposes, such as setting standards for the entry of new students.

To use SQL aggregate functions such as AVG(), MAX(), and MIN():

1. With the College database open in Access, click Queries on the Objects bar, if necessary, and then double-click Create query in Design view. Close the Show Table dialog box, and then change to SQL View.
2. To determine the average grade for the SE301 (Object Oriented Programming I) course, enter the following SQL statement:

```
SELECT AVG(grade)
FROM grades
WHERE course_no = "SE301";
```

3. Execute this statement and verify your results.
4. Enter a new SQL statement to determine the maximum grade achieved for the SE301 course:

```
SELECT MAX(grade)
FROM grades
WHERE course_no = "SE301" ;
```

5. Execute this statement and verify your results.
6. Enter a new SQL statement to determine the minimum grade achieved for the SE301 course:

```
SELECT MIN(grade)
FROM grades
WHERE course_no = "SE301";
```

7. Execute this statement and verify your results.
8. Close the SQL View window, leaving the College database open in Access for the next exercise.

Exercise 2-5

In most cases, the data you retrieve comes from more than one table, and requires you to join tables in the WHERE clause of your SELECT statement. Most relationships, or table joins, require a common column or field to be present in both tables. In the following project, you join the students table to the grades table to produce a listing of grades for each full-time student at ABC College.

To join tables using a WHERE clause:

1. With the College database open in Access, click Queries on the Objects bar, if necessary, and then double-click Create query in Design view. Close the Show Table dialog box, and then change to SQL View.
2. To retrieve a list of full-time students and their grades, enter the following SQL statement:

```
SELECT s.student_id, s.last_name, s.first_name,
   s.middle_initial, g.course_no, g.grade
FROM students s, grades g
WHERE s.student_id = g.student_id
     AND s.full_time = Yes;
```

3. Execute this statement and verify your results.
4. Modify the query to include the course_name instead of the course_no column in your SELECT statement:

```
SELECT s.student_id, s.last_name, s.first_name,
   s.middle_initial, c.course_name, g.grade
FROM students s, grades g, courses c
WHERE s.student_id = g.student_id
     AND g.course_no = c.course_no
     AND s.full_time = Yes;
```

5. Execute this statement and verify your results.
6. Close the SQL View window, and then exit Access.

Web Programming Projects

Project 2-1

A local video rental store has asked you to develop a computerized system for tracking its customers and video rentals. Design and create a database named **video.mdb** to store this information. First, draft a database model and then create your database in Access using your design. Include tables to track customers, video titles, rentals, and any other data that a video rental store might want to track.

Project 2-2

The company president has scheduled an annual sales meeting that all salespeople must attend. During the meeting, the president will review the company's sales figures for the past fiscal year. Your IS manager has asked you to write several queries to provide the information that the company president has requested. Write queries to retrieve the following sales information for both the fiscal year and for each sales quarter. To prepare these queries, you need to use the **sales.mdb** file in the Chap02\Projects folder:

- Total sales for the company
- Region with the highest sales
- Region with the lowest sales
- Salesperson with the highest sales
- Salesperson with the lowest sales
- Average sales

The IS manager has requested these specific figures; however, think of other types of sales statistics you might provide.

Project 2-3

ABC College is expanding by opening new campuses throughout the eastern United States. The college has decided to use one centralized database to track all students, rather than maintain separate databases for each campus. In this Web Programming Project, you alter the existing College database to include changes which will allow for tracking students and courses from multiple campuses.

Start by modifying the College.mdb database that you saved in your Chap02\Exercises folder in your work folder. Save the modified database in your Chap02\Projects folder in your work folder.

The new version of the database should include a table named campus. Revise the other existing tables to include a new column to identify which campus is being referenced (for example, the student table will require a column to indicate at which campus the student is enrolled).

Once you have changed the structure of the College.mdb database, prepare INSERT and UPDATE statements to populate new data. This lets you to test the databases you have made.

CHAPTER

3

XML: PART I

In this chapter you will:

- Create basic XML documents
- Parse XML documents
- Study the rules for well-formed XML documents
- Work with special characters
- Add comments to your XML documents

Extensible Markup Language, or **XML**, is used for creating Web pages and for defining and transmitting data between applications. XML is based on **Standard Generalized Markup Language (SGML)**, which separates the actual content of a document from the way the content is displayed and formatted. Each element in an SGML document is marked according to its type, such as a paragraph, heading, and so on. How individual SGML elements are displayed is up to each target output format. For instance, the paragraphs in a printed document may look quite different in an online help system, although they represent the same type of element.

XML works in the same way, except the user agent that receives the XML document decides how to display it. **User agents** are devices that can retrieve and process documents created in XML and other markup languages such as HTML and XHTML. A user agent can be a traditional Web browser, a mobile phone, or a personal digital assistant (PDA). Understand that a user agent may not display an XML document at all, but instead may store it in a database or use it to perform a calculation.

As you work through this chapter and the next, keep in mind that XML is not really a Web programming tool at all, but a way of structuring your data. Although XML can be used to create and display Web pages, its most common use is in the definition, organization, and transfer of data between applications, including Web applications. Because XML is so commonly used in Web programming, it is considered an intrinsic part of the field and is therefore covered in this book.

XML 1.0 achieved recommendation status in 1998 by the **World Wide Web Consortium (W3C)**, which oversees the development of Web technology standards. XML 1.0 was still current at the time of this writing. XML is a markup language like HTML, but is not a replacement for HTML. XML was designed to describe data while HTML was designed primarily for displaying Web pages.

Creating Basic XML Documents

XML documents are text files, which means you can create them in any text editor such as Notepad or WordPad, or in any word-processing program capable of creating simple text files. If you use a text editor to create an XML document, you cannot view the final result until you open the document in a parser, which you will study in the next section. However, many applications (called XML editors) are designed specifically for creating XML documents. XML editors range from high-end, professional systems such as Arbortext Adept and Adobe FrameMaker+SGML to freeware systems such as Microsoft XML Notepad and IBM alphaWorks Xeena. All these XML editors still create simple text files, but they allow you to create your documents within a visual environment that automatically assists you in structuring your XML code.

An XML editor can greatly simplify the task of creating XML documents; once your XML skills increase, you will definitely want to use one. However, to become truly proficient in XML, you need to thoroughly understand how to structure the tags and attributes that make up an XML document. Unfortunately, XML editors often hide the actual XML document itself and display only the parts of the document that will be visible in a user agent. In other words, with an XML editor, you may not be able to easily see the XML document itself. For instance, Figure 3-1 shows an example of a simple XML document in Notepad. The XML document contains several tags that may be used for storing the information entered into a personal check. Notice that you can clearly see how the document is structured.

The display and formatting of XML in a user agent is accomplished through the use of Cascading Style Sheets (CSS) and Extensible Style Language (XSL). For more information on CSS and XSL, search for these topics on the Course Technology Web site at *www.course.com*.

Figure 3-2 shows the same XML document in XML Notepad. As you can see, XML Notepad does not show the actual structure of the document. Instead, it only shows the values assigned to each tag. For now, do not worry about how the XML tags are structured. The goal of this section is to explain how to create a simple XML document.

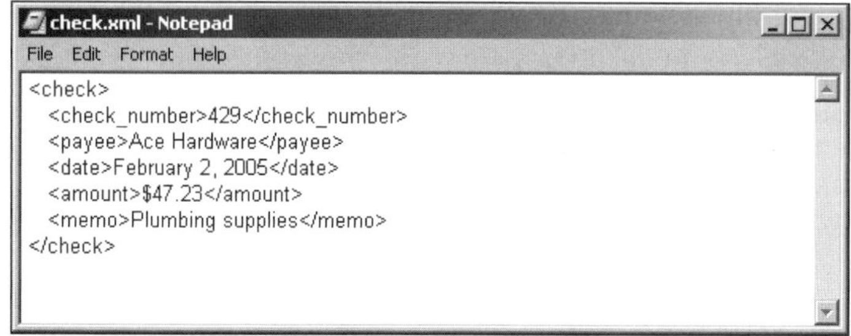

Figure 3-1 XML document in Notepad

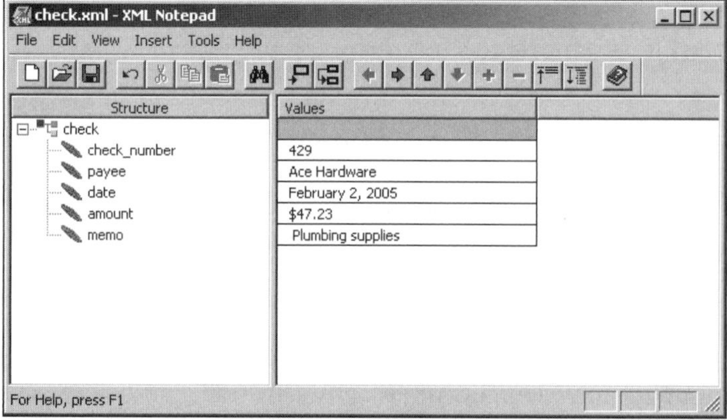

Figure 3-2 XML document in XML Notepad

You can view the underlying XML code in XML Notepad by clicking View on the menu bar and then clicking Source. In fact, almost every XML editor gives you the option of viewing the underlying XML code. As a beginner, however, it is important that you see exactly how an XML document is structured while you are creating it. For this reason, you will create your XML documents in this book using a simple text editor such as Notepad.

Next you will create a simple XML document that contains your mailing address.

To create an XML document that contains personal information:

1. Start your text editor and create a document.
2. Type the following opening tag to begin the document:

```
<Mailing_Address>
```

3. Next, add the following tags that contain your mailing address. Be sure to replace the text within each tag pair with your own information.

```
<Name>your name</Name>
<Address>your address</Address>
<City>your city</City><State>your state</State>
<Zip>your zip code</Zip>
```

4. Type the closing mailing address tag, as follows:

```
</Mailing_Address>
```

5. Save the file as **Ch03XML01.xml** in the Chap03\Chapter folder in your work folder.

XML Elements and Attributes

In XML you refer to a tag pair and the information it contains as an **element**. All elements must have an opening tag and a closing tag, or the document is not well formed. The information contained within an element's opening and closing tags is referred to as its **content**. You can think of elements as the basic building blocks of all XML documents. You use various parameters, called **attributes**, to configure XML elements. Attributes are placed before the closing bracket of the starting tag, and are separated from the tag name or other attributes with a space.

One XML concept that can be difficult to grasp for programmers who know HTML is that XML does not define any elements or attributes. Instead, you define your own tags and attributes to describe the data in your document. For instance, the following XML code defines several tags that describe the data associated with an automobile. The <make> element also defines a manufacturer attribute.

```
<auto>
     <make manufacturer="GM">Chevrolet</make>
     <model>Corvette</model>
     <year>1967</year>
     <color>Red</color>
</auto>
```

The XML Declaration

XML documents should begin with an **XML declaration**, which specifies the version of XML being used. You are not actually required to include an XML declaration because currently only one version of XML exists, version 1.0. However, it's good practice to always include the XML declaration because XML will almost certainly evolve into other versions that will contain features not found in version 1.0. Specifying the version with the XML declaration helps ensure that whatever user agent or application is parsing an XML document knows which version to use (assuming that newer versions will be released).

You can use the following three properties with the XML declaration: version, standalone, and encoding. All of the properties are optional, but you should at least include the version property, which designates the XML version number (currently "1.0"). The following statement is an XML declaration that only includes the version property:

```
<?xml version="1.0"?>
```

The XML declaration is not actually a tag, but a processing instruction, which is a special statement that passes information to the user agent or application that is processing the XML document. You can easily recognize processing instructions because they begin with <? and end with ?>.

The encoding property of the XML declaration designates the language used by the XML document. Although English is the primary language used on the Web, it is certainly not the only one. To be a considerate resident of the international world of the Web, use the encoding property of the XML declaration to designate the character set for your XML document. English and many western European languages use the iso-8859-1 character set. Therefore, you should use the following XML declaration in your documents:

```
<?xml version="1.0" encoding="iso-8859-1"?>
```

The standalone property indicates whether a document requires a **Document Type Definition (DTD)** in order to be rendered correctly. Languages based on SGML use a DTD to define the elements and attributes that can be used in a document. Unlike other SGML-based languages, XML documents do not require a DTD to be rendered correctly. Given that XML does not include any predefined elements, it does not need a DTD to define them. Because the tags associated with an XML document are defined within the document itself instead of a separate DTD, XML is said to be **self-describing**. This is especially important for user agents such as mobile phones and PDAs that do not have the power to process a DTD. However, some XML documents may benefit from a DTD, especially if multiple XML documents share the same elements. If your XML document requires a DTD, then you assign the standalone property a value of "no." However, if you are certain that your XML document will not require a DTD, then you assign the standalone property a value of "yes." For instance, you use the following XML declaration for any XML documents that do not require a DTD:

```
<?xml version="1.0" encoding="iso-8859-1"
standalone="yes"?>
```

You will learn how to define DTDs for your XML documents in Chapter 4.

Next, you will open the Ch03XML01.xml file and add an XML declaration.

To add an XML declaration that includes the version, encoding, and standalone properties:

1. Return to the **Ch03XML01.xml** file in your text editor.
2. At the top of the file, add the following XML declaration that includes the version, encoding, and standalone properties:

```
<?xml version="1.0" encoding="iso-8859-1"
standalone="yes"?>
```

3. Save and close the **Ch03XML01.xml** file. Your file should resemble the statements shown in Figure 3-3.

```
<?xml version="1.0" encoding="iso-8859-1"
     standalone="yes"?>
<Mailing_Address>
     <Name>your name</Name>
     <Address>your address</Address>
     <City>your city</City>
     <State>your state</State>
     <Zip>your zip</Zip>
</Mailing_Address>
```

Figure 3-3 Ch03XML01.xml after adding an XML declaration

PARSING AN XML DOCUMENT

When you open an HTML document that is not written properly, such as a document that does not include the closing </html> tag, the browser simply ignores the error and renders the page anyway. However, XML documents must adhere to some strict rules, the most important being that all tags must be closed. When a document adheres to XML's syntax rules, it is said to be **well formed**. (The W3C actually uses the term "well formedness"; this book uses the term "well formed.") You use a program called a **parser** to check whether an XML document is well formed.

There are two types of parsers: nonvalidating and validating. A nonvalidating parser simply checks whether an XML document is well formed. A validating parser checks whether an XML document is well formed and also whether the document conforms to an associated DTD. In this section, you will learn how to use a nonvalidating parser. You will use a validating parser in the next chapter when you learn how to write DTDs for your XML documents.

Internet Explorer, Netscape, and other browsers have the capability to act as nonvalidating parsers. If a nonvalidating parser finds that a document is well formed, it displays the document's XML tags and data. If an XML document is not well formed, then the parser displays the error. For instance, if you open the XML document containing the automobile data in Internet Explorer and the document is well formed, then Internet Explorer correctly parses and displays the document, as shown in Figure 3-4.

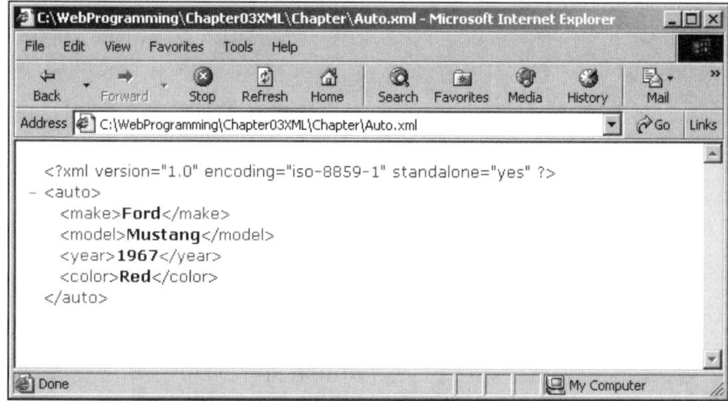

Figure 3-4 XML document in Internet Explorer that is well formed

However, if the automobile XML document is missing the closing </auto> tag, then it is not well formed. In this case, Internet Explorer points to the error, as shown in Figure 3-5.

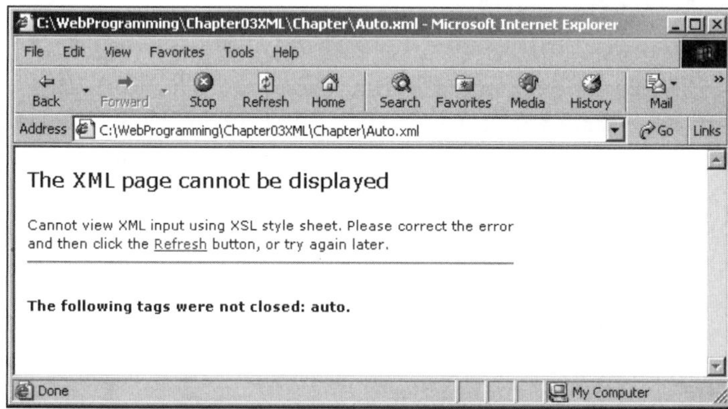

Figure 3-5 XML document in Internet Explorer that is not well formed

Next, you will parse an XML document.

To parse the Ch03XML01.xml document:

1. Open the **Ch03XML01.xml** file in Internet Explorer or another Web browser. If you created the document properly, your Web browser should resemble Figure 3-6. If you did not create the document properly, fix the error that appears in the browser and reload the document.

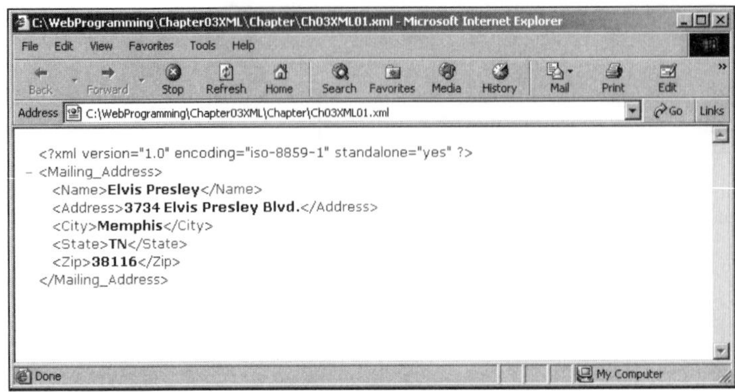

Figure 3-6 Ch03XML01.xml file in Internet Explorer

2. Close your Web browser.

Writing Well-Formed Documents

One reason that XML documents need to be well formed is to allow user agents and Web programs to easily read the document's data. User agents and Web programs expect XML data to be structured according to specific rules, which allow the user agent or Web program to parse the data quickly without worrying whether it contains structural problems.

In this section, you will study the rules for writing well-formed XML documents. The most important of these rules are:

- All XML documents must have a root element.
- XML is case sensitive.
- All XML tags must have a closing tag.
- XML elements must be properly nested.
- Attribute values must be quoted.
- Empty elements must be closed.

Next, you will study each of these rules.

All XML Documents Must Have a Root Element

A **root element** contains other elements on a page. The <html>...</html> element is the root element for HTML documents, although it's not required. XML documents, on the other hand, do require a root element that you define yourself. For instance, the root element for the XML document containing the automobile data is the <auto> element. If you do not include a root element, then the XML document is not well formed. For instance, the following version of the XML automobile document is illegal because it is missing the <auto> root element:

```
<?xml version="1.0" encoding="iso-8859-1"
     standalone="yes"?>
<make>Ford</make><model>Mustang</model>
<year>1967</year><color>Red</color>
```

Next, you will start creating an XML document that stores data associated with fiction and nonfiction books.

To start creating an XML document that stores data:

1. Create a document in your text editor.
2. Type the XML declaration, as follows:

   ```
   <?xml version="1.0" encoding="iso-8859-1"
   standalone="yes"?>
   ```

3. Next, type the opening and closing tag for a root element <books>:

   ```
   <books>
   </books>
   ```

4. Save the file as **Ch03XML02.xml** in the Chap03\Chapter folder in your workfolder, and then open it in Internet Explorer. Your Web browser should look like Figure 3-7.

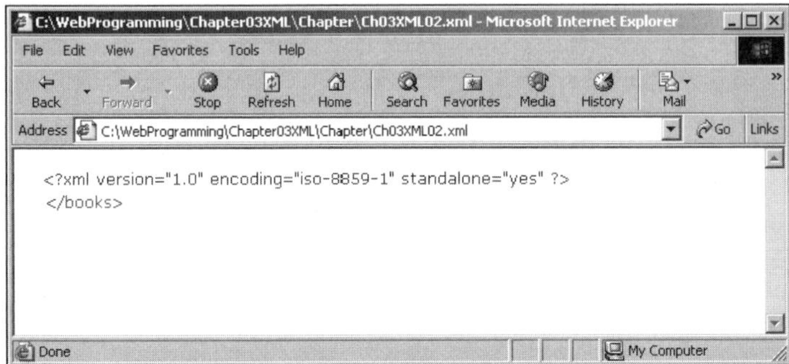

Figure 3-7 Ch03XML02.xml in Internet Explorer

5. Close your Web browser.

XML is Case Sensitive

Unlike HTML tags, XML tags are case sensitive. For instance, in an HTML document it makes no difference whether the bold tag is uppercase or lowercase. Both of the following HTML statements are rendered properly in a Web browser:

```
<B>This line is bold.</B>
<b>This line is also bold.</b>
```

You can even mix and match the cases of tags in an HTML document, as in the following statements:

```
<B>This line is bold.</b>
<b>This line is also bold.</B>
```

With XML, however, you cannot mix the case of tags. For instance, if you have an opening tag named <color> that is all lowercase, you must also use lowercase letters for the closing tag, as follows:

```
<color>Red</color>
```

If you use a different case for an opening and closing tag, they are treated as completely separate tags, resulting in a document that is not well formed. The following statement, for instance, is incorrect because the case of the closing tag does not match the case of the opening tag:

```
<color>Red</COLOR>
```

For practice, you will introduce a case error into your XML document to see the error that is raised in your nonvalidating parser (Internet Explorer).

To introduce a case error into the Ch03XML02.xml document:

1. Return to the **Ch03XML02.xml** file in your text editor.
2. Modify the closing **</books>** tag so it is uppercase. Your file should appear as follows:

```
<?xml version="1.0" encoding="iso-8859-1"
standalone="yes"?>
<books>
</BOOKS>
```

3. Save the **Ch03XML02.xml** file and then open it in Internet Explorer. You should receive the error shown in Figure 3-8. As you can see, the </BOOKS> end tag does not match the <books> start tag.
4. Close your Web browser and change the closing </BOOKS> tag back to lowercase letters.
5. Save the **Ch03XML02.xml** file, and then reopen it in Internet Explorer. The file should open correctly.
6. Close your Web browser.

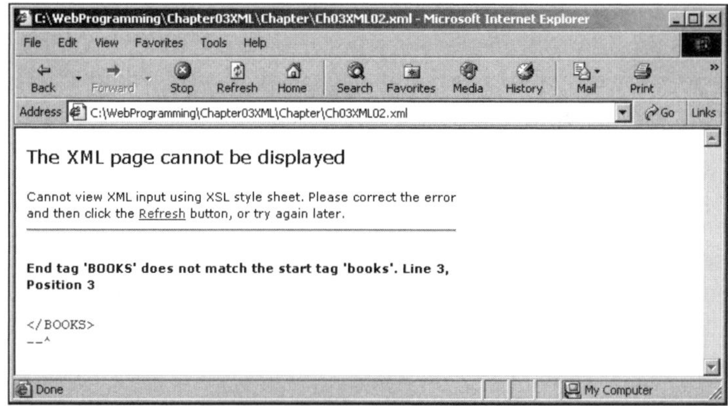

Figure 3-8 Case-sensitivity error raised in Internet Explorer

All XML Tags Must Have a Closing Tag

As mentioned earlier, most Web browsers usually look the other way if the code in an HTML document is not properly structured. One common example is the paragraph tag, <p>. The <p> tag should be used to mark a block of text as a single paragraph by enclosing the text within a <p>...</p> tag pair, as follows:

```
<p>Sacramento is the capital of California.</p>
```

Many Web designers, however, do not follow this convention. They simply place a <p> tag at the end of a block of text to create a paragraph, as follows:

```
Sacramento is the capital of California.<p>
```

One of the reasons this is possible is that Web browsers usually treat HTML documents as text that contains formatting tags. XML, however, is designed to organize data, not display it. For this reason, XML documents consist of tags that contain text, not of text that contains tags. To emphasize this concept, in XML you refer to a tag pair and the information it contains as an element. All elements must have a closing tag or the document is not well formed. For instance, in the XML document you saw earlier for the automobile data, all of the elements have a corresponding closing tag. The following version of the document is illegal because there are no corresponding closing tags for the <make>, <model>, <year>, and <color> elements:

```
<?xml version="1.0" encoding="iso-8859-1"
     standalone="yes"?>
<auto>
     <make>Ford<model>Mustang
     <year>1967<color>Red
</auto>
```

You may have noticed that the XML declaration does not include a closing tag. This is because the XML declaration is not actually part of the document; it only declares the document as an XML document. For this reason, it does not require a closing tag.

Next, you will add two <book> elements to your XML file. Each <book> element will contain the title of a book.

To add two <book> elements to the Ch03XML02.xml file:

1. Return to the **Ch03XML02.xml** file in your text editor.
2. Modify the document as follows to include two <book> elements. Be sure to add the elements within the <books> root element. For now, do not include the closing </book> tag.

```
<?xml version="1.0" encoding="iso-8859-1"
standalone="yes"?>
<books>
     <book>Of Mice and Men
     <book>Diplomacy
</books>
```

3. Save the **Ch03XML02.xml** file, and then open it in Internet Explorer. You should receive the error shown in Figure 3-9. As you can see, the error is raised because Internet Explorer cannot find the ending tag for the <book> element.

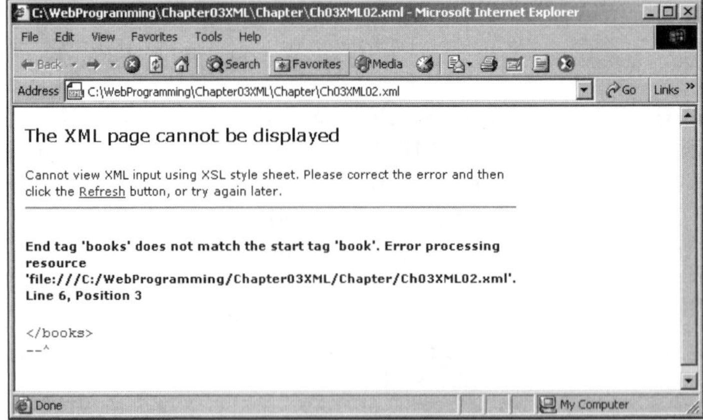

Figure 3-9 Missing closing tag error raised in Internet Explorer

4. Close your Web browser and add the closing **</book>** tags to each of the <book> elements. Your document should appear as follows:

```
<?xml version="1.0" encoding="iso-8859-1"
     standalone="yes"?>
<books>
     <book>Of Mice and Men</book>
     <book>Diplomacy</book>
</books>
```

5. Save the **Ch03XML02.xml** file, and then reopen it in Internet Explorer. Your Web browser should look like Figure 3-10.

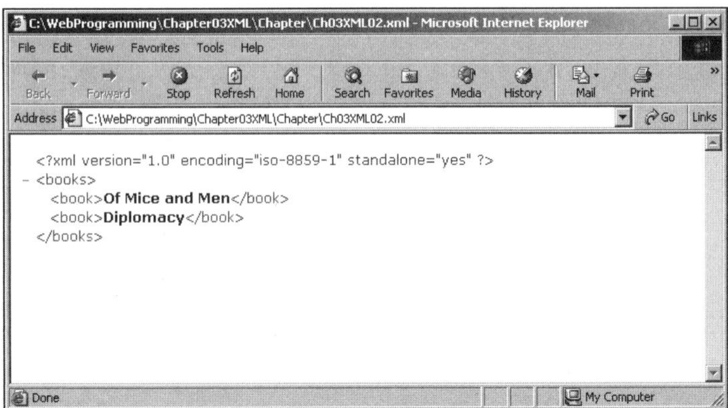

Figure 3-10 Ch03XML02.xml after adding the <book> elements

6. Close your Web browser.

XML Elements Must Be Properly Nested

Nesting refers to how tags are structured in a document. When you write an HTML document, it makes no difference how you nest your tags. Examine the following HTML statement, which applies boldface and italics to the text within a paragraph:

```
<p><b><i>This paragraph is bold and italicized.</b></p></i>
```

Notice in the preceding statement that the third element applied is the <i> tag. This is considered the innermost element. In XML, each innermost element must be closed before another element is closed. In the preceding statement, however, the <b> and <p> tags are closed before the <i> tag is closed. Although this makes no difference in HTML, in XML this statement must be written as follows:

```
<p><b><i>This paragraph is bold and italicized.</i></b></p>
```

As another example, consider the following version of the XML document containing the automobile data. The code is not well formed because the <make> element is improperly nested in the <model> element.

```
<?xml version="1.0" encoding="iso-8859-1"
     standalone="yes"?>
<auto>
     <make>Ford<model>Mustang</make></model>
     <year>1967</year><color>Red</color>
</auto>
```

In order for the preceding code to be well formed, the <model> element must close before the <make> element, as follows:

```
<?xml version="1.0" encoding="iso-8859-1"
     standalone="yes"?>
<auto>
     <make>Ford<model>Mustang</model></make>
     <year>1967</year><color>Red</color>
</auto>
```

Next, you will modify the <book> elements in the Ch03XML02.xml file to include nested elements that describe more detailed information about each book.

To modify the XML file to include nested book elements:

1. Return to the **Ch03XML02.xml** file in your text editor.
2. Replace the <book> element for *Of Mice and Men* with the following nested elements that contain information on the book's title and author. Notice that the <title> and <author> elements are nested within the <book> element, and that the <first_name> and <last_name> elements are nested within the <author> element.

```
<book>
     <title>Of Mice and Men</title>
     <author>
          <first_name>John</first_name>
          <last_name>Steinbeck</last_name>
     </author>
</book>
```

3. Next, replace the <book> element for *Diplomacy* with the following nested elements:

```
<book>
     <title>Diplomacy</title>
     <author>
          <first_name>Henry</first_name>
          <last_name>Kissinger</last_name>
     </author>
</book>
```

4. Save the **Ch03XML02.xml** file, and then open it in Internet Explorer. Your Web browser should look like Figure 3-11.

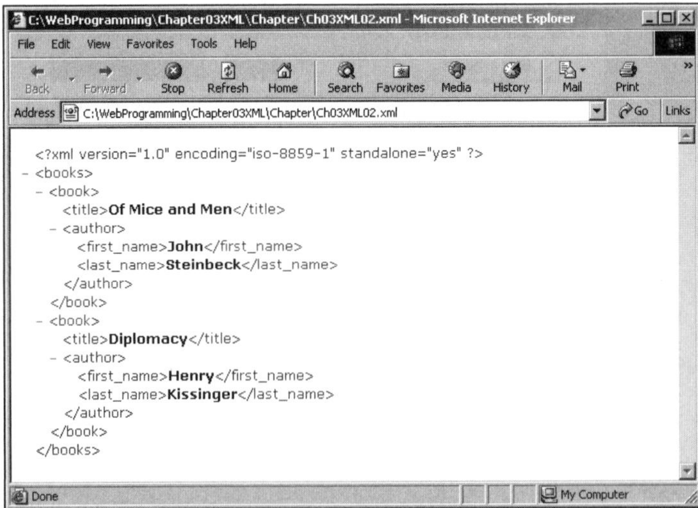

Figure 3-11 Ch03XML02.xml after adding nested elements

5. Close your Web browser.

Attribute Values Must Be Quoted

The value assigned to an attribute in an HTML document can either be contained in quotes or assigned directly to the attribute, provided there are no spaces in the value being assigned. For example, a common HTML attribute is the src attribute of the image tag, <img>. You assign to the src attribute the name of the image file you want to display in your document. The following code shows two <img> tags. Even though the first tag includes quotes around the value assigned to the src attribute and the second tag does not, both statements can function correctly.

```
<img src="dog.gif">Image of a dog</img>
<img src=cat.gif>Image of a cat</img>
```

With XML, you must place quotes around the values assigned to an attribute. For instance, in the XML automobile document you may add an empty <manufacturer> element that includes a single attribute named company, which stores the name of the automobile's manufacturer. You must include quotations around the value assigned to the company attribute using a statement similar to `<manufacturer company="General Motors"/>`. Omitting the quotations in the statement `<manufacturer company=General Motors/>` results in a document that is not well formed.

You cannot include an empty attribute in an element, meaning that you must assign a value to an attribute or exclude it from the element. For instance, the tag `<manufacturer company>` is incorrect because no value is being assigned to the company attribute.

Next, you will add an attribute named `genre` to each of the <book> elements in your example XML document. The `genre` attribute stores a value that describes each book's genre.

To add an attribute named `genre` to each of the <book> elements:

1. Return to the **Ch03XML02.xml** file in your text editor.
2. Modify the opening tag for the *Of Mice and Men* <book> element so it includes the `genre` attribute, assigned a value of "fiction":

```
<book genre="fiction">
```

3. Modify the opening tag for the *Diplomacy* <book> element so it includes the `genre` attribute, assigned a value of "nonfiction":

```
<book genre="nonfiction">
```

4. Save the **Ch03XML02.xml** file, and then open it in Internet Explorer. Your Web browser should look like Figure 3-12.

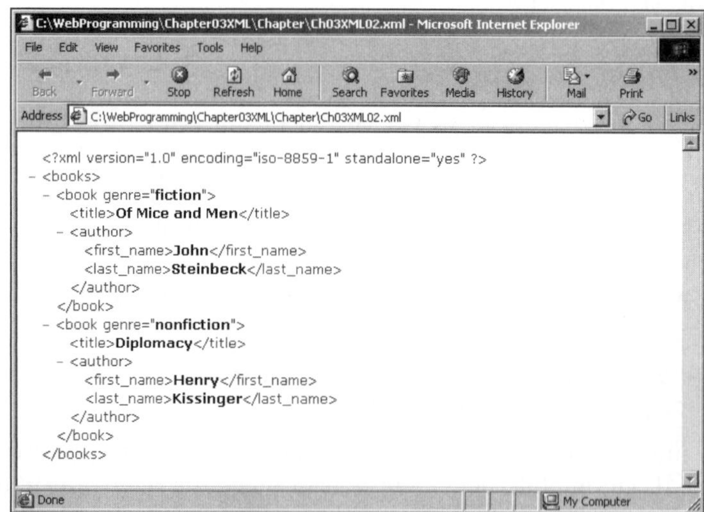

Figure 3-12 Ch03XML02.xml after adding attributes

5. Close your Web browser.

Empty Elements Must Be Closed

A number of elements in HTML do not have corresponding ending tags, including the <hr> tag, which inserts a horizontal rule into the document, and the <br> tag, which inserts a line break. Elements that do not require an ending tag are called **empty elements**. You can also create an empty element in an XML document by adding a single slash (/) before the tag's closing bracket to close the element. Most often, you use an empty element for elements that do not require content between their tag pairs, such as an image. For instance, in the XML document of automobile data, you may create a <photo> tag with a single attribute that stores the name of an image file. This file contains a photograph of the automobile. An example of the <photo> empty element is shown in the following XML code:

```
<?xml version="1.0" standalone="yes"?>
<auto>
     <photo image_name="mustang.jpg"/>
     <make>Ford</make><model>Mustang</model>
     <year>1967</year><color>Red</color>
</auto>
```

Remember that the primary purpose of XML is to structure data. An empty image element such as the one shown in the XML automobile document only provides the name of the associated image file—it does not display it. Although you can display an image from an XML document if you use CSS and XSL, your goal in this chapter and the next is to understand how to structure XML data so it can be transferred between Web applications.

Next, you will add an empty element named `cover_art` to the Ch03XML02.xml file. This element contains a single attribute that stores the name of an image file containing the cover art for each book.

To add an empty element to your example XML document:

1. Return to the **Ch03XML02.xml** file in your text editor.
2. Add an empty `cover_art` element as a nested element to the *Of Mice and Men* <book> element, as follows:

```
<book genre="fiction">
     <cover_art filename="mice_and_men.jpg"/>
     <title>Of Mice and Men</title>
     <author>
          <first_name>John</first_name>
          <last_name>Steinbeck</last_name>
     </author>
</book>
```

3. Now add an empty **`cover_art`** element as a nested element to the *Diplomacy* <book> element, as follows:

```
<book genre="nonfiction">
     <cover_art filename="diplomacy.jpg"/>
     <title>Diplomacy</title>
     <author>
          <first_name>Henry</first_name>
          <last_name>Kissinger</last_name>
     </author>
</book>
```

4. Save the **Ch03XML02.xml** file, and then open it in Internet Explorer. Your Web browser should look like Figure 3-13.

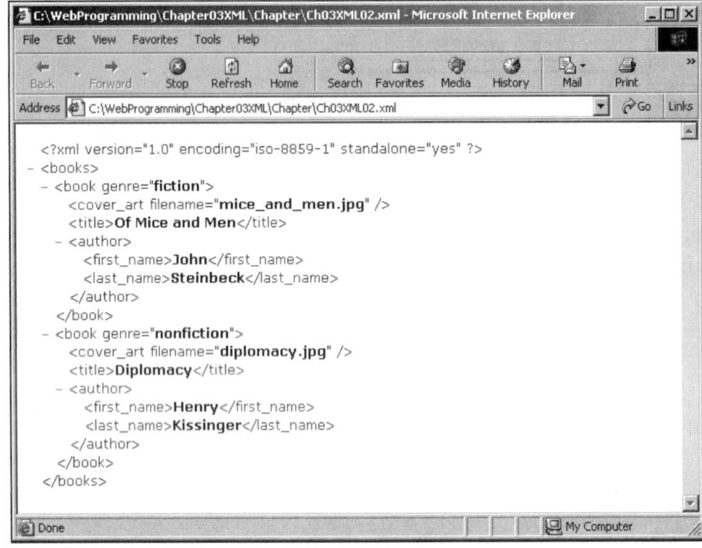

Figure 3-13 Ch03XML02.xml after adding empty elements

5. Close your Web browser.

Working with Special Characters

You will often find it necessary to add special characters to your XML documents, such as a copyright symbol (©) or a foreign character like the Latin capital letter E with a circumflex (Ê). You add special characters to an XML document using predefined character entities or numeric character references.

Predefined Character Entities

Five special symbols are used to help structure an XML document. If you want to display these symbols as content instead, use **predefined character entities**. You display a predefined character entity by preceding the character entity's name with an ampersand (&) and by following the name with a semicolon. Table 3-1 lists the five predefined XML character entities.

Table 3-1 Predefined character entities

Predefined character entity	Represented character
<	< (Less-than symbol)
&	& (Ampersand)
>	> (Greater-than symbol)
"	" (Double quotation)
'	' (Single quotation)

As you know, the less-than and greater-than symbols mark the beginning and end of XML tags, although they are also commonly used in math equations. However, if you add either symbol to the content of an XML element, a user agent or application will try to interpret it as the beginning or ending bracket of an XML tag. The solution is to use the predefined character entity. For instance, the following XML document contains an equation that may be presented in a math quiz. However, the equation will cause an error when it is parsed, because the parser will assume that the less-than symbol is the starting bracket of a tag that did not include a closing bracket.

```
<?xml version="1.0" encoding="iso-8859-1"
      standalone="yes"?>
<Quiz>
      <Question_1>How do you solve the following
            equation?</Question_1>
      <Equation_1>2(x - 1) < 3(2x + 3)</Equation_1>
</Quiz>
```

To fix the problem, you replace the less-than symbol in the equation with the < predefined character entity, as follows:

```
<?xml version="1.0" encoding="iso-8859-1"
      standalone="yes"?>
<Quiz>
      <Question_1>How do you solve the following
            equation?</Question_1>
      <Equation_1>2(x - 1) &lt; 3(2x + 3)</Equation_1>
</Quiz>
```

Finally, you should use predefined character entities for any ampersands or quotations you want to include in your Web pages. Because the ampersand is the starting character for predefined character entities, and quotation marks are used for assigning values to tag attributes, a user agent or application may become confused if it encounters these symbols within the text of an XML document. For instance, the following XML document uses both the & and " predefined character entities:

```
<?xml version="1.0" encoding="iso-8859-1"
standalone="yes"?>
<Company>
     <Name>Sanders &amp; Sons Construction, Inc.</Name>
     <Motto>Our motto is &quot;Pride before
           profit&quot;</Motto>
</Company>
```

Next, you will add a new <book> element to the **Ch03XML02.xml** file for an educational book named *Cultural Anthropology*, 2nd Edition, written by Barbara D. Miller, and published by Allyn & Bacon. You will include a new <publisher> element as part of the <book> element that lists the publisher's name. Because the publisher, Allyn & Bacon, includes an ampersand in its name, you will use the & predefined character entity.

To add a new <book> element to the Ch03XML02.xml file:

1. Return to the **Ch03XML02.xml** file in your text editor.
2. Add the following <book> element just above the closing </books> root tag. Notice that the ampersand in Allyn & Bacon is replaced with the & predefined character entity.

```
<book genre="educational">
     <publisher>Allyn &amp; Bacon</publisher>
     <title>Cultural Anthropology, 2nd Edition</title>
     <author>
           <first_name>Barbara D.</first_name>
           <last_name>Miller</last_name>
     </author>
</book>
```

3. Save the **Ch03XML02.xml** file, and then open it in Internet Explorer. Your Web browser should look like Figure 3-14. Notice that the & predefined character entity appears as an ampersand in the figure.
4. Close your Web browser.

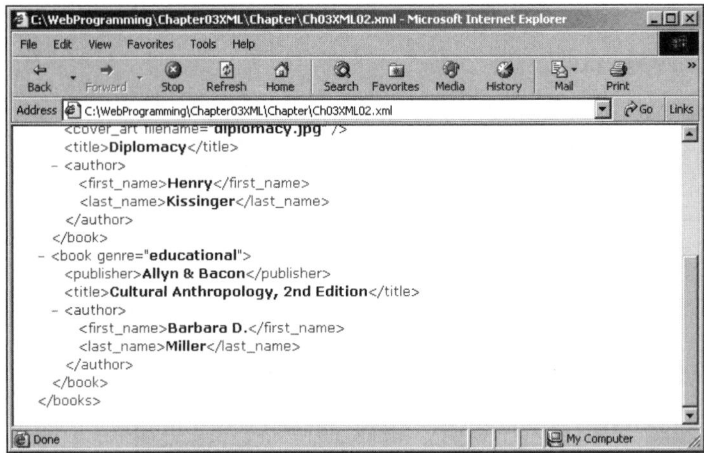

Figure 3-14 Ch03XML02.xml after adding a new <book> element with a predefined character entity

Numeric Character References

What if you need to use a character that is not available on your keyboard or is not one of the predefined character entities? A **numeric character reference** inserts a special character using its numeric position in the Unicode character set. **Unicode** is a standardized character set of numeric representations capable of displaying characters from all the world's languages.

The character set that is most commonly used today is the American Standard Code for Information Interchange, or ASCII, which is a standardized set of numeric representations for English characters. However, the Unicode character set contains the ASCII character set. In fact, Unicode will eventually replace ASCII entirely because of ASCII's limitation to English characters.

A number represents each character in the Unicode character set. You display a character using a numeric character reference by preceding the character's Unicode number with an ampersand (&) and the number sign (#) and by following the number with a semicolon. For instance, the Unicode numbers for the uppercase letters "A," "B," and "C" are 65, 66, and 67, respectively. You could display these letters using the following numeric character references:

```
<?xml version="1.0" encoding="iso-8859-1"
standalone="yes"?>
<Alphabet>
     <Letters>&#65;, &#66;, &#67;</Letters>
</Alphabet>
```

Figure 3-15 shows how the preceding XML document would parse in Internet Explorer.

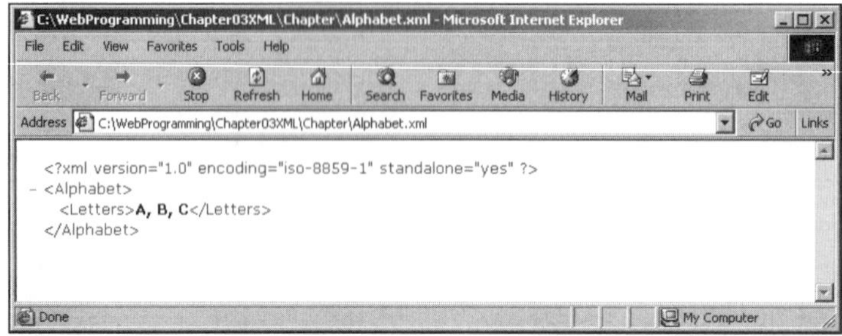

Figure 3-15 XML document with numeric character references

Obviously, you do not need to use numeric character references for letters or numbers. However, you use the same syntax to display special characters in the Unicode character set. For instance, the Unicode number for a copyright symbol is 169. Therefore, you can display the copyright symbol in an XML document using a numeric character reference of `©`.

Table 3-2 lists the numeric character references for some of the more commonly used special characters.

Table 3-2 Numeric character references

Character	Description	Numeric character reference
¢	Cent	¢
£	Pound	£
¥	Yen	¥
©	Copyright	©
®	Registered trademark	®
<	Less than	<
>	Greater than	>
&	Ampersand	&
"	Quotation	"

You can find a complete listing of numeric character references at *www.macchiato.com/unicode/charts.html*.

Next, you will add a new <copyright> element to each of the <book> elements in the Ch03XML02.xml file. The contents of each <copyright> element will contain the copyright symbol (©) along with the publishing year. You will use the © numeric character reference to display the copyright symbol in each <copyright> element's content.

To add a new <copyright> element to each of the <book> elements in the Ch03XML02.xml file:

1. Return to the **Ch03XML02.xml** file in your text editor.
2. Add the following **<copyright>** element immediately after the <title> element for *Of Mice and Men*.

```
<copyright>&#169; 1937</copyright>
```

3. Next, add the following **<copyright>** element immediately after the <title> element for *Diplomacy*.

```
<copyright>&#169; 1994</copyright>
```

4. Finally, add the following **<copyright>** element immediately after the <title> element for *Cultural Anthropology*, 2nd Edition.

```
<copyright>&#169; 2002</copyright>
```

5. Save the **Ch03XML02.xml** file, and then open it in Internet Explorer. Your Web browser should look like Figure 3-16. Notice that the © numeric character references appear as copyright symbols in the figure.

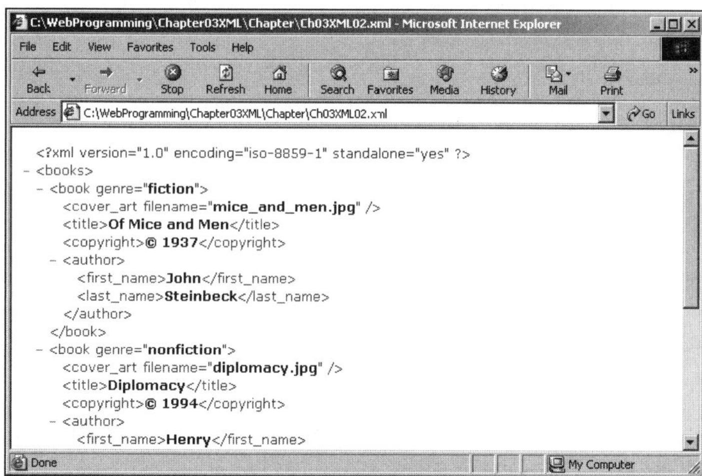

Figure 3-16 Ch03XML02.xml after adding <copyright> elements with numeric character references

6. Close your Web browser.

ADDING COMMENTS

When you work with any kind of programming language, whether a simple markup language such as XML or an advanced language like Java or C++, it is considered good practice to add comments to your code. **Comments** are statements you place in your code to contain various types of remarks, including your name and the date you wrote the code, notes to yourself, copyright information, or instructions to future designers and developers who may need to modify your work. When you are working with long XML documents, comments can make it easier to decipher how the document is structured.

XML comments begin with <!-- and end with -->, the same as HTML comments. A nonvalidating parser ignores any text located between the opening and closing comment tags, although some parsers, such as Internet Explorer, do display any comment text. Keep in mind, however, that Web applications ignore (or should ignore) any text within a comment block while reading an XML document.

You can add comments anywhere in an XML document after the opening XML declaration. The following code displays an XML document containing comments. Figure 3-17 shows the output in Internet Explorer.

```
<?xml version="1.0" encoding="iso-8859-1"
standalone="yes"?>
<Invoice>
   <!-- Customer name -->
   <Name>Don Gosselin</Name>
   <!-- Date of purchase -->
   <Date>February 10, 2005</Date>
   <!-- Invoice number -->
   <Num>10034</Num>
   <!-- Description of item -->
   <Item>Palm PDA</Item>
</Invoice>
```

Next, you will add comments to the Ch03XML02.xml document.

To add comments to the Ch03XML02.xml file:

1. Return to the **Ch03XML02.xml** file in your text editor.
2. Add the following comments immediately after the XML declaration:

```
<!--
XML document that stores data associated with published
books
your name
today's date
-->
```

3. Save and close the **Ch03XML02.xml** file, and then open it in Internet Explorer. Your Web browser should look like Figure 3-18.

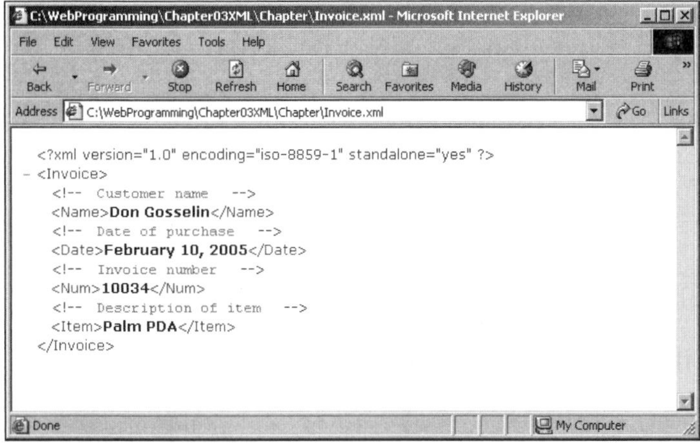

Figure 3-17 XML document with comments displayed in Internet Explorer

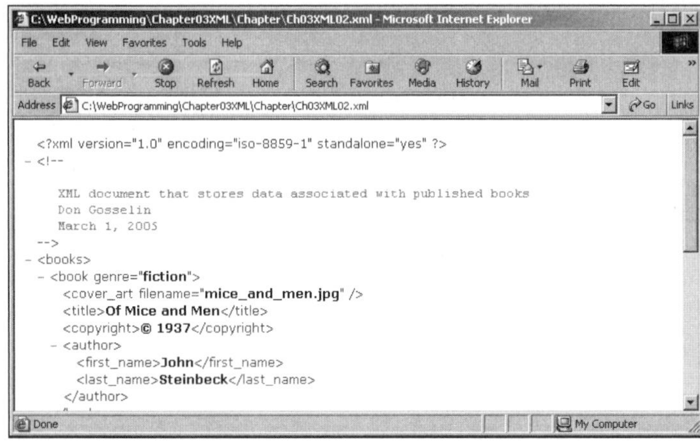

Figure 3-18 Ch03XML02.xml after adding comments

4. Close your Web browser.

Chapter Summary

- Extensible Markup Language, or XML, is used for creating Web pages and for defining and transmitting data between applications.
- User agents are devices that can retrieve and process documents created in XML and other types of markup languages such as HTML and XHTML.

- XML documents are text files, which means you can create them in any text editor such as Notepad or WordPad, or in any word-processing program capable of creating simple text files.
- In XML you refer to a tag pair and the information it contains as an element. The information contained within an element's opening and closing tags is referred to as its content. You use various parameters, called attributes, to configure XML elements.
- Languages based on SGML use a Document Type Definition (DTD) to define the elements and attributes that can be used in a document. Because the tags associated with an XML document are defined within the document itself instead of a separate DTD, XML is said to be self-describing.
- You use a program called a parser to check whether an XML document is well formed.
- When a document adheres to XML's syntax rules, it is well formed. In XML, a well-formed document has a root element, has tags with matching case, has closing tags for all XML tags, and has properly nested XML elements. In addition, all attribute values must be quoted and empty elements must be closed.
- You add special characters to an XML document using predefined character entities or numeric character references.
- Comments are statements you place in your code to contain various types of remarks, including your name and the date you wrote the code, notes to yourself, copyright information, or instructions to future designers and developers who may need to modify your work.

Review Questions

1. XML is based on ________________.
    a. SGML
    b. HTML
    c. XHTML
    d. Java
2. In XML you refer to a tag pair and the information it contains as a(n) ________________.
    a. block
    b. element
    c. tag unit
    d. method

3. The information contained within an element's opening and closing tags is referred to as its ________________.
   a. method
   b. property
   c. content
   d. function
4. Which of the following statements is correct?
   a. XML does not use elements or attributes.
   b. XML does not define any elements or attributes.
   c. XML only defines elements.
   d. XML only defines attributes.
5. What is the correct syntax for an XML declaration that does not require a DTD in order to be rendered correctly?
   a. <xml version="1.0" standalone="yes">
   b. <xml version="1.0" standalone="no">
   c. <?xml version="1.0" standalone="yes"?>
   d. <?xml version="1.0" standalone="no"?>
6. DTD stands for ________________.
   a. Data Transfer Display
   b. Digital Technology Definition
   c. Decimal Type Determinant
   d. Document Type Definition
7. When a document adheres to XML's syntax rules, it is said to be ________________.
   a. well formed
   b. compiled
   c. interpreted
   d. safe
8. Programs that check whether an XML document is well formed are called ________________.
   a. parsers
   b. checkers
   c. compilers
   d. interpreters

9. A ________________ element contains other elements on a page.
   a. master
   b. source
   c. base
   d. root
10. Which of the following statements is considered to be well formed?
    a. <name>Rajesh Singh</name>
    b. <name>Rajesh Singh</NAME>
    c. <NAME>Rajesh Singh</name>
    d. <Name>Rajesh Singh</name>
11. Which of the following is the correct way to write a well-formed element with an attribute?
    a. <organization name=General Motors>
    b. <organization name="General Motors">
    c. <organization "name=General Motors">
    d. <"organization name=General Motors">
12. How do you close the empty element named <account_number> in an XML document?
    a. <account_number\>
    b. <account_number/>
    c. </account_number>
    d. <\account_number>
13. What is the predefined character entity for a less-than symbol (<)?
    a. &<
    b. &<;
    c. <
    d. <
14. What is the numeric character reference for the registered trademark symbol?
    a. ©
    b. ®
    c. ¥
    d. ¢

15. With which characters do XML comments begin and end?
    a. \\...//
    b. <comment>...</comment>
    c. /*...*/
    d. <!--...-->

HANDS-ON EXERCISES

If necessary, use Windows Explorer to create a new folder in the Chap03 folder in your work folder. Name this folder **Exercises**. Save the files that you create in these exercises in the Chap03\Exercises folder in your work folder.

Exercise 3-1

In this exercise, you create an XML document that contains the name and price per pound of coffee beans.

1. Create a document in your text editor and type the opening XML declaration. Be sure to use all three properties of the XML declaration.
2. Type the opening tag for a root element named <coffee_beans>.
3. Within the <coffee_beans> element, create the following nested elements for different types of coffee:

```
<coffee>
     <name>Kona</name>
     <price>$18.95</price>
</coffee>
<coffee>
     <name>Sumatran</name>
     <price>$7.95</price>
</coffee>
<coffee>
     <name>Columbian</name>
     <price>$5.95</price>
</coffee>
```

4. Type the closing tag for the <coffee_beans> root element.
5. Save the XML document as **Ch03XMLEX01.xml** in the Exercises folder for Chapter 3.
6. Validate the **Ch03XMLEX01.html** document in Internet Explorer. If you receive any parsing errors, fix them and then reopen the document.

Exercise 3-2

In this exercise, you identify and fix the problems in an XML document that is not well formed.

1. Create a document in your text editor and type the opening XML declaration. Be sure to use all three properties of the XML declaration.
2. Type the following XML document, but identify and fix each of the errors that prevent it from being well formed.

```
<?xml version="1.0" standalone="yes"?>
<travel>
     <transportation mode=airplane>
          <destination>Paris</destination>
          <depart_date>June 1</depart_date>
          <carrier company=United>
     <transportation mode=train>
          <destination>New Orleans</destination>
          <depart_date>April 15</depart_date>
          <railroad company=Amtrak>
     <transportation mode=automobile>
          <destination>Vancouver</destination>
          <depart_date>August 3</depart_date>
</travel>
```

3. Save the XML document as **Ch03XMLEX02.xml** in the Exercises folder for Chapter 3.
4. Validate the **Ch03XMLEX02.html** document in Internet Explorer. If you receive any parsing errors, fix them and then reopen the document.

Exercise 3-3

In this exercise, you create an XML document that contains foreign phrases.

1. Create a document in your text editor and type the opening XML declaration. Be sure to use all three properties of the XML declaration.
2. Create a root element named <foreign_phrases>.
3. Within the <foreign_phrases> root element, create at least three elements named <phrase> that contain phrases in another language. Search the Internet for phrases you can use. Be sure to find phrases that include foreign characters. Use the appropriate numeric character reference for each foreign character. For instance, for the French phrase *à votre santé* (to your health), you would type the following into the element's content: À votre santé. You can find a complete listing of numeric character references at *www.macchiato.com/unicode/charts.html*. Include within each <phrase> element a language attribute that contains the language of the phrase. The language attribute of the French phrase, for instance, should read `language="French"`.

4. Save the XML document as **Ch03XMLEX03.xml** in the Exercises folder for Chapter 3.
5. Validate the **Ch03XMLEX03.html** document in Internet Explorer. If you receive any parsing errors, fix them and then reopen the document.

Exercise 3-4

In this exercise, you create an XML document that contains airline flight information.

1. Create a document in your text editor and type the opening XML declaration. Be sure to use all three properties of the XML declaration.
2. Create a root element named <airlines>.
3. Within the <airlines> root element, create three nested <carrier> elements for three separate airlines. Each <carrier> element should include a name attribute that stores the name of the airline. Use the names of whatever airline companies you like.
4. Within each <carrier> element, nest at least two <flight> elements that contain the following elements: <departure_city>, <destination_city>, <flight_number>, and <departure_time>. Use whatever information you like for the content of each element.
5. Save the XML document as **Ch03XMLEX04.xml** in the Exercises folder for Chapter 3.
6. Validate the **Ch03XMLEX04.html** document in Internet Explorer. If you receive any parsing errors, fix them and then reopen the document.

Exercise 3-5

In this exercise, you create an XML document that contains grading information for an elementary school class.

1. Create a document in your text editor and type the opening XML declaration. Be sure to use all three properties of the XML declaration.
2. Create a root element named <report_cards>.
3. Within the <report_cards> root element, create at least three <student> elements.
4. Within each <student> element, create the following nested elements. Be sure to nest the <history_grade>, <math_grade>, <geography_grade>, and <english_grade> elements within the <grades> element. Make up some fictitious names and grades for at least three students.

```
<name>content</name>
<grades>
     <history_grade>content</history_grade>
     <math_grade>content</math_grade>
     <geography_grade>content</geography_grade>
     <english_grade>content</english_grade>
</grades>
```

5. Save the XML document as **Ch03XMLEX05.xml** in the Exercises folder for Chapter 3.
6. Validate the **Ch03XMLEX05.html** document in Internet Explorer. If you receive any parsing errors, fix them and then reopen the document.

Web Programming Projects

In the following projects, be sure that each XML document includes an XML declaration and is well formed.

If necessary, use Windows Explorer to create a new folder in the Chap03 folder in your work folder. Name this folder **Projects**. Save the files that you create in these projects in the Chap03\Projects folder in your work folder.

Project 3-1

Create an XML document that contains elements you would find in a business letter. Include elements such as company name, logo, company address, subject, salutation, and body. Nest the recipient's name and address within another element named <to>. Save the XML document as **Ch03XMLProject01.xml** in the Projects folder for Chapter 3.

Project 3-2

Create an XML version of your resume. Include elements such as your name and position desired. Nest each of your former employers within an <employer> element. Also, nest your educational experience within an <education> element. Create any other nested elements that you deem appropriate, such as <references> or <special_skills> elements. Save the XML document as **Ch03XMLProject02.xml** in the Projects folder for Chapter 3.

Project 3-3

Create an XML document that outlines the table of contents for a software reference manual. You can write your manual using any software with which you are proficient. Create elements for each chapter of the manual, along with elements for the appendixes, glossary, and index. Within each chapter, include nested elements for the chapter's main sections, including chapter title, a summary, and major sections of the chapter. Save the XML document as **Ch03XMLProject03.xml** in the Projects folder for Chapter 3.

CHAPTER

4

XML: PART II

In this chapter you will:

- Organize your elements with namespaces
- Define elements with Document Type Definitions (DTDs)
- Validate XML documents against DTDs
- Declare elements in a DTD
- Declare attributes in a DTD

As you learned in Chapter 3, XML has no predefined elements or attributes. Instead, you must define your own elements, attributes, and document structure. Because you have to build everything in your XML documents from the ground up, you are actually writing your own markup language. One of the biggest challenges you face with XML is deciding which elements and attributes to use in your new markup language and how those elements should be structured. Simply creating new elements and attributes each time you need them works fine for XML documents that you will only use once. However, you may want to design an XML document that is used many times, or that should include specific elements, attributes, and structure expected by an application that needs to access the document's data.

In this chapter, you will study namespaces and Document Type Definitions (DTDs) to learn how to organize, define, and structure the elements and attributes in your XML documents. You will also learn how to validate your XML documents against a DTD.

ORGANIZING ELEMENTS WITH NAMESPACES

One of the greatest strengths of XML is that you can define your own elements in your documents. However, it is only a matter of time before you create an XML document containing elements with names that are identical to elements in another XML document. At first, you may not realize that this can cause problems, but remember from Chapter 3 that XML documents commonly define and transfer data between Web applications. If an application accesses two separate XML documents that contain identical element names, the application has no way of differentiating them. Or, you may combine into a single document two separate XML documents, both of which contain elements with the same names, but with different purposes.

For instance, consider an element named `name`. The `name` element could contain the name of a person, an organization, a country, and so on. Suppose you have an XML document that contains multiple `name` elements, with each element storing data with a different meaning. For instance, one of the `name` elements in the document could store customer names, while another `name` element could store product names. Without some way to uniquely identify each `name` element, an application that is accessing the XML document has no way of knowing which `name` element to use. Or, an application may need to access the `name` elements in your XML document along with the `name` elements in someone else's XML document. Again, an application has no way of knowing which `name` elements to use. To solve these problems, you use **namespaces** to organize the elements and attributes of an XML document into separate collections.

Namespaces and URIs

You should already be familiar with the basics of working with the Web, but to review, a **Uniform Resource Identifier (URI)** is a generic term for identifying namespaces and addresses on the World Wide Web. A **Uniform Resource Locator**, or **URL**, is a unique address that identifies a Web page. URLs are also referred to as Web addresses. For instance, *www.course.com* is a typical URL that points to Course Technology's home page. Namespaces are identified by a URI because it is guaranteed to be unique, which means that an associated namespace is also unique. This allows any applications that use an XML document to clearly identify its elements and attributes, resolving any conflicts with identically named elements and attributes in other XML documents.

With URL namespaces, common practice is to include an `ns` folder in the URL name. (The `ns` stands for "namespace.") Beneath the `ns` folder, you create additional folders that uniquely identify individual namespaces. For instance, the following two Course Technology URLs could be used to identify two unique namespaces:

```
http://www.course.com/ns/catalog
http://www.course.com/ns/certification
```

One potentially confusing fact about namespaces is that a URL you use to identify a namespace does not need to exist. In other words, you do not actually need to create an ns folder or any subfolders on your server. If you do create an ns folder and subfolders for namespaces on your server, you can place anything you want into the folder or you can leave it empty; it makes no difference. The point is that a URL associated with a namespace only needs to be a unique name used to identify the namespace; it does not matter if it physically exists as a resource on your Web site.

Default Namespaces

A **default namespace** is applied to all of the elements and nested elements beneath the element that declares the namespace. You select a default namespace for an entire XML document by using the xmlns attribute in the document's root element. The **xmlns** attribute assigns a namespace to an element; to this attribute you assign the URI that you want to use as a namespace. For instance, the following XML document contains the hardware costs associated with the renovation of a company's offices. A default namespace for the document is created by assigning the URL *www.GosselinConsulting.com/ns/renovation* to the xmlns attribute in the renovation root element.

```
<?xml version="1.0" encoding="iso-8859-1" standalone="yes"?>
<renovation xmlns="http://www.GosselinConsulting.com/
          ns/renovation">
   <hardware><description>plumbing</description>
     <cost>$15,000</cost></hardware>
   <hardware><description>electrical</description>
     <cost>$11,000</cost></hardware>
</renovation>
```

You can also apply a namespace to a particular element in an XML document. In this case, the namespace is applied to all of the element's nested elements, with the exception of elements with explicit namespace declarations (which you will study next). For instance, you may want to use separate namespaces for each of the hardware elements in the preceding code. The following code shows how to assign two default namespaces, one for the plumbing <hardware> element and one for the electrical <hardware> element:

```
<?xml version="1.0" encoding="iso-8859-1" standalone="yes"?>
<renovation>
   <hardware xmlns="http://www.GosselinConsulting.com/
         ns/plumbing">
     <description>plumbing</description>
     <cost>$15,000</cost></hardware>
   <hardware xmlns="http://www.GosselinConsulting.com/
         ns/electrical">
     <description>electrical</description>
     <cost>$11,000</cost></hardware>
</renovation>
```

Next you will create a simple XML document that contains weather-related elements. You will apply a default namespace to the weather document's root element.

To create a simple XML document that uses a default namespace:

1. Start your text editor and create a document.
2. Type the opening XML declaration, as follows:

```
<?xml version="1.0" encoding="iso-8859-1" standalone="yes"?>
```

3. Next, type the following root element named <weather> that uses the xmlns attribute to declare a default namespace. Replace the "*Your_Name*" portion of the domain name with your name. This namespace assumes that the weather being reported is for San Francisco. Notice that the default namespace includes an ns folder in the URL name.

```
<weather
     xmlns="http://www.Your_Name.com/ns/SanFrancisco">
```

4. Type the following <weather_reading> element, which contains other nested weather elements:

```
<weather_reading>
     <date>January 27, 2005</date>
     <temperature>48.0</temperature>
     <rainfall>2 inches</rainfall>
     <humidity>70</humidity>
</weather_reading>
```

5. Type the closing tag for the <weather> root element:

```
</weather>
```

6. Save the file as **Ch04XML01.xml** in the Chapter04\Chapter folder.
7. Open the **Ch04XML01.xml** file in Internet Explorer. Your Web browser should look like Figure 4-1. If you did not create the document properly, fix the error that appears in the browser and reload the document.

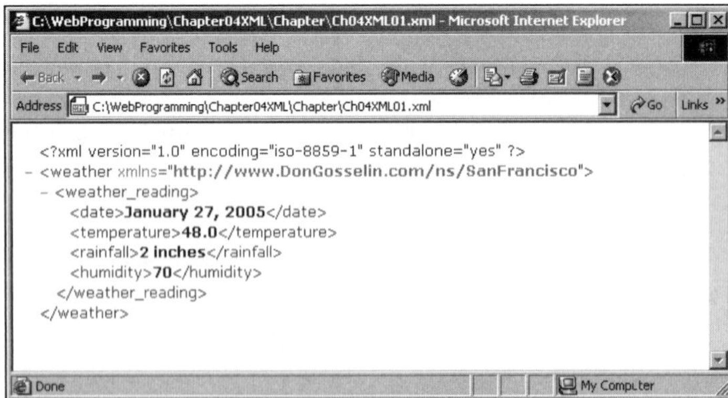

Figure 4-1 Ch04XML01.xml file in Internet Explorer

8. Close your Web browser.

Explicit Namespaces

Sometimes you want to explicitly declare a namespace for a specific element in an XML document. Namespaces that are assigned to individual elements in an XML document are called **explicit namespaces**. For instance, with the renovation XML document, you could probably get by using a single default namespace for the `<hardware>` elements that relate to construction. However, as part of your renovation, you may want to upgrade your computer hardware. If you used `<hardware>` as the element name for your computer hardware, then you would want to use a separate namespace because computer hardware is quite different from construction hardware. To explicitly declare a namespace for a specific element in an XML document, you must assign a prefix to the namespace declaration using the following syntax:

```
xmlns:prefix="URI"
```

The following statement declares a "computers" prefix within the opening `<renovation>` tag for a namespace that represents computer hardware elements:

```
<renovation xmlns:computers="http://www.GosselinConsulting
     /ns/computers">
```

Usually, you place all namespace declarations, including default and explicit namespaces, within the root element of an XML document. For instance, the following code shows how to declare both a default namespace and an explicit namespace within the root element of the renovation XML document.

```
<?xml version="1.0" encoding="iso-8859-1" standalone="yes"?>
<renovation xmlns="http://www.GosselinConsulting
     /ns/construction"
     xmlns:computers="http://www.GosselinConsulting
     /ns/computers">
     <hardware><description>plumbing</description>
          <cost>$15,000</cost></hardware>
     <hardware><description>electrical</description>
          <cost>$11,000</cost></hardware>
     <computers:hardware>
          <computers:description>
          personal computers</computers:description>
          <computers:cost>$25,000</computers:cost>
     </computers:hardware>
</renovation>
```

Next, you will declare an explicit namespace for weather in Los Angeles. You will also add a new `<weather_reading>` element that contains the weather information.

To add an explicit namespace for an element:

1. Return to the **Ch04XML01.xml** file in your text editor.

2. Modify the <weather> root element so it declares an explicit namespace for Los Angeles, as follows:

```
<weather xmlns="http://www.DonGosselin.com/ns/SanFrancisco"
     xmlns:losangeles="http://www.DonGosselin.com/
          ns/LosAngeles">
```

3. Above the closing </weather> element, add the following new <weather_reading> element:

```
<weather_reading>
     <date>January 27, 2005</date>
     <temperature>74.0</temperature>
     <rainfall>0 inches</rainfall>
     <humidity>20</humidity>
</weather_reading>
```

4. Save the **Ch04XML01.xml** file, and then open it in Internet Explorer. The file should look like Figure 4-2.

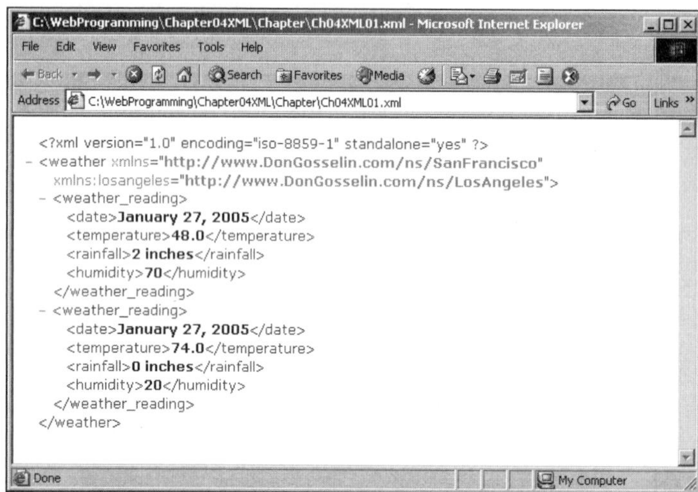

Figure 4-2 Ch04XML01.xml file in Internet Explorer after adding an explicit namespace and new <weather_reading> element

5. Close your Web browser.

To explicitly assign a namespace to a specific element, you must place the namespace's prefix and a colon in an element's opening and closing tag. The following code shows how to assign the computers prefix to a <hardware> element and its nested elements for the computer hardware equipment. Notice that the prefix and colon are applied to both the opening and closing tags for each element.

```
<computers:hardware>
     <computers:description>personal computers
     </computers:description>
     <computers:cost>$25,000</computers:cost>
</computers:hardware>
```

Any elements that do not contain an explicit namespace declaration belong to the default namespace. This means that you must explicitly assign a namespace to any nested elements, even if the element that contains them declares an explicit namespace. For instance, in the following code, the `<description>` and `<cost>` elements belong to the default namespace, even though the `<hardware>` element that contains them declares an explicit namespace:

```
<computers:hardware>
     <description>personal computers</description>
     <cost>$25,000</cost>
</computers:hardware>
```

Next, you will assign the explicit `losangeles` namespace to the new `<weather_reading>` element in the weather XML document.

To assign an explicit namespace to an element in an XML document:

1. Return to the **Ch04XML01.xml** file in your text editor.
2. Modify the new `<weather_reading>` element and its nested elements so that each element is explicitly assigned the `losangeles` namespace, as follows:

```
<losangeles:weather_reading>
     <losangeles:date>January 27, 2005</losangeles:date>
     <losangeles:temperature>74.0</losangeles:temperature>
     <losangeles:rainfall>0 inches</losangeles:rainfall>
     <losangeles:humidity>20</losangeles:humidity>
</losangeles:weather_reading>
```

3. Save the **Ch04XML01.xml** file, and then open it in Internet Explorer. The file should look like Figure 4-3.
4. Close your Web browser.

Remember that the prefix is only a way of referring to a namespace within an XML document—the namespace itself is still identified by a unique URI. Namespaces with the same prefix but different URIs are considered to be separate namespaces. However, namespaces with different prefixes but the same URI are considered to be the same namespace.

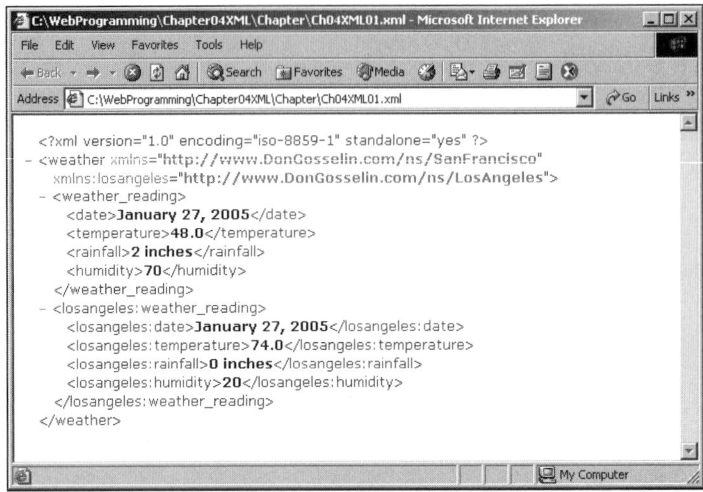

Figure 4-3 Ch04XML01.xml file in Internet Explorer after adding explicit namespace declarations

Defining Elements with DTDs

The XML documents you have created so far have been well formed, but they have not been valid. When an XML document conforms to an associated DTD, it is said to be **valid**. When an XML document does not conform to an associated DTD, it is said to be **invalid**. As you learned in Chapter 3, a DTD is a set of rules that define the elements and attributes you can use in an XML document. A DTD also defines how the elements should be structured in an XML document. You can think of a DTD as the place where you define your own markup language. An XML document must use only the elements and attributes defined in an associated DTD and be structured according to the DTD's rules, or it is not valid. Later in this section, you learn how to use a validating parser to check whether your XML documents conform to their associated DTDs.

An XML document can be well formed but invalid if it does not conform to its associated DTD. Most nonvalidating parsers (such as a Web browser) will render an invalid but well-formed XML document. The only problem with this scenario is that an application may not function properly if it expects an XML document to use specific elements and attributes and be structured in a certain way.

Document Type Declarations

You use the `<!DOCTYPE>` tag to create a **document type declaration**, which defines the structure of a DTD. The syntax for the <!DOCTYPE> tag is as follows:

```
<!DOCTYPE root_element [ element_declarations ]>
```

Do not be confused by a Document Type Definition (DTD) and a document type declaration. The acronym DTD is only used with Document Type Definitions, while the term "document type declaration" refers to the DTD's elements and structure, which are defined within the `<!DOCTYPE>` tag.

You can create two types of DTDs: internal and external. An **internal DTD** is defined within an XML document. Use an internal DTD when you want to define the elements, attributes, and structure for a single XML document, or when you are first developing and testing your DTD. When you create an internal DTD, you place the document type declaration after the XML declaration. The following code shows an example of an XML document with an internal DTD that a museum might use to catalog a collection of artworks:

```
<?xml version="1.0" encoding="iso-8859-1" standalone="no"?>
<!DOCTYPE artwork [
     <!ELEMENT artwork (artist+, title, date, medium)>
     <!ELEMENT artist (#PCDATA)><!ELEMENT title (#PCDATA)>
     <!ELEMENT date (#PCDATA)><!ELEMENT medium (#PCDATA)>
]>
<artwork>
     <artist>Rembrandt van Rijn</artist>
     <title>Lucretia</title><date>1666</date>
     <medium>oil on canvas</medium>
</artwork>
```

For now, do not worry about how the `<!ELEMENT>` tags in the document type declaration are structured—you will study them in the next section. Instead, focus on how the XML document is structured. Notice how the standalone attribute in the XML declaration is assigned a value of "no" because the document requires a DTD to be rendered correctly. Also notice how the <artwork> root element is defined within the document type declaration.

Next, you will create a human resources XML document with an internal DTD.

To create an XML document with an internal DTD:

1. Start your text editor and create a document.
2. Type the opening XML declaration, as follows. Be sure to assign the standalone attribute a value of "no".

   ```
   <?xml version="1.0" encoding="iso-8859-1" standalone="no"?>
   ```

3. Next, declare the following internal DTD, which defines several elements that would be used in a human resources document. Again, do not worry about how the `<!ELEMENT>` tags are structured. You will study them in the next section.

   ```
   <!DOCTYPE human_resources [
        <!ELEMENT human_resources (employee+)>
        <!ELEMENT employee (first_name, last_name,
             position, department)>
   ```

```
        <!ELEMENT first_name (#PCDATA)>
        <!ELEMENT last_name (#PCDATA)>
        <!ELEMENT position (#PCDATA)>
        <!ELEMENT department (#PCDATA)>
]>
```

4. Next, add the following XML document, which declares two employees:

```
<human_resources>
     <employee><first_name>Scott</first_name>
          <last_name>Morinaga</last_name>
          <position>Programmer</position>
          <department>Software Engineering</department>
     </employee>
     <employee><first_name>Raymond</first_name>
          <last_name>Picard</last_name>
          <position>Analyst</position>
          <department>Program Management</department>
     </employee>
</human_resources>
```

5. Save the file as **Ch04XML02.xml** in the Chapter04\Chapter folder.
6. Open the **Ch04XML02.xml** file in Internet Explorer. Your Web browser should look like Figure 4-4. If you did not create the document properly, fix the error that appears in the browser and reload the document.

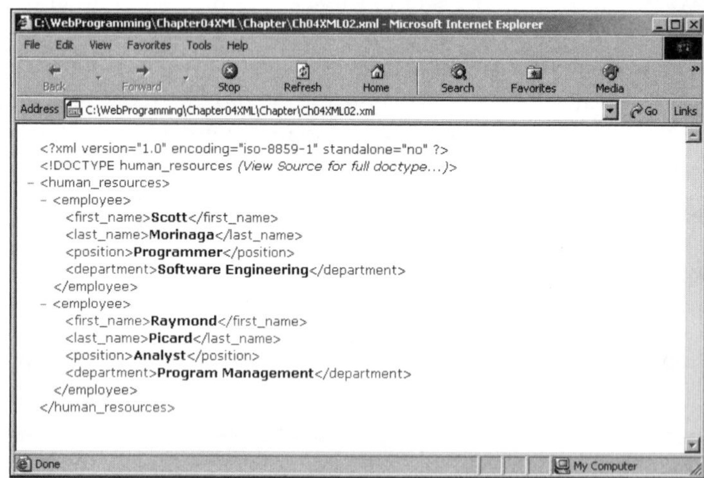

Figure 4-4 Ch04XML02.xml file in Internet Explorer

7. Close your Web browser.

Although an internal DTD is useful when you are first developing and testing a DTD, most of the DTDs you create will be external DTDs that can be shared by multiple XML documents. An **external DTD** is defined in a separate document with an extension of .dtd. One of the main differences between declaring an internal DTD and an external DTD is that you do not include an XML declaration or document type declaration in the external DTD file. Also, you do not place the element declarations inside brackets ([ ]). For instance, the following code shows how you declare an external DTD for the artworks example:

```
<!ELEMENT artwork (artist+, title, date, medium)>
<!ELEMENT artist (#PCDATA)><!ELEMENT title (#PCDATA)>
<!ELEMENT date (#PCDATA)><!ELEMENT medium (#PCDATA)>
```


To declare that an XML document uses an external DTD, you place the document type declaration within the XML document using the following syntax:

```
<!DOCTYPE root_element SYSTEM or PUBLIC "DTD file">
```

You use either the **SYSTEM** or the **PUBLIC** attribute in an external document type declaration. The **SYSTEM** attribute declares that the DTD file is located on a local computer, network server, or corporate intranet. The **PUBLIC** attribute declares that the DTD is publicly available on the Internet. With either the **SYSTEM** or the **PUBLIC** attribute, you can use a URL for the location of the DTD file. For simplicity, this chapter assumes that the DTD files you use are local, so you will use a **SYSTEM** attribute along with a local filename for your DTD files. For instance, if the artworks DTD were named Artworks.dtd, then you would place the following document type declaration in an XML document that uses the DTD:

```
<?xml version="1.0" encoding="iso-8859-1" standalone="no"?>
<!DOCTYPE artwork SYSTEM "Artworks.dtd">
<artwork>
     <artist>Rembrandt van Rijn</artist>
     <title>Lucretia</title><date>1666</date>
     <medium>oil on canvas</medium>
</artwork>
```

Next, you will modify the human resources document so the DTD is defined in a separate document as an external DTD.

To define a DTD in a separate document as an external DTD:

1. Return to the **Ch04XML02.xml** file in your text editor.
2. Modify the <!DOCTYPE> declaration so that it uses the SYSTEM attribute to reference an external DTD named HumanResources.dtd. Before you modify the <!DOCTYPE> declaration, cut the <!ELEMENT> tags to your Clipboard—you will need them when you create the external DTD file. Your modified <!DOCTYPE> declaration should appear as follows:

   ```
   <!DOCTYPE human_resources SYSTEM "HumanResources.dtd">
   ```

3. Save the **Ch04XML02.xml** file.

4. Create a document in your text editor and type or paste the element declarations that were included in the internal DTD:

```
<!ELEMENT human_resources (employee+)>
<!ELEMENT employee (first_name, last_name,
     position, department)>
<!ELEMENT first_name (#PCDATA)><!ELEMENT last_name (#PCDATA)
>
<!ELEMENT position (#PCDATA)><!ELEMENT department (#PCDATA)>
```

5. Save the file as **HumanResources.dtd** in the Chapter04\Chapter folder.
6. Reopen the **Ch04XML02.xml** file in Internet Explorer. The file should look the same in your Web browser as it did in Figure 4-4.
7. Close your Web browser.

VALIDATING XML DOCUMENTS AGAINST DTDS

When you open an XML document in a nonvalidating parser such as Internet Explorer, it only checks to see if the document is well formed; it does not check to see if the document is structured according to an associated DTD. A **validating parser**, on the other hand, checks to see if an XML document is well formed and also compares the document to a DTD to ensure that it adheres to the DTD's rules. There are numerous XML parsers on the market, both validating and nonvalidating. The one you choose is completely up to you, but keep in mind that you must use a validating parser if you want to ensure that an XML document complies with the rules of any given DTD.

You can find a comprehensive list of validating and nonvalidating parsers by searching for "XML parsers" on a search engine such as Google.

This book's CD includes an evaluation copy of Altova's xmlspy 5, a popular XML development tool. xmlspy 5 is a large and comprehensive program with many features that are far too advanced for this chapter's purposes. However, xmlspy 5 is an excellent tool to use as both a validating and nonvalidating parser. You will need a validating parser for the rest of the exercises in this chapter, so be sure to install xmlspy 5 (or some other validating parser) before you continue. The instructions in this chapter assume you are using xmlspy 5, but feel free to use whatever validating parser you like.

Next, you will validate the human resources XML document against its DTD.

To validate an XML document against its DTD:

1. Start **xmlspy 5** and open the Ch04XML02.xml file by clicking **File** on the menu bar and then clicking **Open** and browsing for the file. By default, xmlspy 5 validates a file when you first open it, although you can change this

setting by clicking **Tools** on the menu bar and then clicking **Options**. If xmlspy 5 does not automatically validate the Ch04XML02.xml file when you first open it, click **XML** on the menu bar, and then click **Validate**.

The XML menu also contains a "Check well-formedness" command that you can use to check if an XML document is well formed, but not valid.

2. If your Ch04XML02.xml file is valid, then you should receive a "This file is valid" message box, as shown in Figure 4-5. Click **OK** to close the message box. If your file is not valid, then you receive a message box that points you to the error. You can fix the error directly in xmlspy 5, and then click the **Recheck** button to revalidate the file.

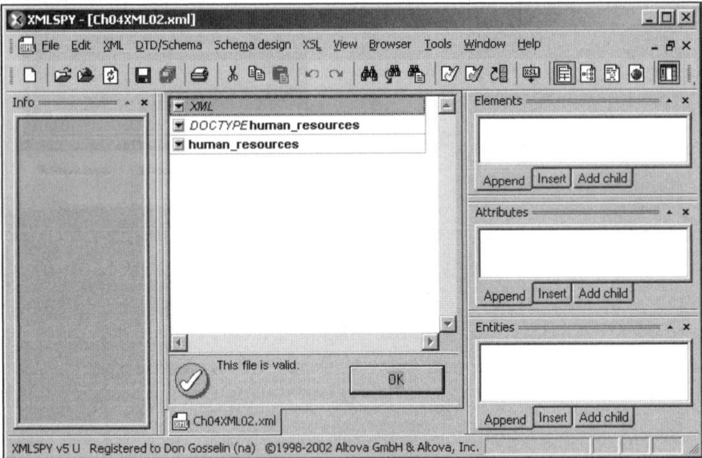

Figure 4-5 Ch04XML02.xml after being validated in xmlspy 5

The easiest way to edit an XML file in xmlspy 5 is to click View on the menu bar, and then click Text view, which opens the XML file in a simple text editor window.

3. Once your Ch04XML02.xml file is valid, close it by clicking **File** on the menu bar and then clicking **Close**. Click **Yes** if you are prompted to save changes to the file.

DECLARING ELEMENTS IN A DTD

As you know, elements are the main building blocks of XML documents. You use an **element declaration** in a DTD to define an element's name and the content it can contain. You create an element declaration using the `<!ELEMENT>` tag with the following syntax:

```
<!ELEMENT name content>
```

While a DTD's element declarations determine the names of the elements you can use in an XML document, they also declare the content (if any) that can be stored in a particular element, along with the elements that must be structured.

The root element must be the first element declaration to follow the document type definition in an internal DTD, or it must be the first element declaration in an external DTD. The root element also cannot be an empty element. (You will learn how to define empty element declarations shortly.) One of the simplest ways to define the root element is to use the **ANY** keyword, which declares that an element can contain any type of content. For instance, the following statement declares the root element for the artworks DTD using the **ANY** keyword:

```
<!ELEMENT artwork ANY>
```

You need to understand, however, that it is considered very bad form to include the **ANY** keyword in any final DTDs because it essentially prevents an element from having any enforceable structure. For any element, including the root element, it is much more preferable to define the exact content that the element can accept. However, when you first start developing a DTD, you may find the **ANY** keyword useful as a placeholder until you determine the exact element structure that will appear in your DTD. Once you finish developing your DTD, remember to replace the **ANY** keyword with the element structure to which you want users of your DTD to adhere.

Next, you will start creating a DTD that defines elements a shipping company may use when shipping a package.

To create a DTD with an element declaration:

1. Create a document in your text editor.
2. Declare the following `<shipping>` root element using the ANY keyword:

   ```
   <!ELEMENT shipping ANY>
   ```

3. Save the file as **Shipping.dtd** in the Chapter04\Chapter folder.

For the rest of this section, you will study other types of content and element structure you can define with an element declaration.

Character Data Elements

You can create a simple element that stores only character data by placing the keyword `#PCDATA` inside parentheses in an element declaration. `PCDATA` stands for "parsed character" data and declares that an XML parser should parse the content of the element. This type of element can only contain character data and not other types of elements. For instance, the following statements declare parsed character elements in the artworks DTD:


```
<!ELEMENT artist (#PCDATA)><!ELEMENT title (#PCDATA)>
<!ELEMENT date (#PCDATA)><!ELEMENT medium (#PCDATA)>
```

Next, you will add parsed character elements to the shipping DTD.

To add parsed character elements to a DTD:

1. Return to the **Shipping.dtd** file in your text editor.
2. Add the following parsed character elements to the end of the file:

   ```
   <!ELEMENT package ANY><!ELEMENT sender (#PCDATA)>
   <!ELEMENT recipient (#PCDATA)><!ELEMENT weight (#PCDATA)>
   <!ELEMENT cost (#PCDATA)>
   ```

3. Save the **Shipping.dtd** file in the Chapter04\Chapter folder.

Next, you will create an XML document that conforms to Shipping.dtd and validate it using xmlspy 5.

To create and then validate an XML document that conforms to a DTD:

1. Create a document in your text editor.
2. Type the opening XML declaration, as follows.

   ```
   <?xml version="1.0" encoding="iso-8859-1" standalone="no"?>
   ```

3. Add the following `<!DOCTYPE>` declaration that uses the `SYSTEM` attribute to reference the Shipping.dtd file.

   ```
   <!DOCTYPE shipping SYSTEM "Shipping.dtd">
   ```

4. Add the following root and body elements that conform to the elements you declared in the Shipping.dtd file:

   ```
   <shipping>
        <package><sender>Rajesh Singh</sender>
             <recipient>Dennis Blair</recipient>
             <weight>2.5 lbs.</weight>
             <cost>$14.95</cost></package>
   </shipping>
   ```

5. Save the file as **Ch04XML03.xml** in the Chapter04\Chapter folder.
6. Validate the **Ch04XML03.xml** file with xmlspy 5. Once the file is valid, close xmlspy 5.

7. Open the **Ch04XML03.xml** file in Internet Explorer. Your Web browser should look like Figure 4-6.

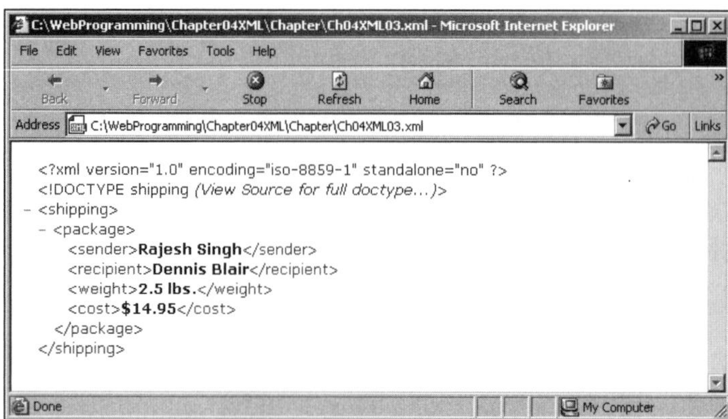

Figure 4-6 Ch04XML03.xml in Internet Explorer

8. Close your Web browser.

Empty Elements

You should be familiar with empty elements, which do not require ending tags and therefore do not include content. A number of elements in HTML do not have corresponding ending tags, including the `<hr>` tag, which inserts a horizontal rule into the document, and the `<br>` tag, which inserts a line break. The example of an empty XML tag you saw in the last chapter was in a document containing automobile data. The document included an empty `<photo>` element with a single attribute that stored the name of an image file containing a photograph of the automobile. Using the same example, you might want to create a `<photo>` element for the artworks DTD that stores the name of an image file containing a photograph of a particular artwork.

You create an empty element declaration in a DTD by using the keyword EMPTY in the content portion of an element declaration. For instance, the following statement declares an empty `<photo>` element for the artworks DTD:

```
<!ELEMENT photo EMPTY>
```

When you use an empty element in XML, you can either use an opening and closing tag or just use the opening tag by adding a single slash (/) before the tag's closing bracket to close the element. For instance, both of the following statements are valid for using the empty `<photo>` element in an XML document:

```
<photo></photo>
<photo/>
```

Keep in mind that even though some empty HTML elements can include content, such as the `<img>` element, empty XML elements cannot. The following statement results in an invalid XML document because content is placed within the opening and closing tags of the empty `<photo>` element:

```
<photo>Rembrandt's "Lucretia"</photo>
```

Next, you will add an empty `<account>` element to Shipping.dtd and to the Ch04XML03.xml file.

To add an empty element to a .dtd file and an .xml file:

1. Return to the **Shipping.dtd** file in your text editor.
2. Add the following empty declaration for the `<account>` element:

   ```
   <!ELEMENT account EMPTY>
   ```
3. Save the **Shipping.dtd** file.
4. Return to the **Ch04XML03.xml** file in your text editor.
5. Add the following empty `<account>` element above the closing `</package>` tag:

   ```
   <account/>
   ```
6. Save the **Ch04XML03.xml** file.
7. Validate the **Ch04XML03.xml** file with xmlspy 5, and then open the file in Internet Explorer. Your Web browser should look like Figure 4-7.

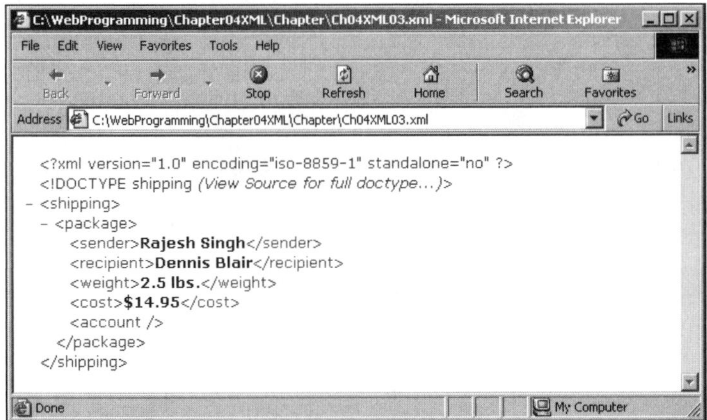

Figure 4-7 Ch04XML03.xml in Internet Explorer after adding an empty element

8. Close your Web browser.

An empty XML element is essentially useless unless it includes attributes. Later in this section, you will learn how to create attribute declarations in your DTDs.

Element Sequences

One of the most important aspects of DTDs is their ability to define the number and order of elements you can add to an XML document. This lets a DTD determine exactly how to structure XML documents that conform to it. For instance, with the artworks DTD, you would want to give an XML document the ability to add multiple artists, and to list multiple works for each artist. However, you would only want to allow each artwork to be given a single title, date, and medium. Or, you may want XML documents that conform to the artworks DTD to nest the elements in a specific order to conform to the requirements of a Web application. You define the number of elements and the order in which they can be added to an XML document using the symbols in Table 4-1.

Table 4-1 Symbols for defining content in element declarations

Symbol	Description
( )	Groups expressions in the content portion of an element declaration
,	Determines the sequence in which elements must appear
+	Requires that at least one instance of the element be included
?	Allows zero or one instance of an element
*	Allows zero or more instances of an element
|	Allows one element from a group of elements to be included

To define an element sequence, you place the elements you want to include in the sequence within parentheses in the content portion of an element declaration. This essentially determines how elements can be nested within an XML document that conforms to the DTD. For instance, you may have an element named `<employee>` within a DTD with a root element of `<company>`. If you want the `<employee>` element to contain a single `<name>`, then you add the following element declarations to your DTD:

```
<!ELEMENT company ANY><!ELEMENT employee (name)>
<!ELEMENT name (#PCDATA)>
```

An XML document that conforms to the DTD in the previous code must include an `<employee>` root element that contains a single `<name>` element. If you want an element to include multiple nested elements, but in a specific order, you separate the element names with a comma. The following code, for instance, shows the same code as the previous example, but includes three required elements for the `<employee>` element: `<first_name>`, `<last_name>`, and `<position>`.

```
<!ELEMENT company ANY>
<!ELEMENT employee (first_name, last_name, position)>
<!ELEMENT first_name (#PCDATA)><!ELEMENT last_name (#PCDATA)>
<!ELEMENT position (#PCDATA)>
```

If you created an XML document that conformed to the preceding DTD, then the document could only contain a single `<employee>`. To require an XML document to include one or more instances of a particular element, you follow the element name with the (+) symbol. Similarly, you use the (?) symbol to allow an XML document to include zero or one instance of an element, and you use the (*) to allow an XML document to include zero or more instances of an element. The following code shows another example of the company DTD. This time, however, the content portion of the `<company>` element declaration includes the employee element name, followed by the (+) symbol, which allows XML documents that conform to the DTD to create one or more `<employee>` elements. Also, the <employee> element includes a new `<middle_name>` element that is optional because its name is followed by the (?) symbol in the `<employee>` element declaration. Finally, the code includes new `<phone>`, `<fax>`, and `<mobile>` elements that are followed by (*) symbols, which means you can include zero or more instances of each of these elements.


```
<!ELEMENT company (employee+)>
<!ELEMENT employee (first_name, middle_name?,
     last_name, position, phone*, fax*, mobile*)>
<!ELEMENT first_name (#PCDATA)><!ELEMENT middle_name (#PCDATA)>
<!ELEMENT last_name (#PCDATA)><!ELEMENT position (#PCDATA)>
<!ELEMENT phone (#PCDATA)><!ELEMENT fax (#PCDATA)>
<!ELEMENT mobile (#PCDATA)>
```

The (|) symbol is useful in that it allows one element from a group of elements to be included. You must enclose the group of elements and (|) symbols within another set of parentheses. For instance, the following code shows another version of the artworks DTD. In this case, the `<medium>` element has been replaced with two new elements: `<painting>` and `<sculpture>`. The `<artwork>` root element requires an XML document to include either the `<painting>` or the `<sculpture>` elements.

```
<!ELEMENT artwork (artist+, title, date, medium,
     (painting | sculpture))>
<!ELEMENT artist (#PCDATA)><!ELEMENT title (#PCDATA)>
<!ELEMENT date (#PCDATA)><!ELEMENT painting (#PCDATA)>
<!ELEMENT sculpture (#PCDATA)>
```

Next, you will add element sequences to the Shipping.dtd file.

To add element sequences to a .dtd file:

1. Return to the **Shipping.dtd** file in your text editor.
2. Modify the `<shipping>` root element declaration so that it can contain multiple `<package>` elements, as follows:

   ```
   <!ELEMENT shipping (package+)>
   ```

3. Next, modify the `<package>` element as follows, so that it must contain the `<sender>`, `<recipient>`, `<cost>`, and `<account>` elements. Make the `<weight>` element optional by following it with a question mark.

   ```
   <!ELEMENT package (sender, recipient, weight?,
        cost, account)>
   ```

4. Save the **Shipping.dtd** file.
5. Validate the **Ch04XML03.xml** file with xmlspy 5, and then open it in Internet Explorer. Your Web browser should look the same as it did in Figure 4-7.
6. Close your Web browser.

Mixed Content Elements

Mixed content elements contain both character data and other elements. A mixed content element is useful when you want to specify the elements that can be nested within the element, but also allow the element to contain character data. Mixed content elements also allow you to define elements that should be nested within another element, but do not require XML documents to follow a specific element sequence. This can be useful when the XML documents that conform to your DTD do not need to be structured as rigidly as they would with element sequences. The syntax for creating a mixed content element is as follows:

```
<!ELEMENT name (#PCDATA | element | element | ... )* >
```

You must use the preceding syntax to create a mixed content element. Specifically, the `#PCDATA` keyword must be the first item in the option list. Also, you must place the (*) symbol after the option list to indicate that the mixed content element is optional and that an XML document can contain more than one instance of it. (Recall that the (*) symbol allows an XML document to create zero or more instances of an element.) Understand that the preceding syntax is required for the DTD to be well formed.

As an example of a mixed content element, consider a DTD that defines travel information elements. You may not need to require XML documents that conform to the DTD to use a specific sequence of elements, and you may want to allow the document to have different types of travel comments. Therefore, you could create the DTD's root element as a mixed content element, as follows:

```
<!ELEMENT travel (#PCDATA | destination | airline |
     travel_dates | cost)* >
<!ELEMENT destination (#PCDATA)><!ELEMENT airline (#PCDATA)>
<!ELEMENT travel_dates (#PCDATA)><!ELEMENT cost (#PCDATA)>
```

The following code shows an XML document that uses the travel information DTD. Notice that the code does not include the `<airline>` element. However, it does include character data that specifies the transportation method for getting to Napa Valley.

```
<?xml version="1.0" encoding="iso-8859-1" standalone="no"?>
<!DOCTYPE travel SYSTEM "Travel.dtd">
<travel>
     <destination>Napa Valley, California</destination>
     Transportation: We drove from Portland, Oregon
     <travel_dates>May 4</travel_dates>
     <cost>$850</cost>
</travel>
```

Keep in mind that with mixed content elements you can include as many or as few of the elements in the option list as you like. For instance, with the travel information DTD, you can include only some character data between the <travel> root element, and the XML document will still be valid:

```
<?xml version="1.0" encoding="iso-8859-1" standalone="no"?>
<!DOCTYPE travel SYSTEM "Travel.dtd">
<travel>Our trip was cancelled.</travel>
```


Or, you can include multiple instances of the same element, as follows:

```
<?xml version="1.0" encoding="iso-8859-1" standalone="no"?>
<!DOCTYPE travel SYSTEM "Travel.dtd">
<travel><destination>Paris, France</destination>
<destination>London, England</destination>
<destination>Rome, Italy</destination></travel>
```

Declaring Attributes in a DTD

As you know, you use attributes to provide additional information about an element. Attributes are placed before the closing bracket of the starting tag and separated from the tag name or other attributes with a space. The value assigned to an attribute must be in quotations. It's important to understand that many attributes can also be created as an element. For instance, the following code shows a <company> element containing a name attribute that stores the name of the company:

```
<company name="Course Technology">
nested elements
</company>
```

However, the name attribute in the preceding code could just as easily be created as an element, as follows:

```
<company><name>Course Technology></name></company>
```

In general, elements should contain information that will be displayed. Attributes, on the other hand, should contain information about the element. For instance, because the company name in the preceding code would probably be displayed, it should be created as an element. By comparison, you may want to record a tax ID number for the <company> element that you do not need displayed. In this case, you could create a `tax_id` attribute, as follows:

```
<company tax_id="12-3456789">
<name>Course Technology></name>
</company>
```

You use an **attribute declaration** in a DTD to declare all of the attributes that are allowed or required for a particular element. You create an attribute declaration using the `<!ATTLIST>` tag with the following syntax:

```
<!ATTLIST element-name
attribute-name attribute-type default-value
attribute-name attribute-type default-value
...
>
```

As you can see in the preceding syntax, the element name to which the attribute declaration applies immediately follows the `<!ATTLIST` portion of the declaration. Then, you create a list of attribute names, types, and default values that are allowed or required for the element.

Attribute Types

Just as you can specify an element's content, you can also specify the values that can be assigned to an attribute by declaring its **type**. Although you can create several types of attributes, the type you will study in this chapter is the CDATA type. The **CDATA attribute type** can accept any combination of character data, with the exception of tags and elements. For instance, the following code declares a CDATA attribute type named `name` for the `<company>` element. The "Course Technology" portion of the attribute declaration is the default value for the attribute, and appears automatically if an XML document does not declare the name attribute in a `<company>` element.

```
<!ATTLIST company
name CDATA "Course Technology"
>
```

Next, you will add an attribute declaration for the empty `<account>` element to the Shipping.dtd file.

To add an attribute declaration for an empty element to a .dtd file:

1. Return to the **Shipping.dtd** file in your text editor.
2. At the end of the file, add the following declaration for an attribute named "number" in the `<account>` element. The attribute declaration includes a default value of unknown.

```
<!ATTLIST account
     number CDATA "unknown"
>
```

3. Save the **Shipping.dtd** file.
4. Validate the **Ch04XML03.xml** file with xmlspy 5, and then open it in Internet Explorer. Your Web browser should look like Figure 4-8. Notice that because no number attribute was declared for the `<account>` element, the default value of "unknown" is added automatically.

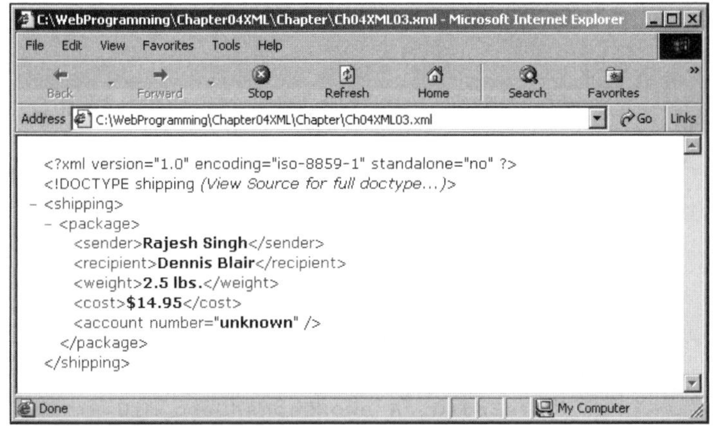

Figure 4-8 Ch04XML03.xml after adding an attribute declaration

5. Close your Web browser.

Attribute Defaults

You can declare a default value for an attribute by placing the value in quotations, as shown in the `name` attribute declaration in the preceding section. If you use an element in an XML document and exclude an attribute that has a default value, then the default value is automatically used by any program that accesses the XML document. For instance, the following code shows a simple internal DTD that defines the `<company>` element and a `parent` attribute. A default value of "Thomson Learning" (Course Technology's parent company) is assigned to the `parent` attribute. Notice that even though the `<company>` element does not include the `parent` attribute, the default value of "Thomson Learning" is automatically added when you open the document in Internet Explorer, as shown in Figure 4-9.

```
<?xml version="1.0" encoding="iso-8859-1" standalone="no"?>
<!DOCTYPE corporation [
<!ELEMENT corporation (company+)>
<!ELEMENT company (#PCDATA)>
<!ATTLIST company
  parent CDATA "Thomson Learning" >
]>
<corporation><company>Course Technology</company>
</corporation>
```

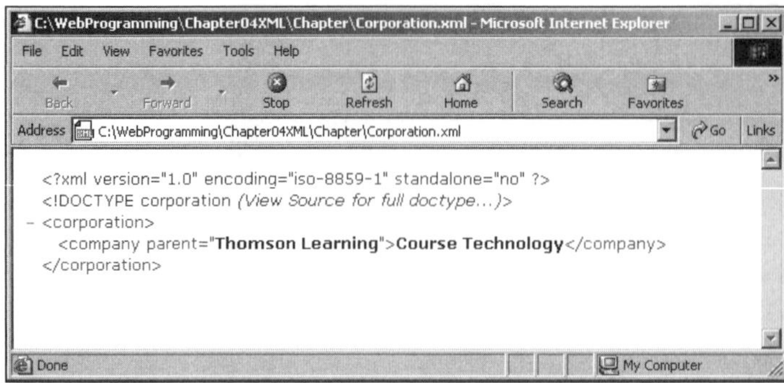

Figure 4-9 Output of an XML document with a default attribute

If you do not want to include a default value for an attribute, then you can use one of the attribute defaults in Table 4-2.

Table 4-2 Attribute defaults

Default	Description
`#REQUIRED`	An XML document must assign the attribute a value each time it is used
`#FIXED`	This assigns a default value to an attribute that cannot be modified
`#IMPLIED`	The attribute is not required and there is no default value

The following code shows an attribute declaration for the `<company>` element that uses the three values listed in Table 4-2. Notice that the `#FIXED` attribute also declares a default value. Even though the `<company>` element does not include the `#FIXED` parent attribute, the default value of "Thomson Learning" is automatically added when you open the document in Internet Explorer, as shown in Figure 4-10.

```
<?xml version="1.0" encoding="iso-8859-1" standalone="no"?>
<!DOCTYPE corporation [
<!ELEMENT corporation (company+)>
<!ELEMENT company (#PCDATA)>
<!ATTLIST company
  tax_id CDATA #REQUIRED
  web_site CDATA #IMPLIED
  parent CDATA #FIXED "Thomson Learning" >
]>
<corporation>
    <company tax_id="12-3456789" web_site="www.course.com">
     Course Technology</company>
</corporation>
```

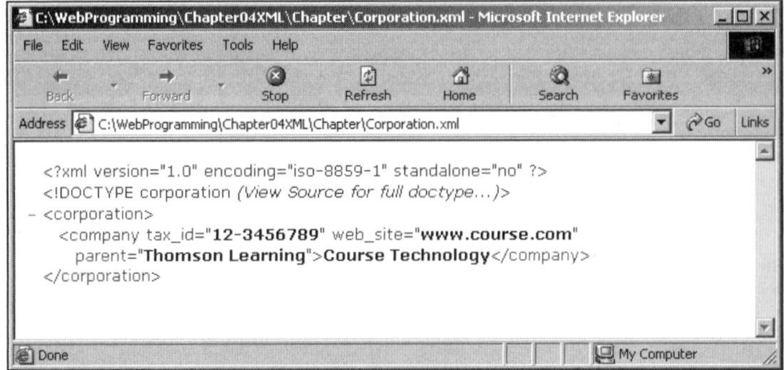

Figure 4-10 Output of an XML document with multiple attribute declarations

Because each shipped package must include an account number, you will now modify the Shipping.dtd file so that the number attribute of the `<account>` element is required.

To modify the example .dtd file so the element's number attribute is required:

1. Return to the **Shipping.dtd** file in your text editor.
2. Modify the declaration for the number attribute so that it uses the `#REQUIRED` attribute default instead of the default value of "unknown," as follows:

```
<!ATTLIST account
     number CDATA #REQUIRED
>
```

3. Save and close the **Shipping.dtd** file.
4. Return to the **Ch04XML03.xml** file in your text editor.
5. Modify the `<account>` element so that it assigns a value to the number attribute as follows:

```
<account number="12-34567"/>
```

6. Save and close the **Ch04XML03.xml** file.
7. Validate the **Ch04XML03.xml** file with xmlspy 5, and then open it in Internet Explorer. Your Web browser should look like Figure 4-11.
8. Close your Web browser.

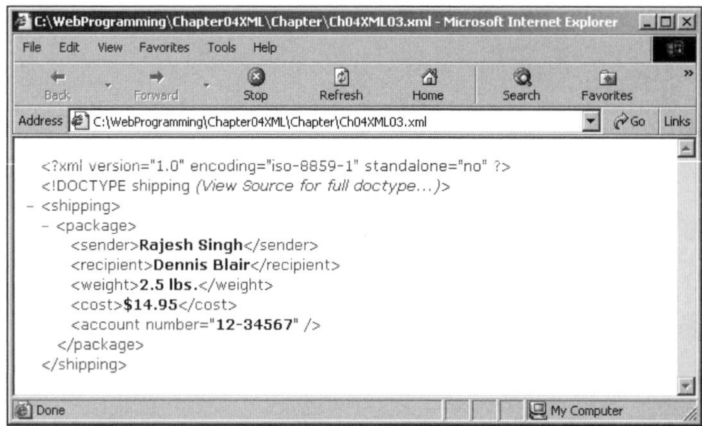

Figure 4-11 Ch04XML03.xml after modifying the attribute declaration

Chapter Summary

- You use namespaces to organize the elements and attributes of an XML document into separate collections. Uniform Resource Identifiers, such as Uniform Resource Locators, are used to identify namespaces.
- A default namespace is applied to all of the elements and nested elements beneath the element that declares the namespace.
- The xmlns attribute assigns a namespace to an element. Namespaces that are assigned to individual elements in an XML document are called explicit namespaces.
- When an XML document conforms to an associated DTD, it is said to be valid.
- You use the <!DOCTYPE> tag to create a document type declaration, which defines the structure of a DTD.
- An internal DTD is defined within an XML document. An external DTD is defined in a separate document with an extension of .dtd.
- A validating parser checks to see if an XML document is well formed and also compares the document to a DTD to ensure that it adheres to the DTD's rules.
- You use an element declaration in a DTD to define an element's name and the content it can contain. Use an attribute declaration in a DTD to declare all of the attributes that are allowed or required for a particular element.
- An attribute's type determines the values that you can assign to the attribute. For example, the CDATA attribute type can accept any combination of character data, with the exception of tags and elements. You can declare a default value for an attribute by placing the value in quotations.

Review Questions

1. Which of the following statements is true?
    a. If an application accesses two separate XML documents that contain identical element names, the application can automatically tell them apart without the use of namespaces.
    b. You must include an `ns` folder in the URL name you want to use as a namespace.
    c. You are not allowed to place any files within an `ns` folder that is part of a URL name.
    d. The URL you use to identify a namespace does not need to exist.
2. A ________________ namespace is applied to all of the elements and nested elements beneath the element that declares the namespace.
    a. default
    b. standard
    c. implied
    d. built-in
3. The ________________ attribute assigns a namespace to an element.
    a. `namespace`
    b. `xmlns`
    c. `xml`
    d. `ns`
4. Namespaces that are assigned to individual elements in an XML document are called ________________ namespaces.
    a. local
    b. nested
    c. explicit
    d. child
5. How do you explicitly assign a namespace to a specific element?
    a. You must place the namespace's prefix and a colon in an element's opening tag.
    b. You must place the namespace's prefix and a colon in an element's closing tag.
    c. You must place the namespace's prefix and a colon in an element's opening and closing tag.
    d. You cannot explicitly assign a namespace to a specific element.

6. When an XML document conforms to an associated DTD, it is said to be ________________.
   a. valid
   b. well formed
   c. intrinsic
   d. correct
7. Which tag do you use to create a document type declaration?
   a. <!DECLARATION>
   b. <!DOC>
   c. <!TYPE>
   d. <!DOCTYPE>
8. Inside which symbols do you place the element and attribute declarations in an internal DTD?
   a. ( )
   b. < >
   c. { }
   d. [ ]
9. Which attribute do you use in an external document type declaration to declare that the DTD file is located on a local computer, network server, or corporate intranet?
   a. PUBLIC
   b. PRIVATE
   c. SYSTEM
   d. LOCAL
10. Which of the following statements about the root element is false?
    a. The root element must be the first element declaration to follow the document type definition in an internal DTD.
    b. The root element must be the first element declaration in an external DTD.
    c. You can declare the root element with the ANY keyword.
    d. The root element can be empty.
11. What is the correct syntax for declaring a <name> element that stores only character data?
    a. <!ELEMENT name (PCDATA)>
    b. <!ELEMENT name (#PCDATA)>
    c. <!ELEMENT name #PCDATA>
    d. <!ELEMENT name CDATA>

12. What is the correct syntax for declaring an empty `<sales>` element?
    a. `<!ELEMENT sales>`
    b. `<!ELEMENT />`
    c. `<!ELEMENT sales EMPTY>`
    d. `<!ELEMENT EMPTY sales>`

13. Which element sequence symbol requires that at least one instance of the element be included?
    a. +
    b. ?
    c. *
    d. |
14. Which symbol must you place after the option list in a mixed content element?
    a. +
    b. ?
    c. *
    d. |
15. Which attribute default value assigns a value that cannot be modified?
    a. #REQUIRED
    b. #FIXED
    c. #IMPLIED
    d. #STATIC

HANDS-ON EXERCISES

If necessary, create a folder named Chapter04\Exercises in your work folder.

Exercise 4-1

In this exercise, you create an XML document that includes default and explicit namespaces.

1. Create a document in your text editor and type the opening XML declaration.
2. Type the opening tag for a root element named <mail_order>. Use the **xmlns** attribute to include a default namespace:

```
<mail_order xmlns="http://www.MailOrderCatalogs.com/
     ns/clothing">
```

3. Create the following nested <catalog> element for a clothing catalog:

```
<catalog>
     <merchandise>clothing</merchandise>
     <customers>children</customers>
     <pages>83</pages>
</catalog>
```

4. Modify the <mail_order> root element so it includes an explicit namespace, as follows:

```
<mail_order xmlns="http://www.MailOrderCatalogs.com/
     ns/clothing"
xmlns:automotive="http://www.MailOrderCatalogs.com/
     ns/automotive">
```

5. At the end of the document, add the following <catalog> element and its nested <catalog> element, along with explicit namespace declarations for each element:

```
<automotive:catalog>
     <automotive:merchandise>auto parts</automotive:merchandise>
     <automotive:customers>mechanics</automotive:customers>
     <automotive:pages>77</automotive:pages>
</automotive:catalog>
```

6. Type the closing tag for the <mail_order> root element.
7. Save the XML document as **Ch04XMLEX01.xml** in the Chapter04\ Exercises folder.
8. Validate the **Ch04XMLEX01.xml** document in Internet Explorer. If you receive any parsing errors, fix them, and then reopen the document.

Exercise 4-2

In this exercise, you create an XML document that includes three explicit namespaces.

1. Create a document in your text editor and type the opening XML declaration.
2. Type the opening tag for a root element named <coffee_house>.
3. Within the <coffee_house> root element, create the following nested elements for different types of coffee:

```
<coffee>
     <name>Kona</name>
     <price>$18.95</price>
</coffee>
<coffee>
     <name>Sumatran</name>
     <price>$7.95</price>
</coffee>
<coffee>
     <name>Columbian</name>
     <price>$5.95</price>
</coffee>
```

4. Type the closing tag for the </coffee_house> root element.
5. Create three explicit namespaces, one for each of the <coffee> elements. Assign the explicit namespaces to the appropriate elements for each <coffee> element.
6. Save the XML document as **Ch04XMLEX02.xml** in the Chapter04\Exercises folder.
7. Validate the **Ch04XMLEX02.xml** document in Internet Explorer. If you receive any parsing errors, fix them, and then reopen the document.

Exercise 4-3

In this exercise, you declare elements in a DTD that will store university information. You also create and validate an XML document against the universities DTD.

1. Create a document in your text editor.
2. Create the following DTD that declares elements for the universities DTD:

```
<!ELEMENT universities (university+)>
<!ELEMENT university (name, location)>
<!ELEMENT name (#PCDATA)>
<!ELEMENT location (#PCDATA)>
```

3. Save the DTD document as **Ch04XMLEX03.dtd** in the Chapter04\Exercises folder for Chapter 4.
4. Create another document in your text editor and type the following XML document that uses the universities DTD:

```
<?xml version="1.0" encoding="iso-8859-1" standalone="no"?>
<!DOCTYPE universities SYSTEM "Ch04XMLEX03.dtd">
<universities>
     <university>
          <name>Harvard University</name>
          <location>Cambridge, MA</location>
     </university>
     <university>
          <name>Yale University</name>
          <location>New Haven, CT</location>
     </university>
     <university>
          <name>Columbia University</name>
          <location>New York, NY</location>
     </university>
</universities>
```

5. Save the XML document as **Ch04XMLEX03.xml** in the Chapter04\Exercises folder.
6. Use xmlspy 5 to validate the **Ch04XMLEX03.xml** document against the **Ch04XMLEX03.dtd** file. If you receive any parsing errors, fix them, and then open the document in Internet Explorer.

Exercise 4-4

In this exercise, you add an attribute declaration to the DTD you created in the last exercise.

1. Open the **Ch04XMLEX03.dtd** file in your text editor and immediately save it as **Ch04XMLEX04.dtd**.
2. In the Ch04XMLEX04.dtd file, add the following declaration for a `name` attribute that will be used in the `<university>` element:

```
<!ATTLIST university
  name CDATA #REQUIRED
>
```

3. Delete the `<name>` attribute declaration.
4. Save and close the **Ch04XMLEX04.dtd** file.
5. Open the **Ch04XMLEX03.xml** file in your text editor and immediately save it as **Ch04XMLEX04.xml**.
6. Modify the three `<university>` elements so they include a name attribute with the name of the university. Also, delete each `<name>` element.
7. Save and close the **Ch04XMLEX04.xml** file.
8. Use xmlspy 5 to validate the **Ch04XMLEX04.xml** document against the **Ch04XMLEX04.dtd** file. If you receive any parsing errors, fix them, and then open the document in Internet Explorer.

Exercise 4-5

In this exercise, you create a DTD for an existing XML document.

1. Create a document in your text editor and type the following XML document:

```
<?xml version="1.0" encoding="iso-8859-1" standalone="no"?>
<!DOCTYPE travel SYSTEM "Ch04XMLEX05.dtd">
<travel>
     <transportation mode="airplane">
          <destination>Paris</destination>
          <depart_date>June 1</depart_date>
          <carrier company="United" />
     </transportation>
     <transportation mode="train">
          <destination>New Orleans</destination>
          <depart_date>April 15</depart_date>
          <railroad company="Amtrak" />
     </transportation>
     <transportation mode="automobile">
          <destination>Vancouver</destination>
          <depart_date>August 3</depart_date>
     </transportation>
</travel>
```

2. Save the XML document as **Ch04XMLEX05.xml** in the Exercises folder for Chapter 4.
3. Create another document in your text editor and create a DTD for the Ch04XMLEX05.xml document.
4. Save the DTD document as **Ch04XMLEX05.dtd** in the Exercises folder for Chapter 4.
5. Use xmlspy 5 to validate the **Ch04XMLEX05.xml** document against the **Ch04XMLEX05.dtd** file. If you receive any parsing errors, fix them, and then open the document in Internet Explorer.

Web Programming Projects

In the following projects, use xmlspy 5 to validate each XML document against its associated DTD. Save the documents in the Projects folder for Chapter 4.

Project 4-1

Create an accounts receivable DTD. Include elements such as `<vendor>`, `<date>`, and `<amount>`. Also, include empty elements for different payment options, such as check, credit card, and cash, but allow only one payment option to be selected. Create unique attributes for each payment option, such as a check number attribute for the check element. Also create an XML document that uses the accounts receivable DTD. Save the DTD document as **Ch04XMLProject01.dtd** and the XML document as **Ch04XMLProject01.xml**.

Project 4-2

Create a DTD that contains elements you find in a business memo. Include elements such as sender, recipient, subject, salutation, and paragraph. Add at least one empty element and one attribute with a default value—but do not use an attribute default. Be sure to set up the element sequence so that XML documents must add each element in the proper order. Also, allow XML documents to include multiple `<paragraph>` elements. Create an XML document that uses the elements and attributes in the DTD. Save the DTD document as **Ch04XMLProject02.dtd** and the XML document as **Ch04XMLProject02.xml**.

Project 4-3

Create a DTD that contains elements you find in a resume. Include elements such as your name and position desired. Create any other nested elements that you deem appropriate, such as `<references>` or `<special_skills>` elements. Be sure to set up the element sequence so that XML documents must add each element in the proper order. Also, allow XML documents to include multiple `<employment>` and `<education>` elements. Save the DTD document as **Ch04XMLProject03.dtd** and the XML document as **Ch04XMLProject03.xml** in the Chapter04\Projects folder.

CHAPTER

5

VISUAL BASIC .NET: PART I

In this chapter you will:

- Understand the basics of Visual Studio .NET
- Use the Visual Studio .NET Integrated Developer Interface (IDE)
- Create the user interface for a program
- Use VB .NET controls
- Examine the structure of a VB .NET module
- Understand VB .NET data types and variables
- Understand event handlers
- Use decision-making statements and repetition statements

In this chapter, you will learn about elemental features of Visual Basic .NET (VB .NET), one of today's most popular languages for programming personal computers. The popularity of VB .NET stems from its ease of use and its capabilities. You can use VB .NET to create desktop applications that work the same way as any other Windows application. That is, the VB .NET applications you create are made up of forms containing buttons that the user clicks, boxes in which the user enters text, and other visual elements including check boxes and list boxes. You can use VB .NET to create applications that run on the Internet or an intranet. In addition, you can create VB .NET applications that work with databases including Microsoft Access, SQL Server, and Oracle. No matter which programming problem you are trying to solve, VB .NET can solve it.

VB .NET is but one programming language that makes up a suite of programming languages called Visual Studio .NET. C# (pronounced "C sharp") and C++ are the other two languages in the Visual Studio .NET family. No matter which Visual Studio .NET language you choose, you can create programs that produce the same results. Language compatibility and interoperability are two of the new features supplied by the Visual Studio .NET development environment.

UNDERSTANDING THE BASICS OF VISUAL STUDIO .NET

VB .NET is an **object-oriented programming** language, which means that you work with reusable components to create programs. For example, in nearly every VB .NET program that you create, you reuse a component called the Button control to provide the user with a clickable button. VB .NET defines thousands of different reusable components, each designed to perform a particular task. Some of these components are visible to the user, while others are accessed through programming statements. Visual Studio .NET organizes each of these predefined components hierarchically. Understanding this organization and how Visual Studio .NET executes the components contained in the hierarchy are the keys to creating .NET applications.

For a user to run any application created in Visual Studio .NET (using VB .NET or another language), the user's computer must have a software component installed known as the **.NET Framework**. The .NET Framework has two parts: the Common Language Specification, and the .NET Framework class library.

The .NET Framework is automatically installed when you install Visual Studio .NET. If you need a copy of the .NET Framework, however, you can download the file named DotNetFx.exe from *www.msdn.microsoft.com*. Executing this file runs the installer for the .NET Framework.

The Common Language Specification

The **Common Language Specification (CLS)** defines a set of standards allowing Visual Studio .NET languages and the applications written using those languages to seamlessly operate with each other. Because of the CLS, it does not matter whether you develop programs in VB .NET, C#, or use another Visual Studio .NET language. The CLS includes the **Common Type System (CTS)** and the **Common Language Runtime (CLR)**.

Visual Studio .NET and the services provided by the .NET Framework form an object-oriented programming environment. At the core of this environment is the concept of a **type**, which is a template from which you create objects. The CTS defines the structure and format for every type. For example, Integers and Strings are types. No matter which Visual Studio .NET programming language you choose, the format of a particular type is the same. For example, a Visual Studio .NET Integer is 32 bits in both VB .NET and C#. A TextBox and a Button are also considered types and work the same way in both VB .NET and C#.

When you compile a Visual Studio .NET application into an executable file, that executable file cannot run unless the .NET Framework is installed on the computer. The reason for this requirement is simple. Visual Studio .NET executable files are not true executable files. A Visual Studio .NET application is compiled into a machine-independent language called **Microsoft Intermediate Language (MSIL)**. The term IL is commonly used for brevity. When the .NET Framework executes an IL program, it translates the machine-independent statements into an executable program that runs on a specific computer's hardware. In Visual Studio .NET, this translation is performed by the **just-in-time (JIT)** compiler. This machine independence allows applications developed in any Visual Studio .NET language to execute on any computer, no matter the type of underlying hardware. That is, a Visual Studio .NET application could run on a Pentium-based computer, or other brand of CPU.

The CLR manages the execution of a running application by translating IL programs into executable programs and managing the memory for running applications. As statements in a program execute and create objects, the CLR allocates memory from the managed heap. The **managed heap** is an area of memory managed by the CLR. The CLR keeps track of the allocated memory, and returns that memory to the managed heap when the object is no longer used. This process of returning memory to the managed heap is called **garbage collection**. The CLR allocates other types of objects from an area in memory called the **program stack**. A program that is executed by the CLR is called **managed code**.

The .NET Framework Class Library

The **.NET Framework class library** contains all of the types defined by the .NET Framework. In Visual Studio .NET, types are built from other types using inheritance. To understand the concept of inheritance, consider the subject of biology. In biology, every organism is classified systematically into a coherent hierarchical order based on the attributes of that organism. For example, the base classification is the kingdom. All species are divided into the plant (Plantae) and animal (Animalia) kingdoms. Each kingdom is divided into phylums. This subdivision of species continues with the class, order, family, genus, and species. Figure 5-1 illustrates the classification of a short list of different species.

Through genetic inheritance, one type expands upon or alters the features supplied by another type. Figure 5-1, for example, shows the systematic classification for humans (homo sapiens), and the black widow spider (Latrodectus mactans).

The .NET Framework organizes types in a manner similar to the preceding biological classification. All of the types belonging to the .NET Framework, along with the types that you create, are organized into a hierarchy. The type at the base of the .NET Framework hierarchy is System.Object. In other words, System.Object lies at the root of the hierarchical tree and is called the **superclass**. Consider System.Object as the kingdom. All other types inherit characteristics from System.Object. The .NET Framework categorizes types derived from System.Object into value types and reference types. **Value types** (System.ValueType) store their data directly in the memory allocated to the variable. The memory for value types is allocated from the program stack. **Reference types** store a memory address in a variable rather than data. This memory address, in turn, points to another memory address in the managed heap, where the object is actually stored. Other types derive from both value types and reference types. For example, data types such as Integer and Single both derive from System.ValueType. Strings are reference types and derive directly from System.Object. Figure 5-2 illustrates a few types in the .NET Framework. (This hierarchy actually contains thousands of elements.)

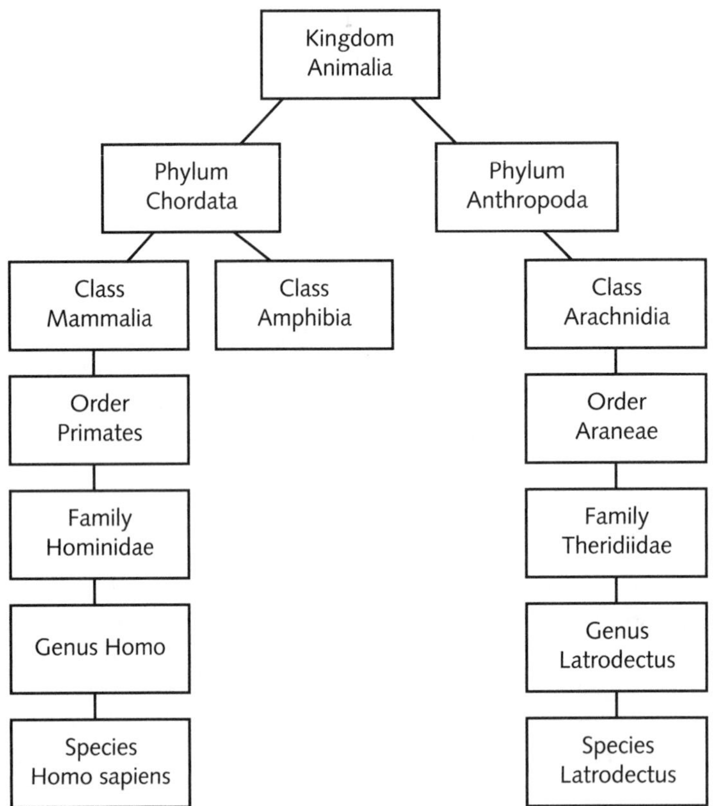

Figure 5-1 Systematic classification of species

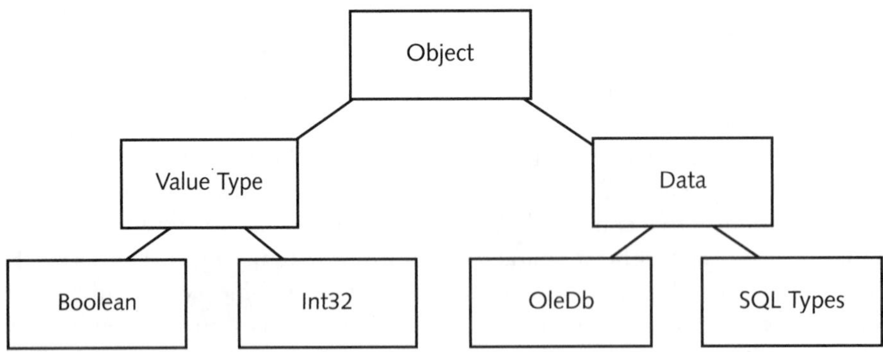

Figure 5-2 Systematic classification of.NET Framework data types

All of the types that make up the .NET Framework are stored in library files that have a .dll extension. These files are called **assemblies**, and they provide the physical organization of the .NET Framework types. In addition to the assemblies that are part of the .NET Framework, the programs that you create are stored in assemblies, too. In fact, every program and .NET component is stored in an assembly. Every assembly contains a manifest. The **manifest** describes the assembly and the modules (files) that form the assembly. The manifest is often referred to as assembly **metadata**. Finally, an assembly contains the code that makes up the component(s) of the assembly.

The following list describes a few .NET Framework assemblies and their purpose. Nearly every desktop form-based application that you create uses these assemblies.

- *System.dll* defines the primary data types such as Integer and Long, and the most elemental types such as System.Object.
- *System.Data.dll* defines the types in ADO.NET, which supplies the database-processing services used by Visual Studio .NET.
- *System.Drawing.dll* contains the types used to draw shapes to an output device, such as the screen or a printer. These shapes include rectangles and lines, among others.
- *System.Windows.Forms.dll* contains the types used to implement the forms used in a desktop application.

Assemblies (physical components) contain one or more logical components called namespaces. **Namespaces** are the primary logical building blocks in the .NET Framework object hierarchy. Namespaces map the physical components stored in an assembly into logical components. Microsoft divides the .NET Framework into two primary namespaces as follows:

- **System namespace**, and those namespaces contained by the System namespace, were created by the Microsoft .NET team.
- **Microsoft namespace**, and those namespaces contained by the Microsoft namespace, were created by Microsoft, but by groups other than the Microsoft .NET team.

VB .NET is not formally considered part of the .NET Framework. Rather, VB .NET is a language that relies on the services provided by the .NET Framework. Therefore, the Microsoft.VisualBasic namespace defines the types unique to the Visual Basic language. Namespaces are organized into a hierarchy. Syntactically, each element in the hierarchy is connected with a period (.). To illustrate, the System namespace contains a class named Convert. The Convert class, in turn, contains a method named ToInt32 that converts a string to an Integer number. Assuming that a variable named mintValue is an Integer number and mstrValue is a string, the following statement explicitly converts the string value into its Integer equivalent.

```
mintValue = System.Convert.ToInt32(mstrValue)
```

Note that the namespace (System), class (Convert), and method (ToInt32) are each connected using a period (.).

Namespaces themselves can be hierarchical. That is, one namespace can contain another namespace, which in turn can contain another namespace. Consider the following statement, which opens a file named C:\Demo.txt for reading:

```
Private pstrCurrent = New System.IO.StreamReader
("C:\Demo.txt")
```

While the meaning of the Private and New keywords will be discussed in more detail later in the chapter, the preceding statement illustrates how hierarchical namespaces are connected. The IO namespace of the System namespace has a class named StreamReader. This class, in turn, contains methods to read a sequential file.

USING THE VISUAL STUDIO .NET INTEGRATED DEVELOPER INTERFACE (IDE)

Visual Studio .NET is an **Integrated Development Environment (IDE)**, which allows you to create, test, debug, and deploy programs. You use the Visual Studio .NET IDE to create computer programs written in Visual Basic, Visual C++, or C#. No matter which Visual Studio .NET programming language you choose, the IDE works the same way; the windows and tools you use to create a program are the same for each Visual Studio .NET language. In this chapter, you create an application in VB .NET.

You use the following common elements to build different types of applications:

- You create desktop applications with Windows forms. Users interact with a desktop application using a **Windows form**, which appears to the user as a rectangular area on the desktop, typically having a border and a title bar. A Windows form contains boxes in which the user enters text, buttons the user clicks, and other visual elements. These visual elements are called **controls**, which belong to the System.Windows.Forms namespace. When you draw a control on a form, you are creating a **control instance** on the form. A form most often has many control instances. For example, a form can have multiple Button control instances. Each Button control instance performs a different task when clicked by the user.
- Using **Web forms**, you create programmable Web pages. With a Web form, you can, for instance, create an application to look up data in a database based on user input, and then display a Web page containing the selected data.
- **Web services** receive requests from clients, and then respond to those requests. For example, a Web service could be used to track a shipment. Your computer, the client, sends a request containing a tracking number to a Web service. The Web service accepts the request and sends the current location and status of the package back to the client, which is your computer. The client can then display the status information on a Web form, a Windows form, or process the data in some other way.

In this chapter, you create a desktop application based on a Windows form that calculates the cost of an insurance policy based on a person's age, tracks whether that person smokes, and records the person's gender. VB .NET refers to an application as a solution. A **solution** consists of several folders containing the files necessary to test, compile, execute, and distribute the application to other computers. In VB .NET, nearly every file is a text file. You could create or modify the files in the solution using any text editor such as Notepad (though this approach would not be the easiest way to create a solution). A typical Windows form solution contains the following files:

- Visual Studio .NET stores every solution in its own folder. Note that VB .NET automatically creates the solution folder when you create the solution. The solution folder, in turn, contains a **solution file** with a .sln extension. The solution file lists the projects in the solution, and how those projects will be compiled into their respective executable files.
- The solution folder contains two folders named bin and obj. The bin folder stores the compiled executable application, which is what the user runs. The obj folder stores intermediate files needed to debug and test the application in the IDE.
- A solution contains one or more projects, each having its own project file. The **project file** lists the references to any namespaces, form modules, and any other type of module used in the project. A project file has a .vbproj extension.
- A **form module** is stored in a file that has a .vb extension. A form module defines the visual control instances that the user sees, and the statements that execute as the user interacts with those control instances. A project may have multiple forms, hence multiple form modules. Each form in a project is typically stored in a separate file.
- VB .NET creates other files that are part of a project. However, as this chapter introduces only selected VB .NET topics, it omits many of the files automatically generated by VB .NET along with files that are specific to certain project types.

In the next section, you start VB .NET and open an existing solution to explore the IDE.

Starting Visual Studio .NET and Opening an Existing Solution

To start VB .NET, you run Visual Studio .NET. If you are creating a VB .NET solution, you then specify VB .NET as the language you are using for the solution. If you are opening a solution, as you do in the following steps, the file you open determines which language Visual Studio .NET uses. In this case, Visual Studio .NET is opening a VB .NET solution.

To start Visual Studio .NET:

1. Click the **Start** button on the Windows desktop, point to **Programs** (point to **All Programs** in Windows XP), point to **Microsoft Visual Studio .NET**, and then click **Microsoft Visual Studio .NET**.

As Visual Studio .NET loads, a splash screen appears listing the Visual Studio .NET language products installed on the computer. Your list may vary, depending on the installed software. The Visual Studio .NET IDE then appears, as shown in Figure 5-3.

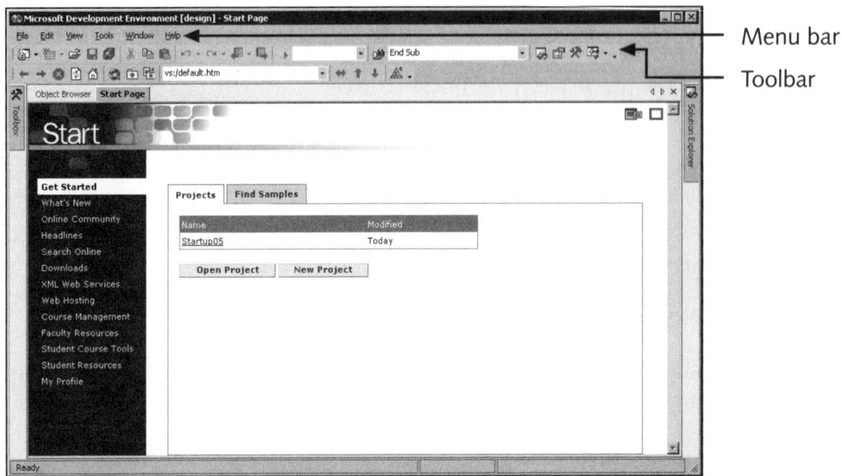

Figure 5-3 Visual Studio .NET IDE

Depending on the configuration of your computer, the appearance and size of the windows in the IDE may differ from those shown in Figure 5-3. In addition, the solutions that appear list the most recently opened solutions on your computer and will also vary. By default, the IDE displays a Start page allowing you to create new applications, and open existing ones. However, the Start page may not appear depending on the configuration of your computer. In addition, as with most applications, a menu bar appears below the title bar and toolbars appear below the menu bar.

So that you can best see how a solution works, in this chapter you open a partially completed solution, explore its contents, and then complete that solution. As mentioned, the solution that you complete calculates the cost of an insurance policy. The steps to open a solution in Visual Studio .NET are similar to the steps to open a document in Microsoft Word. You can double-click the solution file in Windows Explorer or open the solution from Visual Studio .NET. In these steps, you open the solution from Visual Studio .NET.

2. On the Visual Studio .NET menu bar, click **File**, point to **Open**, and then click **Project**. The Open Project dialog box appears.
3. Click the **Look in** list arrow, and then locate and select the folder named **Chap05\Chapter\Startup05** in your work folder.
4. Click the file named **Startup05.sln** to select it. See Figure 5-4.

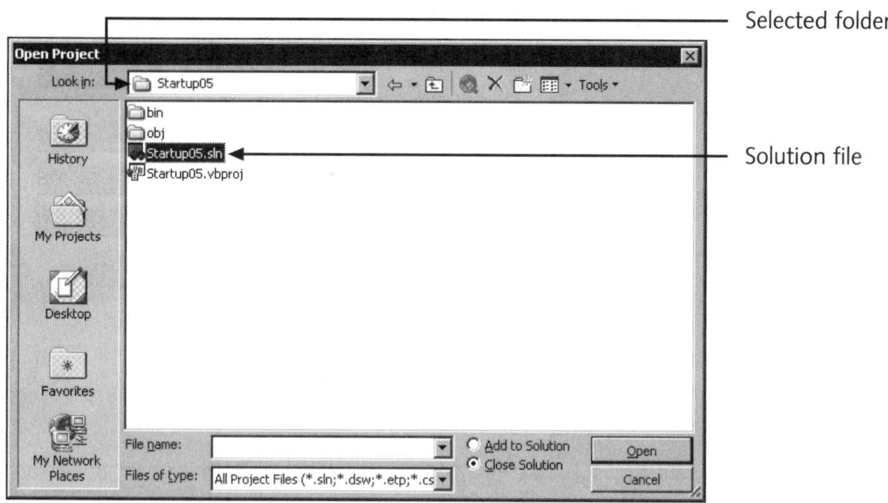

Figure 5-4 Open Project dialog box

5. Click the **Open** button to open the solution file and close the Open Project dialog box. The Startup05 solution opens. See Figure 5-5. (Note that your window may differ slightly.)

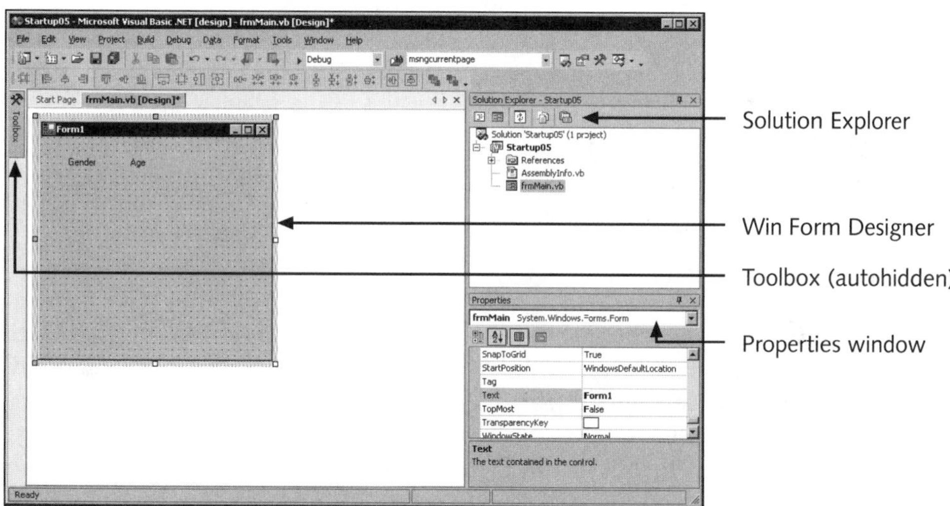

Figure 5-5 Startup05 solution open in Visual Studio .NET

You work in the Win Form Designer to build a form, which is what users interact with when they use your solution. You work in the Code Editor to modify the VB .NET statements that execute when the user interacts with the form.

When you are working in the Win Form Designer, you set properties for forms and control instances in the Properties window, use the Toolbox to add control instances to the form, and manage files using the Solution Explorer.

The following sections discuss these parts of the VB .NET windows in more detail.

6. Open the Solution Explorer, if necessary, by clicking **View** on the VB .NET menu bar, and then clicking **Solution Explorer**.
7. Click the **Show All Files** button in the Solution Explorer to display all of the folders in the solution. (Figure 5-6 shows the Show All Files button.)
8. Expand the folders as necessary by clicking the **plus signs** so that the Solution Explorer resembles Figure 5-6.

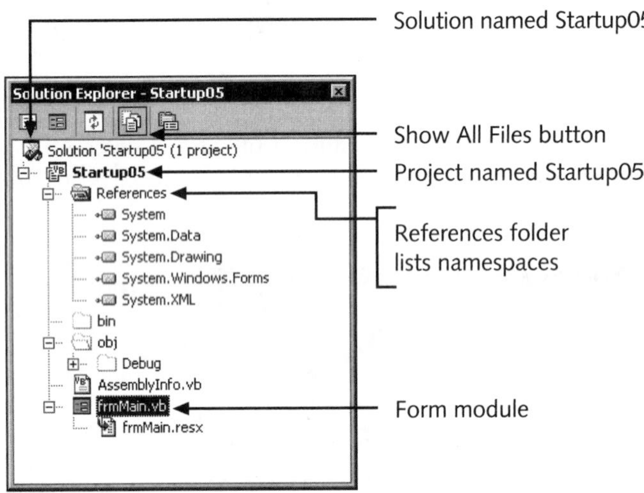

Figure 5-6 Solution Explorer

As shown in Figure 5-6, the Solution Explorer contains a single solution named Startup05 and a single project folder having the same name. The project folder contains a folder named References, which lists the namespaces used by the project. VB .NET provides access to classes through namespaces. Figure 5-6 lists five namespaces. When you create a solution, VB .NET adds to the project references to the most commonly used namespaces.

The project also contains a single form named frmMain.vb. Remember that a form is considered a module, and it corresponds to a physical file on the disk. When you create a new solution (application), VB .NET creates a single blank form for you automatically. The Startup05 solution already contains a form for you to complete. Control instances have already been created on the form.

Figure 5-6 also lists folders named bin and obj. Remember that the bin folder contains the executable file(s) that you distribute to other computers, and the obj folder stores temporary files used to debug and test the solution. The folders shown in Figure 5-6 correspond to physical folders on the disk.

The solution you complete in this chapter, like most Windows applications, consists of two parts. The user interface is the first part of the solution. The **user interface** represents what users see when they run the solution. The second part of the solution contains the statements that execute as the user clicks the buttons and interacts with other control instances on the form. These statements are called the **code behind the form**. First, you explore how to create the visual interface for the solution and the windows that you use to create the visual interface. In the following section, you use the windows of the IDE to configure the form, and then create the control instances on the form.

How and where a window appears inside the IDE depends on its type. Visual Studio .NET divides windows into two types: document windows and tool windows.

Document Windows and Their Role

Document windows appear on group tabs and correspond to the individual files (modules) in a solution. The Win Form Designer and Code Editor are the primary document windows that you use to create desktop VB .NET applications. Visual Studio .NET supports two document windows that allow you to create the visual interface and code for a specific solution.

Figure 5-7 illustrates the IDE with three open document windows appearing on one tab group: the Visual Studio .NET Start Page, the Win Form Designer, and the Code Editor. The Win Form Designer is the active window. The Solution Explorer and Properties window are both tool windows appearing in the figure.

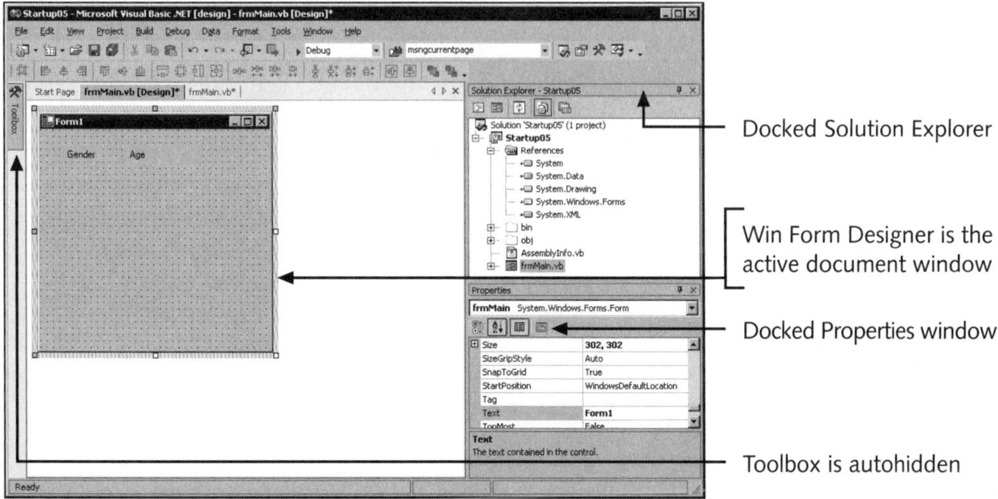

Figure 5-7 Document and tool windows

As shown in Figure 5-7, one tab group appears containing three documents, each appearing as a tab on the tab group. The Win Form Designer is the active document window. To switch between open document windows, you click the tab for the desired document. For example, to activate the Code Editor, click frmMain on the tab group.

Three buttons appear at the right of the tab group. The left and right arrows are used when the tabs representing the open documents do not fit on the tab group. Clicking these arrows scrolls the tabs to the left or right. Clicking the Close button on the tab group closes the active document window.

Tool Windows and Their Role

Tool windows help you manage an application. For example, the Properties window allows you to define the attributes for a form or other object such as a control instance. The Solution Explorer is also a tool window. Tool windows can float on the desktop, be docked along an edge of the IDE, or be autohidden. The same tool windows are used in the creation of all VB .NET solutions. Tool windows appear in one of four ways.

- A tool window may be docked. A **docked** tool window appears anchored along any edge of the IDE. To dock a tool window, right-click the tool window's title bar, and then click Dockable. Then drag the window to the edge of the IDE where you want the window to be docked.
- Tool windows may appear as floating windows. A **floating window** is not docked to another window, and appears anywhere on the desktop. To make a tool window appear as a floating window, right-click the tool window's title bar, disable autohide if necessary, and then click Dockable to remove the check box.
- Docked windows appearing on a specific edge of the IDE parent window may be autohidden. When **autohide** is enabled, the window name appears as a tab along an edge of the IDE window. Moving the mouse over the tab causes the window to be displayed. Moving the mouse off of the autohidden window causes the window to disappear. To autohide a window, first make it dockable, and then dock the window along an edge of the IDE. Next, right-click the title bar and enable the autohide feature.
- Tool windows, such as the Solution Explorer and the Properties window, can also be configured to appear as a document window by dragging the window to a tab group.

When and how the tool windows are displayed is a matter of preference. Configure the IDE to suit your own personal work habits.

Having seen the basics of tool windows and document windows, you now complete the user interface for the partially completed solution that you have already loaded.

Creating the User Interface for a Solution

The user of a VB .NET solution interacts with a form by clicking buttons, entering text into boxes, and so on, just as any user would interact with any other Windows application. Buttons and text boxes appear inside of windows, or forms. Most VB .NET solutions have one or more forms. The collection of forms and the buttons and boxes created on those forms constitute the user interface of a solution.

For the Startup05 project, you are creating a user interface that includes the control instances created on the form. These elements allow the user to enter a person's age and gender, and select whether or not the person smokes. In addition, buttons appear that perform tasks as the user clicks a button. Part of the user interface has already been completed in the form for the Startup05 project. You complete this user interface by customizing the form's size, defining its title, and configuring the form so that it is not resizable.

Setting the Form's Properties

The Startup05 project already contains a partially completed form named frmMain, shown in Figure 5-8.

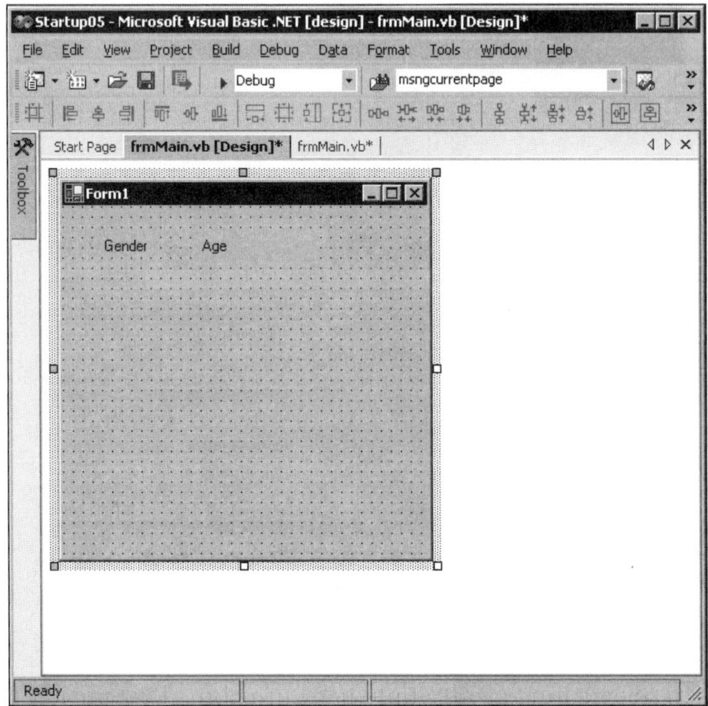

Figure 5-8 frmMain form

Note that this form has two instances of the Label control already created. We have created some of the control instances merely to reduce the number of repetitive tasks that you must perform. In the steps that follow, you create the remaining control instances on the form.

A form and its control instances have properties that define their visual appearance. For this form, you create control instances and set their properties so that the user can calculate the cost of an insurance policy. To change the appearance and position of the form, you set its properties. Because this form will contain additional control instances, you increase its width and height, specify that it opens in the center of the desktop when the user runs the solution, add a descriptive title, and modify the border so that the user cannot resize the form. In the following steps, you use the Properties window to change the properties of the frmMain form.

To define the properties for a form:

1. Activate the Win Form Designer, if necessary, by clicking the form named **frmMain.vb** in the Solution Explorer, clicking **View** on the menu bar, and then clicking **Designer**.

2. Press **F4** to activate the Properties window, if necessary. View the properties alphabetically by clicking the **Alphabetic** button at the top of the Properties window. See Figure 5-9.

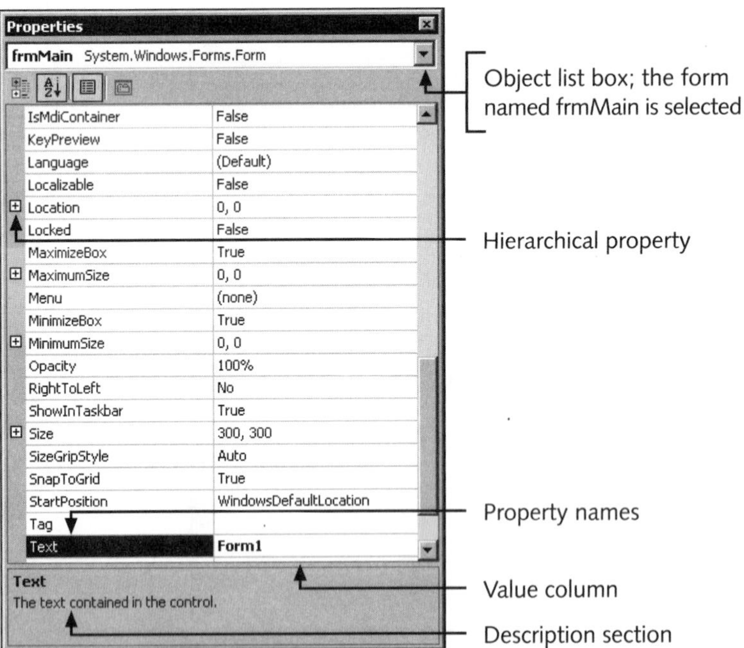

Figure 5-9 Properties window

The Object list box at the top of the Properties window identifies the form or control instance for which you are setting properties. To work with a different form or control instance, you click the Object list arrow, and then select the form or control instance. The Properties window also contains two columns. The first column displays the name of a property related to the current form or control instance. The second column, called the value column, lists the corresponding property value. To change the value of a property, you click in the value column for a property, and then type or select a new value.

3. To change the size of the form, you set its Width and Height properties. Start by locating the Size property in the Properties window, using the scroll bars, if necessary. Click the **plus sign** to the left of the Size property to display the Width and Height properties.
4. In the value column, set the Width property to **470**, and then press **Enter**.
5. In the value column, set the Height property to **390**, and then press **Enter**. (Note that you could also type **470, 390** in the Size property box.)
6. To specify that the form opens in the center of the desktop, click in the value column to the right of the **StartPosition** property. A list arrow appears in the value column. Click the list arrow, and then click **CenterScreen**.
7. To define the border of the form, click the value column for the **FormBorderStyle** property, click the **FormBorderStyle** list arrow, and then click **FixedSingle**. Because the control instances will not resize if the user resizes the form, it is logical to prohibit the user from resizing the form.
8. To change the text that appears in the form's title bar, click in the value column to the right of the **Text** property (which now reads "Form1"), and then type **Insurance Calculator**. This title better describes the purpose of the form. See Figure 5-10.

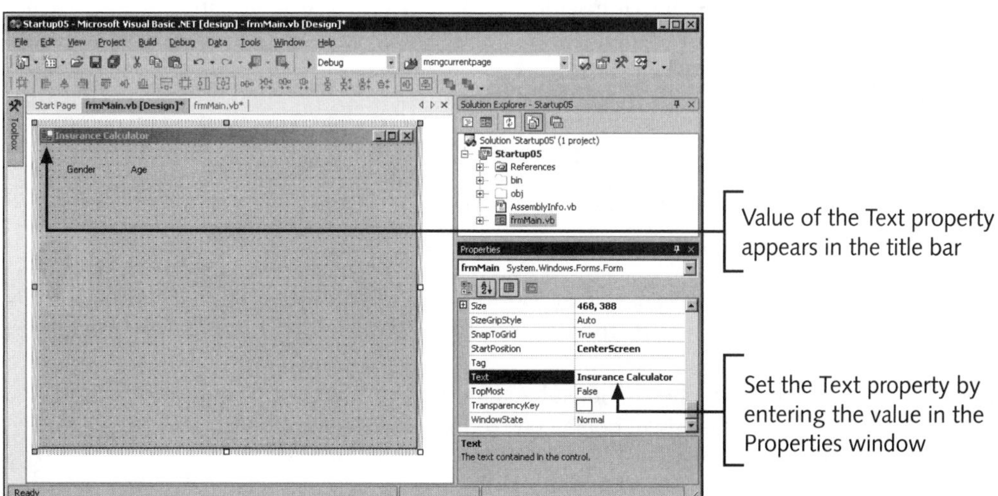

Figure 5-10 Setting the form's Text property

After completing a task, it is a good idea to save your work.

9. On the VB .NET menu bar, click **File**, and then click **Save All**. The solution and all of the files, including the form, that comprise the solution are saved.

Note that the frmMain form already includes Label control instances that are used to describe a list box where users select a gender, and a combo box where users select an age range. In the following sections, you add other types of controls to the form. No matter the type of control instance that you create, the process to create them is exactly the same.

Creating a Control Instance

When you add a control to a form, you are creating an instance of the control from its class. Both the form and each control are considered VB .NET classes. You can create multiple occurrences, or instances, of the same control. For example, the frmMain form already contains two instances of the Label control—the Gender and Age labels. You create a control instance by dragging a control from the Toolbox to the form.

No matter the type of control instance that you create, whether it is a TextBox, Label, or Button, all controls have similar characteristics. VB .NET also assigns a unique name to every control instance when you create it. This unique name is stored in the Name property. To make the programs you write more readable, you should change this default name to a name that explains the purpose of the control instance. Each type of control has a defined set of properties just as a form has properties, although the properties may vary from one type of control to another according to the tasks they perform.

After you create a control instance on the form, you can set its properties. You can reposition or resize a control instance by using the Properties window, or by dragging it on the form. To delete a control instance, click the control instance in the Win Form Designer to select it, and then press Delete.

In the following steps, you create an instance of a Label control on the frmMain form. This label will ultimately display the current date. You write the statements to display the current date later in the chapter.

To create a control instance on a form:

1. Activate the Win Form Designer, if necessary.
2. Activate the Toolbox by pointing to the autohidden Toolbox window along the left side of the VB .NET window.

If the Toolbox is not autohidden along the left side of the window, click View, and then click Toolbox on the menu bar to activate it.

3. Click the **Label** control on the Toolbox. When clicked, the control appears recessed in the Toolbox. See Figure 5-11.

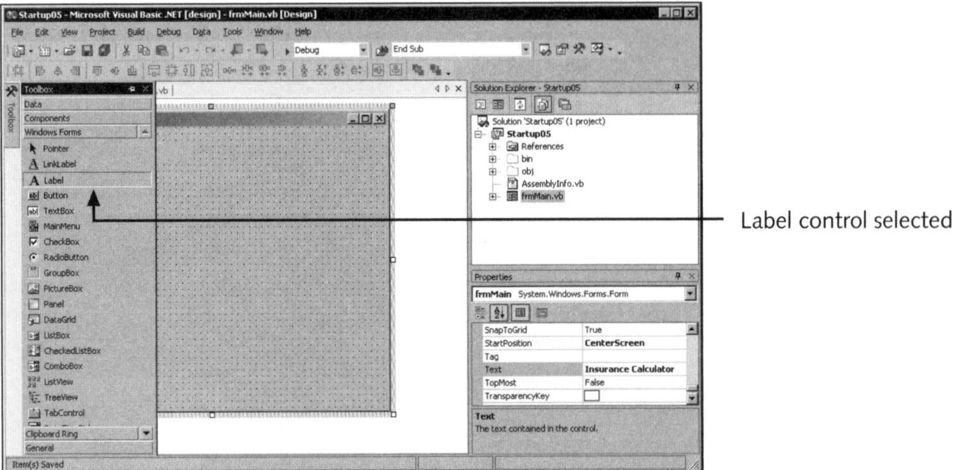

Figure 5-11 Toolbox with Label control selected

4. Drag the **Label** control instance to the lower-right region of the form. You will position the Label control instance in the next set of steps.

Eight small boxes (called sizing handles) surround the border of the Label control instance, indicating that it is selected. You drag a sizing handle to resize a control instance. You drag a selected control instance to move it to a new position on the form. You can also use the Properties window to position and resize a control instance.

To resize and reposition a control instance:

1. If necessary, click the **Label** control instance that you just created to select it.

If you accidentally double-click the control instance, you open the Code Editor. Click View, and then click Designer on the VB .NET menu bar to return to the Win Form Designer.

2. Drag the **Label** control instance to the lower-right corner of the form. An outline of the label appears on the form as you drag, indicating the current position of the control instance. This label will ultimately display the current date. Status information such as the current date typically appears along the bottom of a form.
3. Drag the sizing handles so that the label is approximately two inches wide. The size of the label changes as you drag each sizing handle.
4. Activate the Properties window for the Label control instance.
5. Remove the text from the Text property. You store the current date in the label later in the chapter when the program executes.
6. Set the BorderStyle property to **FixedSingle**. A black border surrounds the control instance.

Another way to set the size and position of a control instance is to set the Size and Location properties using the Properties window. Whether to drag the control instance or use the Properties window is a matter of personal preference. Next, you position and size the control instance so that it appears in the lower-right corner of the form at a precise location and having an exact size so that the label you created matches the one shown in Figure 5-12.

7. Set the Size property to **168, 24**.
8. Set the Location property to **256, 320**.
9. Set the Name property to **lblDate**. See Figure 5-12.

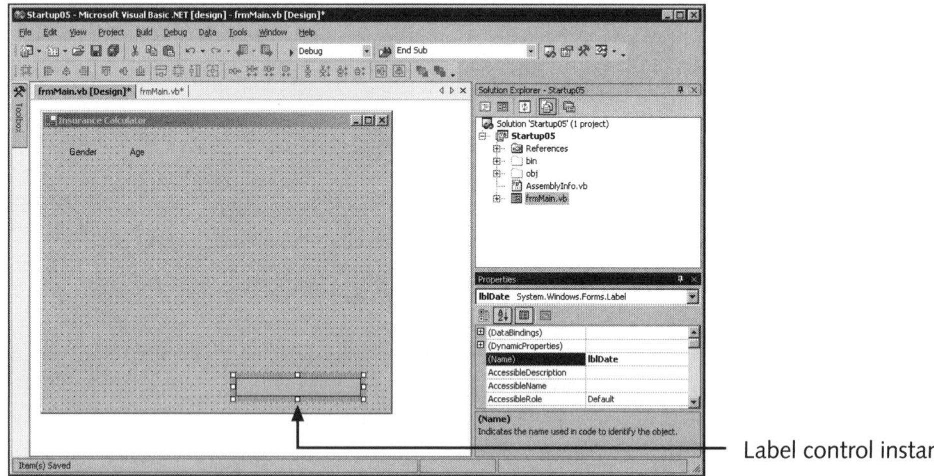

Figure 5-12 Form with Label control instance

10. Save the solution by clicking **File**, and then clicking **Save All**. Again, save your work each time you reach a milestone in your program.

No matter what type control instance you create, the process is the same. That is, whether you are creating a TextBox, Button, or any other control instance, you add them to the form, move them, and resize them using exactly the same techniques. Next, you learn more about other controls and their properties, and then add them to the frmMain form.

Using VB .NET Controls

For each control instance that you create, you assign a unique value to the Name property. So that you, as the developer, can easily identify the type of control instance, you use a standard three-character prefix for the name (the value of the Name property). For example, the three-character prefix for the Button control is btn. Following the three-character prefix, you supply descriptive text to identify the purpose of the control instance. For example, the name of the Calculate button is btnCalculate. The value for the Name property must be unique, must begin with a letter, must not contain any special characters other than the underscore character, and be less than 255 characters in length.

The following list describes the controls you will use in this chapter. Note that you only use a few of the available VB .NET controls as this is an introductory chapter on VB .NET.

- When the user clicks the Button control, statements in your program execute to perform some action.
- The TextBox and Label controls are used to edit and display text, respectively.
- The CheckBox control displays a box that can either be checked or unchecked. The CheckBox control is useful when the user needs to choose between two possible values, such as whether a person is male or female.
- The ComboBox and ListBox controls allow the user to select one or more items from a list of items. These two controls support nearly the same properties.

Creating Button Control Instances

In the following steps, you create two instances of the Button control. The first button, the Calculate button, calculates the cost of the insurance policy when clicked. The second button, the Exit button, lets users exit the solution. You can create the Calculate and Exit buttons by dragging the Button control from the Toolbox to the form, as you did to create a label. Later in the chapter, you write the code to specify what the solution does when the buttons are clicked.

To create buttons on the form:

1. Activate the Toolbox.
2. Click the **Button** control in the Toolbox to create an instance of the control on the form. Drag the button to the right side of the form, as shown in Figure 5-13.
3. Using the Properties window, set the Name property of the button to **btnCalculate**, and set the Text property to **&Calculate**.

   You create a hot key for a button by inserting an ampersand character (&) in the Text property before the character that acts as the hot key. A hot key is a set of keystrokes a user types to produce the same result as clicking the button. The hot key for the Calculate button is Alt+C. Each hot key on a form should be unique.
4. Create a second Button control instance on the form, below the first button. Set the Name property to **btnExit**, and the Text property to **E&xit**. (The hot key for the Exit button is Alt+X.)
5. Position the buttons as shown in Figure 5-13.

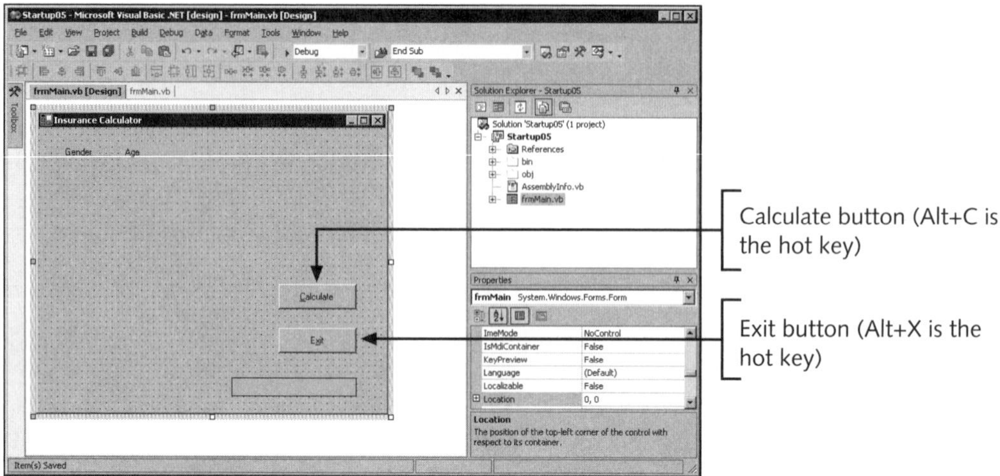

Figure 5-13 Creating buttons

6. On the menu bar, click **File**, and then click **Save All** to save all of the files comprised by the solution and the solution file itself.

So far, you've added three control instances to the user interface of the form: a label that will display the current date, and two buttons that users can click. In the next section, you create a text box in which to display the cost of the insurance policy.

Adding a TextBox Control

The TextBox and Label controls are similar. The Label control displays text, often to identify a particular control instance appearing on the form or to display textual output. In a TextBox control, the user can enter text as well as view the text displayed. For example, in a text box, the user can enter his or her name. A text box can also be used to enter numbers or any other textual data. A text box can also be configured to display textual output appearing on multiple lines. In this solution, you create a text box to display the insurance quotation. This information will not fit on a single line.

To create and format a TextBox control instance:

1. Activate the Win Form Designer, if necessary, and create a TextBox control instance on the form. (You can drag the TextBox control from the Toolbox, or double-click it.) See Figure 5-14.
2. Using the Properties window, set the Name property to **txtOutput**.
3. Remove the text from the Text property. The statements that you write later in the chapter define the text that appears in the text box. This text will contain the insurance quotation.
4. Set the Multiline property to **True** so that the text can span more than one line. (You set this property to False to restrict the text to one line.)

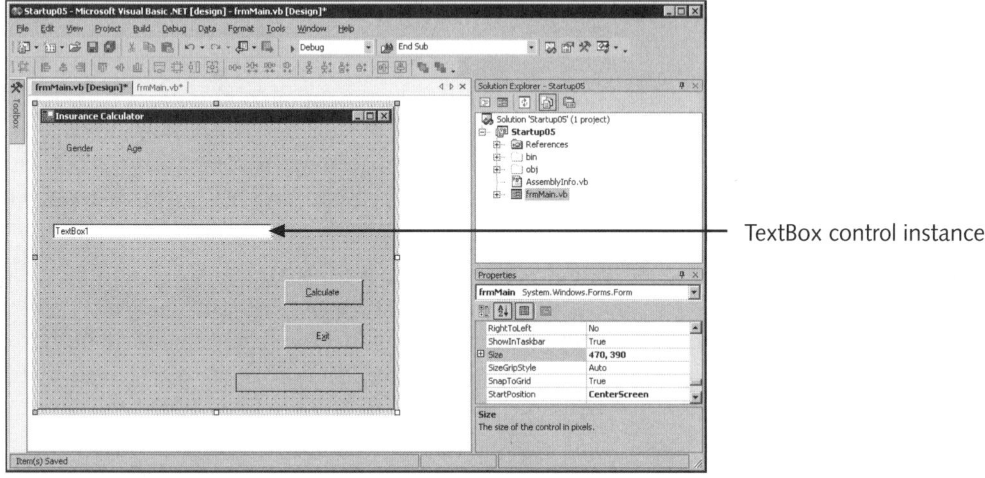

Figure 5-14 Adding a text box

5. Resize the control instance so that it resembles the one shown in Figure 5-15.

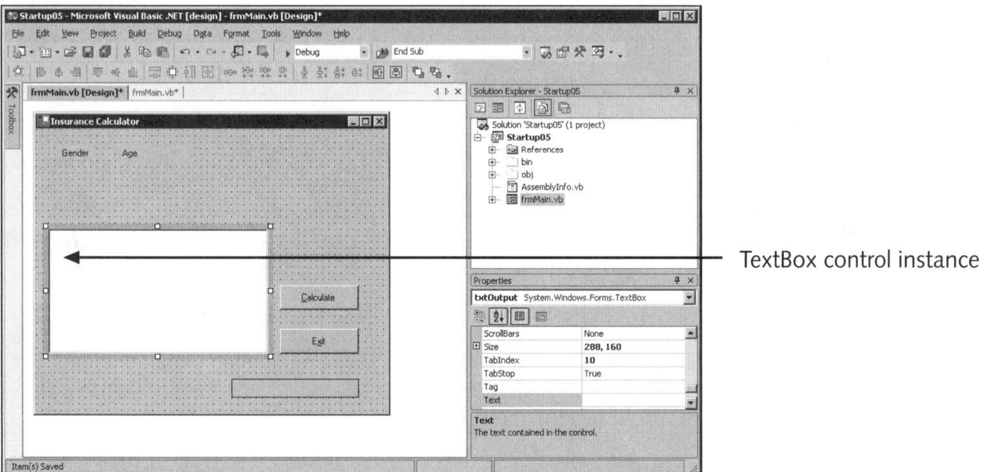

Figure 5-15 Resizing a text box

6. Save the solution by clicking **File**, and then clicking **Save All** on the menu bar.

In addition to the TextBox and Label controls, VB .NET supports other specialized controls. For example, the CheckBox control is useful when the user needs to specify yes/no information.

Adding a CheckBox Control Instance

In cases where a user needs to choose between two possible values, such as yes or no and on or off, the CheckBox control is the most suitable choice, as it is designed for situations in which yes and no are the only choices. The **CheckBox** control creates a box that can be checked or unchecked. It contains three visible regions: a box that indicates whether the box is checked, a descriptive prompt, and an optional icon. The standard prefix for a check box is chk.

The CheckBox control can also be configured to specify a third choice, called indeterminate, which is typically used to indicate that the user has not yet checked or unchecked the box. For example, if the user must explicitly specify whether or not they smoke, then the initial state of the check box should be set to indeterminate indicating that the user has not yet made a selection.

In the following steps, you add a CheckBox control to the form so users can select whether they are a smoker or a nonsmoker.

To add a CheckBox control to the form:

1. Activate the Win Form Designer, if necessary, and create a CheckBox control instance on the form. You create a CheckBox control instance in the same way you created Label and TextBox control instances. Click the **CheckBox** control in the Toolbox, and drag the control instance on to the form.
2. Set the value of the Name property to **chkSmoker**.
3. The value of the Text property appears in the visible region of the control instance to describe its purpose. Set the value of the Text property to **Smoker**.
4. The TextAlign property indicates how the text is aligned within the region of the control instance. Set the value of the TextAlign property to **MiddleCenter** by clicking the list arrow, and then clicking the center box.
5. By default, the CheckBox control allows two possible states indicating on and off. The ThreeState property, if set to True, allows the CheckState property to store three possible values. Remember that this third value is indeterminate. Set the ThreeState property to **True**.
6. The CheckAlign property determines where the box appears within the region of the control instance. Set the CheckAlign property to **MiddleRight**.
7. To indicate that the check box is neither checked nor unchecked set the CheckState property to **Indeterminate**. The configured check box is shown in Figure 5-16.

Your form to calculate the cost of an insurance policy is almost complete. You need to add two other control instances—the ListBox and ComboBox controls. The user interacts with these controls by selecting a value from a list of values. Your form needs a list box so that users can select their gender. You'll add a combo box to the form so that the user can select their age from a predefined list of values. These two input values will be used to determine the cost of the insurance policy.

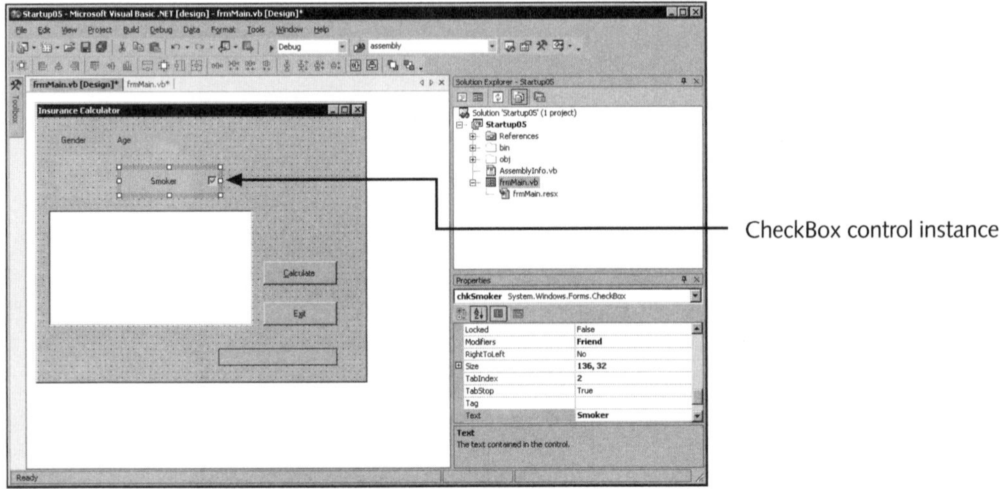

Figure 5-16 Creating a check box

Using ListBox and ComboBox Controls

The ComboBox and ListBox controls display lists of data, such as a list of names. Both controls allow you to sort lists, and determine which item or items the user has selected.

The ListBox and ComboBox controls share many of the same properties. The user cannot enter new items into a list box by typing information. Rather, you must add items at design time by setting the Items property or at run time by calling the Add method. However, the user can enter items into a combo box depending on how the combo box is configured.

The ListBox control, like the ComboBox control, displays a list of items. However, the ComboBox control displays a drop-down list, but the ListBox control does not. The choice of whether to use a list box or combo box is subjective. Primarily, the list box consumes more space on the form. Therefore, when a form contains many control instances and space is limited, use a combo box instead of a list box. The prefix for the ComboBox control is "cbo", and the prefix for the ListBox control is "lst". In this chapter, you create a list box to store a person's gender.

To create a ListBox control instance:

1. Activate the Win Form Designer, if necessary, and create a ListBox control instance on the form. Change the size and position of the ListBox control instance to match the one shown in Figure 5-17.
2. Set the Name property to **lstGender**. Again, remember that the Name of each control instance appearing on the form must be unique.

Next, you add items to the list box that you just created. The ListBox control instance should list two values—Male and Female—so users can specify the gender of the person applying for insurance.

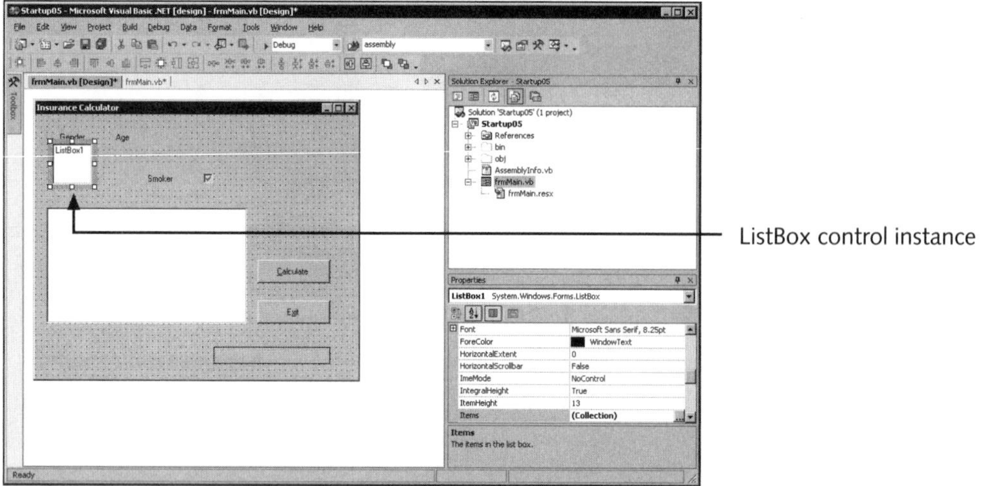

Figure 5-17 Creating a ListBox control instance

To set properties of the ListBox control instance:

1. Click the **value** column for the Items property, and then click the **build** button to display the String Collection Editor dialog box. You use this dialog box to enter the items that appear on each line of the list box.
2. Type **Male** and press **Enter**, and then type **Female** and press **Enter**. See Figure 5-18. Click **OK** to record your changes and close the String Collection Editor dialog box.

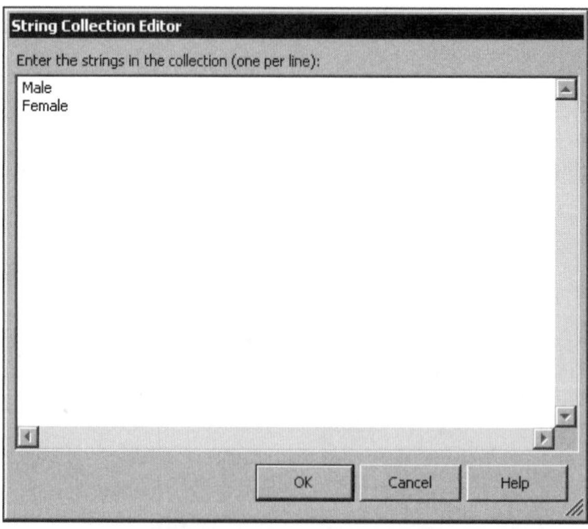

Figure 5-18 String Collection Editor dialog box

3. Save your changes by clicking **File**, and then clicking **Save All**.

Having created the ListBox control instance, you next create the ComboBox control instance. This ComboBox will ultimately display the age of the person applying for the insurance policy.

Combo boxes appear in one of three styles defined by the Style property. Setting the Style property to Dropdown allows a user to select an item from a drop-down list of suggested choices or to type in a new item. No items will appear until the user clicks the list arrow at the right of the combo box. Setting the Style property to Simple displays a text box and a list that does not drop down. Instead, the list shows all choices at all times, causing the combo box to look like a list box. If the list will not fit inside the combo box, a scroll bar appears. The user can then type in a new value not appearing in the list of suggested choices. Setting the Style property to DropDownList allows a user to select an item only from a preset drop-down list of choices. As with the drop-down combo box, this list does not appear until the user clicks the list arrow at the right of the combo box.

To create a ComboBox control instance:

1. Activate the Win Form Designer, if necessary, and create a ComboBox control instance on the form as shown in Figure 5-19.

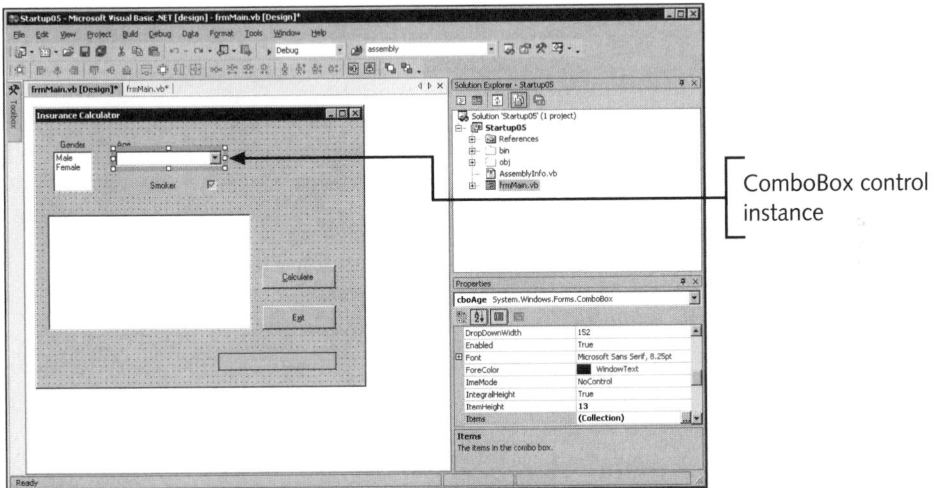

Figure 5-19 Creating a ComboBox control instance

2. Set the Name property to **cboAge**. Remove the text from the Text property.

At this point you have completed creating the user interface for the form. Your form should match the one shown in Figure 5-20. Next, you write the statements that execute as the user interacts with the program.

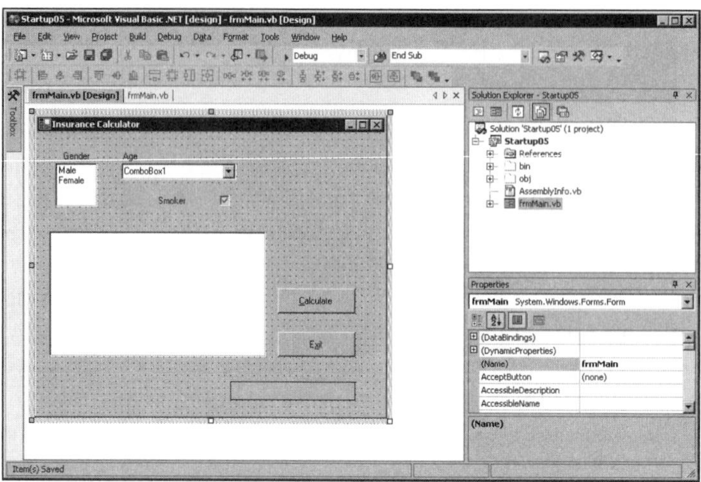

Figure 5-20 Completed user interface for the form

EXAMINING THE STRUCTURE OF A VB .NET MODULE

Every form is stored in a physical file with a .vb extension. This file has a well-defined structure.

A form is a VB .NET class. The `Public Class` and `End Class` keywords mark the beginning and end of the form. In addition, every form that you create inherits all of the capabilities of a Windows form. Therefore, given a form named frmMain, the following statements appear in the form module:

```
Public Class frmMain
    Inherits System.Windows.Forms.Form
End Class
```

The Class keyword defines the name of the class. The statement `Inherits System.Windows.Forms.Form` tells VB .NET that this form inherits from another class. All classes in .NET inherit from other classes and the superclass is System.Object. Finally, the `End Class` statement marks the end of the class.

As you used the Toolbox to create the control instances on your form, VB .NET wrote the corresponding statements in the form module for you. This automatically generated code is, by default, hidden from you. However, you can expand and view these statements if desired. However, do not modify the automatically generated code. If you do, the Win Form Designer may not be able to display the control instances that you created.

In the following steps, you examine the statements automatically generated by the Win Form Designer to explore how to use the Code Editor.

To use the Code Editor to examine statements generated by the Win Form Designer:

1. On the VB .NET menu bar, click **View**, and then click **Code** to activate the Code Editor, shown in Figure 5-21.

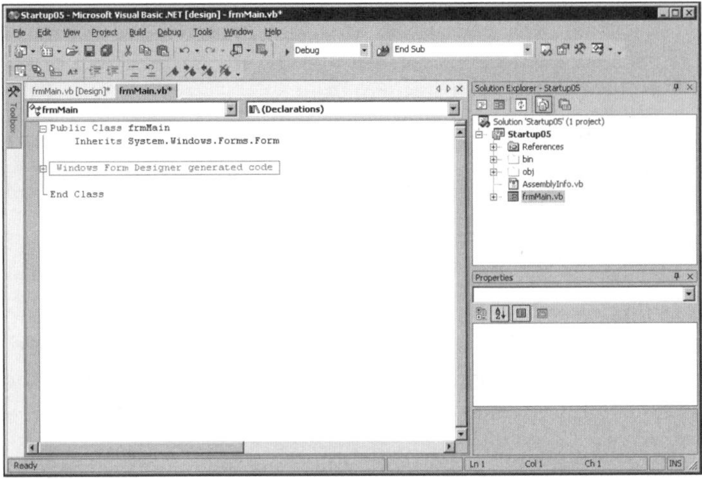

Figure 5-21 Code Editor

As shown in Figure 5-21, the `Class` and `End Class` statements mark the beginning and end of the Form module. In addition, an expandable block appears named Windows Form Designer generated code.

2. Click the **plus sign** to the left of the Windows Form Designer generated code. You see the statements that VB .NET wrote to initialize the form and create the control instances on the form, as shown in Figure 5-22. Note that Figure 5-22 shows only a portion of the code generated by the Win Form Designer.

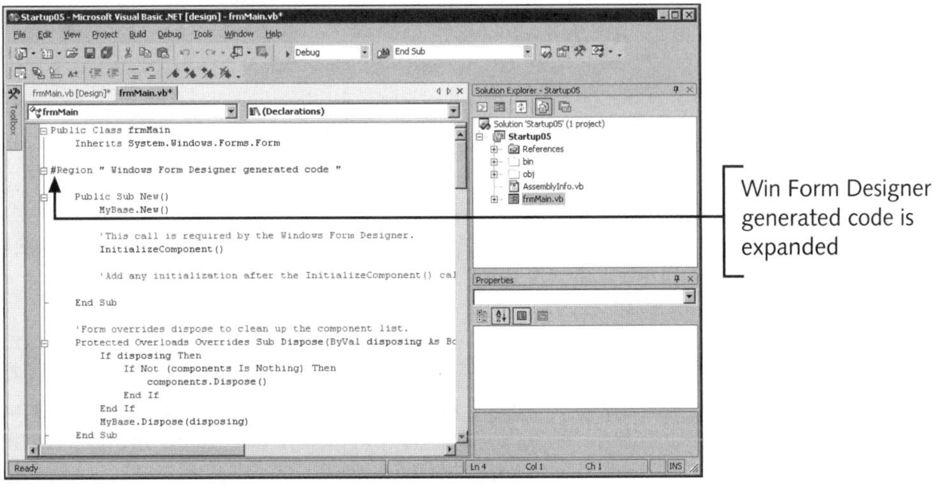

Figure 5-22 Expanded code generated by the Win Form Designer

3. Using the scroll bars, scroll downward through the window until the following line appears:

   ```
   Friend WithEvents chkSmoker As System.Windows.Forms.
   CheckBox
   ```

   The preceding statement was automatically generated by the Win Form Designer. This statement declares a variable to store the CheckBox control instance that you created on the form.

   The following statements set the properties of the CheckBox control instance:

   ```
   Me.chkSmoker.Location = New System.Drawing.Point(120, 72)
   Me.chkSmoker.Name = "chkSmoker"
   Me.chkSmoker.Size = New System.Drawing.Size(136, 32)
   Me.chkSmoker.Text = "Smoker"
   ```

   The first of the preceding statements sets the Location property and defines the position of the check box on the form. The second statement sets the Name property. The third statement defines the size of the check box. The final statement defines the text that appears in the check box.

4. Click the **minus sign** to collapse the code.

Next you will see how to write statements in the Code Editor. In these first statements you write, you declare variables to store information as the program runs.

UNDERSTANDING VB .NET DATA TYPES AND VARIABLES

Like any programming language, VB .NET supports variables that store data while the solution runs. Recall that a variable is simply a unique name that identifies a space in memory (RAM) that stores data such as a number or a string of characters. Just as every control instance has a name (the value of the Name property), every variable has a name. Recall that every variable also has a data type that determines the kind of information it can store. Some data types store numbers while other data types store strings of characters. Numeric data types either store whole numbers or numbers containing decimal points. Other types of variables store dates, or values such as True or False. Each variable should have a prefix that denotes its data type. Table 5-1 lists selected VB .NET data types, their storage sizes in bytes, standard prefixes, and the possible values for each data type.

Choosing the correct data type for a variable is important. For example, if a variable will contain only whole numbers (numbers without a decimal point), you should choose the Short, Integer, or Long Integer data type instead of the Single or Double data types. Operations on Shorts, Integers and Long Integers are faster than comparable operations on the Single and Double data types. Furthermore, if the value of a whole number will always be between -32,768 and 32,767, then you should use a Short instead of an Integer or Long Integer to conserve memory. For data containing a decimal point, you must also choose between the Single and Double data types. If you need more than six digits of decimal precision, choose the Double data type. Otherwise, choose the Single data type to save memory.

Table 5-1 Selected VB .NET data types

Data type	Storage size	Prefix	Possible values
Boolean	2 bytes	bln	True or False
Date	8 bytes	dat	Dates between 1/1/0001 to 12/31/9999
Short	2 bytes	sho	Positive and negative whole numbers between –32,768 and 32,767; a number such as 84 or –1715 can be stored as a Short
Integer	4 bytes	int	Positive and negative whole numbers between –2,147,483,648 and 2,147,483,647
Long Integer	8 bytes	lng	Positive and negative whole numbers between –9,223,372,036,854,775,808 to 9,223,372,036,854,775,807
Single	4 bytes	sng	A number with a decimal point, such as 3.14, –10034.388, or 0.113; the Single data type can store at most six digits to the right of the decimal point
Double	8 bytes	dbl	A number with a decimal point; the Double data type can store at most 14 digits to the right of the decimal point.
String	1 byte per character	str	You can store up to about 2 billion characters in a string; text entries such as "John Doe" or "Pacific Ocean" are stored as strings

Variable names must adhere to certain standards. Variable names must begin with a letter, and must not contain periods, dashes, spaces, or other special characters. Finally, variable names must be unique. As you created control instances, you have assigned them meaningful names such that each control instance begins with a three-character prefix denoting the type of control. This chapter uses the same naming conventions for variables.

In addition to the three-character prefix that denotes a variable's data type, the variable names in this book include a fourth character that denotes a variable's scope. The **scope** of a variable indicates which procedures can use the variable, and when VB .NET allocates the memory for the variable. In this chapter, you create module-level variables. **Module-level variables** can be used by all of the event handlers on a form (class). Event handlers are discussed in a moment. Furthermore, VB .NET allocates the memory for a module-level variable when loading the form, and releases that memory when the form is unloaded. In solutions containing a single form, module-level variables and their values persist when the form is loaded and while the solution is running. Module-level variables have a prefix of "m".

Declaring a Variable

The process of creating a variable is known as declaring a variable. To declare a module-level variable, you use the `Private` keyword, as in `Private mintCounter As Integer`, which declares mintCounter as a module-level variable that has an Integer data type.

When declaring a variable, you can optionally assign it an initial value. If you do not assign an initial value to a numeric variable, VB .NET initializes the variable's value to zero. To declare a variable and assign it an initial value, you write a statement resembling a declaration statement and an assignment statement combined, as shown in the following code segment:

```
Private mintYearTerm As Integer = 30
Private mdblInitialValue As Double = 100000.52
```

The preceding statements resemble the statements to declare Integer and Double variables. The first statement declares the variable mintYearTerm as an Integer and assigns the value 30 to the variable when it is declared. The second statement assigns the value 100000.52 to the variable mdblInitialValue. Note that numeric values cannot contain commas or other formatting characters. For example, the following statements are not valid:

```
Private mdblInitialValue As Double = 100,000.52
Private mdblInitialValue As Double = $100,000.52
```

The first of the preceding statements is invalid because the numeric value on the right side of the assignment statement contains a comma. The second statement is also invalid because the numeric value on the right side contains both a comma and a dollar sign.

In the following steps, you declare the variables that store the information used to perform the calculations in this chapter's example. The variable msngBaseRate will store the base rate of the insurance policy. The variables named msngAgeFactor, msngSmokingFactor, and msngGenderFactor will be used as multipliers to adjust the cost of the insurance policy based on a person's age, whether or not the person smokes, and the person's gender, respectively. Typically, you declare module-level variables immediately after the code that the Windows Form Designer generates in the Code Editor.

To declare variables:

1. Activate the Code Editor by clicking **View**, and then clicking **Code** on the VB .NET menu bar, if necessary.
2. Enter the statements shown in Figure 5-23.
3. On the menu bar, click **File**, and then click **Save All** to save the statements that you just wrote.

Note that the variables should be declared after the code generated by the Win Form Designer, but must appear before the End Class statement. The variables are declared inside the class because they are part of the class.

The variables you declared in the preceding steps all have numeric data types. In addition to numeric variables, data can also be stored as a string.

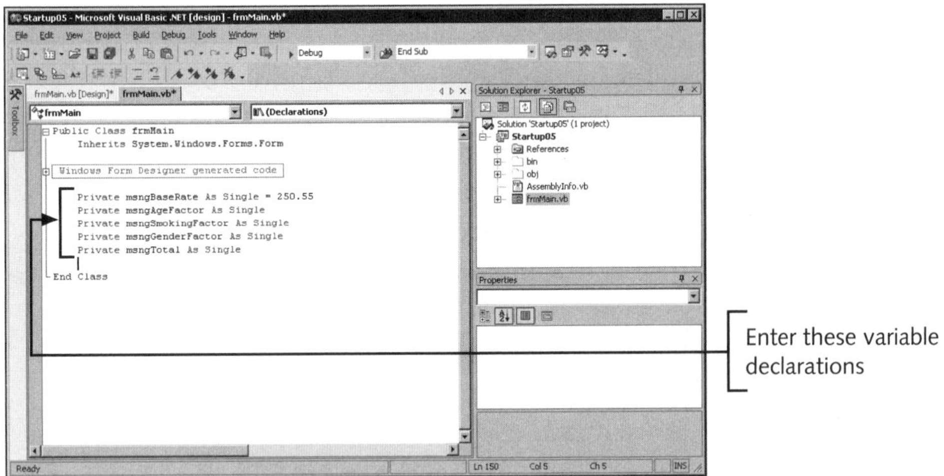

Figure 5-23 Declaring variables in the Code Editor

Using the String Data Type

VB .NET supports a data type named String. Unlike a numeric variable, which stores a number such as an Integer or a Double, string variables store data as a consecutive sequence of characters. You declare a string variable the same way you declare a numeric variable. However, instead of giving the variable a data type of Integer or Double, you give the variable a data type of String, as shown in the following statements:

```
Private mstrDemo As String
Private mstrDemo As String = "Joe Smith"
```

The first of the preceding statements declares a variable having a data type of String. The second statement declares a String variable and initializes the variable to store the value "Joe Smith." When storing a literal value in a string, the literal value is enclosed in double quotation marks. If you omit the quotation marks, a syntax error occurs. Often, you perform operations on strings. While VB .NET supports methods that extract substrings from a string, or determine the length of a string, in this chapter, you simply perform string concatenation. To concatenate strings, you apply the ampersand character (&), which is the string concatenation operator as shown in the following statements:

```
Private mstrDemo1 As String = "First"
Private mstrDemo2 As String = "Second"
Private mstrDemo3 As String
mstrDemo3 = mstrDemo1 & " " & mstrDemo2
```

The preceding statements declare String variables. The variables mstrDemo1 and mstrDemo2 are concatenated. A space character appears between the two String variables. Therefore, the variable mstrDemo3 contains the string "First Second". You write statements to concatenate strings in the next sections.

Using the Boolean Data Type

Recall that Boolean data operates similar to an on/off switch. The keyword "True" signifies on, and the keyword "False" signifies off. Properties such as Visible and Enabled store Boolean values. For example, the following statement makes the Label control instance named lblPrompt visible:

```
lblPrompt.Visible = True
```

VB .NET supports a data type to store Boolean values as shown in the following variable declarations:

```
Private mblnValid As Boolean
Private mblnValid As Boolean = True
```

The preceding statements declare a Boolean variable named mblnValid. In the second statement, the variable is initialized so that it has a value of True. The three-character prefix for a Boolean variable is "bln". The "m" denotes a module-level variable.

Having learned how to declare variables, you now need to learn how to use them in statements that execute as a program runs.

INTRODUCTION TO EVENT HANDLERS

When the user clicks an instance of the Button control as a program runs, statements in a procedure execute in response to the event. This procedure is called an **event handler**. An event handler is nothing more than a procedure that Windows calls automatically when the user performs some activity such as clicking a button. The code you write in the event handler performs an action (executes statements), such as displaying a picture, ending the solution, or any other task that you define. As a user, you have used buttons before, such as when you clicked an OK or Cancel button in a dialog box. Buttons you create in VB .NET work the same way. To create an event handler, you use two list boxes in the Code Editor.

- In the Class Name list box, you select the name of the form or the control instance.
- In the Method name list box, you select an event supported by the form or by the selected control instance.

Forms and controls support events that correspond to the purpose of the form or control. For example, a form supports the Load event, but the Button control does not. Windows calls the Load event handler when the user runs the solution, and the form is loaded into memory. Therefore, you can place statements in the Load event handler that execute as the form is loaded. In this chapter's example, you display the current date in a Label control instance that you already created. This label appears on the form named frmMain.

To create an event handler:

1. Click **View** on the menu bar, and then click **Code** to activate the Code Editor, if necessary.
2. Click the **Class Name** list arrow (the one on the left), and then click **(Base Class Events)**. This selects the events applicable to the form.
3. Click the **Method Name** list arrow (the one on the right), and then click **Load**.

VB .NET creates the event handler as shown in Figure 5-24.

So far, you have created an event handler that executes when VB .NET loads the form. In the next set of steps, you write the statements that execute when Windows calls the event handler.

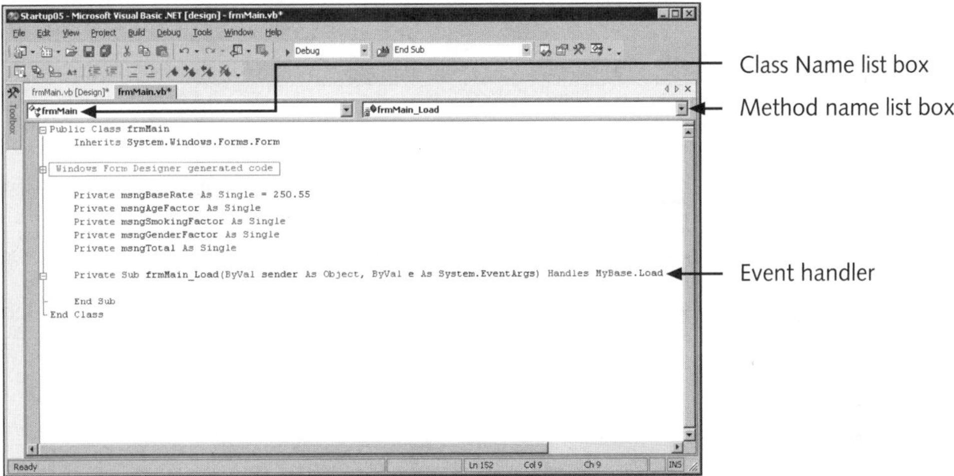

Figure 5-24 Creating an event handler

As shown in Figure 5-24, the event handler begins with the keywords `Private Sub`, followed by the procedure name. In this case, the procedure is named frmMain_Load. VB .NET calls this procedure when the Startup05 solution starts, and the form named frmMain loads. Every event handler contains two arguments. These arguments form the mechanism that VB .NET uses to send information to the event handler. As this is an introductory chapter on VB .NET, you will not use or modify these arguments. If you modify the arguments, then an error will occur.

Controls also support events. For example, the Button control supports a Click event. Windows fires this event when the user clicks a Button control instance created on the form. You can create the Click event handler for a button the same way you created the frmMain_Load event handler. That is, you can select the Button control instance in the Class Name list box, and then select the Click event in the Method Name list box.

However, VB .NET supplies an easy way to create the Click event handler for a button. You simply double-click the button control instance in the Win Form Designer.

To create the Click event handler for a Button control instance:

1. Activate the Win Form Designer, if necessary.
2. In the Win Form Designer, double-click the **Exit Button** control instance. VB .NET creates the Click event handler as shown in Figure 5-25.
3. Enter the following statement in the event handler to end the program. The keyword "Me" is used to reference the form. The form, in turn, supports a method named Close, which closes the form. Because this is the only form in the program, calling the Close method has the effect of ending the program.

   ```
   Me.Close()
   ```

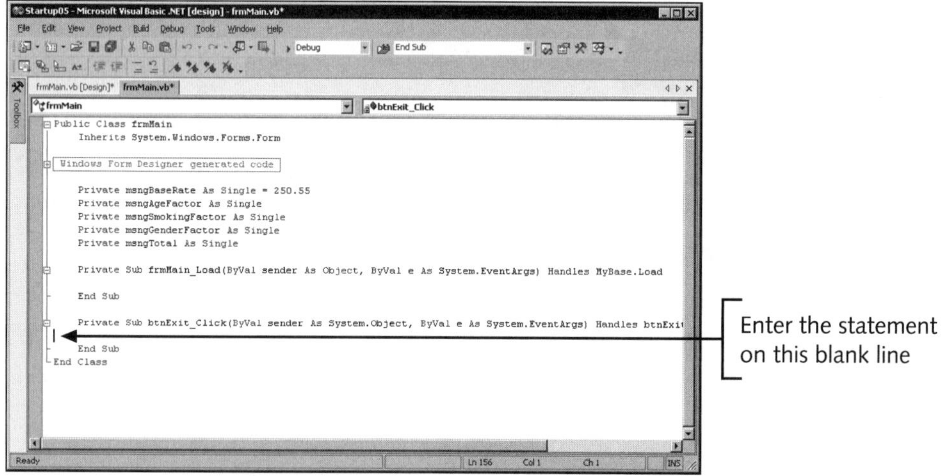

Figure 5-25 Creating a Click event handler

As you develop a program, you should test your work frequently to see that the statements that you write work correctly. That way, if you make a small error, you can correct the error quickly. You will do that now.

To test the program:

1. Run the program by clicking **Debug** on the menu bar, and then clicking **Start**, or by pressing **F5**.

   VB .NET displays the form as the user will see it. See Figure 5-26.
2. Click the **Exit** button on the form. The statement that you just wrote executes, causing the program to exit.

The `Me.Close()` statement performs a task; in this case, unloading a form. In addition, you can write statements that store data in variables, or properties of control instances. These types of statements are called assignment statements.

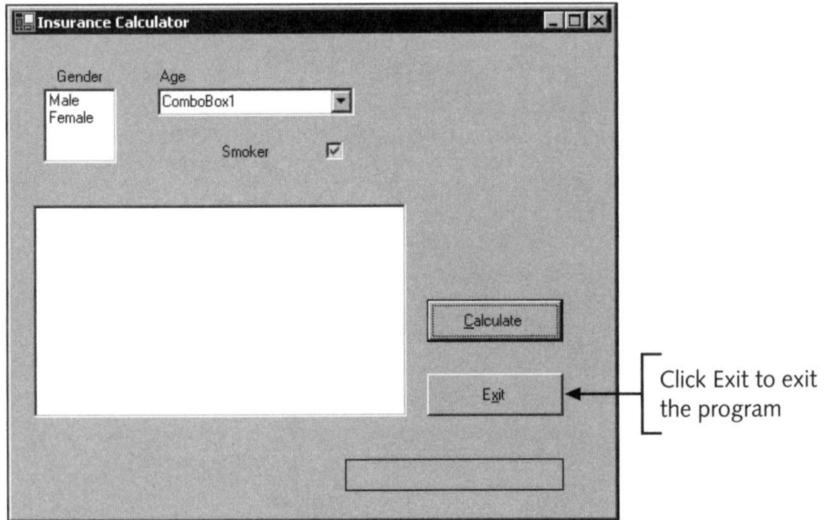

Figure 5-26 Testing the main form

Using Assignment Statements

Executable statements must appear inside of a procedure (event handler). One type of an executable statement is called an assignment statement, which consists of two parts: a left side and a right side separated by an equal sign (=). For example, the following assignment statement makes the text box named txtOutput visible:

```
txtOutput.Visible = True
```

You use an assignment statement to store values in variables or properties. You can write more complex assignment statements to perform arithmetic operations.

VB .NET performs the task on the right side of the equal sign and assigns the result to the variable or property name appearing on the left side. For example, you can write an assignment statement that displays the current date in an instance of the Label control as follows:

```
lblDate.Text = System.DateTime.Today.ToShortDateString()
```

The preceding statement requires careful examination. On the right side of the assignment statement, the Today method of the System.DateTime class is called to get the current date from the system. This value is stored as a DateTime data type. Calling the ToShortDateString method converts the value to a string. This converted result is then stored in the Text property of the label named lblDate.

To write an assignment statement:

1. Activate the Code Editor, if necessary.

2. In the Code Editor, between the Private Sub and End Sub for the frmMain_Load event handler, enter the following statement:

   ```
   lblDate.Text = System.DateTime.Today.ToShortDateString()
   ```

3. Save the solution by clicking **File**, and then clicking **Save All**.
4. Test the program by pressing **F5**. The current date appears in the label at the bottom of the form. Of course, the date you see will differ from the one shown in Figure 5-27. Click the **Exit** button to end the program.

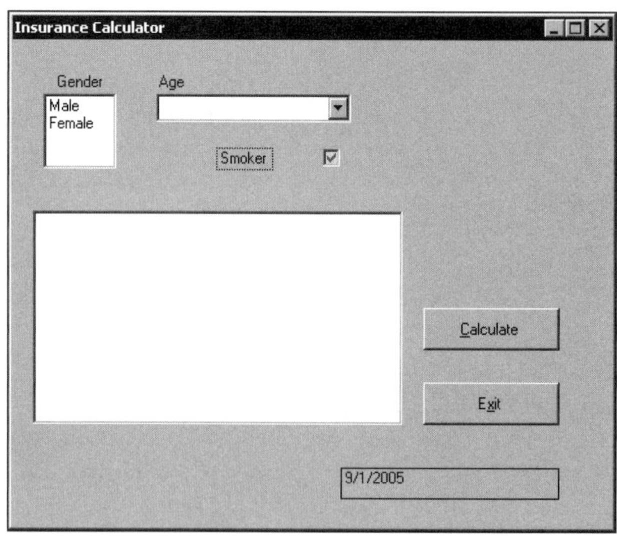

Figure 5-27 Testing the assignment statement

In addition to simple assignment statements you can also write decision-making statements.

WRITING DECISION-MAKING STATEMENTS

In addition to sequentially executing statements in the order that they appear in a procedure, you can write statements that execute different code in different situations. These statements are called **decision-making statements** or **conditional statements**. A conditional statement executes one group of statements when a condition is True and another group of statements when the condition is False. When writing a conditional statement, you use comparison operators on two or more values or expressions. VB .NET supports the following comparison operators: equal to (=), not equal to (<>), less than (<), greater than (>), less than or equal to (<=), and greater than or equal to (>=).

Comparison operators appear in a decision-making statement and always produce a Boolean value as their result. Comparison operators are evaluated from left to right in the order that they appear. The simplest form of an If statement is called a one-way If statement, which is used in the following sample code:

```
If chkSmoker.Checked = True Then
    msngSmokingFactor = 1.5
End If
```

The preceding If statement uses the CheckBox control instance named chkSmoker that you created previously. If the box is checked, then the Checked property has a value of True, and the value 1.5 will be stored in the variable named msngSmokingFactor.

A one-way If statement can be expanded to execute specific statements when a condition is True, and other statements when the condition is False. This type of statement is referred to as an If-Then-Else statement, or a two-way If statement, and is shown in the following code sample:

```
If chkSmoker.Checked = True Then
    msngSmokingFactor = 1.5
Else
    msngSmokingFactor = 1
End If
```

This form of an If statement illustrates a two-way decision (one that has two possible outcomes). If the check box is checked, then the variable msngSmokingFactor is set to 1.5. If the check box is not checked, then the value 1 is stored in the variable msngSmokingFactor.

The final variation of the If statement is the **multiway If statement**, which provides for three or more possible outcomes.

```
If mintGrade > 90 Then
   mstrLetterGrade = "A"
ElseIf mintGrade > 80 Then
   mstrLetterGrade = "B"
ElseIf mintGrade > 70 Then
   mstrLetterGrade = "C"
ElseIf mintGrade > 60 Then
   mstrLetterGrade = "D"
Else
   mstrLetterGrade = "F"
End If
```

The preceding If statement calculates a letter grade based on a numeric grade. The numeric grade is assumed to be an Integer between 0 and 100. The If statement first tests whether the numeric grade is greater than 90. If it is, the letter grade "A" is assigned to the variable mstrLetterGrade. Once a condition is found to be True, the If statement exits, and the statement following the End If statement executes. Therefore, if the grade were 92, the first condition is True, and the statement following the If executes, and then the If statement exits. So, even though 92 is greater than 80, the second condition is never tested, therefore an incorrect grade will not be assigned to the variable. If the numeric grade is not greater than 90, then the first ElseIf condition is tested to determine whether the numeric grade is greater than 80. If it is, the letter grade is a "B." The process continues examining the numeric grade to determine whether it is greater than 70 or greater than 60. If none of the ElseIf conditions are True, then the Else clause executes, and the letter grade assigned is an "F."

You can now write the If statements that will be used to determine the variable information ultimately used to calculate the solutions output. The first If statement determines whether or not a person smokes. In the second If statement, you use the Text property of the list box to get the text for the selected item ("Male" or "Female").

To create an If statement:

1. Activate the Win Form Designer if necessary, and then double-click the **Calculate** button to create the Click event handler for the button.
2. Enter the following statements in the event handler (between the `Private Sub` and the `End Sub` statements):

```
If chkSmoker.Checked = True Then
    msngSmokingFactor = 1.5
Else
    msngSmokingFactor = 1
End If
If lstGender.Text = "Male" Then
    msngGenderFactor = 1.1
Else
    msngGenderFactor = 0.9
End If
```

3. Save the solution by clicking **File**, and then clicking **Save All** on the menu bar.

You will test these statements when you write the statements to perform the calculations to produce the cost of the insurance policy.

USING REPETITION STATEMENTS

VB .NET supports two categories of repetition statements: Do loops and For loops. Recall that a Do loop executes statements repeatedly until some condition becomes True or False. You can write a Do loop in many ways to achieve the same results. That is, you can write any Do While loop as a Do Until loop. Which variation to use is a matter of personal preference. To illustrate the use of a Do loop, examine the following example code that loops ten times and prints a list of numbers to the Output window using the Debug.WriteLine method. The Output window displays output from a program. This window is typically used for debugging purposes. To view the Output window, click View, Other Windows, and then click Output on the menu bar.

```
Dim pintCounter As Integer = 1
Do Until pintCounter > 10
    Debug.WriteLine(pintCounter)
```

```
        pintCounter = pintCounter + 1
    Loop
```

The statements in the preceding Do Until loop execute 10 times. The first time the Do Until statement executes, pintCounter has a value of 1. Because 1 is not greater than 10, the two statements inside the loop execute. The statements inside the loop print the value of pintCounter to the Output window, and then add 1 to the value of the variable. The next time through the loop, the value of pintCounter is 2, and then 3, and so on, until the variable pintCounter has a value greater than 10. When this situation occurs, execution of the statements in the loop ends, and the statement following the Loop statement executes.

Any Do Until loop can be written as a Do While loop as shown in the following code segment:

```
    Dim pintCounter As Integer = 1
    Do While pintCounter <= 10
        Debug.WriteLine(pintCounter)
        pintCounter = pintCounter + 1
    Loop
```

The preceding Do While loop has exactly the same effect as the previous loop written with the Do Until statement. The condition has been reversed, however, so the loop executes while pintCounter is less than or equal to 10. Again, which variation to use is a matter of personal preference.

The preceding Do Until and Do While loops both tested the condition before executing the statements in the loop. Therefore, depending on the value of the condition, the statements inside the loop may never execute.

A For loop executes statements repeatedly. However, a For loop can only be used when the number of iterations (times the loop will execute) is known in advance. A For loop works like a Do loop that uses a counter. Each time the statements in the loop execute, VB .NET automatically increments a counter until the counter reaches some value that you define. Review the following code example:

```
    Dim pintCounter As Integer
    For pintCounter = 1 To 10
        Debug.WriteLine(pintCounter)
    Next pintCounter
```

The For statement uses the variable named pintCounter as the loop's counter. The statement in the loop will execute ten times. Each time the statements in the loop execute, VB .NET automatically increments the variable pintCounter by one, the default.

Next, you create a For loop to initialize the ComboBox control instance created on the form. The values stored in the ComboBox will be whole numbers from 20 to 50, indicating a person's age. To add items to a ComboBox at run time, you call the Add method of the ComboBox's Items collection. You populate the combo box when the form loads.

To add items to a ComboBox at run time:

To set up, calculate, and display the program output:

1. Activate the Code Editor, and then locate the form's Load event handler. Enter the following statements in the event handler:

```
Dim pintCount As Integer
For pintCount = 20 To 50
    cboAge.Items.Add(pintCount)
Next
lblDate.Text = System.DateTime.Today.ToShortDateString()
```

   Next, you write the final calculations to compute the cost of the insurance policy and display the results.

2. In the Code Editor, if necessary, select the **Click** event handler for the Calculate button, and then enter the following statements at the end of the event handler:

```
msngAgeFactor = cboAge.Text * 0.01
msngTotal = msngBaseRate * msngGenderFactor * _
msngSmokingFactor * msngAgeFactor
txtOutput.Text = "The cost of your policy based on the " & _
"input that you specified is " & _
msngTotal.ToString("c") & "."
```

The preceding statements calculate the total insurance policy cost and store the result in the variable msngTotal. String concatenation is used to display the output in the text box. Because the statements are so long, the continuation character, an underscore (_), is used to break up the long lines. The final statement converts the value stored in the variable named msngTotal to a string and formats it with two decimal places.

Finally, you can test the solution to make sure that it works correctly:

To test the completed solution:

1. Run the program, selecting **Female** in the Gender text box, and **24** as the Age. Check the **Smoker** box.
2. Click the **Calculate** button to calculate the output. See Figure 5-28.
3. End the program.
4. Exit Visual Studio .NET.

You have completed the programming for this chapter. You have seen how to use Visual Studio .NET to create the user interface, and how to create the code behind the form that executes as the user interacts with the form.

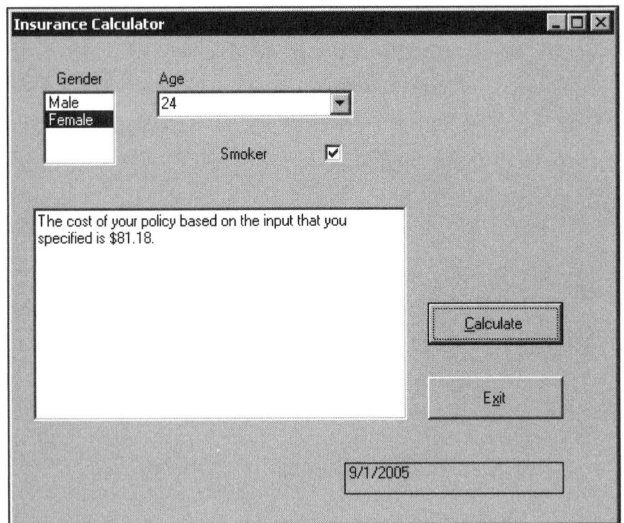

Figure 5-28 Testing the completed solution

5

CHAPTER SUMMARY

- For a user to run any application created in Visual Studio .NET, the .NET Framework must be installed. The .NET Framework defines standards that allow programs written in any Visual Studio .NET language to operate with each other. The .NET Framework also supplies the run-time services that allow a program to execute. Finally, the .NET Framework class library contains all of the type defined by the .NET Framework.
- The Visual Studio .NET IDE allows you to create, test, debug, and deploy programs using two types of windows: document windows and tool windows. The Win Form Designer and Code Editor are document windows. Tool windows, including the Properties window, Toolbox, and Solution Explorer work the same way for all Visual Studio .NET applications.
- To create the user interface for a solution, you use the Toolbox to create the control instances on the form. As you create the control instances on a form, you use the Properties window to configure those control instances.
- Each type of control you create serves a particular purpose. The Button control is used to create a clickable button. The TextBox and Label controls allow the user to edit and display text respectively. The CheckBox control provides the user a box which can be checked or unchecked. The ComboBox and ListBox controls are used to display lists.
- A form is a VB .NET class marked by the `Class` and `End Class` keywords. Between these keywords, the statements to create the control instances on the form appear, along with any event handlers that you create. Do not modify the code automatically generated by the Win Form Designer.

- Like any programming language, VB .NET allows you to declare variables. Module-level variables exist while the form containing the declaration is loaded. Every variable has a data type such as Short, Integer, Long, Single, or Double. You declare a module-level variable with the `Private` statement.
- To create the statements that execute as the user interacts with the control instances created on a form, you create an event handler. Every type of control supports events. For example, the Button control supports a Click event, which Windows executes when the user clicks the button on the form. The form itself supports a Load event which executes when the form loads.
- Like all programming languages, VB .NET supports decision-making and repetition statements. Decision-making statements execute one group of statements while a condition is true and another group of statements when the condition is false. Repetition statements execute the same code over and over again. Do loops and For loops form the repetition statements supported by VB .NET.

Review Questions

1. Which of the following elements make up the Visual Studio .NET Framework?
   a. Common Language Specification
   b. Common Language Runtime
   c. Common Type System
   d. all of these
   e. none of these
2. What is meant by the term IL?
   a. It refers to the instruction language used to compile a .NET application.
   b. It refers to the intermediate language that .NET uses for all applications.
   c. .NET does not support IL.
   d. IL defines the set of instructions understood by the target architecture of a particular computer.
   e. none of these
3. Which of the following statements is true of the memory allocation strategy used by .NET?
   a. Object variables (reference types) are allocated from the managed heap.
   b. Value type variables are allocated from the program stack.
   c. The code component that releases memory is called the garbage collector.
   d. all of these
   e. none of these

4. Which of the following statements correctly describes the relationship between an assembly and a namespace?
   a. A namespace always contains two or more assemblies.
   b. An assembly contains one or more logical components called namespaces.
   c. Most assemblies contain at least one namespace although many do not.
   d. There exists no relationship between assemblies and namespaces.
   e. none of these

5. What is the purpose of a solution file?
   a. A solution file contains the statements used to describe the control instances created on a form, and the code that executes as the user interacts with the control instances on the form.
   b. The solution file lists the properties for the control instances created on the form and the form itself.
   c. The solution file helps you solve errors that arise as you create a program.
   d. A solution is analogous to a VB .NET application and contains various folders that you use to test, compile, execute, and distribute the application.
   e. none of these
6. Which of the following statements describes the two categories of windows that make up the IDE?
   a. Tool windows differ from application to application, and document windows allow you to create textual documents that describe the purpose of an application.
   b. Document windows appear on group tabs and correspond to the modules that make up a solution, while tool windows help you manage an application.
   c. Solution windows are part of a specific solution, while configuration windows help you to manage the contents of solution windows.
   d. Visual windows allow you to define the visual characteristics of an application, while program windows allow you to write the code that executes as the user interacts with a solution.
   e. none of these
7. Which of the following statements describes how a tool window can be displayed?
   a. A tool window can be docked, which means that the window is anchored along an edge of the IDE.
   b. A tool window can be configured as a floating window, meaning that it can appear anywhere on the desktop.
   c. A tool window can be autohidden meaning that it appears as an icon along an edge of the IDE.
   d. all of these
   e. none of these

8. What is the name of the window that you use to create control instances on a form?
   a. Win Form Designer
   b. Form Editor
   c. Window Editor
   d. Control Creator
   e. none of these
9. Which of the following correctly lists the properties applicable to a form?
   a. BorderStyle, Caption, Position, Startup
   b. Border, Title, Position, StartupPosition
   c. BorderType, Caption, Position, StartupLocation
   d. FormBorderStyle, Text, Width, Height, StartPosition
   e. none of these
10. Which of the following statements correctly describes how to create a control instance on a form?
    a. Using the menu bar, select the desired control instance, and then click Create Control on the menu bar. Finally, position the control instance on the form.
    b. Select the control in the Toolbox, and then, using the mouse, draw the control instance on the form.
    c. Using the Properties window, set the desired properties, and then create the control instance on the form.
    d. Using the Solution Explorer, select the desired control instance, and then create it on the form.
    e. none of these
11. Which of the following lists valid VB .NET controls?
    a. Command, Text, Output, Check, List
    b. Button, TextBox, Label, CheckBox, ListBox
    c. CommandButton, Input, Output, Check, Item
    d. Command, Visible, Invisible, Boolean
    e. none of the above
12. Which of the following statements correctly describes a variable?
    a. A variable stores data while a solution runs.
    b. A variable is exactly the same as a property.
    c. All variables store numbers.
    d. Only certain types of variables have a data type.
    e. all of these

13. Which of the following correctly describes an assignment statement?
    a. In VB .NET you can only write assignment statements that assign numbers.
    b. Assignment statements cannot appear inside of an event handler.
    c. An assignment statement has a left side and a right side separated by an equal sign.
    d. all of these
    e. none of these
14. Which of the following is true of decision-making statements?
    a. They are often called conditional statements.
    b. They typically contain a comparison operator.
    c. The result of a decision making statement is a Boolean value.
    d. all of these
    e. none of these
15. Which of the following statements describes the difference between a Do loop and a For loop?
    a. Every Do loop can be written as a For loop, but not the other way around.
    b. Every For loop can be written as a Do loop, but not the other way around.
    c. The counter in both a Do loop and a For loop must always be incremented by a value of 1.
    d. Do loops and For loops cannot appear inside of an event handler.
    e. none of these

HANDS-ON EXERCISES

If necessary, use Windows Explorer to create a new folder in the Chap05 folder in your work folder. Name this folder **Exercises**. Save the solutions that you create in these Exercises in the Chap05\Exercises folder in your work folder.

Exercise 5-1

In this exercise, you create a solution that determines the cost of a printing order. The cost of the printing order is based on the paper size and the number of pages printed. An $8^{1/2} \times 11$-inch copy costs 5 cents. An $8^{1/2} \times 14$-inch copy costs 7 cents, and an 11×17-inch copy costs 9 cents.

To determine the cost of a printing order:

1. Start VB .NET, if necessary, and create a new solution named **Ch05Ex1** in the Chap05\Exercises folder in your work folder. To create a new project, click File on the menu bar, point to New, and then click Project. In the New Project dialog box, click Visual Basic Projects, if necessary. In the Templates pane, click Windows Application. Finally, click Open to create the project.

2. Create the control instances on the form and set the Text property of the form as shown in Figure 5-29.
3. Set the Name property of the control instances as shown in Figure 5-29.

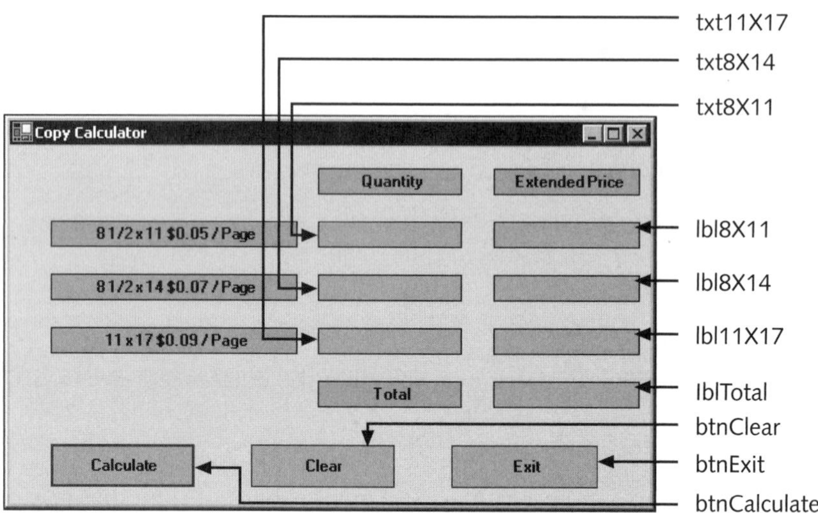

Figure 5-29

4. Declare the following variables:

```
Private mint8x11Qty As Integer
Private mint8x14Qty As Integer
Private mint11x17Qty As Integer
Private mdbl8x11Price As Double
Private mdbl8x14Price As Double
Private mdbl11x17Price As Double
Private mdblTotal As Double
```

5. Create the following statements in the Click event handler for the Calculate button:

```
mint8x11Qty = txt8x11.Text
mint8x14Qty = txt8x14.Text
mint11x17Qty = txt11x17.Text

mdbl8x11Price = mint8x11Qty * 0.05
mdbl8x14Price = mint8x14Qty * 0.07
mdbl11x17Price = mint11x17Qty * 0.09

lbl8X11.Text = mdbl8x11Price.ToString("$###,##0.00")
lbl8X14.Text = mdbl8x14Price.ToString("$###,##0.00")
lbl11X17.Text = mdbl11x17Price.ToString("$###,##0.00")

mdblTotal = mdbl8x11Price + mdbl8x14Price + mdbl11x17Price
lblTotal.Text = mdblTotal.ToString("$###,##0.00")
```

6. Create the following statements in the Click event handler for the Clear button:

```
lbl8X11.Text = ""
lbl8X14.Text = ""
lbl11X17.Text = ""
txt8x11.Text = "0"
txt8x14.Text = "0"
txt11x17.Text = "0"
lblTotal.Text = ""
```

7. Create the following statement in the Click event handler for the Exit button:

```
Me.Close()
```

8. Test the program, then save and close the Ch05Ex1 solution.

Exercise 5-2

In this exercise, you create a solution that converts measurements from U.S. to metric values. To perform these tasks, you need to know that there are 2.54 centimeters per inch.

To convert U.S. and metric value measurements:

1. Start VB .NET and create a new solution named **Ch05Ex2** in the Chap05\Exercises folder in your work folder.
2. Create the control instances on the form and set the Text property of the form as shown in Figure 5-30.

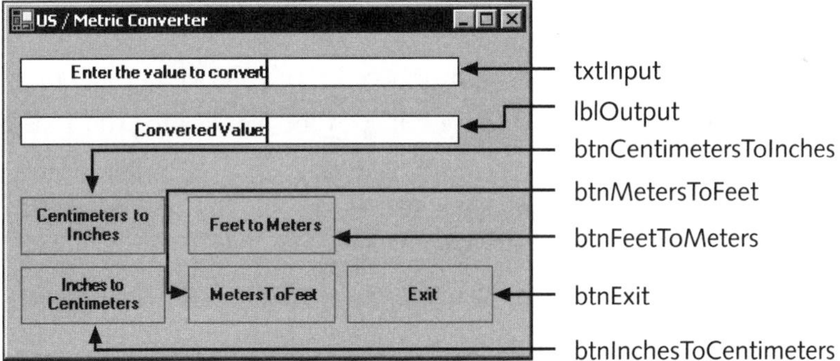

Figure 5-30

3. Set the Name property of the control instances as shown in Figure 5-30.
4. Declare the following variables:

```
Private mdblInput As Double
Private mdblOutput As Double
```

5. Create the following statements in the Click event handler for the button named btnCentimetersToInches:

```
mdblInput = txtInput.Text

mdblOutput = mdblInput * 0.394
lblOutput.Text = mdblOutput.ToString("###,###.###")
```

6. Create the following statements in the Click event handler for the button named btnInchesToCentimeters:

```
mdblInput = txtInput.Text

mdblOutput = mdblInput * 2.54
lblOutput.Text = mdblOutput.ToString("###,###.###")
```

7. Create the following statements in the Click event handler for the button named btnFeetToMeters:

```
mdblInput = txtInput.Text

mdblOutput = mdblInput * 12
mdblOutput = mdblOutput * 2.54
mdblOutput = mdblOutput / 100
lblOutput.Text = mdblOutput.ToString("###,###.###")
```

8. Create the following statements in the Click event handler for the button named btnMetersToFeet:

```
mdblInput = txtInput.Text
mdblOutput = mdblInput * 100
mdblOutput = mdblOutput * 0.394
mdblOutput = mdblOutput / 12
lblOutput.Text = mdblOutput.ToString("###,###.###")
```

9. Create the following statement in the Click event handler for the Exit button:

```
Me.Close()
```

10. Test the program, then save and close the Ch05Ex2 solution.

Exercise 5-3

In this exercise, you create a solution that computes the average of three test scores and displays a letter grade.

To compute a grade average and display a letter grade:

1. Start VB .NET and create a new solution named **Ch05Ex3** in the Chap05\Exercises folder in your work folder.
2. Create the control instances on the form and set the Text property of the form as shown in Figure 5-31.
3. Set the Name property of the control instances as shown in Figure 5-31.

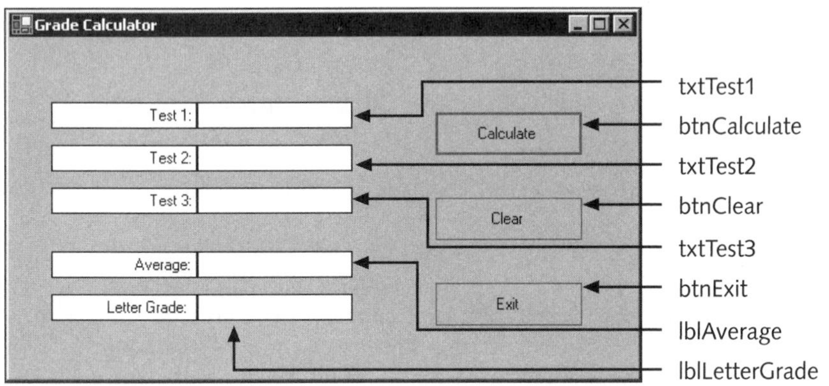

Figure 5-31

4. Declare the following variables:

```
Private mblnValidStudentID As Boolean
Private mblnValidTest1 As Boolean
Private mblnValidTest2 As Boolean
Private mblnValidtest3 As Boolean
Private mdblAverage As Double
Private mdblTest1, mdblTest2, mdblTest3 As Double
Private mstrAverage As String
```

5. Create the following statements in the Click event handler for the **Calculate** button:

```
mdblTest1 = txtTest1.Text
mdblTest2 = txtTest2.Text
mdblTest3 = txtTest3.Text

mdblAverage = (mdblTest1 + mdblTest2 + mdblTest3) / 3
lblAverage.Text = mdblAverage.ToString("###.##")

    If mdblAverage > 90 Then
        mstrAverage = "A"
    ElseIf mdblAverage > 80 Then
        mstrAverage = "B"
    ElseIf mdblAverage > 70 Then
        mstrAverage = "C"
    ElseIf mdblAverage > 60 Then
        mstrAverage = "D"
    Else
        mstrAverage = "F"
End If
lblLetterGrade.Text = mstrAverage
```

6. Create the following statements in the Click event handler for the Clear button:

```
txtTest1.Text = ""
txtTest2.Text = ""
```

5

```
txtTest3.Text = ""
lblAverage.Text = ""
lblLetterGrade.Text = ""
```

7. Create the following statement in the Click event handler for the Exit button:

```
Me.Close()
```

8. Test the program, then save and close the Ch05Ex3 solution.

Exercise 5-4

In this exercise, you create a program that calculates the cost of a hotel room. The cost of the hotel room varies based on the number of guests, the length of the stay, and whether or not guests have meals included. The base cost of the room is $58.24 per day. A $10.00 per day charge is incurred for each guest above two. Meals are charged per guest at a rate of $37.25 per day.

To calculate the cost of a hotel room:

1. Start VB .NET and create a new solution named **Ch05Ex4** in the Chap05\Exercises folder in your work folder.
2. Create the control instances on the form and set the Text property of the form as shown in Figure 5-32.

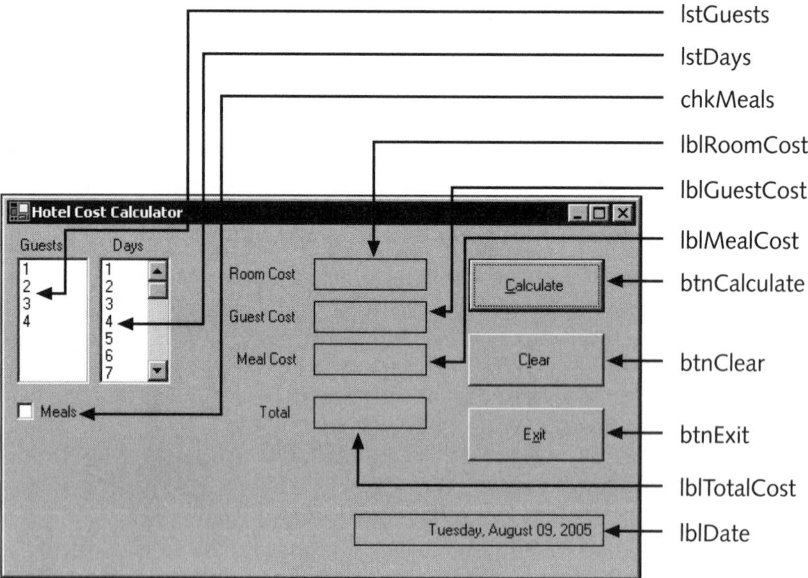

Figure 5-32

3. Set the Name property of the control instances as shown in Figure 5-32.

4. Declare the following variables:

```
Private mintCount As Integer
Private msngBaseRoomCost As Single = 58.24
Private msngExtendedRoomCost As Single
Private msngGuestRoomCost As Single = 10.0
Private msngExtendedGuestRoomCost As Single
Private msngGuestMealCost As Single = 37.25
Private msngExtendedguestMealCost As Single
Private msngTotalCost As Single
```


5. Create the following statements in the Click event handler for the Calculate button:

```
msngExtendedRoomCost = msngBaseRoomCost * lstDays.Text
lblRoomCost.Text = msngExtendedRoomCost.ToString("c")

If lstGuests.Text > 2 Then
    msngExtendedGuestRoomCost = msngGuestRoomCost * _
        (lstGuests.Text - 2) * lstDays.Text
    lblGuestCost.Text = msngExtendedGuestRoomCost.ToString("c")
Else
    msngExtendedGuestRoomCost = 0
    lblGuestCost.Text = ""
End If

If chkMeals.Checked Then
    msngExtendedguestMealCost = msngGuestMealCost * _
        (CInt(lstGuests.Text) * CInt(lstDays.Text))
    lblMealCost.Text = msngExtendedguestMealCost.ToString("c")
Else
    msngExtendedguestMealCost = 0
    lblMealCost.Text = ""
End If

msngTotalCost = msngExtendedRoomCost + _
    msngExtendedGuestRoomCost + msngExtendedguestMealCost
lblTotalCost.Text = msngTotalCost.ToString("c")
```

6. Create the following statements in the Click event handler for the Clear button.

```
lblRoomCost.Text = ""
lblGuestCost.Text = ""
lblMealCost.Text = ""
lblTotalCost.Text = ""
msngTotalCost = 0
msngExtendedRoomCost = 0
msngExtendedGuestRoomCost = 0
msngExtendedguestMealCost = 0
```

7. Create the following statements in the form's Load event handler:

```
For mintCount = 1 To 4
    lstGuests.Items.Add(mintCount)
Next
```

```
For mintCount = 1 To 31
    lstDays.Items.Add(mintCount)
Next
lblDate.Text = System.DateTime.Today.ToLongDateString
```

8. Create the following statement in the Click event handler for the Exit button:

```
Me.Close()
```

9. Test the program, then save and close the Ch05Ex4 solution.

Exercise 5-5

In this exercise, you create a program to calculate a travel expense reimbursement. An employee's daily expenses are based on the number of miles traveled and the meals eaten. An employee receives $0.28 cents per mile of travel, $7.23 for breakfast, $8.92 for lunch, and $16.55 for dinner.

To calculate a travel expense reimbursement:

1. Start VB .NET and create a new solution named **Ch05Ex5** in the Chap05\ Exercises folder in your work folder.
2. Set the form name to Ch05Ex5. Create the control instances on the form and set the Text property of the form as shown in Figure 5-33.

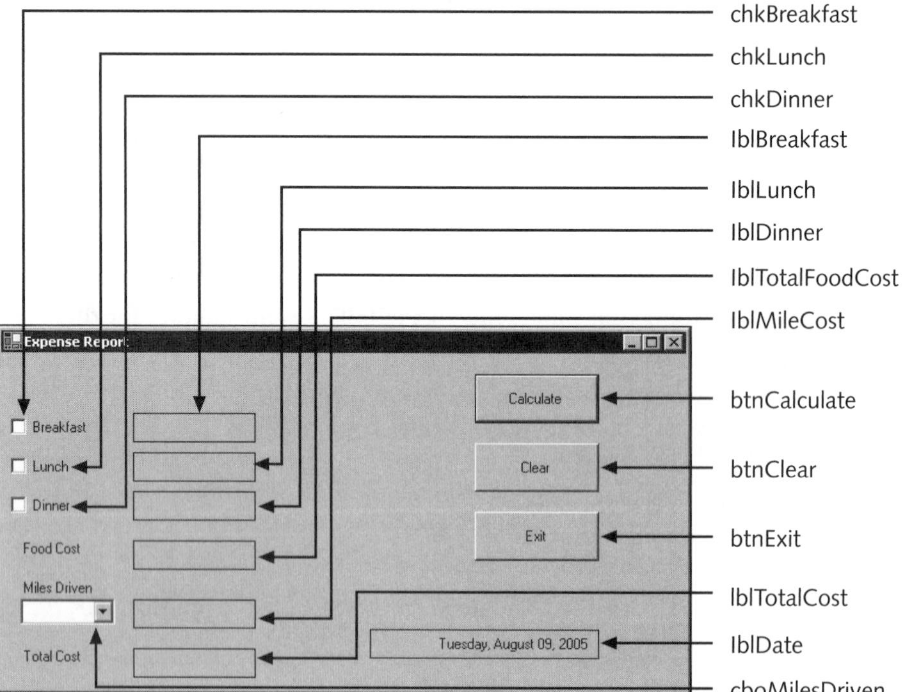

Figure 5-33

3. Set the Name property of the control instances as shown in Figure 5-33.
4. Declare the following variables:

```
Private msngBreakfastRate As Single = 7.23
Private msngLunchRate As Single = 8.92
Private msngDinnerRate As Single = 16.55
Private msngMileRate As Single = 0.28
Private msngFoodCost As Single
Private msngMileCost As Single
Private msngTotalCost As Single
Private mintCount As Integer
```


5. Create the following statements in the Click event handler for the Calculate button:

```
msngFoodCost = 0

If chkBreakfast.Checked = True Then
    lblBreakfast.Text = msngBreakfastRate
    msngFoodCost = msngFoodCost + msngBreakfastRate
Else
    lblBreakfast.Text = ""
End If

If chkLunch.Checked = True Then
    lblLunch.Text = msngLunchRate
    msngFoodCost = msngFoodCost + msngLunchRate
Else
    lblLunch.Text = ""
End If

If chkDinner.Checked = True Then
    lblDinner.Text = msngDinnerRate
    msngFoodCost = msngFoodCost + msngDinnerRate
Else
    lblDinner.Text = ""
End If

lblTotalFoodCost.Text = msngFoodCost.ToString("c")
msngMileCost = msngMileRate * cboMilesDriven.Text
lblMileCost.Text = msngMileCost.ToString("c")
msngTotalCost = msngFoodCost + msngMileCost
lblTotalCost.Text = msngTotalCost.ToString("c")
```

6. Create the following statements in the Click event handler for the Clear button:

```
chkBreakfast.Checked = False
chkLunch.Checked = False
chkDinner.Checked = False
lblBreakfast.Text = ""
lblLunch.Text = ""
lblDinner.Text = ""
lblTotalFoodCost.Text = ""
lblMileCost.Text = ""
lblTotalCost.Text = ""
```

7. Create the following statements in the form's Load event handler:

```
For mintCount = 0 To 500 Step 10
    cboMilesDriven.Items.Add(mintCount)
Next
lblDate.Text = System.DateTime.Today.ToLongDateString()
```

8. Create the following statement in the Click event handler for the Exit button:

```
Me.Code
```

9. Test the program, then save and close the Ch05Ex5 solution.

WEB PROGRAMMING PROJECTS

If necessary, use Windows Explorer to create a new folder in the Chap05 folder in your work folder named **Projects**. Save the solutions that you create in these Projects in the Chap05\Projects folder in your work folder.

Project 5-1

In this project, you calculate the property taxes for a home. The property taxes are based on the square footage of the home, the square footage of the land, and the age of the home. Create the user interface and code behind the form to calculate the property taxes based on the following criteria:

- The rate per square foot of the home is $0.13.
- The rate per square foot for the land is $0.04.
- A deduction of 1/2 of one percent of the tax amount applies to the home for each year of the home's age.
- A deduction of one percent of the tax amount applies to the lands for each year of the home's age.

Project 5-2

In this project, you create a program to calculate a sales commission. The sales commission is based on the amount sold, and the number of years with the company. Create the user interface and code behind the form to calculate the sales commission based on the following criteria:

- Each salesperson receives a base commission of 2.5 percent of their gross sales.
- Each sales person receives 1/10 of one percent of their gross sales for each year that they have worked with the company.
- A salesperson receives a $1,000.00 bonus if they did not call in sick for the sales period.

Project 5-3

In this project, you calculate tuition costs. Create the user interface and code behind the form to calculate the tuition costs based on the following criteria:

- An optional $50.00 orientation fee is charged for new students.
- Undergraduate credits cost $83.00 per credit for resident students.
- Undergraduate credits cost $111 per credit for nonresident students.
- Graduate credits cost $87.00 per credit for nonresident students.
- A nonresident fee of $1000 is assessed for nonresident undergraduate students and $1200.00 is assessed for nonresident graduate students.
- Graduate credits cost $121.00 per credit for nonresident students.

CHAPTER

6

VISUAL BASIC .NET: PART II

In this chapter you will:

- Learn about ADO.NET
- Create a DataAdapter
- Store data in DataSet and DataTable objects
- Bind controls to a DataSet
- Navigate through the records in a database table
- Modify a database record

In this chapter, you develop a VB .NET solution that will work with a Microsoft Access database to manage employee information. (The database itself is complete. You will not be working on it from Microsoft Access.) A database simplifies the task of writing any solution that needs to manage large quantities of data because the database itself takes care of storing, retrieving, and organizing information. In addition, a database makes it easy to add, change, and delete data.

GETTING STARTED

Just as standard prefixes were used for variables in Chapter 5, this chapter uses standard prefixes for database objects. Tables carry a prefix of "tbl", and fields carry a prefix of "fld". The solution in this chapter uses one table named tblEmployees having the following fields:

- fldEmployeeID is an Integer storing a unique employee identification number. This field is called the primary key. Typically, a table has a primary key that uniquely identifies each database record.
- fldFirstName and fldLastName store an employee's first and last name, respectively.
- fldTelephone stores the telephone number of the employee.
- fldDateHired is a date value and stores the date that the employee was hired.
- fldWage contains the hourly wage for the employee.
- fldDeductions contains the number of tax deductions claimed by the employee.
- fldNotes is a string containing notes pertaining to the employee.

This chapter's solution uses a database that was created using Microsoft Access. The database and its table contain an employee list. The solution that you create in this chapter allows the user to navigate through the records in the employee list by clicking buttons to locate the first, previous, next, and last records. In addition, the user will be able to add, change, and delete records by clicking buttons on the form. The database already contains a populated table, as shown in Figure 6-1. (A populated table is one that contains data.)

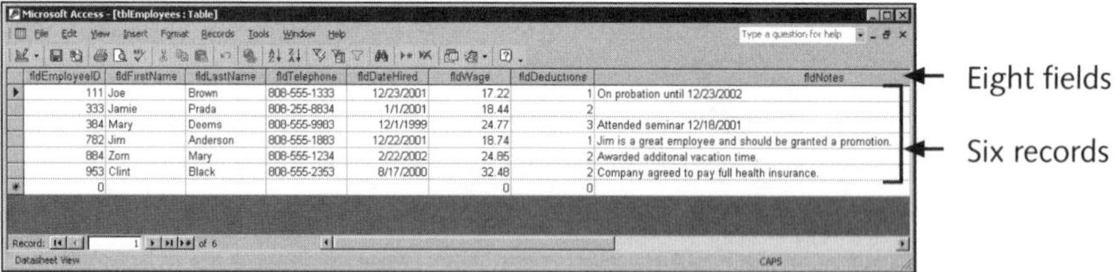

fldEmployeeID	fldFirstName	fldLastName	fldTelephone	fldDateHired	fldWage	fldDeductions	fldNotes
111	Joe	Brown	808-555-1333	12/23/2001	17.22	1	On probation until 12/23/2002
333	Jamie	Prada	808-255-8834	1/1/2001	18.44	2	
384	Mary	Deems	808-555-9983	12/1/1999	24.77	3	Attended seminar 12/18/2001
782	Jim	Anderson	808-555-1883	12/22/2001	18.74	1	Jim is a great employee and should be granted a promotion.
884	Zorn	Mary	808-555-1234	2/22/2002	24.85	2	Awarded additonal vacation time.
953	Clint	Black	808-555-2353	8/17/2000	32.48	2	Company agreed to pay full health insurance.
0					0	0	

Figure 6-1 Populated database table

As shown in Figure 6-1, the database table named tblEmployees has eight fields and six rows called records. The field named fldEmployeeID is the primary key. While this database contains a single table, most databases contain several. For simplicity in this chapter, however, a single table is used.

The database and its table were created in Microsoft Access XP. However, the Access 2000 file format was used to provide compatibility with the largest number of software configurations. Therefore, if you want to examine the table in Microsoft Access, you can use either Access 2000 or Access 2002.

An Overview of ADO.NET

Remember that VB .NET organizes components into namespaces. VB .NET provides database access through another namespace; the System.Data namespace. The classes in the System.Data namespace are collectively referred to as **ActiveX Data Objects (ADO.NET)**.

ADO evolved into ADO.NET, which allows database applications to operate on the desktop, a network, an intranet, or the Internet. ADO.NET provides an in-memory disconnected view of data. In other words, data is retrieved from a data source and stored in the computer's memory. A **data source** is a repository for data. While the data source is most often a database, text files and spreadsheets could be data sources, too. To retrieve data from a database, ADO.NET opens a database connection. After the data is stored in memory, ADO.NET closes the database connection. After changes are made to the in-memory copy of the data, another connection to the database is made, and any changes are then recorded back to the original database. This concept is referred to as a **disconnected architecture**. Using a disconnected architecture, the connection to the data source is open only while data is being retrieved or updated.

Establishing a Database Connection

The first step in retrieving data from a database is to establish a database connection. The ADO.NET Connection class forms a pipeline between your solution and a data source (database) through a provider. Again, the Connection class is just another reusable component supported by VB .NET.

A **provider** establishes a link between an ADO.NET connection and the database. Different providers exist for different databases. For example, ADO.NET supports providers for Access, SQL Server, and Oracle. The Connection class communicates with a database via a provider sending and receiving data to and from a client solution. Figure 6-2 illustrates the relationship between a solution, an ADO.NET connection, and a database provider.

VB .NET supports two controls to establish a database connection. These controls appear in the Toolbox and work similarly to the controls you used in Chapter 5. In this chapter, you will create a connection using the OleDbConnection control. The OleDbConnection control establishes connections with Jet, SQL Server, and Oracle databases. The SQLConnection control operates only with SQL Server databases and is not discussed further in this chapter.

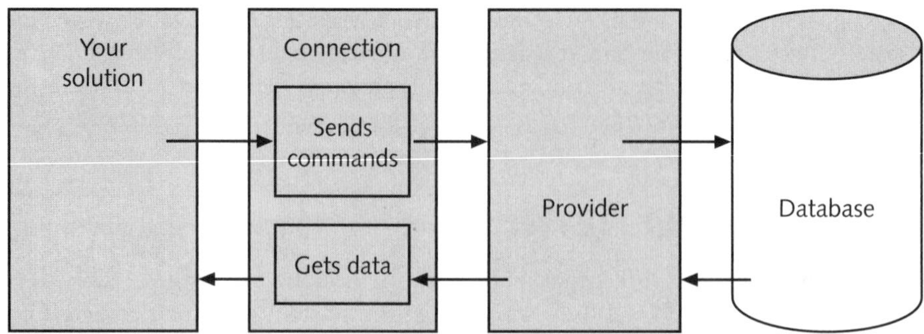

Figure 6-2 Connecting to a database with ADO.NET

Note that Jet is an acronym for Joint Engine Technology, and represents the software component used by Microsoft Access to read and write database data.

When you create an instance of the OleDbConnection control, VB .NET writes the statements to create an instance of the OleDbConnection class, and then configures that class instance much in the same way that VB .NET wrote statements to configure other control instances such as the Button control. Note, however, that you could also write these statements by hand.

Creating a connection with the OleDbConnection control connection involves two steps. First, you specify the provider, and second, you specify the database to which you want to connect.

To create a database connection using the OleDbConnection control:

1. Start Visual Studio .NET, and then open the file named **Startup06.sln** in the Chap06\Chapter\Startup06 folder in your workfolder. The control instances including buttons, labels, and text boxes have already been created on the form.
2. Activate the Win Form Designer for the form named **frmMain** if necessary. To activate the Win Form Designer, remember that you first click the form in the Solution Explorer to select it. Then click **View** on the menu bar, and then click **Designer**.
3. Click the **Data tab** in the Toolbox. Figure 6-3 shows the partially completed solution with the Data tab on the Toolbox active and the OleDbConnection control selected.
4. Create an instance of the **OleDbConnection** control on the form. It does not matter where you place the control instance on the form.

   Unlike the other controls you have used, the OleDbConnection control is not visible to the user at run time. Therefore, the control instance appears in a resizable tray below the form. All invisible control instances work in this same manner. VB .NET assigns the default name of OleDbConnection1 to the control instance. Again, remember that every control instance created on a form must have a unique name. See Figure 6-4.

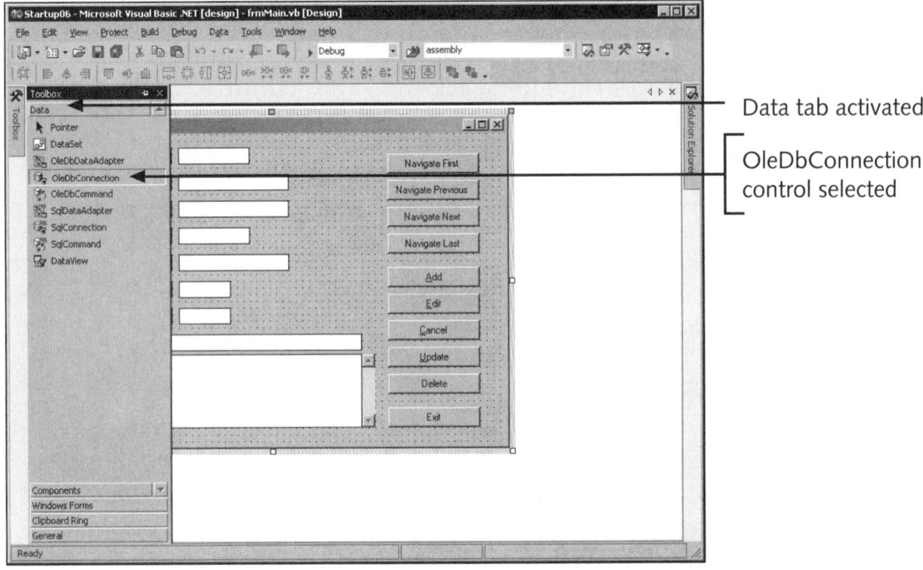

Figure 6-3 Creating an instance of the OleDbConnection control

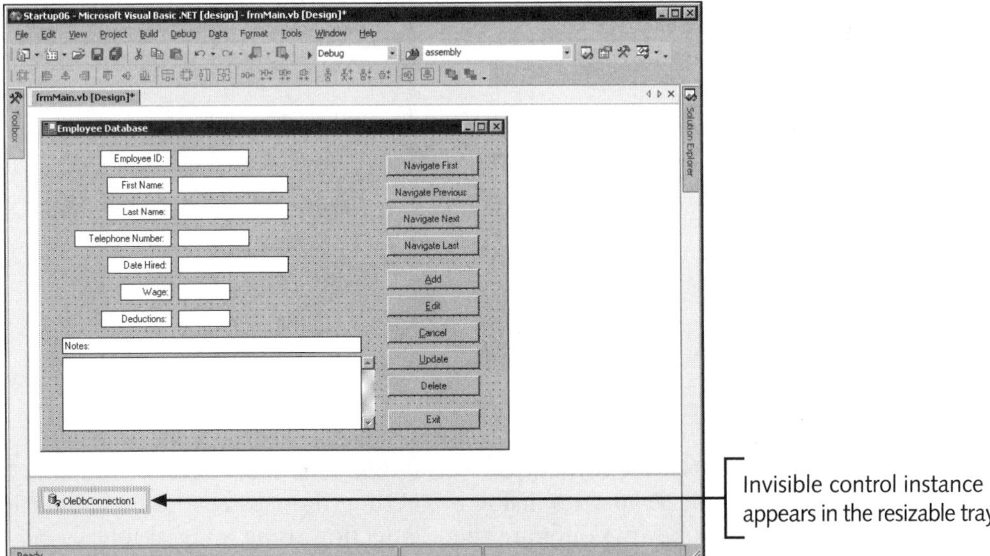

Figure 6-4 OleDbConnection control instance

5. Make sure that the OleDbConnection control instance is selected. To select the control instance, click it in the resizable tray below the form. The selected control instance appears with a hatched border.
6. Activate the Properties window for the control instance by pressing **F4**.
7. Set the Name property to **odbconEmployees**. This chapter uses the prefix "odbcon" for the OleDbConnection control.
8. In the Properties window, click the **value column** for the ConnectionString property; a list arrow appears.
9. Click the **list arrow**. The list drops down and displays the connections currently established on your computer. The list shown in Figure 6-5 shows an empty list because no connections have been established on the computer. However, your list may show existing connections if a connection has already been created. Figure 6-5 shows the Properties window with the drop-down list visible.

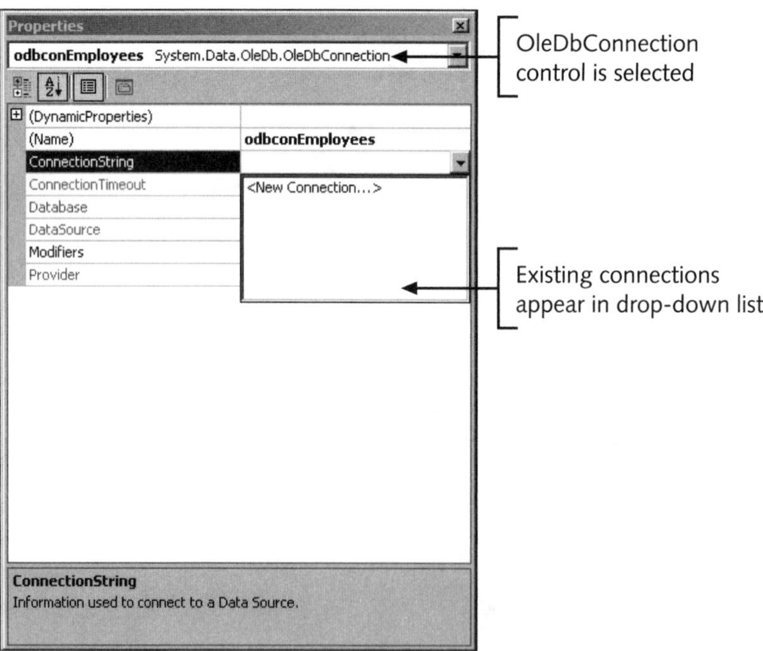

Figure 6-5 Properties window

10. Click **<New Connection>** to define a new connection and activate the Data Link Properties dialog box. Using the tabs on the Data Link Properties dialog box, you configure the connection using a visual interface.
11. Click the **Provider** tab to select a provider, as shown in Figure 6-6. Note that VB .NET supports several providers as illustrated in the list box shown in

Figure 6-6. For example, ADO.NET supports providers for SQL Server and Oracle. The list of providers appearing in the dialog box will vary based on the software installed on your computer.

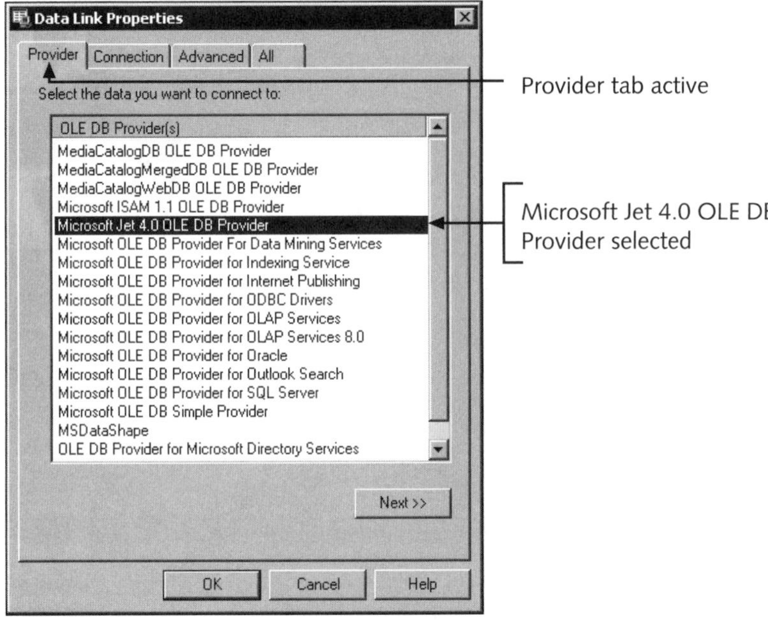

Figure 6-6 Data Link Properties dialog box—Provider tab

12. Click the provider named **Microsoft Jet 4.0 OLE DB Provider**. Again, depending on the software installed on your computer, this list of providers will vary.

13. Click **Next** to activate the Connection tab. The Connection tab allows you to define the database to which your solution will connect. You also specify any login and password information using this tab. The database in this chapter does not have a password, so you need not specify one. Figure 6-7 shows the Data Link Properties dialog box with the Connection tab active.

14. You can define the database name by entering the name in the text box, or by clicking the build button, and then selecting the database. Click the **build** button to display the Select Access Database dialog box, and then select the database named **Chap06\Data\Employees.mdb** from your workfolder, setting the drive designator as necessary. Click **Open** to select the database.

15. Click the **Test Connection** button to verify that the connection is operating properly. A dialog box displaying the text "Test connection succeeded" should appear. See Figure 6-8.

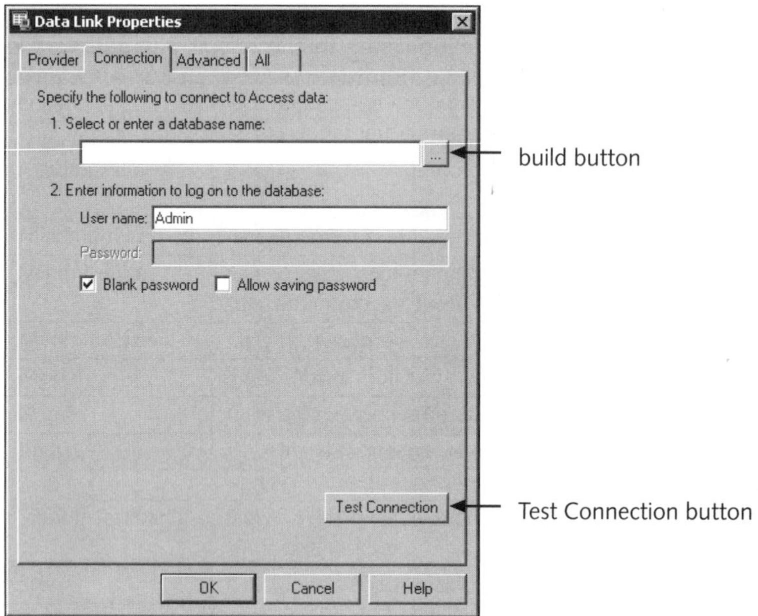

Figure 6-7 Data Link Properties dialog box—Connection tab

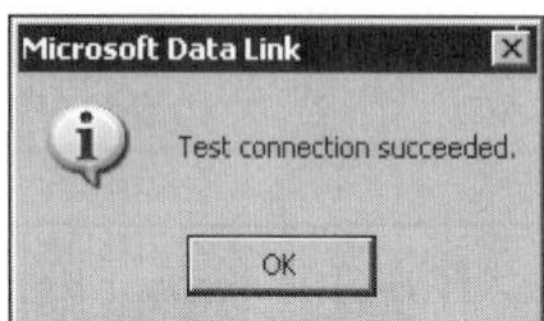

Figure 6-8 Microsoft Data Link dialog box

16. Click **OK** to close the Microsoft Data Link dialog box.
17. Click **OK** on the Data Link Properties dialog box to close it. You have completed building a database connection.
18. On the menu bar, click **File**, and then click **Save All** to save your work.

The Code Behind a Database Connection

When you updated and then closed the Data Link Properties dialog box in the previous set of steps, VB .NET updated the ConnectionString property for the OleDbConnection control instance. VB .NET also wrote the statements to create an instance of the control and configure it. To further study the setting of this property, part of the connection string appears below:

```
Provider=Microsoft.Jet.OLEDB.4.0;Password="";User ID=Admin;
Data Source=D:\Web\Chap06\Data\Employees.mdb;
Mode=ShareDeny None ...
```

Even though the preceding string appears on multiple lines, it is stored as a consecutive string of characters. The ConnectionString property is made up of key value pairs. A key value pair is similar to a variable. Think of the key as the variable, and the value as the data stored in the variable. In code, an equal sign separates the key and value in each pair. A semicolon, in turn, separates each key value pair.

The following list describes selected key value pairs appearing in the previous ConnectionString:

- *Provider key*—Defines the database provider used by the connection. Its current value specifies the Jet provider. Therefore, this connection uses an Access database.
- *User ID and Password keys*—Define authentication information required by the provider. For Access databases, the default User ID is "Admin." The databases used in this book do not have passwords. Therefore, the values are set to an empty string.
- *Data Source key*—Defines the file containing the database. Its value is set to D:\Web\Chap06\Data\Employees.mdb. Note that if you place the database in a different folder or delete the database, the connection will not operate because VB .NET will not be able to locate the database.
- *Mode key*—Defines how the database is shared among other connected users. Its value is set to Share Deny None, meaning that multiple uses can read and write data to the database while the connection is open.

Defining the connection is only the first step in retrieving data from the database. Next, you must specify what data to retrieve. That is, you must specify the database table to use, which fields should be retrieved from that table, and the order in which the rows should be returned.

CREATING THE DATAADAPTER

Having defined the database connection, you are now ready to send requests over that connection. The provider processes those requests and then retrieves data from the database making that data available to your solution. You send and retrieve data over a connection via a DataAdapter. The DataAdapter class of the System.Data.OleDb namespace supplies the methods to send the requests that retrieve data from a database. All of these requests appear in a standard language called the Structured Query Language (SQL).

You create the DataAdapter much in the same way you created the Connection. That is, you create an instance of the OleDbDataAdapter control on the form. Again, because the OleDbDataAdapter control is not visible to the user at run time, it appears in the resizable tray at the bottom of the form. In addition, the OleDbDataAdapter control has a Wizard that helps you configure the control instance. Like any Wizard, you configure the OleDbDataAdapter control instance by completing a series of dialog boxes supplied by the Wizard. In this solution, you will use the Wizard to configure the OleDbDataAdapter control instance to retrieve all of the rows from all of the fields in the table of employees named tblEmployees. Again, you could perform this same task by hand.

To create an instance of the OleDbDataAdapter control:

1. Activate the Toolbox. Click the **Data** tab, if necessary to activate it, and then click the **OleDbDataAdapter** control. Create an instance of the OleDbDataAdapter control on the main form. Again, because the control instance is not visible at run time, it appears in the resizable tray next to the instance of the OleDbConnection control instance. The Data Adapter Configuration Wizard appears, and displays a welcome message. See Figure 6-9.

Figure 6-9 Data Adapter Configuration Wizard—Welcome dialog box

2. Click **Next** to activate the Choose Your Data Connection dialog box.

   The Choose Your Data Connection dialog box allows you to choose an existing connection or create a new one. You will use the connection that you created in the preceding steps for this DataAdapter. See Figure 6-10.

3. Click the list arrow to select the data connection. Select the connection named **ACCESS.D:\Web\Chap06\Data\Employees.mdb.Admin**. Note that drive and path name will vary depending on where you installed the data files corresponding to the book. Furthermore, other connections may exist on your computer. These other connections will appear in the drop-down list.

4. Click **Next** to activate the Choose a Query Type dialog box. See Figure 6-11.

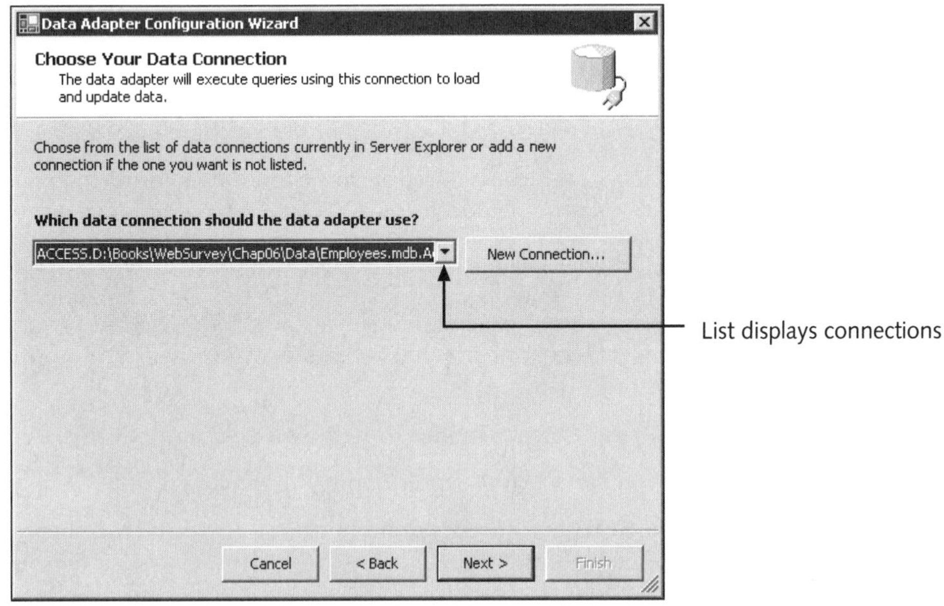

Figure 6-10 Data Adapter Configuration Wizard—Choose Your Data Connection dialog box

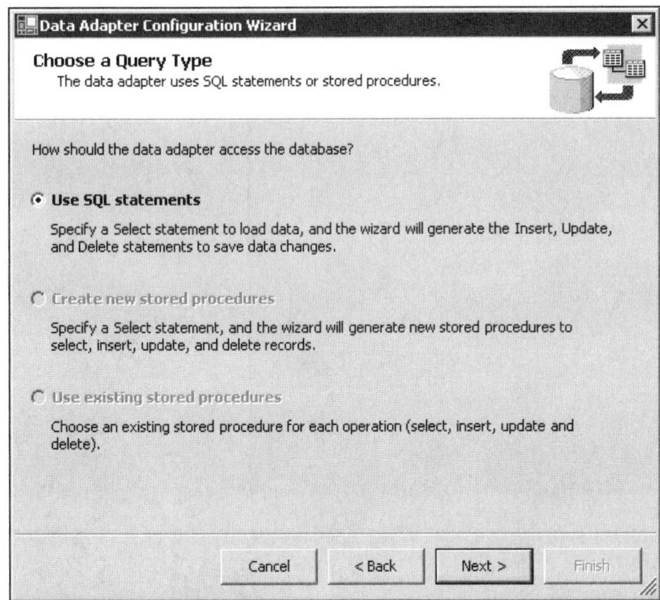

Figure 6-11 Data Adapter Configuration Wizard—Choose a Query Type dialog box

Next you must tell the DataAdapter which data you want to get from the database. You accomplish this task using the Choose a Query Type dialog box. VB .NET supports three query type options. Some query type options may not be available, depending on the provider.

- The Use SQL statements option causes the Wizard to generate the necessary SQL statements to select, add, update, and delete database records.
- The Create new stored procedures option causes the Wizard to create procedures and store them in the database to select, add, update, and delete records. Stored procedures are supported by databases such as SQL Server and Oracle, but are not discussed in this chapter.
- The Use existing stored procedures option causes the Wizard to generate statements that call existing stored procedures. Again, you will not use stored procedures in this chapter.

In this chapter, you use the Query Builder to help you create the SQL statements.

To define the query type for a DataAdapter control instance:

1. Click the **Use SQL statements** radio button if necessary, and then click **Next** to activate the dialog box to generate the SQL statements. See Figure 6-12.

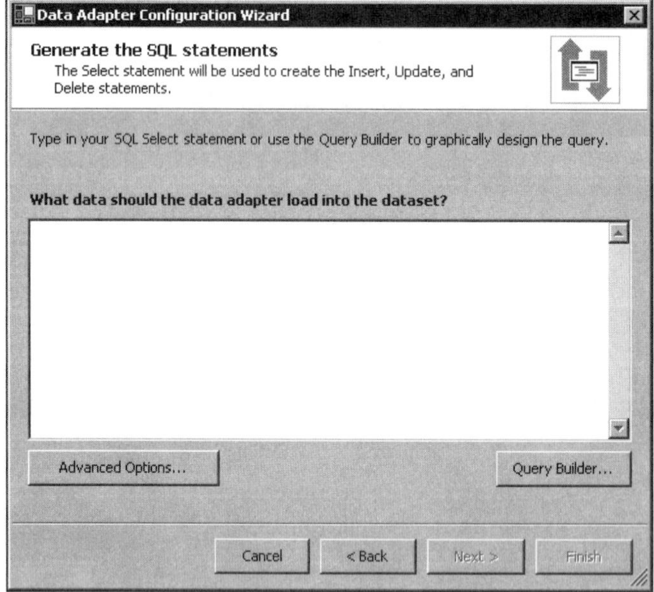

Figure 6-12 Data Adapter Configuration Wizard—Generate the SQL statements dialog box

As shown in Figure 6-12, a text box displays the SQL SELECT statement, which you will create next. The text box is empty because you have not yet created the SQL statement. You can enter the SQL SELECT statement by hand or use the Query Builder to help you define the statement. The Query

Builder supplies the easiest and most intuitive way to define an SQL statement. To use the Query Builder, you specify a database table, and then select the desired columns from the table. The Query Builder generates an SQL statement based on the criteria you specify. In addition, you can use the Query Builder to sort the records.

2. Click the **Query Builder** button on the Generate the SQL statements dialog box to display the Add Table dialog box shown in Figure 6-13.

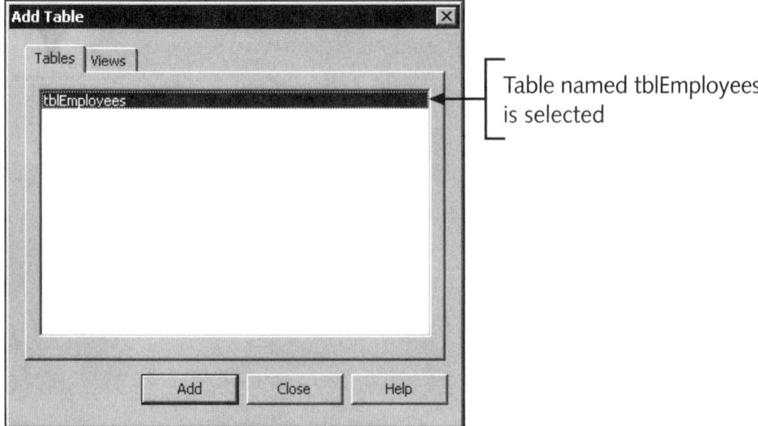

Figure 6-13 Add Table dialog box

The Add Table dialog box allows you to select the table(s) used in the query. Because the Employees database contains only a single table, only one table appears in the Add Table dialog box. However, all the tables that appear in the database will also appear here.

3. Click the table named **tblEmployees**, and then click the **Add** button. The table is added to the Query Builder.
4. Click the **Close** button to close the Add Table dialog box, which activates the Query Builder dialog box shown in Figure 6-14. Note that Figure 6-14 shows the query after it has been built.

As shown in Figure 6-14, the Query Builder dialog box displays the table used in the query.

Next you must define the SQL statement to retrieve data from the table. Again, you use the Query Builder to accomplish this task. As shown in Figure 6-14, the top pane of the Query Builder contains a box listing the columns that make up the table. You can select individual columns, or select all of the columns by checking the All Columns box. The second pane of the Query Builder dialog box allows you to control how the data is sorted and to restrict the number of rows displayed. Because users will likely want the data sorted by the employee's last name and first name, you use the field named fldLastName as the primary sort field and the field named fldFirstName as the secondary sort field.

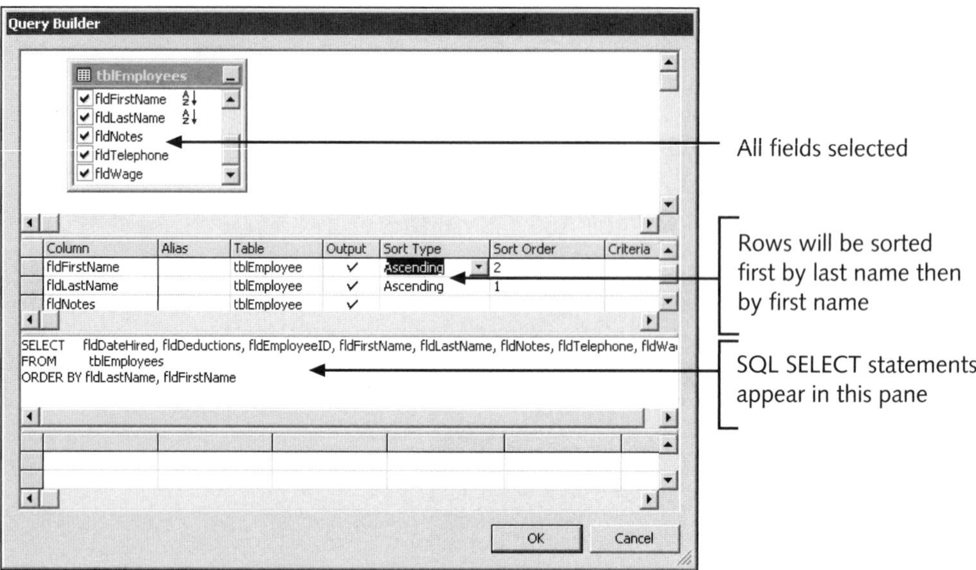

Figure 6-14 Query Builder dialog box

To build an SQL query:

1. Select each of the columns from the table named **tblEmployees** by checking each box. Do not click the (All Columns) check box. As you select each column, it appears in the columnar table shown in the second pane of the Query Builder dialog box. Furthermore, the SQL statement is updated in the third pane of the Query Builder dialog box.
2. In the column named Sort Type, click the row with the caption **fldLastName**. Use the scroll bars if necessary to locate the row. From the list box, click **Ascending**. The rows will appear sorted in ascending order by the employee's last name when the user runs the solution.
3. In the Sort Type column, click the row with the caption **fldFirstName**. From the list box, click **Ascending**. If two employees have the same last name, then the rows will be further sorted by first name.
4. Click **OK** to close the Query Builder and return to the Generate the SQL statements dialog box. Note that the SQL statement you just built appears in the Generate the SQL statements dialog box.
5. Click **Next** to display the View Wizard Results dialog box shown in Figure 6-15.

   The View Wizard Results dialog box lists the tasks that were completed successfully and any tasks that could not be completed. These tasks include writing the SQL SELECT statement to retrieve the rows from the employees table. In addition, SQL INSERT, UPDATE, and DELETE statements are written to add, change, and delete records. All of the statements generated by the Wizard appear in the code region automatically generated by the Win Form Designer. Remember that this region also contains the code to create the control instances. A complete description of these statements is beyond the scope of this chapter, however, and is not discussed in detail.

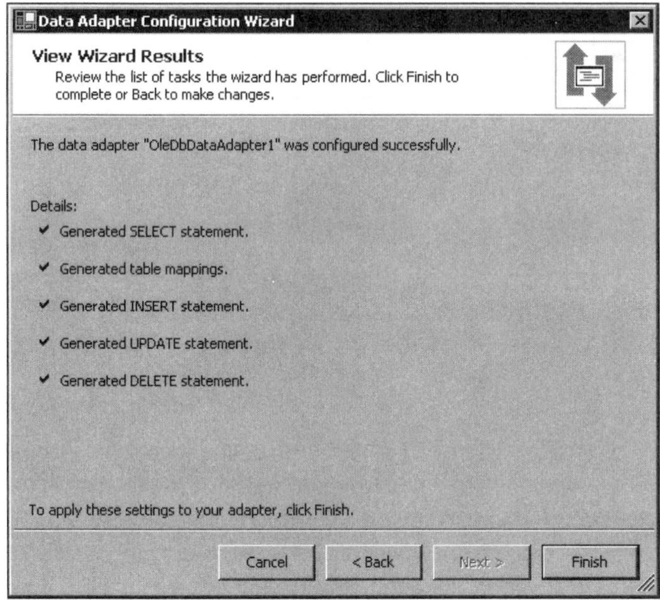

Figure 6-15 View Wizard Results dialog box

6. In the View Wizard Results dialog box, click **Finish** to complete configuration of the DataAdapter. The Wizard closes and the DataAdapter control instance appears in the tray at the bottom of the Win Form Designer.
7. Activate the Properties window for the DataAdapter you just created, and then set the Name property to **odbdaEmployees**.
8. On the menu bar, click **File**, and then click **Save All** to save your work.
9. Click the plus sign (+) to the left of the SelectCommand property to expand it. See Figure 6-16.

Note that the CommandText property contains the SQL SELECT statement that was generated by the Wizard. Clicking the build button activates the Query Builder that you just used. This button provides another means to regenerate the queries in the DataAdapter. If you need to change the configuration of the DataAdapter after creating it, you can also use the Wizard again by right-clicking on the DataAdapter control instance in the Win Form Designer, and then clicking Configure Data Adapter from the pop-up menu. You would need to reconfigure the DataAdapter if the schema (structure) of the database changed. That is, you would need to reconfigure the DataAdapter if you added or removed field(s) from the table named tblEmployees. In addition, you would also need to reconfigure the DataAdapter if you changed the data type of a field.

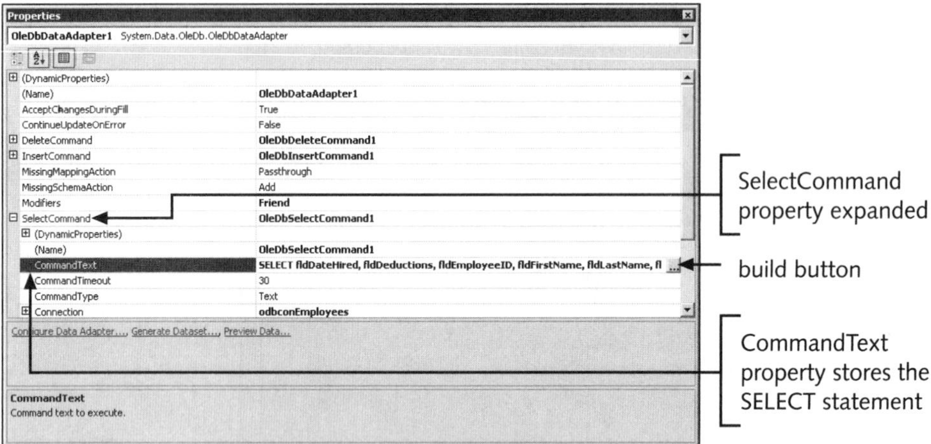

Figure 6-16 Properties window for the DataAdapter

Next, you must tell the DataAdapter to retrieve the data, and where to store the data it retrieves. As shown in Figure 6-17, the DataAdapter sends an SQL SELECT statement over the connection to the provider. The provider then executes the SQL SELECT statement. The table or tables, and the rows in those tables, are sent back over the connection to your solution. These tables are then stored in another object called a DataSet, which is discussed in the next section of this chapter.

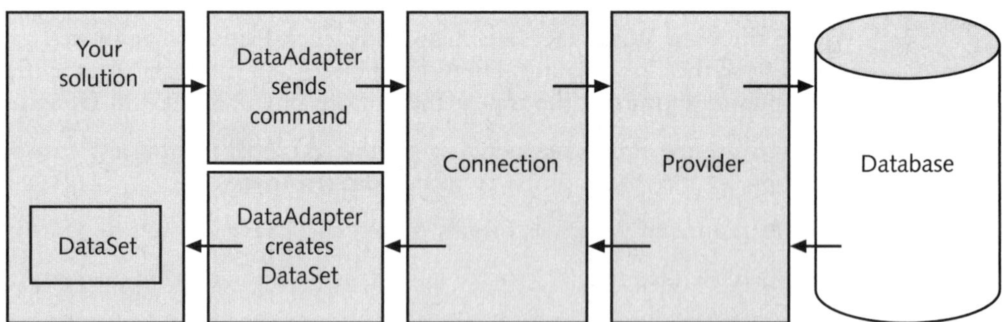

Figure 6-17 Retrieving data from a DataAdapter

STORING DATA IN DATASET AND DATATABLE OBJECTS

The DataAdapter sends a request over a connection to the provider. The provider then processes that request, and then returns the rows in a table into another object called a DataSet. A DataSet stores an in-memory representation of a database table. It is through this DataSet that your program and the control instances in that program display the rows in a table and allow the user to make changes to those rows. In this chapter, the DataSet stores the rows from a single table, but the DataSet can store information for several tables and the rows for those tables. In addition, you can use the DataSet to define relationships between the different database tables.

The easiest way to create a DataSet for a DataAdapter is to select an instance of the DataAdapter control, and then click Data, Generate Dataset from the VB .NET menu bar. You will now, using the DataAdapter that you just created, generate a DataSet so that your solution can display the contents of those rows to the user. Again, you could perform these tasks by hand, but the VB .NET tools simplify the process considerably.

To create a DataSet:

1. Make sure that the OleDbDataAdapter control instance named odbdaEmployees is selected in the Win Form Designer. Select the control instance by clicking the icon in the tray at the bottom of the Win Form Designer. The control instance appears with a hatched border when selected.

If you accidentally double-click the control instance, VB .NET activates the Code Editor. On the VB .NET menu bar, click **View**, and then click **Designer** to return to the Win Form Designer.

2. On the VB .NET menu bar, click **Data**, and then click **Generate Dataset** to open the Generate Dataset dialog box shown in Figure 6-18. Note that if the Win Form Designer is not the active window, then the menu bar will not display the Data menu.

   As shown in Figure 6-18, you can use existing DataSets or create new ones. When you create a new DataSet, you select a table or tables from a configured DataAdapter. In this example, you will create a DataSet based on the table named tblEmployees. If the database had multiple tables, then all of those tables would appear in the Generate Dataset dialog box.

3. In the Generate Dataset dialog box, click the **New** radio button, if necessary. When you click the New button, the text box to the right of the radio button becomes enabled. Enter the text **dsEmployees** to set the name of the DataSet. Conceptually, setting the name of the DataSet is similar to setting the Name property of a control instance. Again, note that the name of the DataSet must be unique.
4. Click the check box **tblEmployees (odbdaEmployees)**, if necessary. This causes the data in the database table to be selected and copied into the DataSet when the user runs the solution.
5. Make sure the **Add this dataset to the designer** check box is checked.
6. Click **OK** to close the dialog box and generate the DataSet.

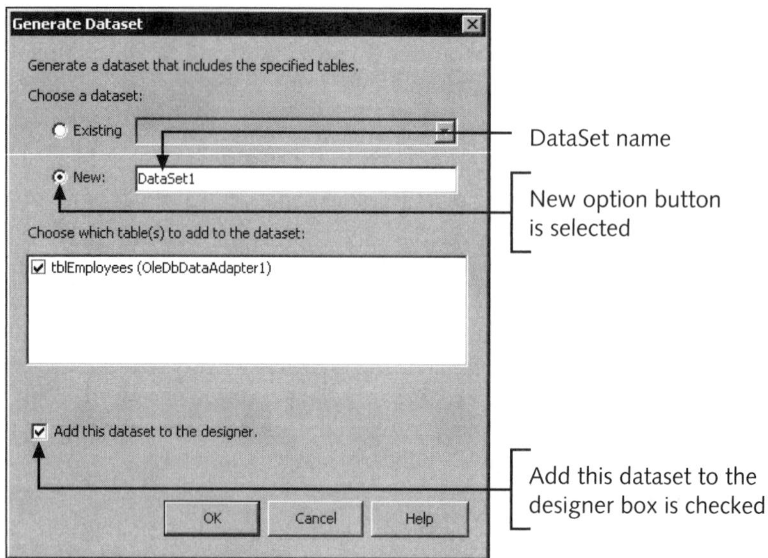

Figure 6-18 Generate Dataset dialog box

7. On the menu bar, click **File**, and then click **Save All** to save your work. If you change the SQL statements in the DataAdapter, you should generate the DataSet again. If you do not, the DataSet generated by VB .NET will not be synchronized with the DataAdapter, and run-time errors will occur.

When you generated the DataSet, VB .NET automatically created a control instance and placed that control instance in the resizable tray at the bottom of the form. Again, the control instance appears in the resizable tray because it is not visible to the user at run time. In addition, VB .NET created two new files that make up the DataSet. Figure 6-19 shows the control instance, and other files that are part of the DataSet.

The following list describes the files that make up the DataSet:

- VB .NET created a new file having the suffix ".xsd" and stored a reference to that file in the Solution Explorer. VB .NET uses this file to configure the DataSet. The .xsd file is called a schema definition file. It contains the XML statements that VB .NET uses to store data into the DataSet. You do not need to modify this file directly.
- VB .NET also created a file named dsEmployees.vb. This file contains several procedures that represent the methods that make up the DataSet. This file should never be modified directly. It should only be modified by the tools that generate the DataSet.

At this point in your solution's development, you have defined the connection using the OleDbConnection control. Using the OleDbDataAdapter control, you have defined the SQL statements that will select, insert, update, and delete records from a database table.

Finally, you have defined the DataSet that will actually store the data from the employees table as the solution runs. Next, you must write a statement that will actually load the DataSet with data when the user runs the solution. To populate a DataSet, you call the overloaded Fill method of the OleDbDataAdapter class. Therefore, you will call the Fill method of odbdaEmployees, the name of the DataAdapter that you created previously.

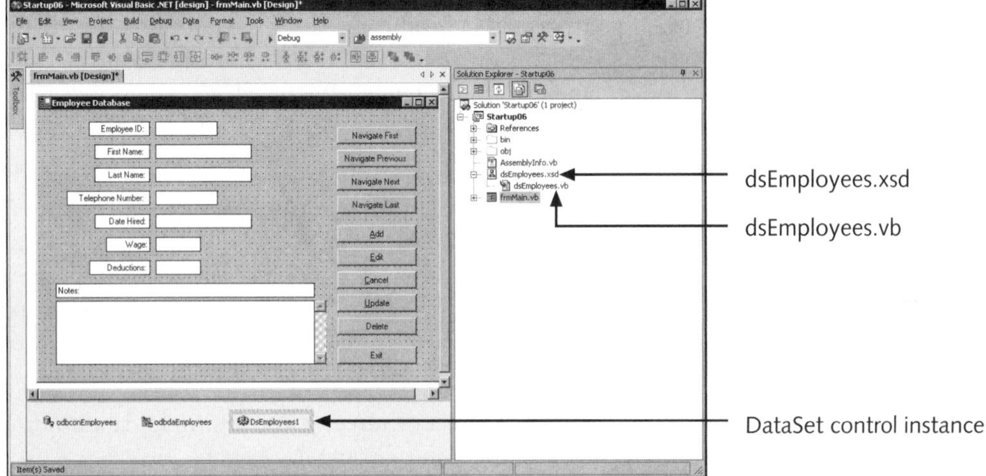

Figure 6-19 DataSet control instance

To fill a DataSet:

1. Activate the Code Editor for the form named **frmMain**. Remember that to activate the Code Editor, you click **View** on the menu bar, and then click **Code**.
2. Create the **frmMain_Load** event handler by clicking **Base Class Events** in the Class Name list box and clicking **Load** in the Method name list box.
3. Enter the following statements between the Private Sub and End Sub statements for the frmMain_Load event handler. The first statement declares a local variable named pintRecords. The second statement populates the DataSet by calling the Fill method of the DataAdapter named odbdaEmployees. The DataSet that you created is passed as an argument to the Fill method. The value stored in pintRecords is the number of records contained in the DataSet.

```
Dim pintRecords As Integer
pintRecords = odbdaEmployees.Fill(DsEmployees1)
```

4. On the menu bar, click **File**, and then click **Save All** to save your work.

If you ran the solution at this point, you would not see any data appear in the control instances already created on the form. This is because although you have filled the DataSet, you still need to configure the control instances on the form so that they will display data for the current record in the text boxes. This process is called data binding. Again, the text boxes were created on the form so that you need not complete steps with which you are already familiar.

BINDING CONTROLS TO A DATASET

When processing database data, users commonly see the data displayed in text boxes or other control instances appearing on the form. The user can add new data or update existing data using those same control instances. In this chapter, you will allow the user to navigate through the records in the employees table, displaying one record at a time in the text boxes already created.

The process of associating a specific property of a control instance, such as the Text property of a text box, to a field in a data source, such as a DataSet, is called **data binding**. When you bind a control instance to a data source, you bind a single property, such as the Text property of a text box, to a field in a DataSet. When the solution is run, VB .NET automatically stores the contents of the field in the bound property. Rows of the DataSet automatically appear in any bound text boxes or other control instance.

When binding a control instance to a data source, you use simple data binding or complex data binding, depending on the type of control.

- Controls, such as text boxes, are **simple bound**, meaning that they display only one row of data at a time. In this chapter, you will use simple bound text boxes to display data.
- Other controls that display multiple data items at once are complex bound. The ListBox, ComboBox, and DataGrid controls are **complex bound** because they display data from multiple rows from a DataSet or DataTable. You will not use complex binding in this chapter.

The Binding Object

To bind a control instance to a data source, you first create a Binding object. When you create a Binding object, you bind a property (such as the Text property of a text box) to a data source (such as a DataSet), by supplying three elements of information:

1. First supply a property name, such as the Text property, to which the field will be bound.
2. Second, supply a data source. This data source can be a DataSet or DataTable.
3. Finally, supply the navigation path to a field in the data source. The concept of a navigation path will be discussed in a moment.

The first step involved in binding a control instance to a DataSet requires that you create an instance of the Binding class of the System.Windows.Forms namespace. The constructor takes three arguments that define the control property that will be bound to the data source and how that property will be bound. The following code segment illustrates the statements to create a binding:

```
Dim pbndTemp As Binding
pbndTemp = New Binding("Text", DsEmployees1, _
    "tblEmployees.fldEmployeeID")
```

The first of the preceding statements declares a variable named pbndTemp to store the binding, while the second statement actually creates the binding. Note that we use the standard prefix of "bnd" to represent a binding. Examining the three arguments, the first argument specifies that the Text property of a control instance will be bound. This argument contains a string. The second argument contains the name of the DataSet that will be bound. This is the same DataSet that you created in the previous steps. The final argument contains a string which specifies the table and the field in that table that will be bound. This information is called a navigation path because it provides the means to navigate to a particular table and field in the underlying DataSet. The table name and field name are separated by a period. In the preceding statements, the employee table named tblEmployees, and the field named fldEmployeeID are bound. These statements are repeated for each control instance that needs to be bound.

After creating the binding, the next step is to associate the binding with a particular control instance as shown in the following statement:

```
txtEmployeeID.DataBindings.Add(pbndTemp)
```

The preceding statement adds the binding named pbndTemp to the DataBindings collection for the TextBox control instance named txtEmployeeID. Again, this step must be performed for each TextBox control instance that needs to be bound.

At this point, you will bind all of the text boxes on the form so that they will display a row from the DataSet you already created.

To create the bindings for the control instances on the form:

1. Activate the Code Editor for the form named **frmMain**. Enter the following statements (shown in bold) within the **Load** event handler:

```
Dim pbndTemp As Binding
Dim pintRecords as Integer
pintRecords = odbdaEmployees.Fill(DsEmployees1)
pbndTemp = New Binding("Text", DsEmployees1, _
    "tblEmployees.fldEmployeeID")
txtEmployeeID.DataBindings.Add(pbndTemp)

pbndTemp = New Binding("Text", DsEmployees1, _
    "tblEmployees.fldLastName")
txtLastName.DataBindings.Add(pbndTemp)

pbndTemp = New Binding("Text", DsEmployees1, _
    "tblEmployees.fldFirstName")
txtFirstName.DataBindings.Add(pbndTemp)
```

```
pbndTemp = New Binding("Text", DsEmployees1, _
    "tblEmployees.fldTelephone")
txtTelephone.DataBindings.Add(pbndTemp)

pbndTemp = New Binding("Text", DsEmployees1, _
    "tblEmployees.fldDateHired")
txtDateHired.DataBindings.Add(pbndTemp)

pbndTemp = New Binding("Text", DsEmployees1, _
    "tblEmployees.fldWage")
txtWage.DataBindings.Add(pbndTemp)

pbndTemp = New Binding("Text", DsEmployees1, _
    "tblEmployees.fldDeductions")
txtDeductions.DataBindings.Add(pbndTemp)

pbndTemp = New Binding("Text", DsEmployees1, _
    "tblEmployees.fldNotes")
txtNotes.DataBindings.Add(pbndTemp)
Call EditState(cblnNotEditing)
```

The preceding statements create a binding for each of the text boxes on the form, and add each binding to the DataBindings collection. The final statement calls the EditState procedure. The code in this procedure disables the text boxes to indicate that a record is not being edited.

2. On the menu bar, click **File**, and then click **Save All** to save your work.
3. Test the solution. When run, your solution should display the first record from the database table. This is the record for Jim Anderson. See Figure 6-20.

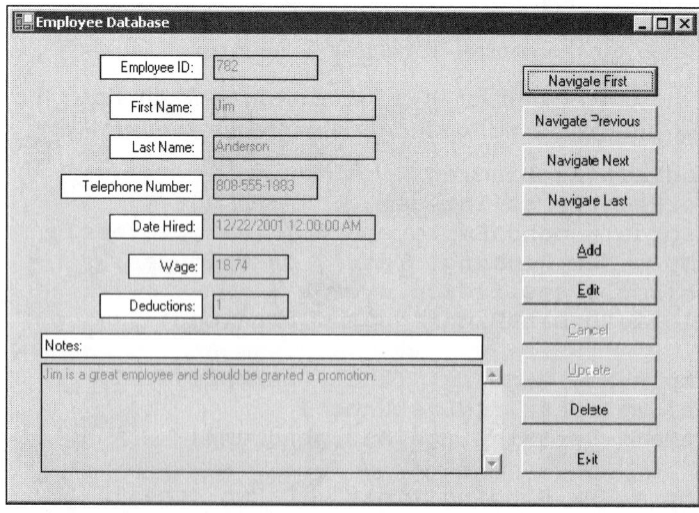

Figure 6-20 Form displaying database records

If you receive a run-time error, VB .NET highlights the statement in error in the Code Editor. Check that the property name and the navigation path are correct. End and run the solution again.

At this point in the solution's development, the text boxes display the first employee record. Although the control instances display data from the current row in the DataSet, you need a way for the user to navigate from record to record, and a way for the user to add, change, and delete records. Each of these tasks is accomplished through the BindingContext property supplied by the Form class.

Navigating Through the Records in a Database Table

When you bind control instances to a DataSet, VB .NET automatically creates two objects: CurrencyManager and BindingContext. These objects keep the control instances synchronized with the data in the DataSet so that they always display data from the same record.

The key to using the CurrencyManager is understanding the purpose of the Position property. By incrementing or decrementing the value of the Position property, the CurrencyManager automatically displays the next or previous record in all of the bound control instances.

The key to using the BindingContext is understanding how VB .NET creates and manages multiple BindingContexts and how to reference a particular BindingContext. In this example, you bound all the control instances to the same DataSet. If control instances are bound to different DataSets, then VB .NET creates a separate BindingContext for each DataSet. A BindingContext, like most collections, references individual objects with the Item method. In the case of the BindingContext, the collection references the BindingManagerBase class. This class, in turn, supports methods to navigate through the data in an underlying data source and modify that data.

You have already bound the control instances to a DataSet. In the steps that follow, you will write the code to navigate through the rows in the DataSet table. This code will execute in response to the menu items you created previously in the chapter.

To position bound controls:

1. Create the **btnNavigateFirst_Click** event handler, and then enter the following statement. Remember that to create the event handler, you can use the Class Name and Method name list boxes in the Code Editor, or you can activate the Win Form Designer, and then double-click the button.

   ```
   Me.BindingContext(DsEmployees1, "tblEmployees").Position = 0
   ```

   The preceding statement locates the first record in the BindingContext. The Me keyword references the current form so the statement fragment

`Me.BindingContext` references the BindingContext collection of the current form. The two arguments contain the name of the DataSet (DsEmployees1), and the name of the table (tblEmployees). Again, these arguments are defining the navigation path to the table in the DataSet. By setting the Position property to 0, the first record is displayed to the user. Note that the Position property is 0-based, so the first record has a position of 0 instead of having a position of 1.

2. Create the **btnNavigatePrevious_Click** event handler, and then enter the following statement:

```
Me.BindingContext(DsEmployees1, "tblEmployees").Position _
    -= 1
```

   This statement works similarly to the preceding statement. However, the Position property is decremented by 1, and thus locates the previous record. Note that if the first record is the current record, then the preceding statement does nothing. That is, VB .NET does not produce a run-time error. Note also that a continuation character appears because the statement does not fit on a single line.

3. Create the **btnNavigateNext_Click** event handler, and then enter the following statement:

```
Me.BindingContext(DsEmployees1, "tblEmployees").Position _
    += 1
```

   This statement works similarly to the previous statement. Instead of decrementing the Position property by 1, the Position property is incremented by 1. Again, VB .NET does not cause a run-time error if the current record is the last record.

4. Create the **btnNavigateLast_Click** event handler, and then enter the following statement:

```
Me.BindingContext(DsEmployees1,"tblEmployees").Position = _

    Me.DsEmployees1.tblEmployees.Rows.Count - 1
```

   Again, the preceding statement appears on multiple lines so the continuation character appears. The preceding statement to locate the last record requires a bit of additional explanation. The Position property is not incremented or decremented. Rather, the statement fragment `Me.DsEmployees1.tblEmployees.Rows.Count` obtains the number of rows in the table named tblEmployees in the DataSet named DsEmployees1. One is subtracted from this value because the Position property is 0-based while the Count property is 1-based. That is, a DataSet having 10 rows would have positions ranging from 0 to 9.

5. On the menu bar, click **File**, and then click **Save All** to save your work.

6. Test the solution. Navigate to the last, first, next, and previous records by clicking the **Last**, **First**, **Next**, and **Previous** buttons on the form. Note that the current record displayed changes as you click each menu item.

At this point in the solution's development, you have seen how to bind control instances to a DataSet. You have also seen how to navigate from one row to another using those bound control instances. One problem remains to be solved. The user must be able to add, change, and delete records from the database.

Adding, Changing, and Deleting Records

The steps to add, change, and delete records are more complex than the steps to navigate from record to record. This complexity arises because you must copy data from the bound controls to the DataSet, and then save those changes in the DataSet back to the database. Before allowing the user to modify database data, however, think about the order of operations that need to be performed.

- When adding a new row, the user must click a button to add a record (employee). The statements in the Click event handler will clear the contents of the text boxes so that the user can enter a new employee. Then, the user must either commit the addition or cancel it. No other operations should be performed while the user is adding an employee. That is, the user should not be able to navigate from record to record when adding an employee.
- When modifying an existing employee, the text boxes on the form must be enabled for editing and the edited record either saved to the database or cancelled. Again, the user should not be able to navigate between records while editing a record.

To prevent the user from attempting a task that may cause a run-time error, the following sub procedure will enable and disable menu items so that the solution operates in one of two modes. If the user is not editing a record, then the menu items to add, edit, delete, and locate records are enabled. If the user is editing a record, then the user must either update or cancel the edit before proceeding. In addition, the subprocedure will enable or disable the form's text boxes.

The following code shows part of the EditState procedure that has already been created in the startup solution:

```
Private Sub EditState(ByVal pblnState As Boolean)
    Select Case pblnState
        Case cblnEditing
            btnAdd.Enabled = False
            btnEdit.Enabled = False
            btnUpdate.Enabled = True
            btnCancel.Enabled = True
            btnDelete.Enabled = False
            ' Code to enable all text boxes.

        Case cblnNotEditing
            btnAdd.Enabled = True
            btnEdit.Enabled = True
```

```
                btnUpdate.Enabled = False
                btnCancel.Enabled = False
                btnDelete.Enabled = True
                ' Code to disable all text boxes.

        End Select
    End Sub
```

Whenever the user tries to add, edit, update, or delete a record, the EditState procedure will be called to enable or disable the menu items accordingly. If editing is enabled, then the user cannot locate a different record and must commit or abandon the edit. If the record is not being edited, then the text boxes are disabled; the user can navigate between records, and add, change, and delete records. You later will write code to call this procedure as the user selects menu items that involve modification of data.

MODIFYING A DATABASE RECORD

Adding or modifying a new or existing record to a DataSet is a three-step process. First, a new record must be created in the BindingContext, then that new record must be saved back to the bound DataSet (DsEmployees1). Finally, the contents of the DataSet must be updated and the new record stored in the underlying database.

The following statement illustrates how to add a new record to a BindingContext:

```
Me.BindingContext(DsEmployees1, "tblEmployees").AddNew()
```

The syntax of the preceding statement is similar to the syntax of the statement to locate a row in the BindingContext. The DataSet and navigation path to a table are supplied as arguments. At the end of the statement, the AddNew method adds a new row to the BindingContext.

After adding the new record to the BindingContext, those changes must be saved to the bound DataSet, then the changes made to the DataSet must be saved to the underlying database table. (Remember that the DataSet is not connected to the database.) You save the data from the BindingContext to the DataSet by calling the EndCurrentEdit method of the BindingContext as shown in the following statement:

```
Me.BindingContext(DsEmployees1, _
   "tblEmployees").EndCurrentEdit()
```

The preceding statement references a single BindingContext within the collection by specifying, as arguments, the DataSet name and the navigation path to the table. This is the same BindingContext that you used to navigate from record to record in the preceding steps. Calling the EndCurrentEdit method indicates that editing is complete for the current record and saves the current record back to the bound DataSet.

Although the DataSet is bound to the control instances on the form, changes made to the DataSet's records are not automatically saved to the underlying database. To accomplish this task, you must explicitly call the Update method to save the DataSet changes back to the database.

In the following sections, you will learn how to, add, update, and delete a record. You will also learn how to cancel an update.

Enabling a Record for Updating

When working with bound controls such as text boxes, they are automatically enabled for updating. So that the user is aware that they are editing a record, the form contains an Edit button. This button enables the text boxes on the form and requires that the user edit the form or abandon it.

To enable a record for editing:

1. Create the **btnEdit_Click** event handler.
2. Enter the following statement:

```
Call EditState(cblnEditing)
```

Once a record has been enabled for editing, it must be updated.

Adding and Updating a Record

Remember that a DataSet represents a disconnected view of one or more database tables. When you add, modify, or delete records from a DataSet, you must explicitly save those changes back to the database using the DataAdapter. To accomplish this task, you find out which records in the DataSet were added, changed, or deleted, and then save those records back to the database. The GetChanges method of the DataSet class creates a second DataSet or DataTable from the records that were added, changed, or deleted in the primary DataSet. The first of the following statements declares a DataSet named pdsChangedRows. The second of the statements gets any and all rows that were added, changed, or deleted, and stores those rows in the DataSet named pdsChangedRows. Therefore, the DataSet named pdsChangedRows will contain only the row in the primary DataSet that was added, changed, or deleted.

```
Dim pdsChangedRows As System.Data.DataSet
pdsChangedRows = DsEmployees1.GetChanges()
```

After identifying the added, changed, or deleted records, those records need to be saved back to the database. To copy the changes made to a DataSet back to the database, you use the DataAdapter once again. Remember that the DataAdapter executes commands that will retrieve, add, change, or delete database records. When you called the Fill method, the DataAdapter retrieved records from the database and filled the DataSet with records. The Update method of the DataAdapter records changes to the database. The method requires one argument, a DataSet containing the rows to update.

The following statement saves the rows from the respective DataSet back to the database:

```
odbdaEmployees.Update(pdsChangedRows)
```

Calling the Update method of the DataAdapter causes VB .NET to open the connection again automatically. Then the SQL UPDATE statement is sent over the DataAdapter and processed by the provider causing the change to be recorded back to the underlying database.

Having saved the DataSet representing the inserted or modified row to the database, you must now advise the DataSet that the changes have been recorded. That is, you must synchronize the in-memory DataSet with the database itself. To accomplish this task, you call the AcceptChanges method pertaining to the DataSet as shown in the following statement:

```
DsEmployees1.AcceptChanges()
```

The preceding statement marks any changed records in the DataSet as unchanged. Note that the preceding statement called the Update method on the primary DataSet named DsEmployees1, rather than the copy (pdsChangedRows). Had you accepted the changes for the copies, you would not have accepted the changes to the original DataSet, you would have accepted changes only for the copies. Figure 6-21 illustrates how changes are recorded to the database.

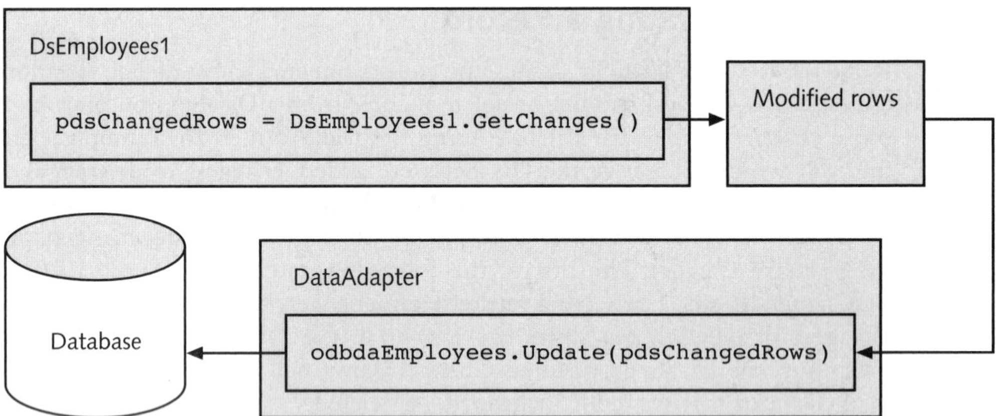

Figure 6-21 Recording changes to the database

You now have the tools to add records and update those newly added records to the underlying database.

To add and update records:

1. Create the **btnAdd_Click** event handler by activating the Win Form Designer and then double-clicking the button. Enter the following statements into the event handler:

   ```
   Call EditState(cblnEditing)
   Me.BindingContext(DsEmployees1, "tblEmployees").AddNew()
   ```

   The first statement calls the procedure that enables the text boxes for editing, and the second statement creates the new record in the BindingContext.

2. Create the **btnUpdate_Click** event handler. Enter the following statements into the event handler.

   ```
   Dim pdsChangedRows As DataSet
   Call EditState(cblnNotEditing)
   Me.BindingContext(DsEmployees1, "tblEmployees").EndCurrentEdit
   pdsChangedRows = DsEmployees1.GetChanges()

   If Not pdsChangedRows Is Nothing Then
       odbdaEmployees.Update(pdsChangedRows)
   End If

   DsEmployees1.AcceptChanges()
   ```

   In the preceding statements the Update button records changes for both added and modified records. The DataSet named pdsChangedRows contains a record if a new record was added or if an existing record was modified. The If statement tests whether a row exists in the DataSet. The DataSet has a value of Nothing when no rows exist. If a row exists, then calling the Update method sends the SQL INSERT or UPDATE statement stored in the DataAdapter's InsertCommand or UpdateCommand property to the provider to add or update the record. Finally, the changes are accepted in the original DataSet, and the DataSet and database are synchronized.

3. On the menu bar, click **File**, and then click **Save All** to save your work.

4. Test the solution. On the form's menu, click **Add**. Enter an ID number of **99877**. Enter your first and last name, your telephone number, and use your birth date as the date hired. Enter **15.99** for the wage and **1** for the deductions. After completing all the fields, click **Update**. The new record that you just added is saved to the database.

Deleting a Record

The process to delete a record from a bound control and its underlying DataSet is simpler than the process to add and update a record. To delete a record, you call the RemoveAt method pertaining to the BindingContext. The RemoveAt method requires one argument, the position of a record in the BindingContext. Next, you call the

GetChanges method of the DataSet to copy the deleted row to a new DataSet. Then you delete the row from the database by calling the Update method of the DataAdapter and then accepting the changes in the DataSet.

You can now write the code to Delete a database record.

To create the statements to delete a record:

1. Create the Click event handler for the menu item named **btnDelete**, and then enter the following statements:

```
Dim pdsDeletedRows As DataSet
Me.BindingContext(DsEmployees1, "tblEmployees"). _
   RemoveAt(Me.BindingContext(DsEmployees1, _
   "tblEmployees").Position)
pdsDeletedRows = DsEmployees1.GetChanges(DataRowState.Deleted)
odbdaEmployees.Update(pdsDeletedRows)
DsEmployees1.AcceptChanges()
```

   The first of the preceding statements declares a local DataSet to store the deleted row. The second statement deletes the current row from the BindingContext and the underlying bound DataSet. The next statement retrieves the deleted row from the DataSet, and the next statement calls the Update method supplied by the DataAdapter with one argument, a DataSet containing the deleted row. Execution of this statement causes the DataAdapter to reestablish a connection with the database and send the SQL DELETE statement stored in the DataAdapter's DeleteCommand property to the provider to delete the record. The final statement synchronizes the database with the DataSet.

2. On the menu bar, click **File**, and then click **Save All** to save your work.
3. Test the solution. Locate the record that you just created (the one with your name).
4. Click the **Delete** button to delete the record.

Canceling an Update

Suppose that the user had started to edit a record, made a mistake, and did not want to save the changes to the DataSet or database. To abandon the editing of bound controls, you call the CancelCurrentEdit method pertaining to the BindingContext as shown in the following statement:

```
Me.BindingContext(DsEmployees1, "tblEmployees"). _
   CancelCurrentEdit()
```

The preceding statement cancels the current edit for the BindingContext used in this chapter. By calling this method, the changes are not saved to the DataSet, and the bound control instances are restored to their original contents before editing began. You can now write the code to cancel an edit.

To cancel a record being edited:

1. Create the Click event handler for the menu item named **btnCancel**, and then enter the following statements:

```
Call EditState(cblnNotEditing)
Me.BindingContext(DsEmployees1, "tblEmployees"). _
CancelCurrentEdit()
```

2. On the menu bar, click **File**, and then click **Save All** to save your work.
3. Test the solution. Click the **Edit** button. Modify the contents of the current record by changing the name to your name.
4. Click the **Cancel** button to cancel the edit and restore the contents of the text boxes.

You have completed the programming for this chapter. You have learned how to perform database operations, to navigate, add, change, and delete records.

CHAPTER SUMMARY

- VB .NET supports database processing though the classes of the System.Data namespace. These objects are collectively referred to as ADO.NET.
- A connection forms the pipeline between your application and a database. To create a connection, create an instance of the OleDbConnection control on the form. Define the connection string by activating the Properties window, selecting the ConnectionString property, and clicking New Connection. In the Provider tab of the Data Link Properties dialog box, select Microsoft Jet 4.0 OLE DB Provider. On the Connection tab, define the database to which you want to connect. Finally, test the connection.
- The DataAdapter provides the means to retrieve data over a connection. Create an instance of the DataAdapter control on the form. When you create the control instance, VB .NET activates a Wizard. First, select the connection that you want to use. Second, use the Query Builder to define the SQL SELECT statement that will execute to retrieve the desired rows from a database table.
- After creating the DataAdapter, the DataSet must be generated. To generate the DataSet, click Data, and then click Generate Dataset on the VB .NET menu bar. In the Generate Dataset dialog box, click the New radio button if necessary. Specify the name of the DataSet, and then make sure that the Add this dataset to the designer check box is checked.
- Fill the DataSet by calling the Fill method of the DataAdapter. The Fill method takes one argument, the name of the DataSet that you want to populate.
- The process of associating a property of a control instance, such as the Text property of a text box, with a data source is called data binding. Some controls are

simple bound while other controls are complex bound. To define a binding, create a new instance of the Binding class. The first argument to the Binding constructor is the name of the property to bind. The second argument contains the name of the DataSet, and the final argument contains the navigation path to the desired table and field in the DataSet.

- After creating the binding, add it to the DataBindings collection for the control instance, such as a text box.
- To navigate from record to record in a DataSet, you use the BindingContext of the form. Set the Position property in the BindingContext to the desired record. This causes the correct record to be displayed in the bound control instance.
- To add a record to the DataSet, call the AddNew method of the BindingContext. Then, call the EndCurrentEdit method of the BindingContext. Next, call the GetChanges methods of the DataSet to get the newly added row. Finally, call the Update method of the DataAdapter with one argument, the name of the DataSet containing the added rows.
- To modify an existing record, call the EndCurrentEdit method of the BindingContext. Again, call the GetChanges method of the DataSet to get the changed row. Finally, call the Update method of the DataAdapter with one argument, the name of the DataSet containing the added rows.
- To delete a record, call the RemoveAt method of the BindingContext. Again, call the GetChanges method of the DataSet, and then call the Update method of the DataAdapter.
- To synchronize the DataSet with the database, call the AcceptChanges method of the DataSet.

Review Questions

1. Which of the following statements is true of ADO.NET?
   a. ADO.NET uses a disconnected architecture meaning that database connections are closed after use.
   b. ADO.NET only works with Access databases.
   c. ADO.NET only works with desktop applications. To create Internet applications that manage data, you use ADOI.NET
   d. all of these
   e. none of these

2. Which of the following statements applies to creating a database connection using ADO.NET?
   a. Because ADO.NET uses a disconnected architecture, connections are not used.
   b. A provider establishes a link between an ADO.NET connection and the database.
   c. To create a connection, you create an instance of the Connection control on the form.
   d. The connection is visible to the user.
   e. none of these

3. What is the purpose of the DataAdapter?
   a. It is used to adapt different type of databases so that they can function with ADO.NET.
   b. ADO.NET does not support the DataAdapter.
   c. To create a DataAdapter, you create an instance of the DataAdapter control on the form, which is visible to the user at run time.
   d. It is used to send commands over a connection to retrieve data.
   e. none of these
4. What is the name of the method of the DataAdapter that you call to populate a DataSet with records?
   a. Populate
   b. Read
   c. Fill
   d. Load
   e. none of these
5. Which of the following statements correctly describes a DataSet?
   a. To create a DataSet, you create an instance of the DataSet control on the form, and then configure it using the DataSet configuration Wizard.
   b. DataSets are of two types, single row DataSets and multiple row DataSets.
   c. A DataSet represents an in-memory disconnected view of one or more database tables.
   d. all of these
   e. none of these

6. What is the difference between complex binding and simple binding?
   a. Complex binding is more difficult to perform than simple binding.
   b. The terms "complex binding" and "simple binding" are synonymous.
   c. Simple bound controls display one row at a time while complex bound controls display multiple rows at a time.
   d. Complex binding allows you to control the order in which rows are displayed in a control instance, but with simple binding the rows are always displayed in alphabetical order.
   e. none of these
7. Which of the following statements is true pertaining to data binding?
   a. To save changes to a database, you call the Save method of the Binding object.
   b. You bind a control instance by setting the Binding property to True and the DataSet property to the name of a DataSet.
   c. The Binding object binds a control property to a field in a DataSet. This Binding is then added to the DataBindings collection for a control instance such as a text box.
   d. You navigate between bound rows by setting the CurrentRow property pertaining to a BindingContext.
   e. all of these
8. Which of the following statements correctly fills the DataSet named of dsDemo1, assuming that the DataAdapter is named odbdaDemo?
   a. odbdaDemo.Populate(DsDemo1)
   b. DsDemo1.Fill()
   c. odbdaDemo.Fill(DsDemo1)
   d. DsDemo1.Fill(odbdaDemo)
   e. none of these
9. Which of the following statements is correct referring to the Position property of a BindingContext?
   a. It is 0-based. Therefore, the first record in the BindingContext has a value of 0.
   b. By incrementing or decrementing the Position property, the records displayed to the user will be changed.
   c. To locate the last record in the BindingContext, you set the Position property to Max.
   d. both a and b
   e. all of these

10. What are the methods used to add, change, and delete records using a BindingContext?
    a. Add, Update, Remove
    b. Add, Modify, Remove
    c. AddNew, Modify, Delete
    d. Add, Change, Delete
    e. AddNew, EndCurrentEdit, RemoveAt
11. What is the purpose of the AcceptChanges method pertaining to the DataSet?
    a. It causes any changed rows to be saved back to the underlying database.
    b. It marks any changed rows as unchanged.
    c. The AcceptChanges method does not apply to the DataSet.
    d. both a and b
    e. none of these
12. Referring to the BindingContext, what is the name of the method that you call to create a new record?
    a. Add
    b. AddNew
    c. Create
    d. CreateRecord
    e. none of these
13. Referring to the BindingContext, what is the name of the method that you call to abandon editing on the current record?
    a. AbortCurrentEdit
    b. AbandonChanges
    c. Cancel
    d. Abort
    e. none of these
14. How do you delete a record using the DataSet and BindingContext?
    a. Call the Remove method of the DataAdapter. Save the removed record back to the Database by calling the SaveChanges method of the DataSet itself.
    b. Call the DeleteRecord method of the DataSet producing a second DataSet containing the deleted record. Save this record by calling the SaveChanges method of the DataSet.
    c. Call the Delete method of the BindingContext. Then call the GetDeletedRecord method of the DataSet to get the deleted row. Finally, call the Update method of the DataAdapter to save the changes back to the database.

d. Call the RemoveAt method of the BindingContext. Then call the GetChanges method of the DataSet to get the deleted row. Finally, call the Update method of the DataAdapter to save the changes back to the database.

e. none of these

15. Which of the following statements is true of updating a record in a DataSet?

a. DataSets are not updatable.

b. When you update a record in a DataSet, the changed records are automatically saved back to the database.

c. When a record in a database is updated, that updated record must be saved back to the database through the DataAdapter.

d. To save the changes to the DataSet, you call the Update method of the DataSet itself.

e. none of these

HANDS-ON EXERCISES

If necessary, use Windows Explorer to create a new folder in the Chap06 folder in your workfolder. Name this folder **Exercises**. Save the solutions that you create in these Exercises in the Chap06\Exercises folder in your workfolder.

Exercise 6-1

In this exercise, you create a solution that uses buttons to locate, add, change, and delete records from a database table. The database and its table have already been created in the database named Chapter06\Data folder. The database is named Factory and the table is named tblParts. Table 6-1 describes the database table:

Table 6-1

Field name	Description	VB .NET Data type
fldPartNumber	Unique identification number	Long Integer
fldDescription	Description of part	String
fldCost	Cost of part	Single
fldSalesPrice	Sales price of part	Single
fldQuantityOnHand	Number of items in inventory	Integer

1. Start VB .NET, if necessary, and create a new solution named **Ch06Ex1** in the Chap06\Exercises folder.
2. Create the control instances on the form as shown in Figure 6-22.
3. Set the Name property of the control instances as shown in Figure 6-22, and set the caption for the form.

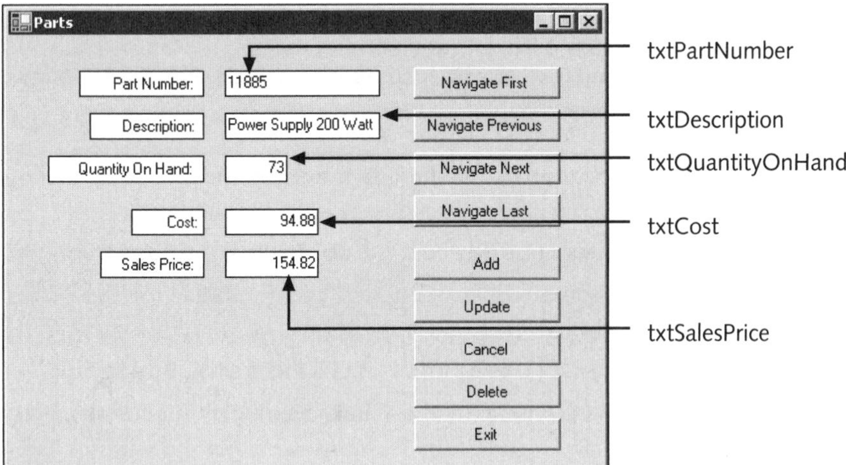

Figure 6-22

4. Using the Data tab on the Toolbox, create an instance of the OleDbConnection control, and configure it so that you establish a connection with the database named Factory.mdb. Set the name of the control instance to odbconParts.
5. Using the Data tab on the Toolbox, create an instance of the DataAdapter control on the form. Using the Wizard, configure the DataAdapter so that it establishes a connection with the database connection you created in the previous step. Use the database table named tblParts. Add all of the columns from the table. Sort the output in ascending order by part number. Set the name of the DataAdapter to odbdaParts.
6. Generate a DataSet for the DataAdapter you just created. Set the DataSet name to dsParts.
7. In the Load event handler for the form, enter the following statements to fill the DataSet and bind the control instances:

```
Dim pintRecords As Integer
Dim bndTemp As Binding

pintRecords = odbdaParts.Fill(DsParts1)

bndTemp = New Binding("Text", DsParts1, "tblParts.fldPartNumber")
txtPartNumber.DataBindings.Add(bndTemp)

bndTemp = New Binding("Text", DsParts1, "tblParts.fldDescription")
txtDescription.DataBindings.Add(bndTemp)

bndTemp = New Binding("Text", DsParts1, "tblParts.fldCost")
txtCost.DataBindings.Add(bndTemp)

bndTemp = New Binding("Text", DsParts1, "tblParts.fldSalesPrice")
```

6

```
txtSalesPrice.DataBindings.Add(bndTemp)

bndTemp = New Binding("Text", DsParts1, "tblParts.fldQuantity
OnHand")
txtQuantityOnHand.DataBindings.Add(bndTemp)
```

8. Create the following statement in the Click event handler for the Navigate First button:

```
Me.BindingContext(DsParts1, "tblParts").Position = 0
```

9. Create the following statement in the Click event handler for the Navigate Previous button:

```
Me.BindingContext(DsParts1, "tblParts").Position -= 1
```

10. Create the following statement in the Click event handler for the Navigate Next button:

```
Me.BindingContext(DsParts1, "tblParts").Position += 1
```

11. Create the following statements in the Click event handler for the Navigate Last button:

```
Me.BindingContext(DsParts1, "tblParts").Position() = _
   Me.DsParts1.Tables("tblParts").Rows.Count - 1
```

12. Create the following statements in the Click event handler for the Add button:

```
Me.BindingContext(DsParts1, "tblParts").AddNew()
```

13. Create the following statements in the Click event handler for the Update button:

```
Dim pdsChangedRows As System.Data.DataSet

Me.BindingContext(DsParts1, "tblParts").EndCurrentEdit()

pdsChangedRows = DsParts1.GetChanges()

If Not pdsChangedRows Is Nothing Then
    odbdaParts.Update(pdsChangedRows)
End If

DsParts1.AcceptChanges()
```

14. Create the following statements in the Click event handler for the Cancel button:

```
Me.BindingContext(DsParts1, "tblParts").CancelCurrentEdit()
```

15. Create the following statements in the Click event handler for the Delete button:

```
Dim pdsDeletedRows As DataSet

Me.BindingContext(DsParts1, "tblparts"). _
   RemoveAt(Me.BindingContext(DsParts1, "tblParts").Position)
```

```
pdsDeletedRows = DsParts1.GetChanges( _
            System.Data.DataRowState.Deleted)

odbdaParts.Update(pdsDeletedRows)

DsParts1.AcceptChanges()
```

16. Create the following statement in the Click event handler for the Exit button:

```
Me.Close()
```

17. Test the program, and then save and close the **Ch06Ex1** solution.

Exercise 6-2

In this exercise, you create a solution that allows the user to add, change, and delete records from a customers table having several fields. Table 6-2 describes the fields in the table named tblCustomers.

Table 6-2

Field name	Description	VB .NET Data type
fldCustomerID	Unique identification number	Long Integer
fldFirstName	First name	String
fldLastName	Last name	String
fldAddress	Customer address	String
fldCity	Customer city	String
fldState	Customer state	String
fldZipCode	Customer Zip code	String
fldAnnualSales	Annual sales amount	Double
fldBalanceDue	Balance due on account	Double
fldCreditLimit	Customer credit limit	Double

1. Start VB .NET and create a new solution named **Ch06Ex2** in the Chap06\Exercises folder.
2. Create the control instances on the form as shown in Figure 6-23.
3. Set the Name property of the control instances as shown in Figure 6-23, and set the title of the form.
4. Using the Data tab on the Toolbox, create an instance of the OleDbConnection control, and configure it so that you establish a connection with the database named Factory.mdb. Set the name of the control instance to odbconFactory.
5. Using the Data tab on the Toolbox, create an instance of the DataAdapter control on the form. Using the Wizard, configure the DataAdapter so that it establishes a connection with the database connection you created in the previous step. Use all of the fields from the database table named tblCustomers. Sort the output in

ascending order by the customer ID number. Set the name of the DataAdapter to odbdaCustomers.

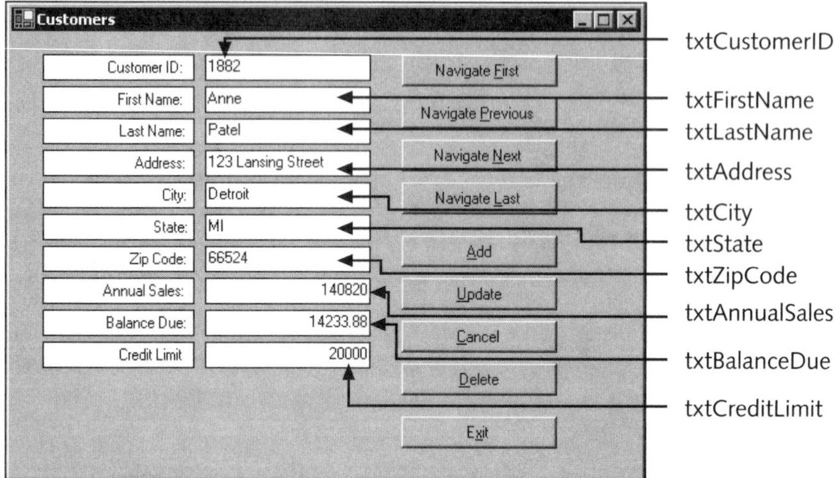

Figure 6-23

6. Generate a DataSet for the DataAdapter you just created. Set the DataSet name to dsCustomers.
7. In the Load event handler for the form, enter the following statements to fill the DataSet and bind the control instances:

```
Dim pintRecords As Integer
Dim bndTemp As Binding

odbdaCustomers.Fill(DsCustomers1)

bndTemp = New Binding("Text", DsCustomers1, _
    "tblCustomers.fldCustomerID")
txtCustomerID.DataBindings.Add(bndTemp)

bndTemp = New Binding("Text", DsCustomers1, _
    "tblCustomers.fldFirstName")
txtFirstName.DataBindings.Add(bndTemp)

bndTemp = New Binding("Text", DsCustomers1, _
    "tblCustomers.fldLastName")
txtLastName.DataBindings.Add(bndTemp)

bndTemp = New Binding("Text", DsCustomers1, _
    "tblCustomers.fldAddress")
txtAddress.DataBindings.Add(bndTemp)
```

```
bndTemp = New Binding("Text", DsCustomers1, _
    "tblCustomers.fldCity")
txtCity.DataBindings.Add(bndTemp)

bndTemp = New Binding("Text", DsCustomers1, _
    "tblCustomers.fldState")
txtState.DataBindings.Add(bndTemp)

bndTemp = New Binding("Text", DsCustomers1, _
    "tblCustomers.fldZipCode")
txtZipCode.DataBindings.Add(bndTemp)

bndTemp = New Binding("Text", DsCustomers1, _
    "tblCustomers.fldAnnualSales")
txtAnnualSales.DataBindings.Add(bndTemp)

bndTemp = New Binding("Text", DsCustomers1, _
    "tblCustomers.fldBalanceDue")
txtBalanceDue.DataBindings.Add(bndTemp)

bndTemp = New Binding("Text", DsCustomers1, _
    "tblCustomers.fldCreditLimit")
txtCreditLimit.DataBindings.Add(bndTemp)
```


8. Create the following statement in the Click event handler for the Navigate First button:

```
Me.BindingContext(DsCustomers1, "tblCustomers").Position = 0
```

9. Create the following statement in the Click event handler for the Navigate Previous button:

```
Me.BindingContext(DsCustomers1, "tblCustomers").Position -= 1
```

10. Create the following statement in the Click event handler for the Navigate Next button:

```
Me.BindingContext(DsCustomers1, "tblCustomers").Position += 1
```

11. Create the following statement in the Click event handler for the Navigate Last button:

```
Me.BindingContext(DsCustomers1, "tblCustomers").Position = _
    Me.DsCustomers1.Tables("tblCustomers").Rows.Count - 1
```

12. Create the following statement in the Click event handler for the Add button:

```
Me.BindingContext(DsCustomers1, "tblCustomers").AddNew()
```

13. Create the following statements in the Click event handler for the Update button:

```
Dim pdsChangedRows As System.Data.DataSet

Me.BindingContext(DsCustomers1, "tblCustomers").EndCurrentEdit()

pdsChangedRows = DsCustomers1.GetChanges()
```

```
If Not pdsChangedRows Is Nothing Then
    odbdaCustomers.Update(pdsChangedRows)
End If

DsCustomers1.AcceptChanges()
```

14. Create the following statements in the Click event handler for the Cancel button:

```
Me.BindingContext(DsCustomers1, _
"tblCustomers").CancelCurrentEdit()
```

15. Create the following statements in the Click event handler for the Delete button:

```
Dim pdsDeletedRows As DataSet

Me.BindingContext(DsCustomers1, "tblCustomers"). _
    RemoveAt(Me.BindingContext(DsCustomers1, _
    "tblCustomers").Position)

pdsDeletedRows = _
    DsCustomers1.GetChanges( _
    System.Data.DataRowState.Deleted)

odbdaCustomers.Update(pdsDeletedRows)

DsCustomers1.AcceptChanges()
```

16. Create the following statement in the Click event handler for the Exit button:

```
Me.Close()
```

17. Test the program, and then save and close the **Ch06Ex2** solution.

Exercise 6-3

In this exercise, you create a solution that navigates through the rows in a DataSet using control instances other than text boxes. You will use Date controls and check boxes to display the information in the database table. Table 6-3 describes the fields in the table named tblTelephoneCalls.

Table 6-3

Field name	Description	VB .NET Data type
fldCallID	Unique identification number	Long Integer
fldCallIn	Call originator	String
fldCallOut	Call destination	String
fldDateTimeStart	Starting date and time of the call	DateTime
fldDateTimeEnd	Ending date and time of call	DateTime
fldPeakNonPeak	Peak call time	Boolean

1. Start VB .NET and create a new solution named **Ch06Ex3** in the Chap06\ Exercises folder.
2. Create the control instances on the form as shown in Figure 6-24.

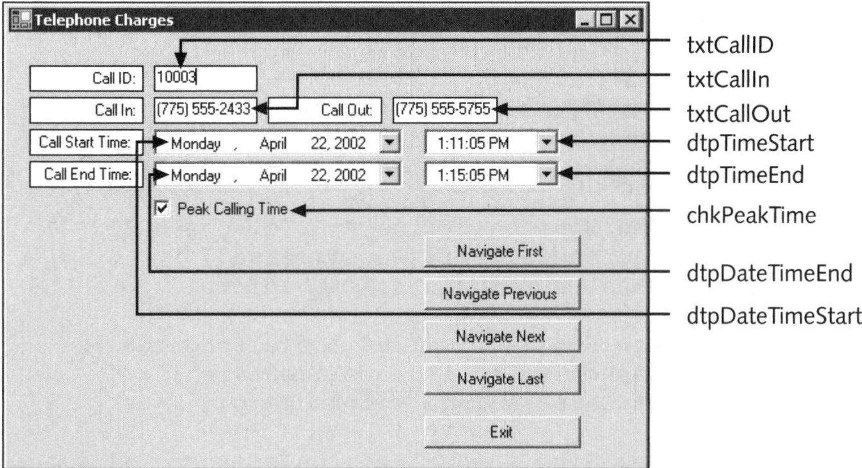

Figure 6-24

3. Set the Name property of the control instances as shown in Figure 6-24, and set the form's title.
4. Using the Data tab on the Toolbox, create an instance of the OleDbConnection control, and configure it so that you establish a connection with the database named Factory.mdb. Set the name of the control instance to odbconFactory.
5. Using the Data tab on the Toolbox, create an instance of the DataAdapter control on the form. Using the Wizard, configure the DataAdapter so that it establishes a connection with the database connection you created in the previous step. Use the database table named tblTelephoneCalls. Sort the output in ascending order by the call ID number. Set the name of the DataAdapter to odbdaTelephoneCalls.
6. Generate a DataSet for the DataAdapter you just created. Set the DataSet name to dsTelephoneCalls.
7. Create the following statements in the form's Load event handler to bind the control instances:

```
Dim pintRecords As Integer
Dim bndTemp As Binding

pintRecords = odbdaTelephoneCalls.Fill(DsTelephoneCalls1)

bndTemp = New Binding("Text", DsTelephoneCalls1, _
    "tblTelephoneCalls.fldCallID")
txtCallID.DataBindings.Add(bndTemp)
```

```
bndTemp = New Binding("Text", DsTelephoneCalls1, _
    "tblTelephoneCalls.fldCallIn")
txtCallIn.DataBindings.Add(bndTemp)

bndTemp = New Binding("Text", DsTelephoneCalls1, _
    "tblTelephoneCalls.fldCallOut")
txtCallOut.DataBindings.Add(bndTemp)

bndTemp = New Binding("Value", DsTelephoneCalls1, _
    "tblTelephoneCalls.fldDateTimeStart")
dtpDateTimeStart.DataBindings.Add(bndTemp)

bndTemp = New Binding("Value", DsTelephoneCalls1, _
    "tblTelephoneCalls.fldDateTimeEnd")
dtpDateTimeEnd.DataBindings.Add(bndTemp)

bndTemp = New Binding("Value", DsTelephoneCalls1, _
    "tblTelephoneCalls.fldDateTimeStart")
dtpTimeStart.DataBindings.Add(bndTemp)

bndTemp = New Binding("Value", DsTelephoneCalls1, _
    "tblTelephoneCalls.fldDateTimeEnd")
dtpTimeEnd.DataBindings.Add(bndTemp)

bndTemp = New Binding("Checked", DsTelephoneCalls1, _
    "tblTelephoneCalls.fldPeakNonPeak")
chkPeakTime.DataBindings.Add(bndTemp)
```

8. Create the following statements in the Click event handler for the Navigate First button:

```
Me.BindingContext(DsTelephoneCalls1, _
    "tblTelephoneCalls").Position = 0
```

9. Create the following statements in the Click event handler for the Navigate Previous button:

```
Me.BindingContext(DsTelephoneCalls1, _
    "tblTelephoneCalls").Position -= 1
```

10. Create the following statement in the Click event handler for the Navigate Next button:

```
Me.BindingContext(DsTelephoneCalls1, _
    "tblTelephoneCalls").Position += 1
```

11. Create the following statement in the Click event handler for the Navigate Last Button:

```
Me.BindingContext(DsTelephoneCalls1, _
    "tblTelephoneCalls").Position = _
    Me.DsTelephoneCalls1.Tables("tblTelephoneCalls"). _
    Rows.Count - 1
```

12. Create the following statement in the Click event handler for the Exit button:

```
Me.Close()
```

13. Test the program, and then save and close the **Ch06Ex3** solution.

Exercise 6-4

In this exercise, you create a program that allows you to navigate, add, change, and delete records from a table containing data of credit and balance owed to suppliers. Table 6-4 describes the fields in the table named tblSuppliers.

Table 6-4

Field name	Description	VB .NET Data type
fldId	Unique identification number	Integer
fldName	Supplier name	String
fldAddress	Supplier address	String
fldCity	Supplier city	String
fldState	Supplier state	String
fldZipCode	Supplier Zip code	String
fldCreditLimit	Supplier credit limit	Single
fldBalanceDue	Supplier balance due	Single

1. Start VB .NET and create a new solution named **Ch06Ex4** in the Chap06\Exercises folder.
2. Create the control instances on the form as shown in Figure 6-25.
3. Set the Name property of the control instances as shown in Figure 6-25, and set the text for the form's title.
4. Using the Data tab on the Toolbox, create an instance of the OleDbConnection control, and configure it so that you establish a connection with the database named Factory.mdb. Set the name of the control instance to odbconFactory.
5. Create an instance of the DataAdapter control on the form. Using the Wizard, configure the DataAdapter so that it establishes a connection with the database connection you created in the previous step. Use all the fields from the database table named tblSuppliers. Sort the output in ascending order by ID number. Set the name of the DataAdapter to odbdaSuppliers.
6. Generate a DataSet for the DataAdapter you just created. Set the DataSet name to dsSuppliers.

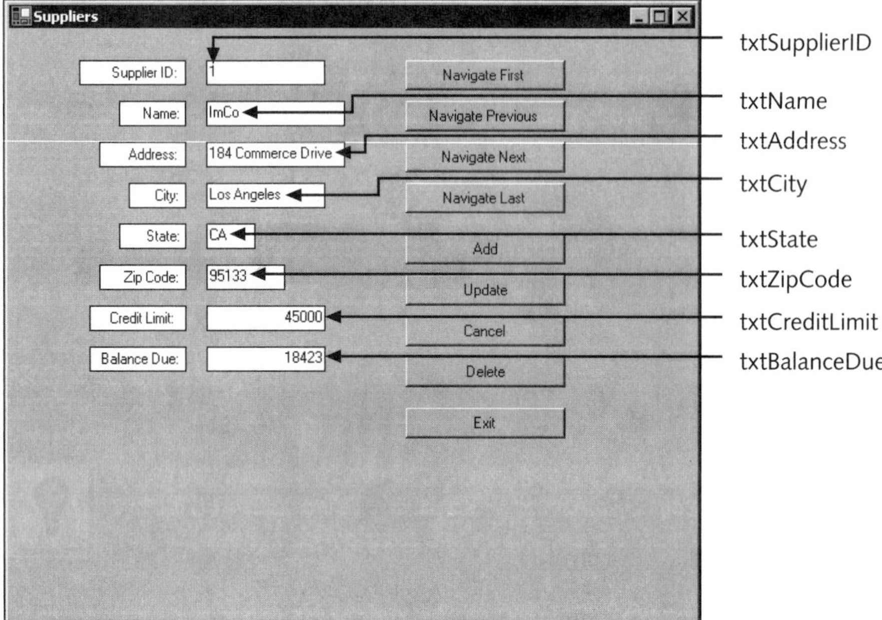

Figure 6-25

7. In the Load event handler for the form, enter the following statements to fill the DataSet and bind the control instances:

```
Dim pintRecords As Integer
Dim bndTemp As Binding

pintRecords = odbdaSuppliers.Fill(DsSuppliers1)


bndTemp = New Binding("Text", DsSuppliers1, _
    "tblsuppliers.fldID")
txtSupplierID.DataBindings.Add(bndTemp)

bndTemp = New Binding("Text", DsSuppliers1, _
    "tblsuppliers.fldName")
txtName.DataBindings.Add(bndTemp)

bndTemp = New Binding("Text", DsSuppliers1, _
    "tblsuppliers.fldAddress")
txtAddress.DataBindings.Add(bndTemp)

bndTemp = New Binding("Text", DsSuppliers1, _
    "tblsuppliers.fldCity")
txtCity.DataBindings.Add(bndTemp)
```

```
bndTemp = New Binding("Text", DsSuppliers1, _
    "tblsuppliers.fldState")
txtState.DataBindings.Add(bndTemp)

bndTemp = New Binding("Text", DsSuppliers1, _
    "tblsuppliers.fldZipCode")
txtZipCode.DataBindings.Add(bndTemp)

bndTemp = New Binding("Text", DsSuppliers1, _
    "tblSuppliers.fldCreditLimit")
txtCreditLimit.DataBindings.Add(bndTemp)

bndTemp = New Binding("Text", DsSuppliers1, _
    "tblSuppliers.fldBalanceDue")
txtBalanceDue.DataBindings.Add(bndTemp)
```


8. Create the following statement in the Click event handler for the Navigate First button:

```
Me.BindingContext(DsSuppliers1, "tblSuppliers").Position = 0
```

9. Create the following statement in the Click event handler for the Navigate Previous button:

```
Me.BindingContext(DsSuppliers1, "tblSuppliers").Position -= 1
```

10. Create the following statements in the Click event handler for the Navigate Next button:

```
Me.BindingContext(DsSuppliers1, "tblSuppliers").Position += 1
```

11. Create the following statements in the Click event handler for the Navigate Last button:

```
Me.BindingContext(DsSuppliers1, "tblSuppliers").Position = _
    Me.DsSuppliers1.Tables("tblSuppliers").Rows.Count - 1
```

12. Create the following statement in the Click event handler for the Add button:

```
Me.BindingContext(DsSuppliers1, "tblSuppliers").AddNew()
```

13. Create the following statements in the Click event handler for the Update button:

```
Dim pdsChangedRows As System.Data.DataSet

Me.BindingContext(DsSuppliers1, "tblSuppliers").EndCurrentEdit()

pdsChangedRows = DsSuppliers1.GetChanges()
If Not pdsChangedRows Is Nothing Then
    odbdaSuppliers.Update(pdsChangedRows)
End If
DsSuppliers1.AcceptChanges()
```

14. Create the following statement in the Click event handler for the Cancel button:

```
Me.BindingContext(DsSuppliers1, "tblSuppliers"). _
    CancelCurrentEdit()
```

15. Create the following statements in the Click event handler for the Delete button:

```
Dim pdsDeletedRows As DataSet

Me.BindingContext(DsSuppliers1, "tblSuppliers"). _
    RemoveAt(Me.BindingContext(DsSuppliers1, _
    "tblSuppliers").Position)

pdsDeletedRows = _
     DsSuppliers1.GetChanges(System.Data.DataRowState.Deleted)

odbdaSuppliers.Update(pdsDeletedRows)

DsSuppliers1.AcceptChanges()
```

16. Create the following statement in the Click event handler for the Exit button:

```
Me.Close()
```

17. Test the program, and then save and close the **Ch06Ex4** solution.

Exercise 6-5

In this exercise, you create a program that allows you to navigate, add, change, and delete records from a table containing payroll information. Table 6-5 describes the fields in the table named tblPayroll.

Table 6-5

Field name	Description	Data type
fldId	Employee number	Integer
fldPayrollID	Unique identification number	Integer
fldHoursWorked	Hours worked	Single
fldDate	Date paid	DateTime

1. Start VB .NET and create a new solution named **Ch06Ex5** in the Chap06\Exercises folder.
2. Set the Name property of the control instances as shown in Figure 6-26, and set the text for the form's title.
3. Using the Data tab on the Toolbox, create an instance of the OleDbConnection control, and configure it so that you establish a connection with the database named Factory.mdb. Set the name of the control instance to odbconFactory.
4. Create an instance of the DataAdapter control on the form. Using the Wizard, configure the DataAdapter so that it establishes a connection with the database connection you created in the previous step. Use all of the fields from the database table named tblPayroll.

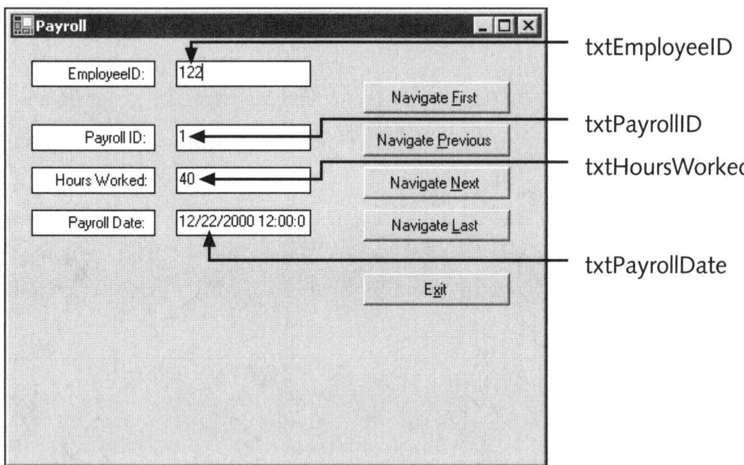

Figure 6-26

5. Generate a DataSet for the DataAdapter you just created. Set the DataSet name to dsPayroll.
6. In the Load event handler for the form, enter the following statements to fill the DataSet and bind the control instances:

```
Dim pintRecords As Integer
Dim bndTemp As Binding

pintRecords = odbdaPayroll.Fill(DsPayroll1)

bndTemp = New Binding("Text", DsPayroll1, _
    "tblpayroll.fldPayrollID")
txtPayrollID.DataBindings.Add(bndTemp)

bndTemp = New Binding("Text", DsPayroll1, "tblPayroll.fldID")
txtEmployeeID.DataBindings.Add(bndTemp)

bndTemp = New Binding("Text", DsPayroll1, _
    "tblPayroll.fldHoursWorked")
txtHoursWorked.DataBindings.Add(bndTemp)

bndTemp = New Binding("Text", DsPayroll1, "tblPayroll.fldDate")
txtPayrollDate.DataBindings.Add(bndTemp)
```

7. Create the following statement in the Click event handler for the Navigate First button:

```
Me.BindingContext(DsPayroll1, "tblPayroll").Position = 0
```

8. Create the following statement in the Click event handler for the Navigate Previous button:

```
Me.BindingContext(DsPayroll1, "tblPayroll").Position -= 1
```

9. Create the following statements in the Click event handler for the Navigate Next button:

```
Me.BindingContext(DsPayroll1, "tblPayroll").Position += 1
```

10. Create the following statements in the Click event handler for the Navigate Last button:

```
Me.BindingContext(DsPayroll1, "tblPayroll").Position = _
    Me.DsPayroll1.tblPayroll.Rows.Count - 1
```

11. Create the following statement in the Click event handler for the Exit button:

```
Me.Close()
```

12. Test the program, and then save and close the **Ch06Ex5** solution.

WEB PROGRAMMING PROJECTS

If necessary, use Windows Explorer to create a new folder in the Chap06 folder in your workfolder. Name this folder **Projects**. Save the solutions that you create in these Projects in the Chap06\Projects folder in your workfolder.

Project 6-1

In this project, you create a database, allow the user to navigate through the records in the database, and allow the user to add, change, and delete the database records. Create a database with the following fields and data types: fldIDNumber – Integer; fldLocation – String; fldXCoordinate – Single; fldYCoordinate – Single; fldZCoordinate – Single; fldDateAdded – DateTime. Create the necessary buttons and code to allow the user to navigate between records. Allow the user to add, change, and delete records.

Project 6-2

In this project, you create a database, allow the user to navigate through the records in the database, and allow the user to add, change, and delete the database records. The database that you create in this exercise will manage an address book. Create a database with the following fields and data types: fldIdNumber – Integer; fldLastName – String; fldFirstName – String; fldAddress – String; fldCity – String; fldState – String; fldZipCode – String; fldEMail – String; fldDateAdded – DateTime; fldTelephone – String; fldFax – String. Create the necessary buttons and code to allow the user to navigate between records. Allow the user to add, change, and delete records.

Project 6-3

In this project, you create a database, allow the user to navigate through the records in the database, and allow the user to add, change, and delete the database records. The database will store computer configuration information. Create the database with the following fields and data types: fldSerialNumber – String; fldHardDiskSize – Integer; fldMemory – Integer; fldPrinter – String; fldMonitor – String. Create the necessary buttons and code to allow the user to navigate between records. Allow the user to add, change, and delete records.

CHAPTER

7

C#: PART I

In this chapter you will:

- Write a C# program that produces output
- Compile and execute a C# program from the command line and using the Visual Studio IDE
- Add comments to a C# program
- Use the System namespace
- Declare and use variables, including performing arithmetic and accepting input
- Make decisions
- Write methods
- Create and use a `MessageBox`

The **C#** (pronounced "C sharp") **programming language** was developed as an object-oriented and component-oriented language. It exists as part of Visual Studio .NET, a package that contains a platform for developing applications for the Windows family of operating systems. Unlike other programming languages, in C# every piece of data can be treated as an object and employ the principles of object-oriented programming. C# provides constructs for creating components with properties, methods, and events, making it an ideal language for twenty-first-century programming, where building small, reusable components is more important than building huge, stand-alone applications.

C# contains a GUI interface that makes it similar to Visual Basic. However, Visual Basic is not fully object oriented. C# is truly object oriented, yet it is simpler to use than many other object-oriented languages. C# is modeled after the C++ programming language, but some of the most difficult features to understand in C++ have been eliminated in C#. For example, pointers are not used in C#, object destructors and forward declarations are not needed, and using #include files is not necessary. Multiple inheritance, which causes many C++ programming errors, is not allowed in C#. (Technically, you can use pointers in C#, but only in a mode called unsafe, which seldom is used.)

C# is also very similar to Java, because Java was based on C++ as well. In Java, simple data types are not objects; therefore, they do not work with built-in methods. In C#, every piece of data is an object, providing all data with the functionality of true objects. Additionally, in Java, parameters must be passed by value, which means a copy must be made of any data that is sent to a method for alteration, and the copy must be sent back to the original object. C# provides the convenience of passing by reference, which means the actual object can be altered by a method without a copy being passed back. If you have not programmed before, the difference between C# and other languages means little to you. However, experienced programmers can appreciate the thought that the developers of C# put into its features.

WRITING A C# PROGRAM THAT PRODUCES OUTPUT

At first glance, even the simplest C# program involves a fair amount of confusing syntax. Consider the simple program in Figure 7-1. This program is written on seven lines, and its only task is to print "This is my first C# program" on the screen.

```
public class FirstClass
{
        public static void Main()
        {
                System.Console.Out.WriteLine
                        ("This is my first C# program");
        }
}
```

Figure 7-1 First console application

The statement `System.Console.Out.WriteLine("This is my first C# program");` is a single statement that you can write on a single line. As with many other statements in this chapter, it is spread across two lines here only to fit the page size of this book.

The statement that does the actual work in this program is in the middle of the figure: `System.Console.Out.WriteLine("This is my first C# program");`. The statement ends with a semicolon because all C# statements do.

The text "This is my first C# program" is a **literal string** of characters, that is, a series of characters that will appear exactly as entered. Any literal string in C# appears between double quotation marks.

The string "This is my first C# program" appears within parentheses because the string is a **parameter** or an **argument** to a method, and parameters to methods always appear within parentheses. Parameters represent information that is needed by a method in order to perform its task. Within the statement `System.Console.Out.WriteLine("This is my first C# program");`, the method to which you are passing the string "This is my first C# program" is named `WriteLine()`. The `WriteLine()` method prints a line of output on the screen, positions the cursor on the next line, and stands ready for additional output.

The `Write()` method is very similar to the `WriteLine()` method. With `WriteLine()`, the cursor appears on the following line after the message is displayed. With `Write()`, the cursor does not advance to a new line; it remains on the same line as the output.

Within the statement `System.Console.Out.WriteLine("This is my first C# program");`, `Out` is an object. The `Out` object represents the screen on the terminal or computer where you are working. Of course, not all objects have a `WriteLine()` method (for instance, you can't write a line to a computer's mouse), but the creators of C# assumed you frequently would want to display output on the screen at your terminal. Therefore the `Out` object was created and endowed with the method named `WriteLine()`.

The C# programming language is case sensitive—the object named `Out` is a completely different object than one named `out`, `OUT`, or `oUt`.

Within the statement `System.Console.Out.WriteLine("This is my first C# program");`, `Console` is a class. Therefore, it defines the attributes of a collection of similar Console objects. (You might guess that another `Console` object is `In`. The `In` object represents the keyboard.)

Within the statement `System.Console.Out.WriteLine("This is my first C# program");`, `System` is a namespace. A **namespace** is a scheme that provides a way to group similar classes. To organize your classes, you can (and will) create your own namespaces. The `System` namespace is built into your C# compiler, and holds commonly used classes.

An advantage to using Visual Studio .NET is that all its languages use the same namespaces. In other words, everything you learn about any namespace in C# is knowledge you can transfer to Visual C++ and Visual Basic.

The dots (periods) in the statement `System.Console.Out.WriteLine("This is my first C# program");` are used to separate the names of the namespace, class, object, and method. You use this same namespace-dot-class-dot-object-dot-method format repeatedly in your C# programs.

The statement `System.Console.Out.WriteLine("This is my first C# program");` lies within a method named `Main()`. Every method in C# contains a header and a body. The body of every method is contained within a pair of curly braces. In the program in Figure 7-1, there is only one statement between the curly braces of the `Main()` method. Soon, you will write methods with many additional statements. For every opening curly brace ({) in a C# program, there must be a corresponding closing curly brace (}).

The **method header** for the `Main()` method contains four words. In the method header `public static void Main()`, the word `public` is an access modifier. As opposed to the case in which a method is `private`, the access modifier `public` indicates that other classes may use this method.

If you do not use an access modifier within a method header, then the method is `private` by default.

In the English language, the word "static" means showing little change or stationary. In C#, the reserved keyword `static` has the same meaning, and indicates that you do not need to create an object of type `FirstClass` to use the `Main()` method defined within `FirstClass`.

In English, the word "void" means empty. When the keyword `void` is used in the `Main()` method header, it does not indicate that the `Main()` method is empty, but that the method does not return any value when called. This doesn't mean that `Main()` doesn't produce output—it does. The `Main()` method does not send any value back to any other method that might call it. You will learn more about return values when you study methods in greater detail.

In the method header, the name of the method is `Main()`. All C# applications must include a method named `Main()`, and most C# applications have additional methods with other names. When you execute a C# application, the compiler always executes the `Main()` method first.

You will write many C# *classes* that do not contain a `Main()` method. However, all executable *applications* must contain a `Main()` method.

Every method that you use within a C# program must be part of a **class**. To create a class, you use a class header and curly braces in much the same way you use a header and braces for a method within a class. When you write `public class FirstClass`, you are defining a class named `FirstClass`. In Figure 7-1, the line `public class FirstClass` contains the keyword `class`, which identifies `FirstClass` as a class. The reserved word `public` is an access modifier. An **access modifier** defines the circumstances under which a class can be accessed. Public access is the most liberal type of access.

Entering a C# Program into a Text Editor

Now that you understand the basic framework of a program written in C#, you are ready to enter your first C# program into a text editor so you can execute it. It is a tradition among programmers that the first program you write in any language produces "Hello, world!" as its output. You will create such a program now. To create a C# program you can use the editor that is included as part of the Microsoft Visual Studio Integrated Development Environment, or IDE. (The C# compiler, other language compilers, and many development tools also are contained in the IDE.) Alternatively, you can use any text editor. There are advantages to using the C# editor to write your programs, but to get started, using a plain text editor is simpler.

To write your first C# program:

1. Start any text editor, such as Notepad, WordPad, or any word-processing program. Open a new document, if necessary.
2. Type the class header `public class Hello`. In this example, the class name is `Hello`.
3. Press **Enter** and type the class-opening **curly brace** `{`.
4. Press **Enter** again, then press **Tab** to indent.
5. Write the Main() method header: `public static void Main()`. Then press **Enter**.
6. Press **Tab** twice, type `{`, press **Enter**, and then press **Tab** three times to indent. Then type the one executing statement in this program: `System.Console.Out.WriteLine ("Hello, world!");`
7. Press **Enter**, press **Tab** twice, type a closing **curly brace** for the Main() method, press **Enter**, and type `}` for the class. Your code should look like Figure 7-2.

```
public class Hello
{
     public static void Main()
        {
           System.Console.Out.WriteLine("Hello, world!");
        }
}
```

Figure 7-2 The Hello class

8. Save the program as **Hello.cs** in the Chap07\Chapter folder in your work folder. It is important that the file extension is .cs, which stands for "C Sharp." If it is not, the compiler for C# does not recognize the program as a C# program.

Many text editors attach their own filename extension (such as .txt or .doc) to a saved file. Double-check your saved file to ensure that it does not have a double extension (as in Hello.cs.txt). If the file has a double extension, rename it. If you explicitly type quotes surrounding a filename (as in "Hello.cs"), most editors save the file as you specify, without adding their own extension. If you use a word-processing program as your editor, select the option to save the file as a plain text file.

Compiling and Executing a Program from the Command Line

After you write and save a program, you must perform two more steps before you can view the program output.

1. You must compile the program you wrote (called the **source** code) into **intermediate language** (called **IL**).
2. You must use the C# **just in time (JIT)** compiler to translate the intermediate code into executable statements.

When you compile a C# program, you translate your source code into intermediate language. The JIT compiler converts IL instructions to native code at the last moment, and appropriately, for each different type of computer on which the code might eventually be executed. In other words, the same set of IL can be JIT compiled and executed on any supported architecture.

To compile your source code from the command line, you type `csc` followed by the name of the file that contains the source code. The command csc stands for "C Sharp compiler." For example, to compile a file named Hello.cs, you would type `csc Hello.cs` and then press Enter. There will be one of three outcomes:

- You receive an operating system error message such as "Bad command or file name" or "csc is not recognized as an internal or external command."
- You receive one or more program language error messages.
- You receive no error messages (only a copyright statement from Microsoft Corporation), meaning the program has compiled successfully.

If you receive an operating system message such as "Bad command or file name," "csc is not recognized...," or "Source file could not be found," it may mean that:

- You misspelled the command `csc`.
- You misspelled the filename.
- You forgot to include the extension .cs with the filename.
- You didn't use the correct case. If your filename is `Hello.cs`, then `csc hello.cs` does not compile.

- You are not within the correct subdirectory or folder on your command line.
- The C# compiler was not installed properly.
- You need to set a path command. To locate the C# compiler with the name "csc.exe," use Explorer or click Start and then click Search. At the command line, type `path =`, followed by the complete path name that describes where csc.exe is stored. Then try to execute the Hello program again. For example, you might type `path = c:\winnt\Microsoft.net\framework\v1.0.2914` and press Enter. Then type `csc Hello.cs`, and press Enter again.

If you receive a programming language error message, it means there are one or more syntax errors in the source code. A **syntax error** occurs when you introduce typing errors into your program. For example, if the first line within your program begins with "Public" (with an uppercase P), you get an error message such as `A namespace does not directly contain members such as fields or methods` after compiling the program, because the compiler won't recognize Hello as a class with a Main() method. If this occurs, you must reopen the text file that contains the source code and make the necessary corrections.

7

The C# compiler issues warnings as well as errors. A warning is less serious than an error; it means the compiler has determined that you have done something unusual, but not illegal. If you know you have purposely introduced a warning situation to test a program, for example, then you can ignore the warning. Usually, however, you should treat a warning message just as you would an error message and attempt to remedy the situation.

If you receive no error messages after compiling the code in a file named Hello.cs, then the program compiled successfully and a file named Hello.exe is created and saved in the same folder as the program text file. To run the program from the command line, you simply type the program name `Hello`.

To compile and execute your Hello program from the command line:

1. Go to the command prompt on your system. In Windows 2000, click **Start**, point to **Programs**, point to **Accessories**, and then click **Command Prompt**. Change the current directory to your work folder that holds Chap07\Chapter.

If your command prompt indicates a path other than the one you want, you can type `cd\` and then press Enter to return to the root directory. Then you can type `cd` *`<work folder>`* (where *work folder* is the name of your work folder) to change the path to the one where your work folder resides. Type `cd Chap07` to change the path to the Chap07 folder in the work folder. Then type `cd Chapter` to change the path to the Chapter folder in the Chap07 folder. The command `cd` is short for "*change directory*."

2. Type the command that compiles your program: `csc Hello.cs`. If you do not receive any error messages and the prompt returns, it means that the compile was successful, that a file named Hello.exe has been created, and that you can execute the program. If you do receive error messages, check every character of the program you typed to make sure it matches Figure 7-2. Remember, C# is case sensitive, so all casing must match exactly. When you have corrected the errors, compile the program again.

3. You can verify that a file named Hello.exe was created in several ways:
   - At the command prompt, enter `dir` to view a directory of the files stored in the Chap07\Chapter folder in your work folder. Both Hello.cs and Hello.exe should appear in the list.
   - Use Windows Explorer to view the contents of the Chap07\Chapter folder.
   - Double-click the My Computer icon, double-click the icon for your work folder, double-click the Chap07 folder, double-click the Chapter folder, and view the contents.

4. At the command prompt, type the name of the program (the name of the executable file), `Hello`, and press **Enter**. Alternatively, you can type the full filename Hello.exe, but typing the .exe extension isn't necessary. The output should look like Figure 7-3.

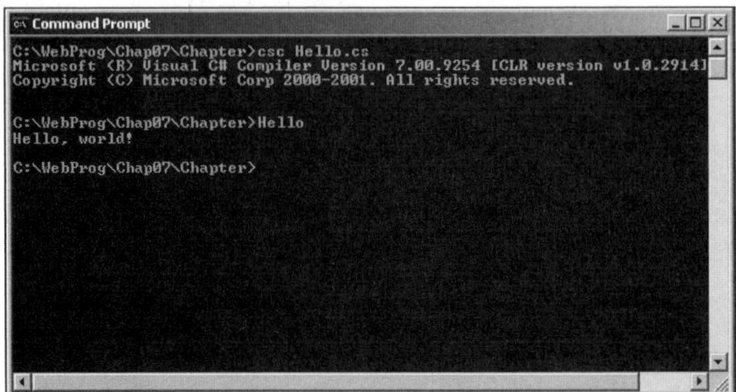

Figure 7-3 Output of Hello program

You can use the **/out** compiler option between the csc command and the name of the .cs file to indicate the name of the output file. For example, if you type `csc /out:Hello.exe Hello.cs` you create an output file named Hello.exe. By default, the name of the output file is the same as the name of the .cs file. Usually, this is your intention, so most often you omit the /out option.

ADDING COMMENTS TO A PROGRAM

Program comments are nonexecuting statements that you add to document a program. Programmers use comments to leave notes for themselves and for others who might read their programs in the future. Comments also can be useful when you are developing a program. If a program is not performing as expected, you can **comment out** various statements and subsequently run the program to observe the effect. When you comment out a statement, you turn it into a comment so that the compiler does not execute its command. This helps you pinpoint the location of errant statements in malfunctioning programs.

There are three types of comments in C#:

- **Line comments** start with two forward slashes (//) and continue to the end of the current line. Line comments can appear on a line by themselves, or at the end of a line following executable code.
- **Block comments** start with a forward slash and an asterisk (/*) and end with an asterisk and a forward slash (*/). Block comments can appear on a line by themselves, on a line before executable code, or after executable code. Block comments also can extend across as many lines as needed.
- C# also supports a special type of comment used to create documentation from within a program. These comments, called **XML-documentation format**, involve using a special set of tags within angle brackets. (XML stands for eXtensible Markup Language.) You will learn more about this type of comment as you continue your study of C#.

The forward slash (/) and the backslash (\) characters often are confused, but they are distinct characters. You cannot use them interchangeably.

Next you add comments to your Hello.cs program.

To add comments to your program:

1. Position your cursor at the top of the file, press **Enter** to insert a new line, press the **Up** arrow key to go to that line, and then type the following comments at the top of the file. Press **Enter** after typing each line. Insert your name and today's date where indicated by angle brackets.

```
// Filename Hello.cs
// Written by <your name>
// Written on <today's date>
```

2. Scroll to the line that reads `public class Hello` and press **End** to position the insertion point at the end of the line. Press **Enter**, and then type the following block comment in the program.

```
/*  This program demonstrates the use of the WriteLine()
          method to print the message Hello, world!  */
```

3. Save the file, replacing the old Hello.cs file with this new, commented version.

4. At the command line, compile the program using the command `csc Hello.cs`. When the program compiles successfully, execute it with the command `Hello`. Adding program comments does not make any difference in the execution of the program.

Compiling and Executing a Program Using the Visual Studio IDE

Instead of using the command line, you can compile and write your program within the Visual Studio Integrated Development Environment. There are several advantages to this approach:

- Some of the code you need is already created for you.
- The code is displayed in color, so you can more easily identify parts of your program. Reserved words appear in blue, comments in green, and identifiers in black.
- If error messages appear when you compile your program, you can double-click on an error message and the cursor moves to the line of code that contains the error.
- Other debugging tools are available. You will become more familiar with these tools as you develop more sophisticated programs.

Next, you use the C# compiler environment to compile and execute the same Hello program you ran from the command line.

To compile and execute the Hello program:

1. Within the text editor you used to write the Hello program, select the entire program. In Notepad, for example, you can highlight all the lines of text with your mouse or press **Ctrl+A**. Next, copy the text to the clipboard for temporary storage by clicking **Edit** on the menu bar, and then clicking **Copy**, or by pressing **Ctrl+C**.

2. Open **Visual Studio**. If there is a shortcut icon on your desktop, you can double-click it. Alternatively, you can click the **Start** button, point to **Programs** (point to **All Programs** in Windows XP), and click **Microsoft Visual Studio .NET 7.0**, as shown in Figure 7-4.

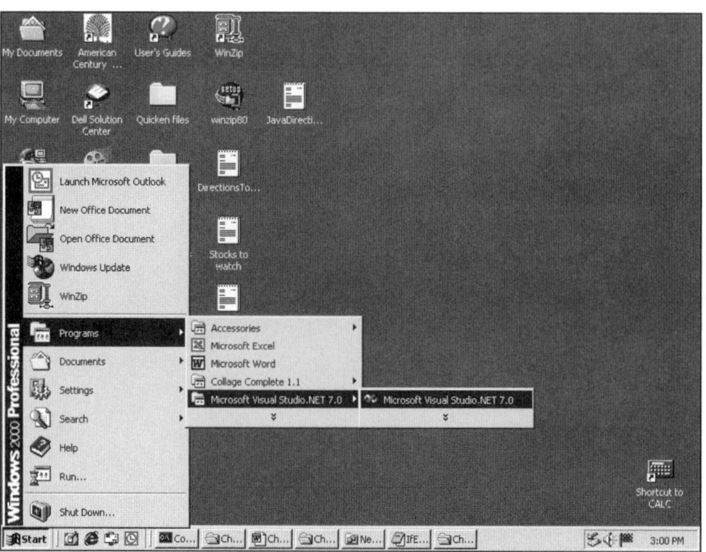

Figure 7-4 Navigating to Visual Studio .NET

3. If you see a Start window, click **New Project**. If you do not see a Start window, click **File** on the menu bar, point to **New**, and then click **Project**, as shown in Figure 7-5.

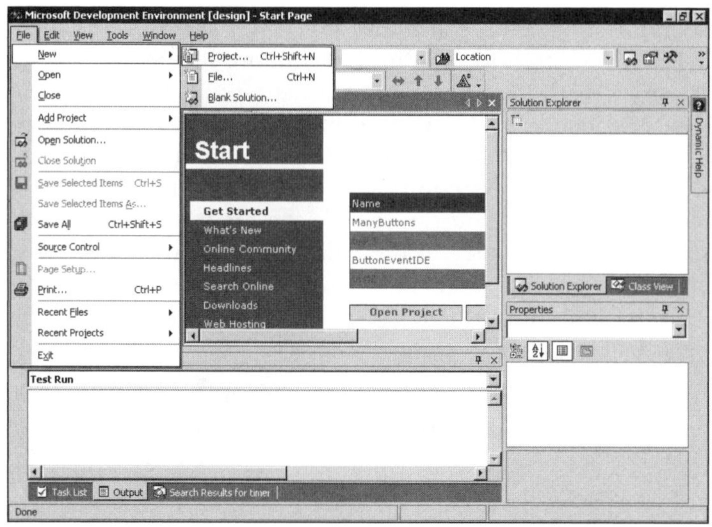

Figure 7-5 Creating a project

4. In the New Project window, click **Visual C# Projects** in the Project Types list, if necessary. Under Templates, click **Console Application**. Enter **Hello** as the Name for this project. For the location, select the **Chap07\Chapter** folder in your work folder. Finally, click **OK**. See Figure 7-6.

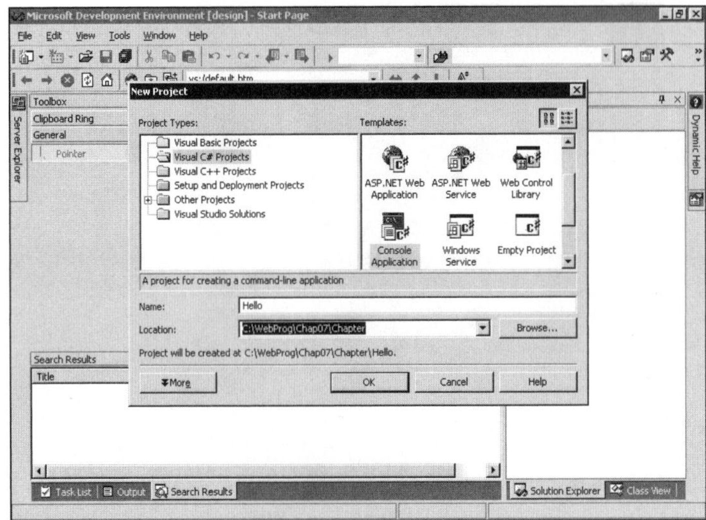

Figure 7-6 Selecting project options

5. The Hello application editing window appears, as shown in Figure 7-7. A lot of code is already written for you in this window, including a class named Hello, a `Main()` method, many comments, and other features. You could leave the class header, `Main()` method header, and other features, and just add specific statements you need. You would save a lot of typing and prevent typographical errors. However, in this case you have already written a functioning Hello program, so you can replace the prewritten code with your Hello code. Select all the code in the editor window by highlighting it with your mouse or by pressing **Ctrl+A**. Then press **Delete**. Paste the previously copied Hello program into the editor by pressing **Ctrl+V** or by clicking **Edit** on the menu bar, and then clicking **Paste**.
6. Save the file by clicking **File** on the menu bar, and then clicking **Save Class1.cs**, or by clicking the **Save** icon on the toolbar.
7. To compile the program, click **Build** on the menu bar, and then click the **Build** option. You should receive no error messages, as shown in Figure 7-8.

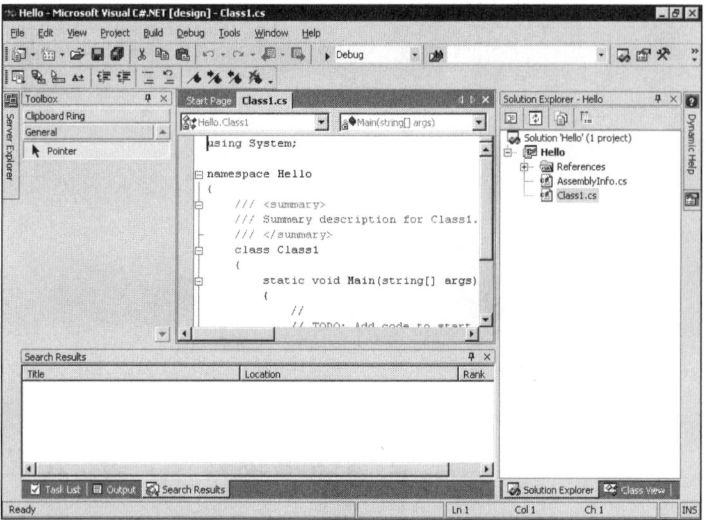

Figure 7-7 The console application template

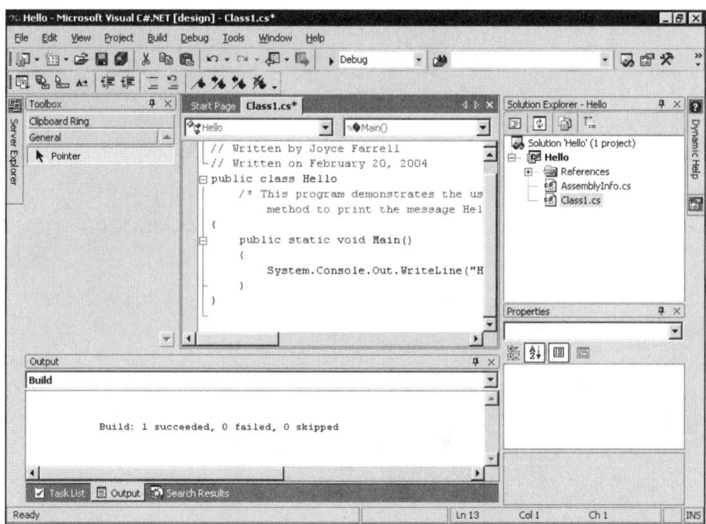

Figure 7-8 Output screen after compiling the Hello program

8. Next, click **Debug** on the menu bar, and then click **Start without debugging**. The output that appears in Figure 7-9 is identical to that of running the program from the command line.

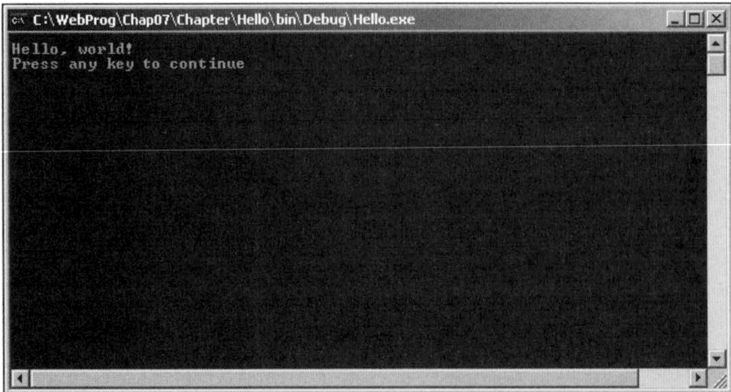

Figure 7-9 Output of the Hello program as run from within the Visual Studio IDE

9. Close the command prompt window, and then close Visual Studio .NET by clicking **File** on the menu bar, and then clicking **Exit**, or by clicking the **Close** button in the upper-right corner of the Visual Studio window.

10. When you create a C# program using an editor such as Notepad and compiling with the csc command, only two files are created—Hello.cs and Hello.exe. When you create a C# program using the Visual Studio editor, many additional files are created. You can view these files in several ways:

    - At the command prompt, type **dir** to view a directory of the files stored in the Chap07\Chapter folder of your work folder. Within the Chapter folder, a new folder named Hello has been created. Type the command **cd Hello** to change the current path to include this new folder, then type **dir** again. Figure 7-10 shows the list created using this method.

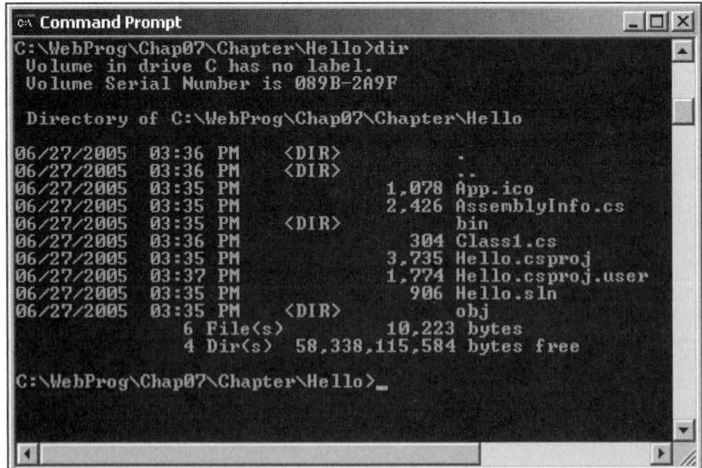

Figure 7-10 List of Hello program files

- Use Windows Explorer to view the contents of the Hello folder within the Chapter folder.
- Double-click the My Computer icon, double-click your work folder, double-click the Chap07 folder, double-click the Chapter folder, double-click the Hello folder, and view the contents.

The Hello folder contains a Bin folder, an Obj folder, and seven additional files. If you explore further, you find that the Bin folder contains a Debug folder, which contains additional files. Using the Visual Studio editor to compile your programs creates a lot of overhead. These additional files become important as you create more sophisticated C# projects. For now, while you learn C# syntax, using the command line to compile programs is simpler.

Using the System Namespace

A program can contain as many statements as you want. For example, the program in Figure 7-11 produces the three lines of output shown in Figure 7-12. A semicolon separates each program statement.

```
public class ThreeLines
{
  public static void Main()
    {
        System.Console.Out.WriteLine("Line one");
        System.Console.Out.WriteLine("Line two");
        System.Console.Out.WriteLine("Line three");
    }
}
```

Figure 7-11 A program that produces three lines of output

The program in Figure 7-11 shows a lot of repeated code—the phrase "System.Console.Out.WriteLine" appears three times. When you use the name of the object `Out`, you are indicating the console screen. However, `Out` is the default output object. That is, if you write `System.Console.WriteLine("Hi");` without specifying a `Console` object, the message "Hi" goes to the default `Console` object, which is `Out`. Most C# programmers usually use the `WriteLine()` method without specifying the `Out` object.

When you need to repeatedly use a class from the same namespace, you can shorten the statements you type by using a clause that indicates a namespace where the class can be found. You use a namespace with a using clause, as you will do in the next steps.

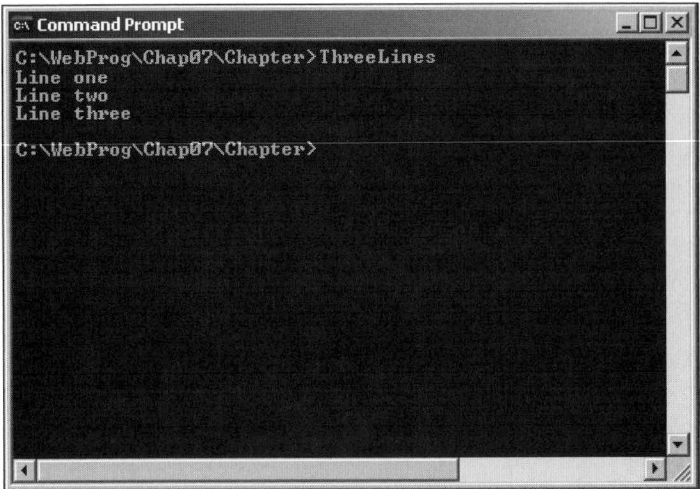

Figure 7-12 Output of ThreeLines program

To use a namespace with a using clause:

1. Type the code shown in the program in Figure 7-13. By typing `using System;` prior to the class definition, the compiler knows to use the System namespace when it encounters the `Console` class.

```
using System;
public class ThreeLines
{
    public static void Main()
        {
            Console.WriteLine("Line one");
            Console.WriteLine("Line two");
            Console.WriteLine("Line three");
        }
}
```

Figure 7-13 A program that uses a using `System` clause

2. Save the file as **ThreeLines.cs** in the Chap07\Chapter folder of your work folder. Compile and execute the program. The output of the program in Figure 7-13 is identical to that produced by the code in Figure 7-11, in which `System` was repeated with each `WriteLine()` statement. You need less typing, and the program is easier to read.

DECLARING VARIABLES

You can categorize data as variable or constant. A data item is **constant** when it cannot be changed after a program is compiled; in other words, when it cannot vary. For example, if you use the number 347 within a C# program, then 347 is a constant. Every time you execute this program, the value 347 is used. You can refer to the number 347 as a **literal constant**, because its value is taken literally at each use. On the other hand, when you want a value to be able to change, you can create a variable. A **variable** is a named location in computer memory that can hold different values at different points in time.

Whether it is stored as a constant or in a variable, all data you use in a C# program has a data type. A **data type** describes the format and size of a piece of data. C# provides for 14 basic, or **intrinsic types**, of data, as shown in Table 7-1. Of these built-in data types, the ones most commonly used are `int`, `double`, `char`, `string`, and `bool`. Each C# intrinsic type is an **alias**, or other name for, a class in the `System` namespace.

You name variables using the same rules for identifiers as you use for class names. Basically, that means variable names must start with a letter, cannot include embedded spaces, and cannot be a reserved keyword. You must declare all variables you want to use in a program. A **variable declaration** includes:

- The data type that the variable stores
- An identifier that is the variable's name
- An optional assignment operator and assigned value when you want a variable to contain an initial value
- An ending semicolon

Variable names usually begin with lowercase letters to distinguish them from class names, which usually begin with uppercase letters. You should follow these conventions when naming your variables and classes.

Table 7-1 C# data types

Type	System type	Bytes	Description	Largest value	Smallest value
byte	Byte	1	Unsigned byte	255	0
sbyte	Sbyte	1	Signed byte	127	-128
short	Int16	2	Signed short	32,767	-32,768
ushort	UInt16	2	Unsigned short	65,535	0
int	Int32	4	Signed integer	2,147,483,647	-2,147,483,648
uint	UInt32	4	Unsigned integer	4,294,967,295	0
long	Int64	8	Signed long integer	Over 900,000 trillion	Less than -900,000 trillion
ulong	UInt64	8	Unsigned long integer	Over 18 million trillion	Less than -18 million trillion
float	Single	4	Floating point number	A number that is greater than 3 followed by 38 zeros	A number that is less than -3 followed by 38 zeros
double	Double	8	Double-precision floating-point number	A number that is greater than 1 followed by 308 zeros	A number that is less than -1 followed by 308 zeros
decimal	Decimal	8	Fixed precision number	A number that is greater than 7 followed by 28 zeros	A number that is less than -7 followed by 28 zeros
string	String		Unicode string	There is no highest String value; for any two Strings, the one with the higher Unicode character values in an earlier position is considered higher than the other	Although the String type has no true minimum, you can think of the empty String "" as being the "lowest" String
char	Char		Unicode character	0xFFFF	0x0000
bool	Boolean		Boolean value (true or false)	Although the Boolean type has no true maximum, you can think of true as the "highest" Boolean value	For the same reason, you can think of false as the "lowest" Boolean value

A variable name can be any legal C# identifier that adheres to the following rules:

- An identifier must begin with an underscore or a letter. (Letters include foreign-alphabet letters such as π and Σ, which are contained in the set of characters known as Unicode.)
- An identifier can contain only letters or digits, not special characters such as #, $, or &.
- An identifier cannot be a C# reserved keyword, such as public or class. See Table 7-2 for a complete list of reserved keywords. (Actually, you can use a keyword as an identifier if you precede it with an "at" sign, as in @class. This feature allows you to use code written in other languages that do not have the same set of reserved keywords. However, when you write original C# programs, you should not use the keywords as identifiers.)

Table 7-2 C# reserved keywords

abstract	float	return
as	for	sbyte
base	foreach	sealed
bool	goto	short
break	if	sizeof
byte	implicit	stackalloc
case	in	static
catch	int	string
char	interface	struct
checked	internal	switch
class	is	this
const	lock	throw
continue	long	true
decimal	namespace	try
default	new	typeof
delegate	null	uint
do	object	ulong
double	operator	unchecked
else	out	unsafe
enum	override	ushort
event	params	using
explicit	private	virtual
extern	protected	void

Table 7-2 C# reserved keywords (continued)

false	public	volatile
finally	readonly	while
fixed	ref	

You can display a variable's value by including it within the parentheses of a `WriteLine()` statement, as in `Console.WriteLine(someMoney);`. Another way to display variables is to use a **format string**, which is a string of characters that contains one or more place holders for variable values. A **place holder** consists of a pair of curly braces containing a number that indicates the desired variable's position in a list that follows the string. The first position is always position 0. In the next steps you write a program that uses several variables.

To write a program that declares and uses variables:

1. Open a new file in your text editor. Use the System namespace, name the class **DemoVariables**, and type the class-opening **curly brace**.

```
using System;
public class DemoVariables
{
```

2. In the `Main()` method, declare the following two variables (an integer and an unsigned integer) and assign the given values to them.

```
public static void Main()
{
  int anInt = -123;
  uint anUnsignedInt = 567;
```

3. Next, add the following two statements to display the two values.

```
Console.WriteLine
      ("The int is {0} and the unsigned int is {1}.",
      anInt, anUnsignedInt);
```

4. Add two closing **curly braces**—one that closes the `Main()` method and one that closes the `DemoVariables` class. Align each closing curly brace vertically with the opening brace that is its partner. In other words, the first closing brace aligns with the brace that opens `Main()`, and the second aligns with the brace that opens `DemoVariables`.

5. Save the program as **DemoVariables.cs** in the Chap07\Chapter folder of your work folder. Compile the program. If you receive any error messages, correct the errors and compile again. When the file is error free, execute the program. The output should look like Figure 7-14.

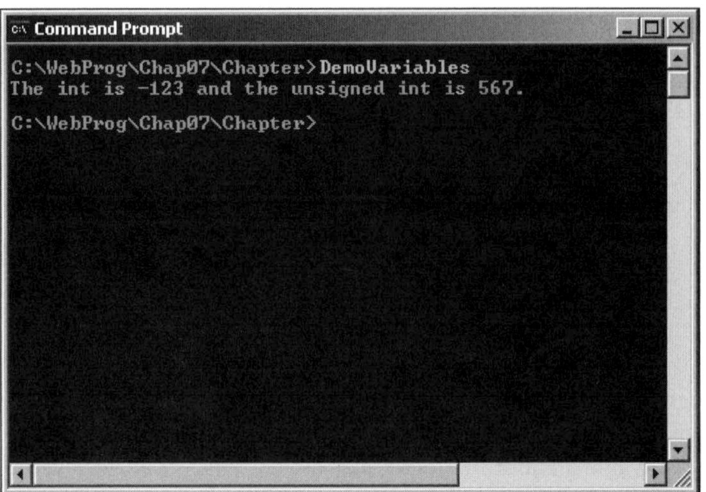

Figure 7-14 Output of DemoVariables.cs

6. Now experiment with the program by introducing invalid values for the named variables. For example, change the value of `anUnsignedInt` to **–567** by typing a minus sign in front of the constant value. Compile the program. You receive an error message: *Constant value '-567' cannot be converted to a 'uint'*. Correct the error either by removing the minus sign or by changing the data type of the variable to **int**, and compile again. You should not receive any error messages.
7. Next, change the value of `anInt` from –123 to **–123456789000**. When you compile the program, the following error message appears: *Cannot implicitly convert type 'long' to 'int'*. The value is a `long` type because it is greater than the highest allowed int value. Correct the error either by using a lower value or by changing the variable type to **long**, and compile again. You should not receive any error messages.
8. Experiment with other changes to the variables. Include some variables of each of the other types listed in Table 7-1, and experiment with their values.

Using the Standard Binary Arithmetic Operators

Table 7-3 describes the five most commonly used binary arithmetic operators. You use these operators to manipulate values in your programs. The operators are called **binary** because you use two arguments with each—one value to the left of the operator and another value to the right of it.

Table 7-3 Binary arithmetic operators

Operator	Description	Example
+	Addition	45 + 2, the result is 47
-	Subtraction	45 - 2, the result is 43
*	Multiplication	45 * 2, the result is 90
/	Division	45 / 2, the result is 22 (not 22.5)
%	Remainder (modulus)	45 % 2, the result is 1 (that is, 45 / 2 = 22 with a remainder of 1)

The operators (/) and (%) deserve special consideration. When you divide two integers, whether they are integer constants or integer variables, the result is an *integer*. In other words, any fractional part of the result is lost. For example, the result of 45 / 2 is 22, even though the result is 22.5 in a mathematical expression. When you use the remainder operator with two integers, the result is an integer with the value of the remainder after division takes place—so the result of 45 % 2 is 1 because 2 "goes into" 45 twenty-two times with a remainder of 1.

In the following steps you add some arithmetic statements to the DemoVariables.cs program.

To use arithmetic statements in a program:

1. Open a new C# program file named **DemoVariables2**, and enter the following statements to start a program that demonstrates arithmetic operations:

```
using System;
public class DemoVariables2
{
     public static void Main()
     {
```

2. Write a statement that declares seven integer variables. You assign initial values to two of the variables; the values for the other five variables are calculated. Because all these variables are the same type, you can use a single statement to declare all seven integers, insert commas between variable names, and place a single semicolon at the end. You can place line breaks wherever you want for readability. (Alternatively, you could use up to seven separate declarations.)

```
int value1 = 43, value2 = 10,
      sum, diff, product, quotient, remainder;
```

3. Write the arithmetic statements that calculate the sum of, difference between, product of, quotient of, and remainder of the two assigned variables.

```
sum = value1 + value2;
diff = value1 - value2;
product = value1 * value2;
quotient = value1 / value2;
remainder = value1 % value2;
```

4. Next, include five `WriteLine()` statements to display the results.

```
Console.WriteLine
    ("The sum of {0} and {1} is {2}",
    value1,value2,sum);
Console.WriteLine
    ("The difference between {0} and {1} is {2}",
    value1,value2,diff);
Console.WriteLine("The product of {0} and {1} is {2}",
    value1,value2,product);
Console.WriteLine("{0} divided by {1} is {2}",
    value1,value2,quotient);
Console.WriteLine
    ("and the remainder is {0}",remainder);
```

5. Add two `}` — one for the `Main()` method and the other for the `DemoVariables2` class.

6. Save the file in the Chap07\Chapter folder of your work folder. Compile and execute the program. The output should look like Figure 7-15.

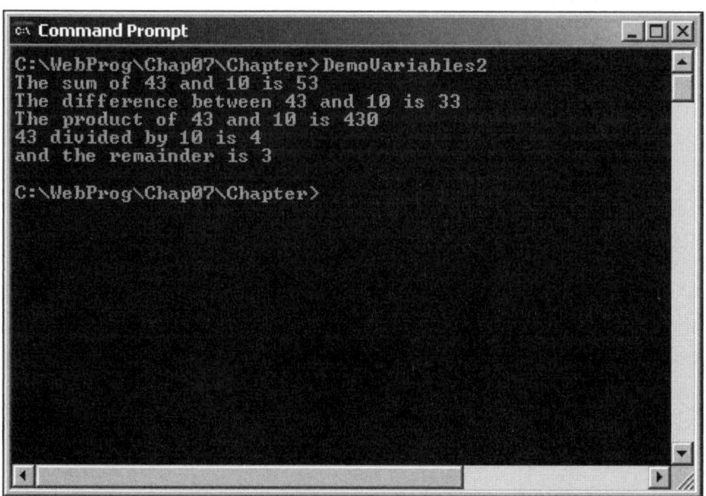

Figure 7-15 Output of DemoVariables2 program

7. Vary the values of the `value1` and `value2` variables and run the program again. Analyze the output to make sure you understand the arithmetic operations.

USING FLOATING-POINT DATA TYPES

A **floating-point** number is one that contains decimal positions. C# supports three floating-point data types: `float`, `double`, and `decimal`. A `double` can hold larger values than a `float`, and a `decimal` provides more accuracy. Just as an integer constant such as 178 is an `int` by default, a floating-point number constant such as 18.23 is a `double` by default. To explicitly store a value as a float, you may place an "F" after the number, as in `float pocketChange = 4.87F;`. Either a lowercase or uppercase "F" can be used. You can also place a "D" (or "d") after a floating-point value to indicate it is a `double`, but even without the "D" it is stored as a `double` by default. To explicitly store a value as a `decimal`, use an "M" (or "m") after the number. ("M" stands for Monetary; "D" can't be used for `decimal`s because it indicates `Double`.)

As with `int`s, you can add, subtract, multiply, and divide with floating-point numbers, but unlike `int`s, you cannot perform modulus operations. (Floating-point division results in a floating-point answer, so there is no remainder.)

If you store a value that is too large in a floating-point variable, you see output expressed in **scientific notation**. Values expressed in scientific notation include an "E" (for Exponent). For example, if you declare `float f = 1234567890f;`, the value is displayed as *1.234568E9*, meaning that it is approximately 1.234568 times 10 to the ninth power, or 1.234568 with the decimal point moved nine positions to the right.

By default, C# always displays floating-point numbers in the most concise way it can while maintaining the correct value. For example, if you declare a variable as `double myMoney = 14.00;`, then display it on the screen with a statement such as `Console.WriteLine("The amount is {0}", myMoney);`, the output appears as "The amount is 14." The two zeros to the right of the decimal point are not displayed because they add no mathematical information. To see the decimal places, you can convert the floating-point value to a string using a standard numeric format string.

Standard numeric format strings are strings of characters expressed within double quotes that indicate a format for output. They take the form *X0*, where *X* is the format specifier and *0* is the precision specifier. The **format specifier** can be one of nine, built-in format characters that define the most commonly used numeric format types. The **precision specifier** controls the number of significant digits or zeros to the right of the decimal point. Table 7-4 lists the nine format specifiers.

Table 7-4 Format specifiers

Format character	Description	Default format (if no precision is given)
C or c	Currency	$XX,XXX.XX ($XX,XXX.XX)
D or d	Decimal	[-]XXXXXXX
E or e	Scientific (exponential)	[-]X.XXXXXXE+xxx [-]X.XXXXXXe+xxx [-]X.XXXXXXE-xxx [-]X.XXXXXXe-xxx
F or f	Fixed-point	[-]XXXXXXX.XX
G or g	General	Variable; either general or scientific
N or n	Number	[-]XX,XXX.XX
P or p	Percent	Represents a passed numeric value as a percentage
R or r	Round trip	Ensures that numbers converted to strings have the same value when they are converted back into numbers
X or x	Hexadecimal	Minimum hexadecimal (base 16) representation

You can use a format specifier with the `ToString()` method to convert a number to a string that has the desired format. For example, you can use "C" as the format specifier when you want to represent a number as a currency value. Currency values display with a dollar sign and appropriate commas as well as the desired number of decimal places, and negative values display within parentheses. The integer you use following the "C" indicates the number of decimal places; if you do not use an integer, two decimals are assumed. For example, the following code:

```
double moneyValue = 456789;
Console.WriteLine(moneyValue.ToString("C"));
```

produces $456,789.00.

Currency displays with a dollar sign and commas in the English **culture**, a set of rules that determines how culturally dependent values such as money and dates are displayed. You can change a program's culture using the CultureInfoClass. The .NET framework supports over 200 culture settings such as Japanese, French, Urdu, and Sanskrit.

USING THE STRING DATA TYPE TO ACCEPT CONSOLE INPUT

In C#, you use the **char** data type to hold a single character and the **string** data type to hold a series of characters. The value of a character is expressed in single quotes while the value of a string is always expressed within double quotes. For example, the following statements declare a character and a string and assign values to them.

```
char firstInitial = 'J';
string firstName = "Jane";
```

When you compare strings, you use the `Equals()` method, which requires two string arguments and returns true or false.

You can use the **`Console.ReadLine()` method** to accept user input from the keyboard. This method accepts all the characters a user enters until the user presses Enter. The characters can be assigned to a string. For example, the statement `myString = Console.ReadLine();` accepts a user's input and stores it in the variable `myString`. If you want to use the data as a string—for example, if the input is a word—then you simply use the variable to which you assigned the value. However, if you want to use the data as a number, then you must use a Convert method to convert the input string to the proper type.

The `Console.Read()` method is similar to the `Console.ReadLine()` method. `Console.Read()` reads just one character from the input stream, but `Console.ReadLine()` reads every character in the input stream until the user presses the Enter key.

Table 7-5 shows Convert class methods you can use to change strings into more useful data types. The methods use the System types (also called runtime types) in their names. For example, recall from Table 7-1 that the "formal" name for an `int` is `Int32`, so the method you use to convert a string to an integer is named `Convert.ToInt32()`.

Table 7-5 Selected convert class methods

Method	Description
ToBoolean()	Converts a specified value to an equivalent Boolean value
ToByte()	Converts a specified value to an 8-bit unsigned integer
ToChar()	Converts a specified value to a Unicode character
ToDecimal()	Converts a specified value to a decimal number
ToDouble()	Converts a specified value to a double-precision, floating-point number
ToInt16()	Converts a specified value to a 16-bit signed integer
ToInt32()	Converts a specified value to a 32-bit signed integer
ToInt64()	Converts a specified value to a 64-bit signed integer
ToSByte()	Converts a specified value to an 8-bit signed integer
ToSingle()	Converts a specified value to a single-precision, floating-point number

Table 7-5 Selected convert class methods (continued)

Method	Description
ToString()	Converts the specified value to its equivalent String representation
ToUInt16()	Converts a specified value to a 16-bit unsigned integer
ToUInt32()	Converts a specified value to a 32-bit unsigned integer
ToUInt64()	Converts a specified value to a 64-bit unsigned integer

In the next steps you write an interactive program that allows the user to enter two integer values. The program then calculates and displays their sum.

To write the interactive addition program:

1. Open a new file in your editor. Type the following for the first few lines needed for the `Main()` method of an InteractiveAddition class:

```
using System;
public class InteractiveAddition
{
   public static void Main()
   {
```

2. Add these variable declarations for the two strings that will accept the user's input values, and then declare three integers for the numeric equivalents of the string input values and their sum:

```
string name, firstString, secondString;
int first, second, sum;
```

3. Type the following lines of code to prompt the user for his or her name, accept it into the name string, and then display a personalized greeting to the user, along with the prompt for the first integer value:

```
Console.WriteLine("Enter your name");
name = Console.ReadLine();
Console.WriteLine("Hello {0}! Enter the first integer",
  name);
```

4. Next, type the following to accept the user's input as a string, and then convert the input string to an integer:

```
firstString = Console.ReadLine();
first = Convert.ToInt32(firstString);
```

5. Add these statements that prompt for and accept the second integer and convert it to a string:

```
Console.WriteLine("Enter the second integer");
secondString = Console.ReadLine();
second = Convert.ToInt32(secondString);
```

6. Type the following code to assign the sum of the two integers to the sum variable and then display all the values. Finally, add the closing **curly brace** for the `Main()` method and the closing **curly brace** for the class.

```
            sum = first + second;
            Console.WriteLine
            ("{0}, the sum of {1} and {2} is {3}",
            name, first, second, sum);
        }
    }
```

7. Save the file as **InteractiveAddition.cs** in the Chap07\Chapter folder of your work folder. Compile and run the program. When you are prompted, supply your name and any integers you want, and confirm that the result displays correctly. Figure 7-16 shows a typical run of the program.

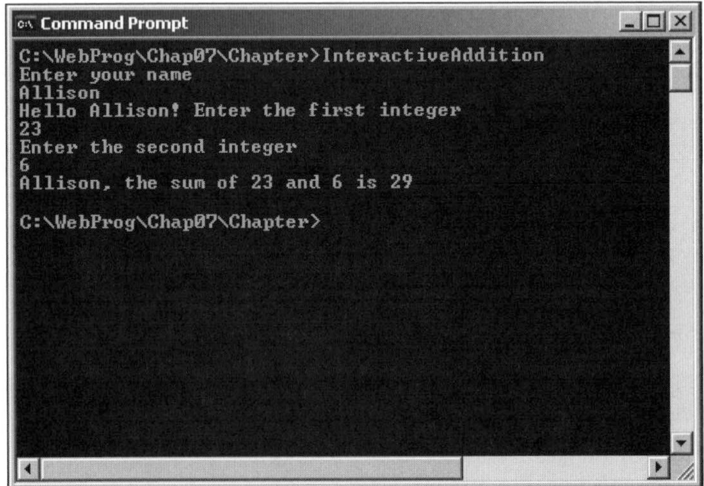

Figure 7-16 Typical run of InteractiveAddition program

MAKING DECISIONS

You make decisions within C# programs using an `if` statement, for example `if(a > 10) Console.WriteLine("The number is over 10");`. Within an `if` statement, you use a **comparison operator**, which compares two items and results in a true or false, or **Boolean**, value. Table 7-6 describes the six comparison operators that C# supports.

Table 7-6 Comparison operators

Operator	Description	true example	false example
<	Less than	3 < 8	8 < 3
>	Greater than	4 > 2	2 > 4
==	Equal to	7 == 7	3 == 9
<=	Less than or equal to	5 <=5	8 <= 6
>=	Greater than or equal to	7 >= 3	1 >= 2
!=	Not equal to	5 != 6	3 != 3

When you use any of the operators that require two keystrokes (==, <=, >=, or !=), you cannot place any whitespace between the two symbols.

Some decisions you make are **dual-alternative decisions**; they have two possible outcomes. If you want to perform one action when a Boolean expression evaluates as `true` and an alternate action when it evaluates as `false`, you can use an `if-else` statement. The `if-else` statement takes the form:

```
if (expression)
   statement1;
else
   statement2;
```

You can code an `if` without an `else`, but it is illegal to code an `else` without an `if`.

Next, you write a program that requires using multiple, nested `if-else` statements to accomplish its goal—determining whether any of the three integers entered by a user are equal.

To write a program with multiple nested `if-else` statements:

1. Open a new text file and then enter the following method, which prompts a user for an integer and then returns it to the calling method. The `Main()` program can call this method three times to get each of the three integers that you compare. You learn more about constructing methods in the next section.

```
public static int GetANumber()
{
    string numberString;
    int number;
    Console.Write("Enter an integer ");
    numberString = Console.ReadLine();
    number = Convert.ToInt32(numberString);
    return number;
}
```

2. Above the `GetANumber()` method, at the top of the file, write the first lines necessary for a `CompareThreeNumbers` class:

```
using System;
public class CompareThreeNumbers
{
```

3. Begin a `Main()` method by declaring three integers and obtaining values for them using the `GetANumber()` method.

```
public static void Main()
{
    int num1, num2, num3;
    num1 = GetANumber();
    num2 = GetANumber();
    num3 = GetANumber();
```

4. If the first number and the second number are equal, there are two possibilities: either the first is also equal to the third, in which case all three numbers are equal, or the first is not equal to the third, in which case only the first two numbers are equal. Insert the code:

```
if(num1 == num2)
  if(num1 == num3)
    Console.Out.WriteLine("All three numbers are equal");
  else
    Console.Out.WriteLine
      ("The first two numbers are equal");
```

Often, programmers mistakenly use a single equal sign rather than the double equal when attempting to determine equivalency. For example, the expression `number = HIGH` does not compare `number` to HIGH. Instead, it attempts to assign the value HIGH to the `number` variable. When it is part of an `if` statement, this assignment is illegal.

5. If the first two numbers are not equal, but the first and third are equal, print an appropriate message. Insert the following code: (For clarity, the `else` should vertically align under `if(num1 == num2)`.)

```
else
  if(num1 == num3)
     Console.Out.WriteLine
        ("The first and last numbers are equal");
```

6. When `num1` and `num2` are not equal, and `num1` and `num3` are not equal, but `num2` and `num3` are equal, insert the following code that displays an appropriate message. (For clarity, the `else` should vertically align under `if(num1 == num3)`.)

```
else
    if(num2 == num3)
       Console.Out.WriteLine
         ("The last two numbers are equal");
```

7. Finally, type the following code that describes when none of the pairs (num1 and num2, num1 and num3, and num2 and num3) are equal and displays an appropriate message. (For clarity, the `else` should vertically align under `if(num2 == num3)`.)

```
else
   Console.Out.WriteLine
     ("No two numbers are equal");
```

8. Add a closing **curly brace** for the `Main()` method. At the end of the file, below the closing brace for the `GetANumber()` method, add a closing **curly brace** for the class.

9. Save the file as **CompareThreeNumbers.cs** in the Chap07\Chapter folder in your work folder. Compile the program, then execute it several times, providing different combinations of equal and nonequal integers when prompted. Figure 7-17 shows several executions of the program.

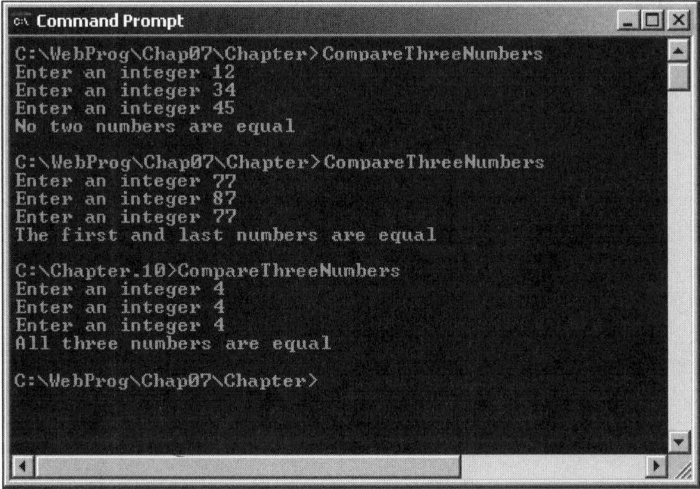

Figure 7-17 Three executions of `CompareThreeNumbers`

WRITING METHODS

A **method** is a series of statements that carry out a task. Any class can contain an unlimited number of methods. So far, you have written classes that contain a `Main()` method, and in the last section you wrote a method named `GetANumber()`. You also have used, or **invoked**, or **called**, other methods such as `WriteLine()` and `Convert.ToInt32()`. You can easily identify method names because they are always followed by a set of parentheses. Depending on the method, there might be an **argument** within the parentheses. For example, when you call the `WriteLine()` method, you usually provide a string argument. When you call the `WriteLine()` method, you use a method that has already been created for you. Because the creators of C# knew you would often want to write a message to the output screen, they created a method that you could call. This method takes care of all the hardware details of producing a message on the output device; you simply call the method and pass the desired message to it. The creators of C# were able to predict many of the methods you would like to use within your programs, and you use many of these methods when using C#. However, your programs often require you to create custom methods that the creators of C# could not have predicted you would need or want.

There are two major reasons why you want to create methods:

1. First, if you add a method call instead of multiple new statements, the `Main()` method remains short and easy to follow.
2. More importantly, a method is easily *reusable*. After you create a method, you can use it in any program. In other words, you do the work once, and then you can use the method many times.

In C#, a method must include:

- A method declaration (or header or definition)
- An opening curly brace
- A method body
- A closing curly brace

The method declaration contains:

- Optional declared accessibility
- An optional `static` modifier
- The return type for the method
- The method name
- An opening parenthesis
- An optional list of method arguments (you separate the arguments with commas if there are more than one)
- A closing parenthesis

The optional declared accessibility for a method can be any of the following modifiers: `public`, `protected internal`, `protected`, `internal`, or `private`. If you do not provide an accessibility modifier for a method, the method is `private` by default. When you begin to create your own class objects, you often provide them with `private` methods. For now, you create methods that are `public`.

Additionally, a method can be declared to be `static` or non-`static`. If you use the keyword modifier `static`, you indicate that a method can be called without referring to an object. If you do not indicate that a method is `static`, it is non-`static` by default. When you begin to create your own class objects, you will write many non-static methods; for now, all methods are static.

Every method has a return type, indicating a value that the method returns to any other method that calls it. If a method does not return a value, its return type is void. If you do not indicate a return type for a method, its return type is int by default. When you wrote the GetANumber() method in the last section, you created its return type to be int because the method's purpose was to return an integer to the calling method.

Every method has a name that must be a legal C# identifier—that is, it must not contain spaces and must begin with a letter of the alphabet or an underscore.

Every method name is followed by a set of parentheses. Sometimes, these parentheses contain arguments, but in the simplest methods, the parentheses are empty. You can place a method in its own file or within the file of a program that uses it, but not within any other method.

CREATING A MESSAGEBOX

The Visual Studio environment includes many built-in objects that contain their own prewritten methods. A MessageBox is a GUI object that can contain text, buttons, and symbols that inform and instruct a user. You use the static class method Show() to display a MessageBox. The MessageBox class contains 12 versions of the Show() method; the simplest version accepts a string argument that is displayed within the MessageBox, for example MessageBox.Show("Hello!");. This would contain a title bar at the top, a Close button in the upper-right corner, the message "Hello!", and an "OK" button. When the user clicks either the Close button or the OK button, the MessageBox disappears. Because Visual Studio .NET contains the MessageBox class, you do not have to design all these standard MessageBox features and capabilities yourself when you write a program. Instead, you simply use the MessageBox class and concentrate on the message you want to convey within the MessageBox.

Besides a simple string, you can pass additional arguments to the MessageBox.Show() method when you want to display a caption in a MessageBox's title bar, or add buttons and an icon. Table 7-7 summarizes the features of six of the 12 versions of the MessageBox.Show() method. (The other six versions each correspond to one in the table, with the addition of naming a component in front of which you want the MessageBox to be displayed.) When you use a version of the Show() method, you must provide a value in the correct order for each argument listed in the table.

Table 7-7 Arguments used with the `MessageBox.Show()` method

Argument to MessageBox.Show()	Explanation
String	Displays a message box with the specified text
String, string	Displays a message box with the specified text and caption
String, string, MessageBoxButtons	Displays a message box with specified text, caption, and buttons
String, string, MessageBoxButtons, MessageBoxIcon	Displays a message box with specified text, caption, buttons, and icon
String, string, MessageBoxButtons, MessageBoxIcon, MessageBoxDefaultButton	Displays a message box with the specified text, caption, buttons, icon, and default button
String, string, MessageBoxButtons, MessageBoxIcon, MessageBoxDefaultButton, MessageBoxOptions	Displays a message box with the specified text, caption, buttons, icon, default button, and options

For example, the program in Figure 7-18 uses two string arguments to the `MessageBox.Show()` method. Figure 7-19 shows the execution; notice that the second string argument passed to the `Show()` method in the program displays in the title bar of the `MessageBox`.

```
using System;
using System.Windows.Forms;
public class MessageBox2
{
       public static void Main()
       {
              MessageBox.Show("Hello!","MessageBox2 program");
       }
}
```

Figure 7-18 Using two string parameters with `MessageBox.Show()`

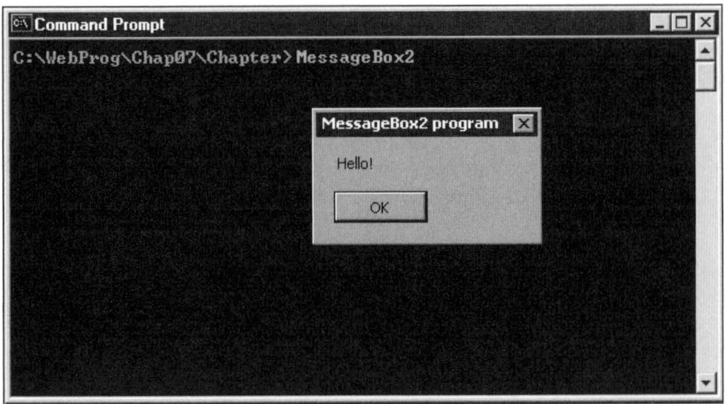

Figure 7-19 Output of program using two string arguments to `MessageBox.Show`

Besides strings, the `MessageBox.Show()` method can also accept `MessageBoxButtons`, `MessageBoxIcon`, `MessageBoxDefaultButton` and `MessageBoxOptions` arguments. Tables 7-8 through 7-11 describe all the possible values for each of these arguments. Using all the possible `MessageBox.Show()` arguments provides you with a wide variety of possible appearances for your `MessageBox` objects.

The `MessageBoxOptions` values are not used frequently. They are listed in Table 7-11 but won't be used in this chapter.

Table 7-8 `MessageBoxButtons` values

Member name	Description
AbortRetryIgnore	The message box contains Abort, Retry, and Ignore buttons
OK	The message box contains an OK button
OKCancel	The message box contains OK and Cancel buttons
RetryCancel	The message box contains Retry and Cancel buttons
YesNo	The message box contains Yes and No buttons
YesNoCancel	The message box contains Yes, No, and Cancel buttons

Table 7-9 `MessageBoxIcon` values

Member name	Description
Asterisk	The message box contains a symbol consisting of a lowercase letter "i" in a circle
Error	The message box contains a symbol consisting of a white X in a circle with a red background

Table 7-9 `MessageBoxIcon` values (continued)

Member name	Description
Exclamation	The message box contains a symbol consisting of an exclamation point in a triangle with a yellow background
Hand	The message box contains a symbol consisting of a white X in a circle with a red background
Information	The message box contains a symbol consisting of a lowercase letter "i" in a circle
None	The message box contains no symbols
Question	The message box contains a symbol consisting of a question mark in a circle
Stop	The message box contains a symbol consisting of a white X in a circle with a red background
Warning	The message box contains a symbol consisting of an exclamation point in a triangle with a yellow background

The description of each `MessageBoxIcon` is of a typical representation of the symbol. The actual graphic displayed is a function of the operating system in which the program is running.

Table 7-10 `MessageBox` default `Button` values

Member name	Description
Button1	The first button on the message box is the default button
Button2	The second button on the message box is the default button
Button3	The third button on the message box is the default button

Table 7-11 `MessageBoxOptions` values

Member name	Description
DefaultDesktopOnly	The message box displays on the active desktop
RightAlign	The message box text is right-aligned
RtlReading	Specifies that the message box text displays with right-to-left reading order
ServiceNotification	The message box displays on the active desktop

You can combine `MessageBoxOptions` values by placing an ampersand (&) between them. The ampersand is the bitwise AND operator; it allows you to combine bits within a single byte that controls which options are active.

In the next steps you experiment with `MessageBox.Show()` method arguments.

To use `MessageBox.Show()` method arguments:

1. Open a new file in your text editor. Enter the following first few lines of a program that instantiates several `MessageBox` objects:

```
using System;
using System.Windows.Forms;
public class MessageBoxExperiment
{
```

2. Add a `Main()` method that declares two strings to serve as the `MessageBox` messages and captions, and an integer count to keep track of the number of `MessageBox` objects displayed.

```
public static void Main()
    {
        string message = "This is message ";
        string caption = "Message box experiment";
        int count = 1;
```


3. Create a `MessageBox` with a single string argument containing the `count` value.

```
MessageBox.Show(message + count);
```

4. Add 1 to the `count` using the C# shortcut increment operator ++. Then display a `MessageBox` containing the message with the new `count` value and a caption for the title bar.

```
++count;
MessageBox.Show(message + count, caption);
```

5. Add 1 again to the `count` and display a `MessageBox` containing three defined features: a message, a caption, and some buttons. Add 1 again to the `count` and display a `MessageBox` containing four features: a message, a caption, some buttons, and an icon.

```
++count;
MessageBox.Show(message + count, caption,
  MessageBoxButtons.OKCancel);
++count;
MessageBox.Show(message + count, caption,
  MessageBoxButtons.RetryCancel, MessageBoxIcon.Warning);
```

6. For the last `MessageBox`, add 1 to the `count` and create a `MessageBox` that employs five options, including naming `Button3` as the default button.

```
++count;
MessageBox.Show(message + count, caption,
  MessageBoxButtons.YesNoCancel,
  MessageBoxIcon.Information,
  MessageBoxDefaultButton.Button3);
```

7. Add two `}` — one for the `Main()` method and one for the class.
8. Save the file as **MessageBoxExperiment.cs** in the Chap07\Chapter folder of your work folder. Compile and execute the program. The first `MessageBox` appears as shown in Figure 7-20. Notice that the string "This is message " and the `count` value 1 have been combined to create the `MessageBox` message. No caption appears in the `MessageBox` title bar, but a Close button is available in the upper-right corner of the `MessageBox`. A `MessageBox` is a **modal dialog box**, meaning that the program can progress no farther until you dismiss the box. Whether you click OK or Close, the second `MessageBox` appears, including the caption and updated `count` value, as shown in Figure 7-21. Notice that this `MessageBox` is slightly wider than the first one in order to accommodate the title bar caption.

Figure 7-20 First `MessageBox` of `MessageBoxExperiment` program

Figure 7-21 Second `MessageBox` of `MessageBoxExperiment` program

9. Whether you click OK or Close in the second `MessageBox`, the third `MessageBox` appears, containing OK and Cancel buttons as shown in Figure 7-22. The OK button has a darker outline than the Cancel button; this means that this button has focus. When a button has focus, not only is the user's attention drawn to it, but if the user presses the Enter key, the button executes. If you press Tab, or use the right and left arrow keys on your keyboard, you can change the focus from one button to the other. Whether you dismiss this `MessageBox` by pressing Enter, closing the box, or clicking one of the two buttons, the fourth `MessageBox` is displayed, as shown in Figure 7-23.

If your computer has speakers, you might hear a different sound when the Warning icon displays. Because you normally would use the Warning icon in a "dangerous" situation, this sound is intended to get the user's attention.

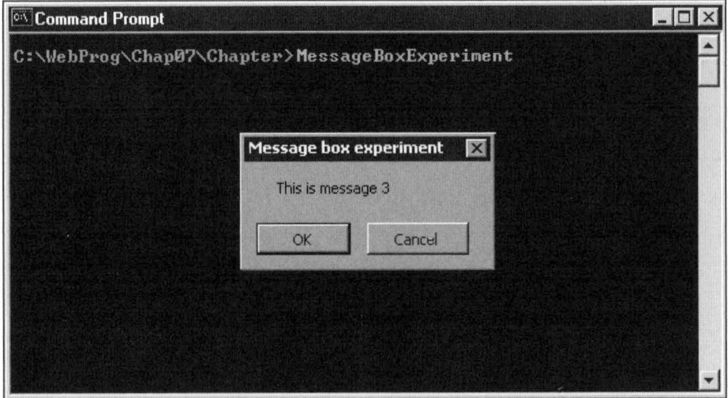

Figure 7-22 Third `MessageBox` of `MessageBoxExperiment` program

Figure 7-23 Fourth `MessageBox` of `MessageBoxExperiment` program

10. The fourth `MessageBox` contains Retry and Cancel buttons and the Warning icon. Again, you can change the focus of the buttons, and proceed to the next `MessageBox` using either of the option buttons, the Enter key, or the Close button. Figure 7-24 shows the last `MessageBox`. When this box is displayed, the focus is on the far right of the three buttons because you selected `MessageBoxDefaultButton.Button3` when creating the `MessageBox`. Dismiss this last `MessageBox`.

Figure 7-24 Fifth `MessageBox` of `MessageBoxExperiment` program

11. Run the program several times and experiment with using the different buttons.
12. Resave the program as **MessageBoxExperiment2.cs** in the Chap07\Chapter folder of your work folder, then experiment using different values for the message, caption, `MessageBoxButtons`, `MessageBoxIcon`, `MessageBox DefaultButton`, and `MessageBoxOptions` for the individual `MessageBox`es.

Adding Functionality to MessageBox Buttons

`MessageBox` objects provide an easy way to display information to a user in a GUI format. When you use a `MessageBox` to display some text you want the user to read, it makes sense to include only an OK button that the user can click after reading the text. However, including multiple `MessageBoxButtons` that all dismiss the `MessageBox` doesn't make sense. Usually you want to determine users' interactions with a `MessageBox`'s buttons and take appropriate action based on the users' choices. A `DialogResult` is an **enumeration**, or list of values that correspond to a user's potential `MessageBox` button selections. Table 7-12 contains `DialogResult` values you can use to compare to a `MessageBox`. The `DialogResult` member names correspond to the button labels available within a `MessageBox`.

Table 7-12 DialogResult values

Member name	Description
Abort	The dialog box return value is Abort
Cancel	The dialog box return value is Cancel
Ignore	The dialog box return value is Ignore
No	The dialog box return value is No
None	Nothing is returned from the dialog box; this means that the modal dialog box stays open
OK	The dialog box return value is OK
Retry	The dialog box return value is Retry
Yes	The dialog box return value is Yes

Figure 7-25 shows a program written for a fast-food restaurant. Its **MessageBox** asks the user to click Yes or No to a standard fast-food question. If the user clicks the Yes button, the price increases by 0.75; otherwise, the price remains at $3.00. Whichever button the user chooses, a new **MessageBox** displays the final meal price. Figures 7-26 and 7-27 show the **MessageBox** that contains the question and the result when the user clicks Yes.

```
using System;
using System.Windows.Forms;
public class HamburgerAddition
{
       public static void Main()
       {
            string question = "Do you want fries with that?";
            string caption = "Hamburger addition";
            double price = 3.00;
            if(MessageBox.Show(question, caption,
                 MessageBoxButtons.YesNo, MessageBoxIcon.Question)
                 == DialogResult.Yes)
                 price += 0.75;
             MessageBox.Show("Total is " + price.ToString("C"));
       }
}
```

Figure 7-25 HamburgerAddition program

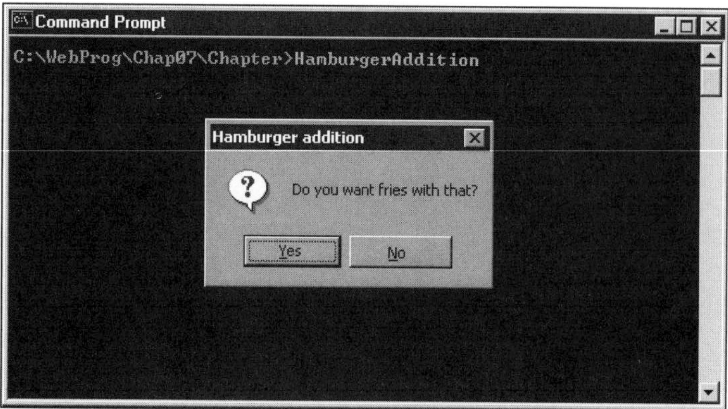

Figure 7-26 First `MessageBox` of `HamburgerAddition` program

Figure 7-27 Second `MessageBox` of `HamburgerAddition` program

Instead of the following single `if` statement:

```
if(MessageBox.Show(question, caption,
   MessageBoxButtons.YesNo, MessageBoxIcon.Question)
   == DialogResult.Yes)
```

you can create a `DialogResult` object and assign the result of the `MessageBox.Show()` method to it, as in the following code:

```
DialogResult dr = MessageBox.Show(question, caption,
  MessageBoxButtons.YesNo, MessageBoxIcon.Question);
```

Then the `if` statement becomes simpler:

```
if( dr == DialogResult.Yes)
```

Additionally, when you use this technique, you can compare the `DialogResult` named `dr` to different values one at a time.

Chapter Summary

- The C# programming language was developed as an object-oriented and component-oriented language. To write a C# program that produces a line of console output, you must pass a literal string as a parameter to the `System.Console.Out.WriteLine()` method. `System` is a namespace, `Console` is a class, and `Out` is an object. The `WriteLine()` method call lies within the `Main()` method of a class you create.
- To create a C# program you can use the Microsoft Visual Studio environment, but you can also use any text editor, such as Notepad, WordPad, or any word-processing program. After you write and save a program, you must compile the source code into intermediate and machine language. From the command line, you use the csc command to create an executable file. Then you type the program's name to execute it. Instead of using the command line, you can compile and write your program within the Visual Studio Integrated Development Environment. The IDE provides some prewritten code, uses color to identify program components, and provides easier debugging.
- Program comments are nonexecuting statements that you add to document a program or to disable statements when you test a program. There are three types of comments in C#: line comments, block comments, and XML-documentation comments.
- When you need to repeatedly use a class from the same namespace, you can shorten the statements you type by using a clause that indicates a namespace where the class can be found.
- Data is constant when it cannot be changed after a program is compiled; data is variable when it might change. C# provides for 14 basic, built-in types of data; a variable declaration includes a data type, an identifier, an optional assigned value, and a semicolon.
- You use the binary arithmetic operators (+, -, *, /, and %) to manipulate values in your programs.
- C# uses the `if` and `if-else` statements to make decisions. C# supports six comparison operators: (>), (<), (>=), (<=), (==), and (!=). An expression containing a comparison operator has a Boolean value.
- You create methods by providing a method header, curly braces, and a method body. The header contains an optional declared accessibility, optional `static` modifier, the return type for the method, the method name, an opening parenthesis, an optional list of method arguments, and a closing parenthesis.
- A `MessageBox` is a GUI object that can contain text, buttons, and symbols that inform and instruct a user. You use the static class method `Show()` to display a `MessageBox`. You can pass a string message, caption, buttons, and an icon to the `MessageBox.Show()` method. A `DialogResult` is an enumeration, or list of values that correspond to a user's potential `MessageBox` button selections.

7

REVIEW QUESTIONS

1. Of the following languages, which is least similar to C#?
   a. Java
   b. Visual Basic
   c. C++
   d. COBOL
2. A series of characters that appears in double quotes is a(n) ______________.
   a. parameter
   b. interface
   c. argument
   d. literal string
3. The C# method that prints a line of output on the screen and then positions the cursor on the next line is ______________.
   a. WriteLine()
   b. PrintLine()
   c. DisplayLine()
   d. OutLine()
4. Which of the following is an object?
   a. System
   b. Console
   c. Out
   d. WriteLine
5. In C#, a scheme that groups similar classes is a(n) ______________.
   a. superclass
   b. method
   c. namespace
   d. identifier
6. Which of the following is a method?
   a. namespace
   b. public
   c. Main()
   d. static

7. Which is true of identifiers?
   a. An identifier must begin with an underscore.
   b. An identifier can contain digits.
   c. An identifier must be no more than 16 characters long.
   d. An identifier can contain only lowercase letters.
8. A comment in the form `/* this is a comment */` is a(n) ________________.
   a. XML comment
   b. block comment
   c. executable comment
   d. line comment

9. If a programmer inserts `using System;` at the top of a C# program, which of the following can the programmer use as an alternative to `System.Console.Out.WriteLine("Hello");`?
   a. `System("Hello");`
   b. `WriteLine("Hello");`
   c. `Console.WriteLine("Hello");`
   d. `Console.Out("Hello");`
10. Assuming you have declared a variable as `int number = 5;`, what is produced by the following code:

```
if (number > 3)
     Console.WriteLine("Number is valid");
else
     Console.WriteLine("Number is too low");
```

   a. Number is valid.
   b. Number is too low.
   c. both of these
   d. none of these
11. A method's header is `int Compute(double amount)`. The method's return type is ________________.
   a. int
   b. double
   c. void
   d. impossible to tell

12. Which is true of the `MessageBox` class?
    a. You cannot create a new instance of this class.
    b. Its constructor is `public`.
    c. Its methods cannot be overloaded.
    d. A single version of its `Show()` method exists.
13. A programmer who uses a `MessageBox` must ________________.
    a. determine the message that appears on the OK button
    b. write the message that appears in the `MessageBox`
    c. write an overloaded version of the `Show()` method
    d. select an icon to display within the `MessageBox`
14. Optionally, a programmer can select all of the following for a `MessageBox` except ________________.
    a. a message within the `MessageBox`
    b. a caption in the title bar of the `MessageBox`
    c. a default button for the `MessageBox`
    d. the modality of the `MessageBox`
15. A `MessageBox` is modal, meaning ________________.
    a. it can appear in several different styles
    b. the program does not progress until a user dismisses the `MessageBox`
    c. it is always rectangular with a title bar
    d. it appears in Windows style so all components have the same look and feel

HANDS-ON EXERCISES

If necessary, use Windows Explorer to create a new folder in the Chap07 folder in your work folder. Name this folder **Exercises**. Save the programs that you create in these Exercises in the Chap07\Exercises folder in your work folder.

Exercise 7-1

Write, compile, and test a program that displays your first name on the screen. Save the program as **Name.cs** in the Chap07\Exercises folder in your work folder.

Exercise 7-2

Write, compile, and test a program that displays your full name, street address, city, and state on three separate lines on the screen. Save the program as **Address.cs** in the Chap07\Exercises folder in your work folder.

Exercise 7-3

Write, compile, and test a program that displays your favorite quotation on the screen. Include the name of the person to whom the quote is attributed. Use as many display lines as you feel are appropriate. Save the program as **Quotation.cs** in the Chap07\Exercises folder in your work folder.

Exercise 7-4

Write, compile, and test a program that displays a pattern similar to the following on the screen:

```
   X
  XXX
 XXXXX
XXXXXXX
   X
```

Save the program as **Tree.cs** in the Chap07\Exercises folder in your work folder.

Exercise 7-5

Write a C# program that declares variables to represent the length and width of a room in feet. Assign appropriate values to the variables, such as `length = 15` and `width = 25`. Compute and display the floor space of the room in square feet (area = length * width). As output, do not display only a value; display explanatory text with the value, such as `The floor space is 375 square feet.`. Save the program as **Room.cs** in the Chap07\Exercises folder in your work folder.

Web Programming Projects

If necessary, use Windows Explorer to create a new folder in the Chap07 folder in your work folder. Name this folder **Projects**. Save the programs that you create in these Projects in the Chap07\Projects folder in your work folder.

Project 7-1

Write a program for an Internet provider that displays a `MessageBox` asking users to choose whether they want unlimited access. Display a second `MessageBox` showing the prices: $10.95 a month for limited access and $19.95 a month for unlimited access. Save the program as **InternetAccess.cs** in the Chap07\Projects folder in your work folder.

Project 7-2

Write a program for an Internet provider that displays a `MessageBox` asking users whether they want to read the company's usage policy. If the user chooses Yes, display a short usage policy. If the user chooses No, remind the user to read the policy later. If the user chooses Cancel, end the program. Save the program as **Policy.cs** in the Chap07\Projects folder in your work folder.

Project 7-3

Write a program that simulates an Internet connection error. Display a `MessageBox` that notifies the user of the error and provide three buttons: Abort, Retry, and Ignore. If the user chooses Retry, display a message indicating that the connection succeeded. If the user chooses Ignore, display a message indicating that the user can work offline. If the user chooses Abort, end the program. Save the program as **Connection.cs** in the Chap07\Projects folder in your work folder.

CHAPTER

8

C#: PART II

In this chapter you will:

- Create a simple `Form`
- Use the Visual Studio IDE to design a `Form` and examine the automatically generated code
- Add functionality to a `Button` on a `Form`
- Use the Visual Studio Help Search function
- Understand `Controls`
- Work with `Labels` and `Color` on a `Form`
- Add `CheckBox`, `RadioButton`, and `PictureBox` objects to a `Form`

`MessageBox`es provide a large, but not infinite, number of ways to interact with users. They provide information and can allow a user to select one of two or three button options. However, some applications require more components than a few buttons; they require additional buttons, lists of available options from which to select, or text fields in which to type. **`Forms`** provide an interface for collecting, displaying, and delivering such information, and are a key component of GUI programs. You use a `Form` to represent any window you want to display within your application. Although they are not required, `Forms` often contain controls such as text fields, buttons, and check boxes that users can manipulate to interact with a program.

CREATING A Form

Figure 8-1 shows a program that creates the simplest Form possible, and Figure 8-2 shows the output. The object form1 is an instance of the Form class. The ShowDialog() method displays the form as a modal dialog box, so the user must dismiss the box before the program proceeds. The Form contains neither a caption nor components, but possesses a title bar with an icon. You can use your mouse to minimize, restore, resize (by dragging on the Frame borders), and close the Form, as you can with most of the Forms you have ever encountered when using programs written by others.

```
using System;
using System.Windows.Forms;
using System.Drawing;
public class CreateForm1
{
 public static void Main()
 {
  Form form1 = new Form();
  form1.ShowDialog();
 }
}
```

Figure 8-1 CreateForm1 program

Figure 8-2 Output of CreateForm1

You can change the appearance, size, color, and window management features of a Form by setting its instance fields or properties. The Form class contains about 100 properties (many of which it inherits from the Control class); Table 8-1 lists just some of them.

For example, setting the **Text** property allows you to specify the caption of the **Frame** in the title bar. The **Size** and **DesktopLocation** properties allow you to define the size and position of the window when it is displayed.

If you use the Visual Studio .NET Search option, you can find descriptions for all the Form class properties. Additionally, if you highlight a property and press F1 or click a property name, you see a description of the property at the bottom of the Properties list.

Not every property you can use with a Form appears in the Properties list within the Visual Studio IDE—only those most frequently used are listed.

Table 8-1 Properties of Forms

Member name	Description
AcceptButton	Gets or sets the button on the form that is clicked when the user presses Enter
AllowDrop	Gets or sets a value indicating whether the control can accept data that the user drags and drops into it
BackColor	Gets or sets the background color for this control
BackgroundImage	Gets or sets the background image displayed in the control
Bottom	Gets the distance between the bottom edge of the control and the top edge of its container's client area
CancelButton	Gets or sets the button control that is clicked when the user presses the Esc key
CanFocus	Gets a value indicating whether the control can receive focus
ContainsFocus	Gets a value indicating whether the control, or one of its child controls, currently has the input focus
ControlBox	Gets or sets a value indicating whether a control box is displayed in the caption bar of the form
DesktopBounds	Gets or sets the size and location of the form on the Windows desktop
DesktopLocation	Gets or sets the location of the form on the Windows desktop
DialogResult	Gets or sets the dialog result for the form
Focused	Gets a value indicating whether the control has input focus
Font	Gets or sets the current font for the control
ForeColor	Gets or sets the foreground color of the control
Height	Gets or sets the height of the control
HelpButton	Gets or sets a value indicating whether a Help button should be displayed in the caption box of the form
Icon	Gets or sets the icon for the form
Left	Gets or sets the x-coordinate of a control's left edge in pixels

Table 8-1 Properties of `Forms` (continued)

Member name	Description
Location	Gets or sets the coordinates of the upper-left corner of the control relative to the upper-left corner of its container
MaximizeBox	Gets or sets a value indicating whether the Maximize button is displayed in the caption bar of the form
MaximumSize	Gets the maximum size to which the form can be resized
MinimizeBox	Gets or sets a value indicating whether the Minimize button is displayed in the caption bar of the form
MinimumSize	Gets the minimum size to which the form can be resized
Modal	Gets a value indicating whether this form is displayed modally
Name	Gets or sets the name of the control
Right	Gets the distance between the right edge of the control and the left edge of its container
ShowInTaskbar	Gets or sets a value indicating whether the form is displayed in the Windows taskbar
Size	Gets or sets the size of the form
TabStop	Gets or sets a value indicating whether the user can give the focus to this control using Tab
Text	Gets or sets the text associated with this control
Top	Gets or sets the top coordinate of the control
Visible	Gets or sets a value indicating whether the control is visible
Width	Gets or sets the width of the control

Creating a `Form` That Is the Main Window of a Program

You can instantiate a `Form` within an application and use the `ShowDialog()` method to display it, as in the program in Figure 8-1. Alternatively, you can create a child class from `Form` that becomes the main window of an application. When you create a new main window, you must complete two steps:

- You must derive a new custom class from the base class `System.Windows.Forms.Form`.
- You must write a `Main()` method that calls the `Application.Run()` method, and you must pass an instance of your newly created `Form` class as an argument. This starts the program and makes the form visible.

Figure 8-3 shows the simplest program you can write that creates a new main window for a program. You must include the `using System.Windows.Forms;` statement at the top of the program. In Figure 8-3, the class name is `Window1`; it extends the `Form` class.

```
using System;
using System.Windows.Forms;
public class Window1 : Form
{
 public static void Main()
 {
  Application.Run(new Window1());
 }
}
```

Figure 8-3 `Window1` class

The `Window1` class in Figure 8-3 contains a single method: a `Main()` method that calls the `Application.Run()` method, passing a new instance of the `Window1` object. Figure 8-4 shows the output. The `Form` created has no title and contains no components, but possesses a title bar that displays an icon.

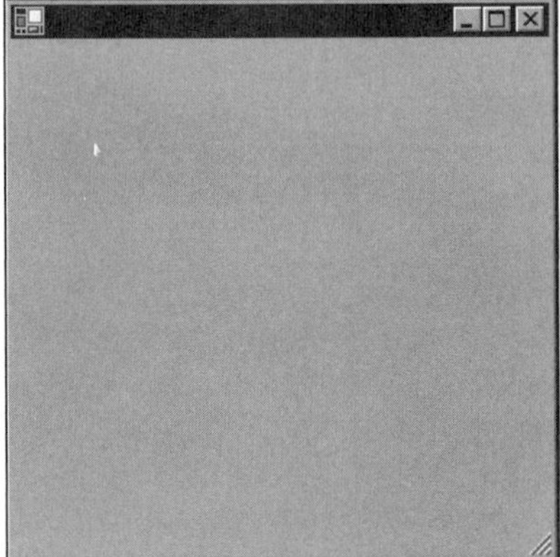

Figure 8-4 The `Window1` object

The `Application.Run()` method processes messages from the operating system to the application. Without the call to `Application.Run()`, the program would compile and execute, but the program would end without displaying the window.

When you want to add property settings to the main window of a program, you can do so within the class constructor (the method with the same name as the class that follows `new`). Figure 8-5 shows a `Window2` class in which the `Size` and `Text` attributes of a window are set. The keyword `this` in the constructor method refers to "this `Form` being constructed"; you could eliminate `this` and the constructor would work in the same way. The `Size` field uses the `System.Drawing.Size()` method, which takes two parameters. The first indicates the horizontal size, or width, of a component; the second indicates the vertical size (or height) of a component. Setting the `Size` to `System.Drawing.Size(500,100)` creates a window that is five times wider than it is tall. The **Text** field supplies the caption that appears in the title bar of the window. Figure 8-6 shows the created **Window2** object.

```
using System;
using System.Windows.Forms;
public class Window2 : Form
{
 public Window2()
 {
  this.Size = new System.Drawing.Size(500,100);
  this.Text = "This is a Window2 Object";
 }
 public static void Main()
 {
  Application.Run(new Window2());
 }
}
```

Figure 8-5 `Window2` class

Figure 8-6 The `Window2` object

PLACING A Button ON A WINDOW

Although it has interesting dimensions, the window in Figure 8-6 is not yet as useful as a **MessageBox**. However, a window is more flexible than a **MessageBox** because you can place manipulatable window components wherever you like in the window. You identify these components as a **Form**'s **Controls**.

One type of object the user can manipulate is a **Button**. A **Button** is a GUI object you can click to cause some action. (Alternatively, you can press Enter if the **Button** has focus.) You can create your own **Button** objects by using the **Button** class. The class contains more than 60 properties; two of the most useful are its **Text** and

`Location` properties. You use the `Text` property to set a `Button`'s label. You can use the `Location` property to position a `Button` relative to the upper-left corner of the `Form` (or any other `ContainerControl` object) holding it.

When you use the `Location` property you supply two integer arguments to the `System.Drawing.Point()` method. The first argument represents the number of horizontal pixels to the right of the upper-left corner of a `Form` (or other container). The second argument represents the vertical position down from the top. You use the `System.Drawing.Point()` method in the next set of steps you complete in this chapter.

For a `Button` to be clickable, you need to use the `System.Windows.Forms.Control` class, which implements very basic functionality required by any classes that display GUI objects to the user. The class handles user input through the keyboard and pointing device. To use the class, you can create an array of GUI components (such as `Buttons`) and add them to a `Form`'s `Control` property with the `AddRange()` method. The statement that adds components to the list of a `Form`'s controls takes the following form:


```
this.Controls.AddRange
 (new System.Windows.Forms.Control[]
 {this.button1});
```

It takes a fair amount of code to make a `Form`'s `Button` clickable; it is easiest to show an example of such a `Form`. In the next steps, you create a `Form` containing a `Button`.

To create a `Form` containing a `Button`:

1. Start any text editor, such as Notepad, WordPad, or any word-processing program. Open a new document, if necessary, and start a `WindowWithButton` class that descends from the `Form` class as follows:

```
using System;
using System.Windows.Forms;
public class WindowWithButton : Form
{
```

2. Create a `Button` object named `button1`.

```
Button button1 = new Button();
```

3. Add a `WindowWithButton` constructor that sets the `Size` and `Text` fields for the `Form` as well as the `Text` field for the `Button`. Then use a `Controls.AddRange()` method to indicate that the `Button` you created becomes one of the `Form`'s usable controls. Finally, locate the `Button` at position 100, 50 on the `Form`.

```
public WindowWithButton()
{
 this.Size = new System.Drawing.Size(300,300);
 this.Text = "Window Object With Button";
 button1.Text = "Press";
```

```
    this.Controls.AddRange
     (new System.Windows.Forms.Control[]
     {this.button1});
    this.button1.Location = new
     System.Drawing.Point(100, 50);
  }
```

4. Add the following `Main()` method to execute the application:

```
public static void Main()
{
 Application.Run(new WindowWithButton());
}
```

5. Add a closing curly brace for the class. Save the file as **WindowWithButton.cs** in the Chap08\Chapter folder of your work folder.

6. Compile and execute the program. Figure 8-7 shows the output. Notice that the upper-left corner of the `Button` you placed in location 100, 50 is about one-third of the distance from the left edge of the 300 × 300 form, and about one-sixth of the distance vertically from the top.

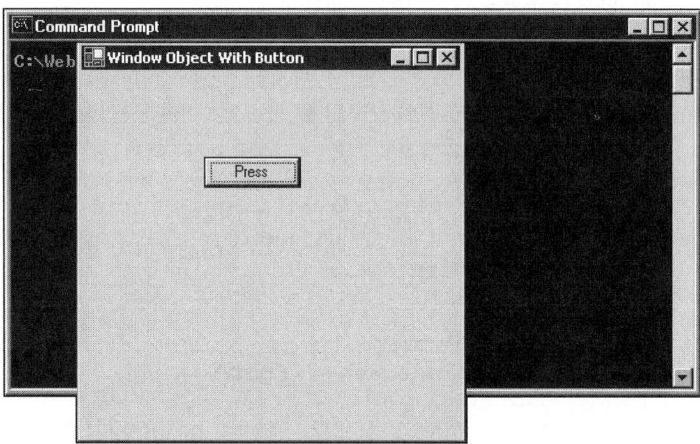

Figure 8-7 Output of `WindowWithButton` program

7. Click the `Button`. Nothing happens because you have not yet added the code necessary for the `Button` to cause some action.

8. In the statement `this.button1.Location = new System.Drawing.Point(100, 50);`, experiment by changing the horizontal and vertical coordinates to any new values you choose. Save, compile, and execute the program several times until you can accurately predict where the `Button` will be located on the `Form`.

USING THE VISUAL STUDIO IDE TO DESIGN A `Form`

The window in Figure 8-7 consists of only a `Form` and a `Button`, and even though the `Button` doesn't do anything yet, there are scores of more options available to you. The program in Figure 8-6 sets only two attributes for the `Form` (`Size` and `Text`), yet Table 8-1 shows dozens of additional properties you can set, and that table lists fewer than half the available properties. Likewise, the program in Figure 8-6 sets only two `Button` properties (`Text` and `Location`); by the time you create a full-blown Windows application, you might want to set several more properties for the existing `Button`, add more `Button`s, and set all their properties. You might want to add other components to the window, and supply locations and appropriate resulting actions for each of them, as well. Just determining an attractive and useful layout in which to position all the components on your `Form` can take many lines of code and a lot of trial and error. Even a simple but fully functional GUI program might require several hundred statements. Therefore, coding such a program can be tedious.

The Visual Studio Integrated Development Environment (IDE) provides a wealth of tools to help make the `Form` design process easier. Rather than having to write multiple assignment statements and guess at appropriate component locations, the Visual Studio IDE provides you with a graphical environment for designing your `Forms`. You most easily can understand the Visual Studio environment by using it. In the next steps, you use the IDE to graphically create a `Form` with a `Button`.

Designing aesthetically pleasing, functional, and user-friendly `Forms` is an art; entire books are devoted to the topic.

To create a `Form` with a `Button`:

1. Open **Microsoft Visual Studio .NET**. You might have a desktop shortcut you can double-click, or you might click **Start** on the taskbar, point to **Programs** (point to **All Programs** in Windows XP), point to **Microsoft Visual Studio .NET 7.0**, and then click **Microsoft Visual Studio .NET 7.0**. If you are using a school network, you might be able to select Visual Studio from the school's computing menu.
2. Click **File** on the menu bar, point to **New**, and then click **Project**.
3. A New Project dialog box appears on your screen, as shown in Figure 8-8. In the window under Project Types, click **Visual C# Projects**, if necessary. Under Templates, click **Windows Application**. Near the bottom of the New Project dialog box, click in the Name text box and insert **WindowCreatedWithIDE** as the name for your application. Make sure the Location text box contains the name of the Chap08\Chapter folder in your work folder.

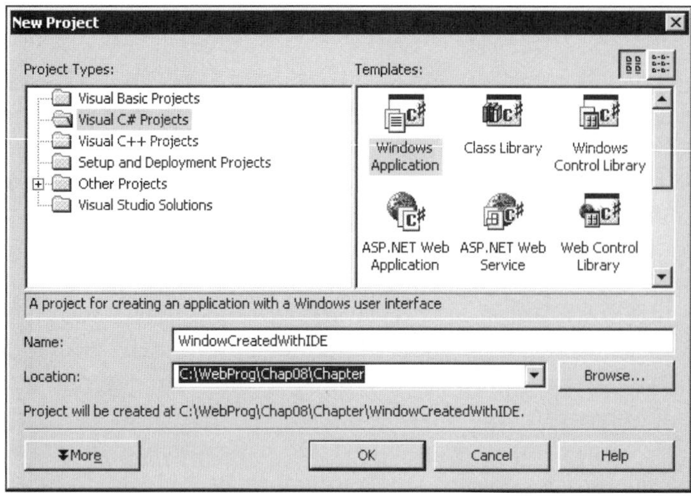

Figure 8-8 New Project dialog box

4. Click **OK** at the bottom of the dialog box. Figure 8-9 shows the design screen that appears. (If necessary, click the Form1 title bar to make it active.) The blank `Form` in the center of the screen has an empty title bar. The lower-right corner of the screen contains a Properties window that holds a list of the `Form`'s properties. In Figure 8-9 you can see some of the properties of Form1 listed in the Settings box in the lower-right pane. Take a minute to scroll through the Properties list and notice the values of the properties of the `Form`. For example, the `Text` property is "Form1" and the `Size` property is "300, 300".

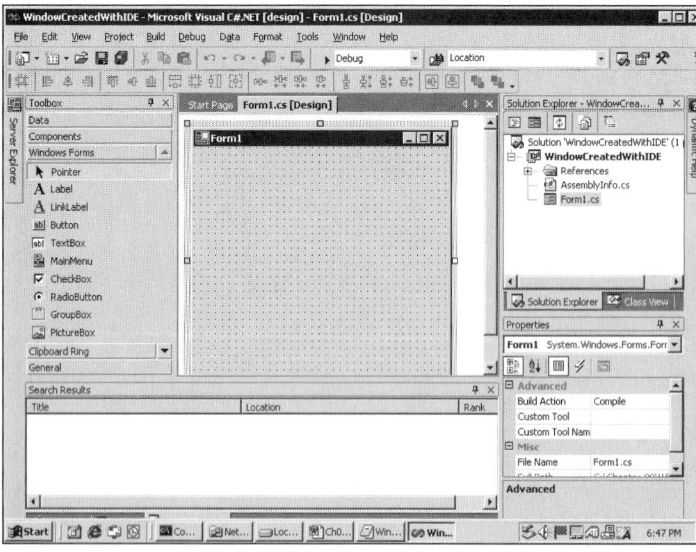

Figure 8-9 Design screen for Form1

5. In the Properties list, click the description **Form1** in the Settings box for the `Text` property. Delete **Form1** and type **My IDE Form**. Press **Enter**; the title of the `Form` in the center of the screen changes to "My IDE Form". See Figure 8-10.

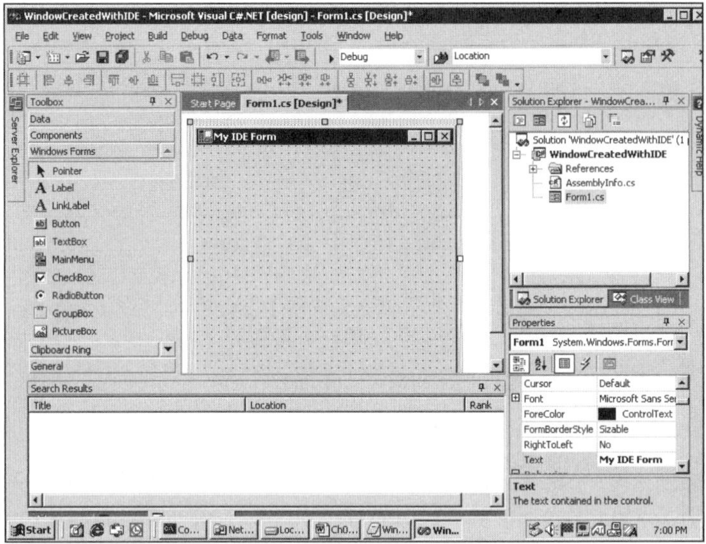

Figure 8-10 Changing the `Text` of a `Form`

6. At the left side of the design screen, you see a list of tools you can use and add to a `Form`, including `Pointer`, `Label`, `LinkLabel`, `Button`, and so on. Click `Button` and drag a `Button` onto the `Form`, as shown in Figure 8-11. When you release your mouse button, the `Button` appears on the `Form` and contains the text "button1".

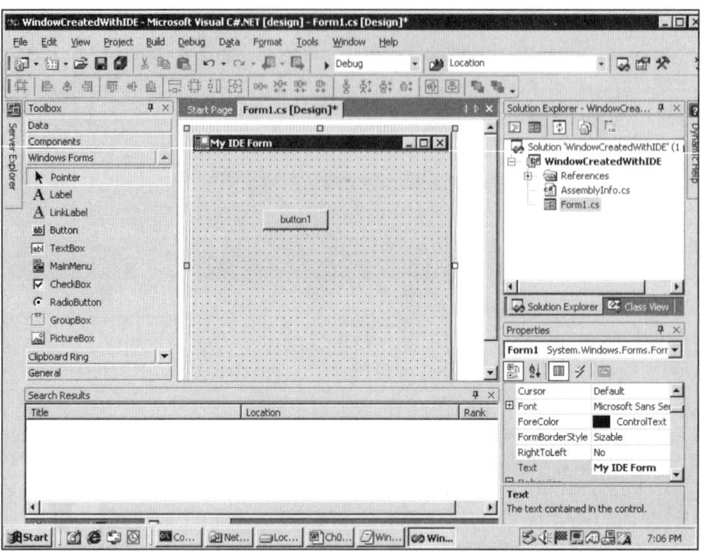

Figure 8-11 A `Button` placed on the `Form`

7. The Properties list box on the right side of the screen shows the component for which you are viewing the properties. If the properties for `button1` are not showing, click the Properties list arrow and then click `button1`. Change the `Text` property of `button1` to **Press**, then press **Enter**. The text of the `Button` on the `Form` changes to "Press". See Figure 8-12.

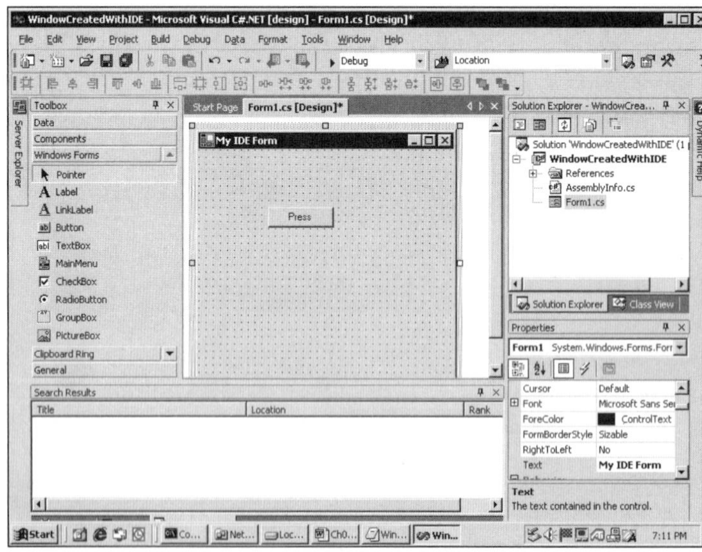

Figure 8-12 Changing the `Text` property of the `Button`

8. Scroll through the other `button1` properties. In Figure 8-13, notice that the value in the Settings box for the `Location` property is 80, 64. Your `Location` property might be different, depending on where you released the `Button` when you dragged it onto the `Form`. Drag the button across the `Form` to a new position. Each time you release your mouse button, the value of the button's `Location` property is updated to reflect the new location. Try to drag the `Button` to Location **80, 64**. Alternatively, delete the contents of the `Location` property field and type **80, 64**. The `Button` moves to the requested location on the `Form`.

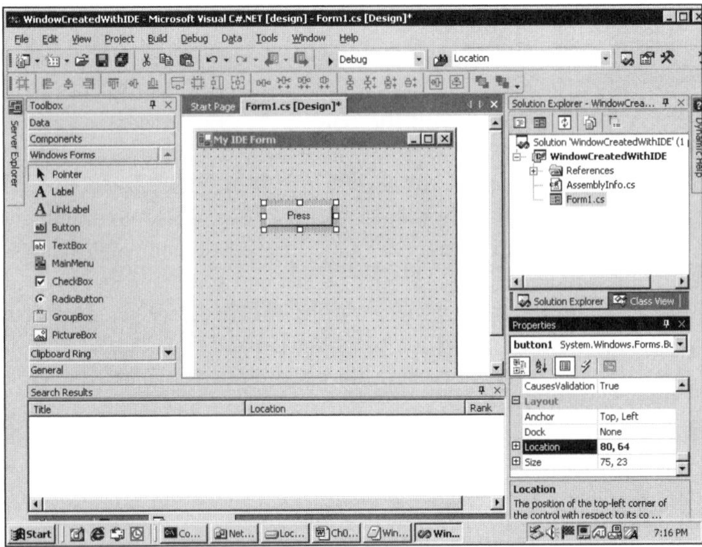

Figure 8-13 Examining the `Location` property of `button1`

8

9. Save the form you have created by clicking **File** on the menu bar, then clicking **Save All**. Alternatively, you can click the **Save All** button on the toolbar (its icon is a stack of floppy disks).

10. Although the `Form` you have designed doesn't do much yet, you can execute the program you have designed. Click **Debug** on the menu bar, and then click **Start Without Debugging**, or press **Ctrl+F5**. The Output window at the bottom of the screen shows 0 errors, and the `Form` is displayed, as shown in Figure 8-14. You can drag, minimize, and restore it and click its button just as you could with the `Forms` you developed earlier in this chapter by writing all the code.

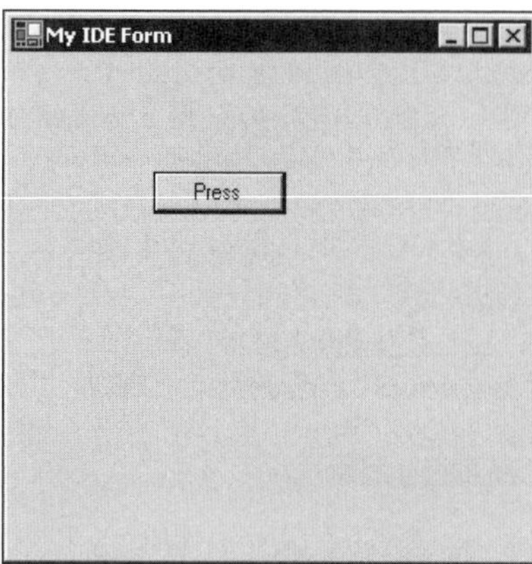

Figure 8-14 The `Form1 form` created with the IDE

11. Close the form. Click **View** on the menu bar, then click **Code**. In Figure 8-15 you can see part of the code. Scroll through the code on your computer as you continue to read this discussion of it. There are over 80 lines of code, and much of it looks confusing. However, if you examine it closely, you can find many familiar statements. For example, locate the class header for the `Form1` class at about the 12th line of code: `public class Form1 : System.Windows.Forms.Form`. This header shows that the `Form1` class descends or inherits from `System.Windows.Forms.Form`. You could shorten the header to `public class Form1 : Form` because the `using` statement, `using System.Windows.Forms;`, appears at the top of the file; however, the C# IDE uses the fully qualified version in the code for clarity.

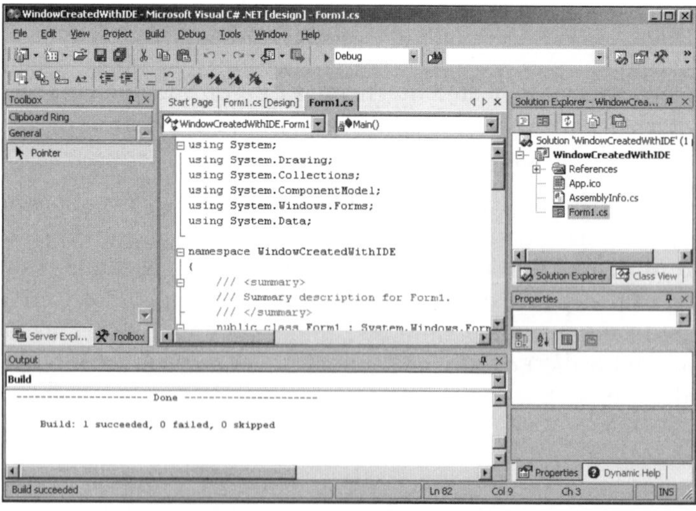

Figure 8-15 Viewing the code for the `WindowCreatedWithIDE` program

A discussion of the other statements in this code follows the completion of these steps.

12. The code in the WindowCreatedWithIDE program was created for you when you used the IDE. Still, it is simply code. You can make changes to it just as you can to code you type yourself. Take some time to experiment with this code. For example, locate the `InitializeComponent()` method and find the statement that sets the location of the button. (You might have to expand the code to see this statement.)

    ```
    this.button1.Location = new System.Drawing.Point(80, 64);
    ```

    Change the `Location` coordinates to **200, 150**, then execute the program again. The button appears in a new location, further to the right and down from its first location. Find the statement that sets the button's text:

    ```
    this.button1.Text = "Press";
    ```

    Change the text from "Press" to **Press Me**. When you run the program, the change takes effect.

When you use the IDE, you can work visually or with the code text, whichever you find easier or more appropriate to the task at hand. Click **View** on the menu bar, then click **Designer** if you want to switch back to the Designer view. When you want to work with the code, click **View** on the menu bar, then click **Code**. By pressing **F7** or **Shift+F7** you can also switch from Designer view to Code view and back.

13. Exit Visual Studio by clicking the **Close** button in the upper-right corner of the screen, or by clicking **File** on the menu bar, and then clicking **Exit**. If you have made changes since the last time you saved in Step 9, you are asked if you want to save your changes. Choose **No** to exit the program.

UNDERSTANDING THE CODE CREATED BY THE IDE

When using the Visual Studio IDE it is easy to create elaborate forms with a few keystrokes. However, if you don't understand the code behind the forms you create, you cannot say you have truly mastered the C# language. Everything you have learned to this point has prepared you to understand the code that lies behind a visually designed form. The generated code is simply a collection of C# statements and method calls similar to ones you have been using throughout this book. When you use the Designer in the IDE to design your forms, you save a lot of typing, which reduces the errors you may create. As you saw when you scrolled through the WindowCreatedWithIDE program, it takes quite a bit of code to create even a simple form containing a single button. In the next steps, you examine the code piece by piece.

To examine the code in the `WindowCreatedWithIDE` program:

1. Reopen **Visual Studio**, then open the **WindowCreatedWithIDE** project. Select **Code View** so you can see the generated code.

Because the IDE generates so much code automatically, it is often more difficult to find and correct errors in programs created by the IDE than in programs you code by hand.

2. Locate the first section of the code in WindowCreatedWithIDE which contains a list of `using` statements as follows:

```
using System;
using System.Drawing;
using System.Collections;
using System.ComponentModel;
using System.Windows.Forms;
using System.Data;
```

You have placed many statements such as these within your programs. These statements simply list the classes that the program uses.

3. Scroll to the next code segment that creates a namespace using the name you supplied when you began to create this C# Windows project. The namespace declaration is followed by an opening curly brace and three comments that describe the next section of code.

```
namespace WindowCreatedWithIDE
{
 /// <summary>
 /// Summary description for Form1.
 /// </summary>
```

C# uses three slashes (///) to begin an XML comment. When C# inserts the tag pairs `<summary>` and `</summary>` within the code, it allows the IntelliSense feature within Visual Studio to display additional information about the members contained between the tags. The IntelliSense feature provides automatic statement completion for you within the Visual Studio IDE. Recall that XML stands for eXtensible Markup Language. For more information, search XML in the Visual Studio Help facility. It directs you to several articles that discuss XML.

4. Find the next code segment that declares the `Form1` class. The name `Form1` was supplied by default; you can change this name using the form's `Name` property if you want. The `Form1` class header shows that the class descends from the `Form` class. The class header is followed by an opening curly brace.

```
public class Form1 : System.Windows.Forms.Form
{
```

5. Notice the next statement that defines a `Button` object named `button1`:

```
private System.Windows.Forms.Button button1;
```

This object declaration was added to the code when you dragged the `Button` onto the `Form`'s surface. You can change the `Button`'s access from `private` to `public` if you like, but it is defined as `private` because it is used only within this class. You also can eliminate the fully qualified `System.Windows.Forms.Button` class name and replace it with `Button` because the `using` statement at the top of the file includes `System.Windows.Forms`. You also can change the name of `button1` to any other legal identifier you choose. However, if you delete `button1` in the declaration and replace it with a new name, then you must be sure to change every instance of `button1` in the program. The safer alternative is to change `button1`'s `Name` property in the IDE, either in the code or in the Setting box for the `Name` field in the Properties list of the Designer view. Either way, every instance of `button1` is replaced with its new identifier.

If you change `button1`'s `Name` property within the code, switch to Designer view, then double-click the button to switch back to Code view. You will find every instance of `button1` has been changed to use the new name you assigned.

6. After the `button1 Button` is declared, three comments appear, followed by a declaration of a `Container` object named `components`, set to `null`, or nothing.

```
/// <summary>
/// Required designer variable.
/// </summary>
private System.ComponentModel.Container components = null;
```

7. Continue to scroll through the code and locate the definition for the `Form1` constructor. The `Form1` constructor looks similar to many constructor methods you have created:

```
public Form1()
{
  //
  // Required for Windows Form
  // Designer support
  //
  InitializeComponent();

  //
  // TODO: Add any constructor code after
  // InitializeComponent call
  //
}
```

The `Form1` constructor contains several comments and a single method call to a method named `InitializeComponent()`. The tasks performed by `InitializeComponent()` can be performed directly within the constructor; `InitializeComponent()` is simply used as a helper method to organize all the component initialization tasks in one location. The comments following `InitializeComponent()` begin with "TODO". These are not XML comments, but plain C# line comments. C# uses comments beginning with "TODO" to remind you of tasks you might need to do. If your application requires any additional constructor statements for `Form1`, you place them here.

You learned about the `bool` data type in Chapter 7. In this code, `disposing` is a `bool` variable, meaning it holds either `true` or `false`.

8. Continue to scroll and find the `Dispose()` method. The IDE provides the form with a `Dispose()` method as follows:

```
/// <summary>
/// Clean up any resources being used.
/// </summary>
protected override void
 Dispose( bool disposing )
{
 if( disposing )
 {
  if (components != null)
  {
   components.Dispose();
  }
 }
 base.Dispose( disposing );  }
```

   This method contains any clean-up activities you need when a `Form` is dismissed. When you write an application that leaves open files or other unfinished business, you might want to add statements to this method. For now, you can let C# take care of the clean-up tasks that are invisible to you.

9. The next statement in the code, `#region`, is a preprocessor directive. Any code placed between `#region` and `#endregion` statements forms a group that can be used by some of the IDE's automated tools. The `#region` and `#endregion` statements do not affect the way the code operates; for now you can ignore the statements.

```
#region Windows Form Designer generated code
/// <summary>
/// Required method for Designer support
/// - do not modify the contents of this method
/// with the code editor.
/// </summary>
```

```
private void InitializeComponent()
{
 this.button1 = new System.Windows.Forms.Button();
 this.SuspendLayout();
 //
 // button1
 //
 this.button1.Location = new
    System.Drawing.Point(80, 64);
 this.button1.Name = "button1";
 this.button1.TabIndex = 0;
 this.button1.Text = "Press";
 //
 // Form1
 //
 this.AutoScaleBaseSize = new
  System.Drawing.Size(5, 13);
 this.ClientSize = new System.Drawing.Size(292, 273);
 this.Controls.AddRange
    (new System.Windows.Forms.Control[]
               {this.button1});
 this.Name = "Form1";
 this.Text = "My IDE Form";
 this.ResumeLayout(false);

}
#endregion
```

The statements within the preceding `InitializeComponent()` method should look familiar to you. These statements reflect the code generated by the properties you have selected for the `Form`. For example, the `button1.Text` and `Form this.Text` fields contain values you typed into the Settings boxes in the Properties list.

10. Scroll to the last section of the program that contains a `Main()` method that runs the application. Two curly braces follow—one ends the `Form1` class and the other ends the `WindowCreatedWithIDE` namespace.

```
  /// <summary>
  /// The main entry point for the application.
  /// </summary>
  [STAThread]
  static void Main()
  {
      Application.Run(new Form1());
  }
 }
}
```

8

Just above `Main()`, `[STAThread]` indicates that this program uses the Single Threaded Apartment Thread model. You will learn more about threads as you continue to study C#.

11. Exit Visual Studio. If you have made changes while examining this code, you are asked if you want to save your changes. Choose **No** to exit the program.

ADDING FUNCTIONALITY TO A `Button` ON A `Form`

In most cases it is easier to design a `Form` using the IDE than it is to write by hand all the code a `Form` requires. Adding functionality to a `Button` is particularly easy using the IDE. In the next steps, you make the `Button` on the `WindowCreatedWithIDE` form functional by making it display a `MessageBox` when the user clicks it.

To display a `MessageBox` when the user clicks the `Button`:

1. Start **Visual Studio**. Click **File** on the menu bar, point to **Open**, and then click **Project**, as shown in Figure 8-16. Make sure the Look in: box at the top of the screen indicates that you are looking in the Chap08\Chapter folder of your work folder.

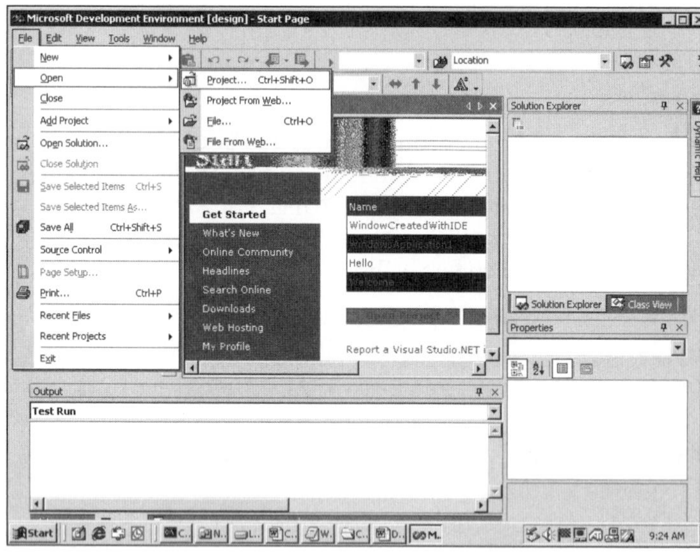

Figure 8-16 Opening an existing project

2. Double-click the **WindowCreatedWithIDE** folder. Click the **WindowCreatedWithIDE** C# source code file. See Figure 8-17.

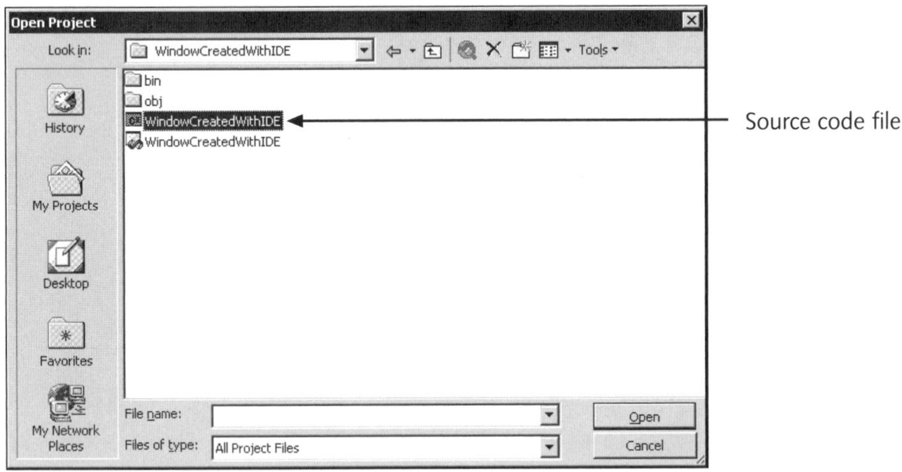

Figure 8-17 Selecting the source file

3. The `Form` you created should appear. If you see the code behind the `Form` instead of the `Form`, click **View** on the menu bar, and then click **Designer**, or press **Shift+F7**. Double-click the **Press** button on the `Form`. The program code appears, revealing a newly created method:

```
private void button1_Click
 (object sender, System.EventArgs e)
{
}
```

4. The method named `button1_Click()` contains the code that identifies the actions you want to perform when a user clicks `button1`. The method receives two arguments—an object named `sender` and an `EventArgs` object named `e`. Next, you add some code that will display a `MessageBox` when the user clicks `button1`. Place your insertion point between the curly braces of the `button1_Click()` method and add the following:

```
MessageBox.Show("Thank you");
```

5. Save the file, then run the program by clicking **Debug** on the menu bar and clicking **Start Without Debugging**, or press **Ctrl+F5**. When `My IDE Form` appears, click the **Press** `Button`. The `MessageBox` containing "Thank you" appears, as shown in Figure 8-18.

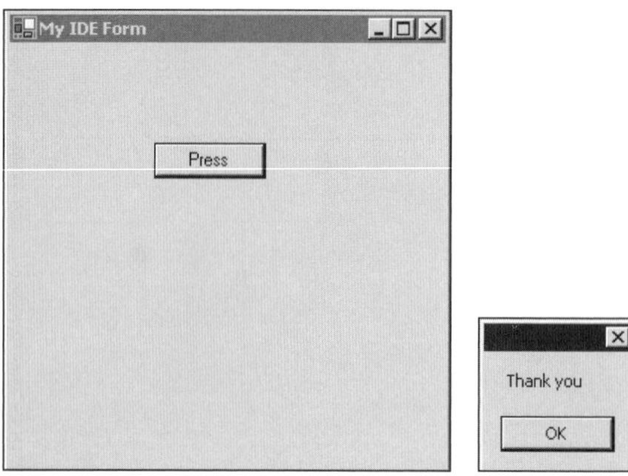

Figure 8-18 `MessageBox` that appears after clicking "Press"

6. Dismiss the `MessageBox`, then close the `Form`.
7. Examine the code for the `Form`. In the `InitializeComponent()` method, a new statement has been added:

```
this.button1.Click +=
   new System.EventHandler(this.button1_Click);
```

This statement associates the `button1_Click()` method with the `button1.Click` event that is generated when a user clicks the `button1Button`.

Adding a Second Button to a Form

`Form`s often contain multiple `Button` objects; a `Form` can contain as many `Button`s as you need. Because each `Button` has a unique identifier, you can provide unique methods to execute when a user clicks each `Button`.

In the next steps, you create a form that allows a pizzeria customer to select one of two buttons identifying two types of pizza—Cheese or Sausage. The form then displays one of two pizza prices—$10 or $12, depending on the user's selection.

To create a form with two buttons:

1. If it is not still open, open **Visual Studio .NET**. Click **File** on the menu bar, point to **New**, click **Project**, and then click **Visual C# Projects** and **Windows Application**. Change the Name of the project to **WindowWithTwoButtons** and make sure the Chap08\Chapter folder of your work folder is designated as the storage Location, as in Figure 8-19. Then click **OK**.

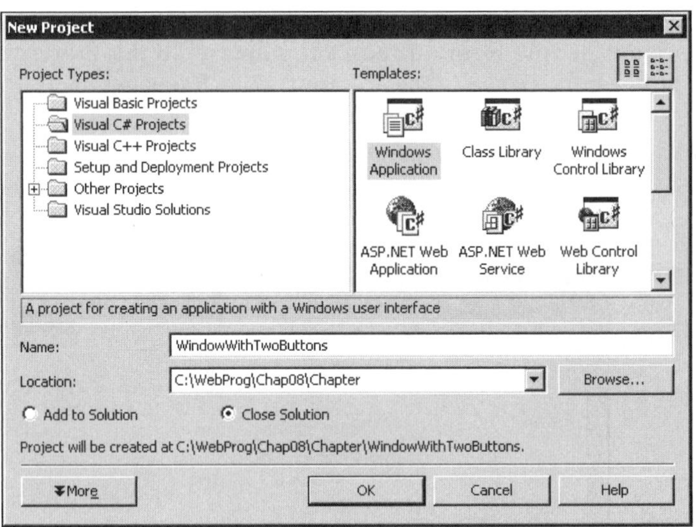

Figure 8-19 Starting the `WindowWithTwoButtons` project

2. Click the **title bar** of the form designer that appears. Then in the `Form`'s Properties list, change the text of the form to **Make a Choice**. When you press **Enter**, "Make a Choice" appears in the `Form`'s title bar. Drag a `Button` onto the `Form`. Release your mouse button to deposit the `Button` on the surface of the `Form`, then drag a second `Button` onto the `Form`. The `Buttons` automatically contain the text labels `button1` and `button2`, as shown in Figure 8-20.

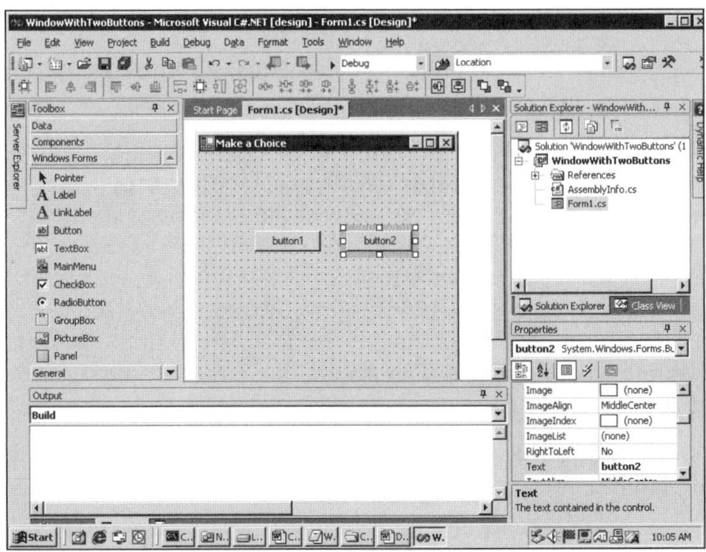

Figure 8-20 Two `Buttons` on a `Form`

3. In the Properties window, click the list box, and then click `button1`. Change its `Text` property setting from `button1` to **Cheese**. In the Properties list box, click `button2`. Change its `Text` property to **Sausage**. See Figure 8-21.

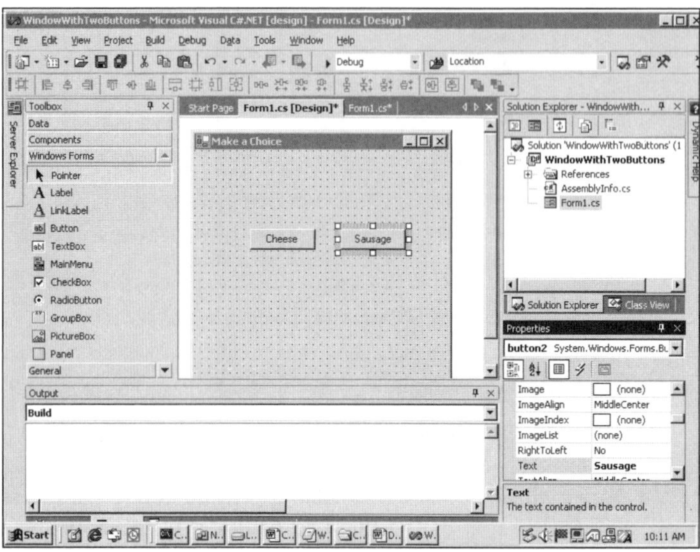

Figure 8-21 Two `Buttons` containing `Text` properties "Cheese" and "Sausage"

4. Double-click the **Cheese** `Button` to view the code for the `button1_Click()` method. Between the curly braces, type:

```
MessageBox.Show("Price is $10");
```

5. Return to Designer view. Double-click the **Sausage** `Button`. Between the curly braces of the method, add `MessageBox.Show("Price is $12");`

6. Save the file, and then run the program using **Ctrl+F5** or by clicking **Debug** on the menu bar and clicking **Start Without Debugging**. When the `Form` appears, notice the Cheese `Button` has a darker outline than the Sausage `Button`. This means the Cheese `Button` has focus. When a `Button` has **focus**, it appears darker than other `Buttons`, and you can activate it by clicking it or pressing Enter. By default, the first `Button` you place on a `Form` has focus. The user can press Tab to change the focus from one `Button` to the next. Experiment with pressing **Tab**, then click either of the `Buttons` and confirm that the correct price message is displayed.

7. Dismiss the `MessageBox`, and click the other button. Again, the correct price is displayed. Figure 8-22 shows the result when the user selects Sausage.

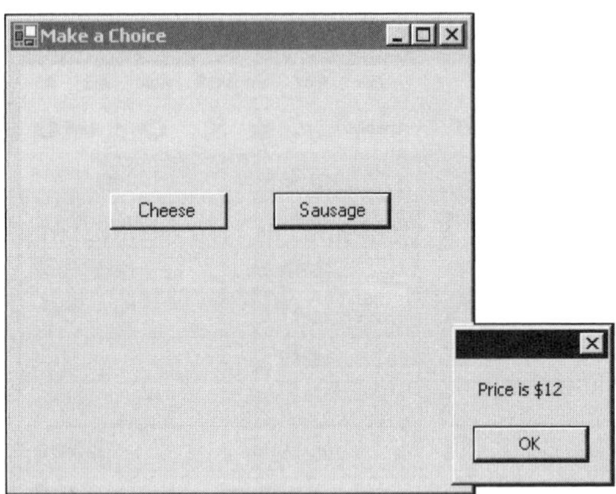

Figure 8-22 Make a Choice `Form` after user clicks "Sausage" `Button`

8. Dismiss the `MessageBox`, and close the `Form`. In the IDE, switch to Code view, if necessary. Within the `InitializeComponent()` method, locate the statements that set the `button1.TabIndex` property: `this.button1.TabIndex = 0;` and `this.button2.TabIndex = 1;`. The `TabIndex` property specifies the order (0, 1, 2, and so on) in which `Button` objects receive focus when the user presses Tab. (If you set both `Buttons` to the same `TabIndex`, the last one set receives the focus.)

Using the Visual Studio Help Search Function

When working with a class that is new to you, such as `Button` or `Form`, no book can answer all your questions. The ultimate authority on the classes available in C# is the Visual Studio Search facility. You want to use this tool often as you continue to learn about C# in particular and the Visual Studio products in general. In the next steps, you search for information on the `Button` class.

To search for information on the `Button` class:

1. In the Visual Studio IDE, click **Help** on the menu bar, then click **Search**. (Alternatively, you can press **Ctrl+Alt+F3**.) See Figure 8-23.

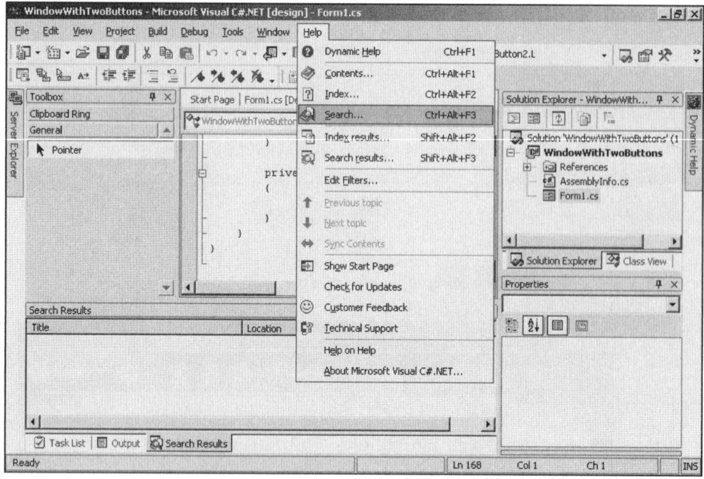

Figure 8-23 Using Search

2. In the Search dialog box near the top right of the screen, type a term for which you want to search. (You can choose Visual C# and Related in the Filtered by list box to narrow the search from the superset of all Visual Studio topics.) For example, type **Button**. Press **Enter** and a list of topics appears at the bottom of the screen. See Figure 8-24.

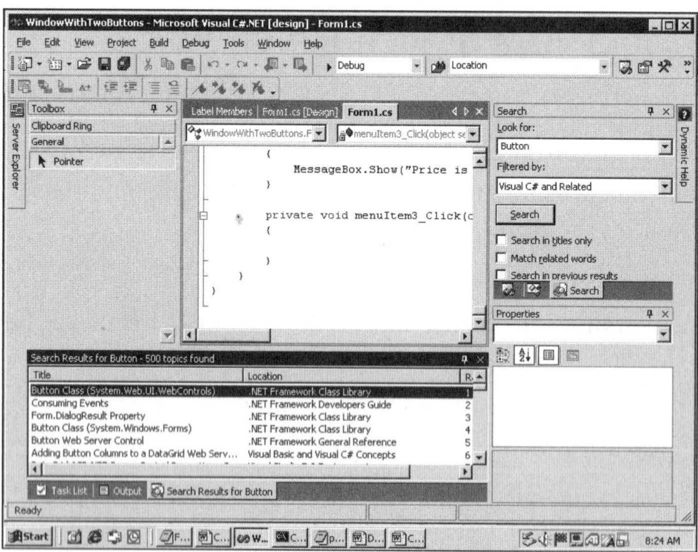

Figure 8-24 Topics found after searching for `Button`

3. Double-click the topic you want to pursue (for example, Button Class). (Depending on your version of Visual Studio .Net, you might be prompted to insert a CD at this point.) Documentation appears in the Visual Studio main window. See Figure 8-25.

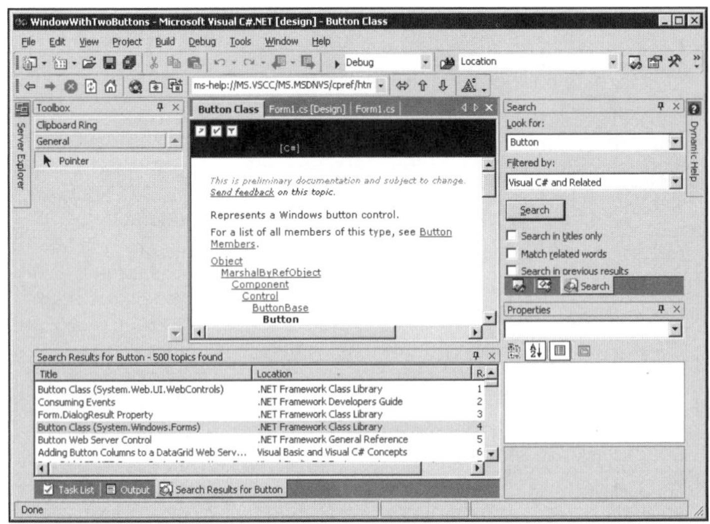

Figure 8-25 Button class documentation

4. Scroll through the documentation. You can read a definition of `Button`, examine its inheritance hierarchy, see how its constructor is configured, and so on. At the bottom of the `Button` information, the *See Also* section provides you with links to appropriate related topics, such as all the `Button` members, that is, all the properties and methods associated with `Buttons`.

5. Experiment by searching for other topics you have studied. When you are done, close the Visual Studio IDE.

UNDERSTANDING Controls

When you design a `Form` you can place `Buttons` and other controls such as `Labels`, `CheckBoxes`, and `RadioButtons` on the `Form` surface. The `Control` class provides the definitions for these GUI objects.

Table 8-2 shows some of the properties associated with `Controls` in general.

Table 8-2 Some `Control` properties

Property	Function
Anchor	Gets or sets which edges of the control are anchored to the edges of its container
BackColor	Gets or sets the background color for this control
BackgroundImage	Gets or sets the background image displayed in the control
BorderStyle	Gets or sets the border style for the control
Bottom	Gets the distance between the bottom edge of the control and the top edge of its container's client area
CanFocus	Gets a value indicating whether the control can receive focus
CanSelect	Gets a value indicating whether the control can be selected
Container	Returns the `Container` that contains the `Component`
ContainsFocus	Gets a value indicating whether the control, or one of its child controls, currently has the input focus
ContextMenu	Gets or sets the shortcut menu associated with this control
Controls	Gets or sets the collection of controls contained within the control
Cursor	Gets or sets the cursor that is displayed when the user moves the mouse pointer over this control
Dock	Gets or sets to which edge of the parent container a control is docked
Enabled	Gets or sets a value indicating whether the control is enabled
Focused	Gets a value indicating whether the control has input focus
Font	Gets or sets the current font for the control
ForeColor	Gets or sets the foreground color of the control
HasChildren	Gets a value indicating whether the control contains one or more child controls
Height	Gets or sets the height of the control
IsAccessible	Gets or sets a value indicating whether the control is visible to accessibility applications
Left	Gets or sets the x-coordinate of a control's left edge in pixels
Location	Gets or sets the coordinates of the upper-left corner of the control relative to the upper-left corner of its container
Name	Gets or sets the name of the control
Right	Gets the distance between the right edge of the control and the left edge of its container
Size	Gets or sets the height and width of the control
TabIndex	Gets or sets the tab order of this control within its container
Text	Gets or sets the text associated with this control
Top	Gets or sets the top coordinate of the control
TopLevelControl	Gets the top-level control that contains the current control
Visible	Gets or sets a value indicating whether the control is visible
Width	Gets or sets the width of the control.

CREATING A Form WITH Labels

A Label is one of the simplest GUI Control objects you can place on a Form. The Label class descends directly from Control. Typically, you use a Label control to provide descriptive text for another Control object (for example, to tell the user what pressing a Button accomplishes) or to display other text information on a Form.

Just as with Buttons, it is easier to create Forms containing Labels using the Visual Studio Integrated Development Environment (IDE). In the next steps, you begin to create an application for Bailey's Bed and Breakfast. The main Form allows the user to select one of two different suites and discover the amenities and the prices. You start by placing two Labels on a Form.

The screen images you see in the next steps represent a typical Visual Studio environment. Based on options selected in your installation, your screen might vary from the figures.

To begin to create an application for Bailey's Bed and Breakfast:

1. Open Microsoft Visual Studio. NET. You might have a desktop shortcut, or you might click **Start** on the taskbar, point to **Programs** (point to **All Programs** in Windows XP), click **Microsoft Visual Studio .NET 7.0**, and then click **Microsoft Visual Studio .NET 7.0** again.
2. Click **File** on the menu bar, point to **New**, and then click **Project**.
3. A New Project dialog box appears. In the window under Project Types, click **Visual C# Projects**. Under Templates, click **Windows Application**. Near the bottom of the New Project dialog box, click in the **Name** text box and insert **BedAndBreakfast** as the name for your application. Make sure the Location text box contains the name of the Chap08\Chapter folder of your work folder. See Figure 8-26.

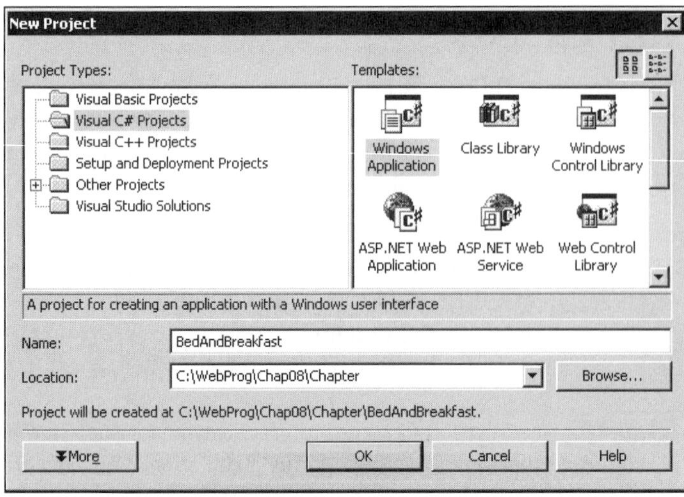

Figure 8-26 Opening a new project named BedAndBreakfast

4. Click **OK** at the bottom of the dialog box. Figure 8-27 shows the design screen that appears. The blank `Form` in the center of the screen has an empty title bar. Click on the `Form`. The lower-right corner of the screen contains a Properties window that holds a list of the `Form`'s properties. In Figure 8-27 you can see that the `Text` property is set to "Form1."

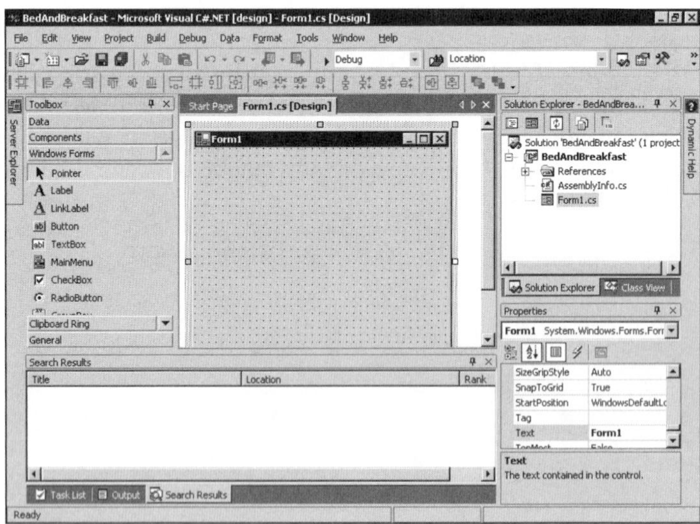

Figure 8-27 Design screen

5. In the Properties list, click on the description **Form1** in the Settings box for the `Text` property. Delete **Form1** and type **Bailey's Bed and Breakfast**. Press **Enter**; the title of the `Form` in the center of the screen changes to "Bailey's Bed and Breakfast."

6. At the left side of the design screen, you see a list of components that can be added to the `Form`. Click `Label` and drag a `Label` onto the `Form`. When you release your mouse button, the `Label` appears on the `Form` and contains the text "label1." At the right side of the screen, under Properties, make sure the list box shows that you are viewing the properties for `label1`. Change the `Text` property of `label1` to **Welcome to Bailey's**, then press **Enter**. The text of the `Label` on the `Form` changes. Drag and resize the `Label` so it is close to the position and size of the `Label` in Figure 8-28. (If you prefer to set the `Label`'s attributes manually in the Properties list, the `Location` is **64, 40** and the `Size` is **144, 23**.)

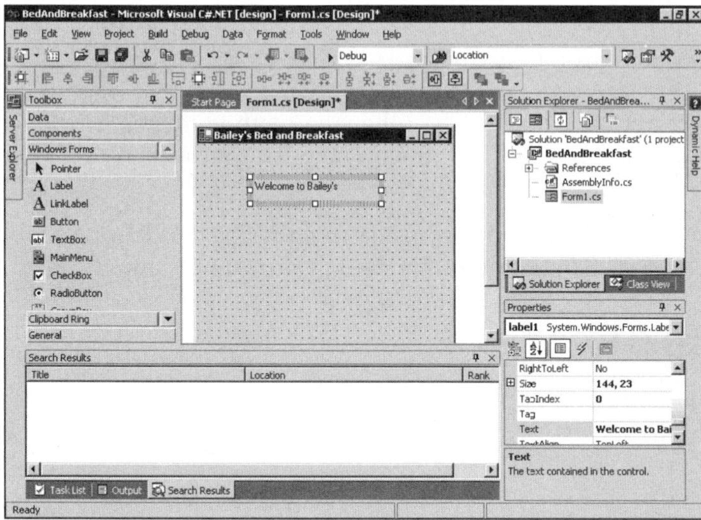

Figure 8-28 "Welcome to Bailey's" `Label`

7. Drag a second `Label` onto the `Form` as shown in Figure 8-29, then set its `Text` property to **Check our rates**. (If you prefer to set the `Label`'s attributes manually in the Properties list, the `Location` is **64, 80** and the `Size` is **100, 23**.)

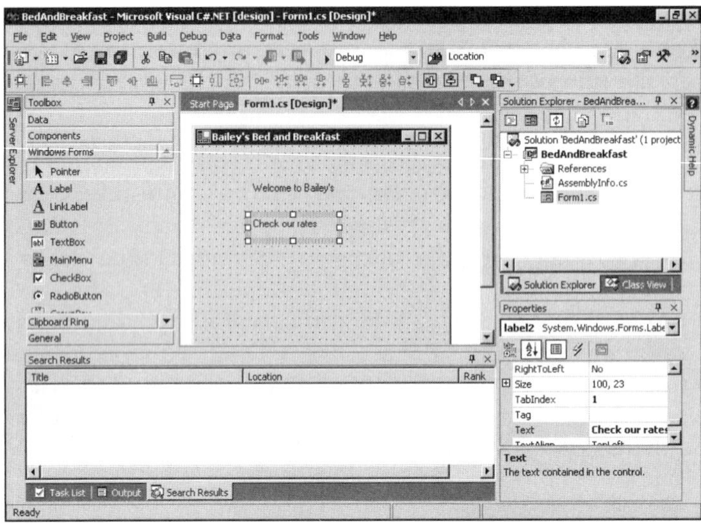

Figure 8-29 "Check our rates" `Label` added to `Form`

8. Save the project using one of the following methods: Click **File** on the menu bar and then click **Save All**, click the **Save All** button that resembles a stack of diskettes, or press **Ctrl+Shift+S**.
9. Click **Debug** on the menu bar, and then click **Start Without Debugging**, or press **Ctrl+F5**. The `Form` is displayed as shown in Figure 8-30.

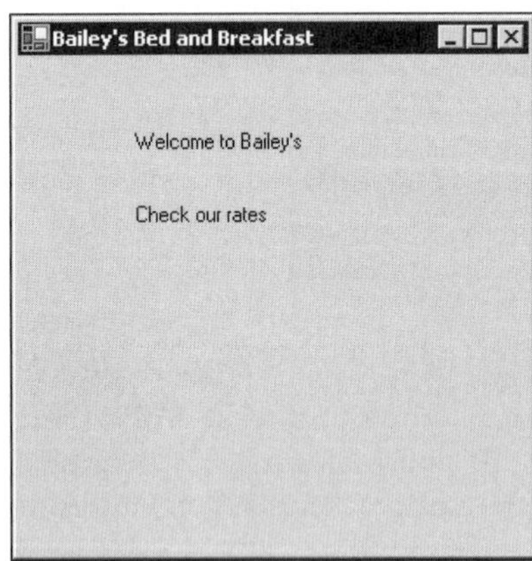

Figure 8-30 Bailey's `Form` with two `Labels`

10. Dismiss the `Form` by clicking the **Close** button in the upper-right corner of the `Form`.

SETTING A Label's Font

You use the Font class to change the appearance of printed text on your Forms. The Font class has a number of overloaded constructors. For example, you can create a Font using two arguments (a type and size) as follows:

```
Font myFavoriteFont = new Font("Times Roman", 12.5F);
```

You also can type the fully qualified Font class name, as in the following example:

```
System.Drawing.Font myFavoriteFont =
      new System.Drawing.Font("Times Roman", 12.5F);
```

However, if you include using System.Drawing; at the top of your file, you can use the shortened version of the class name.

The Font name you pass to the Font constructor is a string. The second value is a float that represents the font size. Notice that you must use an "F" (or an "f") following the Font size value constant when it contains a decimal point so the constant is recognized as a float and not a double. The Font constructor argument list contains a float variable for size; if you use a double you generate a compiler error indicating a double cannot be converted to a float.

Alternatively, you can create a Font using three arguments, adding a FontStyle, as in the following example:

```
Font aFancyFont = new Font("Arial", 24, FontStyle.Italic);
```

Table 8-3 shows a list of the available FontStyles. You can combine multiple styles using the pipe (|) (which is also called the bitwise operator). For example, the following creates a Font that is bold and underlined:

```
Font boldAndUnderlined = new
 Font("Helvetica",10, FontStyle.Bold | FontStyle.Underline);
```

Table 8-3 FontStyle enumeration

Member name	Description
Bold	Bold text
Italic	Italic text
Regular	Normal text
Strikeout	Text with a line through the middle
Underline	Underlined text

Once you have defined a Font, you can set a Label's Font with a statement such as the following:

```
label1.Font = myFavoriteFont;
```

Alternatively, you can create and assign a Font in one step without providing an identifier for the Font, as in this example:

```
label1.Font = new System.DrawingFont("Times Roman",
  12.5F);
```

If you don't provide an identifier for a Font, you can't reuse it; you have to create it again if you want to use it with additional Controls.

Of course, you can also create a Font from within the Visual Studio IDE. In the next steps, you change the Font of the Labels you have already placed on the Bailey's Bed and Breakfast Form.

To change the Font of the Labels:

1. Within the BedAndBreakfast project, click the **Welcome to Bailey's** Label on the Form. (Alternatively, select label1 from the list box under Properties in the lower-right corner of the screen.)
2. Locate the Font property in the Properties list, and click to select it, if necessary. Currently, it lists the default Font, Microsoft Sans Serif, 8.25 pt. Notice the ellipsis (three dots) at the right of the Font type. Click the ellipsis to display the Font dialog box, as shown in Figure 8-31. It shows 8 pt, Regular, Microsoft Sans Serif as the selected Font.

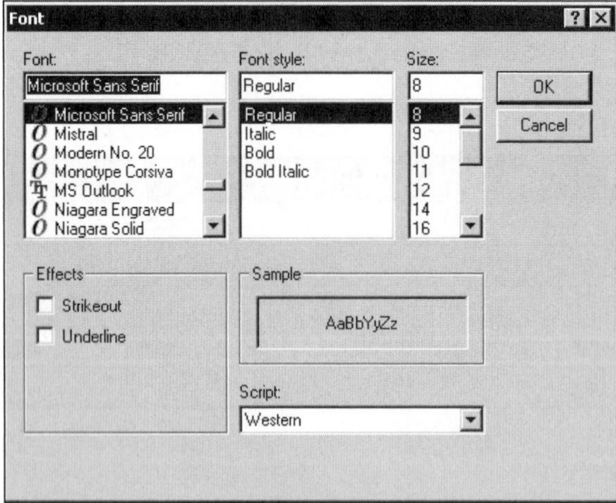

Figure 8-31 Font dialog box

3. Scroll through the Font choices and select **Lucida Calligraphy**, **Bold**, and **16** as the `Font`, `FontStyle`, and `Size`. Then click **OK**. (If Lucida Calligraphy is not available on your system, choose any other font you like.)

4. The "Welcome to Bailey's" `Label` text no longer fits in the display area allotted on the `Form`. Click the `Label` and use your mouse to drag the left, right, top, and bottom arrows until the entire welcome message appears. Figure 8-32 shows the `Form` at `Location` **16, 32** and `Size` **256, 32**.

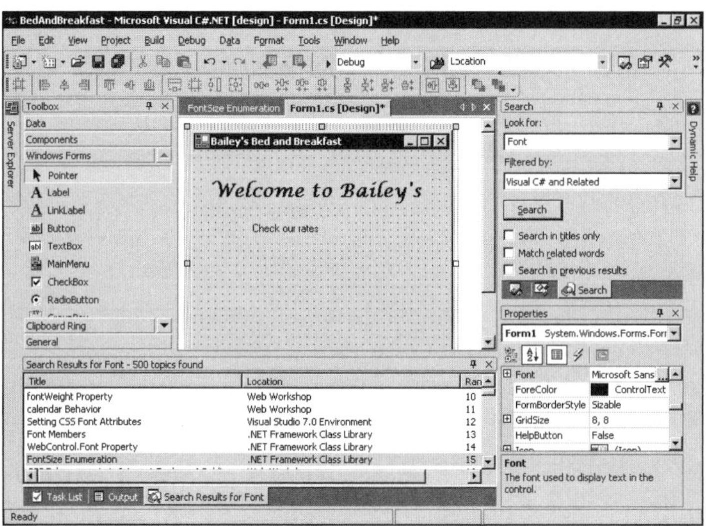

Figure 8-32 "Welcome to Bailey's" `Label` with new `Font`, `FontStyle`, and `Size`

5. Click **View** on the menu bar, and then click **Code** (or press **F7**) to view the code. Locate the line of code in which the `label1 Font` is set:

```
this.label1.Font = new System.Drawing.Font
("Lucida Calligraphy", 15.75F,
 System.Drawing.FontStyle.Bold,
 System.Drawing.GraphicsUnit.Point,
 ((System.Byte)(0)));
```

You can easily locate a line of code in a long listing by clicking Edit on the IDE menu bar and then clicking Find and Replace. Next, click Find, type in a key phrase to search for, and click the Find Next button.

The IDE creates an unnamed instance of the `Font` you selected. It uses the fully qualified `Font` class name (`System.Drawing.Font`) and a string representing the `Font` name. Notice that the point value is "15.75F" instead of 16; the IDE selects an appropriate size close to your choice. If you want the point size to be exactly 16, you can click the Expand box (+) to the left of the `Font` property in the Properties list. The list expands so you can change the `Size` property to any size you like. For now, leave it at 15.75.

The IDE also uses a more thorough version of the constructor, which includes arguments representing a `GraphicsUnit` and a byte value representing a character set. These default values can be eliminated without any change in the resulting program.

6. Change the `label2` object so its `Font` is **Lucida Sans**, **Italic**, **8**. (Choose a similar font if this one is not available.)
7. Click **View** on the menu bar, click **Designer** to return to the Designer view, if necessary, and then save the project.

ADDING `Color` TO A `Form`

The `Color` class contains a wide variety of predefined `Colors` that you can use with your `Controls`. Some of the 140 `Color` properties you can use have names such as `AliceBlue`, `FloralWhite`, and `ForestGreen`. You can search for all the available `Color` names using the Visual Studio Help Search facility.

As examples of how to use `Colors`, you can declare a `Label`'s `BackColor` and `ForeColor` properties with such statements as:

```
label1.BackColor = System.Drawing.Color.Blue;
label1.ForeColor = System.Drawing.Color.Gold;
```

Next, you change the `BackColor` property of the Bailey's Bed and Breakfast `Form`.

To change the `BackColor` property of a `Form`:

1. In the Designer view for the BedAndBreakfast project within the Visual Studio IDE, make sure **`Form1`** is selected in the Properties list.
2. Change the `BackColor` option to **`Yellow`** by clicking the `BackColor` property field, typing **Yellow** and pressing **Enter**, or by clicking the list arrow, clicking the **Web** tab, and clicking **Yellow** from the list of available colors.
3. View the code and confirm that the `Form`'s `BackColor` property is set to `Yellow`.
4. Save the project.

USING `CheckBox` AND `RadioButton` OBJECTS

You have already placed `Button` objects on a `Form`. The `Button` class derives from the `ButtonBase` class. The `ButtonBase` class has two other descendants: `CheckBox` and `RadioButton`.

CheckBox objects are GUI widgets (short for "windows gadgets") the user can click to select or deselect an option. When a Form contains multiple CheckBoxes, any number of them can be checked or unchecked at any time. RadioButtons are similar to CheckBoxes, except that when they are placed on a Form, only one RadioButton can be selected at a time—selecting any RadioButton automatically deselects the others. You can place multiple groups of RadioButtons on a Form by using a GroupBox. If you place several GroupBox Controls on a Form and place several RadioButtons in each, then, at any point in time, one RadioButton can be selected from each GroupBox; in other words, each GroupBox operates independently from any others.

Both CheckBox and RadioButton objects have a Checked property the value of which is true or false. For example, if you create a CheckBox named extraToppings and you want to add $1.00 to a pizzaPrice value when the user checks the box, you can write:

```
if (extraToppings.Checked)
 pizzaPrice = pizzaPrice + 1.00;
```


Both CheckBox and RadioButton objects also have a CheckedChanged() method that occurs when a user clicks any CheckBox or RadioButton.

In the next steps, you add two RadioButtons to the BedAndBreakfast Form so the user can select a specific, available room and view information about the room.

To add two RadioButtons to a Form:

1. In the Designer view of the BedAndBreakfast project in the Visual Studio IDE, drag a RadioButton onto the Form below the "Check our rates" Label. (See Figure 8-33 for approximate placement.) Change the Text property of the RadioButton to **BelleAire Suite**.
2. Drag a second RadioButton onto the Form beneath the first one. Change its Text property to **Lincoln Room**. See Figure 8-33.

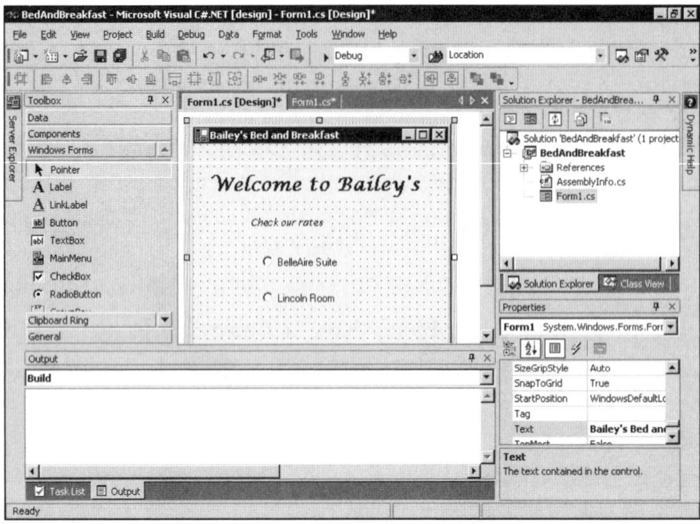

Figure 8-33 Bed and Breakfast `Form` containing two `RadioButtons`

3. Next you create two new `Forms`. One is displayed when the user selects the BelleAire Suite `RadioButton` and the other is displayed when the user selects the Lincoln Room `RadioButton`. Click **File** on the menu bar, then click **Add New Item**. From the Templates window, click **Windows Form**, and then click **Open**. A new `Form` named `Form2` appears, as shown in Figure 8-34.

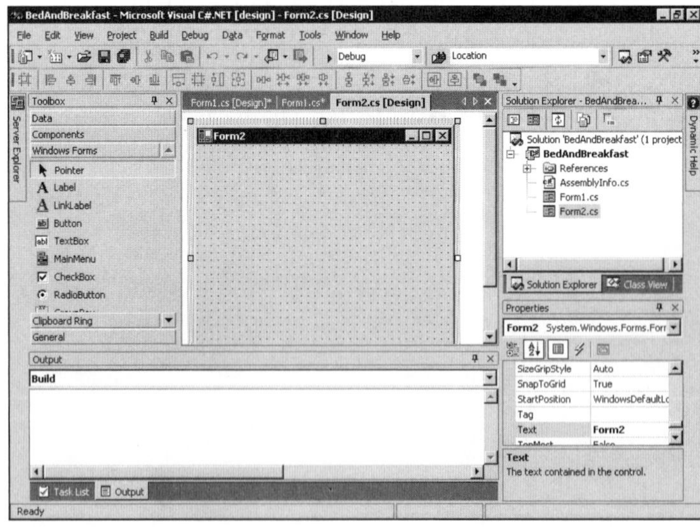

Figure 8-34 Form2

4. Change the `Text` property of the second `Form` to **BelleAire Suite**.

5. Drag a **Label** onto the Form using Figure 8-36 as a guide to approximate placement. Change the Text property of the Label to contain: **The BelleAire Suite has two bedrooms, two baths, and a private balcony**. Adjust the size of the Label so all the text is visible.
6. Drag a second **Label** onto the Form and type the price as the Text property: **$199.95 per night**.
7. Change the BackColor property of Form2 to **Yellow**.
8. In the Solution Explorer at the right of the screen, double-click **Form1**. Double-click the **BelleAire Suite** RadioButton. The program code appears in the IDE main window. Within the radioButton1_CheckedChanged() method, add an if statement that determines whether radioButton1 is checked. If it is checked, create a new instance of Form2 and display it.

```
private void radioButton1_CheckedChanged
 (object sender, System.EventArgs e)
{
 if(radioButton1.Checked)
 {
  Form2 belleAireForm = new Form2();
  belleAireForm.ShowDialog();
 }
}
```

9. Execute the program. When the BedAndBreakfast Form appears, it looks like Figure 8-35.

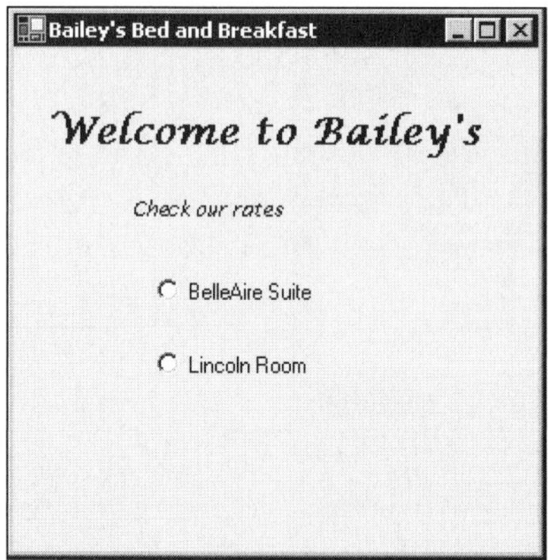

Figure 8-35 Bed and Breakfast form with RadioButtons

10. Click the **BelleAire Suite RadioButton**. The BelleAire Suite Form appears as in Figure 8-36.

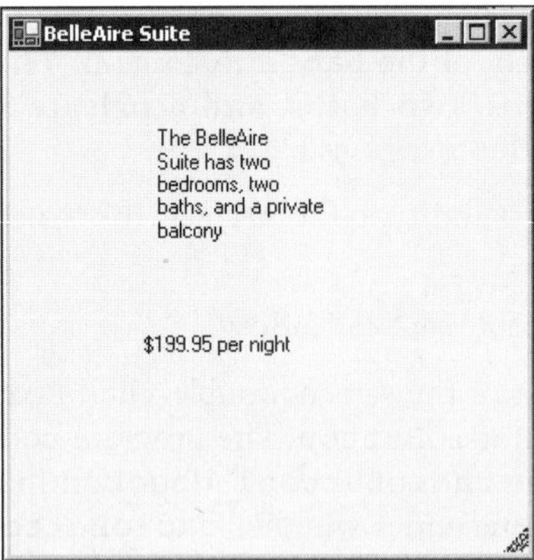

Figure 8-36 BelleAire Suite `Form`

11. Dismiss the BelleAire `Form`, then on the BedAndBreakfast `Form`, click the **Lincoln Room `RadioButton`**. Nothing happens because you have not created any action to accompany the user clicking here. Close the main form.
12. Click **File** on the menu bar, and then click **Add New Item**. Click **Windows Form** and then click **Open**. When `Form3` appears, change its `Text` property to **Lincoln Room**. Then add two `Labels` to the `Form`. The first says: **Return to the 1850s in this lovely room with private bath**. The second says: **$110.00 per night**. Change the `Form's` `BackColor` property to **White**. Resize the labels as necessary. See Figure 8-37.

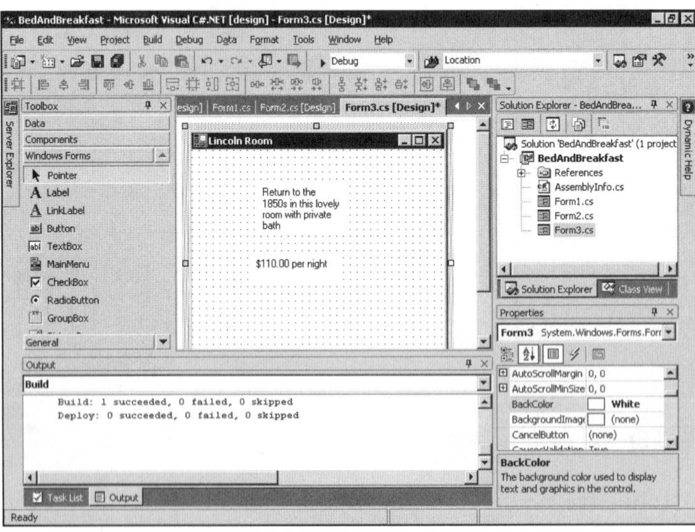

Figure 8-37 The Lincoln Room `Form`

13. In the Solution Explorer, double-click **Form1**, double-click **radioButton2** (Lincoln Room), and add the following **if** statement to the radioButton2_CheckChanged() method:

```
private void radioButton2_CheckedChanged
 (object sender, System.EventArgs e)
{
 if(radioButton2.Checked)
 {
  Form3 lincolnForm = new Form3();
  lincolnForm.ShowDialog();
 }
}
```

14. Save the project; then execute it. When the BedAndBreakfast Form appears, click either RadioButton—the appropriate informational Form is displayed. Dismiss it and click the other RadioButton. Again, the appropriate Form is displayed. Close any open forms.

Adding a PictureBox to a Form

A PictureBox is a Control in which you can display graphics from a bitmap, icon, JPEG, GIF, or other image file type. Just like a Button or a Label, you can easily add a PictureBox to a Form by dragging a Control onto the Form in the Visual Studio IDE. In the next steps, you add a PictureBox to the BedAndBreakfast application.

To add a PictureBox:

1. In the BedAndBreakfast project in the IDE, select the Lincoln Form object (**Form3**).
2. From the list of Controls on the left side of the screen, select a **PictureBox** control. (You might have to scroll down the list of controls using the down arrow key to locate the PictureBox Control.) Drag a **PictureBox Control** onto the Form.
3. Arrange the components as in Figure 8-38 so the picture box is to the left and the two labels sit to the right.

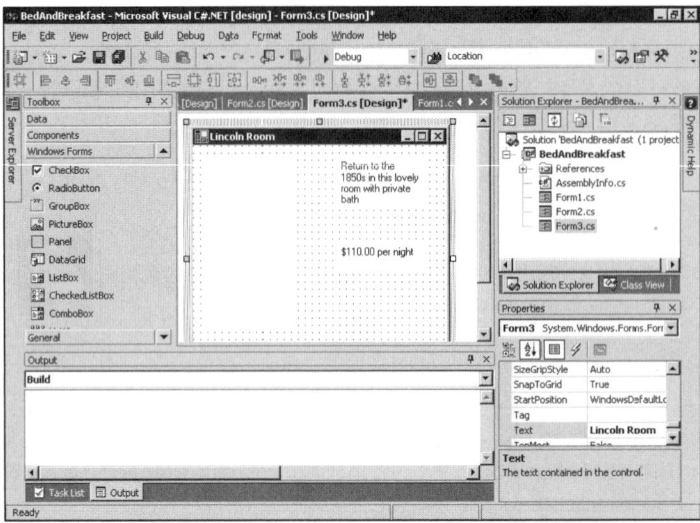

Figure 8-38 The Lincoln `Form` containing an empty `PictureBox`

4. In the Properties list for **`pictureBox1`**, select the **`Image`** property. Click the ellipsis and browse for an image. The Chap08\Chapter folder in your work folder contains a file named Lincoln_4. Click **Open** to select it. The Lincoln_4 file was obtained at *www.free-graphics.com*. You can visit the site and download other images to use in your own applications.
5. Adjust the size of the **`PictureBox`** so you can see the entire image, then save the project.
6. Execute the project. At the BedAndBreakfast **`Frame`**, click the **`RadioButton`** representing the Lincoln room. Figure 8-39 shows the result.

Figure 8-39 The Lincoln `Form` with `Image`

7. Dismiss the Lincoln Room `Form`. Dismiss the BedAndBreakfast `Form`.
8. Within the IDE, examine the code until you are comfortable with each section.
9. Exit Visual Studio.

Chapter Summary

- `Forms` provide an interface for collecting, displaying, and delivering user information. You use a `Form` to represent any window you want to display within your application. `Forms` often contain controls such as text fields, buttons, and check boxes that users can manipulate to interact with a program. You can change the appearance, size, color, and window management features of a `Form` by setting its instance fields or properties.
- Using the Visual Studio IDE, it is easy to create elaborate forms with very few keystrokes. When you use the Designer in the IDE to design your forms, you save a lot of typing, which reduces the errors you may create. However, you should attempt to understand each line of code generated.
- `Forms` often contain multiple `Button` objects; a `Form` can contain as many `Buttons` as you need. Because each `Button` has a unique identifier, you can provide unique methods to execute when a user clicks each `Button`.
- Typically, you use a `Label` control to provide descriptive text for another `Control` object.
- The `Button`, `CheckBox`, and `RadioButton` classes all descend from `ButtonBase`. `CheckBox` objects are GUI widgets the user can click to select or deselect an option.
- A `PictureBox` is a `Control` in which you can display graphics from a bitmap, icon, JPEG, GIF, or other image file type.

8

Review Questions

1. The `Form` class descends from the ________________ class.
   a. `Object`
   b. `Component`
   c. `Control`
   d. all of these

2. The `Form` class contains ______________ properties.
   a. 0
   b. 4
   c. about 100
   d. over 4,000
3. When you create a new main window, you must ______________.
   a. derive a new custom class from the base class `System.Windows.Forms.Form`
   b. write a `Main()` method that calls the `Application.Run()` method
   c. either a or b, but not both
   d. both a and b
4. When used with a component, the `System.Drawing.Size()` method takes two parameters representing ______________.
   a. width and height
   b. line thickness and horizontal position
   c. height and degrees of rotation
   d. horizontal position and width
5. A `Form`'s `Controls` are its ______________.
   a. static methods
   b. nonstatic methods
   c. manipulatable components
   d. parents
6. For a `Button` to be clickable, you ______________.
   a. need only to add the `Button` to a `Form`
   b. use the `System.Windows.Forms.Control` class
   c. include a `GUIImplement()` method within your program
   d. write a method named `ClickButton()`
7. The main reason to use the Visual Studio Integrated Development Environment is to ______________.
   a. use methods that are not available when you write code by hand
   b. have access to the Studio's private data types
   c. make the program design process easier
   d. all of these

8. When you begin to create a `Form` using the Visual Studio IDE, the default `Form` name is ________________.
   a. MyForm
   b. IDEForm
   c. Form1
   d. null
9. When you design a `Form` using the IDE, ________________.
   a. much less code is generated than when you design a `Form` by hand
   b. the generated code is written in machine language so you cannot read it
   c. you cannot alter the generated code
   d. none of these
10. If a `Form` contains a `Button` named `agreeButton`, then you code the actions to be performed when the user clicks the `Button` in a method named ________________.
    a. `ButtonClick()`
    b. `Button_Click()`
    c. `agreeButtonClick()`
    d. `agreeButton_Click()`
11. All `Control` objects descend from the ________________ class.
    a. `Form`
    b. `Component`
    c. `ButtonBase`
    d. all of these
12. The `Control` you use to provide descriptive text for another `Control` object is a ________________.
    a. `Form`
    b. `Label`
    c. `CheckBox`
    d. `MessageBox`
13. Which of the following creates a `Label` named `firstLabel`?
    a. `firstLabel = new firstLabel();`
    b. `Label = new firstLabel();`
    c. `Label firstLabel = new Label();`
    d. `Label firstLabel = Label();`

14. The property that determines what the user reads on a `Label` is the ________________ property.
    a. `Text`
    b. `Label`
    c. `Phrase`
    d. `Setting`
15. Assume you have created a `Label` named `myLabel`. Which of the following sets `myLabel`'s background color to green?
    a. `myLabel = BackColor.System.Drawing.Color.Green;`
    b. `myLabel.BackColor = System.Drawing.Color.Green;`
    c. `myLabel.Green = System.DrawingColor;`
    d. `myLabel.Background = new Color.Green;`

Hands-on Exercises

If necessary, use Windows Explorer to create a new folder in the Chap08 folder in your work folder. Name this folder **Exercises**. Save the programs that you create in these Exercises in the Chap08\Exercises folder in your work folder.

Exercise 8-1

Using the Visual Studio IDE, create a `Form` that contains a button labeled "About". When a user clicks the button, display a `MessageBox` containing your personal copyright statement for the program. Save the program as **About.cs**.

Exercise 8-2

Create a `Form` containing two buttons for a book publisher. If a user selects the "Paperback" button, display a `MessageBox` that contains a book price of $6.99. If the user selects "Hardback," display $24.99. Save the program as **Book.cs**.

Exercise 8-3

Create a game `Form` containing six buttons. Display different prizes depending on the button the user selects. Save the program as **Game.cs**.

Exercise 8-4

Create a `Form` containing two `Buttons`, one labeled "Stop" and one labeled "Go". Add a `Label` telling the user to press a button. When the user presses Stop, change the `BackColor` of the `Form` to `Red`; when the user presses Go, change the `BackColor` of the `Form` to `Green`. Save the program as **StopGo.cs**.

Exercise 8-5

Create a `Form` containing at least five `RadioButton` objects, each labeled with a color. When the user selects a `RadioButton`, change the `BackColor` of the `Form` appropriately. Save the program as **FiveColors.cs**.

WEB PROGRAMMING PROJECTS

If necessary, use Windows Explorer to create a new folder in the Chap08 folder in your work folder. Name this folder **Projects**. Save the programs that you create in these Projects in the Chap08\Projects folder in your work folder.

Project 8-1

Create a `Form` for a video store. The `Form` contains a `ListBox` that lists the titles of at least eight videos available to rent. Allow users to select as many videos as they want. When they press a `Button` indicating they are done, display the total rental price, which is $2.50 per video. Save the file as **Video.cs**.

8

Project 8-2

Create a `Form` with two `ListBox`es—one contains at least four `Font` names and the other contains at least four `Font` sizes. Let the first item in each list be the default selection if the user fails to make a selection. When the user selects a new `Font` or size, display "Hello" in the selected `Font` and size. Save the program as **FontSelector.cs**.

Project 8-3

Create a `Form` for a car rental company. Allow the user to choose a car model (compact, standard, or luxury) and a number of days (1 through 7). After users make their selections, display the total rental charge, which is $19.95 per day for a compact car, $24.95 per day for a standard car, and $39.00 per day for a luxury car. Save the file as **CarRental.cs**.

CHAPTER

9

ASP.NET: PART I

In this chapter you will:

- Build Web forms using ASP.NET
- Explore ASP.NET server controls
- Use ASP.NET controls to build Web forms
- Understand the code behind the page

ASP.NET dramatically simplifies building powerful forms-based Web pages. When building these pages, you can use ASP.NET server controls to create user interfaces that appear as HTML forms on your browser. You can then write server-side code to access the forms and implement application logic. ASP.NET server controls enable you to build Web pages with far less code than when using traditional ASP, CGI, and PERL programming. ASP.NET server controls make it easy to display data, validate user input, access databases, and upload files, tasks that would otherwise require programs with hundreds of lines of code. The first time an ASP.NET Web page is required, it is compiled into a .NET class, and then the resulting class is used to process incoming requests, which improves the performance of your Web applications.

ASP.NET also lets you leverage your current programming language skills. You can write ASP.NET Web applications in any .NET compatible language, including Visual Basic .NET, C#, and JScript .NET

In this chapter, you learn how to convert existing HTML files into ASP.NET pages and how to use ASP.NET server controls to build Web forms. You learn how to handle events to respond to users interacting with your Web forms, and you learn how to bind database tables to list controls and use these controls to display data in the tables. You also learn how to use code behind the page to separate the code associated with a Web page code from its content.

Building Web Forms Using ASP.NET

ASP.NET Web pages are text files with an .aspx filename extension. The first time a browser requests an ASP.NET page, the page is compiled into a .NET class. Then the Web server uses the resulting class to process incoming requests. When you request the same ASP.NET page in the future, the corresponding class file is executed to process requests.

You can create an ASP.NET page simply by changing the extension of an HTML file to .aspx; you do not need to modify the code. In the following section, you will create your first ASP.NET page.

Writing Your First ASP.NET Page

The first ASP.NET page you will write displays a greeting and the current date and time on the Web server.

To create a simple greeting on an ASP.NET page:

1. If necessary, use Windows Explorer to create a new folder in the Chap09 folder in your work folder. Name this folder **Chapter**.
2. Open a new document in a text editor, such as Notepad, and type the following code:

```
<%@ Page language="VB" %>
<html>
<head>
<title>Welcome to ASP.NET</title>
<script runat="server">
  sub Page_Load(source as Object, e as EventArgs)
    TimeLabel.Text = DateTime.Now.ToString()
  end sub
</script>
</head>
<body>
<h2>Welcome to ASP.NET!</h2>
The current date and time on the Web server are:
<asp:Label id="TimeLabel" runat="server" />
</body>
</html>
```

3. Save the file as **example1.aspx** in the Chap09\Chapter folder in your work folder.

When you save a file with Notepad, be sure to click the Save as type list arrow in the Save As dialog box and then select All Types as the value. Otherwise, Notepad automatically adds the extension .txt to the name of your file. You can also explicitly type quotation marks around a filename (as in "example1.aspx"). Most editors save the file as you specify, without adding their own extension.

The page example1.aspx contains HTML tags and some ASP.NET code. The first line `<%@ Page language="VB" %>` uses a page directive to specify the language used for this page. **Page directives** enable you to select settings that apply to the entire page. For example, you can use page directives to set the default language for the ASP.NET page, enable or disable the session state, or choose to buffer the contents of the page before sending it to the client. If you use a page directive, it must be located in the first line of an ASP.NET page. A page directive always contains <% %> tags and begins with the @ character. Following is the syntax used for page directives:

<%@ *Page attribute="value"* [*attribute="value"* ...] %>

For example, you can use the buffer attribute to determine whether HTTP response buffering is enabled. Setting buffer to true enables page buffering; setting it to false disables page buffering.

You can write ASP.NET code by using any programming language that the .NET platform supports. For example, you can use VB .NET, C#, or JScript to code your ASP.NET pages. The ASP.NET chapters in this book primarily use VB .NET and C# examples. The example1.aspx is written in VB .NET; following is its C# version:

9

```
<%@ Page language="C#" %>
<html>
<head>
<title>Welcome to ASP.NET</title>
<script runat="server">
  void Page_Load(Object sender, EventArgs e)
   {
    TimeLabel.Text = DateTime.Now.ToString();
   }
</script>
</head>
<body>
<h2>Welcome to ASP.NET!</h2>
The current date and time on the Web server are:
<asp:Label id="TimeLabel" runat="server" />
</body>
</html>
```

Consider the following code in example1.aspx:

```
<script runat="server">
  sub Page_Load(source as Object, e as EventArgs)
    TimeLabel.Text = DateTime.Now.ToString()
  end sub
</script>
```

This VB .NET code defines scripts that are executed in the Web server. To execute scripts on the Web server, you must use the `runat="server"` attribute within the opening <script> tag. Inside the script tags, a procedure called Page_Load is defined, which is the first method called on any ASP.NET page whenever it is loaded. Within the procedure, the execution of the code `TimeLabel.Text = DateTime.Now.ToString()` retrieves the current date and time on the Web server, and the date and time are converted into a string and then assigned to the Label control.

The line `<asp:Label id="TimeLabel" runat="server" />` defines a server control in ASP.NET. **Server controls** are elements of ASP.NET Web pages that you can access with server-side code; they are covered in more detail later in this chapter. The `runat="server"` attribute means that ASP.NET is responsible for turning the tag into a command that the Web browser can understand. You will examine how the ASP.NET does so in the following section.

Next, you learn how ASP.NET pages are processed on the Web server and produce output to client browsers.

Processing Client Requests

When you type a URL in the address box or location box of a Web browser and press Enter, or when you click a text or image link on a Web page, you are sending a page request to a Web server. A **Web server** is simply a computer that provides services, such as locating the requested file and sending it back to a client on the Internet or a local intranet or extranet. A Web server can accept and process requests for Web pages, images, executable programs, and other files. The Web server responds to each request differently, based on the requested file type. When a Web server receives a request for a Web page, it first checks to see whether the page exists in the server system (either on disk or memory). If the page is an HTML file (with extension .html or .htm), an image file, or text file, the Web server sends the page to the client browser, which then interprets and displays the page. If the page is an ASP.NET Web page, the ASP.NET code is executed on the Web server and creates regular HTML, which is sent to the client browser. Test the first example to see what it displays on your browser.

To test the example1.aspx Web page:

1. Open your browser.
2. In the Address box, type the following text:
   http://*localhost*/*workfolder*/Chap09/Chapter/example1.aspx
   Be sure to replace *localhost* with the name of your server. For example, if your server's name is www.course.com, replace *localhost* with www.course.com. Similarly, if your server's name is localhost, then replace *localhost* with localhost. Also replace *workfolder* with the name of your work folder.
3. Press **Enter**. The page is displayed as shown in Figure 9-1. The current date and time on the Web server are displayed on your browser.

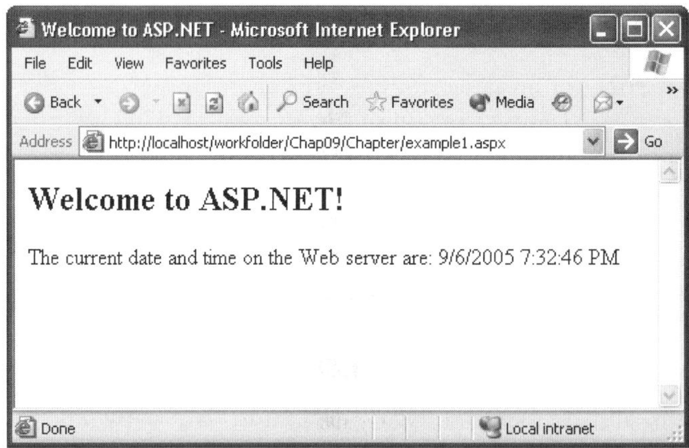

Figure 9-1 Current date and time on the Web server

4. Reload this page by pressing the **F5** key or by clicking the **Refresh** button on the browser's toolbar. The Web server time is updated on the page.

The browser requests the example1.aspx page by sending a URL to the Web server. When the Web server receives the request, it retrieves the page from the Chap09\Chapter folder, the code is executed on the server, and the output is sent to your browser. Figure 9-2 shows the source code displayed on your browser.

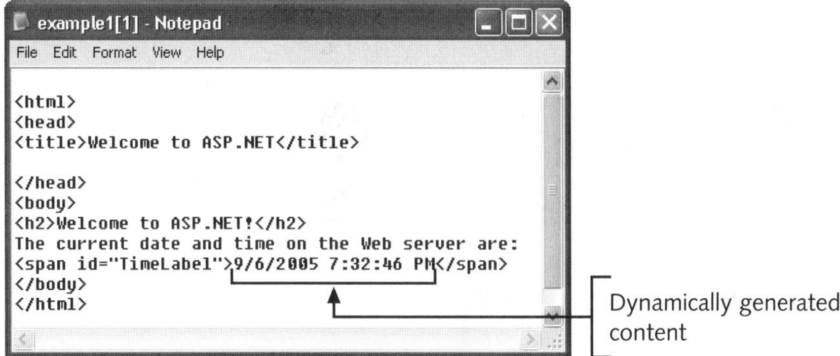

Figure 9-2 Source code sent to your browser

The content sent to your browser is nothing more than regular HTML. However, part of the content is dynamically generated upon request. In this example, the dynamic content is the current date and time on the Web server. You may wonder how the dynamic content is generated. As mentioned earlier, the method Page_Load is automatically invoked every time this page is loaded, and the execution of the code within this method generates the current date and time on the Web server and assigns them to the Label control.

Exploring ASP.NET Server Controls

ASP.NET server controls are reusable components that can perform the same work as traditional HTML controls. However, unlike traditional HTML controls, you can access the ASP.NET controls through a .NET programming language using server-side code, just as you can any other .NET object or class. This can be helpful when you want to respond to events and get or set properties, for example. ASP.NET server controls use a taglike syntax for declaring the various controls used on an ASP.NET Web page. For example, in example1.aspx, a Label server control, `<asp:Label id="TimeLabel" runat="server" />`, uses server-side code to display the time.

ASP.NET provides several controls, including the HTML server control, Web form controls, validation controls, and list controls. ASP.NET controls provide the dynamic and interactive portions of the user interface for your Web pages. These controls render the content, usually HTML, which is sent and displayed on client browsers. In the following steps, you work with an ASP.NET control that renders HTML.

To create a simple ASP.NET page with an ASP.NET control:

1. Open a new document in Notepad and type the following code:

```
<html>
<head>
<title>A simple ASP.NET control</title>
</head>
<body>
<form runat="server">
<asp:TextBox id="txtControl" runat="server" />
<asp:Button id="btnControl" runat="server"
   Text="A button control"/>
</form>
</html>
```

2. Save this file as **example2.aspx** in the Chap09\Chapter folder of your work folder. Then close the document.

3. Load this page using the following URL. Be sure to replace *localhost* with the name of your server and substitute the name of your work folder where *workfolder* appears.

   http://*localhost*/*workfolder*/Chap09/Chapter/example2.aspx

   The page is displayed, as shown in Figure 9-3.

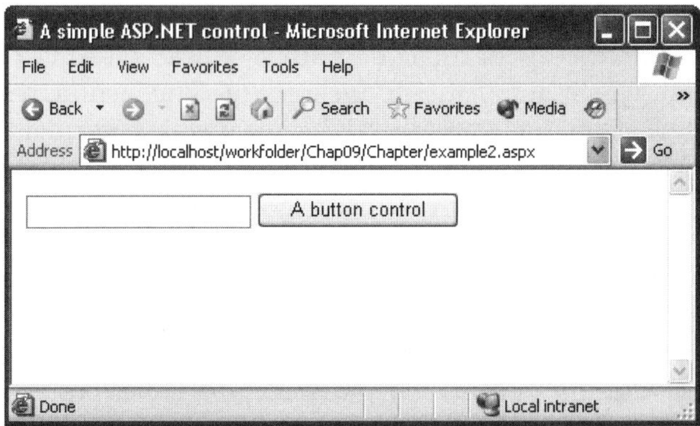

Figure 9-3 Simple ASP.NET button control

In the code used to create this page, the attribute `runat="server"` is added to the form tag. Some ASP.NET controls must be placed within form tags; otherwise, the Web page is not compiled. For example, if you remove the `runat="server"` attribute of the form and reload this page, you receive an error message. The elements placed in the form tags are ASP.NET TextBox and Button controls:

```
<asp:TextBox id="txtControl" runat="server" />
<asp:Button id="btnControl" runat="server"
    Text="A button control" />
```

Now examine the source code on your browser, shown in Figure 9-4.

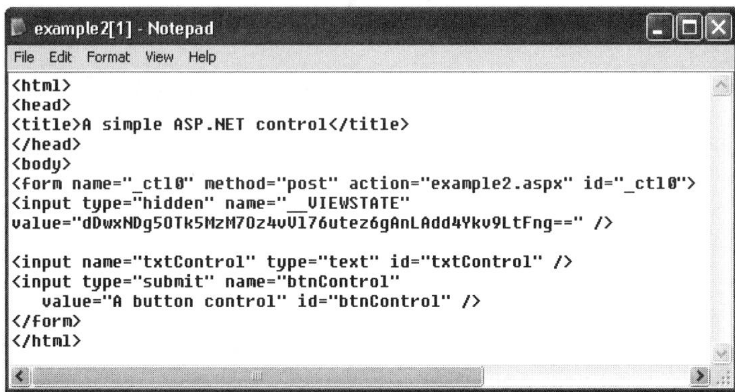


```
<html>
<head>
<title>A simple ASP.NET control</title>
</head>
<body>
<form name="_ctl0" method="post" action="example2.aspx" id="_ctl0">
<input type="hidden" name="__VIEWSTATE"
value="dDwxNDg5OTk5MzM7Oz4vVl76utez6gAnLAdd4Ykv9LtFng==" />

<input name="txtControl" type="text" id="txtControl" />
<input type="submit" name="btnControl"
   value="A button control" id="btnControl" />
</form>
</html>
```

Figure 9-4 HTML code rendered by an ASP.NET control

To view source code in Internet Explorer, click View on the menu bar, and then click Source. If you use Netscape Navigator, click View on the menu bar, and then click Page Source.

Note that the server controls are converted to their HTML equivalents. For example, the server-side form, which is specified with the code `<form runat="server">`, is converted to an HTML form, which automatically includes method, action, name, and id attributes. You can add these attributes in an ASP.NET page if you want to, although they are not necessary. If you do not specify the method attribute, POST is used by default. This is in contrast to ASP, the previous Active Server Pages technology, where the default method for forms is GET. Note that you cannot change the action attribute in ASP.NET. If you set the action attribute of a server-side form, it is ignored. The TextBox control is converted into a standard Text input field and the Button control is converted into a standard submit button. Also, instead of the name attribute in each control, you use the id attribute. For each control with the runat=server attribute, the server processes it before sending it to the browser. The result of this server processing is shown in the HTML code that is sent when the page is requested for the first time. Although you can programmatically access these controls on the server, doing so doesn't affect how the code is presented on the client. It's still standard HTML, with standard forms and elements.

In the rendered HTML page, ASP.NET adds a hidden input field, which contains the state of the server controls. This is called the **ViewState**, which ASP.NET uses to manage the content of the controls. With ViewState, when you submit a server-side form, the data entered into (or programmatically assigned to) all ASP.NET controls is preserved when the form is displayed again. For example, if you enter data into the text input box and then click the button on the page, the ViewState automatically preserves the form information you entered. The ViewState is preserved only if a server-side form is posted back to itself; otherwise, all the ViewState information is lost. Only ASP.NET controls can preserve ViewState information. Regular HTML elements cannot preserve previously entered data. In the following steps, you examine the difference between ASP.NET controls and regular HTML controls.

To test whether a regular HTML control can preserve ViewState data:

1. In Notepad or another text editor, open **example3.txt**, which is located in the Chap09\Chapter folder in your work folder.
2. Save the file as **example3.aspx** in the same location.
3. Add the code that appears bold in Figure 9-5.
4. Save the file and close the document.
5. Load this page using the following URL. Be sure to replace *localhost* with the name of your server, and *workfolder* with the name of your work folder.

   http://*localhost*/*workfolder*/Chap09/Chapter/example3.aspx

   The page is displayed, as shown in Figure 9-6.

```
<html>
<head>
<title>ASP.NET control & regular HTML control</title>
</head>
<body>
<form id="form1" runat="server" >
ASP.NET control:<asp:TextBox id="txtControl" runat="server" /><br>
Regular HTML control:<input type="text" name="txtHTMLctl"><br>
<asp:Button id="btnControl" runat="server"
   Text="Submit"/>
</form>
</html>
```

Figure 9-5 Example3.aspx code

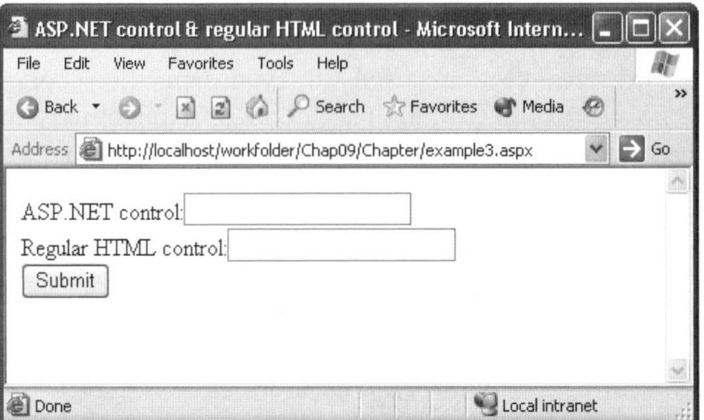

Figure 9-6 View state of an ASP.NET control and regular HTML control

6. Enter data into both the ASP.NET control text box and the regular HTML text box, and then click the **Submit** button to submit the form. The data entered into the ASP.NET control is preserved when this page is displayed again, while the data entered into the regular HTML control is lost.

Handling Control Events

Like any visual programming language, ASP.NET is an event-driven, server-side programming language. In other words, ASP.NET controls can generate events when clients interact with them. When a user interacts with an ASP.NET control, it triggers an event corresponding to that control. For example, a Button control triggers an onClick event after being clicked; a ListBox control triggers an onSelectedIndexChanged event when its list selection changes; a TextBox control triggers an onTextChanged event when its text changes, and a DropDown List control triggers an onSelectedIndexChanged event when its list selection changes. You can assign event handlers to respond to events that an ASP.NET server control may trigger. An **event handler** is a method called as a result of specific events. To execute code in response to the events an ASP.NET server control triggers, you include the code in its event handler.

Events and event handlers are extremely useful for Web applications because they provide a mechanism for dynamically responding to events when clients interact with your Web pages. You can write event handlers to perform any special logic or processing that the form or control calls for. The syntax to handle an event is as follows:

Event = "*event handler*"

For example, you can use the following code to handle an onClick event of a button with an event handler called btnClickHandler:

```
<asp:Button id="btnSubmit" runat="server"
     onClick="btnClickHandler" Text="Submit"/>
```

An event handler is a method that follows certain rules. By convention, event handlers accept two parameters of the Object and EventArgs types. The first parameter passed to an event handler represents the source that raised the event, and the second parameter is the data about the event. You can use the first parameter to determine who raised the event. Therefore, an event handler takes the following form in VB .NET:

Sub *EventHandlerName*(source as Object, e as EventArgs)
  'Code goes here.
End Sub

An event handler takes the following form in C#:

void *EventHandlerName*(Object source, EventArgs e){
  //Code goes here.
}

In the following steps, you write an event handler to execute code that responds to the OnClick event, which is triggered when the button is clicked. Specifically, your page displays a message to inform a user that the code in the event handler is executed when the user clicks the button.

To write an event handler using VB .NET syntax:

1. Open a new document in Notepad and type the following code:

```
<html>
<head>
<script runat="server">
Sub Button_Click(s as Object, e as EventArgs)
  lblMessage.Text = "Hi " & txtName.Text & ":" & _
    " You have clicked the button and the handler " & _
    "is called to respond to the OnClick event."
End Sub
</script>
<html>
<head>
```

```
<title>Event and event handler</title>
</head>
<body>
<form runat="server" >
Name:<asp:TextBox id="txtName" runat="server" columns="10" />
<asp:Button id="btnControl" runat="server"
   Text="Click Me!" OnClick="Button_Click" />
<br><br>
<asp:Label id="lblMessage" runat="server" />
</form>
</body>
</html>
```

2. Save this file as **example4.aspx** in the Chap09\Chapter folder in your work folder.

3. Load this page using the following URL. Be sure to enter your server name and work folder as appropriate.

   http://*localhost*/*workfolder*/Chap09/Chapter/example4.aspx

4. Enter your name in the Name input box, and then click the **Click Me** button. A page similar to Figure 9-7 appears.

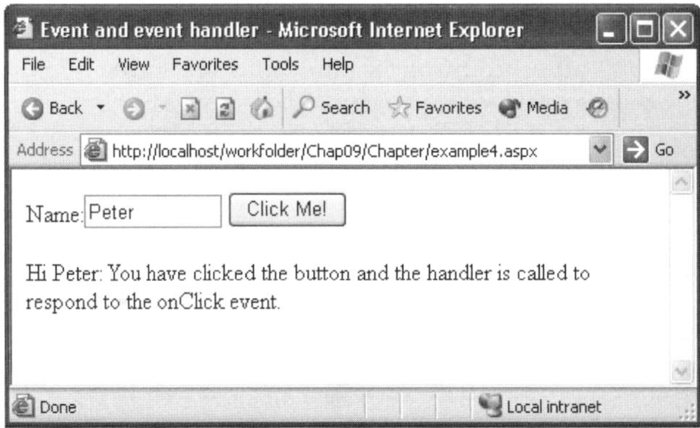

Figure 9-7 Event handler

In this example, the code declares three ASP.NET controls. The TextBox control allows users to provide their names; the Button control is for submitting the form and triggering the onClick event when the button is clicked; and the Label control is used to display a message. The code `<asp:Button id="btnControl" runat="server" Text= "Click Me!" onClick="Button_Click" />` handles the onClick event raised by the button by associating the event handler, Button_Click, with the event. When the button is clicked, it raises the onClick event and its event handler is invoked. To associate an event handler with an event, you simply assign the event handler name to the event without providing parameters for the method.

In this example, you defined the event handler Button_Click to update the label text as follows:

```
Sub Button_Click(s as Object, e as EventArgs)
  lblMessage.Text = "Hi " & txtName.Text & ":" & _
    " You have clicked the button and the handler " & _
    "is called to respond to the onClick event."
End Sub
```

The code within the method gets the user's name combined with existing text and assigns the message to the Text property of the Label control. The symbol & (ampersand) is the string-concatenating operator in VB .NET, which is used to combine strings. The symbol _ (underscore) is the line-continuation character. To improve readability, the line-continuation character splits the long line over several lines.

To programmatically access an ASP.NET control, the id attribute must be set to that control, as in `<asp:Button id="btnControl" runat="server"/>`. Then you use the id attribute to access that control with ASP.NET code.

The following code shows the C# version of example4.aspx:

```
<script language="C#" runat="server">
void Button_Click(Object s, EventArgs e){
  lblMessage.Text = "Hi " + txtName.Text + ":" +
    " You have clicked the button and the handler " +
    "is called to respond to the onClick event.";
}
</script>
<html>
<head>
<title>Event and event handler</title>
</head>
<body>
<form runat="server" >
Name:<asp:TextBox id="txtName" runat="server" columns="10" />
<asp:Button id="btnControl" runat="server"
   Text="Click Me!" onClick="Button_Click" />
<br><br>
<asp:Label id="lblMessage" runat="server" />
</form>
</body>
</html>
```

USING ASP.NET SERVER CONTROLS TO CREATE WEB FORMS

ASP.NET controls fall into two categories: HTML server controls and ASP.NET Web controls. ASP.NET server controls run on the server and determine the user interface and other related functionality, which greatly enhances the Web forms.

Building Forms with HTML Server Controls

HTML server controls correspond directly to various HTML tags. They offer the following features:

- You can access HTML server controls programmatically on the Web server using object-oriented programming language techniques. Each HTML control is an object; you can access its various properties and methods with ASP.NET code.
- You can use HTML controls to write event handlers that execute code in response to certain events.
- When data is posted to the server, the data entered into the HTML controls is automatically maintained by participating in the ViewState.
- HTML controls enable you to separate the design content of a page from the application logic by using code behind the page (covered in this chapter).
- HTML controls can detect browser types and maintain browser compatibility.
- You can use validation controls to validate HTML controls.

You can convert any HTML page to an ASP.NET page by simply changing the .htm or .html filename extension to .aspx. However, HTML elements within an ASP.NET file are treated as literal text, so you cannot programmatically access these HTML elements. To do so, you need to convert the elements to HTML server controls. You can convert any HTML tag into its corresponding HTML server control by adding the `runat="server"` attribute to the tag. However, to reference an HTML server control in a program, you must set the id attribute for the control. By converting existing HTML tags to HTML server controls, you can access controls from the server.

All HTML server controls must be placed within a <form> tag with the runat="server" attribute.

HTMLInputText is a common server-side control that maps to the <input type=text> and <input type=password> HTML elements, and allows you to create a single-line text box to receive user input.

You can use server-side code to access the HTMLInputText controls. As with standard HTML, you can use these controls to enter user names and passwords in HTML forms.

You can use this control with the HTMLInputButton, HTMLInputImage, or HTMLButton control to process user input on the server.

The syntax to create HTMLInputText control is as follows:

```
<input type=text | password
    id=“control_ID”
    maxLength=“max#ofcharacters”
    size=“widthoftextbox”
    value=“defaulttextboxcontents”
   onServerChange=“serverChangeEventHandler”
    runat=“server” >
```

Among the various attributes, id and runat are required and all others are optional. The maxlength attribute controls the number of characters that can be entered; the size attribute controls the width of the control displayed on browser; and the value attribute specifies the content of the control. The HTMLInputText control contains a ServerChange event that is raised when the contents of the control change between posts to the server. This event is often used to validate the text entered in the control.

HTMLTextArea creates a server-side control that maps to the <textarea> HTML element and allows you to create a multi-line text box. The syntax to create an HTMLTextArea is as follows:

```
<TextArea id=“control_ID”
      cols=“numberofcolsintextarea”
      rows=“numberofrowsintextarea”
      onserverchange=“onserverchangehandler”
      runat=“server” >
      TextArea content goes here
</TextArea>
```

This control allows you to create a multi-line text box. The dimensions of the text box are controlled by the Cols and Rows properties. The Cols property determines the width of the control, while the Rows property determines the height of the control.

You use HTMLInputButton to create a server-side control that maps to the <input type=button>, <input type=submit>, and <input type=reset> HTML elements to create a command button, submit button, or reset button, respectively.

The syntax to create the HTMLInputButton is as follows:

```
<input type=button | submit | reset
    id=“control_ID”
    OnServerClick=“onserverclickhandler”
   value=“buttonlabel”
    runat=“server” >
```

When a user clicks an HTMLInputButton control, the form containing the control is posted to the server and processed. A response is then sent back to the requesting browser.

The HTMLInputButton control contains a serverClick event that is raised when the control is clicked. By providing a custom event handler for the serverClick event, you can perform a specific set of instructions when the control is clicked.

A reset button does not support the serverClick event. When a reset button is clicked, all input controls on the page are not necessarily cleared. Instead, they are returned to their original value when the page was loaded. For example, if a text box originally contained the value "ASP.NET," clicking the reset button would return the text box to this value.

In the following steps, you create a page to collect comments from clients. This page contains two input fields and a button. The text input field accepts a client's e-mail address; the TextArea is for entering comments.

To create a page using HTML server controls:

1. Open the file **example5.txt** located in the Chap09\Chapter folder in your work folder.
2. To create HTML server controls, add the code that appears bold in Figure 9-8.

```
<%@ Page Language="VB" %>
<html>
<script runat="server">
Sub SubmitBtn_Click(sender As Object, e as EventArgs)
  message.visible = true
  message.InnerHTML = ""
  if(email.Value = "")
    message.InnerHTML = "<li>E-mail address is required!</li>"
  end if
  if(comments.value = "")
    message.InnerHTML = message.InnerHTML & _
        "<li>Please enter your comments.</li>"
  end if
  if(Message.InnerHTML = "")
     myform.visible = false
     message.InnerHtml = "Thanks for your comments."
  else
     message.InnerHtml = "Error message:<br>" & message.InnerHtml
  end if
End Sub
</script>
<body>
<form id="myform" runat="server">
  E-mail address:
  <input id="email" type=text size=20 runat="server"><br>
  Comments:<br>
  <TextArea id="comments" cols=30
    rows=4 runat="server"></TextArea><br>
  <input type=submit value="Submit"
      OnServerClick="SubmitBtn_Click" runat="server">
  <input type=reset runat="server">
</form>
<span id="message" runat="server" visible="false"></span>
</body>
</html>
```

Figure 9-8 Example5.aspx code

3. Save the file as **example5.aspx** in the same location.
4. Load this page using the following URL. Be sure to replace the italicized text with your server name and work folder as appropriate.

   http://*localhost*/*workfolder*/Chap09/Chapter/example5.aspx

   The page is displayed, as shown in Figure 9-9.

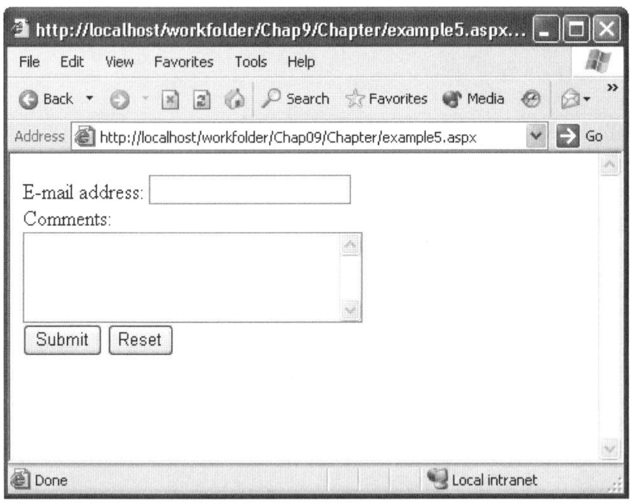

Figure 9-9 HTML server control form

5. Click the **Submit** button without entering any data to the form. An error message appears on the bottom of the page.
6. Enter your e-mail address and some comments, and then click the **Submit** button. The page displays "Thanks for your comments."

In the previous steps, the following code created the HTML server controls:

```
<input id="email" type=text size=20 runat="server">
<TextArea id="comments" cols=30 rows=4 runat="server"></TextArea>
<input type=submit value="Submit"
   onServerClick="SubmitBtn_Click" runat="server">
<input type=reset runat="server">
<span id="message" runat="server" visible="false"></span>
```

The id attributes of the Text, TextArea, and span are provided. To access the HTML server controls in the server-side code, the id attributes of the controls must be set. Then you use their ids to reference these controls. When these server controls are rendered into their corresponding regular HTML controls, ASP.NET adds name attributes and uses the id as the name attribute value. For example, the HTML server control `<input id="email" type=text size=20 runat="server">` outputs the HTML code: `<input name="email" id="email" type="text" size="20" />`. By using the HTML server controls in your Web form, you can manipulate these controls in the server-side code as the event handler does in the steps.

The following shows the C# version of the code:

```
<%@ Page Language="C#" %>
<html>
<script runat="server">
```

```
void SubmitBtn_Click(Object s, EventArgs e){
  message.Visible = true;
  message.InnerHtml = "";
  if(email.Value == ""){
    message.InnerHtml = "<li>E-mail address is required!</li>";
  }
  if(comments.Value == ""){
    message.InnerHtml  = message.InnerHtml +
        "<li>Please enter your comments.</li>";
  }
  if(message.InnerHtml  == ""){
     myform.Visible = false;
     message.InnerHtml = "Thanks for your comments.";
  }else{
     message.InnerHtml = "Error message:<br>" + message.InnerHtml;
  }
}
</script>
<body>
<form id="myform" runat="server">
  E-mail address:
  <input id="email" type=text size=20 runat="server"><br>
  Comments:<br>
  <TextArea id="comments" cols=30 rows=4 runat="server"></TextArea><br>
  <input type=submit value="Send"
      OnServerClick="SubmitBtn_Click" runat="server">
  <input type=reset runat="server">
</form>
<span id="message" runat="server" visible="false"></span>
</body>
</html>
```

Building Forms Using ASP.NET Web Controls

When you build an ASP.NET page with ASP.NET controls, you have a choice. Either you can use HTML server controls, or you can use the Web controls. In fact, you can mix HTML server controls and ASP.NET server controls within your Web forms. For the most common HTML tags, ASP.NET provides corresponding HTML server controls and Web controls. The HTML server controls were designed to be server-side duplicates of the standard HTML tags so that you can easily convert an existing HTML page into an ASP.NET page. However, the Web controls do not necessarily correspond to HTML elements and may represent more complex elements. The syntax for creating a Web server control is:

<asp:*control_name* *id*="*control_id*" runat="server" />

or

<asp:*control_name* *id*="*control_id*" runat="server" ></asp:*control_name*>

When you add a Web control to a page, you must always explicitly close the tag with the trailing forward slash (/) or closing tag, as in `</asp:control_name>`. For example, the following text boxes are identical.

```
<asp:TextBox id="txtField" Text="Default text" runat="server" />
```

or

```
<asp:TextBox id="txtField" Text="Default text"
runat="server"></asp:TextBox>
```

or

```
<asp:TextBox id="txtField" runat="server" />Default text</asp:TextBox>
```

In this section, you explore the power that Web controls can add to your Web pages. In the following steps, you use a Web control to create a fully functional calendar on your Web page.

To use the Calendar Web control:

1. Open a new document in Notepad and type the following code:

```
<html>
<head>
<script runat="server">
Sub Selection_Change(s As Object, e As EventArgs)
  Label1.Text = "The selected date is " & _
       Calendar1.SelectedDate.ToShortDateString()
End Sub
</script>
</head>
<body>
<form runat="server">
<h3>Calendar Web control</h3>
<asp:Calendar ID="Calendar1" runat="server"
  OnSelectionChanged="Selection_Change" />
<br>
<asp:Label id="Label1" runat=server />
</form>
</body>
</html>
```

2. Save the file as **example6.aspx** in the Chap09\Chapter folder in your work folder.

3. Load this page using the following URL. Be sure to replace the italicized text with your Web server name and work folder as appropriate.

   http://*localhost*/*workfolder*/Chap09/Chapter/example6.aspx

   The page is displayed, as shown in Figure 9-10.

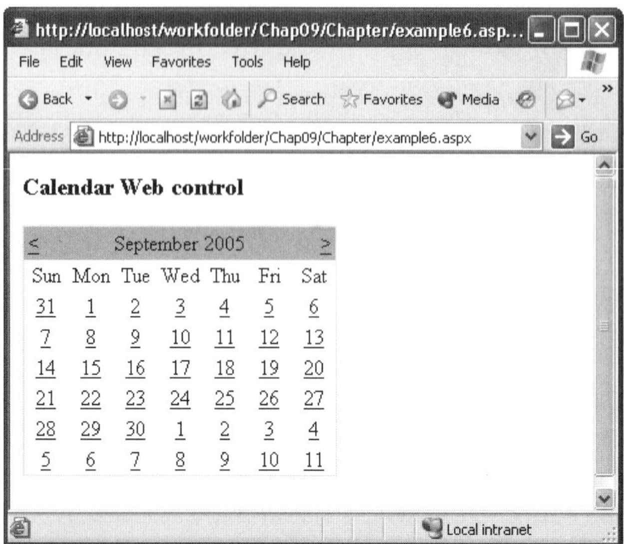

Figure 9-10 Using the Calendar Web control

4. Click a date on the calendar; the selected date appears on your browser.

To add a calendar to your Web page, you create a Web control using the following code:

```
<asp:Calendar ID="Calendar1" runat="server"
   OnSelectionChanged="Selection_Change" />
```

Without using Web controls, you need to write many lines of code to create a calendar like the one displayed on your browser. A Calendar control provides the selectionChanged event when a date is selected. The code `OnSelectionChanged="Selection_Change"` associates the event with its event handler: Selection_Change, in this case. When you click to select a date, the event handler method is invoked, which assigns the selected date to the Label control. You can also customize the Calendar control to meet your needs.

The following shows the C# version of the calendar code:

```
<%@ Page language="C#" %>
<html>
<head>
<script runat="server">
void Selection_Change(Object s, EventArgs e){
  Label1.Text = "The selected date is " +
       Calendar1.SelectedDate.ToShortDateString();
}
</script>
</head>
<body>
<form runat="server">
```

```
<h3>Calendar Web control</h3>
<asp:Calendar ID="Calendar1" runat="server"
  OnSelectionChanged="Selection_Change" />
<br>
<asp:Label id="Label1" runat=server />
</form>
</body>
</html>
```

Using DropDownList and ListBox Controls

You use a drop-down list to represent a set of mutually exclusive options; users can select one item at one time from the list. A DropDownList control shows only the selected item in a box, along with a drop-down button. When users click the button, a list of items is displayed.

A ListBox control allows users to select one or more items from a predefined list. It differs from a DropDownList control in that it can display multiple items. A list box allows users to select one item at a time or multiple items at the same time.

There are three ways to add options to a DropDownList or a ListBox control:

- List options when you declare the DropDownList.
- Add items directly to the control.
- Bind a data source to the control.

To list options when you declare a DropDownList or a ListBox control, you use the following format. This example lists two states and their abbreviations.

```
<asp:DropDownList id="ddlist" runat="server" >
    <asp:ListItem Text="Virginia" Value="VA"/>
    <asp:ListItem Text="South Carolina" Value="SC"/>
</asp:DropDownList>
<asp:ListBox id="list" runat="server" >
    <asp:ListItem Text="Virginia" Value="VA"/>
    <asp:ListItem Text="South Carolina" Value="SC"/>
</asp:ListBox>
```

To add items to the control, you use the following syntax:

List_control_ID.Items.Add(new ListItem("*item_Text*", "*item_Value*"))

or

list_control_ID.Items.Add("*item_Text*")

You can also bind a list control to a data source such as a database table or an existing collection. You will see examples shortly.

Each item in a list control such as a DropDownList, ListBox, RadioButtonList, and CheckBoxList has Text and Value properties. The Text property is the text displayed on the controls. You can access both properties from a program. If you do not specify the value property when you add an item, then the Value and Text properties have the same value. In the following steps, you create and use a DropDownList in your ASP.NET Web pages.

To list options when you declare a DropDownList control:

1. Open the file **example7.txt** in the Chap09\Chapter folder in your work folder.
2. Add the bold code shown in Figure 9-11 to declare a DropDownList control with a few options listed.

```
<script runat="server">
sub Selection_Change(s as Object, e as EventArgs)
  label1.Text = ddlist.SelectedIndex
  label2.Text = ddlist.SelectedItem.Text
  label3.Text = ddlist.SelectedItem.Value
end sub
</script>
<html>
<head>
<title>DropDownList Web control</title>
</head>
<body>
<form runat="server">
<h3>DropDownList Web control[1]</h3>
<asp:DropDownList id="ddlist" runat="server"
  AutoPostBack="true" Width="150"
  OnSelectedIndexChanged="Selection_Change">
<asp:ListItem Text="Virginia" Value="VA"/>
<asp:ListItem Text="South Carolina"/>
<asp:ListItem Text="Texas" Value="TX"/>
<asp:ListItem Text="North Carolina" Value="NC"/>
</asp:DropDownList><br>
Selected item index: <asp:Label id="label1" runat="server"/><br>
Selected item text: <asp:Label id="label2" runat="server"/><br>
Selected item value: <asp:Label id="label3" runat="server"/><br>
</form>
</body>
</html>
```

Figure 9-11 Example7.aspx

3. Save the file as **example7.aspx** in the Chap09\Chapter folder in your work folder, and then close the document.

4. Load this page using the following URL. Be sure to replace the italicized text with your server name and work folder as appropriate.

   http://*localhost*/*workfolder*/Chap09/Chapter/example7.aspx

   The page is displayed, as shown in Figure 9-12.

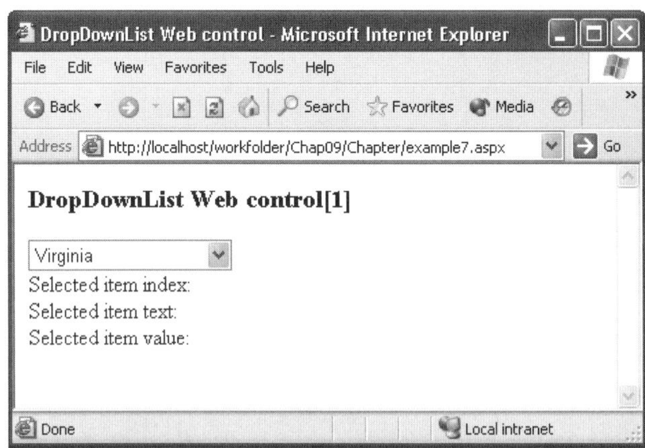

Figure 9-12 Using DropDownList Web control

5. Select an item from the drop-down list, and the data about the selected item appears on the page.
6. Click **South Carolina** on the list. Both the text and value of the selected item are the same.

In the previous steps, you list four options when you create a DropDownList control using the following code:

```
<asp:DropDownList id="ddlist" runat="server"
  AutoPostBack="true" Width="150"
  onSelectedIndexChanged="Selection_Change">
<asp:ListItem Text="Virginia" Value="VA"/>
<asp:ListItem Text="South Carolina"/>
<asp:ListItem Text="Texas"  Value="TX"/>
<asp:ListItem Text="North Carolina" Value="NC"/>
</asp:DropDownList>
```

Except for the second option, you add the other three options by specifying the text and value attributes. You have seen that an item's Value property takes the Text property value if the Value property is not specified when you add the item.

A DropDownList control provides the SelectedIndexChanged event, which is triggered when a new option is selected in the list. The code `OnSelectedIndexChanged ="Selection_Change">` handles the event with the event handler `"Selection _Change"`, which processes the selected item and displays its data on the page. The code

`AutoPostBack="true"` causes the form to be posted whenever a new option is selected.

In the following steps, you add items directly to a DropDownList control.

To add items to a DropDownList control:

1. Open the file **example8.txt** in the Chap09\Chapter folder in your work folder.
2. Add the code that appears bold in Figure 9-13. This code adds items to the DropDownList control when the method is called.

```
<script runat="server">
sub AddNewItem(s as Object, e as EventArgs)
  if Not itemText.Text="" then
    ddlist.Items.Add(itemText.Text)
    itemText.Text=""
  end if
end sub
</script>
<html>
<head>
<title>DropDownList Web control</title>
</head>
<body>
<form runat="server">
<h3>DropDownList Web control[2]</h3>
<asp:TextBox id="itemText" runat="server" Columns="20"/>
<asp:Button runat="server" Text="Add Item"
   OnClick="AddNewItem" /><br><br>
<asp:DropDownList id="ddlist" Width="150" runat="server" />
</form>
</body>
</html>
```

Figure 9-13 Example8.aspx

3. Save the file as **example8.aspx** and close the document.
4. Load this page using the following URL. Be sure to replace the italicized text with your server name and work folder as appropriate.

   http://*localhost*/*workfolder*/Chap09/Chapter/example8.aspx

   The page is displayed, as shown in Figure 9-14.

Figure 9-14 Adding items to the DropDownList control

5. Enter an item in the input box, and then click the **Add Item** button. The item is added to the DropDownList control.

You can bind a data source to a list control and add items to the control from the data source. A data source can be a collection object such as an ArrayList or a database table. In the following steps, you bind an ArrayList to a ListBox control.

To bind an ArrayList to a ListBox control:

1. Open a new document in Notepad and type the following code:

```
<script runat="server">
sub Page_Load
  Dim itemArrayList as New ArrayList
  if Not IsPostBack then
    itemArrayList.Add("Visual Basic .NET")
    itemArrayList.Add("ASP.NET")
    itemArrayList.Add("JavaServer Pages")
    lstbox.DataSource = itemArrayList
    lstbox.DataBind()
  end if
end sub
</script>
<html>
<head><title>ListBox Web control</title></head>
<body>
<form runat="server">
<h3>ListBox Web control</h3>
<asp:ListBox id="lstbox" SelectionMode="Multiple"
      Width="200" runat="server"/>
</form>
</body>
</html>
```

2. Save the file as **example9.aspx** in the Chap09\Chapter folder in your work folder.
3. Load this page using the following URL. Be sure to replace the italicized text with your server name and work folder as appropriate.

   http://*localhost*/*workfolder*/Chap09/Chapter/example9.aspx

   The page is displayed, as shown in Figure 9-15.

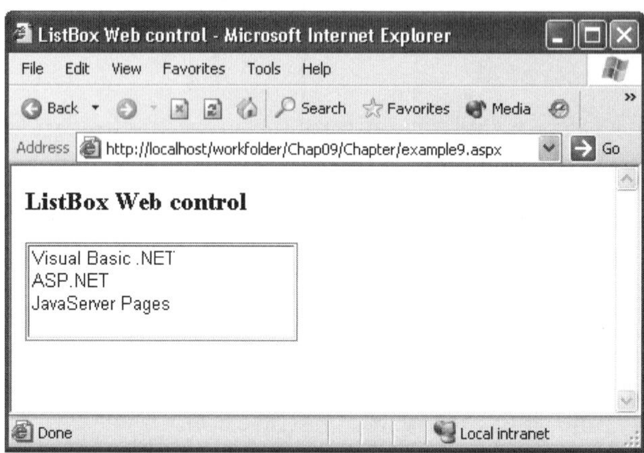

Figure 9-15 ListBox control

In example9.aspx, an ArrayList collection object is declared, which is bound to the ListBox control. The following code adds items to the collection object:

```
itemArrayList.Add("Visual Basic .NET")
itemArrayList.Add("ASP.NET")
itemArrayList.Add("JavaServer Pages")
```

The code `lstbox.DataSource = itemArrayList` assigns the ArrayList object to the control's DataSource property, and the DataBind() method of the control is called to bind the data source to the control. After the DataBind() method is called, all the items in the ArrayList are added to the ListBox control list. You use the Boolean property of the Page object to check whether the form is submitted or if it has been loaded once. Using this property guarantees the item list is constructed only once when the page is loaded.

In the following steps, you process selected items when multiple selections are allowed.

To create a ListBox control with multiple selections:

1. Open the file **example10.txt** in the Chap09\Chapter folder in your work folder.
2. Add the code that appears bold in Figure 9-16 to add a ListBox control with multiple selections.

```
<script runat="server">
sub Button_Clicked(s as Object, e as EventArgs)
  Dim lstItem as ListItem
  Dim strList  as string
  for each lstItem in lstlanguages.Items
    if lstItem.Selected then
       strList &= "<li>" & lstItem.Text
    end if
  Next
  lblItems.Text=strList
end sub
</script>
<html>
<head><title>ListBox Web control</title></head>
<body>
<form runat="server">
<h3>ListBox Web control</h3>
<asp:ListBox id="lstlanguages" SelectionMode="Multiple"
    Width="200" runat="server">
<asp:ListItem Text="Visual Basic .NET"/>
<asp:ListItem Text="C#"/>
<asp:ListItem Text="JavaServer Pages"/>
<asp:ListItem Text="ASP.NET"/>
</asp:ListBox>
<asp:Button runat="server" Text="Get selected items"
    OnClick="Button_Clicked"/><br>
Selected item(s):<br>
<asp:Label id="lblItems" runat="server"/>
</form>
</body>
</html>
```

Figure 9-16 Example10.aspx

3. Save the file as **example10.aspx** and close the file.
4. Load this page using the following URL. Be sure to replace the italicized text with your server name and work folder as appropriate.

   http://*localhost*/*workfolder*/Chap09/Chapter/example10.aspx

   The page is displayed, as shown in Figure 9-17.

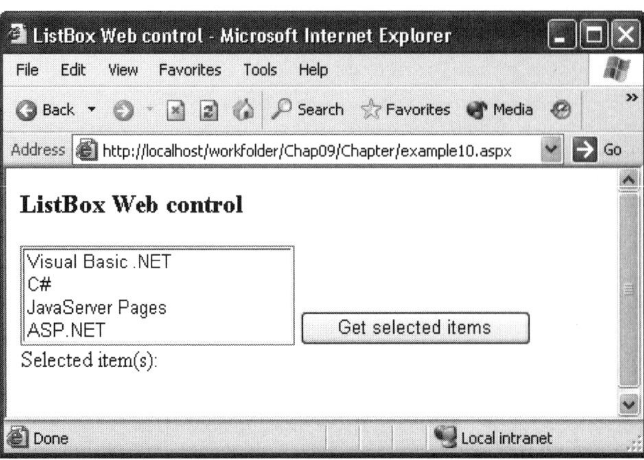

Figure 9-17 ListBox with multiple selections

5. Select items from the list. To select multiple items, press and hold the **Shift** or **Ctrl** key and then click items on the list.
6. Click the **Get selected items** button to display the selected items.

To allow multiple selections, you set the SelectionMode property to Multiple. To detect all selected items, you use the "for each/next" repetition structure. This structure iterates all items in the ListBox control and checks whether an item is selected. If an item is selected, its Text property is retrieved and attached to the String Object. The String Object is assigned to the Label control to display all selected items.

Using RadioButtonList and CheckBoxList Controls

The RadioButtonList control represents a list of radio buttons (often called option buttons). The RadioButtonList control allows you to create a single-selection radio button group. The CheckBoxList control creates a group of check boxes; users can select one or more check boxes from the group. You can set up a Web page to automatically generate the items in the RadioButtonList and CheckBoxList controls by binding the controls to a data source. In this section, you learn how to bind a database source to the RadioButtonList and CheckBoxList controls to create a radio button group and check box group.

In the following steps, you use a database table as data source and then bind the data source to a RadioButtonList control.

To bind a database table to a RadioButtonList control:

1. Make sure the Chap09\Chapter folder in your work folder contains the mydb.mdb database file. Open a new document in Notepad, and save it as **example11.aspx** in the Chap09\Chapter folder in your work folder.

2. When you work with databases, you need to use classes from certain namespaces. When you work with a Microsoft Access database, you need to import the System.Data.OleDB namespace. Type the following page directive at the beginning of the example11.aspx document:

```
<%@ Import Namespace="System.Data.OleDB" %>
```

Add the following code to create and open a database connection when the page is loaded.

```
<script runat="server">
sub Page_Load(s as Object, e as EventArgs)
Dim conn As OleDBConnection
Dim cmd As OleDBCommand
Dim connstr As string
connstr = "Provider=Microsoft.Jet.OLEDB.4.0;" & _
  "Data Source=F:\ASPBook\work folder\Chap09\Chapter\mydb.mdb"
conn = New OleDBConnection(connstr)
conn.Open()
```

The shaded code creates a connection to the database and then opens the connection so you can use a database table as data source. Replace the shaded code with the full path to the mydb.mdb file in your computer.

3. Add the following code to create an instance of the OleDbCommand object and then a data source by calling the method ExecuteReader of the OleDbCommand object. Then assign the data source to the DataSource property of the RadioButtonList control.

```
cmd = New OleDbCommand("select * from States", conn)
rblist.DataSource = cmd.ExecuteReader()
```

4. Add the following code to use the DataTextField and DataValueField properties to specify which field in the data source to bind to the Text and Value properties, respectively, of each list item in the control.

```
rblist.DataTextField ="State"
rblist.DataValueField="Abbreviation"
```

5. Next, use the Control.DataBind method to bind the data source to the RadioButtonList control. Then close the connection to the database.

```
rblist.DataBind()
conn.Close()
End Sub
</script>
```

6. Add the following code to create a server-side form:

```
<html>
<head><title>RadioButtonList Web control</title></head>
<body>
<form runat="server">
```

```
<h3>Binding a database table to a RadioButtonList Web control</h3>
<asp:RadioButtonList id="rblist" runat="server"/>
</form>
</body>
</html>
```

7. Save and close this file.

8. Load this page using the following URL. Be sure to replace the italicized text with your server name and work folder as appropriate.

   http://*localhost*/*workfolder*/Chap09/Chapter/example11.aspx

   The page is displayed, as shown in Figure 9-18.

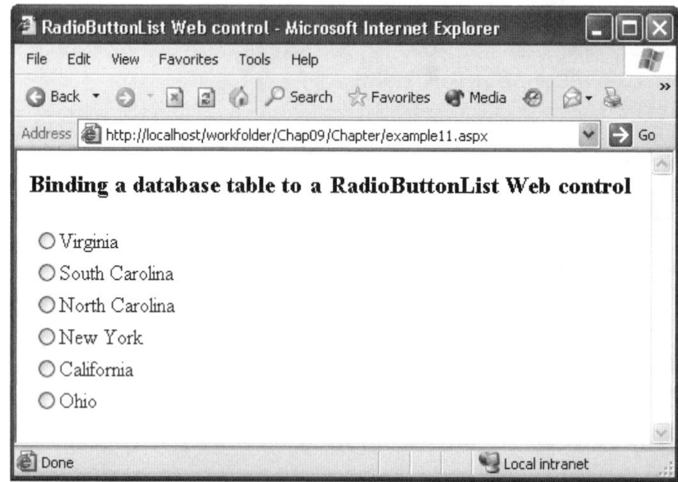

Figure 9-18 Binding a database table to a RadioButtonList control

9. Click the radio buttons on this page. Note that you cannot select more than one button.

Now you can use an ArrayList as a data source and bind it to a CheckBoxList control.

To use an ArrayList to create a CheckBoxList:

1. Open the file **example12.txt** in the Chap09\Chapter folder in your work folder. Then save it as **example12.aspx** in the same folder.

2. Add the bold code shown in Figure 9-19.

```
<%@ Page Language="VB" %>
<script runat="server">
sub Page_Load(s as Object, e as EventArgs)
  Dim itemArrayList as New ArrayList
  if Not IsPostBack then
    itemArrayList.Add("Classical music")
    itemArrayList.Add("Rock music")
    itemArrayList.Add("Country music")
    cblist.DataSource = itemArrayList
    cblist.DataBind()
  end if
end sub
</script>
<html>
<head><title>CheckBoxList Web control</title></head>
<body>
<form runat="server">
<h3>CheckBoxList Web control</h3>
<asp:CheckBoxList id="cblist" runat="server"/>
</form>
</body>
</html>
```


Figure 9-19 Example12.aspx

3. Save and close the file.
4. Load this page using the following URL. Be sure to replace the italicized text with your server name and work folder as appropriate.

   http://*localhost*/*workfolder*/Chap09/Chapter/example12.aspx

   The page is displayed, as shown in Figure 9-20.

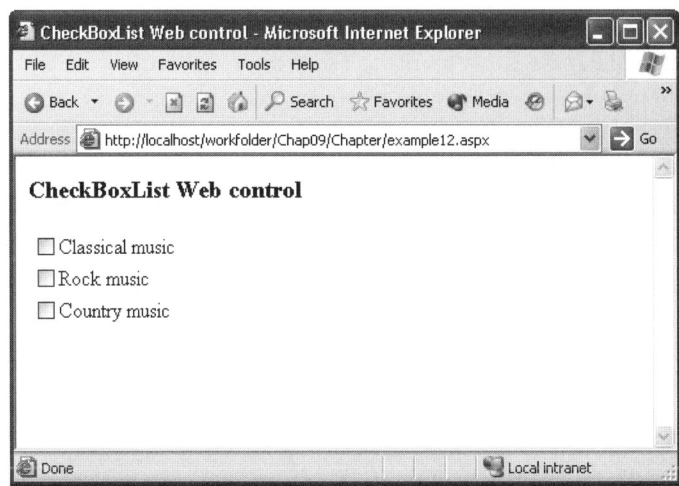

Figure 9-20 Binding an ArrayList to a CheckBoxList control

5. Click the check boxes on the page. Note that you can select all the check boxes.

The following code declares an ArrayList collection object, and adds three items to the object:

```
sub Page_Load(s as Object, e as EventArgs)
  Dim itemArrayList as New ArrayList
  if Not IsPostBack then
    itemArrayList.Add("Classical music")
    itemArrayList.Add("Rock music")
    itemArrayList.Add("Country music")
    cblist.DataSource = itemArrayList
    cblist.DataBind()
  end if
end sub
```

After the items are added to the object, the ArrayList object is bound to the CheckBoxList.

Using DataList and DataGrid Controls

The DataList Web server control displays rows of database information in a format you can customize. It can display items in columns and lets users select and edit items. The DataList control is a template-driven list control. It supports header, footer, and separator templates to let you customize the overall appearance of the DataList. You use templates to define the layout of the items by including HTML text and controls. The DataGrid Web server control is a multi-column, data-bound grid. It displays data in a tabular layout. By default, the DataGrid lets you only view the data, but you can display the data in controls so users can edit data in the DataGrid at run time. In the following steps, you display database table information by using a DataList control.

To bind a data source to a DataList control:

1. Make sure the Chap09\Chapter folder in your work folder contains the employee.mdb database file. Open the file **example13.txt** in the Chap09\Chapter folder in your work folder. Save the file as **example13.aspx** in the same folder.

2. Add the bold code segments shown in Figure 9-21. The shaded line should show the path to the employee.mdb file on your system. The bold code binds the data source to the control and uses the ItemTemplate to specify the items to display.

```
<%@ Import Namespace="System.Data.OleDB" %>
<script runat="server">
sub Page_Load(s as Object, e as EventArgs)
Dim conn As OleDBConnection
Dim cmd As OleDBCommand
Dim connstr As string
connstr = "Provider=Microsoft.Jet.OLEDB.4.0;" & _
  "Data Source=F:\ASPBook\workfolder\Chap09\Chapter\employee.mdb"
conn = New OleDBConnection(connstr)
conn.Open()
cmd = New OleDbCommand("select * from employee", conn)
dlstemployee.DataSource = cmd.ExecuteReader()
dlstemployee.DataBind()
conn.Close()
End Sub
</script>
<html>
<head><title>Binding a table to a DataList control</title>
</head>
<body>
<asp:DataList id="dlstemployee" runat="server">
<HeaderTemplate>
<table cellpadding=5 bgcolor="#eeeeee">
 <tr><th>Name</th><th>E-mail</th></tr>
</HeaderTemplate>
<ItemTemplate>
<%# Container.DataItem("Lname")%>
<%# Container.DataItem("fname")%></td><td>
<%# Container.DataItem("email")%>
</ItemTemplate>
<FooterTemplate>
</table>
</FooterTemplate>
</asp:DataList>
</body>
</html>
```

Figure 9-21 Example13.aspx

3. If necessary, replace the shaded Data Source with the full path to the **employee.mdb** database file on your computer.
4. Save and close the file.
5. Load this page using the following URL. Be sure to replace the italicized text with your server name and work folder as appropriate.

   http://*localhost*/*workfolder*/Chap09/Chapter/example13.aspx

   The page is displayed, as shown in Figure 9-22.

9

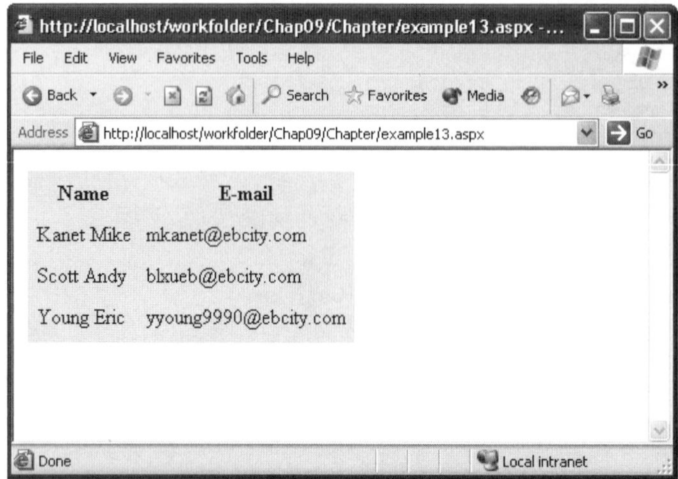

Figure 9-22 Binding a table to a DataList control

In the previous steps, you used three templates to format how the data is to be displayed. The header template adds a column title to the example file. The ItemTemplate property controls the contents of the items in the DataList control. For example, the code specifies that only the employee's first name, last name, and e-mail should be displayed. The footer template controls the contents of the footer section.

In the following steps, you use a DataGrid control to display a database table.

To bind a DataGrid control to a database table:

1. Make sure the Chap09\Chapter folder in your work folder contains the events.mdb database file. Open the file **example14.txt** in the Chap09\Chapter folder in your work folder.

2. Save the file as **example14.aspx** in the same folder.

3. Replace the Data Source with the full path to the events.mdb database on your computer.

4. Add the code that appears bold in Figure 9-23. This code binds the data source to the DataGrid control. The shaded line indicates the Data Source path to events.mdb.

```
<%@ Import Namespace="System.Data.OleDB" %>
<script runat="server">
sub Page_Load(s as Object, e as EventArgs)
Dim conn As OleDBConnection
Dim cmd As OleDBCommand
Dim connstr As string
connstr = "Provider=Microsoft.Jet.OLEDB.4.0;" & _
  "Data Source=F:\ASPBook\workfolder\Chap09\Chapter\events.mdb"
conn = New OleDBConnection(connstr)
conn.Open()
cmd = New OleDbCommand("select * from events", conn)
dgevents.DataSource = cmd.ExecuteReader()
dgevents.DataBind()
conn.Close()
End Sub
</script>
<html>
<head><title>Binding a table to a DataGrid control</title>
</head>
<body>
<asp:DataGrid id="dgevents" runat="server" />
</body>
</html>
```

Figure 9-23 Example14.aspx

5. Save and close the file.
6. Load this page using the following URL. Be sure to replace the italicized text with your server name and work folder as appropriate.

   http://*localhost*/*workfolder*/Chap09/Chapter/example14.aspx

   The page is displayed, as shown in Figure 9-24.

9

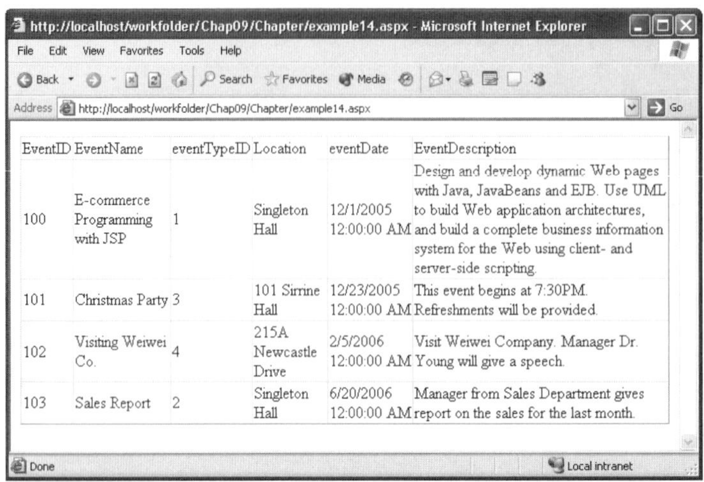

EventID	EventName	eventTypeID	Location	eventDate	EventDescription
100	E-commerce Programming with JSP	1	Singleton Hall	12/1/2005 12:00:00 AM	Design and develop dynamic Web pages with Java, JavaBeans and EJB. Use UML to build Web application architectures, and build a complete business information system for the Web using client- and server-side scripting.
101	Christmas Party	3	101 Sirrine Hall	12/23/2005 12:00:00 AM	This event begins at 7:30PM. Refreshments will be provided.
102	Visiting Weiwei Co.	4	215A Newcastle Drive	2/5/2006 12:00:00 AM	Visit Weiwei Company. Manager Dr. Young will give a speech.
103	Sales Report	2	Singleton Hall	6/20/2006 12:00:00 AM	Manager from Sales Department gives report on the sales for the last month.

Figure 9-24 Displaying the database table with the DataGrid control

UNDERSTANDING THE CODE BEHIND THE PAGE

When you create a Web page, you are unlikely to design and to code the page at the same time. In most cases, you or someone else designs the Web page first and then inserts the server-side code to implement the application logic to allow users to interact with the page. With ASP.NET, you can implement the application logic in a separate file by a technique called "code behind the page." Using this technique allows you to build an ASP.NET page from two files—a presentation file (.aspx) that takes care of the Web site GUI, and a separate file (the code behind the page file) that contains the application logic and page event handlers. Building a single page from two files in this manner allows you to completely separate the code and content.

Using code behind the page has several benefits. First, the code is better organized: every file is either an .aspx file or a code behind the file. Second, because the content (.aspx) and the code are separated, the Web page designer and developer can work separately, which is a more efficient arrangement.

In the following steps, you use the code behind the page technique to separate code and content.

To use the code behind the page technique:

1. Use Notepad to open the file **Example15CodeBehind.vb** from the Chap09\Chapter\components folder in your work folder.
2. Modify the Data Source to reflect the full path to the database mydb.mdb on your computer.
3. Save and close the file.
4. Open the file **example15.txt** in the Chap09\Chapter folder in your work folder.

5. Add the code that appears bold in Figure 9-25.

```
<%@Page Language="VB" Inherits="MyClass1"
 Src="Components/Example15CodeBehind.vb" %>
<html>
<head>
<title>DropDownList Web control</title>
</head>
<body>
<form runat="server">
<h3>DropDownList Web control</h3>
<asp:DropDownList id="ddlist" runat="server"
  AutoPostBack="true" Width="150"
  OnSelectedIndexChanged="Selection_Change"/>
<br>
Selected item index: <asp:Label id="label1" runat="server"/><br>
Selected item text: <asp:Label id="label2" runat="server"/><br>
Selected item value: <asp:Label id="label3" runat="server"/><br>
</form>
</body>
</html>
```

Figure 9-25 Example15.aspx code

6. Save the page as **example15.aspx** and close the file.
7. Load this page using the following URL. Be sure to replace the italicized text with your server name and work folder as appropriate.

   http://*localhost*/*workfolder*/Chap09/Chapter/example15.aspx

   The page is displayed, as shown in Figure 9-26.

Figure 9-26 Code behind the page example

8. Select an item from the drop-down list. The data of the selected item appears on the page.

The following code is the page directive that specifies the name of the code behind the file and the actual class name inside that file.

```
<%@Page Language="VB" Inherits="MyClass1"
Src="Components/Example15CodeBehind.vb" %>
```

In this example, the filename is Example15CodeBehind.vb and the class name is MyClass1. Therefore, the application logic and event handler are implemented in the code behind the page file, Example15CodeBehind.vb.

To create the code behind the page file, you need to define a class in the file. Also define all member variables that correspond to Web controls in the ASP.NET page. To declare such variables, you need to use the controls' ids as variable names. For example, the Label control in example15.aspx is defined as `<asp:Label id="label1" runat="server"/>`. To access this control from the code behind the page file, a variable called label1 must be declared. If you declare a variable using a statement such as `Protected WithEvents label1 As System.Web.UI.WebControls.Label`, you can access this Label control from the code behind the page file.

You can use any programming language that .NET framework supports to write the code behind the page file. The extension of these files varies depending on the language you use. Typical extensions are .cs for C#, .vb for VB .NET, and .js for JScript .NET.

Chapter Summary

- You can use any text editor to create ASP.NET Web pages, and different programming languages to write ASP.NET Web pages. To convert existing HTML Web pages into ASP.NET pages, you change the filename extension to .aspx.
- All regular HTML tags can be converted to their corresponding HTML server controls by adding the `runat="server"` attribute. Place the tags in the server-side form.
- ASP.NET controls can be programmatically accessed, just like any other .NET object or class; they can respond to events, get and set properties, and do all the other things objects can do.
- There are three ways to add items to a list control: list all items when you declare a list control, write code to add items programmatically, or bind a data source to the control.
- A DropDownList control is used to represent a set of mutually exclusive options. It allows users to select one item at one time from a list. A ListBox control allows users to select one or more items from a predefined list. It differs from a DropDownList control in that it can display multiple items, and allows a user to select one item at a time or select multiple items.
- The RadioButtonList control represents a list of radio buttons. The RadioButtonList control allows you to create a single-selection radio button group.

The CheckBoxList control creates a multiselection check box group. The items in the RadioButtonList and CheckBoxList controls can be dynamically generated by binding them to a data source.

- The DataList Web server control displays rows of database information in a customizable format. It can display items in columns and lets users select and edit items. The DataGrid Web server control is a multi-column, data-bound grid. It displays data in a tabular layout. By default, the DataGrid control displays data in read-only mode, but the DataGrid control is also capable of automatically displaying the data in editable controls at run time.
- The DataList and DataGrid controls are template-driven list controls. They support many templates to let you customize the overall appearance of data bound to these controls.
- Using the code behind the page allows you to build an ASP.NET page from two files—a presentation file (.aspx) takes care of the Web site GUI, while the application logic and page's event handlers are stored in a separate file (the code behind the page file). Building a single page from two files in this manner allows you to completely separate the code and content.

Review Questions

1. The file extension for ASP.NET Web pages is:
   a. .asp
   b. .aspn
   c. .vb
   d. .aspx
2. To convert a regular HTML tag into an HTML server control, which of the following attribute/value pairs must be set?
   a. `Name="aName"`
   b. `Id="ctlID"`
   c. `Runat="server"`
   d. `Value="default value"`
3. To programmatically access a server control, which of the following attributes must be set?
   a. name
   b. id
   c. ext
   d. value

4. Which of the following is *not* an attribute of an HTML server control?
   a. id
   b. value
   c. text
   d. runat
5. Which of the following is *not* an attribute of an ASP.NET Web control?
   a. id
   b. value
   c. text
   d. runat
6. Which of the following attributes of a TextBox server control is overwritten if specified when the control is declared?
   a. name
   b. id
   c. text
   d. runat
7. Which of the following controls can handle click events on the client side?
   a. `<asp:TextBox runat="server"/>`
   b. `<asp:Label runat="server"/>`
   c. `<input type=text runat="server"/>`
   d. none of these
8. Which of the following tags execute the method named Button_Click when a user clicks on the button?
   a. `<asp:Button onClick="call Button_Click" runat="server"/>`
   b. `<asp:Button onClick="Button_Click()" runat="server"/>`
   c. `<asp:Button onClick="Button_Click" runat="server"/>`
   d. none of these
9. In VB .NET, which of the following symbols is used to concatenate strings?
   a. ampersand (&)
   b. equal sign (=)
   c. underscore (_)
   d. dot (.)

10. In C#, which of the following symbols is used to concatenate strings?
    a. ampersand (&)
    b. equal sign (=)
    c. plus sign (+)
    d. dot (.)
11. Which of the following controls represents a set of mutually exclusive options?
    a. DropDownList
    b. ListBox
    c. CheckBoxList
    d. none of these
12. Which of the following objects can serve as a data source that can be bound to a RadioButtonList control?
    a. Label
    b. String
    c. ArrayList
    d. none of these
13. Which of the following controls supports multiple selections?
    a. ListBox
    b. DropDownList
    c. RadioButtonList
    d. none of these
14. A database table cannot be bound to which of the following controls?
    a. Label
    b. ListBox
    c. DropDownList
    d. DataList
15. To access a control from a code behind the page file, which is declared as : `<asp:Label id="label1" runat="server"` in the .aspx file, a variable called ________________ must be declared.
    a. Label
    b. myLabel
    c. label1_behind
    d. label1

HANDS-ON EXERCISES

If necessary, use Windows Explorer to create a new folder in the Chap09 folder in your work folder. Name this folder **Exercises**. Save the files that you create in these Exercises in the Chap09\Exercises folder in your work folder.

Exercise 9-1

In this exercise, you bind an ArrayList to a ListBox.

To bind an ArrayList to a ListBox:

1. Open a new document in Notepad and save the file as **exercise1.aspx** in the folder Chap09\Exercises in your work folder.
2. Add the following code to declare an ArrayList object inside the Page_Load subroutine. Then add items to the ArrayList and bind it to the ListBox called lstbox.

```
<script runat="server">
sub Page_Load
  Dim itemArrayList as New ArrayList
  if Not IsPostBack then
    itemArrayList.Add(New ListItem("Virginia","VA"))
    itemArrayList.Add(New ListItem("South Carolina","SC"))
    itemArrayList.Add(New ListItem("North Carolina","NC"))
    lstbox.DataSource = itemArrayList
    lstbox.DataBind()
  end if
end sub
</script>
```

3. Using Figure 9-27 as reference, design a server-side form containing a ListBox control named as lstbox. Set the properties of the ListBox so it allows multiple selections.
4. Save and close the file.
5. Load this page using the following URL. Be sure to replace the italicized text with your server name and work folder as appropriate.

   http://*localhost*/*workfolder*/Chap09/Exercises/exercise1.aspx

   The page is displayed, as shown in Figure 9-27.

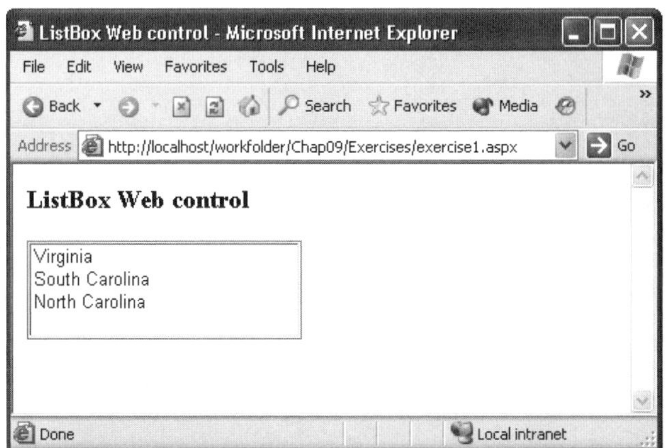

Figure 9-27

Exercise 9-2

In this exercise, you bind an ArrayList data source to a RadioButtonList.

To bind an ArrayList to a RadioButtonList:

1. Open a new document in Notepad and save it as **exercise2.aspx** in the folder Chap09\Exercises in your work folder.
2. Add the following code to specify the language to use in this page and to create script tags and set the `runat="server"` attribute:

```
<%@ Page language="VB" %>
<script runat="server">
</script>
```

3. Add a sub procedure that performs the following tasks: first, this sub procedure is called when this page is loaded. Second, create a new instance of the ArrayList object named itemArrayList; third, add three items using the following code:

```
itemArrayList.Add(New ListItem("Virginia","VA"))
itemArrayList.Add(New ListItem("South Carolina","SC"))
itemArrayList.Add(New ListItem("North Carolina","NC"))
```

4. Add code to bind the ArrayList to a RadioButtonList called rblst.
5. Add the following code to create a server-side form:

```
<html>
<head><title>RadioButtonList Web control</title></head>
<body>
<form runat="server">
<h3>RadioButtonList Web control</h3>
<asp:RadioButtonList id="rblst" runat="server"
 BorderColor="red" BorderWidth="1px"/>
```

```
</form>
</body>
</html>
```

6. Save and close the file.
7. Load this page using the following URL. Be sure to replace the italicized text with your server name and work folder.

   http://*localhost*/*workfolder*/Chap09/Exercises/exercise2.aspx

Exercise 9-3

In this exercise, you create two ListBox controls on the form and then move items on one ListBox control to another one.

To use ListBox controls:

1. Open the file **exercise3.txt** in the folder Chap09\Exercises in your work folder. The VB .NET code contained in this file moves items from one ListBox to another one.
2. Save the file as **exercise3.aspx** in the same folder.
3. Add the following code to create a server-side form:

```
<html>
<head><title>ListBox Web control</title></head>
<body>
<form runat="server">
<h3>ListBox Web control</h3>
<table><tr>
 <td><asp:ListBox id="lstleft" Width="200" runat="server"/></td>
 <td valign="middle">
     <asp:Button Text=">>" id="toright"
         runat="server" onClick="Button_Clicked"/><br>
     <asp:Button Text="<<" id="toleft"
         runat="server" onClick="Button_Clicked"/>
 </td>
 <td><asp:ListBox id="lstright" Width="200" runat="server">
       <asp:ListItem Text="Rock music" />
       <asp:ListItem Text="Country music"/>
     </asp:ListBox>
 </td>
</tr></table>
</form>
</body>
</html>
```

4. Save and close the file.

5. Load this page using the following URL. Be sure to replace the italicized text with your server name and work folder.

   http://*localhost*/*workfolder*/Chap09/Exercises/exercise3.aspx

   The page is displayed, as shown in Figure 9-28.

Figure 9-28

6. Select the item from the ListBox on the left, then click the >> button to move the selected item to the ListBox on the right.

Exercise 9-4

In this exercise, you use code behind the page to separate the code and content.

To separate code and content:

1. Open the file **Exercise4CodeBehind.txt**, which is located in the folder Chap09\Exercises in your work folder.
2. Save the file as **Exercise4CodeBehind.vb** in the same folder.
3. Add code that appears bold in Figure 9-29.

```
Imports System
Imports System.Collections
Imports System.Web.UI
Imports System.Web.UI.WebControls
Public Class Exercise4Class
   Inherits System.Web.UI.Page
   Protected WithEvents lstleft As System.Web.UI.WebControls.ListBox
   Protected WithEvents lstright As System.Web.UI.WebControls.ListBox
   Protected WithEvents toright As System.Web.UI.WebControls.Button
   Protected WithEvents toleft As System.Web.UI.WebControls.Button
   sub Page_Load
     Dim itemArrayList as New ArrayList
     if Not IsPostBack then
      itemArrayList.Add("Classical music")
      lstleft.DataSource = itemArrayList
      lstleft.DataBind()
     end if
   end sub

   sub Button_Clicked(s as Object, e as EventArgs)
     Dim lstItem as ListItem
     Dim source as ListBox, dest as ListBox
     source = lstright
     dest = lstleft
     if s.ID = "toright" then
       source = lstleft
       dest = lstright
     end if
     if source.SelectedIndex = -1 then
       exit sub
     end if
     lstItem = source.SelectedItem
     source.Items.Remove(lstItem)
     dest.Items.Add(lstItem)
     dest.ClearSelection()
   end sub
End Class
```

Figure 9-29

4. Save and close the file.
5. Open the file **exercise4.txt**, which is located in the folder Chap09\Exercises in your work folder.
6. Save the file as **exercise4.aspx** in the same folder.
7. Add the following code at the top of the page:

```
<%@Page Language="VB" Debug="true" Inherits="Exercise4Class"
 Src="Exercise4CodeBehind.vb" %>
```

8. Save and close the file.

9. Load this page using the following URL.

   http://*localhost*/*workfolder*/Chap09/Exercises/exercise4.aspx

   Be sure to replace the italicized text with your server name and work folder.

Exercise 9-5

In this exercise, you use code behind the page to bind a database table to a DataList control and use templates to format the data to be displayed.

To use code behind the page to bind a database table to a DataList control:

1. In a text editor, open the code behind the page file **Exercise5CodeBehind.vb** located in the folder Chap09\Exercises in your work folder.
2. Change the data source to reflect the full path of the database employee.mdb in your system. Save the file.
3. Open the file **exercise5.txt**, which is located in the folder Chap09\Exercises in your work folder. Then rename the file to **exercise5.aspx**.
4. Add the bold code in Figure 9-30 to add templates to format data to be displayed.

9

```
<%@Page Language="VB" Debug="true" Inherits="Exercise5Class"
 Src="Exercise5CodeBehind.vb" %>

<asp:DataList id="dlstemployee" runat="server">
<HeaderTemplate>
 <table cellpadding=5
bgcolor="yellow"><tr><th>Name</th><th>Address</th>
   <th>Zip code</th><th>Phone</th><th>E-mail</th></tr>
</HeaderTemplate>
<ItemTemplate>
<%# Container.DataItem("Lname")%>
<%# Container.DataItem("fname")%></td><td>
<%# Container.DataItem("address")%></td><td>
<%# Container.DataItem("zipcode")%></td><td>
<%# Container.DataItem("phone")%></td><td>
<%# Container.DataItem("email")%>
</ItemTemplate>
<FooterTemplate>
</table>
</FooterTemplate>
</asp:DataList>
```

Figure 9-30

5. Save and close the file.
6. Load this page using the following URL. Be sure to replace the italicized text with your server name and work folder.

   http://*localhost*/*workfolder*/Chap09/Exercises/exercise5.aspx

   This page is displayed as shown in Figure 9-31.

http://localhost/workfolder/Chap9/Exercises/exercise5.aspx - Microsoft Intern...

File Edit View Favorites Tools Help

Address http://localhost/workfolder/Chap09/Exercises/exercise5.aspx

Name	Address	Zip code	Phone	E-mail
Kanet Mike	215 Newcastle Drive	29635	123-4567	mkanet@ebcity.com
Scott Andy	215A Blvd	23806	524-6728	blxueb@ebcity.com
Young Eric	500 Newcastle Drive	56321	520-5236	yyoung9990@ebcity.com

Done Local intranet

Figure 9-31

WEB PROGRAMMING PROJECTS

If necessary, use Windows Explorer to create a new folder in the Chap09 folder in your work folder. Name this folder **Projects**. Save the files that you create in these projects in the Chap09\Projects folder in your work folder.

Project 9-1

You are asked to create a guest book for a Web site. The guest book should meet the following requirements:

- When a user signs in your guest book, the data is stored to a file named guestdata.
- A user can view guests who have already signed the guest book. The data is obtained from the file guest.data.

Use ASP.NET and the techniques you learned in this chapter to create the guest book. Save the file as **GuestBook.aspx** in the Chap09\Projects folder in your work folder.

Project 9-2

A local pizza place named Joe's Pizzeria is interested in reaching customers through the Internet. You are hired to develop a Web page that allows customers to place orders online. On the Web page, the customer is asked to specify the following information:

- Pizza size (small, medium, or large)
- Number of pizzas
- Preferred toppings
- Delivery (pickup, deliver)

After the client provides all the information and submits this form, the information collected from the form is displayed.

Use ASP.NET and the techniques you learned in this chapter to create the Web page. Save the file as **Pizza.aspx** in the Chap09\Projects folder.

Project 9-3

Design a Web page to allow users to list attendees who register for a particular event. Use the event name from the events table in the events.mdb file (in the Chap09\Chapter folder) to create a drop-down list using the DropDownList control. When a user selects an event from the list, persons registered for that event are displayed. Save the file as **Attendees.aspx** in the Chap09\Projects folder in your work folder.

CHAPTER

10

ASP.NET PART II

In this chapter you will:

- Work with user controls
- Expose user control properties and methods
- Use ASP.NET server controls in user controls
- Use validation controls to improve Web forms
- Upload files to a Web server

Server controls are components that enable you to develop simple but powerful Web pages. You have learned how to use HTML server controls and Web server controls in your ASP.NET pages. You can also build your own controls and use them on your pages just like you use ASP.NET server controls.

Typically, you let users enter data on Web forms and then process the data on the Web server. You might also want to validate the data that users provide. For example, suppose you design a Web form to collect client contact phone numbers for an online banking system. You expect clients to type their phone numbers in a certain format so you can check to be sure they are valid phone numbers. You could write code to perform either client-side or server-side validation, but it requires a lot of effort. Instead, you can use ASP.NET, which provides validation controls so you can easily make sure the data that users enter is valid.

In this chapter, you learn how to create and use user controls and their properties and methods. You also learn to use validation controls to ensure data is entered appropriately in a field by checking that a value falls within a specific range of values, for example. You also learn how to use the file upload control so that users can post files on your Web site.

Working With User Controls

In Chapter 9, you learned that the ASP.NET server controls greatly enhance your Web page by allowing you to use encapsulated properties and methods. However, ASP.NET server controls cannot cover every situation you might encounter. You can supplement the server controls that are provided with ASP.NET by defining your own controls. ASP.NET enables you to easily define controls as necessary for your applications, using the same programming techniques that you use to write ASP.NET Web pages. You can even convert an ASP.NET Web page you have developed into a user control.

Creating ASP.NET Web User Controls

You create user controls much the same way that you create normal ASP.NET Web pages. To specify that a text file is a user control, you save the file with an .ascx extension to indicate that this file cannot be executed as a stand-alone ASP.NET Web page.

When you design a Web application, you often want to provide the same navigation links and footer on each page. For example, suppose you want to place navigation links on every page as shown in Figure 10-1. To do so, you could write the code for these elements on each page. However, this is tedious because you must remember to put these elements on each page, and then make sure they are correct and identical. When you need to modify the footers or add more navigation links, you must edit them on each page. You can avoid this extra work by using user controls to create the navigation links on each page. The advantage of using user controls to display the same content on multiple pages is that you can easily update the content if it changes. The following example demonstrates how to create a user control to render navigation links on Web pages.

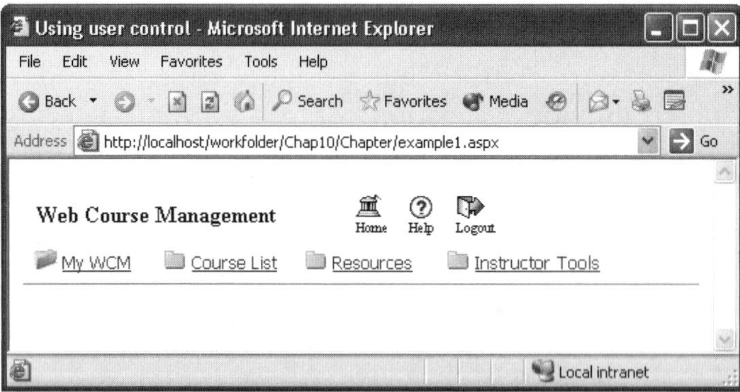

Figure 10-1 Common navigation links

To create a user control to display navigation links:

1. If necessary, use Windows Explorer to create a new folder in the Chap10 folder in your work folder. Name this folder **Chapter**.

2. Open the file **navigation.txt**, which is located in the Chap10\Chapter folder in your work folder. This file contains the code to display navigation links on each page.
3. Save this file as **navigation.ascx** in the same folder.
4. Close the file.

You have created a user control named navigation.ascx. The next section demonstrates how to use the user control in ASP.NET Web pages.

Using User Controls

After you create a user control, you can include it in any other ASP.NET Web page. To include a user control in an ASP.NET Web page, you need to insert the Register directive, which takes the following syntax:

<%@ Register TagPrefix="*TP*" TagName="*TN*"
 src="*virtualPathOftheUserControlFile*" %>

The Register directive supports several attributes. The TagPrefix determines a unique namespace for the user control and differentiates between multiple user controls with the same name. Because of this, you can have different controls with the same name as long as they have different TagPrefixes. The TagName is the unique name for the user control, and may be any name you like. The src attribute is the virtual path to the user control, such as Navigation.ascx or /mycontrols/Navigation.ascx, depending on where the user control file is located.

10

After registering the user control, you place the user control tag in the Web forms page just as you would an ordinary server control. A user control tag takes the following form:

<*theTagPrefix*:*theTagName id*="*controlID*" runat="server"/>

Like any other ASP.NET server control, you must include `runat="server"`. In the following steps, you use the user control navigation.ascx to place common navigation links in a Web page.

To use a user control:

1. Open a new document in Notepad and save it as **example1.aspx** in the Chap10\Chapter folder in your work folder.
2. Add the following code to make the user control available to the ASP.NET Web page by using the Register directive.

```
<%@ Register TagPrefix="WCM" TagName="NavigationLinks"
                src="navigation.ascx" %>
```

3. Add the following code and content to the file:

```
<html>
<head>
<title>Using a user control</title>
</head>
<body>
```

4. Add the following tag to use the user control:

```
<WCM:NavigationLinks Runat="server"/>
```

5. Add the following closing tags to finish this page:

```
</body>
</html>
```

6. Save and close the file.
7. Load this page using the following URL. Be sure to replace the italicized text with your server name and work folder name.

   http://*localhost*/*workfolder*/Chap10/Chapter/example1.aspx

   This page is displayed, as shown earlier in Figure 10-1.

When you need to add or remove links from this page, you edit only the user control file, and the modification is reflected the next time the page is requested.

After a user control is registered, you can use it as many times as you want in an ASP.NET Web page.

Exposing User Control Properties and Methods

You have learned that ASP.NET server controls have properties (or attributes) and methods. For example, when you declare a TextBox server control, you can set the text attribute as follows:

```
<asp:TextBox id="txtUserName" Text="Enter your user name here."
Runat="server"/>
```

In this code, you use the text attribute to set a value to be displayed. You can also create user controls that have attributes, and then use these attributes in the same way as ASP.NET server controls on the Web page. There are two ways to define a property: either declare a property as a public data member or use the property accessor function. To use the accessor function to declare a property, you need to provide a Get accessor and a Set accessor. The Get accessor is used to retrieve the property, and the Set accessor to modify the property. For example, to add a string property called Description, you can use one of the following statements:

```
Public Dim description as string
```

Or

```
Dim desc as string
Public Property description as string
    Get
        Return desc
   End get
   Set
        desc = value
    End set
End Property
```

In the following steps, you create a user control to provide a uniform address format.

To create a user control for an address:

1. Open a new document in Notepad and type the following code:

```
<script Runat="server">
Public UserName as string
Public Address as string
Public City as string
Public State as string
Public ZipCode as string
</script>
<font face="Arial" size="1">
<%= UserName %><br>
<%= Address %><br>
<%= City %>, <%= State %> <%= ZipCode %><br>
</font>
```

2. Save the file as **address.ascx** in the Chap10\Chapter folder in your work folder.

3. Close the file.

To have ASP.NET recognize the properties in a user control, you use public variables. This technique is called exposing the properties. For example, the following code defines five public variables to expose five properties of the user control.

```
<script Runat="server">
Public UserName as string
Public Address as string
Public City as string
Public State as string
Public ZipCode as string
</script>
```

To access these variables within any page that contains the user control, you have to declare them as public.

There are two ways to execute code within the HTML or text content of your ASP.NET page: using inline code or an inline expression. The inline expression begins with the characters <% and ends with the characters %>, with no space between < or > and %. For example, the code segment `<%= UserName %>` is an inline expression. When the expression is executed, the value of the variable is inserted into the output stream.

You can write server-side code within <% and %> tags, and the code is executed on the server before output is sent to the client browser. For example, you could replace the code `<%= UserName %>` with `<% Response.write(UserName) %>`, which uses the write method of the `Response` object to output the value of the variable passed as a parameter.

You can assign default values for each property. For example, to assign a default value for the State property, you can declare the State variable as follows: `Public State as string="Virginia"`

If no other value is assigned to a property, it displays the default value. In the following steps, you use these properties definitions in the address.ascx user control.

To use the properties of the address.ascx user control:

1. Open a new document in Notepad and save the file as **example2.aspx** in the Chap10\Chapter folder in your work folder.
2. Type the following code to use the Register directive to make the user control available to the page:

```
<%@ Register TagPrefix="WCM" TagName="Address"
             src="address.ascx" %>
```

3. Type the following code to set the properties of the user control.

```
<html>
<head>
<title>Using a user control</title>
</head>
<body>
<WCM:Address UserName="Mike Davis"
             Address="215A Newcastle Drive"
             City="Clemson"
             State="SC"
             ZipCode="29634"
Runat="server"/>
</body>
</html>
```

4. Save and close the file.

5. Load this page using the following URL. Be sure to replace the italicized text with your server name and work folder name.

   http://*localhost*/*workfolder*/Chap10/Chapter/example2.aspx

   This page is displayed, as shown in Figure 10-2.

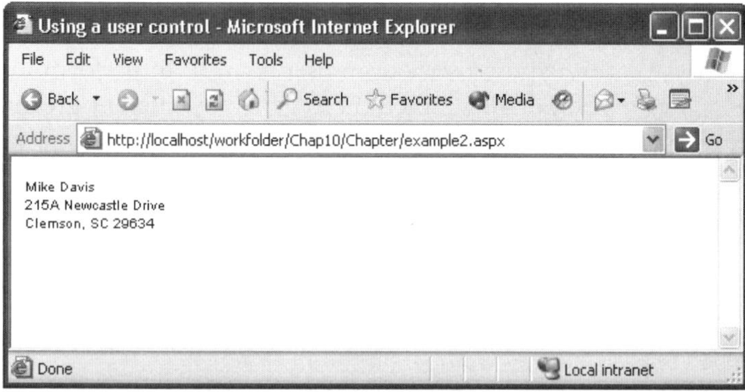

Figure 10-2 Using user control properties

The address information is provided when the user control tag is declared. Each property value is assigned within the declaration of the Address user control. In this example, the values are assigned as follows:

```
Address="215A Newcastle Drive"
City="Clemson"
State="SC"
ZipCode="29634"
```

You can also use a program to access these properties within server-side script tags, a block of inline code, or a block of inline expressions. For example, the following code renders the same page as example2.aspx.

```
<%@ Register TagPrefix="WCM" TagName="Address"
             src="address.ascx" %>
<script runat="server">
  sub Page_Load
    ctladdr.UserName="Mike Davis"
    ctladdr.Address="215A Newcastle Drive"
    ctladdr.City="Clemson"
    ctladdr.State="SC"
    ctladdr.ZipCode="29634"
  end sub
</script>
<html>
<head>
<title>Using a user control</title>
```

```
</head>
<body>
<WCM:Address id="ctladdr" Runat="server"/>
</body>
</html>
```

Note that the id attribute is set. To access a user control in your code, the id attribute must be set for that control, and you use the id to reference that control.

In many cases, you may want to expose methods in user controls to perform some tasks. In the following steps, a user control defines a method to generate different greeting messages according to the time of the day.

To define a Greeting user control:

1. Open a new document in your text editor and type the following code:

```
<script Runat="server">
 Public Dim userName as string="there:"
 sub greeting()
   Dim currTime as Date = now()
   Response.write("<h3>Hi " & userName & ",</h3>")
   if hour(currTime) < 12 then
      Response.write("<font size=4 color=red>Good morning!</font>")
   else if hour(currTime) < 18 then
      Response.write("<font size=4 color=blue>Good afternoon!</font>")
   else
      Response.write("<font size=4 color=black>Good night!</font>")
   end if
 end sub
</script>
```

2. Save the file as **greeting.ascx** in the Chap10\Chapter folder in your work folder.

3. Close the file.

The user control contains a method called Greeting that generates different greeting messages based on the time of the day. In the following steps, you use the method defined in the user control.

To use the method in the user control:

1. Open a new document in Notepad and save the file as **example3.aspx** in the Chap10\Chapter folder in your work folder.

2. Type the following code to use the Register directive to make the control available in the page:

```
<%@ Register TagPrefix="WCM" TagName="Greeting"
             src="greeting.ascx" %>
```

3. Type the following code to call the method defined in the control when this page is loaded:

```
<script runat="server">
  sub Page_Load
    ctlgreeting.greeting()
  end sub
</script>
```

4. Add the following code to use the user control:

```
<html>
<head>
<title>Using a user control method</title>
</head>
<body>
<WCM:Greeting id="ctlgreeting" userName="Mike Davis" runat="server"/>
</body>
</html>
```

5. Save and close the file.

6. Load this page using the following URL. Be sure to replace the italicized text with your server name and work folder name.

http://*localhost*/*workfolder*/Chap10/Chapter/example3.aspx

A page similar to Figure 10-3 is displayed.

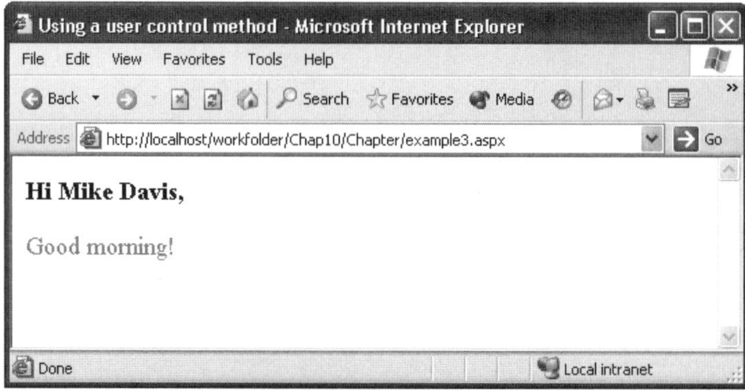

Figure 10-3 Using the user control method

Letting User Controls Handle Events

You can have a user control handle events. For example, if you add the Page_Load method to a user control, the method executes before the control is displayed on the Web page. This type of event handling allows you to write controls that execute code automatically when the controls are declared. For example, you can create a user control to connect a database and bind tables to other list controls. In the following steps, you use the Page_Load method to execute code automatically when a user control is declared.

To define the Page_Load routine in a user control:

1. Open a new document in Notepad and save the file as **userControlEvent.ascx** in the Chap10\Chapter folder in your work folder.
2. Add the following code to define a simple user control with the Page_Load event handler.

```
<script runat="server">
  sub Page_Load
    tb1.Text = "Simply demonstrate that the Page_Load " & _
          "method in the user control " & _
          "is called when it is declared. " & _
          "The current time is: " & _
          Now.ToLongTimeString()
  end sub
</script>
<asp:TextBox id="tb1" TextMode="Multiline" Columns="35"
     Rows="5" runat="server" BackColor="#99ffcc"
     ForeColor="#ff0099" Font-Underline="True" />
```

3. Save and close the file.

Next, you write an ASP.NET page to declare the user control that is examined when the Page_Load method is called.

To use the user control:

1. Open a new document in Notepad and type the following code:

```
<%@ Register TagPrefix="WCM" TagName="UCEvent"
             src="userControlEvent.ascx" %>
<form runat="server">
<WCM:UCEvent runat="server"/><br>
</form>
```

2. Save the file as **example4.aspx** in the Chap10\Chapter folder in your work folder.
3. Load this page using the following URL. Be sure to replace the italicized text with your server name and work folder name.

   http://*localhost*/*workfolder*/Chap10/Chapter/example4.aspx

   The page is displayed, as shown in Figure 10-4.

You see the message displayed in the text box, which is the result of the execution of the code defined in the Page_Load method in the user control.

This simple user control demonstrates that the Page_Load method is called automatically when the user control is declared. In the following section, you will see how a user control handles events generated by its components.

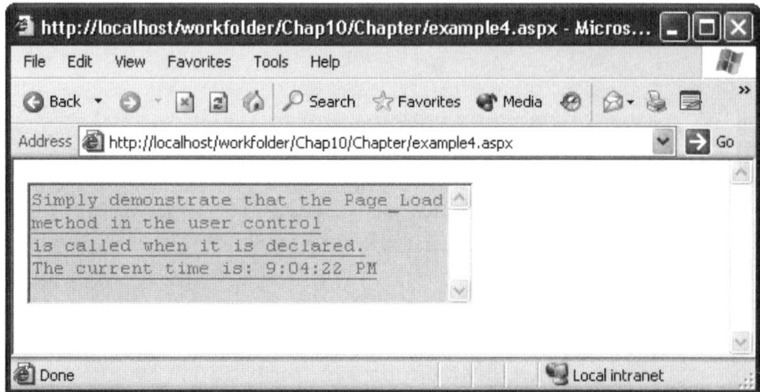

Figure 10-4 User control handles an event

USING ASP.NET SERVER CONTROLS IN USER CONTROLS

You could include any ASP.NET server controls in a user control. For example, you can place several ASP.NET server controls in a user control and use them as a single user control. Throughout your Web application, you may need to use the same group of Web controls in different Web pages. Instead of adding these controls on each page, you can group these controls in one user control, and use the single user control on your Web pages. In the following steps, you create a Calendar user control that can be used in a Web form to allow users to select a date and expose the selected date as a property.

To create the Calendar user control:

1. Open a new document in Notepad and save the file as **mycalendar.ascx** in the Chap10\Chapter folder in your work folder.
2. Add the following code to expose the description and selectedDate attributes of the user control:

```
<script runat="server">
Public Property description as string
  Get
    Return lblDesc.Text
  End Get
  Set
    lblDesc.Text=Value
  End Set
End Property
Public Property selectedDate as string
  Get
    Return selDate.Text
  End Get
  Set
```

```
      selDate.Text=Value
    End Set
  End Property
```

3. Add the following code to handle the selectionChanged event of the Calendar control used in the user control.

```
sub Selection_Change(s as Object, e as EventArgs)
      selDate.Text = Calendar1.SelectedDate.ToShortDateString()
end sub
</script>
```

4. Add the following code to add a Label and a TextBox control to display the selected date.

```
<asp:Label id="lblDesc" Text="Selected date" runat="server"/>:
<asp:TextBox id="selDate" runat="server"/><br>
```

5. Add the following code to add a Calendar control to the user control.

```
<asp:Calendar id="Calendar1"
  OnSelectionChanged="Selection_Change" runat="server"/>
```

6. Save and close the file.

Now you can use the user control to allow users to select a date, and then display the selected date in the text box. You can also access the selected date via the control's property. In the following steps, you write the code to employ the user control.

To use the Calendar user control:

1. Open a new document in Notepad and type the following code:

```
<%@ Register TagPrefix="WCM" TagName="MC"
             src="mycalendar.ascx" %>
<script runat="server">
  sub getSelectedDate(s as Object, e as EventArgs)
     lblDate.Text = mycalendar.selectedDate
  end sub
</script>
<form runat="server">
<WCM:MC id="mycalendar" description="Birthday" runat="server"/><br>
<asp:Button onClick="getSelectedDate" Text="Submit"
runat="server"/><br>
The date you selected:
<asp:Label id="lblDate" runat="server" ForeColor="red"/>
</form>
```

2. Save this file as **example5.aspx** in the Chap10\Chapter folder in your work folder.

3. Load this page using the following URL. Be sure to replace the italicized text with your server name and work folder name.

   http://*localhost*/*workfolder*/Chap10/Chapter/example5.aspx

   This page is displayed, as shown in Figure 10-5.

4. Select a date using the calendar; the selected date is displayed in the Birthday text box.
5. Click the **Submit** button. The selected date is processed and displayed next to the "The date you selected:" label.

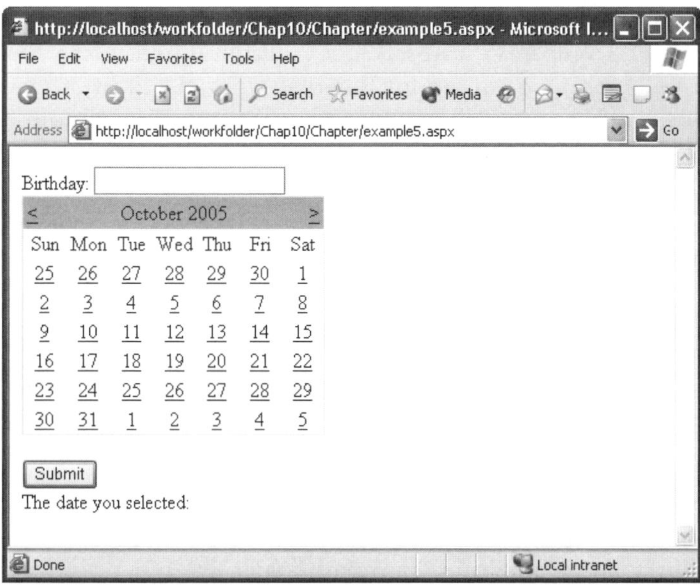

Figure 10-5 Using the Calendar user control

To access a user control's properties within server-side code, you must assign the id attribute to the control, and use the id as reference to access that control's properties, as you have seen in this example.

Using Validation Controls to Improve Web Forms

When you want the information that a user provides to match the requirements of your application, you can validate data on a form before doing further processing. For example, you may want to validate whether the data entered into the text box is a valid phone number, e-mail address, or social security number. Validation can be performed either on the client or on the server. In practice, a client-side script, such as one created in JavaScript, is often used for validation to reserve server resources for other tasks. Client-side validation reduces the number of requests the server receives and therefore reduces the amount of work the server must perform. But, when you write a client-side script for validation, you might find that the client's browser does not support the script you use. For this reason, many Web pages perform validations on the server, even though the server has to process extra requests.

10

ASP.NET offers a better solution. It provides several validation controls you can use when you need to validate a form. Best of all, the validation controls can automatically detect whether the client browser supports the script generated by these controls. If the browser supports them, the validations are performed on the client-side; otherwise, the server automatically performs the validations.

You can use five Web server controls to validate input on your Web pages: RequiredFieldValidator, CompareValidator, RangeValidator, RegularExpressionValidator, and CustomValidator. Each type is used for different types of validation, such as range checking or pattern matching. In addition, the CustomValidator is a custom control that you can use to establish your own validation criteria. You will learn how to use the first three types of validation controls to validate your form in this chapter.

Using the RequiredFieldValidator

You use the RequiredFieldValidator control to ensure that the user does not skip a required field when entering data on a Web form. You can specify that a user must provide information in a specific control by associating a RequiredFieldValidator control with it. In the following steps, you use a RequiredFieldValidator control to ensure a value must be entered into a text box.

To use RequiredFieldValidator controls:

1. Open a new document in Notepad and save the file as **example6.aspx** in the Chap10\Chapter folder in your work folder.
2. Type the following code to add two TextBox controls—one for user name and the other for a message—and one Button control so that users can submit the form.

```
<form runat="server">
User name:
<asp:TextBox id="txtUser" runat="server"/><br>
Comments:<br>
<asp:TextBox id="txtMsg" TextMode="MultiLine"
     Columns="26" Rows="5" runat="server"/>
<asp:Button Text="Submit" runat="server"/><br><br>
```

3. Add the following code to validate the two TextBox controls.

```
<asp:RequiredFieldValidator runat="server"
     ControlToValidate="txtUser"
     ErrorMessage="You must enter your user name!"/><br>
<asp:RequiredFieldValidator runat="server"
     ControlToValidate="txtMsg"
     ErrorMessage="You must enter some comments!"/>
</form>
```

4. Save and close the file.

5. Load this page using the following URL. Be sure to replace the italicized text with your server name and work folder name.

   http://*localhost*/*workfolder*/Chap10/Chapter/example6.aspx

6. Without providing any data on the form, click the **Submit** button. Figure 10-6 shows the messages indicating that both the user name and comments are required.

7. Enter appropriate data into the User name and Comments text boxes, and then click the **Submit** button. The error message does not appear.

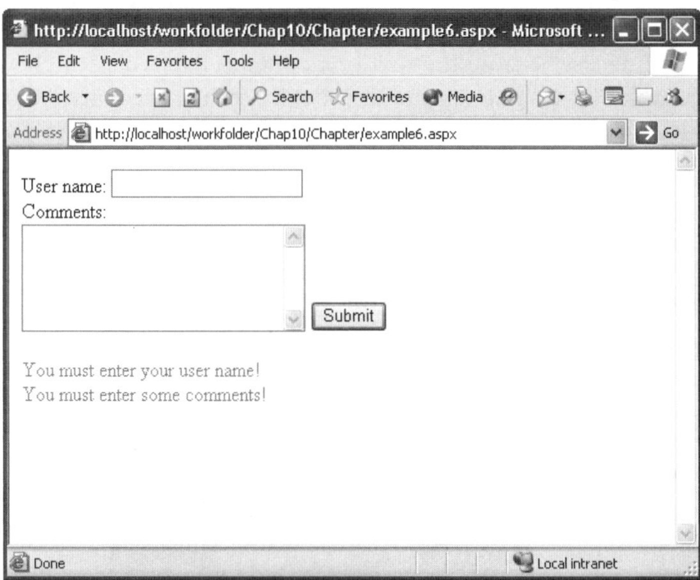

Figure 10-6 Validating required fields with the RequiredFieldValidator control

To validate a required field using the RequiredFieldValidator control, you use the following syntax:

<asp:RequiredFieldValidator runat="server"
ControlToValidate="*ID_of_the_control_to_validate*"
Text="*Message to display if the error occurs*"/>

The ControlToValidate attribute uses the control's id to link the RequiredFieldValidator control to the control you want to validate. The ErrorMessage attribute specifies the error message you want to display if the user does not provide a value in the validated control when the user tries to submit the form. The following code links two RequiredFieldValidator controls to the user name and message text fields, respectively.

```
<asp:RequiredFieldValidator runat="server"
    ControlToValidate="txtUser"
```

```
        ErrorMessage="You must enter your user name!"/><br>
    <asp:RequiredFieldValidator runat="server"
        ControlToValidate="txtMsg"
        ErrorMessage="You must enter some comments!"/>
```

If you failed to provide data into the User name field or Comments field, this page displays error messages and the form is not processed further. By default, the error message is displayed in red text. You can determine how the error message is formatted by using the formatting properties.

In some cases, you may want to provide informative text to remind users to enter data. For example, you may want to set the value of the text attribute of the message TextBox control in the previous example to "Please enter your comments here." The Comments text box passes the validation because the text box contains data. You can check whether a user has entered a value other than an initial value by setting the InitialValue property of the RequiredFieldValidator control. For example, you can modify the previous validator as follows:

```
    <asp:RequiredFieldValidator runat="server"
        ControlToValidate="txtMsg"
       InitialValue="Please enter your comments here."
        ErrorMessage="You must enter some comments!"/>
```

Then the validated field expects data other than the initial value.

Using the CompareValidator

You use the CompareValidator control to compare a user's entry against another value, such as a constant value, the property value of another control, or a database value. For example, a user must enter an integer value greater than or equal to zero. You can use the CompareValidator control to check whether data entered into one control meets the conditions specified in the corresponding CompareValidator control. The condition is constructed using logical operators. Using the CompareValidator takes the following form:

<asp:CompareValidator
  ControlToValidate="*id_of_the_control_to_validate*"
  ControlToCompare="*id_of_the_control_for_comparing or a constant value*"
  ErrorMessage="*error message to display*"
  Operator="*comparison operator*"
  Type="*set the data type used when comparing values*"
  runat="server" />

The Operator attribute can take one of the following values: Equal, NotEqual, GreaterThan, GreaterThanEqual, LessThan, LessThanEqual, and DataTypeCheck. When the comparison is performed, the id specified in the ControlToValidate serves as the first operand, and the ControlToCompare serves as the second operand. The Type attribute may be set to Currency, Date, Double, Integer, and String. For example, in the following steps, you use the CompareValidator control to ensure the employment date for an employee is later than the birth date.

To use the CompareValidator control:

1. Open a new document in Notepad and type the following code:

```
<form runat="server">
Birth date: <asp:TextBox id="bdate" runat="server"/><br>
Employment date: <asp:TextBox id="edate" runat="server"/><br>
<asp:Button Text="Submit" runat="server"/><br><br>
<asp:CompareValidator
    ControlToValidate="bdate"
    ControlToCompare="edate"
    ErrorMessage=
     "The employment date must be greater than the birth date."
    Operator="LessThan"
    Type="Date"
    runat="server" />
</form>
```

2. Save the file as **example7.aspx** in the Chap10\Chapter folder in your work folder.
3. Close the file.
4. Load this page using the following URL. Be sure to replace the italicized text with your server name and work folder name.

   http://*localhost*/*workfolder*/Chap10/Chapter/example7.aspx

5. Enter **05/08/2005** in the Birth date text box and **10/12/1976** in the Employment date text box. Then click the **Submit** button. This page is displayed as shown in Figure 10-7. The error message indicates the employment date must be greater than the birth date.

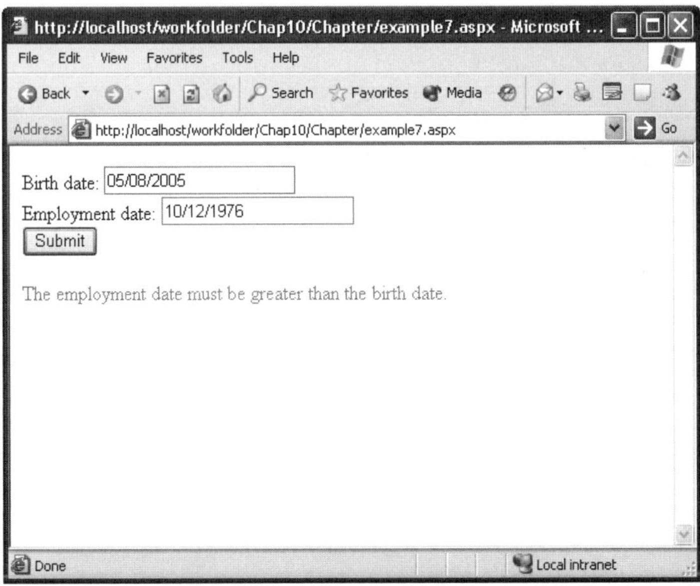

Figure 10-7 Using the CompareValidator control

You can also use the CompareValidator to check whether a form field contains a particular data type. For example, you can use the control to check whether a user entered a valid date, number, or currency value. In the following steps, you check to determine whether a user entered a valid currency value.

To use the CompareValidator control to check a valid currency value:

1. Open a new document in Notepad and type the following code:

```
<form runat="server">
Amount of deposit: <asp:TextBox id="txtCurr" runat="server"/><br>
<asp:Button Text="Submit" runat="server"/><br><br>
<asp:CompareValidator
    ControlToValidate="txtCurr"
    ErrorMessage="Please enter a valid currency value."
    Operator="DataTypeCheck"
    Type="Currency"
    runat="server" />
</form>
```

2. Save the file as **example8.aspx** in the Chap10\Chapter folder in your work folder.
3. Close the file.
4. Load the page using the following URL. Be sure to replace the italicized text with your server name and work folder name.

   http://*localhost*/*workfolder*/Chap10/Chapter/example8.aspx

5. Enter **256.8902** in the Amount of deposit text box, and then click the **Submit** button. A page similar to Figure 10-8 is displayed, indicating that the value entered is not a valid currency value.
6. Change the value to **256.89**, then click the **Submit** button. The error message does not appear.

The CompareValidator control does not check whether values are actually entered into the controls that it is comparing. If the controls to be compared are left blank, the form still passes the validation check.

Using the RangeValidator Control

You use the RangeValidator control to check whether data entered is between specified upper and lower bounds, such as between two numbers, two dates, or two alphabetic characters. You set the upper and lower bounds of the range as properties of a RangeValidator control. The RangeValidator control may take the following form:

<asp:RangeValidator
  ControlToValidate="*id_of_the_control_to_validate*"
  ErrorMessage="*error message to display*"
  MaximumValue="*the maximum value in the range of values*"

MinimumValue="*the minimum value in the range of values*"
Type="*set the data type used when comparing values*"
runat="server" />

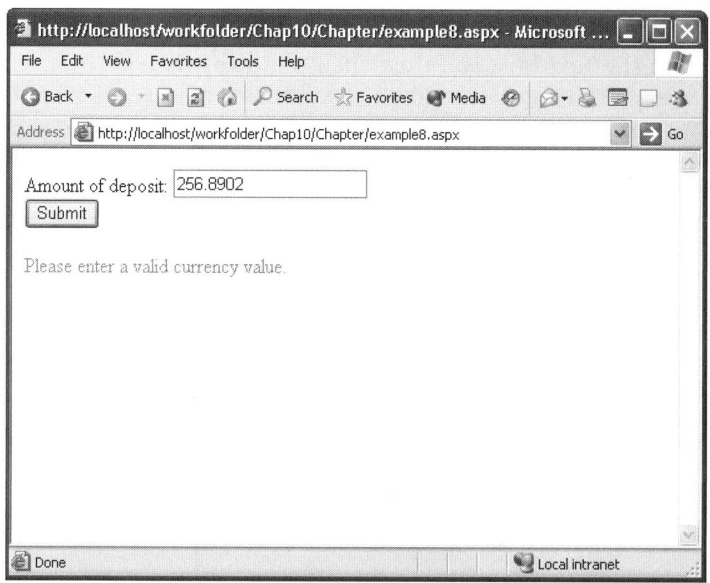

Figure 10-8 Validating a currency value

In the following steps, you use a RangeValidator control to validate that the data falls between two numbers.

To use the RangeValidator control:

1. Open a new document in Notepad and save the file as **example9.aspx** in the Chap10\Chapter folder in your work folder.
2. Add the following code to link a RangeValidator control to a TextBox control:

```
<form runat="server">
Enter a number between 1 and 365
<asp:TextBox id="txtNum" runat="server"/><br>
<asp:Button Text="Submit" runat="server"/><br><br>
<asp:RangeValidator
    ControlToValidate="txtNum"
    ErrorMessage="Please enter a number between 1 and 365: "
    MaximumValue="365"
    MinimumValue="1"
    Type="Integer"
    runat="server" />
</form>
```

3. Save and close the file.

10

4. Load this page using the following URL. Be sure to replace the italicized text with your server name and work folder name.

   http://*localhost*/*workfolder*/Chap10/Chapter/example9.aspx

   This page is displayed, as shown in Figure 10-9.

5. Enter **456** in the text box, and then click the **Submit** button. An error message informs you that you should enter a number between 1 and 365.

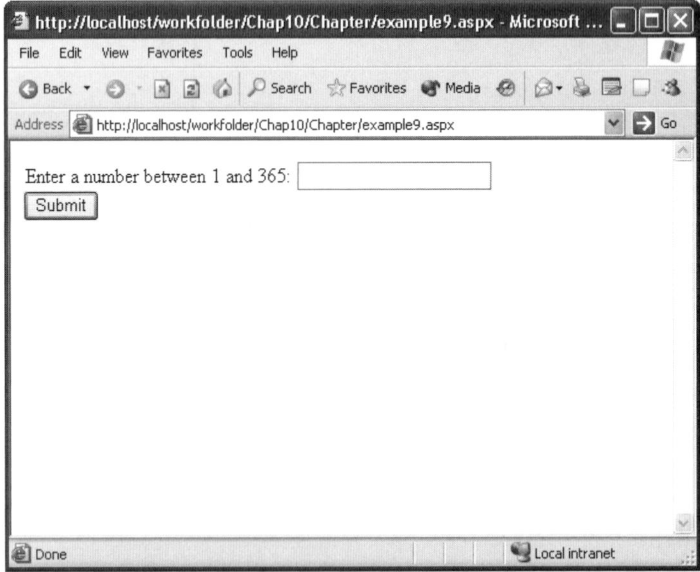

Figure 10-9 Using the RangeValidator control

Note that the range includes the minimum and maximum values. In the preceding example, you must enter a number greater than or equal to 1 and less than or equal to 365. If you enter a non-numerical value, the error message is also displayed.

Using the ValidationSummary Control

You have seen that validation error messages are displayed where the corresponding validator control is declared. If you have a form with 20 fields, error messages may appear anywhere on your page. Fortunately, ASP.NET provides another control, ValidationSummary, which you can use to organize any error messages.

The ValidationSummary control allows you to summarize all errors at the top of the page, or wherever else you wish. It also allows you to format the messages. In the following steps, you display error messages on the top of the page in a bulleted list.

To use the ValidationSummary control:

1. Open the file **example10.txt**, which is located in the Chap10\Chapter folder in your work folder.
2. Save the file as **example10.aspx** in the same folder.
3. Add the bold code shown in Figure 10-10 to declare a ValidationSummary control.

```
<form runat="server">
<asp:ValidationSummary
   HeaderText="The errors are listed here:"
   runat="server"/>
User name:
<asp:TextBox id="txtUser" runat="server"/>
<asp:RequiredFieldValidator runat="server"
     ControlToValidate="txtUser"
     ErrorMessage="You must enter your user name!"/><br>
Comments:<br>
<asp:TextBox id="txtMsg" TextMode="MultiLine"
     Columns="26" Rows="5" runat="server"/>
<asp:RequiredFieldValidator runat="server"
     ControlToValidate="txtMsg"
     ErrorMessage="You must enter some comments!"/><br>

Between 1 and 365:
<asp:TextBox id="txtNum" Columns="10" runat="server"/>
<asp:RangeValidator
    ControlToValidate="txtNum"
    ErrorMessage="Please enter a number between 1 and 365: "
    MaximumValue="365"
    MinimumValue="1"
    Type="Integer"
    runat="server" />
<br>
<asp:Button Text="Submit" runat="server"/><br><br>
</form>
```

Figure 10-10 Example10.aspx

4. Save and close the file.
5. Load the page using the following URL. Be sure to replace the italicized text with your server name and work folder name.

   http://*localhost*/*workfolder*/Chap10/Chapter/example10.aspx

6. Click the **Submit** button without entering any data. The page is displayed, as shown in Figure 10-11.
7. Enter valid values in all of the input fields, and then click the **Submit** button. No error messages appear.

10

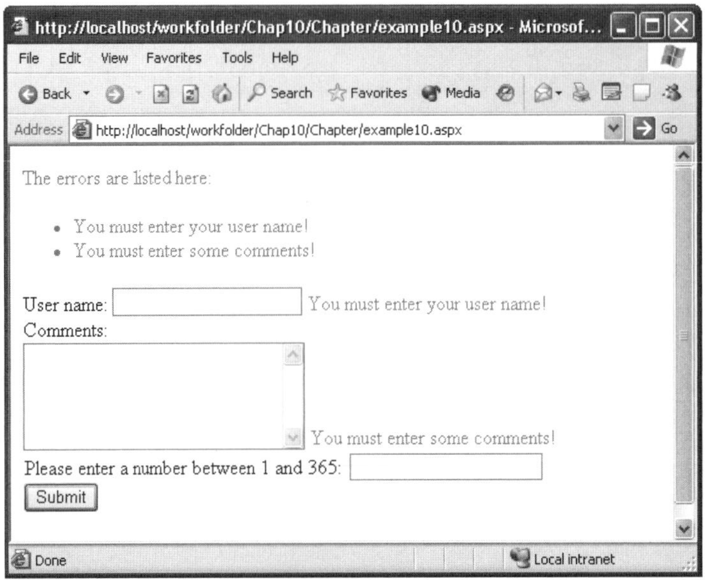

Figure 10-11 Using the ValidationSummary control to organize error messages

UPLOADING FILES TO A WEB SERVER

Many Web applications provide file-uploading capabilities on their Web site. With ASP.NET, you can easily provide such capability to your Web site. In this section, you create an ASP.NET page to allow users to upload files to the Web server.

To upload files, you need to use the InputFile HTML server control. This control renders an input box and a browse button. You can enter the full path of the file to be uploaded, or browse the local file system and select a file by clicking the Browse button. The syntax to use the InputFile HTML server control follows:

<input type="*file*" id="*controlID*" runat="server" />

To upload files, you also need to set the encType attribute of the server-side form to support multipart MIME (Multipurpose Internet Mail Extension) data, which allows the browser to send lots of different types of files to the Web server as one bundle. The syntax is as follows:

<form enctype="*multipart/form-data*" runat="server">
</form>

Now you are ready to develop a simple file-uploading page.

To create a file-uploading ASP.NET page:

1. Open a new document in Notepad and save the file as **example11.aspx** in the Chap10\Chapter folder in your work folder.

2. Add the following code to upload the file to the Web server. To specify the folder where you want to save the files, you change the dirFile value (C:\uploadedfiles in the following code):

```
<script language="VB" runat="server">
  Dim dirFile as string="C:\uploadedfiles"
  sub Page_Load
    if Dir(dirFile, vbDirectory) = "" then
       MkDir(dirFile)
    end if
  end sub
  sub Upload_Click(s as Object, e as EventArgs)
     Dim strFileFullName as string
     strFileFullName = myFile.PostedFile.FileName
     Dim strFileName as string
     strFileName = System.IO.Path.GetFileName(strFileFullName)
     myFile.PostedFile.SaveAs(dirFile & "\" & strFileName)
  end sub
</script>
```

3. Add the following code to add the form to upload the file:

```
<html>
<head><title>Uploading a file</title></head>
<body>
<b>File-uploading tool</b>
<form enctype="multipart/form-data" runAt="server">
 Select a file to upload:
 <input id="myFile" type="file" runat="server" size="20"><br><br>
 <asp:Button Text="Upload file" OnClick="Upload_Click" runat="server"/>
</form>
</body>
</html>
```

4. Save and close the file.

5. Load this page using the following URL. Be sure to replace the italicized text with your server name and work folder name.

   http://*localhost*/*workfolder*/Chap10/Chapter/example11.aspx

   This page is displayed, as shown in Figure 10-12.

6. Click the **Browse** button to open the Open dialog box, and then use this dialog box to locate and select a file to upload, such as an image file.

7. Click the **Upload file** button to upload the file to your Web server.

8. Open the folder where you saved the files to see whether the file uploaded successfully.

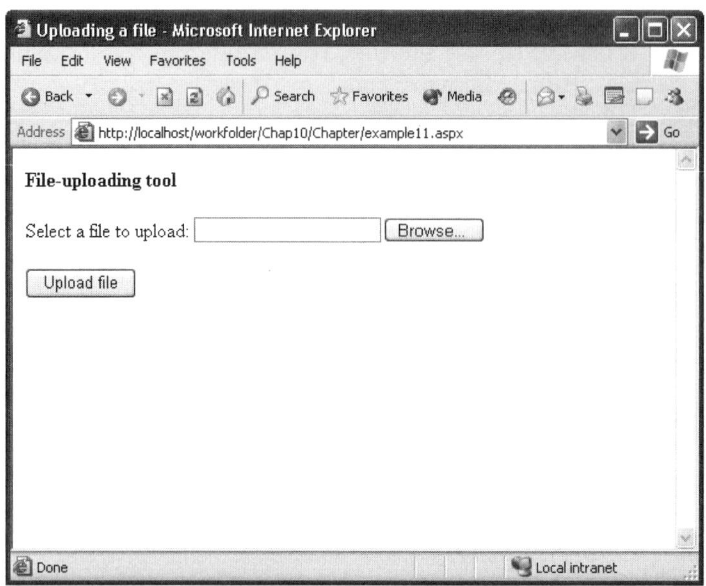

Figure 10-12 Using the file-uploading tool

In the server-side script block, you declare a public variable to specify where to save the file `Dim dirFile as string="C:\uploadedfiles"`. Before uploading a file, you want to make sure the C:\uploadedfiles folder exists by adding the following code in the Page_Load procedure:

```
sub Page_Load
  if Dir(dirFile, vbDirectory) = "" then
     MkDir(dirFile)
  end if
end sub
```

If the folder C:\uploadedfiles does not exist, the method `Dir(dirFile, vbDirectory)` returns an empty string. Calling the method `MkDir(dirFile)` creates the folder, which is passed as a parameter. You can use the Dir method to check whether certain files or folders exist. You write the event handler to perform the actual uploading of the file to the Web server:

```
sub Upload_Click(s as Object, e as EventArgs)
   Dim strFileFullName as string
   strFileFullName = myFile.PostedFile.FileName
   Dim strFileName as string
   strFileName = System.IO.Path.GetFileName(strFileFullName)
   myFile.PostedFile.SaveAs(dirFile & "\" & strFileName)
end sub
```

You can upload files in ASP.NET with a single line of code, as follows:

```
myFile.PostedFile.SaveAs(dirFile & "\" & strFileName)
```

The code uses the name of the HTML InputFile control to access the **`PostedFile`** object's SaveAs method. The PostedFile is an instance of the HTTPPostedFile that accesses the file to be uploaded. The SaveAs method of the **`PostedFile`** object takes as parameter the path and filename. You use the FileName property of the **`PostedFile`** object to get the fully qualified name of the file on the client's computer (for example "C:\temp\me.gif"). Then use the method `System.IO.Path.GetFileName(strFileFullName)` to get the filename.

The **`PostedFile`** object provides various properties that you can use to retrieve information about the file to be uploaded, such as the size of the file, MIME content type, and so on. Table 10-1 lists these properties.

Table 10-1 `PostedFile` object properties

Properties	Description
ContentLength	Gets the size in bytes of an uploaded file
ContentType	Gets the MIME content type of a file sent by a client
FileName	Gets the fully qualified name of the file on the client's computer (for example "C:\temp\me.gif")

The example11.aspx provides a simple file-uploading tool. In the following steps, you create a robust version of the file-uploading tool by creating a file-upload user control, which provides a property to allow you to specify where to save files. 10

To create a file-upload user control:

1. Open the **fileupload.txt** file in the Chap10\Chapter folder in your work folder.
2. Save the file as **fileupload.ascx** in the same folder.
3. Add the code shown in bold in Figure 10-13 to add an attribute so you can specify where to save files in your ASP.NET Web page. The default is C:\uploadedfiles.
4. Save and close the file.

This page also contains a TextBox control, which you can use to specify the filename. Now you can create an ASP.NET Web page to provide a more robust file-uploading tool for your Web site.

To use the file-upload user control:

1. Open a new document in Notepad and type the following code:

```
<%@ Page EnableViewState="false" %>
<%@ Register TagPrefix="WCM" TagName="Upload" src="fileupload.ascx" %>
<html>
<head><title>Uploading a file</title></head>
<body>
<WCM:Upload dirFile="c:\temp" runat="server"/>
</body>
</html>
```

```
<script language="VB" runat="server">
  Public Dim dirFile as string="C:\uploadedfiles"
  sub Page_Load
    if Dir(dirFile, vbDirectory) = "" then
       MkDir(dirFile)
    end if
  end sub
  sub Upload_Click(s as Object, e as EventArgs)
     Dim strFileFullName as string=myFile.PostedFile.FileName
     Dim strFileName as string = txtFileName.Text
     if strFileName = "" then
       strFileName = System.IO.Path.GetFileName(strFileFullName)
     end if
     try
        myFile.PostedFile.SaveAs(dirFile & "\" & strFileName)
        span1.InnerHTML="File uploaded successfully."
        span2.InnerHTML="File name: " + strFileFullName
        span3.InnerHtml="ContentType: " + myFile.PostedFile.ContentType
        span4.InnerHtml="ContentLength: " +
myFile.PostedFile.ContentLength.ToString()
     catch exc as exception
        span1.InnerHtml="Uploading failed."
     end try
     txtFileName.Text=""
  end sub
</script>

<form enctype="multipart/form-data" runat="server">
 <table>
 <tr><td colspan=2><b>File uploading tool</b></td></tr>
 <tr><td>Select file:</td>
     <td><input id="myFile" type="file" size="25"
            runat="server" ></td></tr>
 <tr><td>Save as:</td>
     <td><asp:TextBox columns="25"
          id="txtFileName" runat="server"/></td></tr>
 <tr><td colspan=2>
     <asp:Button Text="Upload a file" OnClick="Upload_Click"
 runat="server"/>
      </td></tr>
 <tr><td valign=top>Status:</td>
     <td>
     <span id="status" runat="server" visible="true">
       <span id="span1" runat="server"/><br>
       <span id="span2" runat="server"/><br>
       <span id="span3" runat="server"/><br>
       <span id="span4" runat="server"/>
     </span>
     </td></tr>
 </table>
</form>
```

Figure 10-13 fileupload.ascx

2. Save the file as **example12.aspx** in the Chap10\Chapter folder in your work folder.

3. Load this page using the following URL. Be sure to replace the italicized text with your server name and work folder name.

   http://*localhost*/*workfolder*/Chap10/Chapter/example12.aspx

   This page is displayed, as shown in Figure 10-14.

4. Click the **Browse** button and use the Choose file dialog box to locate and select a file, and then click the **Upload file** button to upload the file.

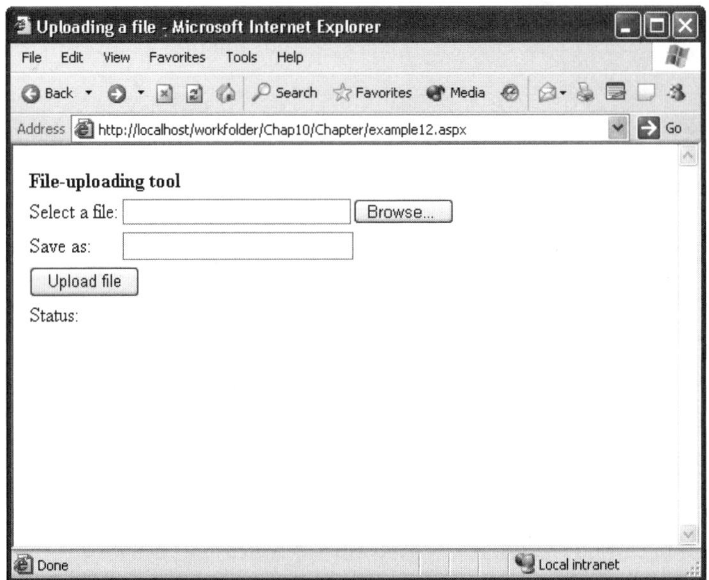

Figure 10-14 Using the file-upload user control

With the file-upload user control, you can specify where to save the uploaded files. You can also specify the filename to save instead of using the original filename on the client computer. The control also displays the file information if uploading succeeds. Otherwise, the page displays an error message indicating that the upload failed.

CHAPTER SUMMARY

- User controls are reusable components that act like ASP.NET server controls. You can build user controls by using the same techniques you have learned to develop Web Forms.
- Before you can include user controls in your ASP.NET Web pages, you need to use the Register directive to make them available.
- You can expose user control properties and methods by declaring public data members and public procedures in the control. You can also provide event handlers in the control so the control itself can handle certain events.

- Validation can be performed either on the client or server. ASP.NET provides various validation controls to facilitate the validation process.
- Validation controls can detect whether the client browser supports the script generated. If the client browser supports the script, the validation can be performed on the client; otherwise, all validations are performed on the server.
- ASP.NET provides five types of validation controls: RequiredFieldValidator, CompareValidator, RangeValidator, RegularExpressionValidator, and CustomValidator.
- ASP.NET provides the HTTPPostedFile class, which enables you to create file-uploading tools easily.
- To upload files, you need to use the InputFile HTML server control. You also need to set the encType attribute of the server-side form to support multipart MIME form data to allow the browser to send files to the Web server.

REVIEW QUESTIONS

1. A user control file discussed in this chapter has the extension of __________________.
   a. .aspx
   b. .asp
   c. .ascx
   d. .txt
2. To access a user control's property, which of the following attributes must be set when the control is declared?
   a. name
   b. runat
   c. id
   d. none of these
3. Which of the following code examples can be used to set an attribute called description, which is accessible from the page where it is declared?
   a. `Public Description as string`
   b. `Public Dim Description as string`
   c. `Dim Description as string`
   d. `Description as string`

4. To register a user control by using the Register directive, all of the following attributes must be set *except*:
   a. TagPrefix
   b. TagName
   c. src
   d. name
5. Assume you declared a user control and set the `id="control1"`. To access the control's Description property, which syntax do you use?
   a. Description
   b. Control1.Description
   c. Description of control1
   d. Control1[Description]
6. Assume you declared a user control and set the `id="control1"`. To use the GetNumber method of the control, which syntax do you use?
   a. GetNumber()
   b. control1.GetNumber
   c. control1.GetNumber()
   d. none of these
7. Which of the following code samples works without triggering errors? (SelDate is a TextBox Web control, and Calendar1 is a Calendar Web control.)
   a. SelDate.Text=calendar1.SelectedDate
   b. SelDate.Text=calendar1.SelectedDate().ToString()
   c. SelDate.Text=calendar1.SelectedDate.ToString()
   d. SelDate.Text=calendar1.SelectedDate()
8. To ensure that the user does not skip a required field when entering data on a Web form page, which of the following validation controls is most appropriate?
   a. RequiredFieldValidator
   b. CompareValidator
   c. RangeValidator
   d. RegularExpressionValidator
9. To compare a user's entry against another value, which of the following validation controls is most appropriate?
   a. RequiredFieldValidator
   b. CompareValidator
   c. RangeValidator
   d. RegularExpressionValidator

10. To check whether a form field contains a particular data type, which of the following validation controls is most appropriate?
    a. RequiredFieldValidator
    b. CompareValidator
    c. RangeValidator
    d. RegularExpressionValidator
11. To check whether data entered is between a specific range of values, which of the following validation controls is most appropriate?
    a. RequiredFieldValidator
    b. CompareValidator
    c. RangeValidator
    d. RegularExpressionValidator
12. To upload files, which of the following server controls must you use on the form?
    a. Button
    b. TextBox
    c. HTTPInputFile
    d. Label
13. To upload files, which of the following attributes must be set on the server-side form?
    a. name
    b. id
    c. enctype
    d. method
14. The `PostedFile` object provides all of the following properties *except*:
    a. ContentType
    b. ContentLength
    c. FileName
    d. ClientComputerIP
15. Which of the following specifies the size of the file to be uploaded in bytes?
    a. FileByte
    b. ContentInByte
    c. ContentLength
    d. none of these

HANDS-ON EXERCISES

If necessary, use Windows Explorer to create a new folder in the Chap10 folder in your work folder. Name this folder Exercises. Save the files that you create in these exercises in the Chap10\Exercises folder in your work folder.

Exercise 10-1

In this exercise, you write a user control to encapsulate rules to convert a number to a corresponding letter grade, and then use the user control to create a grade converter.

To create a Converter user control:

1. Open the file **exercise1.txt** in the Chap10\Exercises folder in your work folder.
2. Save the file as **exercise1.ascx** in the same folder.
3. Add the bold code in Figure 10-15 to add the rules to convert a number to a letter grade.

```
<script runat="server">
 sub Button_Click(s as Object, e as EventArgs)
  Dim grade as Integer
  grade = CInt(txtGrade.Text)
  if grade >= 90 then
    lblGrade.Text="A"
  else if grade >= 80 then
    lblGrade.Text="B"
  else if grade >= 70 then
    lblGrade.Text="C"
  else if grade >= 60 then
    lblGrade.Text="D"
  else
    lblGrade.Text="F"
  end if
 end sub
</script>
<form runat="server">
Enter a grade and then click "Get letter grade"<br><br>
Your grade:<asp:TextBox id="txtGrade" runat="server" columns=5/>
<br>
<asp:Button Text="Get letter grade" runat="server" OnClick="Button_Click"/>
<br><br>
<b>Your letter grade: </b>
<asp:Label id="lblGrade" runat="server"/>
</form>
```

Figure 10-15

4. Save and close the file.

10

5. Open a new document in Notepad and type the following code:

```
<%@ Register TagPrefix="WCM" TagName="Grade" src="exercise1.ascx" %>
<WCM:Grade runat="server"/>
```

6. Save the file as **exercise1.aspx** in the Chap10\Exercises folder in your work folder.
7. Load the page using the following URL. Be sure to replace the italicized text with your server name and work folder name.

   http://*localhost*/*workfolder*/Chap10/Exercises/exercise1.aspx
8. Enter a number and click the "Get letter grade" button. Its corresponding letter grade should be displayed on the page.

Exercise 10-2

In Exercise 10-1, if you enter a nonnumerical value and click the button, you receive an error message. In this exercise, you use a validation control to validate whether the value entered is a valid number.

To improve the user control:

1. Open the file **exercise2.txt**, which is located in the Chap10\Exercises folder in your work folder.
2. Save the file as **exercise2.ascx** in the same folder.
3. Add the CompareValidator control as shown in the bold code in Figure 10-16.
4. Save and close the file.
5. Open a new document in Notepad and type the following code:

```
<%@ Register TagPrefix="WCM" TagName="Grade" src="exercise2.ascx" %>
<WCM:Grade runat="server"/>
```

6. Save the file as **exercise2.aspx** in the Chap10\Exercises folder in your work folder.
7. Load this page to test the user control.
8. Enter a nonnumerical value. Instead of raising an exception, the validation control displays an error message indicating that a numerical value is expected.

```
<script runat="server">
 sub Button_Click(s as Object, e as EventArgs)
  Dim grade as Integer
  grade = CInt(txtGrade.Text)
  if grade >= 90 then
    lblGrade.Text="A"
  else if grade >= 80 then
    lblGrade.Text="B"
  else if grade >= 70 then
    lblGrade.Text="C"
  else if grade >= 60 then
    lblGrade.Text="D"
  else
    lblGrade.Text="F"
  end if
 end sub
</script>
<form runat="server">
Enter a grade and then click "Get letter grade"<br><br>
Your grade:<asp:TextBox id="txtGrade" runat="server" columns=5/>
<asp:CompareValidator
   ControlToValidate="txtGrade"
   Operator="DataTypeCheck"
   ErrorMessage="Please enter a numerical value!"
   Type="Integer"
   runat="server"/>
<br>
<asp:Button Text="Get letter grade" runat="server"
OnClick="Button_Click"/>
<br><br>
<b>Your letter grade: </b>
<asp:Label id="lblGrade" runat="server"/>
</form>
```

Figure 10-16

Exercise 10-3

Although you have improved the letter grade converter in Exercise 10-2 by checking whether the value entered is a numerical value, you still can enter numbers less than 1 or greater than 100. In this exercise, you use a validator to ensure the number entered is between 1 and 100.

To improve the user control:

1. Open the file **exercise3.txt**, which is located in the Chap10\Exercises folder in your work folder.
2. Save the file as **exercise3.ascx** in the same folder.
3. Add the RangeValidator control, as shown in the bold text in Figure 10-17.

```
<script runat="server">
 sub Button_Click(s as Object, e as EventArgs)
  Dim grade as Integer
  grade = CInt(txtGrade.Text)
  if grade >= 90 then
    lblGrade.Text="A"
  else if grade >= 80 then
    lblGrade.Text="B"
  else if grade >= 70 then
    lblGrade.Text="C"
  else if grade >= 60 then
    lblGrade.Text="D"
  else
    lblGrade.Text="F"
  end if
 end sub
</script>
<form runat="server">
Enter a grade and then click "Get letter grade"<br><br>
Your grade:<asp:TextBox id="txtGrade" runat="server" columns=5/>
<asp:CompareValidator
   ControlToValidate="txtGrade"
   Operator="DataTypeCheck"
   ErrorMessage="Please enter a numerical value!"
   Type="Integer"
   runat="server"/>
<asp:RangeValidator
    ControlToValidate="txtGrade"
    ErrorMessage="Please enter a number between 1 and 100."
    MaximumValue="100"
    MinimumValue="1"
    Type="Integer"
    runat="server" />
<br>
<asp:Button Text="Get letter grade" runat="server"
OnClick="Button_Click"/>
<br><br>
<b>Your letter grade: </b>
<asp:Label id="lblGrade" runat="server"/>
</form>
```

Figure 10-17

4. Save and close the file.
5. Write an ASP.NET Web page to test the new version of the user control.

Exercise 10-4

In this exercise, you create an enhanced Calendar user control using the TextBox and Calendar ASP.NET server controls, and then handle the event within the user control.

To create an enhanced Calendar user control:

1. Open the file **exercise4.txt**, which is located in the Chap10\Exercises folder in your work folder.
2. Save the file as **exercise4.ascx** in the same folder.
3. Add the code shown in bold in Figure 10-18 to handle events in the control.

```
<script runat="server">
sub Selection_Change(s as Object, e as EventArgs)
      selDate.Text = Calendar1.SelectedDate.ToShortDateString()
end sub
</script>

Selected date: <asp:TextBox id="selDate" runat="server"/><br>
<asp:Calendar id="Calendar1" Width="350px" Height="190px"
  BorderColor="White" BorderWidth="1px" NextPrevFormat="FullMonth"
  BackColor="White" ForeColor="Black" Font-Size="9pt"
  Font-Names="Verdana" runat="server" VisibleDate="2002-09-13"
  OnSelectionChanged="Selection_Change">
  <TodayDayStyle BackColor="#CCCCCC"></TodayDayStyle>
  <NextPrevStyle Font-Size="8pt" Font-Bold="True"
   ForeColor="#333333" VerticalAlign="Bottom"></NextPrevStyle>
  <DayHeaderStyle Font-Size="8pt" Font-Bold="True"></DayHeaderStyle>
  <SelectedDayStyle ForeColor="White"
BackColor="#333399"></SelectedDayStyle>
  <TitleStyle Font-Size="12pt" Font-Bold="True" BorderWidth="4px"
   ForeColor="#333399" BorderColor="Black"
BackColor="White"></TitleStyle>
  <OtherMonthDayStyle ForeColor="#999999"></OtherMonthDayStyle>
</asp:Calendar>
```

Figure 10-18

4. Save and close the file.
5. Write an ASP.NET Web page to test the new version of the user control.

10

Exercise 10-5

When you provide file-uploading capability on your Web site, you can reserve disk space on the Web server by setting the maximum file size to be uploaded. In this exercise, you modify the user control you developed in this chapter so it does not allow a file to be saved to your Web server if the file size exceeds the maximum limit you specified.

To set a size limit in the file-upload user control:

1. Open the file **fileupload.txt**, which is located in the Chap10\Exercises folder in your work folder.
2. Save the file as **fileupload.ascx** in the same folder.
3. Add the code shown in bold in Figure 10-19 to set the size limit.

```
<script language="VB" runat="server">
  Public Dim dirFile as string="C:\uploadedfiles"
  Public Dim maxSize as Integer = 1048576
  sub Page_Load
    if Dir(dirFile, vbDirectory) = "" then
      MkDir(dirFile)
    end if
  end sub
  sub Upload_Click(s as Object, e as EventArgs)
     Dim strFileFullName as string=myFile.PostedFile.FileName
     Dim strFileName as string = txtFileName.Text
     if strFileName = "" then
       strFileName = System.IO.Path.GetFileName(strFileFullName)
     end if
     try
        if myFile.PostedFile.ContentLength > maxSize then
          span1.InnerHTML="The file exceeds the size limit."
          exit sub
        end if
        myFile.PostedFile.SaveAs(dirFile & "\" & strFileName)
        span1.InnerHTML="File uploaded successfully."
        span2.InnerHTML="File name: " + strFileFullName
        span3.InnerHtml="ContentType: " + myFile.PostedFile.ContentType
        span4.InnerHtml="ContentLength: " +
myFile.PostedFile.ContentLength.ToString()
     catch exc as exception
        span1.InnerHtml="Uploading failed."
     end try
     txtFileName.Text=""
  end sub
</script>

<form enctype="multipart/form-data" runat="server">
 <table>
 <tr><td colspan=2><b>File-uploading tool</b></td></tr>
 <tr><td>Select file:</td>
     <td><input id="myFile" type="file" size="25"
             runat="server" ></td></tr>
 <tr><td>Save as:</td>
     <td><asp:TextBox columns="25"
           id="txtFileName" runat="server"/></td></tr>
 <tr><td colspan=2>
     <asp:Button Text="Upload a file" OnClick="Upload_Click"
runat="server"/>
     </td></tr>
```

Figure 10-19

```
  <tr><td valign=top>Status:</td>
      <td>
      <span id="status" runat="server" visible="true">
        <span id="span1" runat="server"/><br>
        <span id="span2" runat="server"/><br>
        <span id="span3" runat="server"/><br>
        <span id="span4" runat="server"/>
      </span>
      </td></tr>
  </table>
</form>
```

Figure 10-19 (continued)

4. Save and close the file.
5. Open a new document in Notepad and type the following code to test the new version of the file-upload user control.

```
<%@ Page EnableViewState="false" %>
<%@ register TagPrefix="WCM" TagName="Upload" src="fileupload.ascx" %>
<html>
<head><title>Uploading a file</title></head>
<body>
<WCM:Upload dirFile="c:\temp" maxSize="2000000" runat="server"/>
</body>
</html>
```

6. Save the file as **exercise5.aspx** in the Chap10\Exercises folder in your work folder.
7. Load this page using the following URL. Be sure to replace the italicized text with your server name and work folder name.

   http://*localhost*/*workfolder*/Chap10/Exercises/exercise5.aspx
8. Try to upload a file over 2 MB. If the file size exceeds 2 MB, an error message appears, indicating that the file would not be saved to the Web server.

10

WEB PROGRAMMING PROJECTS

If necessary, use Windows Explorer to create a new folder in the Chap10 folder in your work folder. Name this folder Projects. Save the files that you create in these projects in the Chap10\Projects in your work folder.

Project 10-1

You are asked to provide file-upload capability to your Web site. But only image files, such as .gif, and .jpg, can be saved to the Web server. Modify the file-upload user control you developed to accomplish this project.

Project 10-2

You want to provide a guest book on your Web site. The guest book contains three input fields to enter the user name, e-mail address, and comments. All three fields are required, so you decide to use validation controls to validate these fields before processing the form. If the user skips any field, the page should display an informative message to remind the user to provide data for that field. Save the file in the Chap10\Projects folder in your work folder. Load and test this page to make sure it meets the specified requirements.

Project 10-3

A car dealer pays its salespeople a commission. Salespeople receive $320 per week plus two percent of their gross sales for that week. Write a user control to implement this policy. After you create the user control, create an ASP.NET Web page to use the user control to help salespeople to calculate earnings.

CHAPTER

11

CGI/PERL: PART I

In this chapter you will:

- Create a CGI script using the Perl language
- Test a Perl CGI script
- Debug a Perl CGI script
- Create a link to a CGI script
- Use a link to send one item of data to a CGI script
- Parse data sent to a Perl CGI script
- Use a link to send multiple items of data to a CGI script

Web pages can be either static or dynamic. A **static Web page** is an HTML document whose content is established at the time the page is created. Any time you access a static Web page, the same information appears. The information changes only when someone—typically the document's creator or a Web programmer—manually updates the HTML file stored on the server. Static Web pages are useful for displaying information that does not change often and that must be updated by hand, such as a college catalog or a list of the current exhibits at a museum.

Unlike a static Web page, a **dynamic Web page** is interactive; it can accept information from the user and also retrieve information for the user. If you have ever completed an online form—say, for example, to purchase merchandise or submit a resume—then you have used a dynamic Web page.

Whereas a static Web page is simply an HTML document, a dynamic Web page usually requires both an HTML document and a script. A **script** is a set of instructions written in a scripting language that tells a computer how to perform a task. A script associated with a dynamic Web page, for example, tells the computer how to process the data submitted by or retrieved for the user.

Several technologies are available for creating dynamic Web pages; examples include CGI, Active Server Pages (ASP), and Java applets. CGI is one of the most popular of these technologies. **CGI**, which stands for **Common Gateway Interface**, is the protocol that allows a Web server to communicate with CGI scripts. A **CGI script** is a script that follows the standards specified by the CGI protocol. CGI scripts send their output—typically HTML—to the Web server. The Web server transmits the HTML to your Web browser, which renders the Web page.

The most widely used language for creating CGI scripts is **Perl (Practical Extraction and Report Language)**. Perl is popular because it is powerful, yet easy to learn, and is available free of charge. (You can obtain a free copy of Perl from the ActiveState Web site at *www.activestate.com* or the Perl Web site at *www.perl.com*.)

WRITING YOUR FIRST CGI SCRIPT IN PERL

The first CGI script you write in Perl creates a Web page that contains the word "Welcome!" You can use any text editor to enter the Perl instructions for your script; for example, you can use Notepad or WordPad.

To create a Perl CGI script:

1. If necessary, use Windows Explorer to create a new folder in the Chap11 folder in your work folder. Name this folder **Chapter**.
2. Open a text editor, and then enter the text shown in Figure 11-1. Be sure to type each line exactly as shown, as Perl commands are case sensitive.

```
#Hart.pl – creates a Web page
print "Content-type: text/html\n\n";
#generate HTML
print "<HTML>\n";
print "<HEAD><TITLE>Hart Industries</TITLE></HEAD>\n";
print "<BODY>Welcome!</BODY>\n";
print "</HTML>\n";
```

Figure 11-1 Perl CGI script

Although most of the popular browsers allow you to omit the HTML, HEAD, and BODY tags from your HTML code, it is a good practice to include these tags for browsers that require them.

3. Save the script as **Hart.pl** in the Chap11\Chapter folder in your work folder. (The *pl* stands for Perl.)

Many text editors attach their own filename extension (such as .txt or .doc) to a saved file. Double-check your saved file to ensure that it does not have a double extension (as in Hart.pl.txt). If the file has a double extension, rename it. If you explicitly type quotes surrounding a filename (as in "Hart.pl"), most editors save the file as you specify, without adding their own extension.

Study closely each line in the script shown in Figure 11-1. The first line, `#Hart.pl - creates a Web page`, is a **comment**, which is simply internal documentation. Comments in a Perl script always begin with the sharp symbol (#). The Perl interpreter ignores any text appearing after the sharp symbol on that line. It is a good programming practice to include comments in your scripts as reminders for yourself and others who may have to maintain your script. In this case, the comment indicates the script's filename and purpose.

A CGI script must perform two important tasks. First, the script must specify the type of document it is sending to the browser (through the server), and second, the script must output the document. A CGI script uses an HTTP header line, called the **Content-type header**, to perform the first task, and typically uses HTML tags to perform the second task.

The syntax of the Content-type header is **print "Content-type:** ***type*****\n\n";**, where only the letter C in Content-type is capitalized. The Content-type header begins with the Perl `print` function, whose task is to send the text enclosed in quotation marks to the browser. In the syntax, *type* is the type of document the script is sending to the browser. Most scripts send an HTML document; therefore, you typically use `text/html` as the *type* in the Content-type header. The Content-type header shown as the second line in the Hart.pl script, for example, indicates that the script will send an HTML document to the browser.

11

Other *types* commonly found in the Content-type header include `text/plain` (for sending a text document that does not include HTML tags) and `image/gif` (for sending a gif image document).

Notice that `\n\n` follows the *type* in the Content-type header's syntax. A backslash (\) followed by the letter n is called the **newline character** in Perl, and is used to send a new line to the browser. The newline character creates a new line by inserting a carriage return at the end of the current line. The first newline character in the Content-type header's syntax identifies the end of the Content-type header, and ensures that the header appears on a line by itself. The second newline character inserts a blank line below the header; this signals the browser that it has reached the end of the header information. (A script can contain more than one header.) Both newline characters are necessary; otherwise, the browser will not be able to display the document it receives from the script.

The last character in a Content-type header is the semicolon (;). The Content-type header is considered a **statement**, which is simply an instruction that can be executed by the Perl interpreter. All Perl statements must end with a semicolon.

The Perl interpreter is the language translation software that translates the Perl instructions into machine language—the 0s and 1s the computer can understand.

The third line in the script, `#generate HTML`, is a comment that describes the purpose of the last four lines of code. In this case, the purpose of the code is to generate the HTML necessary to create a Web page. Note that each of the four lines begins with the Perl `print` function, which sends the text enclosed in quotation marks to the browser. The lines end with a semicolon, because they are considered Perl statements.

Look closely at the four statements that create the Web page. The statement `print "<HTML>\n";` sends the <HTML> tag, which denotes the beginning of a Web page, and a newline character to the browser. Although the newline character is not required when entering HTML, it makes the HTML code generated by the CGI script easier to read when the code is viewed in a browser. You observe the effect of the newline character later in this chapter.

The next statement in the script, `print "<HEAD><TITLE>Hart Industries </TITLE></HEAD>\n";`, sends the beginning and ending HEAD and TITLE tags, along with the title (which will appear in the browser's title bar) and a newline character. The next statement, `print "<BODY>Welcome!</BODY>\n";`, sends the beginning and ending BODY tags, together with the text to display on the Web page and a newline character. The last statement in the script, `print "</HTML>\n";`, sends the </HTML> tag and a newline character to the browser. The </HTML> tag denotes the end of the Web page.

Next, you learn how to test a script from both the command line and browser.

TESTING A PERL CGI SCRIPT

Before testing a script from a browser, it is a good idea to test it from the command line to verify that it does not contain any syntax errors. The term **syntax** refers to the rules of a language. A syntax error occurs when you fail to follow one or more of the rules.

To test a Perl CGI script from the command line:

1. In Windows 2000, click **Start**, point to **Programs**, point to **Accessories**, and then click **Command Prompt**. A Command Prompt window opens and displays the command prompt, as shown in Figure 11-2. (The default colors for the Command Prompt window shown in Figure 11-2 were changed from the default, which is white text on a black background, to black text on a gray background.)

You can change the color of the text and background displayed in the Command Prompt window by right-clicking the window's title bar, clicking Properties to open the Command Prompt Properties dialog box, and then clicking the Colors tab.

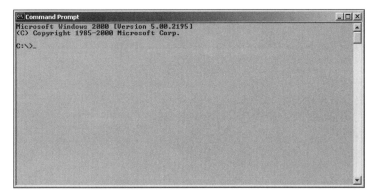

Figure 11-2 Command Prompt window showing the command prompt

Now make the Chap11\Chapter folder the current folder.

2. Type **`cd`** ***`path`*** after the command prompt, where *path* is the path to the Chap11\Chapter folder. For example, if the Chap11\Chapter folder is contained in the WebProg folder on the C drive, the appropriate instruction to type is `cd c:\webprog\chap11\chapter`. Press **Enter**.
3. Type **`perl -c hart.pl`** after the command prompt and press **Enter**. (Be sure to enter the `-c` using a lowercase letter c.) The word `perl` in the command starts the Perl interpreter. The `-c`, referred to as an option or switch, tells the Perl interpreter to check for syntax errors in the Hart.pl script, and then exit without executing the script.

   If you typed the script instructions correctly, the Perl interpreter responds with the message "hart.pl syntax OK." (In the next section, "Debugging a Perl CGI Script," you introduce an error in the Hart.pl script so that you can view a sample message produced by the `-c` switch.)

If the Perl interpreter displays an error message, an instruction in the script is probably mistyped and needs to be corrected. Usually, the error message includes a line number that indicates which instruction is causing the error. You can compare the instruction you entered with the corresponding instruction shown in Figure 11-1. Look for a missing semicolon, or a word entered using the wrong case. If you cannot find an error in the instruction, look at the instructions that precede it in the script. After correcting the error, try Step 3 again.

The `-c` switch checks the script for syntax errors only. However, not all errors in a script are syntax errors. Some errors surface only when the script is executed; to catch these errors, you use the `-w` switch. The `-w` switch tells the Perl interpreter to check for errors as it is executing the script.

4. Type **`perl -w hart.pl`** after the command prompt and press **Enter**. Your screen will look similar to Figure 11-3.

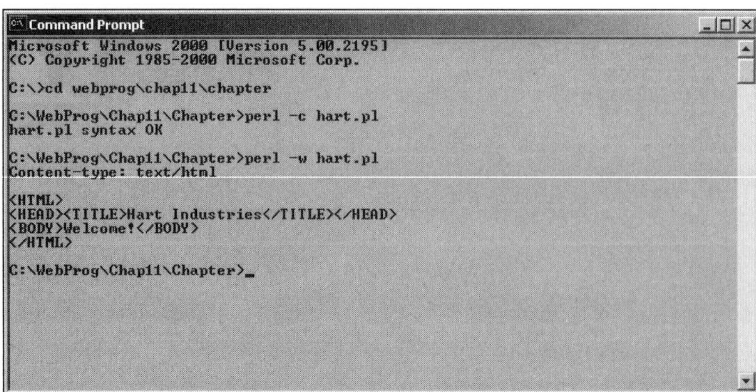

Figure 11-3 Command Prompt window showing the result of the `-c` and `-w` switches

Notice that the screen displays the information contained in each of the `print` functions in the script. For example, it displays the Content-type header line, followed by a blank line. (Recall that the Content-type header contains two newline characters: the first ensures that the header appears on its own line, and the second inserts a blank line below the header.) The screen also displays the HTML entered in the script.

5. Minimize the Command Prompt window.

Now that you know that the script does not contain any errors, and you have some idea of what the script's output will look like, you can test the script using your browser.

To test the Hart.pl script using a browser:

1. Open your browser.

   Next, type the Hart.pl script's URL in the Address box of the browser.

2. Type **http://*yourservername*/webprog/chap11/chapter/hart.pl** in the Address box. Be sure to replace *yourservername* with the name of your server. For example, if your server's name is www.course.com, then replace *yourservername* with www.course.com. Similarly, if your server's name is localhost, then replace *yourservername* with localhost.

3. Press **Enter**. The browser submits the URL to the server, which goes to the Chap11/Chapter folder and runs the Hart.pl script, using the Perl interpreter to convert the instructions into machine language. When the script is finished running, it sends its output to the server. The server sends the output to the browser, which renders the Web page shown in Figure 11-4.

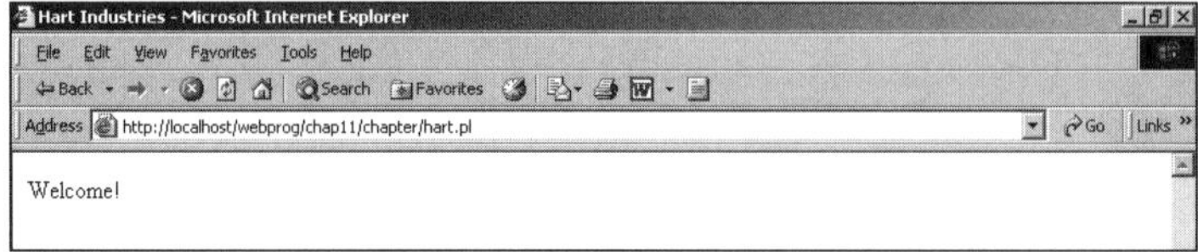

Figure 11-4 Output from the Hart.pl script

Now view the source code used to create the Web page. The source code is the HTML code generated by the Hart.pl script.

4. Click **View** on the browser's menu bar, and then click **Source**. The HTML code generated by the Hart.pl script appears in a separate window, as shown in Figure 11-5.

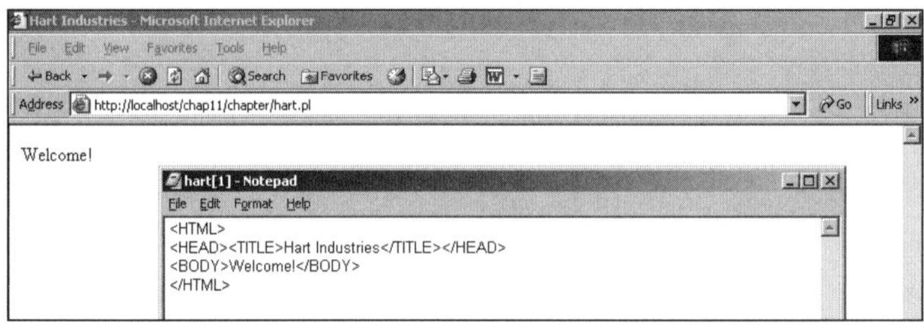

Figure 11-5 HTML code generated by the Hart.pl script

Compare the HTML code shown in Figure 11-5 with the `print` statements shown in Figure 11-1. Notice that each statement appears on a separate line in Figure 11-5. This happens because you included a newline character (\n) in each `print` statement. Without the newline character, the HTML code would appear on one line in the window and would be difficult to read.

5. Close the window containing the source code, then minimize the browser window.

Next, you introduce an error in the Hart.pl script. This will allow you to view a sample error message produced by the `-c` switch.

Debugging a Perl CGI Script

It is extremely easy to make a typing error when entering Perl instructions in a CGI script. A typing error typically results in a syntax error, because the Perl interpreter cannot understand the instruction. As you learned earlier, you can use the `-c` switch to tell the Perl interpreter to check a script for syntax errors. If the interpreter finds an error in the script, it displays a message that describes the error and also gives the error's location (by line number) in the script. You observe how this works in the next set of steps.

11

To introduce a syntax error in the Hart.pl script, and then use the `-c` switch to locate the error:

1. Return to the Hart.pl script in your text editor.
2. Delete the semicolon that appears at the end of the instruction `print "<BODY>Welcome!</BODY>\n";`. The instruction should now be `print "<BODY>Welcome!</BODY>\n"`.
3. Save the script.
4. Restore the Command Prompt window, which you minimized in an earlier set of steps. The Chap11\Chapter folder should be the current folder.
5. Type **`cls`** after the command prompt and press **Enter** to clear the contents of the Command Prompt window.
6. Type **`perl -c hart.pl`** after the command prompt and press **Enter**. The Perl interpreter displays a syntax error message similar to the one shown in Figure 11-6.

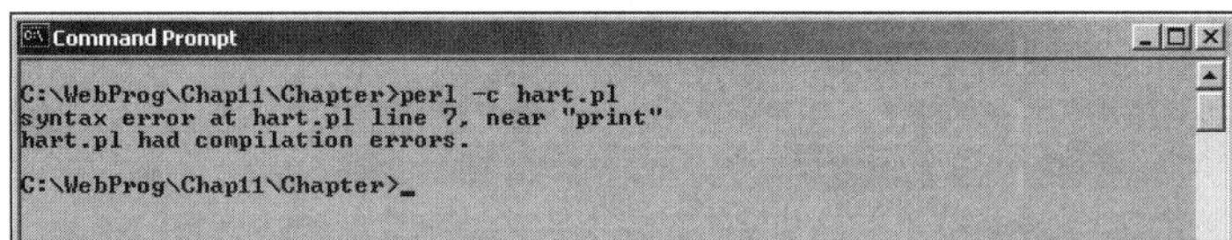

Figure 11-6 Error message displayed by the Perl interpreter

The message indicates that the error is on line 7 in the script, near the `print` function. However, line 7 contains the statement `print "</HTML>\n";`, which is correct. If you cannot find an error in the line identified in the error message, look at the line that precedes it in the script. In this case, the error is actually in the statement entered on the preceding line—line 6; recall that you deleted the semicolon from the statement.

7. Minimize the Command Prompt window.
8. Return to the Hart.pl script in your text editor. Enter the missing semicolon at the end of the `print "<BODY>Welcome!</BODY>\n"` statement.
9. Save the script.

In the next section, you learn how to use a hyperlink to send information to a CGI script.

CREATING A LINK TO A CGI SCRIPT

Most Web pages contain text, images, and hyperlinks. Hyperlinks, or links, typically appear on a Web page as different colored or underlined text or as clickable images. Links allow you to navigate the Internet, moving from one resource on the Internet to another. Examples of Internet resources include HTML documents, images, video files, and CGI scripts. In the following set of steps, you create the Willow Health Club Web page shown in Figure 11-7. You will use the Web page to observe how a text link to a CGI script works. In this case, you will link each of the three sport names on the Web page to a CGI script named Willow.pl, which you create later in the chapter.

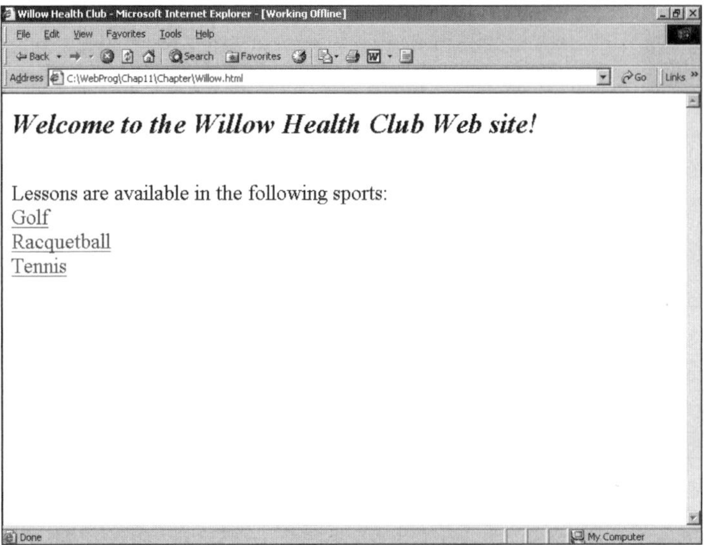

Figure 11-7 Willow Health Club Web page

The syntax for creating a text link to a CGI script is **<A HREF=***URL***>***hyperlinkText***</A>**. In the syntax, *URL* is the URL of the script, and *hyperlinkText* is the word or phrase that you click to activate the link.

To create the Willow Health Club Web page:

1. Open a new document in your text editor, and then enter the following HTML code. Replace *yourservername* in the three URLs with the name of your server. See Figure 11-8.

```
<!Willow.html>
<HTML>
<HEAD><TITLE>Willow Health Club</TITLE><BASEFONT SIZE=5></HEAD>
<BODY>
<B><I><H1>Welcome to the Willow Health Club Web site!</H1></I></B><BR>
Lessons are available in the following sports:<BR>
<A HREF="http://yourservername/webprog/chap11/chapter/willow.pl">Golf</A><BR>
<A HREF="http://yourservername/webprog/chap11/chapter/willow.pl">Racquetball</A><BR>
<A HREF="http://yourservername/webprog/chap11/chapter/willow.pl">Tennis</A><BR>
</BODY>
</HTML>
```

Figure 11-8 HTML code for the Willow Health Club Web page

2. Save the document as **Willow.html** in the Chap11\Chapter folder in your work folder.

   Now view the document in your Web browser.

3. Restore the browser window, which you minimized in an earlier set of steps. Use the browser's File menu to open the Willow.html file. A Web page similar to the one shown earlier in Figure 11-7 appears in the browser window.

4. Minimize the browser window.

Before you can test the three links on the Willow Health Club Web page, you need to create the Willow.pl script. The script will create a dynamic Web page that displays the message "You have linked to the Willow.pl script."

To create the Willow.pl script:

1. Open a new document in your text editor. Enter a comment that includes the script's name and purpose, and then enter the Content-type header, which alerts the browser that it will be receiving HTML.

```
#Willow.pl – creates a dynamic Web page
print "Content-type: text/html\n\n";
```

2. Next, enter the code to display the message "You have linked to the Willow.pl script." on a Web page.

```
#generate HTML
print "<HTML>\n";
print "<HEAD><TITLE>Willow Health Club</TITLE><BASEFONT SIZE=5></HEAD>\n";
print "<BODY>\n";
print "You have linked to the Willow.pl script.\n";
print "</BODY>\n";
print "</HTML>\n";
```

3. Save the document as **Willow.pl** in the Chap11\Chapter folder in your work folder.

   Now test the script for errors.

4. Restore the Command Prompt window, which you minimized in an earlier set of steps. The Chap11\Chapter folder should be the current folder.

5. Type **`cls`** and press **Enter** to clear the contents of the window, then type **`perl -c willow.pl`** and press **Enter** to check the script for syntax errors. If necessary, correct any syntax errors in the script before continuing to the next step.

6. Type **`perl -w willow.pl`** and press **Enter**. Recall that the `-w` switch tells the Perl interpreter to check the script for errors as it is executing the script. If necessary, correct any errors in the script before continuing to the next step. See Figure 11-9.

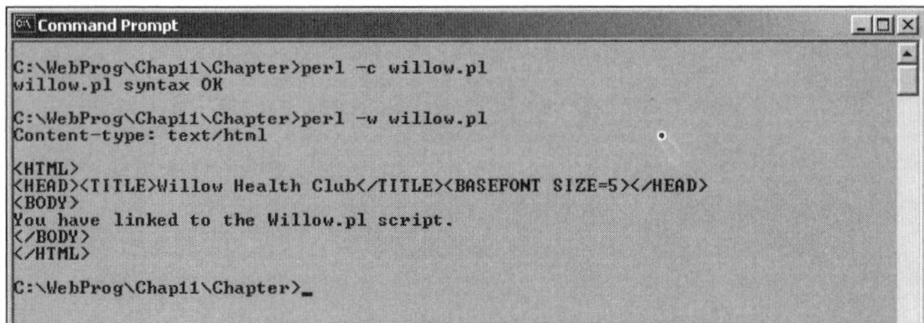

Figure 11-9 Command Prompt window showing the result of testing the Willow.pl script

7. Minimize the Command Prompt window.

Now that you have created the Willow.pl script, you can test the three links contained on the Willow Health Club Web page.

To test the three links contained on the Willow Health Club Web page:

1. Restore the browser window, which you minimized in an earlier set of steps.
2. Click **Golf** on the Willow Health Club Web page. The browser passes the URL of the Willow.pl script to the server. The server runs the script and sends the script's output—in this case, HTML—to the browser, which renders the dynamic Web page shown in Figure 11-10. Notice that the script's URL appears in the Address box in the browser window.

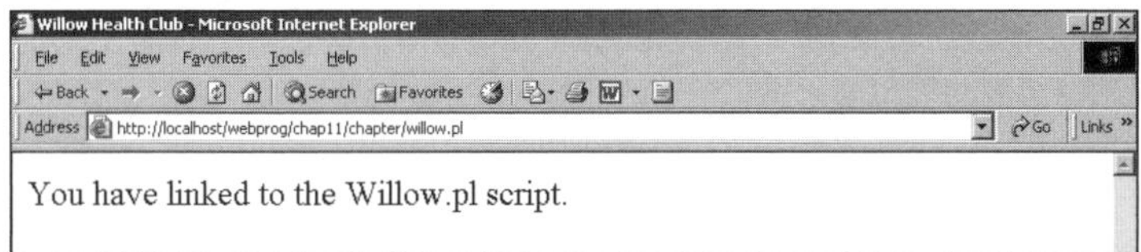

Figure 11-10 Dynamic Web page created by the Willow.pl script

3. Click the **Back** button on the toolbar to return to the Willow Health Club Web page.
4. On your own, verify that the Racquetball and Tennis links display the Web page shown in Figure 11-10.
5. Return to the Willow Health Club Web page, then minimize the browser window.

Now that you know how to create a link to a CGI script, you can learn how to use the link to send information to a script.

USING A LINK TO SEND ONE ITEM OF DATA TO A CGI SCRIPT

Currently, the Willow.pl script creates a Web page that displays the message "You have linked to the Willow.pl script." Assume you want to change the message to "You selected *sport*.", where *sport* is the name of the sport whose link you selected on the Willow Health Club Web page. For the script to display such a message, each link on the Web page needs to send the script the appropriate sport name. For example, the Golf link should send the sport name *golf*, the Racquetball link should send the sport name *racquetball*, and the Tennis link should send the sport name *tennis*.

To send data using a link, you append the data to the link's URL, which is specified in the anchor tag's HREF property. You can send one or more items of data to a script; however, in this section you learn how to send one item only. You learn how to send multiple items later in the chapter.

Figure 11-11 shows the syntax and three examples of sending one item of data using a link. The data sent to the script is shaded in each example. Notice that you use a question mark (?) to separate the URL from the data.

Syntax

<A HREF=*URL?key=value***>***hyperlinkText***</A>**

Examples

```
<A HREF="http://yourservername/webprog/chap11/chapter/willow.pl?sport=golf">Golf</A>
<A HREF="http://yourservername/webprog/chap11/chapter/willow.pl?cost=45">Golf</A>
<A HREF="http://yourservername/webprog/chap11/chapter/willow.pl
      ?contact=Mary+Williams">Golf</A>
```

Figure 11-11 Syntax and examples of sending one item using a link

Each item of data passed to a script has a *key* and a *value*. As the syntax indicates, you use an equal sign (=) to separate the *key* from the *value*. The *key* is simply a one-word name that you assign to the *value*. In Figure 11-11, for example, `sport` is the *key* (name) assigned to the *value* `golf`. Likewise, `cost` is the *key* assigned to the *value* `45`, and `contact` is the *key* assigned to the *value* `Mary+Williams`. Notice the plus sign that appears between the first name Mary and the last name Williams. If a *value* contains more than one word, you replace the space that separates the words with a plus sign.

The *key* allows you to refer to the *value* in a CGI script. For instance, to refer to the *value* `golf` in a script, you use its *key*, which is `sport`.

In the next set of steps, you modify the links on the Willow Health Club Web page so that each sends the name of its associated sport to the Willow.pl script.

To send the sport name using a link:

1. Open the Willow.html file in your text editor, then modify the three URLs so that each passes the appropriate sport name to the Willow.pl script. The modifications you should make to the URLs are shaded in Figure 11-12.

```
<!Willow.html>
<HTML>
<HEAD><TITLE>Willow Health Club</TITLE><BASEFONT SIZE=5></HEAD>
<BODY>
<B><I><H1>Welcome to the Willow Health Club Web site!</H1></I></B><BR>
Lessons are available in the following sports:<BR>
<A HREF="http://yourservername/webprog/chap11/chapter/Willow.pl?sport=golf">Golf</A><BR>
<A HREF="http://yourservername/webprog/chap11/chapter/Willow.pl?sport=racquetball">Racquetball</A><BR>
<A HREF="http://yourservername/webprog/chap11/chapter/Willow.pl?sport=tennis">Tennis</A><BR>
</BODY>
</HTML>
```

Figure 11-12 Modified URLs shown in the Willow.html document

2. Save the document.
3. Restore the browser window, which you minimized in an earlier set of steps. Click the **Refresh** button on the toolbar to reopen the Willow.html file in your browser.
4. Click **Golf**. See Figure 11-13. Notice that, in addition to the script's URL, the data passed to the script—in this case, `sport=golf`—also appears in the Address box of the browser window.

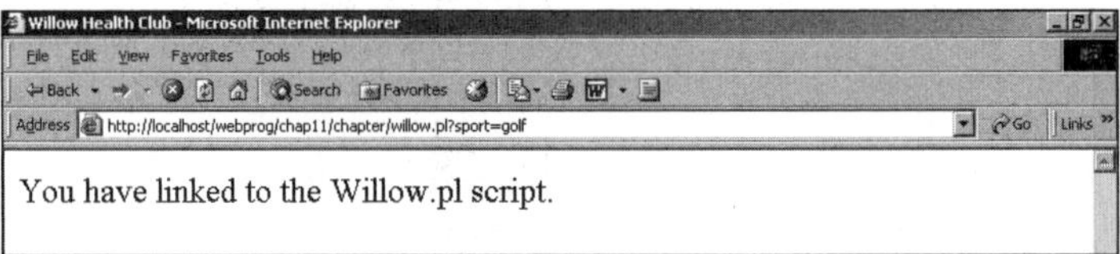

Figure 11-13 Address box showing the script's URL and the data passed to the script

5. Click the **Back** button to return to the Willow Health Club Web page.
6. Verify that the Racquetball and Tennis links send the appropriate sport name to the script.
7. Return to the Willow Health Club Web page, then minimize the browser window.

Before a script can use the data sent to it, it must parse the data. The term **parse** refers to the process of splitting the data's *key* from its *value*.

PARSING THE DATA SENT TO A PERL CGI SCRIPT

The Perl code needed to parse a script's incoming data is fairly complex and especially difficult to understand when you are first learning Perl. Fortunately, many Perl programmers have written parsing routines that you can use—for free—in your CGI scripts. One such parsing routine is contained in a Perl module named CGI.pm. A **module** is simply a collection of prewritten code stored in a file. Module filenames in Perl usually end with *pm*, which stands for *perl module*.

The CGI.pm module was created by Lincoln Stein and is part of the standard Perl distribution. The module also contains routines for other tasks commonly performed by CGI scripts, such as creating cookies, generating HTML, and uploading files.

To use the CGI.pm module to parse a script's incoming data, you enter the statement `use CGI qw(:standard -debug);` in a script. The `qw` in the statement is a Perl function and stands for *quote words*. The **qw function** tells the Perl interpreter to treat each word within the parentheses that follow the function as though the word were entered in single quotation marks. In other words, the statement `use CGI qw(:standard -debug);` is equivalent to the statement `use CGI ':standard, '-debug'`, but the former statement is more commonly used by Perl programmers.

Notice that you do not include the ".pm" part of the module name in the `use` statement.

The `:standard` part of the `use CGI qw(:standard -debug);` statement is called an **import tag**. The `:standard` import tag tells the Perl interpreter to import (make available to the script) only the standard features of the CGI.pm module; for most scripts, the standard features are sufficient.

You can learn about other import tags by typing `perldoc CGI.pm` after the command prompt.

The `-debug` in the `use CGI qw(:standard -debug);` statement is called a **pragma**, which is simply a special type of Perl module. The `-debug` pragma tells the CGI.pm module to pause the execution of a script to allow you to enter information from the keyboard.

Typically, the `use CGI qw(:standard -debug);` statement is entered at the beginning of the script, below the Content-type header.

To use the CGI.pm module's standard features in the Willow.pl script:

1. Open the Willow.pl file in your text editor.
2. Position the cursor at the end of the Content-type header, then press **Enter** to insert a blank line below the header.
3. In the blank line, type **`use CGI qw(:standard -debug);`** and press **Enter**. Be sure to type CGI using uppercase letters. Also be sure to type the colon after the opening parentheses, as well as the hyphen before the word *debug* and the semicolon at the end of the statement.

The CGI.pm module automatically parses the data sent to a script. In other words, the module splits the data's *key* from its *value*. You then can use the **param function**, which is one of the features provided by the `:standard` import tag, to access the *value* associated with a *key*. For example, you can use the `param` function to access the sport name passed to the Willow.pl script. Recall that the sport name *value* is associated with the `sport` *key*.

11

The syntax of the `param` function is **param(*key*)**, where *key* is enclosed in either single or double quotation marks. In other words, you can use either `param('sport')` or `param("sport")` to access the *value*—in this case, the sport name—associated with the `sport` *key*. However, single quotation marks are more commonly used in the `param` function, and this is the convention you will follow in this book.

Recall that you want the Willow.pl script to create a dynamic Web page that displays the message "You selected *sport*.", where *sport* is the sport name passed to the script. Before you can make the appropriate modifications to the script, you need to learn more about the `print` function.

The `print` Function

As you already know, you can use the Perl `print` function to generate a script's output. To do so, you use the `print` function in a Perl statement that follows the syntax **print** *output*;, where *output* is the expression, or a list of expressions separated by commas, that you want the script to output. Table 11-1 shows examples of using the `print` function to output strings (groups of characters enclosed in quotation marks) and the *value* accessed by the `param` function.

Table 11-1 Examples of using the `print` function

Examples	Results
`print "Good morning\n";`	Outputs the message "Good morning" and a newline character
`print "Good ", "morning", "\n";`	Same as above
`print "You selected ", param('sport'), ".\n";`	Outputs the message "You selected ", followed by the sport name passed to the script and accessed by the `param` function, followed by a period and the newline character

The first and second examples shown in Table 11-1 output the same information: the message "Good morning" followed by a newline character. Notice that the first example contains one string, whereas the second example contains three strings separated by commas. The third example shown in Table 11-1 outputs the string "You selected ", followed by the sport name passed to the script and accessed by the `param` function, followed by a period and the newline character.

Now you can make the appropriate modifications to the Willow.pl script.

To modify the message displayed by the Willow.pl script, and to then test the script:

1. Change the `print "You have linked to the Willow.pl script.\n";` statement to **`print "You selected ", param('sport'), ".\n";`**. The modified script is shown in Figure 11-14.

```
#Willow.pl - creates a dynamic Web page
print "Content-type: text/html\n\n";
use CGI qw(:standard -debug);

#generate HTML
print "<HTML>\n";
print "<HEAD><TITLE>Willow Health Club</TITLE><BASEFONT SIZE=5></HEAD>\n";
print "<BODY>\n";
print "You selected ", param('sport'), ".\n";
print "</BODY>\n";
print "</HTML>\n";
```

Figure 11-14 Modified Willow.pl script

2. Save the document.
3. Restore the Command Prompt window, which you minimized in an earlier set of steps. The Chap11\Chapter folder should be the current folder. Type **`cls`** after the command prompt, and press **Enter** to clear the contents of the window.

4. Type **`perl -c willow.pl`** and press **Enter**. If necessary, correct any syntax errors in the script before continuing to the next step.

   As you observed earlier in Figure 11-13, the browser sends data to the script using the format *key=value*. When testing a script from the command line, you also use the *key=value* format to send data to the script. You can include the data on the same line as the command that executes the script, as shown in Step 5.

5. Type **`perl -w willow.pl sport=golf`** and press **Enter**. (Be sure to include a space between the script's name and the data, but do not type any spaces before or after the equal sign.) See Figure 11-15.

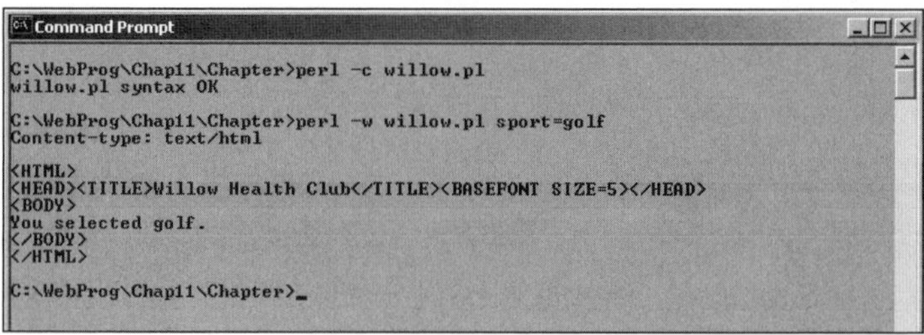

Figure 11-15 Result of including the data on the same line as the `-w` switch

   If you have a lot of data to pass to a script, you might find it more convenient to send each item of data on a separate line, rather than on the same line as the command that executes the script. This is shown in Step 6.

6. Type **`cls`** and press **Enter** to clear the contents of the Command Prompt window, then type **`perl -w willow.pl`** and press **Enter**. The message "(offline mode: enter name=value pairs on standard input)" appears on the screen, as shown in Figure 11-16. (Standard input refers to the keyboard.)

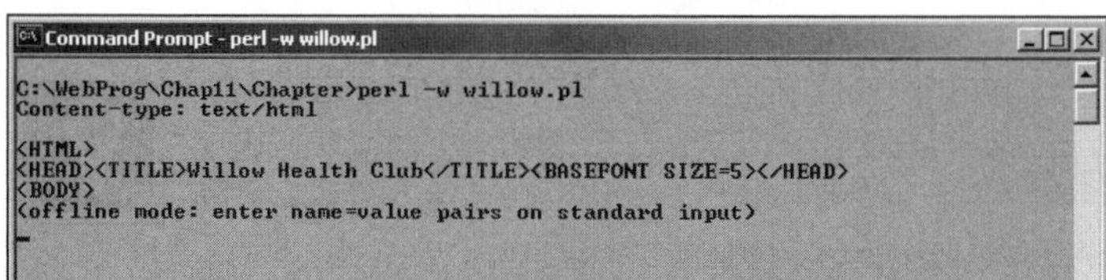

Figure 11-16 Command Prompt window showing the offline mode message

7. Type **`sport=golf`** and press **Enter**.

   You indicate that you have finished entering the input data by pressing Ctrl+z.

8. Press and hold down the **Ctrl** key as you type the letter **z**, then release the **Ctrl** key. ^Z appears on the screen. Press **Enter**. See Figure 11-17.

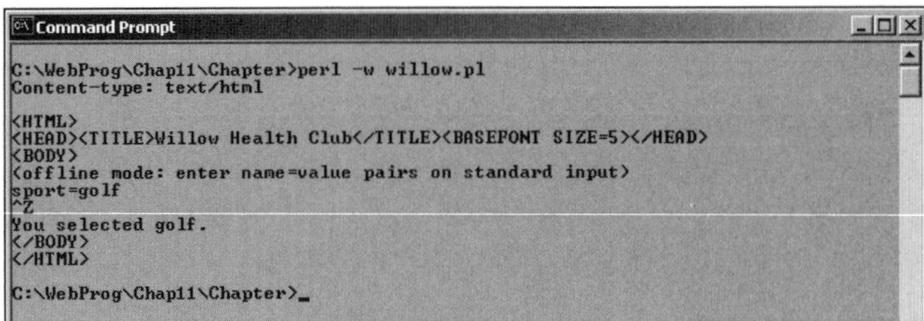

Figure 11-17 Command Prompt window showing the input data entered on a separate line

9. Minimize the Command Prompt window.

Now test the script by clicking the sport name links on the Willow.html Web page.

To test the Willow.pl script from the Willow.html Web page:

1. Restore the browser window, which you minimized in an earlier set of steps. Click **Golf** on the Willow.html Web page. The Willow.pl script creates the dynamic Web page shown in Figure 11-18. Notice that the Web page contains the sport name passed to the script.

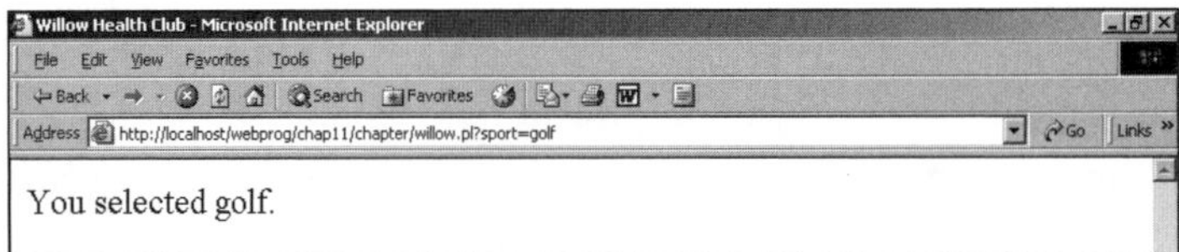

Figure 11-18 Dynamic Web page showing the sport name

Now view the dynamic Web page's source code.

2. Click **View** on the browser's menu bar, then click **Source**. See Figure 11-19.

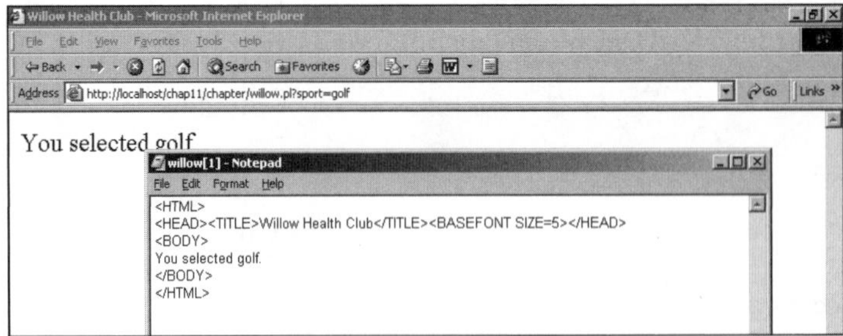

Figure 11-19 Source code for the dynamic Web page

Notice that the source code contains the sport name passed to the script; in this case, it contains *golf*.

3. Close the window containing the source code.
4. Click the **Back** button to return to the Willow Health Club Web page.
5. On your own, verify that the Racquetball and Tennis links display the appropriate sport name on the dynamic Web page.
6. Return to the Willow Health Club Web page, then minimize the browser window.

Next, you learn how to send more than one item of data to a script.

USING A LINK TO SEND MULTIPLE ITEMS OF DATA TO A CGI SCRIPT

Assume that, rather than displaying the message "You selected *sport*." on a Web page, you want the Willow.pl script to display the message "For *sport* information, contact *contact*.", where *sport* is the name of the sport whose link you clicked and *contact* is the name of the appropriate contact person at the health club. For the script to display such a message, each link on the Web page needs to send the script two items of data: the name of the sport and the name of the contact person. The Golf link, for example, should send the sport name *golf* together with the contact name *Mary Williams*. The Racquetball link should send the sport name *racquetball* together with the contact name *Jeff Gonzales*, and the Tennis link should send the sport name *tennis* together with the contact name *Pat Woo*.

11

As you learned earlier, you send data using a link by simply appending the data to the link's URL. Recall that the syntax for sending one item of data is **<A HREF=***URL***?***key***=***value***>***hyperlinkText***</A>**. To send more than one item of data, you use the syntax **<A HREF=***URL***?***key1***=***value1***&***key2***=***value2*...**&***keyN***=***valueN***>** *hyperlinkText***</A>**. Notice that you use an ampersand (&) to separate one data item (*key* and *value* pair) from the next. You can send as many data items as desired, but keep in mind that some browsers limit the amount of data that can be attached to a URL.

Now you will modify the Willow.html file so that each link on the Willow Health Club Web page sends the name of the sport and the name of the appropriate contact person. You also will modify the Willow.pl file to display the message "For *sport* information, contact *contact*."

To modify the Willow.html and Willow.pl files:

1. Open the Willow.html file in your text editor, then modify the three URLs as shown in Figure 11-20. The modifications you should make are shaded in the figure.

```
<!Willow.html>
<HTML>
<HEAD><TITLE>Willow Health Club</TITLE><BASEFONT SIZE=5></HEAD>
<BODY>
<B><I><H1>Welcome to the Willow Health Club Web site!</H1></I></B><BR>
Lessons are available in the following sports:<BR>
<A HREF="http://yourservername/webprog/chap11/chapter/willow.pl
      ?sport=golf&contact=Mary+Williams">Golf</A><BR>
<A HREF="http://yourservername/webprog/chap11/chapter/willow.pl
      ?sport=racquetball&contact=Jeff+Gonzales">Racquetball</A><BR>
<A HREF="http://yourservername/webprog/chap11/chapter/willow.pl
      ?sport=tennis&contact=Pat+Woo">Tennis</A><BR>
</BODY>
</HTML>
```

Figure 11-20 Willow.html code showing the modified URLs

Recall that if you are sending a *value* that contains more than one word, you replace the space that separates the words with a plus sign (+).

2. Save the document.
3. Open the Willow.pl script in your text editor. Change the `print "You selected ", param('sport'), ".\n";` statement to **`print "For ", param('sport'), " information, contact ", param('contact'), ".\n";`**. The modified code is shown in Figure 11-21.

```
#Willow.pl - creates a dynamic Web page
print "Content-type: text/html\n\n";
use CGI qw(:standard -debug);

#generate HTML
print "<HTML>\n";
print "<HEAD><TITLE>Willow Health Club</TITLE><BASEFONT SIZE=5></HEAD>\n";
print "<BODY>\n";
print "For ", param('sport'), " information, contact ", param('contact'), ".\n";
print "</BODY>\n";
print "</HTML>\n";
```

Figure 11-21 Willow.pl document showing the modified `print` statement

4. Save the document.
5. Restore the Command Prompt window, which you minimized in an earlier set of steps. The Chap11\Chapter folder should be the current folder.

6. Type **`cls`** after the command prompt, and press **Enter** to clear the contents of the Command Prompt window.
7. Type **`perl -c willow.pl`** and press **Enter**. If necessary, correct any syntax errors in the script before continuing to the next step.
8. Type **`perl -w willow.pl`** and press **Enter**. When the message "(offline mode: enter name=value pairs on standard input)" appears, type **`sport=golf`** and press **Enter**, then type **`contact=Mary+Williams`** and press **Enter**.
9. Press **Ctrl+z** and then press **Enter** to indicate that you are finished entering the input data. As Figure 11-22 shows, the Command Prompt window displays the message "For golf information, contact Mary Williams."

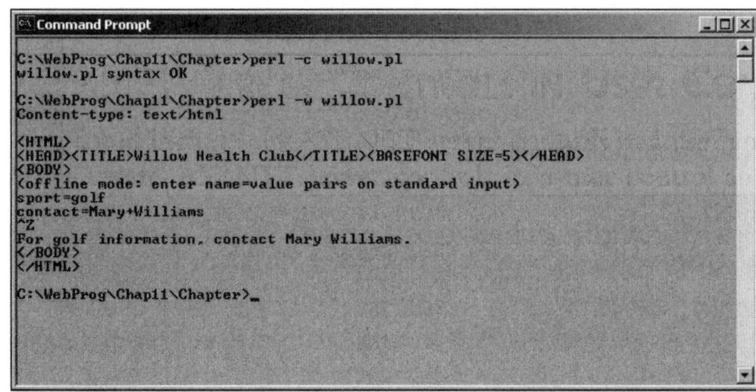

Figure 11-22 Command Prompt window showing the names of the sport and contact person

10. Minimize the Command Prompt window.

Now test the script by clicking the sport name links on the Willow.html Web page.

To test the Willow.pl script from the Willow.html Web page:

1. Restore the browser window, which you minimized in an earlier set of steps. Click the **Refresh** button to reopen the Willow.html file.
2. Click **Golf**. The message "For golf information, contact Mary Williams." appears on a Web page, as shown in Figure 11-23.

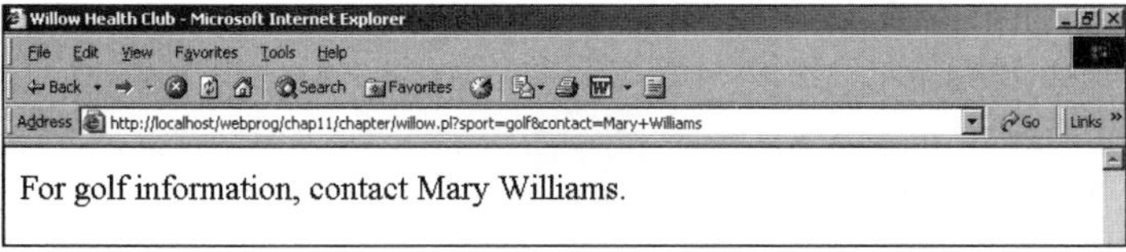

Figure 11-23 Sport and contact person names displayed on the Web page

Notice that, in addition to the script's URL, the data passed to the script—in this case, `sport=golf&contact=Mary+Williams`—also appears in the Address box of the browser window.

3. Click the **Back** button to return to the Willow Health Club Web page.
4. Verify that the Racquetball and Tennis links display the appropriate sport and contact person names on the dynamic Web page.
5. Close the browser and all open windows.

CHAPTER SUMMARY

- You can use any text editor to create a Perl CGI script. Keep in mind that Perl commands are case sensitive.
- In Perl, you use the sharp symbol (#) to designate that a line of text is a comment. The newline character is `\n`. Perl statements must end with a semicolon (;).
- To send HTML output to a browser, a script must contain the Content-type header line `print "Content-type: text/html\n\n";`.
- The command `perl -c` ***`scriptname`*** tells the Perl interpreter to check for syntax errors in a script, but not run the script. The command `perl -w` ***`scriptname`*** tells the Perl interpreter to check for errors in a script as the script is being run. If the Perl interpreter finds an error in a script, it displays a message that describes the error. It also gives the error's location (by line number) in the script.
- The syntax for creating a text link to a CGI script is **<A HREF=***URL***>** *hyperlinkText***</A>**. In the syntax, *URL* is the URL of the script, and *hyperlinkText* is the word or phrase that you click to activate the link. To pass one item of data to a script using a link, you use the syntax **<A HREF=***URL***?***key***=***value***>***hyperlinkText* **</A>**, where *key* is the name of the *value* you are sending. To pass more than one item of data to a script using a link, you use the syntax **<A HREF=***URL***?***key1***=** *value1***&***key2***=***value2***...&***keyN***=***valueN***>***hyperlinkText***</A>**.
- To use a link to pass a value that contains a space, replace the space with a plus sign (+).
- You use the CGI.pm module to automatically parse the data passed to a CGI script. To do so, you include the statement `use CGI qw(:standard -debug);` in the script. You can use the CGI.pm module's `param` function to access the *value* portion of each item of data passed to a script. The syntax of the `param` function is **param(***key***)**, where *key* is enclosed in either single or double quotation marks.
- When testing a script from the command line, you enter the data that you want sent to the script using the format *key*=*value*. You can enter the data on the same line as the command that executes the script. You also can enter each item of data on a separate line.

- You use the `print` function in a Perl script to generate HTML instructions to send to a Web browser through a Web server. The `print` function's syntax is **print** *output*;, where *output* is the expression, or a list of expressions separated by commas, that you want the script to output.

REVIEW QUESTIONS

1. CGI stands for ______________.
   a. Cool Gateway Interface
   b. Common Gateway Interface
   c. Common Gateway Internet
   d. Content Gateway Interface
2. Which of the following is the newline character?
   a. \n
   b. /n
   c. !n
   d. #n
3. Which of the following commands tells the Perl interpreter to check for syntax errors in the sample.pl script and then exit without executing the script?
   a. `perl -c sample.pl`
   b. `perl -w sample.pl`
   c. `perl -x sample.pl`
   d. none of these
4. A comment in Perl must begin with the ______________ symbol.
   a. asterisk (*)
   b. dollar sign ($)
   c. exclamation (!)
   d. sharp (#)
5. Perl statements must end with a ______________.
   a. colon (:)
   b. period (.)
   c. semicolon (;)
   d. space

6. Which of the following links the phrase "Click here" to the city.pl script?
   a. <A HREF="http://*yourservername*/webprog/chap11/chapter/city.pl">Click here</A>
   b. <A LINK="http://*yourservername*/webprog/chap11/chapter/city.pl ">Click here</A>
   c. <A HLINK="http://*yourservername*/webprog/chap11/chapter/city.pl ">Click here</A>
   d. <A HREF="http://*yourservername*/webprog/chap11/chapter/city.pl>Click here"</A>
7. Which of the following statements indicates that a script's output is HTML?
   a. print "Content text/html";
   b. print "Content-type html/text\n";
   c. print "Content-type: text/html\n\n";
   d. none of these
8. You use the statement ________________ to import the standard features of the CGI.pm module.
   a. use CGI.pm qw(:standard -debug);
   b. use CGI qw(standard -debug);
   c. use CGI "(standard -debug)";
   d. none of these
9. When an item of data is sent to a script, the ________________ character separates the item's *key* from its *value*.
   a. ampersand (&)
   b. equal sign (=)
   c. plus sign (+)
   d. question mark (?)
10. When using a link to send data to a script, you use the ________________ character to separate the URL from the data.
   a. ampersand (&)
   b. equal sign (=)
   c. plus sign (+)
   d. question mark (?)

11. When sending multiple items of data to a script, the ______________ character separates one item from the next item.
    a. ampersand (&)
    b. equal sign (=)
    c. plus sign (+)
    d. question mark (?)
12. If you are using a link to send a value that contains a space, you replace the space with a(n) ______________.
    a. ampersand (&)
    b. equal sign (=)
    c. plus sign (+)
    d. question mark (?)
13. The ______________ function tells the Perl interpreter to treat the text within the parentheses that follow the function as though the text were entered in single quotation marks.
    a. `qu`
    b. `quote`
    c. `qw`
    d. `qword`
14. You use the CGI.pm module's ______________ function to access the *value* associated with a *key*.
    a. `access`
    b. `key`
    c. `param`
    d. `value`
15. The process of splitting the data's *key* from its *value* is called ______________.
    a. dividing
    b. parsing
    c. parting
    d. separating

HANDS-ON EXERCISES

If necessary, use Windows Explorer to create a new folder in the Chap11 folder in your work folder. Name this folder **Exercises**. Save the Perl scripts and HTML documents that you create in these Exercises in the Chap11\Exercises folder in your work folder.

Exercise 11-1

In this exercise, you create a CGI script that displays a message on a Web page.

To display a message on a Web page:

1. Use a text editor to create the script shown in Figure 11-24. Save the script as **Message.pl** in the Chap11\Exercises folder in your work folder.

```
#Message.pl - displays a message on a Web page
print "Content-type: text/html\n\n";
#generate HTML
print "<HTML>\n";
print "<HEAD><TITLE>My Message</TITLE></HEAD>\n";
print "<BODY>Perl statements \n";
print "end with a semicolon.</BODY>\n";
print "</HTML>\n";
```

Figure 11-24

2. Open a Command Prompt window, then make the Chap11\Exercises folder the current folder.
3. Test for syntax errors in the script. Correct any syntax errors before continuing to the next step.
4. Run the script from the command line.
5. Open your Web browser. Enter the script's URL in the Address box. The message "Perl statements end with a semicolon." appears on a Web page. (Notice that the message prints on one line, even though the script contains two `print` statements.)

Exercise 11-2

In this exercise, you include another link on the Willow Health Club Web page that you created in the chapter.

To add a link to the Willow Health Club Web page:

1. Open the **Willow.pl** file in a text editor. The file is contained in the Chap11\Chapter folder in your work folder.
2. Change the filename in the first line from Willow.pl to **Willow2.pl**. Save the file as **Willow2.pl** in the Chap11\Exercises folder in your work folder.

3. Open the **Willow.html** file in a text editor. The file is contained in the Chap11\Chapter folder in your work folder.
4. Change the filename in the first line from Willow.html to **Willow2.html**. Save the file as **Willow2.html** in the Chap11\Exercises folder in your work folder.
5. Modify the URLs so that each passes the required information to the **Willow2.pl** script, which is contained in the Chap11\Exercises folder in your work folder.
6. Add another link to the Web page. Use the word "Basketball" as the *hyperlinkText*. Pass the sport name (basketball) and contact person name (Mike Johnson) to the Willow2.pl script.
7. Save the **Willow2.html** document.
8. Open your Web browser. Use the browser's File menu to open the **Willow2.html** file. Click the Basketball link. The message "For basketball information, contact Mike Johnson." should appear on the Web page.

Exercise 11-3

In this exercise, you modify the links contained on the Willow.html Web page that you created in the chapter. Each link will now send three items of data to the script: the sport name, the contact person name, and the cost (per hour) of a lesson. You also modify the message displayed by the Willow.pl script. The script should now display the message "The hourly rate for a *sport* lesson is $*cost*. Contact *contact* for an appointment."

To modify the links contained on the Willow.html Web page, and modify the message displayed by the Willow.pl script:

1. Open the **Willow.html** file in a text editor. The file is contained in the Chap11\Chapter folder in your work folder.
2. Change the filename in the first line from Willow.html to **Willow3.html**. Save the file as **Willow3.html** in the Chap11\Exercises folder in your work folder.
3. Modify the URLs so that each refers to the **Willow3.pl** file contained in the Chap11\Exercises folder in your work folder, and each passes the appropriate data. (The hourly rate for a golf lesson is $45. The hourly rate for a racquetball lesson is $20, and the hourly rate for a tennis lesson is $40.)
4. Save the **Willow3.html** file.
5. Open the **Willow.pl** file in your text editor. The file is contained in the Chap11\Chapter folder in your work folder.
6. Change the filename in the first line from Willow.pl to **Willow3.pl**. Save the file as **Willow3.pl** in the Chap11\Exercises folder in your work folder.
7. Modify the message displayed by the script. [*Hint:* To include a dollar sign ($) in a message, you must type \$ (a backslash followed by the dollar sign)].
8. Save the **Willow3.pl** script.
9. Test the script from the command line.

10. Open your Web browser. Use the browser's File menu to open the **Willow3.html** file. Verify that each link displays the appropriate Web page.

Exercise 11-4

In this exercise, you create an HTML document and a script. The HTML document uses links to pass information to a script, which then displays the information on a Web page.

To use links to pass information to a script, and then display the information on a Web page:

1. Use a text editor to create an HTML document that contains the following five English words defined as links: Hello, Good-bye, Love, Cat, and Dog. Each of the five links should pass both the English word and its Spanish equivalent (Hola, Adios, Amor, Gato, Perro) to the Spanish.pl script. For example, if the user clicks the Hello link, the link should pass the English word "Hello" and the Spanish word "Hola" to the script.
2. Save the HTML document as **Spanish.html** in the Chap11\Exercises folder in your work folder.
3. Create a script that displays the message "The Spanish word for *<display the English word here>* is *<display the Spanish word here>*."
4. Save the script as **Spanish.pl** in the Chap11\Exercises folder in your work folder.
5. Test the script from the command line.
6. Open your Web browser. Use the browser's File menu to open the **Spanish.html** file. Verify that each link displays the appropriate Web page.

Exercise 11-5

In this exercise, you create an HTML document and a script. The HTML document uses links to pass information to a script, which then displays the information on a Web page.

To use links to pass information to a script, and then display the information on a Web page:

1. Use a text editor to create an HTML document that contains the following four course numbers defined as links: CIS100, BIOL100, ENG100, and HIST100. Each of the four links should pass the course number, course name, and instructor name to the Course.pl script. The course and instructor names corresponding to each course number are as follows:

Course number	Course name	Instructor name
CIS100	Introduction to Computers	Harriet Stewart
BIOL100	Biology	John Marshalls
ENG100	English Composition	Samuel Johnson
HIST100	History	Khalid Patel

2. Save the HTML document as **Course.html** in the Chap11\Exercises folder in your work folder.

3. Create a script that displays the message "The instructor for <*display the course number here*> (<*display the course name here*>) is <*display the instructor name here*>."
4. Save the script as **Course.pl** in the Chap11\Exercises folder in your work folder.
5. Test the script from the command line.
6. Open your Web browser. Use the browser's File menu to open the **Course.html** file. Verify that each link displays the appropriate Web page.

WEB PROGRAMMING PROJECTS

If necessary, use Windows Explorer to create a new folder in the Chap11 folder in your work folder. Name this folder **Projects**. Save the Perl scripts and HTML documents that you create in these Projects in the Chap11\Projects folder in your work folder.

Project 11-1

Create an HTML document and a script for Jackson Elementary School. Name the HTML document **Jackson.html** and name the script **Jackson.pl**. Save the HTML document and script in the Chap11\Projects folder in your work folder. The HTML document should display a Web page that lists the numbers 1 through 10. Each of the ten numbers should be a link to the Jackson.pl script. Each link should pass to the script the name of the president that corresponds to the number. For example, the number 1 link should pass the name "George Washington", the number 2 link should pass the name "John Adams". The script should display a Web page that contains the data passed to the script. (The third through tenth presidents were Thomas Jefferson, James Madison, James Monroe, John Quincy Adams, Andrew Jackson, Martin Van Buren, William Henry Harrison, and John Tyler.)

11

Project 11-2

Create an HTML document and a script for Carlton Enterprises. Name the HTML document **Carlton.html** and name the script **Carlton.pl**. Save the HTML document and script in the Chap11\Projects folder in your work folder. The HTML document should display a Web page that lists the 12 months in a year. Each of the 12 months should be a link to the Carlton.pl script. Each link should pass to the script the name of the month and a message that indicates the number of days in the month. For example, the January link should pass "January" and the message "31 days". The February link should pass "February" and the message "28 or 29 (leap year) days". The script should display a Web page that contains the data passed to the script.

Project 11-3

Create an HTML document and a script for the Henry Clyde Library. Name the HTML document **Library.html** and name the script **Library.pl**. Save the HTML document and script in the Chap11\Projects folder in your work folder. The HTML document should display a Web page that lists the following four state names: Alabama, Alaska, Arizona, and Arkansas. Each of the four state names should be a link to the Library.pl script. Each link should pass to the script the state name and capital name. For example, the Alabama link should pass the state name "Alabama" and the capital name "Montgomery". The script should display a Web page that contains the appropriate state and capital names. (The capital of Alaska is Juneau. The capital of Arizona is Phoenix, and the capital of Arkansas is Little Rock.)

CHAPTER

12

CGI/PERL: PART II

In this chapter you will:

- Use a CGI script to process form data
- Plan a CGI script
- Declare scalar variables in Perl
- Use assignment statements to assign values to variables
- Use arithmetic operators in Perl
- Access the values received from an online form
- Associate a form with a script
- Include a dollar sign in a number
- Use the `printf` function

In Chapter 11, you used a hyperlink to send information to a CGI script named Willow.pl. Recall that the script displayed the information it received—the sport and contact names—on a dynamic Web page. In addition to using a hyperlink, you can use an online form to send information to a CGI script.

An online form is created with HTML and is the electronic equivalent of a paper form that you fill out by hand. As with paper forms, you can use online forms to purchase products or services, submit inquiries, or respond to surveys. However, unlike paper forms, which you typically send back through the mail, you send back online forms by clicking a special button, referred to as a submit button. Usually, the submit button is located at the bottom of the form and labeled "Submit", "Send", or something similar.

When you click a form's submit button, the data entered on the form typically is given to a CGI script for processing. In most cases, the script outputs a dynamic Web page that contains an appropriate response to the person submitting the form—such as an acknowledgment of an order or an answer to an inquiry. In this chapter, you learn how to use an online form to send information to a CGI script. You also learn how to plan and create a CGI script that processes the form data it receives.

Using a CGI Script to Process Form Data

Assume that your Web browser displays an Annuity Calculator form that allows you to enter your name, the size of each payment in the annuity, the interest rate (compounded continuously), the term of the annuity (in years), and the number of payments per year. An example of a completed Annuity Calculator form is shown in Figure 12-1.

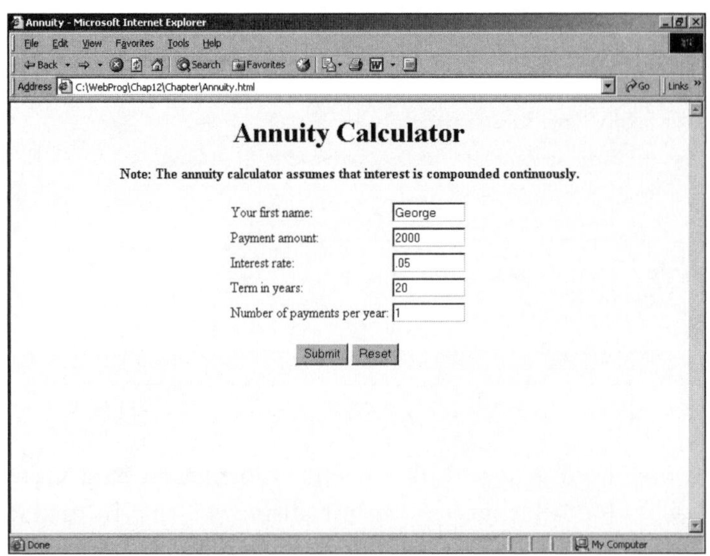

Figure 12-1 Completed Annuity Calculator form

An annuity is a sequence of payments made at regular time intervals. Examples of annuities include regular deposits to a savings account and monthly home mortgage payments. The information shown in Figure 12-1 indicates that George will be making one payment of $2,000 per year for 20 years.

After entering your information, you click the form's Submit button. Almost immediately, the browser displays a personalized Web page that contains the amount of your annuity, as shown in Figure 12-2.

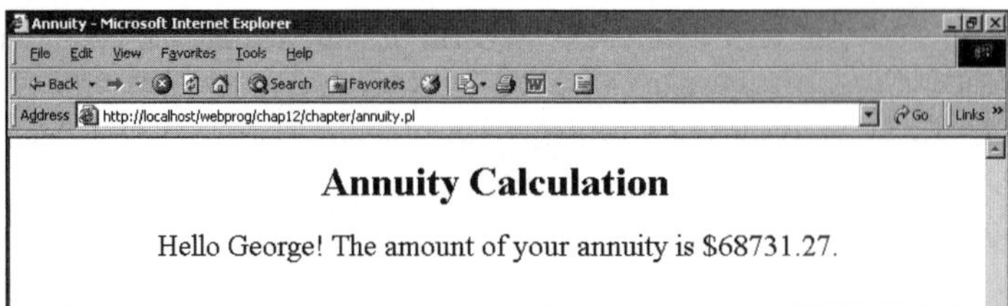

Figure 12-2 Personalized Web page

The amount of an annuity is the sum of the annuity payments plus the interest earned. In this case, if George saves $2,000 per year for 20 years at a 5% interest rate (compounded continuously), the amount of his annuity—in other words, the amount he accumulates—will be $68,731.27.

Did you ever wonder what happens to the data you enter on a form when the form is submitted, or how a personalized Web page is created? The answer to both questions can be found in the form processing procedure shown in Figure 12-3.

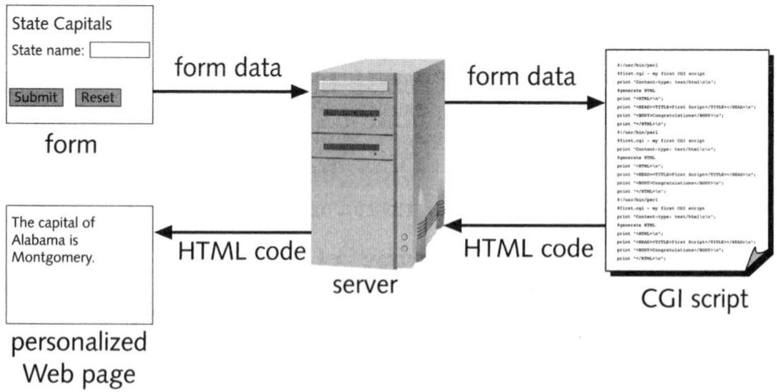

Figure 12-3 Form processing procedure

When you click the Submit button (or a similarly named button) on a form, the browser sends the form data to the server. In the case of the Annuity Calculator form, for example, the browser sends the name, payment amount, interest rate, term, and number of payments entered on the form. If the form is associated with a CGI script, the server forwards the form data to the script for processing. The amount and type of processing a script performs varies with each script and is determined by the programmer. Examples of tasks performed by CGI scripts include making calculations, saving data to and retrieving data from a database, and preparing output (typically HTML code) to send to the server. The CGI script associated with the Annuity Calculator form, for example, calculates the amount of the annuity and prepares the HTML code for the personalized Web page shown in Figure 12-2.

When a CGI script has finished processing, it sends its output—in this case, HTML code—to the server. The server transfers the HTML code to the browser, which renders the personalized Web page on the screen.

In the next section, you learn the steps involved in planning a CGI script that processes form data.

Planning a CGI Script

Most CGI scripts are not as simple as the ones that you created in Chapter 11; most perform many more tasks and contain many more instructions. CGI scripts that perform more than one task, or those that contain more than a few lines of code, should be planned before they are created. The importance of planning cannot be emphasized enough. If you do not take the time to plan a script, the script typically will contain errors that are difficult to find and expensive to correct.

When planning a script, you first determine the script's input and output. The input for a script that processes form data is the form data itself. The Annuity Calculator script's input, for example, is the name, payment amount, interest rate, term, and number of payments entered on the Annuity Calculator form.

A script's output is the purpose for writing the script. The Annuity Calculator script's output is the personalized Web page shown earlier in Figure 12-2. Notice that the Web page contains one of the input items (the name) as well as the amount of the annuity.

After determining the script's input and output, you list the steps the script must follow to transform the input into the output. The list of steps, referred to as an **algorithm**, typically is written in either pseudocode or flowchart form. Table 12-1 shows the input, output, and algorithm (written in pseudocode) for the Annuity Calculator script.

Table 12-1 Input, output, and algorithm for the Annuity Calculator script

Input	Output
name payment amount interest rate (compounded continuously) term (in years) number of payments per year	Web page containing the name and the amount of the annuity
Algorithm	
1. assign the input items to variables 2. calculate the amount of the annuity and assign the result to a variable 3. create a dynamic Web page that displays the name and the amount of the annuity	

An algorithm is a set of step-by-step instructions that solve a problem. Pseudocode consists of short English statements. A flowchart, on the other hand, is composed of standardized symbols.

As its algorithm indicates, the Annuity Calculator script first assigns the five input items (name, payment amount, interest rate, term, and number of payments) to variables. The script then calculates the amount of the annuity and assigns the result to a variable.

Finally, the script creates a dynamic Web page that displays the name and the annuity amount.

After planning a script, you code the script's algorithm using a language that the computer can understand—such as the Perl scripting language. However, before you can begin coding the algorithm shown in Table 12-1, you need to learn about variables in Perl.

DECLARING SCALAR VARIABLES IN PERL

A **variable** is a location (within the computer's internal memory) where a script can temporarily store data. The data may come from a form, be read in from a file, or be the result of a calculation made by the computer.

Every variable has a data type, which determines the kind of data the variable can store. Perl provides three basic data types for variables: scalar, array, and hash. A **scalar variable**, which you learn about in this chapter, can store precisely one value—typically a number or a string. Array and hash variables, on the other hand, store lists or sets of values. Coverage of array and hash variables in Perl is beyond the scope of this book.

Unlike many programming languages, Perl does not have separate data types for integers, floating-point numbers, and strings.

In addition to a data type, every variable also has a name. The name of a scalar variable in Perl must begin with a dollar sign ($) followed by a letter and then, optionally, one or more letters, numbers, or underscores. Examples of valid names for scalar variables include `$city`, `$income2004`, and `$inc_tax`. Keep in mind that variable names in Perl are case sensitive; so the names `$city`, `$CITY`, and `$City` do not refer to the same location in the computer's internal memory. It is important to use the exact capitalization of a name throughout the entire Perl script; otherwise, the script will not work correctly.

The dollar sign ($) indicates the variable's data type: scalar. An easy way to remember that scalar variable names begin with a dollar sign ($) is to associate the $ with the letter "S" in the word "Scalar".

Although variable names can include both uppercase and lowercase letters, most Perl programmers use lowercase letters when naming variables.

You should assign a descriptive name to each variable the script will use. The name should help you remember the purpose of the variable—in other words, the meaning of the value stored therein. For example, the names `$length` and `$width` are much more meaningful than are the names `$x` and `$y`, because `$length` and `$width` remind you that the amounts stored in the variables represent a length and width measurement, respectively.

Unlike many programming languages, Perl does not require you to explicitly declare the variables used in a script. By default, variables in Perl are created "on the fly" and spring into existence upon their first use in a script. It is considered a good programming practice to prevent a programming language from creating variables "on the fly"—in other words, from creating variables that you have not explicitly declared. You prevent Perl from creating undeclared variables using the statement **`use strict;`**. The **`use strict;`** statement typically is entered near the beginning of the script, before any statements that declare variables.

To prevent Perl from creating undeclared variables in a script:

1. Open a text editor, and then enter the following text. Be sure to type each line exactly as shown, as Perl commands are case sensitive.

```
#Annuity.pl - calculates and displays the amount of an annuity
print "Content-type: text/html\n\n";

#prevent Perl from creating undeclared variables
use strict;
```

2. Save the script as **Annuity.pl** in the Chap12\Chapter folder in your work folder.

To explicitly declare one or more variables in Perl, you use a statement that follows the syntax **my (*variablelist*);**, where *variablelist* is a comma-separated list of variable names. When you declare a variable, the computer creates the variable in its internal memory. For example, the statement `my ($length, $width, $area);` declares (creates) three scalar variables named `$length`, `$width`, and `$area`.

If you have only one variable to declare, you can omit the parentheses in the declaration statement. For example, you can use either the statement `my ($area);` or the statement `my $area;` to declare the `$area` variable.

The Annuity Calculator script uses six variables: five to store the input items (name, payment amount, interest rate, term, and number of payments) and one to store the annuity amount. You will name the variables `$name`, `$payment`, `$rate`, `$term`, `$number`, and `$annuity`. Typically, variable declaration statements are entered below the `use strict;` statement in a script.

To declare the six variables:

1. In the blank line below the `use strict;` statement, type **`#declare variables`** and press **Enter**.

2. Type **`my ($name, $payment, $rate, $term, $number, $annuity);`** and press **Enter** twice.

After declaring a variable, you can use an assignment statement to assign a value to the variable.

USING ASSIGNMENT STATEMENTS TO ASSIGN VALUES TO VARIABLES

You can use an assignment statement to assign (or change) the value stored in a variable. The syntax of an assignment statement is *variable* = *value*;, where *variable* is the variable's name and *value* is the number or string you want stored in the variable. Table 12-2 shows examples of assignment statements that assign values to scalar variables.

Table 12-2 Examples of assignment statements

Assigning numeric values	Results
`$hours = 32;`	Assigns the number 32 to the `$hours` variable
`$gross_pay = $hours * 10;`	Assigns the number 320 (32 * 10) to the `$gross_pay` variable
Assigning double-quoted strings	**Results**
`$first = "Sue";`	Assigns the string "Sue" to the `$first` variable
`$msg = "Her name is $first.";`	Assigns the string "Her name is Sue." to the `$msg` variable
Assigning single-quoted strings	**Results**
`$first = 'Sue';`	Assigns the string 'Sue' to the `$first` variable
`$msg = 'Her name is $first.';`	Assigns the string 'Her name is $first.' to the `$msg` variable

12

The first two examples in Table 12-2 assign a number to a scalar variable: the first example assigns the number 32 to the `$hours` variable, and the second example assigns the result of a calculation—in this case, the number 320—to the `$gross_pay` variable. The 320 is calculated by multiplying the contents of the `$hours` variable (32) by the number 10.

The third and fourth examples shown in Table 12-2 assign a double-quoted string to a scalar variable. The third example assigns the string "Sue" (without the double quotation marks) to the `$first` variable. The fourth example assigns the string "Her name is Sue." to the `$msg` variable. Notice that the variable name (`$first`) in the fourth example is replaced with the contents of the variable (Sue) before the string is assigned to the `$msg` variable. When the name of a variable appears within double quotation marks in a statement, Perl replaces the variable's name with the variable's contents—a process referred to as **interpolation**.

Tip

Any statement that contains a variable's name enclosed in double quotation marks is subject to interpolation. You will see more examples of interpolation later in this chapter.

The last two statements in Table 12-2 assign a single-quoted string to a scalar variable. Unlike double quotation marks, single quotation marks indicate that no interpolation should be performed in the string; rather, the string should be treated verbatim. For example, the fifth statement shown in the table, `$first = 'Sue';`, assigns the string 'Sue' (without the single quotation marks) to the `$first` variable. Notice that the statement produces the same result as the statement `$first = "Sue";`, which is the third statement shown in the table; this is because neither statement contains the name of a variable in quotation marks. However, notice that the statement `$msg = 'Her name is $first.';` (the last example) does not produce the same result as the statement `$msg = "Her name is $first.";` (the fourth example). Unlike the latter statement, the former statement does not replace the variable name (`$first`) with its contents; rather, it assigns the string 'Her name is $first.' verbatim.

Now that you have learned about assignment statements, you can begin coding the Annuity Calculator script's algorithm. The first step in the algorithm, shown earlier in Table 12-1, is to assign the input items (name, payment amount, interest rate, term, and number of payments) to variables. Recall that the script will receive the input items from an online form. When you first create a script, it is helpful to assign sample values to the input variables rather than worrying about assigning the form values themselves; doing this allows you to test the script without the form. When the script is working correctly, you then replace the sample values with the form values. In this case you will assign "George" to the `$name` variable, 2000 to the `$payment` variable, .05 to the `$rate` variable, 20 to the `$term` variable, and 1 to the `$number` variable.

To assign sample values to the input variables in the Annuity.pl script:

1. Verify that the cursor is located two lines below the variable declaration statement, and then type the following comment and assignment statements. Press **Enter** twice after typing the last assignment statement.

```
#assign values to variables
$name = "George";
$payment = 2000;
$rate = .05;
$term = 20;
$number = 1;
```

2. Save the Annuity.pl document.

Step 2 in the script's algorithm is to calculate the amount of the annuity, and then assign the result to a variable. Before you can code this step, you need to learn about the arithmetic operators available in Perl.

USING ARITHMETIC OPERATORS IN PERL

Table 12-3 lists the arithmetic operators that you can use to perform calculations in a Perl statement, along with their precedence numbers. The precedence numbers indicate the order in which Perl performs the arithmetic operations in an expression. Operations with a precedence number of 1 are performed before operations with a precedence number of 2, which are performed before operations with a precedence number of 3, and so on. However, you can use parentheses to override the order of precedence, because operations within parentheses always are performed before operations outside parentheses.

Table 12-3 Perl arithmetic operators and their order of precedence

Operator	Operation	Precedence number
()	Override normal precedence rules	1
**	Exponentiation	2
-	Negation	3
*, /, %	Multiplication, division, and modulus arithmetic	4
+, -	Addition and subtraction	5

The difference between the negation and subtraction operators shown in Table 12-3 is that the negation operator is unary, whereas the subtraction operator is binary. *Unary* and *binary* refer to the number of operands required by the operator. Unary operators require one operand. For example, the negative number -3 contains the negation operator (-), which is unary, and one operand—the number 3. Unlike unary operators, binary operators require two operands. For example, the expression 4 * 3 contains the multiplication operator (*), which is binary, and two operands: the number 4 and the number 3.

Notice that some operators shown in Table 12-3 have the same precedence number. For example, both the addition and subtraction operator have a precedence number of 5. If an expression contains more than one operator having the same priority, those operators are evaluated from left to right. In the expression 3 + 12 / 3 - 1, for instance, the division (/) is performed first, then the addition (+), and then the subtraction (-). In other words, the computer first divides 12 by 3, then adds the result of the division (4) to 3, and then subtracts 1 from the result of the addition (7). The expression evaluates to 6.

You can use parentheses to change the order in which the operators in an expression are evaluated. For example, the expression 3 + 12 / (3 - 1) evaluates to 9, not 6. This is because the parentheses tell the computer to subtract 1 from 3 first, then divide the result of the subtraction (2) into 12, and then add the result of the division (6) to 3.

One of the arithmetic operators listed in Table 12-3, the modulus arithmetic operator (%), might be less familiar to you. The modulus arithmetic operator is used to divide two integers, and results in the remainder of the division. For example, 211 % 4 (read 211 mod 4) equals 3, which is the remainder of 211 divided by 4. One use for the modulus operator is to determine whether a year is a leap year—one that has 366 days rather than 365 days. As you may know, if a year is a leap year, then its year number is evenly divisible by the number 4—in other words, if you divide the year number by 4 and the remainder is 0 (zero), then the year is a leap year. You can determine whether the year 2004 is a leap year by using the expression 2004 % 4. This expression evaluates to 0 (the remainder of 2004 divided by 4), so the year 2004 is a leap year. Similarly, you can determine whether the year 2005 is a leap year by using the expression 2005 % 4. This expression evaluates to 1 (the remainder of 2005 divided by 4), so the year 2005 is not a leap year.

Years ending in 00 are not leap years unless they also are evenly divisible by 400.

Using the arithmetic operators shown in Table 12-3, the formula for calculating the amount of an annuity (assuming the interest is compounded continuously) is Annuity = Number of payments per year * Payment amount / Interest rate * (2.7182818 ** (Interest rate * Term) - 1). You will store the result of the calculation in the `$annuity` variable.

The number 2.7182818 is the value of e rounded to seven decimal places.

To calculate the annuity amount and assign the result to a variable:

1. Verify that the cursor is located two lines below the last assignment statement, type **`#calculate annuity amount`** and then press **Enter**.
2. Type **`$annuity = $number * $payment / $rate * (2.7182818 ** ($rate * $term) - 1);`** and press **Enter** twice.
3. Save the Annuity.pl document.

The last step in the script's algorithm is to create the dynamic Web page shown earlier in Figure 12-2. Recall that the Web page displays the name that you entered on the form, as well as the annuity amount calculated by the script.

To create the dynamic Web page, then test the script:

1. Verify that the cursor is located two lines below the statement that calculates the annuity, and then type the following code.

   ```
   #create Web page
   print "<HTML>\n";
   print "<HEAD><TITLE>Annuity</TITLE><BASEFONT SIZE=5></HEAD>\n";
   print "<CENTER><H1>Annuity Calculation</H1>\n";
   print "<BODY>\n";
   ```

   Now display a message that contains the name stored in the `$name` variable (George).

2. Type **`print "Hello $name!\n";`** and press **Enter**. This statement will display the string "Hello George!" on a Web page. As you learned earlier, when the name of a variable appears within double quotation marks in a statement, Perl replaces the variable's name with the variable's contents—a process referred to as interpolation.

   Next, display a message that contains the annuity amount, which is stored in the `$annuity` variable, and then enter the ending BODY, CENTER, and HTML tags.

3. Type **`print "The amount of your annuity is $annuity.\n";`** and press **Enter**.

4. Type **`print "</BODY></CENTER>\n";`** and press **Enter**, then type **`print "</HTML>\n";`** and press **Enter**. Figure 12-4 (on the next page) shows the code entered in the Annuity.pl script.

5. Save the Annuity.pl document.

   Now test the script from the command line.

6. Open a Command Prompt window, and then make the Chap12\Chapter folder the current folder.

7. Type **`perl -c annuity.pl`** and press **Enter** to check the script for syntax errors. If necessary, correct any syntax errors in the script before continuing to the next step.

```
#Annuity.pl - calculates and displays the amount of an annuity
print "Content-type: text/html\n\n";

#prevent Perl from creating undeclared variables
use strict;
#declare variables
my ($name, $payment, $rate, $term, $number, $annuity);

#assign values to variables
$name = "George";
$payment = 2000;
$rate = .05;
$term = 20;
$number = 1;

#calculate annuity amount
$annuity = $number * $payment / $rate * (2.7182818 ** ($rate * $term) - 1);

#create Web page
print "<HTML>\n";
print "<HEAD><TITLE>Annuity</TITLE><BASEFONT SIZE=5></HEAD>\n";
print "<CENTER><H1>Annuity Calculation</H1>\n";
print "<BODY>\n";
print "Hello $name!\n";
print "The amount of your annuity is $annuity.\n";
print "</BODY></CENTER>\n";
print "</HTML>\n";
```

Figure 12-4 Code entered in the Annuity.pl script

8. Type **`perl -w annuity.pl`** and press **Enter** to execute the script. See Figure 12-5.

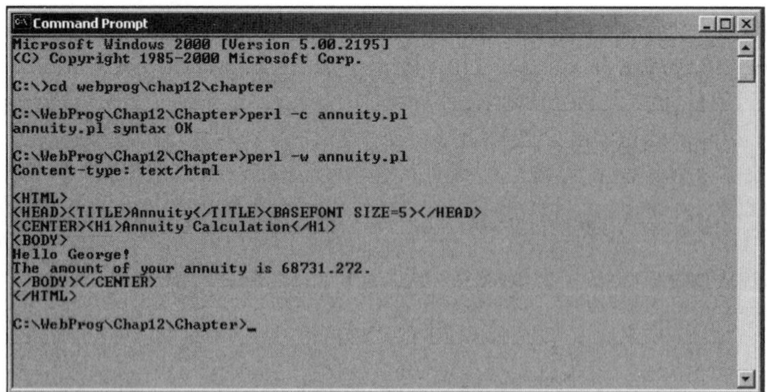

Figure 12-5 Result of testing the script from the command line

Notice that Perl replaces the variable names in the `print` statements with the contents of the variables.

9. Minimize the Command Prompt window.

Now that you know the script is working correctly, you can replace the sample values in the assignment statements with the values received from the online form.

ACCESSING THE VALUES RECEIVED FROM AN ONLINE FORM

As you learned in Chapter 11, each item of data passed to a script by a hyperlink has a *key* and a *value*. Online forms also use *keys* and *values* to pass data to a script. The *key* is simply a one-word name that you assign to the *value*. In the case of a hyperlink, recall that you append the *key* and *value* to the link's URL, which is specified in the anchor tag's HREF property. In the case of an online form, the *key* is the name of the form element containing the *value* entered by the user. Figure 12-6 shows the *keys* (names) assigned to the five text boxes on the Annuity Calculator form. (When you create the Annuity Calculator form later in this chapter, you will learn how to assign a *key* to a text box.)

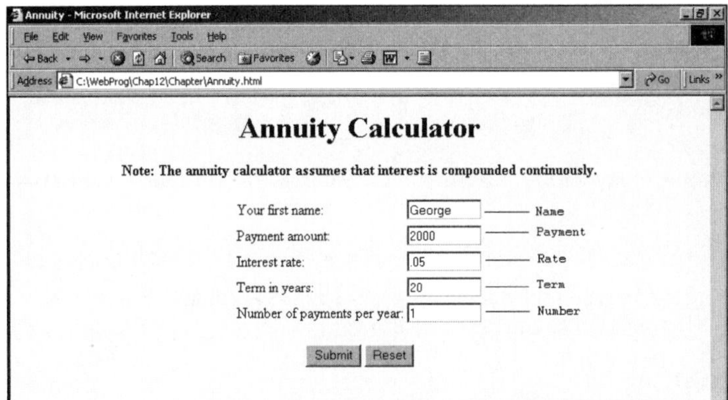

Figure 12-6 *Keys* assigned to the text boxes on the Annuity Calculator form

Form *keys* and *values* are passed automatically to a script when you click the form's submit button. For example, when you click the Submit button on the Annuity Calculator form, the *keys* (Name, Payment, Rate, Term, and Number) along with their *values* (George, 2000, .05, 20, and 1) will be sent to the Annuity.pl script.

As is true of data sent using a hyperlink, data sent using an online form must be parsed by the script when it is received. You can use the parsing routine contained in the CGI.pm module to parse the data. Recall that to do so, you first enter the statement `use CGI qw(:standard -debug);` in the script. You then use the `param` function, whose syntax is **param**(*key*), to access the parsed data.

To parse the data sent by the Annuity Calculator form, then test the script:

1. In the blank line below the Content-type statement in the Annuity.pl script, type **`use CGI qw(:standard -debug);`** and then press **Enter**.

   Now use the `param` function to access the form values.

2. Replace the sample values assigned to the input variables with the values received from the form. The modifications you should make are shaded in Figure 12-7.

```
#Annuity.pl - calculates and displays the amount of an annuity
print "Content-type: text/html\n\n";
use CGI qw(:standard -debug);

#prevent Perl from creating undeclared variables
use strict;
#declare variables
my ($name, $payment, $rate, $term, $number, $annuity);

#assign values to variables
$name = param('Name');
$payment = param('Payment');
$rate = param('Rate');
$term = param('Term');
$number = param('Number');

#calculate annuity amount
$annuity = $number * $payment / $rate * (2.7182818 ** ($rate * $term) - 1);

#create Web page
print "<HTML>\n";
print "<HEAD><TITLE>Annuity</TITLE><BASEFONT SIZE=5></HEAD>\n";
print "<CENTER><H1>Annuity Calculation</H1>\n";
print "<BODY>\n";
print "Hello $name!\n";
print "The amount of your annuity is $annuity.\n";
print "</BODY></CENTER>\n";
print "</HTML>\n";
```

Figure 12-7 Modified statements shown in the script

3. Save the Annuity.pl document.

4. Return to the Command Prompt window, which you minimized in an earlier set of steps. Type **`cls`** after the command prompt and press **Enter** to clear the contents of the Command Prompt window.

5. Type **`perl -c annuity.pl`** and press **Enter** to check the script for syntax errors. If necessary, correct any syntax errors in the script before continuing to the next step.
6. Type **`perl -w annuity.pl`** and press **Enter** to execute the script.
7. When the offline mode message appears, type **`Name=George`** and press **Enter**, and then type **`Payment=2000`** and press **Enter**. Type **`Rate=.05`** and press **Enter**, and then type **`Term=20`** and press **Enter**. Type **`Number=1`** and press **Enter**.
8. Press **Ctrl+z** and then press **Enter** to indicate that you are finished entering the input data. Figure 12-8 shows the result of testing the Annuity.pl script from the command line.

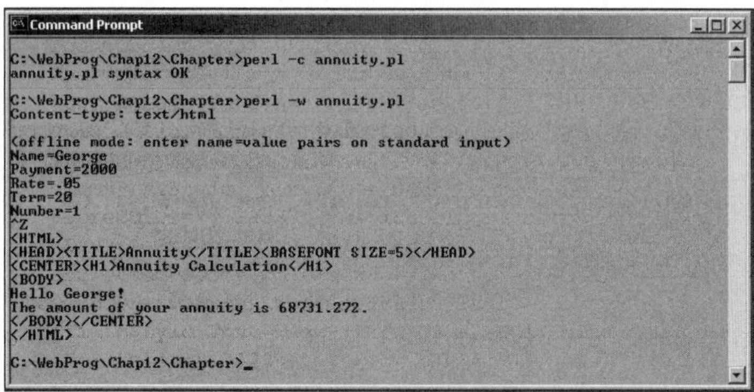

Figure 12-8 Result of testing the Annuity.pl script from the command line

9. Close the Command Prompt window.

Next you learn how to associate a form with a script.

12

Associating a Form With a Script

Now that the Annuity Calculator script is working correctly from the command line, you can create the Annuity Calculator form (shown earlier in Figure 12-1), and then associate the form with the script.

To create the Annuity Calculator form:

1. Open a new document in your text editor, and then enter the following HTML code.

```
<!Annuity.html>
<HTML>
<HEAD><TITLE>Annuity</TITLE></HEAD>
<BODY BGCOLOR=#FFFFCC>
```

```
<CENTER><H1>Annuity Calculator</H1>
<H4>Note: The annuity calculator assumes that interest is
compounded continuously.</H4>
<FORM>
<TABLE>
<TR>      <TD>Your first name:</TD>
          <TD> <INPUT NAME=Name SIZE=10></TD></TR>
<TR>      <TD>Payment amount:</TD>
          <TD><INPUT NAME=Payment SIZE=10></TD></TR>
<TR>      <TD>Interest rate:</TD>
          <TD><INPUT NAME=Rate SIZE=10></TD></TR>
<TR>      <TD>Term in years:</TD>
          <TD><INPUT NAME=Term SIZE=10></TD></TR>
<TR>      <TD>Number of payments per year:</TD>
          <TD><INPUT NAME=Number SIZE=10></TD></TR>
</TABLE>
<P><INPUT TYPE=submit VALUE=Submit> <INPUT TYPE=reset></P>
</FORM></CENTER></BODY></HTML>
```

Notice the *keys* (names) assigned to the text boxes: Name, Payment, Rate, Term, and Number. Recall that these are the *keys* you used in the `param` function in the Annuity.pl script.

2. Save the document as **Annuity.html** in the Chap12\Chapter folder in your work folder.

The <FORM> and </FORM> tags in the Annuity.html document are necessary to create a form. The <FORM> tag marks the beginning of the form, and the </FORM> tag marks the end of the form. The <FORM> tag provides two properties, ACTION and METHOD, that allow you to specify how the form data should be handled. The **ACTION property** indicates the name of the CGI script that will process the form data, and the **METHOD property** controls how your Web browser sends the form data to the Web server running the CGI script. The METHOD property can be set to either GET or POST.

As you will observe shortly, the **GET method**, which is the default value for the METHOD property, appends the form data to the end of the URL specified in the ACTION property, and is similar to sending the data using a hyperlink. The server retrieves the data from the URL and stores it in a text string for processing by the CGI script. The **POST method**, on the other hand, sends the form data in a separate data stream, allowing the Web server to receive the data through what is called "standard input." Because it is more flexible, the POST method is considered the preferred way of sending data to the server. It also is safer, because some Web servers limit the amount of data sent by the GET method and will truncate the URL, cutting off valuable information. You will observe the use of both methods in the next set of steps.

To complete the Annuity Calculator form, then use it to test the Annuity Calculator script:

1. Change the <FORM> tag in the Annuity.html document to **<FORM ACTION="http://*yourservername*/webprog/chap12/chapter/annuity.pl" METHOD=GET>**. Replace *yourservername* in the URL with the name of your server.
2. Save the Annuity.html document.
3. Open your Web browser. Use the browser's File menu to open the Annuity.html file. The Annuity Calculator form should look similar to the one shown earlier in Figure 12-1.
4. Enter **George** as the name, **2000** as the payment amount, **.05** as the interest rate, **20** as the term, and **1** as the number of payments per year. Click the **Submit** button. Figure 12-9 shows the result of using the GET method to send the form data.

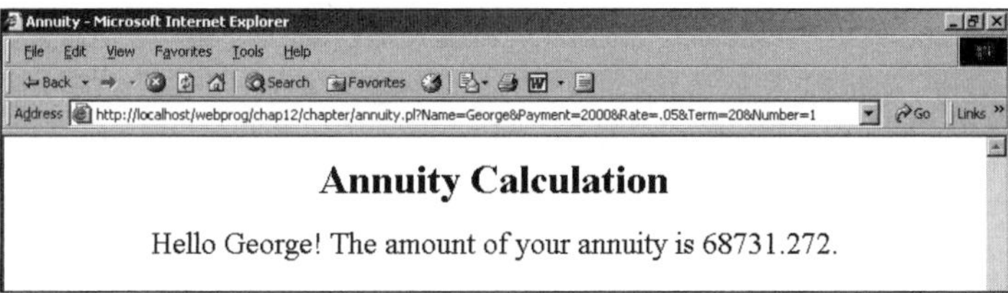

Figure 12-9 Result of using the GET method to send the form data

12

Notice that the form data is appended to the URL and appears in the browser's Address box, just as it does when data is sent using a hyperlink.

Now see the effect of changing the METHOD property to POST.

5. Return to the Annuity.html document in your text editor. Change GET to **POST** in the <FORM> tag.
6. Save the Annuity.html document.
7. Use your browser's File menu to open the Annuity.html document. Enter **George** as the name, **2000** as the payment amount, **.05** as the interest rate, **20** as the term, and **1** as the number of payments per year. Click the **Submit** button. Figure 12-10 shows the result of using the POST method to send the form data.

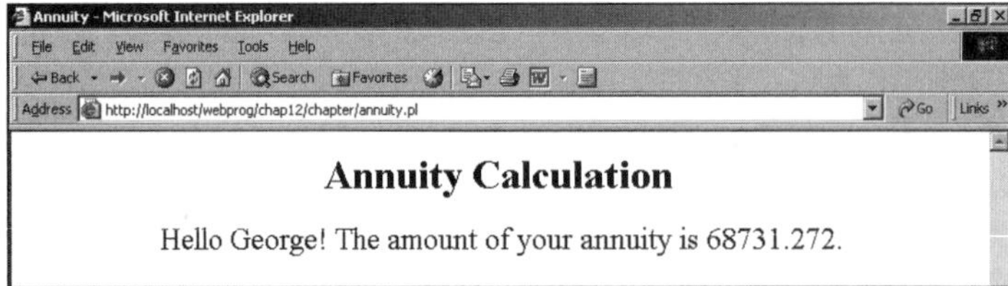

Figure 12-10 Result of using the POST method to send the form data

Notice that the form data does not appear in the browser's Address box when you use the POST method.

8. Click the **Back** button to return to the Annuity Calculator form, then minimize the browser window.

Now that you know that the Annuity.pl script is working correctly, you can begin improving the appearance of the Web page it creates. First, you learn how to include a dollar sign ($) in a number that represents money.

Including a Dollar Sign in a Number

Displaying a dollar sign ($) at the beginning of a number makes it obvious that the number represents money. You display a dollar sign in Perl by including a backslash (\) followed by a dollar sign ($) in a `print` statement, as shown in Table 12-4. The backslash (\) is necessary because the dollar sign ($) has special meaning in Perl. The backslash alerts Perl to ignore the special meaning and simply treat the dollar sign verbatim.

You already learned about the dollar sign's function in creating variables in Perl. The dollar sign also is used in pattern matching, which is beyond the scope of this book.

Table 12-4 Examples of including a dollar sign in a `print` statement

Examples	Results
`print "You earned \$100.\n";`	Displays the text "You earned $100."
`print "Price: \$$price\n";`	Assuming the `$price` variable contains the number 35, this displays the text "Price: $35"
`print "\$$bill due\n";`	Assuming the `$bill` variable contains the number 150.75, this displays the text "$150.75 due"

The first `print` statement shown in Table 12-4, `print "You earned \$100.\n";`, displays the text "You earned $100". Notice that Perl replaces `\$` in the statement with $.

The second `print` statement shown in Table 12-4 displays the text "Price: $35", and the last `print` statement displays the text "$150.75 due". Here again, Perl replaces `\$` in both statements with $. Perl also replaces the variable names (`$price` and `$bill`) with the contents of the variables (35 and 150.75).

In the next set of steps, you include a dollar sign before the annuity amount displayed by the Annuity.pl script.

To include a dollar sign before the annuity amount:

1. Open the **Annuity.pl** file in a text editor. The file is contained in the Chap12\Chapter folder in your work folder.
2. Change the `print "The amount of your annuity is $annuity.\n";` statement to **`print "The amount of your annuity is \$$annuity.\n";`**.
3. Save the Annuity.pl document.
4. Restore the browser window, which you minimized in an earlier set of steps.
5. Click the **Reset** button to clear the data from the Annuity Calculator form. Assume that Jeff deposits $200 each month in his savings account. Calculate the annuity amount using an interest rate of 4% and a term of 10 years.
6. Enter **Jeff** as the name, **200** as the payment amount, **.04** as the interest rate, **10** as the term, and **12** as the number of payments per year. Click the **Submit** button. A dollar sign appears before the annuity amount on the Web page, as shown in Figure 12-11.

12

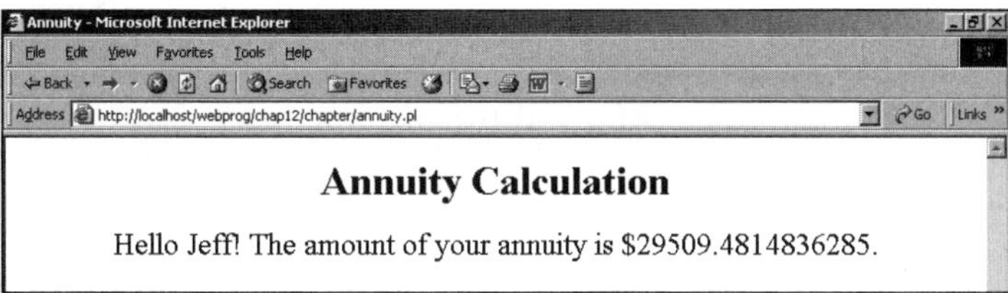

Figure 12-11 Web page showing a dollar sign before the annuity amount

Notice that the annuity amount ($29509.4814836285) contains 10 decimal places. Most times, a number that represents money is displayed with either zero or two decimal places. You can use the Perl `printf` function to specify the number of decimal places to display in a number.

7. Click the **Back** button to return to the Annuity Calculator form, and then minimize the browser window.

USING THE `printf` FUNCTION

In all of the scripts you have created so far, you used the `print` function to display data on a Web page. Perl also provides the **`printf` function** for displaying data on a Web page. Unlike the `print` function, the `printf` function allows you to format the data it displays. For example, the `printf` function allows you to specify the number of decimal places to include in a number. It also allows you to display a plus sign (+) before positive numbers, and a minus sign (-) before negative numbers.

The syntax of the `printf` function is **printf** *formatstring*, *list*;. In the syntax, *list* is a comma-separated list of items—typically variables—whose values you want to format, and *formatstring* is a string that controls the appearance of each item in the *list*. *Formatstring* can contain text and one or more format fields, as indicated in Figure 12-12. (For now, do not worry about understanding the meaning of the numbers, letters, and symbols that appear in the format fields shown in Figure 12-12. You learn more about format fields later in the chapter.)

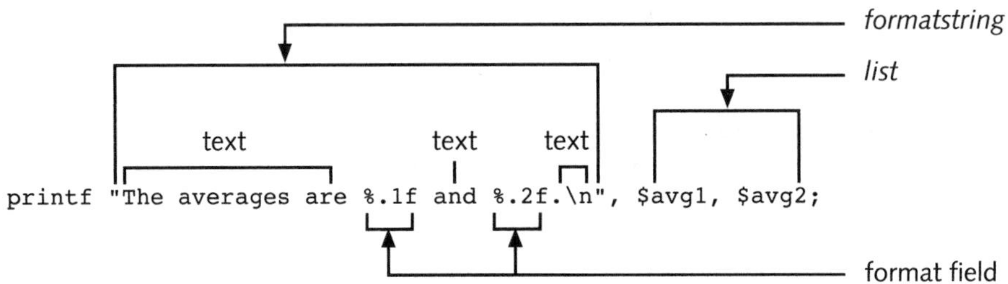

Figure 12-12 Example of a `printf` function

Notice that the *formatstring* shown in Figure 12-12 is enclosed in double quotation marks, and that a comma separates the *formatstring* from the *list*. A comma also is used to separate one item in the *list* from the next. Additionally, notice that the *formatstring* contains two format fields (`%.1f` and `%.2f`), and the *list* contains two items (the variable names `$avg1` and `$avg2`). You should include in the *formatstring* a separate format field for each item in the *list*. The `printf` function uses the first format field in the *formatstring* to format the first item in the *list*, the second format field to format the second item, and so on. In this case, the `printf` function uses the `%.1f` format field to format the value stored in the `$avg1` variable, and uses the `%.2f` format field to format the value stored in the `$avg2` variable. As you will learn shortly, the `%.1f` format field tells the `printf` function to display the value as a floating-point number (f) with one (1) decimal place. A value of 98, for example, will be displayed as 98.0. Notice that the `printf` function appends the decimal point and a 0 to the end of the number so that the number contains one decimal place.

Similarly, the `%.2f` format field tells the `printf` function to display the value as a floating-point number (f) with two (2) decimal places. A value of 45.3, for example, will be displayed as 45.30, and a value of 75.1267 will be displayed as 75.13.

In the next section, you learn about the parts of a format field.

Parts of a Format Field

Each format field is composed of five parts, three of which are optional. The five parts are described in Table 12-5.

Table 12-5 Parts of a format field

Parts	Description
%	The percent sign is required; it indicates the beginning of a format field
Modifier	The modifier is optional; the two modifiers most commonly used to display numbers on a Web page are the plus sign (+) and the number 0; the purpose of each modifier is listed below Modifier — Purpose + — Display a + sign before a positive number, and a – sign before a negative number 0 — Pad the left side of a number with zeroes instead of spaces
Minimum field width	The minimum field width is optional; when used, it is a number that indicates the minimum number of characters you want displayed in the field
Precision	The precision is optional; when used, it is expressed as a period (.) followed by a number; the precision indicates the number of digits you want displayed to the right of the decimal point in a number
Format type	The format type is required; it indicates the format to use when displaying the field data; the two most commonly used format types are `d` (decimal number) and `f` (floating-point number)

As Table 12-5 indicates, the first part of a format field is a percent sign (`%`) and is required; every format field must begin with a percent sign. The second part of the format field, the modifier, is optional. The modifiers most commonly used when displaying numbers on a Web page are the plus sign (+) and the number `0`. The plus sign modifier tells the `printf` function to display a plus sign (+) before a positive number, and a minus sign (-) before a negative number. You can use the number `0` modifier to pad the left side of a number with zeros instead of spaces—for example, to display the number 5 as 05.

The third part of a format field is the minimum field width, which is optional. When used, it is a number that indicates the minimum number of characters you want displayed in the field. The fourth part of a format field is the precision, which also is optional. The precision is expressed as a period (.) followed by a number—for example, .4. The precision indicates the number of digits to display to the right of the decimal point in a numeric value. For example, applying a precision of .4 to the number 45.3 results in the number 45.3000.

The last part of a format field is the format type and is required. The most commonly used format types for displaying numeric values are `d` and `f`. A format type of `d`, which stands for *decimal number*, indicates that the numeric value should be displayed as a whole number (a number without any decimal places). A format type of `f`, which stands for *floating-point number*, indicates that the numeric value should be displayed with zero or more decimal places. Recall that the number of decimal places to display is specified in the precision part of the format field.

The `printf` function also provides the `s` format type for displaying strings, such as product or employee names. The `s` stands for *string*. When displaying a string, the precision part of the format field specifies the number of characters to display from the string. For example, applying a precision of .4 to the string "Jackie" results in the string "Jack".

The `printf` function is a powerful function that gives you a lot of control over the appearance of data displayed on a Web page. Unfortunately, the function can be difficult to master without a lot of practice. To aid in your learning of the `printf` function, Table 12-6 shows the function's syntax and several examples of using the function. The format field in each example is shaded in the figure.

You also can use the Perl `sprintf` function to format numbers. The syntax of the `sprintf` function is similar to the syntax of the `printf` function; it is *variable* = **sprintf** *formatstring*, *list*;, where *formatstring* and *list* have the same meaning as in the `printf` function. The difference between the two functions is that the `printf` function sends the formatted data to a Web page, whereas the `sprintf` function assigns the formatted data to a variable, which then can be printed using a simple `print` statement. You can practice with the `sprintf` function by completing Exercise 5 at the end of this chapter.

The format field shaded in Example 1 (`%.2f`) contains the percent sign (%), precision (.2), and format type (f); it does not contain a modifier or the minimum field width. Recall that the percent sign and format type are required parts of the format field; the precision, modifier, and minimum field width are optional. The format field `%.2f` tells the `printf` function to display the contents of the `$price` variable as a floating-point number with two digits to the right of the decimal point. Assuming the `$price` variable contains the number 9.5, Example 1's `printf` function will display "The price is $9.50". Notice that the `printf` function appends a zero to the end of the number to give the number two decimal places.

Table 12-6 Syntax and examples of the printf function

Syntax
printf *formatstring, list;*
Examples and results
Example 1 `printf "The price is \$%.2f\n", $price;` Result Assuming the $price variable contains the number 9.5, the printf function will display "The price is $9.50"
Example 2 `printf "The averages are %d and %d.\n", $avg, $tot/3;` Result Assuming the $avg and $tot variables contain the numbers 85.6 and 270, respectively, the printf function will display "The averages are 85 and 90."

Example 3
`printf "%04d\n", $num1;`
`printf "%04d\n", $num2;`
Result
Assuming the $num1 and $num2 variables contain the numbers 7500 and 900, respectively, the printf functions will display the following two lines:
7500
0900

Example 4 `printf "Bonus percentage: %.1f%%\n", $rate;` Result Assuming the $rate variable contains the number 5, the printf function will display "Bonus percentage: 5.0%"

To display a percent sign, you must type two percent signs

12

The two format fields shaded in Example 2, %d, contain only the required parts of a format field: the percent sign and the format type. The %d format fields tell the printf function to display as decimal (whole) numbers both the contents of the $avg variable and the result of dividing the contents of the $tot variable by three. Assuming the $avg and $tot variables contain the numbers 85.6 and 270, respectively, the printf function shown in Example 2 will display "The averages are 85 and 90." Notice that the `printf` function truncates (removes or drops off) the decimal portion of the number 85.6 before displaying the number. Also notice that a *list* item can be a calculation, such as `$tot/3`. The `printf` function displays the result of the calculation, rather than the calculation itself.

The two format fields shaded in Example 3 contain the percent sign (%), a modifier (0), the minimum field width (4), and the format type (d). The `%04d` format field tells the `printf` function to display the *list* value as a decimal number containing at least four digits. If the value does not contain four digits, the `printf` function should pad the left side of the value with one or more zeros. Assuming the `$num1` and `$num2` variables contain the numbers 7500 and 900, respectively, the `printf` functions in Example 3 will display the numbers 7500 and 0900, as indicated in the example. Notice that the `printf` function pads the left side of the three-digit number 900 with a zero to give the number four digits.

Example 4 in Table 12-6 (`printf "Bonus percentage: %.1f%%\n", $rate;`) shows how you can use the `printf` function to display a percent sign at the end of a number. To do so, you must type two percent signs (`%%`) after the format field, as shown in the example.

You will use the `printf` function in the Annuity.pl script to format to two decimal places the annuity amount displayed on the dynamic Web page.

Using the `printf` Function in the Annuity Calculator Script

Although the Annuity.pl script is working correctly, the Web page it creates would look more professional if the annuity amount included two decimal places rather than 10 decimal places.

To include the `printf` function in the Annuity.pl script:

1. Return to the Annuity.pl document in your text editor.
2. Change the `print "The amount of your annuity is \$$annuity.\n";` statement to **`printf "The amount of your annuity is \$%.2f.\n", $annuity;`**. (Be sure to change the word `print` to `printf` in the statement.) Figure 12-13 shows the completed Annuity.pl script.
3. Save the Annuity.pl document.
4. Return to your browser, which you minimized in an earlier set of steps. The Annuity Calculator form should show Jeff as the name, 200 as the payment amount, .04 as the interest rate, 10 as the term, and 12 as the number of payments per year.

```
#Annuity.pl - calculates and displays the amount of an annuity
print "Content-type: text/html\n\n";
use CGI qw(:standard -debug);

#prevent Perl from creating undeclared variables
use strict;
#declare variables
my ($name, $payment, $rate, $term, $number, $annuity);

#assign values to variables
$name = param('Name');
$payment = param('Payment');
$rate = param('Rate');
$term = param('Term');
$number = param('Number');

#calculate annuity amount
$annuity = $number * $payment / $rate * (2.7182818 ** ($rate * $term) - 1);

#create Web page
print "<HTML>\n";
print "<HEAD><TITLE>Annuity</TITLE><BASEFONT SIZE=5></HEAD>\n";
print "<CENTER><H1>Annuity Calculation</H1>\n";
print "<BODY>\n";
print "Hello $name!\n";
printf "The amount of your annuity is \$%.2f.\n", $annuity;
print "</BODY></CENTER>\n";
print "</HTML>\n";
```

Figure 12-13 Completed Annuity.pl script

5. Click the **Submit** button. The script displays the formatted annuity amount on a Web page, as shown in Figure 12-14.

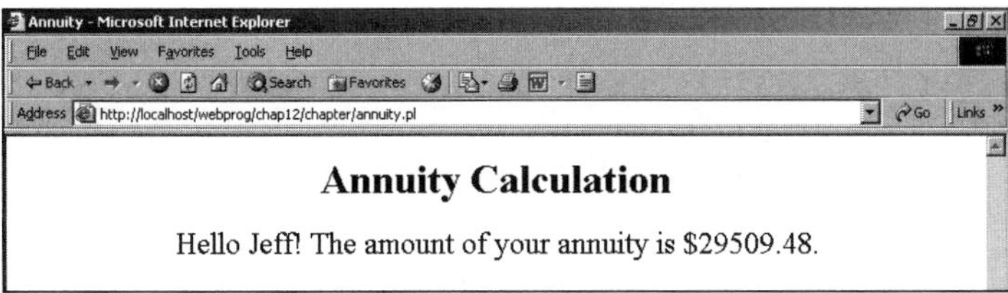

Figure 12-14 Dynamic Web page showing the formatted annuity amount

6. Close the browser and all open windows.

12

Chapter Summary

- When you click the submit button on a form, the browser sends the form data to the server. If the form is associated with a CGI script, the server forwards the form data to the script for processing. When a CGI script has finished processing, it sends its output—typically HTML—to the server, which transfers the output to the browser.
- Planning a CGI script involves determining the script's input, output, and algorithm.
- A variable is a location (within the computer's internal memory) where a script can temporarily store data. Every variable has a data type and a name.
- A scalar variable can store precisely one value—typically a number or a string. The name of a scalar variable must begin with a dollar sign ($) followed by a letter and then, optionally, one or more letters, numbers, or underscores. Variable names in Perl are case sensitive.
- The statement `use strict;` prevents Perl from creating variables "on the fly" and forces you to explicitly declare each variable in the script. You explicitly declare one or more variables using a statement that follows the syntax **my (***variablelist***);**, where *variablelist* is a comma-separated list of variable names.
- The syntax of an assignment statement, which you can use to assign (or change) the value stored in a variable is *variable* = *value*;, where *variable* is the variable's name and *value* is the number or string you want stored in the variable.
- When the name of a variable appears within double quotation marks in a statement, Perl replaces the variable's name with the variable's contents—a process referred to as interpolation. Single quotation marks around a string indicate that no interpolation should be performed in the string.
- You can use the parsing routine contained in the CGI.pm module to parse the data submitted to a script using an online form.
- You use the FORM tag's ACTION property to specify the name of the CGI script that will process the form data. You use the FORM tag's METHOD property to control how your Web browser sends the form data to the Web server running the CGI script. The METHOD property can be set to GET or POST.
- You display a dollar sign in Perl by including a backslash (\) followed by a dollar sign ($) in a `print` or `printf` statement.
- You can use the `printf` function to format data displayed on a Web page. The syntax of the `printf` function is **printf** *formatstring***,** *list*;, where *list* is a comma-separated list of items whose values you want to format, and *formatstring* is a string that controls the appearance of each item in the *list*. *Formatstring* can contain text and one or more format fields. A format field in a `printf` function's *formatstring* is composed of five parts: %, modifier, minimum field width, precision, and format type. Only the % and format type parts are required.

REVIEW QUESTIONS

1. The variable names `$state` and `$State` refer to the same location in the computer's internal memory.

   a. True

   b. False

2. Assuming the form is associated with a CGI script, the form *keys* and *values* are passed automatically to the script when you click the form's submit button.

   a. True

   b. False

3. Which of the following statements creates a scalar variable named `$height`?

   a. `my ($height As Scalar);`

   b. `my (Scalar &height);`

   c. `my $height as scalar;`

   d. none of these

4. When the name of a variable appears within double quotation marks in a statement, Perl uses a process referred to as ________________ to replace the variable's name with the variable's contents.

   a. interpolation

   b. replacement

   c. substitution

   d. none of these

5. Which of the following statements prevents Perl from creating variables "on the fly"?

   a. `declare vars;`

   b. `explicit declare;`

   c. `use explicit;`

   d. `use strict;`

6. Which of the following statements creates three variables named `$employee`, `$age`, and `$pay_rate`?

   a. `my ($employee, $age, $pay_rate);`

   b. `my $employee, $age, $pay_rate;`

   c. `$employee, $age, $pay_rate As Variables;`

   d. `create($employee, $age, $pay_rate);`

7. Which of the following statements assigns the name "Jack" to the `$employee` variable?

   a. `$employee = Jack;`

   b. `$employee = 'Jack';`

   c. `$employee = "Jack";`

   d. both b and c

8. Assuming that the `$name` variable contains the name "Jacob", which of the following statements assigns the message "Hello Jacob" to the `$msg` variable?

   a. `$msg = Hello $name;`

   b. `$msg = 'Hello $name';`

   c. `$msg = "Hello $name";`

   d. both b and c

9. Assuming that the `$total` variable contains the number 78.5, which of the following statements displays the message "The total due is $78.50" on a Web page?

   a. `print "The total due is \$$total\n";`

   b. `printf "The total due is \$%.2f\n, $total";`

   c. `printf "The total due is \$%.2f\n", $total;`

   d. `printf "The total due is \$$total\n", %.2f;`

10. Assuming that the `$age` variable contains the number 35, which of the following statements displays the message "Age: 35" on a Web page?

    a. `print "Age: $age\n";`

    b. `printf "Age: %d\n", $age;`

    c. `printf "Age: %d, $age\n";`

    d. both a and b

11. Which of the following statements multiplies the `$sales` variable by .1, and then assigns the result to the `$commission` variable?

    a. `$commission = $sales * .1;`

    b. `$commission = $sales ** .1;`

    c. `$commission = $sales X .1;`

    d. `$commission = "$sales * .1";`

12. Which of the following is the exponentiation operator in Perl?

    a. `*`

    b. `**`

    c. `^`

    d. none of these

13. The ________________ property indicates the name of the CGI script that will process the form data.
    a. ACTION
    b. FORM
    c. METHOD
    d. URL
14. The default value for the METHOD property is ________________.
    a. GET
    b. GO
    c. POST
    d. SEND
15. The ________________ method is considered the preferred way of sending data to a server.
    a. GET
    b. GO
    c. POST
    d. SEND

HANDS-ON EXERCISES

If necessary, use Windows Explorer to create a new folder in the Chap12 folder in your work folder. Name this folder **Exercises**. Save the Perl scripts and HTML documents that you create in these Exercises in the Chap12\Exercises folder in your work folder.

Exercise 12-1

In this exercise, you modify the Web page displayed by the Annuity.pl script created in the chapter.

To modify the Web page displayed by the Annuity.pl script:

1. Open the **Annuity.html** file in a text editor. The file is contained in the Chap12\Chapter folder in your work folder.
2. Change the filename in the first line from Annuity.html to **Annuity2.html**.
3. Modify the ACTION property so that it refers to the **Annuity2.pl** script contained in the Chap12\Exercises folder in your work folder.
4. Save the file as **Annuity2.html** in the Chap12\Exercises folder in your work folder.

5. Open the **Annuity.pl** file in a text editor. The file is contained in the Chap12\Chapter folder in your work folder.
6. Change the filename in the first line from Annuity.pl to **Annuity2.pl**. Save the file as **Annuity2.pl** in the Chap12\Exercises folder in your work folder.
7. Modify the Annuity.pl script to output a Web page similar to the one shown in Figure 12-15.

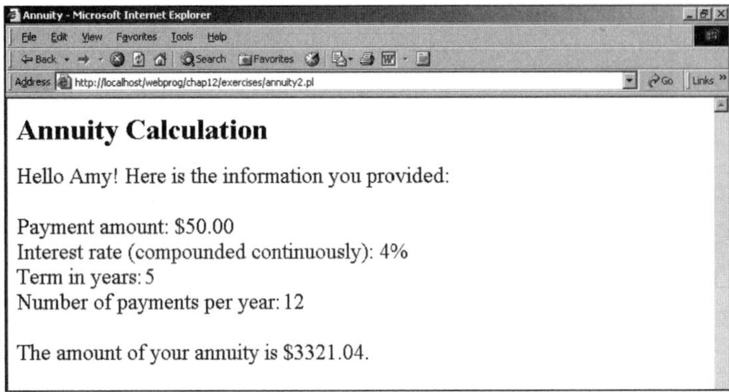
Annuity - Microsoft Internet Explorer
File Edit View Favorites Tools Help
Back Search Favorites
Address http://localhost/webprog/chap12/exercises/annuity2.pl
Go Links
Annuity Calculation
Hello Amy! Here is the information you provided:
Payment amount: $50.00
Interest rate (compounded continuously): 4%
Term in years: 5
Number of payments per year: 12
The amount of your annuity is $3321.04.

Figure 12-15

8. Save the **Annuity2.pl** script.
9. Open your Web browser. Use the browser's File menu to open the **Annuity2.html** file.
10. Enter Amy as the name, 50 as the payment amount, .04 as the interest rate, 5 as the term, and 12 as the number of payments per year. Click the Submit button. The browser should display a Web page similar to the one shown in Figure 12-15.

Project

Exercise 12-2

In this exercise, you create an online form and a script that processes the form data (name, hours, and rate). The script calculates the gross pay amount and displays the form data and the gross pay amount on a dynamic Web page.

To create an online form and a script that processes the form data:

1. Open a new document in your text editor. Type <!Payroll.html> and press Enter. Save the document as **Payroll.html** in the Chap12\Exercises folder in your work folder.
2. Use the Payroll.html document to create the form shown in Figure 12-16. The form data will be processed by the Payroll.pl script contained in the Chap12\Exercises folder in your work folder. Use the POST method.

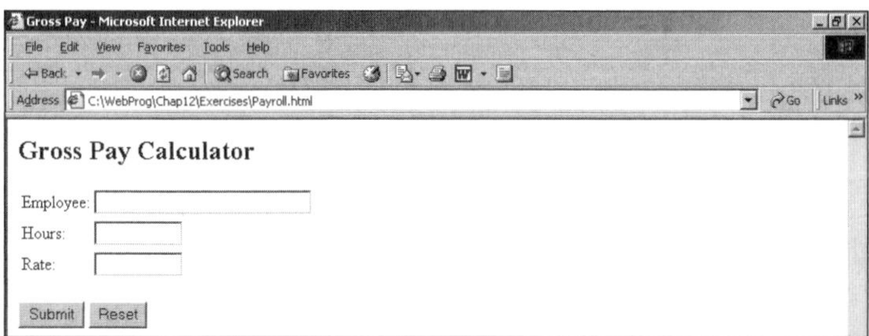

Figure 12-16

3. Save the **Payroll.html** document.
4. Open a new document in your text editor. Type #Payroll.pl and press Enter. Save the document as **Payroll.pl** in the Chap12\Exercises folder in your work folder.
5. The Payroll.pl script should output a Web page similar to the one shown in Figure 12-17. Code the script appropriately. (You do not have to worry about calculating overtime pay, because all hours worked are paid at the regular pay rate.)

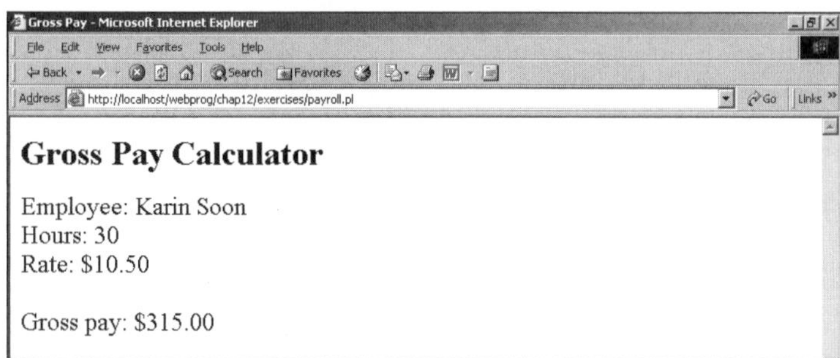

Figure 12-17

6. Save the **Payroll.pl** document.
7. Test the Payroll.pl script from the command line.
8. Open your Web browser. Use the browser's File menu to open the **Payroll.html** file. Enter Karin Soon as the employee name, 30 as the hours, and 10.5 as the pay rate, then click the Submit button. The browser should display a Web page similar to the one shown in Figure 12-17.

Exercise 12-3

In this exercise, you create an online form and a script that processes the form data (length and width). The script calculates the area of a rectangle and displays the form data and the area on a dynamic Web page.

To create an online form and a script that processes the form data:

1. Open a new document in your text editor. Type <!Area.html> and press Enter. Save the document as **Area.html** in the Chap12\Exercises folder in your work folder.
2. Use the Area.html document to create the form shown in Figure 12-18. The form data will be processed by the Area.pl script contained in the Chap12\Exercises folder in your work folder. Use the GET method.

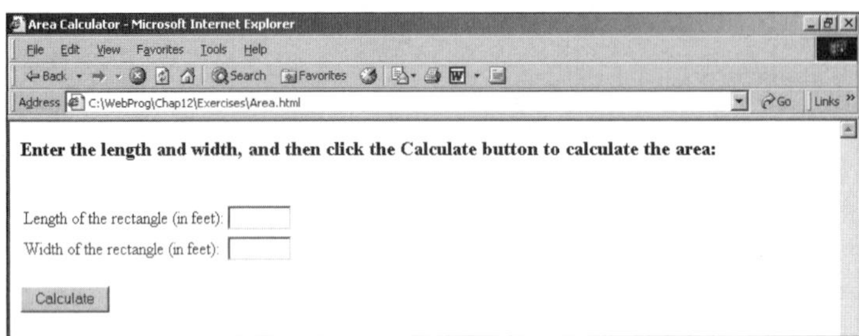

Figure 12-18

3. Save the **Area.html** document.
4. Open a new document in your text editor. Type #Area.pl and press Enter. Save the document as **Area.pl** in the Chap12\Exercises folder in your work folder.
5. The Area.pl script should produce a Web page similar to the one shown in Figure 12-19. Code the script appropriately. (*Hint*: Display the data using a table. Align the numbers using the <TD> tag's `ALIGN` property.)

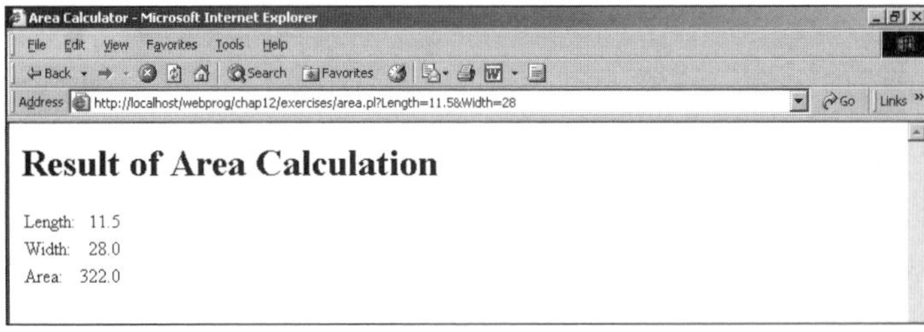

Figure 12-19

6. Save the **Area.pl** document.
7. Test the Area.pl script from the command line.
8. Open your Web browser. Use the browser's File menu to open the **Area.html** file. Enter 11.5 as the length and 28 as the width. Click the Calculate button. The browser should display a Web page similar to the one shown in Figure 12-19.

Exercise 12-4

In this exercise, you create an online form and a script that processes the form data (name and number of hours worked during the month). The script calculates the number of weeks, days, and hours worked during the month. It then displays the form data and the results of the calculations on a dynamic Web page.

To create an online form and a script that processes the form data:

1. Use a text editor to create a Web page for Temp Employers. The Web page should allow the user to enter his or her name and the number of hours he or she worked during the month. The form data will be processed by the Temp.pl script contained in the Chap12\Exercises folder in your work folder. Use the POST method.
2. Save the HTML document as **Temp.html** in the Chap12\Exercises folder in your work folder.
3. Open a new document in your text editor. Type #Temp.pl and press Enter. Save the document as **Temp.pl** in the Chap12\Exercises folder in your work folder.
4. The Temp.pl script should calculate the number of weeks (assume a 40-hour week), days (assume an eight-hour day), and hours worked. For example, if you work 70 hours during the month, then you have worked one week, three days, and six hours. The script should display a Web page that contains the form data and the results of the calculations. Code the script appropriately. (*Hint*: Consider using the modulus arithmetic operator from Table 12-3.)
5. Save the **Temp.pl** document.
6. Test the Temp.pl script from the command line.
7. Open your Web browser. Use the browser's File menu to open the **Temp.html** file. Test the script using Jacob Miller as the name and 70 as the number of hours worked during the month. The browser should display the form data and the results of the calculations made by the script.

Exercise 12-5

In this exercise, you create an online form and a script that processes the form data (original price and discount rate). The script calculates a discount amount and a sale price, and then displays the form data, the discount amount, and the sale price on a dynamic Web page.

To create an online form and script that calculate and display the discount amount and sale price:

1. Use a text editor to create a Web page for The Paper Tree. The Web page should allow the user to enter the original price of an item and the discount rate. The form data will be processed by the PaperTree.pl script contained in the Chap12\Exercises folder in your work folder. Use the POST method.

2. Save the HTML document as **PaperTree.html** in the Chap12\Exercises folder in your work folder.
3. Open a new document in your text editor. Type #PaperTree.pl and press Enter. Save the document as **PaperTree.pl** in the Chap12\Exercises folder in your work folder.
4. The PaperTree.pl script should calculate the amount of the discount and the new sale price. The script should display the form data, the discount, and the new sale price on a Web page, as shown in Figure 12-20.

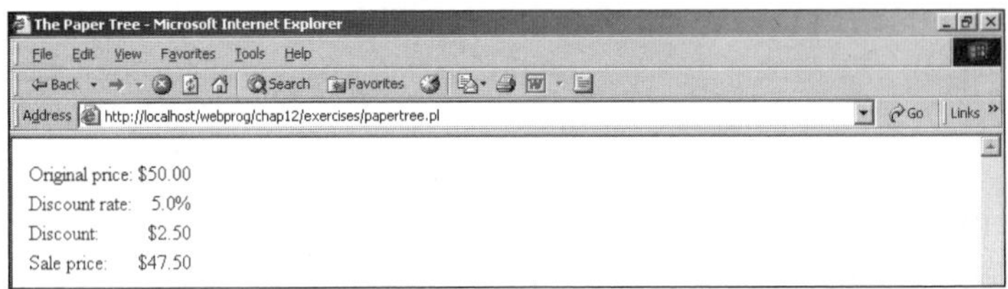

Figure 12-20

5. Save the **PaperTree.pl** document.
6. Test the PaperTree.pl script from the command line.
7. Open your Web browser. Use the browser's File menu to open the **PaperTree.html** file. Test the script using 50 as the original price and .05 as the discount rate. The browser should display a Web page similar to the one shown in Figure 12-20.
8. Press the Back button in the browser to return to the form.
9. Enter 50.50 as the original price and .05 as the discount rate. Click the form's submit button. The browser displays a Web page that shows the correct discount amount ($2.53), but an incorrect sale price ($47.98); the sale price should be $47.97. The error occurs because 50.50 multiplied by .05 gives a discount amount of 2.5250, and 50.50 minus 2.5250 results in a sale price of 47.9750. The `%.2f` format fields in the `printf` statements that display the discount amount and sale price round the 2.5250 and 47.9750 to two decimal places, giving 2.53 and 47.98. You can use the Perl `sprintf` function to fix this problem. The syntax of the `sprintf` function is similar to the syntax of the `printf` function; it is *variable* = **sprintf** *formatstring*, *list*;, where *formatstring* and *list* have the same meaning as in the `printf` function. The difference between the two functions is that the `printf` function sends the formatted data to a Web page, whereas the `sprintf` function sends the formatted data to a variable. You will use the `sprintf` function to round the discount amount to two decimal places before subtracting the amount from the original price.

10. Return to the PaperTree.pl document in your text editor. Modify the statement that calculates the discount amount as follows: `discount = sprintf "%.2f", originalprice * discount-rate;`, where *discount*, *originalprice*, and *discountrate* are the names of the variables used in your script.
11. Save the **PaperTree.pl** script.
12. Return to the PaperTree.html form in your browser. Click the form's submit button to calculate the discount amount and sale price based on an original price of 50.50 and a discount rate of .05. The Web page shows $2.53 as the discount amount and $47.97 as the sale price.

WEB PROGRAMMING PROJECTS

If necessary, use Windows Explorer to create a new folder in the Chap12 folder in your work folder. Name this folder **Projects**. Save the Perl scripts and HTML documents that you create in these Projects in the Chap12\Projects folder in your work folder.

Project 12-1

Create an HTML document and a script for Lake College. Name the HTML document **Lake.html**, and name the script **Lake.pl**. Save the HTML document and script in the Chap12\Projects folder in your work folder. The HTML document should display a Web page that allows the user to enter a student's name and the number of hours the student is enrolled for the semester. The script should calculate the total due by multiplying the number of hours enrolled by $100 and then adding the room and board fee ($1800) to the result. The script then should display the form data and the total due on a Web page.

12

Project 12-2

Create an HTML document and a script for The Regal wallpaper store. Name the HTML document **Regal.html**, and name the script **Regal.pl**. Save the HTML document and script in the Chap12\Projects folder in your work folder. The HTML document should display a Web page that allows the user to enter the length, width, and height dimensions of a room; each dimension should be entered in feet. The Web page also should allow the user to enter the number of square feet a single roll of wallpaper will cover. The script should calculate the required number of single rolls of wallpaper the customer will need to purchase to cover the room. The script should display the form data and the required number of single rolls of wallpaper on a Web page. Display the length, width, height, and coverage values with one decimal place. Display the required number of single rolls as a whole number. For example, if you enter 10 as the length, 12 as the width, 8 as the height, and 30 as the coverage, the script should display the numbers 10.0, 12.0, 8.0, and 30.0. It also should display the number 12 as the required number of single rolls of wallpaper.

Project 12-3

Create an HTML document and a script for Colfax Industries. Name the HTML document **Colfax.html**, and name the script **Colfax.pl**. Save the HTML document and script in the Chap12\Projects folder in your work folder. The HTML document should display a Web page that allows the user to enter the name of an item in inventory, the quantity of the item in inventory, and how many units of the item can be packed in a box for shipping. The script should calculate the number of full boxes that can be packed from the quantity on hand, and the quantity of items left over. It then should display the form data and the results of the calculations on a Web page.

CHAPTER

13

JAVA: PART I

In this chapter you will:

- Explore the Java programming language
- Learn about variables and constants
- Use GUI objects to produce output and accept input
- Use decision and repetition techniques
- Create and use methods
- Create and use classes and objects

The **Java programming language** is an object-oriented, event-driven language. It was developed by Sun Microsystems as an object-oriented language that is used both for general-purpose business programs and interactive Web-based Internet programs. As an object-oriented language, Java uses classes and objects and takes advantage of the principles of inheritance and polymorphism. In this chapter, you learn about many features of the Java programming language and you create your own Java applications.

See Chapter 1 for a description of object-oriented language features and terminology.

EXPLORING THE JAVA PROGRAMMING LANGUAGE

Java is an extremely popular language for writing programs as well as for learning about object-oriented programming principles that you can apply to other languages. Specific characteristics that have made the Java programming language so popular in recent years are its security features, and the fact that it is **architecturally neutral**, which means that you can write a program using Java and it can run on any platform. A machine that runs a program written in the Java programming language only needs to have a special program called an **interpreter** to translate the program for the host machine. In contrast, when using some other programming languages, software vendors often must produce multiple versions of the same product (DOS version, Windows 3.1 version, Windows 2000 version, Macintosh version, and so on) so all users can run the program. With the Java programming language, one program version runs on all these platforms. A program written in the Java programming language is compiled into Java Virtual Machine Code, called **bytecode**. The compiled bytecode is subsequently interpreted on the machine where the program is executed. Any compiled program runs on any machine that has a Java programming language interpreter.

Writing a Java Program that Produces Output

At first glance, even the simplest Java program involves a fair amount of confusing syntax. Consider the program in Figure 13-1. This program is written on seven lines, and its only task is to print "Hello, World!" on the screen.

```
public class Hello
{
    public static void main(String[] args)
   {
      System.out.println("Hello, World!");
   }
}
```

Figure 13-1 Java program that prints a string

It is a tradition among programmers that the first program you write in any language produces "Hello, World!" as its output. In the next set of steps, you create the program shown in Figure 13-1. You can use any text editor, such as Notepad, WordPad, or any word-processing program.

To create the Hello, World program:

1. Start any text editor and then open a new document, if necessary.
2. Type the class header **`public class Hello`**. In this example, the class name is `Hello`. You can use any valid name you want for the class. If you choose "Hello," you must refer to the class as "Hello," and not as "hello," because the Java programming language is case sensitive.

Everything that is used within a Java program must be part of a **class**. When you write `public class Hello`, you are defining a class named `Hello`. You can define a Java class using any name or identifier you need, as long as it meets the following requirements:

- A class name must begin with a letter of the alphabet. In Java underscores, dollar signs, and foreign letters such as α or π are all considered to be letters.
- A class name can contain only letters or digits.
- A class name cannot be a Java language reserved keyword, such as `public` or `class`. (See Table 13-1 for a list of reserved keywords.)
- A class name cannot be one of the following words: `true`, `false`, or `null`, which are values.

Table 13-1 Java reserved keywords

abstract	double	int	strictfp
Boolean	else	interface	super
break	extends	long	switch
byte	final	native	synchronized
case	finally	new	this
catch	float	package	throw
char	for	private	throws
class	goto	protected	transient
const	if	public	try
continue	implements	return	void
default	import	short	volatile
do	instanceof	static	while

Java is based on Unicode, which is an international system of character representation. The term "letter" indicates English-language letters, as well as characters from Arabic, Greek, and a variety of other alphabets.

13

A programming convention is that class names in the Java programming language begin with an uppercase letter and employ other uppercase letters as needed to improve readability. For example, `TextField` is a conventional class name.

In Figure 13-1, the line `public class Hello` contains the keyword `class`, which identifies `Hello` as a class. The reserved word `public` is an access modifier. An **access modifier** defines the circumstances under which a class can be accessed. Public access is the most liberal type of access.

To continue to write the `Hello` class:

1. With the insertion point at the end of the `Hello` class header, press **Enter** once to start a new line. Type an opening curly brace (`{`) to start the class.
2. Press **Enter** again, and then type a closing curly brace (`}`) to end the class. Later, you add statements between these curly braces.

You enclose the contents of all classes within curly braces ({ and }). Between the braces, a class can contain any number of data items and methods. In Figure 13-1, the class `Hello` contains only one method. The name of the method is `main()`, and the `main()` method contains its own set of braces and only one statement—the `println()` statement.

In general, whitespace is optional in the Java programming language. Whitespace is any combination of spaces, tabs, and carriage returns (blank lines). However, you cannot use whitespace within any identifier or keyword. You can insert whitespace between words or lines in your program code by typing spaces, tabs, or blank lines because the compiler ignores these extra spaces. You use whitespace to organize your program code and make it easier to read.

The **method header** for the `main()` method of the `Hello` class is quite complex. In the method header `public static void main(String[] args)`, the word `public` is an access modifier. In the English language, the word "static" means showing little change or stationary. In the Java programming language, the reserved keyword **`static`** also means unchanging and indicates that the `main()` method "goes with" the `Hello` class and not any `Hello` class objects that might eventually be created.

In English, the word "void" means empty. When the keyword **`void`** is used in the `main()` method header, it does not indicate that the `main()` method is empty, but rather that the `main()` method does not return any value when it is called. This doesn't mean that `main()` doesn't produce output—because it does. Instead, it means the `main()` method does not send any value back to any other method that might use it.

To add a `main()` method to your `Hello` application:

1. To include the `main()` method header between the `Hello` class's curly braces, place the insertion point to the right of the opening curly brace of the `Hello` class, and press **Enter** to start a new line. For readability and to

show that the `main()` method is contained within the `Hello` class, indent the `main()` method header a few spaces to the right of the alignment for the class header, then type the header:

```
public static void main(String[] args)
```

2. Following the `main()` method header, but before the closing curly brace of the `Hello` class, add a pair of curly braces for the `main()` method.

All Java applications must include a method named `main()`, and most Java applications also have additional methods. When you execute a Java application, the compiler always executes the `main()` method first.

In the method header `public static void main(String[] args)`, the contents between the parentheses `(String[] args)` represent a **parameter** or **argument** passed to the `main()` method. In Java, parameters to methods always appear within parentheses. Parameters consist of information that is needed by a method in order to perform its task. Every Java `main()` method you write requires an argument of `String[] args`; other methods require different arguments.

Within the `main()` method argument, `String` represents a Java class that can be used to contain character strings. The square brackets indicate that the argument is an array of `Strings`. The identifier `args` is used to name the array of `Strings` that might be sent to the `main()` method. The `main()` method *could* do something with those parameters, such as print them, but in the `Hello` program the `main()` method does not actually use the `args` identifier. Nevertheless you must place an identifier within the `main()` method header's parentheses. The identifier does not need to be named `args`—it could be any legal Java identifier—but the name `args` is traditional.

13

The statement that does the actual work in the `Hello` program is `System.out.println("Hello, World!");`. The statement ends with a semicolon because all Java programming language statements end with a semicolon. The text "Hello, World!" is a **literal string** of characters; that is, it is a series of characters that will appear exactly as entered. Any literal string in Java appears between double quotation marks. The string "Hello, World!" appears within parentheses because the string is a parameter to the `println()` method in the same way that `String[] args` is a parameter to the `main()` method.

Next, add the statement within the `main()` method's braces that produces the output "Hello, World!"

To add a statement that produces "Hello, World!":

1. Between the `main()` method's curly braces, add the statement that produces the output.

```
System.out.println("Hello, World!");
```

2. Your program should match Figure 13-1. Compare your program to the figure and make any corrections.

Within the statement `System.out.println("Hello, World!");`, the `println()` method prints a line of output on the screen and positions the cursor on the next line. Any subsequent output appears on the next line. Java also supports a method named `print()`. With `print()`, the cursor does not advance to a new line; it remains on the same line as the output.

Within the statement `System.out.println("Hello, World!");`, `out` is an object. The `out` object represents the screen. Several methods, including `println()`, are available with the `out` object. Of course, not all objects have a `println()` method (for instance, you can't print to a keyboard), but the Java creators assumed you frequently would want to display output on a screen. Therefore the `out` object was created and endowed with the method named `println()`. Later in this chapter, you create your own objects and endow them with your own methods.

Within the statement `System.out.println("Hello, World!");`, `System` is a class. Therefore, it defines the attributes of a collection of similar `System` objects. One of the `System` objects is `out`. (You can probably guess that another is the object `in`, and that it represents an input device.)

The Java programming language is case sensitive—the class named "System" is a completely different class from one named "system," "SYSTEM," or even "sYsTeM."

The dots (periods) in the statement `System.out.println("Hello, World!);` are used to separate the names of the class, object, and method. You use this same class-dot-object-dot-method format repeatedly in your Java programs.

To save your completed program:

1. Save the program as **Hello.java** in the Chap13\Chapter folder of your work folder. It is important that the file extension is .java. If it is not, the compiler for the Java programming language cannot recognize the program.

Many text editors attach their own filename extension (such as .txt or .doc) to a saved file. Double-check your saved file to ensure that it does not have a double extension (as in Hello.java.txt). If the file has a double extension, rename the file. If you explicitly type quotes surrounding a filename, (as in "Hello.java"), most editors save the file as you specify, without adding their own extension.

Adding Comments to a Java Program

As you can see, even the simplest Java program takes several lines of code and contains somewhat perplexing syntax. Large programs that perform many tasks include much more code, and, as you write longer programs, it becomes increasingly difficult to remember why you included steps, or how you intended to use particular variables. **Program comments** are nonexecuting statements that you add to a program for the purpose of documentation. Programmers use comments to leave notes for themselves and for others who might read their programs in the future. At the very least, your programs should include comments indicating who wrote the program, the date, and the program's name or function.

The forward slash (/) and the backslash (\) characters often are confused, but they are two distinct characters. You cannot use them interchangeably.

There are three types of comments in the Java programming language:

- **Line comments** start with two forward slashes (//) and continue to the end of the current line. Line comments can appear on a line by themselves, or at the end of a line following executable code.
- **Block comments** start with a forward slash and an asterisk (/*) and end with an asterisk and a forward slash (*/). Block comments can appear on a line by themselves, on a line before executable code, or after executable code. Block comments also can extend across as many lines as needed.
- A special case of block comments are **javadoc** comments. They begin with a forward slash and two asterisks (/**) and end with an asterisk and a forward slash (*/). Javadoc comments can be used to generate documentation with a program named javadoc.

The Java Development Kit (JDK) includes the javadoc tool, which contains classes that you can use when writing programs in the Java programming language.

13

Figure 13-2 shows how comments are used in code; the only statement that executes in Figure 13-2 is the statement on the fifth line that prints "Hello".

```
// Demonstrating comments
/* This shows
   that these comments
         don't matter  */
System.out.println("Hello");  // This line executes
//  up to where the comment started
/**  Everything but System.out.println(Hello) line
  is a comment. */
```

Figure 13-2 Using comments within a program

To add comments to your Hello.java program:

1. Position your cursor at the top of the file, press **Enter** to insert a new line, press the **Up arrow** key to go to that line, and then type the following comments at the top of the file. Press **Enter** after typing each line. Insert your name and today's date where indicated.

```
// Filename Hello.java
// Written by <your name>
// Written on <today's date>
```

2. Scroll to the line that reads `public class Hello`, press **Enter**, and then type the following block comment in the program.

```
/*  This program demonstrates the use of the println()
    method to print the message Hello, World!  */
```

3. Save the file, replacing the old Hello.java file with this new, commented version.

Running a Program

After you write and save your program, two steps must occur before you can view the program output.

- You must compile the program you wrote (called the **source** code) into bytecode.
- You must use the Java interpreter to translate the bytecode into executable statements.

When compiling, if the source code file is not in the same directory as indicated by the command prompt, you may use a full path with the filename—for example, `javac c:\java\myprograms\Hello.java`.

To compile your source code from the command line, you type `javac` followed by the name of the file that contains the source code. For example, to compile a file named Hello.java, you type `javac Hello.java`, and then press Enter. There will be one of three outcomes:

- You receive a message such as "Bad command or file name."
- You receive one or more program language error messages.
- You receive no messages, meaning the program has compiled successfully.

If you receive a message such as "Bad command or file name" it may mean that:

- You misspelled the command `javac`.
- You misspelled the filename.
- You are not within the correct subdirectory or folder on your command line.
- The Java programming language was not installed properly.

If you receive a programming language error message, it means there are one or more syntax errors in the source code. A **syntax error** is a programming error that occurs when you introduce typing errors into your program. For example, if your class name is "hello" (with a lowercase "h") in the source code, but you save the file as Hello.java, you receive an error message such as `public class first should not be defined in Hello.java` after compiling the program, because "hello" and "Hello" are not the same in a case-sensitive language. If this occurs, you must reopen the text file that contains the source code and make the necessary corrections.

If you receive no error messages after compiling the code in a file named Hello.java, then the program compiled successfully and a file named Hello.class is created and saved in the same folder as the program text file. After a successful compile, you can run the class file on any computer that has a Java language interpreter. To do so, you use the `java` command followed by the class name.

When you run a Java program using the `java` command, do not add the .class extension to the filename. If you type `java Hello`, the interpreter looks for a file named Hello.class. If you type `java Hello.class`, the interpreter incorrectly looks for a file named Hello.class.class.

To compile and interpret your Hello.java program:

1. Go to the command-line prompt for the drive and folder or subdirectory in which you saved Hello.java.
2. At the command line, type **`javac Hello.java`**. If you receive an error message, find its cause and then make the necessary corrections. Save the file again, and then repeat Steps 1 and 2 until your program compiles successfully.
3. When the compile is successful, execute your program by typing **`java Hello`** at the command line. The output should appear on the next line, as shown in Figure 13-3.

13

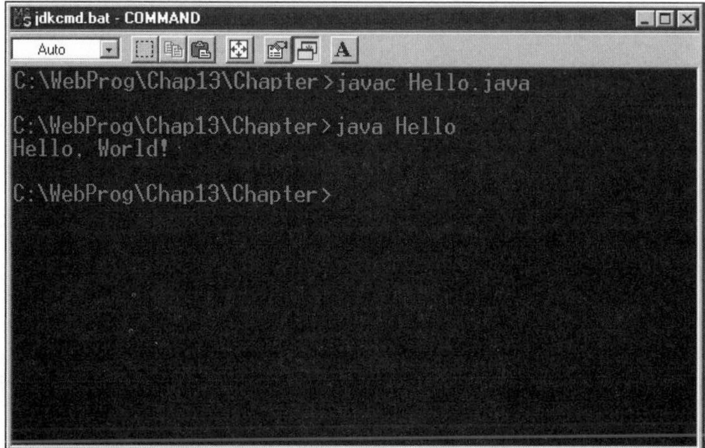

Figure 13-3 Output of `Hello` program

Understanding Variables and Constants

You can categorize program data as variable or constant. Data is **constant** when it cannot be changed after a program is compiled; data is **variable** when it might change. For example, if you include the following statement in a Java program: `System.out.println("Hello");`, the string "Hello" is a constant. Every time the program containing the constant "Hello" is executed, the value "Hello" is displayed. You can refer to "Hello" as a **literal constant**, because its value is taken literally at each use.

On the other hand, if you create a variable named `greeting`, and include the following statement within a Java program: `System.out.println(greeting);`, then different values might be displayed when the program is executed multiple times, depending on what value is stored in `greeting` during each run of the program.

Notice that no quotes appear around `greeting` in the statement `System.out.println(greeting);`. If you use quotes, then the word "greeting" prints literally. The absence of quotes lets Java know that `greeting` is not literal.

Variables are named memory locations that your program can use to store values. The Java programming language provides for eight **primitive types** of data:

- `boolean`
- `byte`
- `char`
- `double`
- `float`
- `int`
- `long`
- `short`

You name variables using the same naming rules for legal class identifiers. Basically, that means variable names must start with a letter and cannot be any reserved keyword. You must declare all variables you want to use in a program. A **variable declaration** includes:

- A data type that identifies the type of data that the variable stores
- An identifier that is the variable's name
- An optional assigned value, when you want a variable to contain an initial value
- An ending semicolon

Variable names usually begin with lowercase letters to distinguish variable names from class names. However, variable names can begin with either an uppercase or a lowercase letter.

For example, the variable declaration `int myAge = 25;` declares a variable of type `int` named `myAge` and assigns it an initial value of 25. This is a complete statement that ends in a semicolon. The equal sign (=) is the **assignment operator**. Any value to the right of the equal sign is assigned to the variable on the left of the equal sign. An assignment made when a variable is declared is an **initialization**.

The variable declaration `int myAge;` also declares a variable of type `int` named `myAge`, but no value is assigned at the time of creation. Although you can create a variable without an initial value, you must assign a value to a variable before you can display it or use it as part of an arithmetic calculation within a program.

You can declare multiple variables of the same type in separate statements on different lines. For example, the following statements declare two variables—the first variable is named `myAge` and its value is 25. The second variable is named `yourAge` and its value is 19.

```
int myAge = 25;
int yourAge = 19;
```

You also can declare two variables of the same type in a single statement, by separating the variable declarations with a comma, as shown in the following statement:

```
int myAge = 25, yourAge = 19;
```

However, if you want to declare variables of different types, you must use a separate statement for each type. The following statements declare two variables of type `int` (`myAge` and `yourAge`) and two variables of type `double` (`mySalary` and `yourSalary`).

```
int myAge, yourAge;
double mySalary, yourSalary;
```


Using the `int` Data Type

In the Java programming language, you use variables of type `int` to store (or hold) **integers**, or whole numbers. An integer can hold any whole number value from –2,147,483,648 to 2,147,483,647. When you assign a value to an `int` variable, you do not type any commas; you type only digits, and, optionally, a plus or minus sign to indicate a positive or negative integer.

The types **`byte`**, **`short`**, and **`long`** are all variations of the integer type. You can save space in memory by using `byte` or `short` if you know a variable only needs to hold small values. You use `long` if you know you are working with very large values. Table 13-2 shows the upper and lower value limits for each of these types. It is important to choose appropriate types for the variables you use in a program.

If you use a literal constant integer in a program, such as 932, it is an `int` by default. If you need to use a constant higher than 2,147,483,648, you must follow the number with an "L" to indicate `long`. For example, `long mosquitosInTheNorthWoods = 2444555888L;` stores a number that is greater than the maximum limit for the `int` type. You can type either an uppercase or lowercase "L" to indicate the `long` type, but the uppercase "L" is preferred to avoid confusion with the number "1."

Table 13-2 Limits on integer values by type

Type	Minimum value	Maximum value	Size in bytes
byte	–128	127	1
short	-32,768	32,767	2
int	-2,147,483,648	2,147,483,647	4
long	-9,223,372,036,854,775,808	9,223,372,036,854,775,807	8

To write a program to declare and display numeric values:

1. Open a new document in your text editor.
2. Create a class header and an opening and closing curly brace for a new class named `DemoVariables1` by typing the following:

```
public class DemoVariables1
{
}
```

3. Position the insertion point after the opening curly brace, press **Enter**, then type the following `main()` method and its curly braces:

```
public static void main(String[] args)
{
}
```

4. Position the insertion point after the opening curly brace in the `main()` method, press **Enter**, and then type **`int oneInt = 315;`** to declare a variable of type `int` named `oneInt` with a value of 315.

Variables may be declared at any point within a method prior to their first use. However, it is common practice to declare variables first, and place method calls second.

5. Press **Enter** at the end of the `oneInt` declaration statement, indent the line, and then type the following two output statements. The first statement uses the `print()` method to output "The int is " and leaves the cursor on the

same output line. The second statement uses the `println()` method to output the value of `oneInt` and advance the cursor to a new line.

```
System.out.print("The int is ");
System.out.println(oneInt);
```

When your output contains a literal such as "The int is" you should type a space before the closing quotation mark so there is a space between the end of the literal and the value that prints.

6. Save the file as **DemoVariables1.java** in the Chap13\Chapter folder in your work folder.
7. Compile the file from the command line by typing **`javac DemoVariables1.java`**. If necessary, correct any errors, save the file, and then compile again.
8. Execute the program from the command line by typing **`java DemoVariables1`**. The output should be `The int is 315`.

Next you declare two more variables in your program.

To declare two more variables:

1. Return to the DemoVariables1.java file in the text editor. Change the class name to **DemoVariables2**, then save the file as **DemoVariables2.java**.
2. Position the insertion point at the end of the line that contains the `oneInt` declaration, press **Enter**, and then type the following variable declarations on separate lines:

```
short oneShort = 23;
long oneLong = 123456789876543L;
```

3. Position the insertion point at the end of the line that contains the `println()` method that displays the oneInt value, press **Enter**, and then type the following statements to display the values of the two new variables:

```
System.out.print("The short is ");
System.out.println(oneShort);
System.out.print("The long is ");
System.out.println(oneLong);
```

4. Save the program using the same filename in the Chap13\Chapter folder in your work folder.
5. Compile the program by typing **`javac DemoVariables2.java`**. If necessary, correct any errors, save the file, and then compile again.
6. Execute the program by typing **`java DemoVariables2`**. Your output should match Figure 13-4.

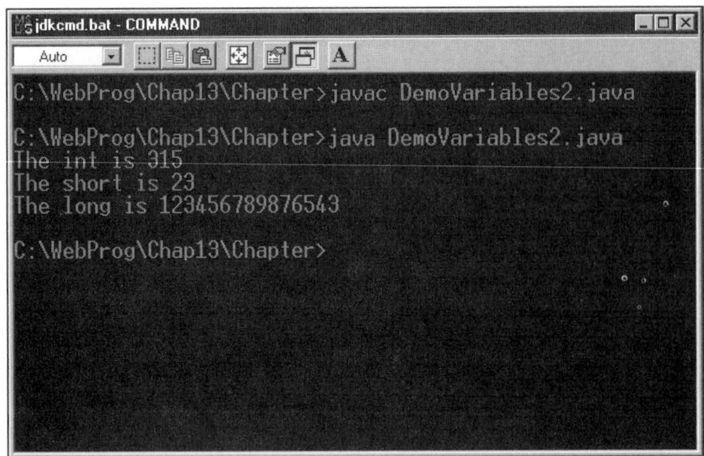

Figure 13-4 Output of `DemoVariables2` program

In the previous program, you used two print methods to print a compound phrase with the following code:

```
System.out.print("The long is ");
System.out.println(oneLong);
```

To reduce the amount of typing, you can use one method and combine the arguments with a plus sign using the following statement: `System.out.println("The long is " + oneLong);`. It doesn't matter which format you use—the result is the same, as you see next.

To change the two print method calls in your program so they become a single statement:

1. Open the **DemoVariables2.java** text file. Change the class name to **DemoVariables3**, and save the file as **DemoVariables3.java** in the Chap13\Chapter folder in your work folder.
2. Use the mouse to select the two statements currently used to print "The int is " and the value of oneInt, and press **Delete** to delete them. In place of the deleted statements, type the following `println()` statement: `System.out.println("The int is " + oneInt);`.
3. Select the two statements that produce output for the short variable, press **Delete** to delete them, and then type the statement `System.out.println("The short is " + oneShort);`.
4. Finally, select the two statements that produce output for the long variable, delete them, and replace them with `System.out.println("The long is " + oneLong);`.
5. Save, compile, and test the program. The output should be the same as what is shown in Figure 13-4.

Using Arithmetic Statements

Table 13-3 describes the five standard arithmetic operators for integers. You use the arithmetic operators to manipulate values in your programs.

Table 13-3 Integer arithmetic operators

Operator	Description	Example
+	Addition	45 + 2, the result is 47
-	Subtraction	45 - 2, the result is 43
*	Multiplication	45 * 2, the result is 90
/	Division	45 / 2, the result is 22 (not 22.5)
%	Modulus (remainder)	45 % 2, the result is 1 (that is, 45 / 2 = 22 with a remainder of 1)

The operators (/) and (%) deserve special consideration. When you divide two integers, whether they are integer constants or integer variables, the result is an *integer*. In other words, any fractional part of the result is lost. For example, in Java the result of 45 / 2 is 22, even though in a mathematical expression the result is 22.5. When you use the modulus operator with two integers, the result is an integer with the value of the remainder after division takes place—so the result of 45 % 2 is 1 because 2 "goes into" 45 twenty-two times with a remainder of 1.

To add arithmetic statements to the DemoVariables3.java program:

1. Open the **DemoVariables3.java** file in your text editor. Change the class name to **DemoVariables4**, and save the file as **DemoVariables4.java**.

13

2. Position the insertion point on the last line of the current variable declarations, press **Enter**, and then type the following declarations:

```
int value1 = 43,  value2 = 10,  sum, difference,
product,
    quotient, modulus;
```

3. Position the insertion point after the statement that prints the `oneLong` variable, press **Enter**, and then type the following statements on separate lines:

```
sum = value1 + value2;
difference = value1 - value2;
product = value1 * value2;
quotient = value1 / value2;
modulus = value1 % value2;
```

4. Press **Enter** and then type the following output statements:

```
System.out.println("Sum is " + sum);
System.out.println("Difference is " + difference);
System.out.println("Product is " + product);
System.out.println("Quotient is " + quotient);
System.out.println("Modulus is " + modulus);
```

5. Save the program in the Chap13\Chapter folder in your work folder using the same filename (DemoVariables4.java).
6. Compile and run the program. Your output should look like Figure 13-5. Analyze the output and confirm that the arithmetic is correct.

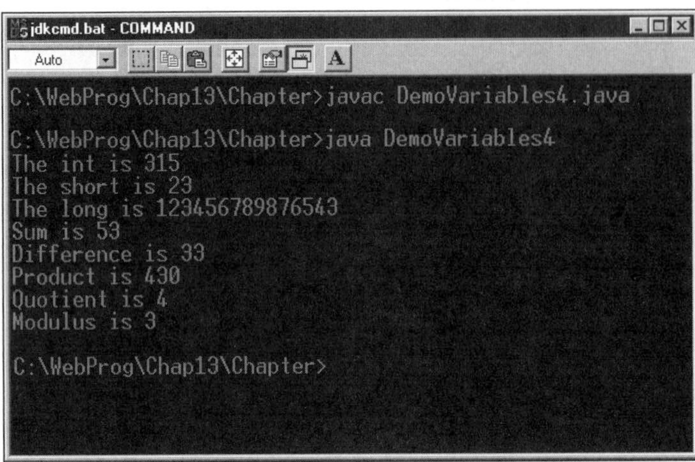

Figure 13-5 Output of `DemoVariables4` program

When you combine mathematical operations in a single statement, you must understand **operator precedence**, or the order in which parts of a mathematical expression are evaluated. Multiplication, division, and modulus always take place prior to addition or subtraction in an expression.

Using the Other Primitive Data Types

Integers are useful for storing whole number values. Java also provides data types that can hold Boolean, floating-point, and character data.

The `boolean` Data Type

Boolean logic is based on true-or-false comparisons. Whereas an `int` variable can hold millions of different values (at different times), a **`boolean` variable** can hold only one of two values—`true` or `false`. The following statements declare and assign appropriate values to `boolean` variables:

```
boolean isItPayday = false;
boolean areYouBroke = true;
```

You also can assign values based on the result of comparisons to `boolean` variables. The Java programming language supports six comparison operators. A **comparison operator** compares two items; an expression containing a comparison operator has a `boolean` value. Table 13-4 describes the comparison operators.

When you use any of the operators that have two symbols (==, <=, >=, or !=), you cannot place any whitespace between the two symbols.

Table 13-4 Comparison operators

Operator	Description	true example	false example
<	Less than	3 < 8	8 < 3
>	Greater than	4 > 2	2 > 4
= =	Equal to	7 = = 7	3 = = 9
<=	Less than or equal to	5 <=5	8 <= 6
>=	Greater than or equal to	7 >= 3	1 >= 2
!=	Not equal to	5 != 6	3 != 3

Assigning values to `boolean` variables becomes meaningful in situations similar to the following examples. In the first statement, the `hours` variable is compared to a constant value of 40. If the `hours` variable is not greater than 40, then the expression is evaluated as `false`. In the second statement, the income variable must be greater than 100000 for the expression to have the value `true`.

```
boolean overtime = (hours > 40);
boolean highTaxBracket = (income > 100000);
```

To add two `boolean` variables to the DemoVariables.java file:

1. Open the **DemoVariables4.java** file in your text editor. Change the class name to **DemoVariables5**, and save the file as **DemoVariables5.java**.
2. Position the insertion point at the end of the line with the integer variable declarations. Press **Enter**, and then type **`boolean isProgrammingFun = true, isProgrammingHard = false;`** to add two new `boolean` variables to the program.
3. Next, add some print statements to display the values. Press **Enter**, and then type the following statements:

```
System.out.println("The value of isProgrammingFun is "
   + isProgrammingFun);
System.out.println("The value of isProgrammingHard is "
   + isProgrammingHard);
```

4. Save the file, compile it, and then test the program.

Floating-Point Data Types

A **floating-point** number is one that contains decimal positions. The Java programming language supports two floating-point data types: `float` and `double`. A **`float`** data type can hold values of up to six or seven significant digits of accuracy. A **`double`** data type can hold 14 or 15 significant digits of accuracy. The term **significant digits** refers to the mathematical accuracy of a value. For example, a `float` given the value 0.324616777 is displayed as 0.324617 because it is only accurate to the sixth decimal position. Table 13-5 shows the minimum and maximum values for each data type.

A value written as $-3.4 * 10^{38}$ indicates that the value is -3.4 multiplied by 10 to the 38th power, or 10 with 38 trailing zeros—a very large number.

Table 13-5 Limits on floating-point values

Type	Minimum	Maximum	Size in bytes
float	$-3.4 * 10^{38}$	$3.4 * 10^{38}$	4
double	$-1.7 * 10^{308}$	$1.7 * 10^{308}$	8

Just as an integer constant such as 178 is an `int` by default, a floating-point number constant such as 18.23 is a `double` by default. To explicitly store a value as a float, you may place an "F" after the number, as in `float pocketChange = 4.87F;`. Either a lowercase or uppercase "F" can be used.

As with `ints`, you can perform the mathematical operations of addition, subtraction, multiplication, and division with floating-point numbers, but unlike `ints`, you should not perform modulus operations. (Floating-point division results in a floating-point answer, so there is no remainder.)

To add some floating-point variables to the DemoVariables5.java file and perform arithmetic with them:

1. Open the **DemoVariables5.java** file in your text editor. Change the class name to **DemoVariables6**, and save the file as **DemoVariables6.java**.
2. Position the insertion point after the line where the boolean variables are declared, press **Enter**, and then type **`double doubNum1 = 2.3, doubNum2 = 14.8, doubResult;`** to add some new floating-point variables.
3. Place the insertion point at the end of the statement that prints the value of `isProgrammingHard`. Press **Enter**, and then type the following statements to perform arithmetic and produce output:

```
doubResult = doubNum1 + doubNum2;
System.out.println("The sum of the doubles is " +
doubResult);
doubResult = doubNum1 * doubNum2;
System.out.println("The product of the doubles is "
   + doubResult);
```

4. Save the file, compile it, and then run the program.

The `char` Data Type

You use the **`char`** data type to hold any single character. You place constant character values within single quotation marks because the computer stores characters and integers differently. For example, the statements `char aCharValue = '9';` and `int aNumValue = 9;` are legal. The statements `char aCharValue = 9;` and `int aNumValue = '9';` are illegal. A number can be a character, in which case it must be enclosed in single quotation marks and declared as a `char` type. An alphabetic letter, however, cannot be stored in a numeric type. The following code shows how you can store any character string using the `char` data type:

```
char myInitial = 'J';
char percentSign = '%';
char numThatIsAChar = '9';
```

A variable of type `char` can hold only one character. To store a string of characters, such as a person's name, you must use a class called a **`String`**. Unlike single characters, which use single quotes, `String` constants are written between double quotation marks. For example, the expression that stores the name Audrey as a `String` in a variable named `firstName` is `String firstName = "Audrey";`.

As is the convention with other classes, `String` begins with an uppercase letter.

You can store any character—including nonprinting characters such as a backspace or a tab—in a `char` variable. To store these characters you must use an **escape sequence**, which always begins with a backslash. For example, the following code stores a backspace character and a tab character in the char variables `aBackspaceChar` and `aTabChar`:

```
char aBackspaceChar = '\b';
char aTabChar = '\t';
```

13

In the preceding code, the escape sequences indicate a value for each character other than the letters "b" or "t". Table 13-6 describes some common escape sequences that are used in Java.

Table 13-6 Common escape sequences

Escape sequence	Description
\b	Backspace
\t	Tab
\n	Newline or linefeed
\f	Form feed
\r	Carriage return
\"	Double quotation mark
\'	Single quotation mark
\\	Backslash

The characters used in Java are represented in **Unicode**, which is a 16-bit coding scheme for characters. For example, the letter "A" actually is stored in computer memory as a set of 16 zeros and ones as 0000 0000 0100 0001 (the spaces inserted after every set of four digits are for readability).

To add statements to your DemoVariables6.java file to use the '\n' and '\t' escape sequences:

1. Open the **DemoVariables6.java** file in your text editor. Change the class name to **DemoVariables7**, and save the file as **DemoVariables7.java**.
2. Position the insertion point after the last method line in the program, press **Enter**, and then type the following:

```
System.out.println
    ("\nThis is on one line\nThis on another");
System.out.println("This shows\thow\ttabs\twork");
```

3. Save, compile, and test the program. Your output should look like Figure 13-6.

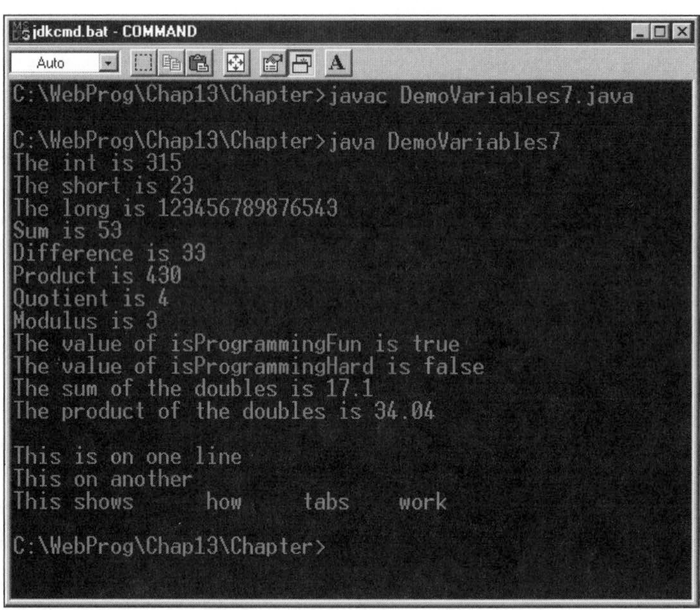

Figure 13-6 Output of `DemoVariables7` demonstrating escape sequences

Using GUI Objects to Produce Output and Accept Input

You can write a wide variety of useful programs using primitive variables, arithmetic statements, and the `println()` method. However, your applications look dull; when you execute all the programs you have written so far, output is displayed from a lack-luster command prompt. Most modern applications, and certainly all programs used on the Internet, use more visually pleasing graphic objects when they interact with users. These **Graphical User Interface**, or **GUI**, objects include the buttons, check boxes, and toolbars you are accustomed to controlling with a mouse when you interact with Windows-type programs.

Java provides you with a number of built-in classes that you can use to produce output. One of the easiest to use is `JOptionPane`. In order to fully understand how `JOptionPane` works, you must understand Java classes and objects. However, just as you can drive a car without fully understanding how the engine operates, you can use Java GUI programs without understanding the complete nature of objects. In the next steps, you create a program that uses GUI output.

You learn more about creating classes and objects later in this chapter.

In the next steps, you modify the `Hello` program you created earlier in this chapter so it uses a `JOptionPane` object to produce output.

To modify the `Hello` program:

1. Open the **Hello.java** file in your text editor. Change the class name to **`GUIHello`**, and save the file as **GUIHello.java**.
2. Add a new statement as the first line in the file:

```
import javax.swing.JOptionPane;
```

`JOptionPane` is a member of a group of classes called `Swing` classes that is stored in a Java package named `javax.swing`. This `import` statement makes the `Swing` classes available to the program. You need import statements for many of the Java classes you use. (When you use the `System` class, for example in a `System.out.println()` statement, you do not have to import it because its package, java.lang, is imported automatically to every Java program.)

3. Delete the line that begins with `System.out.println` and replace it with:

```
JOptionPane.showMessageDialog(null,"Hello Everyone!");
```

4. The comment at the top of the file indicates the filename is Hello.java. Although comments do not affect the operation of a program, it is a good idea to keep comments current when you modify a program. Change the filename within the comments to **GUIHello.java**.
5. The comment within the program indicates the program demonstrates the `println()` method. Change the comment to read:

```
/* this program demonstrates the use of the
   showMessageDialog() method to print
   the message Hello Everyone!  */
```

13

`JOptionPane` is a class, like `System` (Swing classes begin with the letter "J"), and `showMessageDialog()` is a method, like `println()`.The `showMessageDialog()` method contains two arguments, separated by a comma. The first argument to `showMessageDialog()` is "null". Null means "nothing" or "empty". If you provide a first argument for `JOptionPane.showMessageDialog()`, it represents the name of the window in which you want the message to be displayed. When you provide `null` as an argument it means, "There is no specified window to use. Just use the center of the screen."The second argument to `showMessageDialog()` holds the string of characters that are displayed.

The `println()` method requires an object, `out`, but the `showMessageDialog()` method requires no object; `println()` is a non-static method and `showMessageDialog()` is a static method.

6. Insert a new line below the `JOptionPane` line and above the closing curly braces. Insert the statement:

   `System.exit(0);`

This line is required in any program that uses a graphical user interface to terminate the program. You are already familiar with `System`—it is the same class that contains the `println()` method.The `exit()` method takes an integer argument.You could use any integer as an argument, but by convention programmers use 0 to mean the program ended seamlessly—with no error conditions being generated.

7. Save the program and compile it. If necessary, fix any errors and compile again. Then execute the program. For reference, the entire program without comment lines should now look like Figure 13-7. Figure 13-8 shows the output.

```
import javax.swing.JOptionPane;
public class GUIHello
{
    public static void main(String[] args)
    {
       JOptionPane.showMessageDialog(null,"Hello Everyone!");
       System.exit(0);
    }
}
```

Figure 13-7 The `GUIHello` program

8. All `JOptionPane` dialog boxes are **modal**, meaning all other program execution stops until the user takes action. You have two options to dismiss the `JOptionPane`: either click the OK button on the surface of the pane, or click the Close button in the upper-right corner of the pane.

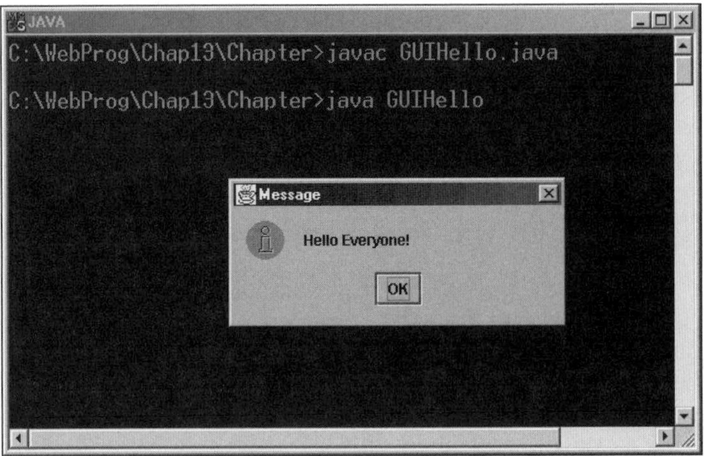

Figure 13-8 Output of `GUIHello` program

You can use the `showInputDialog()` method of the `JOptionPane` class to accept user input. When you use `showInputDialog()`, you place a `String` prompt between the method's parentheses, and you assign the method to a `String` variable that contains the user's response. In other words, the `showInputDialog()` method **returns**, or gives back, a `String` value that you can use as you would any other `String`.

You create your own methods that return values later in the chapter.

13

For example, the following statements declare a `String` named `userName`, display a `JOptionPane` that requests the user's name, and assign the entered name to the `userName` variable.

```
String userName;
userName = JOptionPane.showInputDialog
   ("Please type your name");
```

Next, you modify the `GUIHello` program to accept user input and display it.

To modify the `GUIHello` program:

1. Open the **GUIHello** file in your text editor. Change the class name to **GUIUserName**, and immediately save the program as **GUIUserName.java**. Change the comments that refer to GUIHello so they reflect the new filename.
2. Insert a new line just after the `JOptionPane.showMessageDialog (null,"Hello Everyone!");` statement and enter the following set of

statements that declares a `userName` variable, asks the user to enter a name, and displays a personal greeting containing the `userName` value.

```
String userName;
userName = JOptionPane.showInputDialog
   ("Please type your name");
JOptionPane.showMessageDialog(null,"Hello " + userName);
```

3. Save the program, then compile and execute it. Dismiss the box containing "Hello Everyone!", then enter your name where prompted. Figures 13-9 and 13-10 show the prompt and output.

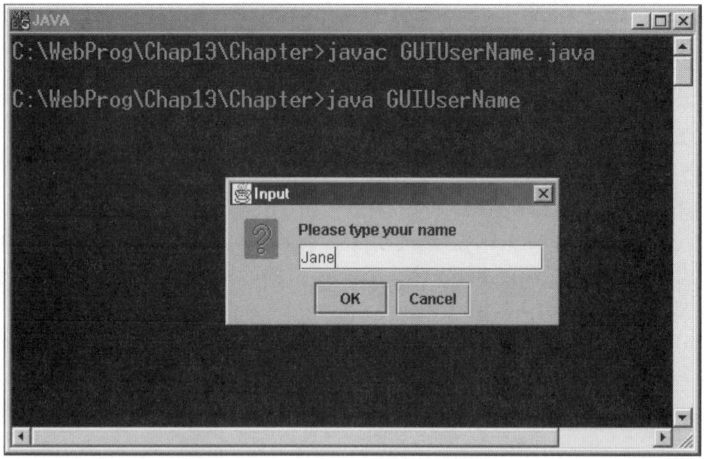

Figure 13-9 `InputDialog`

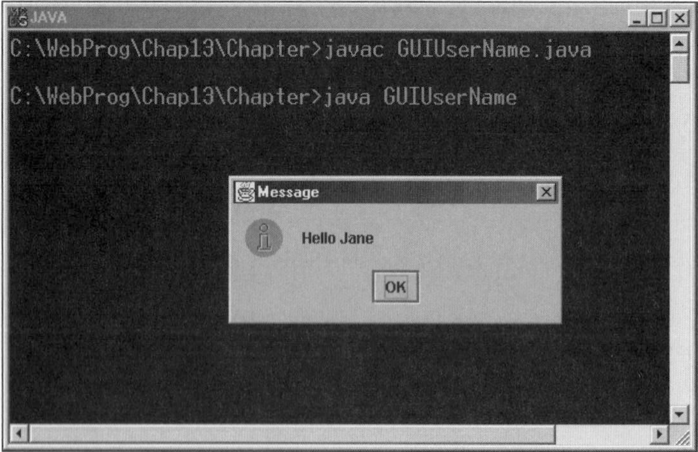

Figure 13-10 `MessageDialog` including user's name

4. Close the final dialog box.

USING DECISION AND REPETITION TECHNIQUES

You already can write a program that produces different output based on input; for example, a user who types "Jane" into the `GUIUserName` program receives different output than a user who types "John". Additionally, after you learn to write programs that can accept input, you gain a powerful new capability—you are able to alter the events that occur within a program based on user input. Now you can make decisions.

You use loops to repeatedly execute a block of statements based on the results of the evaluation of a Boolean expression. In this section, you learn how to write programs that make decisions and use loops.

Making Decisions

Making a **decision** involves choosing between two alternative courses of action based on some value within a program.

In Java, you can use the `if` statement to make decisions. The `if` is followed by parentheses containing a `boolean` expression. If the expression evaluates to `true`, the remainder of the statement following the parentheses, up to the semicolon, executes. For example, in the following statement the `JOptionPane` message is displayed only when the value of the `number` variable is greater than 10.

```
if (number > 10)
      JOptionPane.showMessageDialog(null, "Big number");
```

There is no semicolon at the end of the first line of the `if` statement `if(number > 10)` because the statement does not end there. The statement ends after the `JOptionPane` line.

13

Java provides an **`if...else` statement** to perform one action when a `boolean` expression evaluates as `true` and perform a different action when a `boolean` expression evaluates as `false`.

You can code an `if` without an `else`, but it is illegal to code an `else` without an `if`.

Next, you modify the `GUIUserName` program to include a decision.

To add a decision to the `GUIUserName` program:

1. Open the **GUIUserName.java** file in your text editor. Change the class name to **Decision** and immediately save the file as **Decision.java**. Also change the comment that shows the filename.

2. Insert a new line just above `JOptionPane.showMessageDialog(null, "Hello " + userName");` and type:

   `if(userName.equals("Jane"))`

Although you can use two equal signs (==) to compare primitive objects, you must use the `equals()` method to compare `Strings` and other objects.

3. Indent the line containing `JOptionPane.showMessageDialog(null, "Hello " + userName");` a few spaces. This is not required for the program to operate correctly, but shows that the greeting depends on the correct name being entered.
4. Save the program, then compile and execute it. When you see the prompt, type **Jane** and receive the greeting.
5. Execute the program again. Type any name other than Jane, and the program ends.
6. Insert a new line after the line that displays the "Hello" greeting, and insert an `else` clause as follows:

```
else
    JOptionPane.showMessageDialog
       (null, "Sorry – invalid name");
```

7. Save, compile, and execute the program again. When you enter **Jane** at the prompt, you receive the greeting. Execute the program again. When you enter any other name, you receive the error message.

Often there is more than one action to take following the evaluation of a `boolean` expression within an `if` statement. For example, you might want to print several separate lines of output or perform several mathematical calculations. To execute more than one statement that depends on the evaluation of a `boolean` expression, you use a pair of curly braces to place the dependent statements within a block. You can block statements to depend on an `if`, and you also can block statements to depend on an `else`.

When you create a block using curly braces, you do not have to place multiple statements within it. It is perfectly legal to block a single statement.

Executing Loops

A **loop** is a structure that allows repeated execution of a block of statements. Within a looping structure, a `boolean` expression is evaluated. If it is `true`, a block of statements, called the **loop body**, executes and then the `boolean` expression is evaluated again. As long as the expression is `true`, the statements in the loop body continue to execute. When the `boolean` evaluation is `false`, the loop ends.

In Java, you can use a **`while`** statement to execute a body of statements continuously while some condition continues to be `true`. A `while` loop consists of the keyword `while` followed by a `boolean` expression within parentheses, followed by the body of the loop, which can be a single statement or a block of statements surrounded by curly braces.

When you begin to create loops, you risk creating an infinite loop, one that never ends. If you think your program is in an infinite loop, you can press Ctrl+C.

For example, the code shown in Figure 13-11 shows a variable named `loopCount` being set to a value of 1. The `while` tests `loopCount`, and if it is less than 3, then the loop body executes. The loop body shown in Figure 13-11 consists of two statements made into a block by surrounding them with curly braces. The first statement prints "Hello," and then the second statement adds 1 to `loopCount`. The next time `loopCount` is evaluated, it is 2, which is still less than 3, so the loop body executes again. "Hello" prints a second time and `loopCount` becomes 3. Now when the expression `loopCount < 3` is evaluated, it is `false`, so the loop ends. Program execution would continue with any subsequent statements.

```
loopCount = 1;
while (loopCount < 3)
{
        System.out.println("Hello");
        loopCount = loopCount + 1;
}
```

Figure 13-11 A simple loop that executes twice

Notice that if the curly braces are omitted from the code shown in Figure 13-11, the `while` loop ends at the end of the "Hello" statement. Adding 1 to the `loopCount` is no longer part of the loop, so an infinite situation is created.

13

Next, you alter the `Decision` program so that execution continues while the user enters any name other than "Jane".

To change the `Decision` program:

1. Open the **Decision** file in your text editor. Change the class name to **Loop**, and change the filename in the comment. Immediately save the file as **Loop.java**.
2. Remove the `if-else` statement from the file either by deleting it or by placing two comment slashes (//) in front of each line in the statement. (The statement begins with `if(userName.equals("Jane"))` and ends with `JOptionPane.showMessageDialog(null, "Sorry - invalid name");`.) Insert a new line just above the `System.exit(0);` statement and enter the following loop, which executes until the user enters the correct name. The exclamation point means "not," so the loop continues while the `userName` is not "Jane" and ends when the `userName` becomes "Jane".

```
while(!userName.equals("Jane"))
{
```

```
    userName = JOptionPane.showInputDialog
        (null, "Sorry - there is only one valid
        name\nEnter it now.");
}
```

3. Save, compile, and execute the program. You can enter invalid names as many times as you want. The program continues to prompt you until you type the required name of "Jane".

CREATING AND USING METHODS

A **method** is a series of statements that carry out some task. Any class can contain an unlimited number of methods. Within a class, the simplest methods you can invoke don't require any arguments or return any values. For example, consider the simple Hello class you created at the beginning of this chapter (see Figure 13-1). Suppose you want to add three more lines of output to this program to display your name and address. Of course, you can simply add three new `println()` statements to the class, but you might choose instead to create a method to display the three lines.

A method you create must include the following elements:

- A declaration (or header or definition)
- An opening curly brace
- A body
- A closing curly brace

The method declaration contains:

- Optional access modifiers
- The return type for the method
- The method name
- An opening parenthesis
- An optional list of method arguments (you separate the arguments with commas if there is more than one)
- A closing parenthesis

Most often, methods are given `public` access. Endowing a method with public access means any class can use it. Additionally, as with `main()`, any method that can be used from anywhere within the class (that is, a classwide method) requires the keyword modifier `static`. Therefore, you can write the `nameAndAddress()` method shown in Figure 13-12. According to its declaration, it is `public` and `static`. It returns nothing, so its return type is `void`. It receives nothing, so its parentheses are empty. Its body, consisting of three `println()` statements, appears within curly braces.

```
public static void nameAndAddress()
{
        System.out.println("Lynn Greenbrier");
        System.out.println("8900 U.S. Hwy 14");
        System.out.println("Crystal Lake, IL 60014");
}
```

Figure 13-12 The `nameAndAddress()` method

You place the entire method within the class or program that uses it, but not within any other method. Figure 13-13 shows where you can place a method in the **`Hello`** class (modified using the new name **`Hello2`**).

```
public class Hello2
{
// You can place additional methods here, outside the main() method
       public static void main(String[] args)
       {
            System.out.println("Hello, World!");
       }
// You can place additional methods here, outside the main() method
}
```

Figure 13-13 Placement of methods

If the `main()` method calls the `nameAndAddress()` method, then you simply use the `nameAndAddress()` method's name as a statement within the body of `main()`. Figure 13-14 shows the complete program.


```
public class Hello2
{
       public static void main(String[] args)
       {
            nameAndAddress();
            System.out.println("Hello, World!");
       }
       public static void nameAndAddress()
       {
            System.out.println("Lynn Greenbrier");
            System.out.println("8900 U.S. Hwy 14");
            System.out.println("Crystal Lake, IL 60014");
       }
}
```

Figure 13-14 `Hello2` class `main()` method calling the `nameAndAddress()` method

The output from the program shown in Figure 13-14 appears in Figure 13-15. Because the `main()` method calls the `nameAndAddress()` method before it prints the phrase "Hello, World!", the name and address appear first in the output.

If you want to use the `nameAndAddress()` method in another program, one additional step is required. In the Java programming language, the new program, with its own `main()` method, is a different class. If you place the method named `nameAndAddress()` within the new class, the compiler does not recognize it unless you write it as `Hello2.nameAndAddress()` to notify the new class that the method is located in the `Hello2` class. Notice the use of the class name followed by a dot and then followed by the method. You already used similar syntax for the `System.out.println()` method.

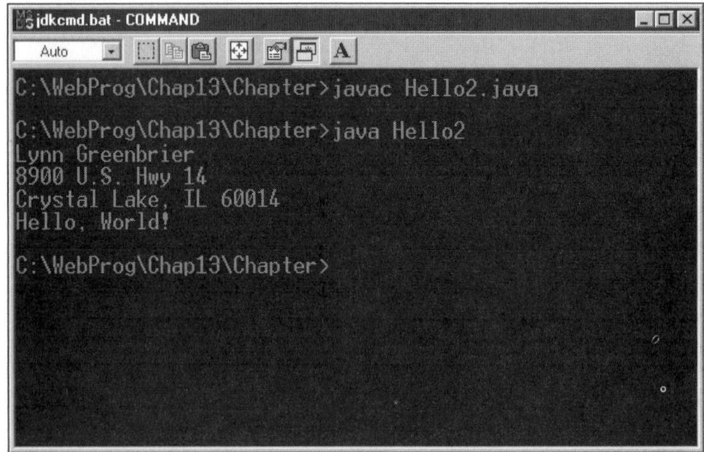

Figure 13-15 `Hello2` class calling `nameAndAddress()`

Some methods require additional information. If a method could not receive communications from you, called **arguments**, then you would have to write an infinite number of methods to cover every possible situation. For example, at any call, the `println()` method can receive any one of an infinite number of arguments. No matter what message is sent to `println()`, the message displays correctly.

When you write the method declaration for a method that can receive an argument, you need to include the following items within the method declaration parentheses:

- The type of the argument
- A local name for the argument

For example, the declaration for a public method named `predictRaise()`, which displays a person's salary plus a 10% raise, could have the declaration `public void predictRaise(double moneyAmount)`. You can think of the parentheses in a method declaration as a funnel into the method—data arguments listed there are "dropping in" to the method. The argument `double moneyAmount` within the parentheses indicates that the `predictRaise()` method receives a value of type `double`. Within the method, the value of any double passed to the method is known as `moneyAmount`. Figure 13-16 shows a complete method.

```
public void predictRaise(double moneyAmount)
{
        double newAmount;
        newAmount = moneyAmount * 1.10;
        System.out.println("With raise salary is " + newAmount);
}
```

Figure 13-16 The `predictRaise()` method

The `predictRaise()` method is a `void` method because it does not need to return any value to any class that uses it—its only function is to receive the `moneyAmount` value, multiply it by 1.10 (resulting in a 10% salary increase), and then display the result.

A method can require more than one argument. You can pass multiple arguments to a method by listing the arguments within the call to the method and separating them with commas. The declaration for a method that receives two or more arguments must list the type for each argument separately, even if the arguments have the same type.

Many methods you create will not be `void` methods; rather, they will return a value. The return type for a method can be any type used in Java, which includes the primitive (or scalar) types `int`, `double`, `char`, and so on, as well as class types (including class types you create). You include a method's return type in the method header and include a **return** statement as the last statement in the method. If a method returns a value, then when you call the method, you usually use the returned value, although you are not required to do so. For example, when you invoke a method with the header `public double calculateRaise()`, you might want to assign the returned value to a `double` variable named `myNewSalary`, as in `myNewSalary = calculateRaise();`.

Next, you create a `DemoMethods` class that demonstrates how a `main()` method can call several other methods.

To create a `DemoMethods` class:

1. Open a new file in your text editor and type the following start of the `DemoMethods` class:

   ```
   public class DemoMethods
   {
   ```

2. Type a `main()` method that declares a variable named `number` and passes it to methods named `methodOne()`, `methodTwo()`, and `methodThree()`.

13

Between passes, the value of number is displayed so you can track the effects of the methods.

```
public static void main(String[] args)
{
   int number = 12;
   methodOne();
   System.out.println("After method One the number is "
      + number);
   methodTwo(number);
   System.out.println("After method Two the number is "
      + number);
   number = methodThree(number);
   System.out.println
      ("After method Three the number is " + number);
}
```

3. The first method takes no parameters and returns no parameters. It contains a local variable named number, which is an entirely different variable than the one with the same name in the main() method. Even though methodOne() assigns a new value to number, the new value does not affect the variable in the main() method.

```
public static void methodOne()
{
   int number = 100;
   System.out.println("Inside method One the number is "
      + number);
}
```

4. The second method accepts the number from main() and correctly displays its original value. Then it assigns a new value to number and displays it. When the program returns to main(), the original value is unaffected.

```
public static void methodTwo(int number)
{
   System.out.println
      ("Inside method Two first the number is "
      + number);
   number = 200;
   System.out.println("...then it becomes " + number);
}
```

5. The last method alters the number and returns it. This time, the number in main() is altered.

```
public static int methodThree(int number)
{
   number = 300;
   System.out.println
      ("Inside method Three the number is " + number);
   return number;
}
```

6. Add a closing curly brace for the class.
7. Save the file as **DemoMethods.java**, then compile and execute it. The output looks like Figure 13-17.

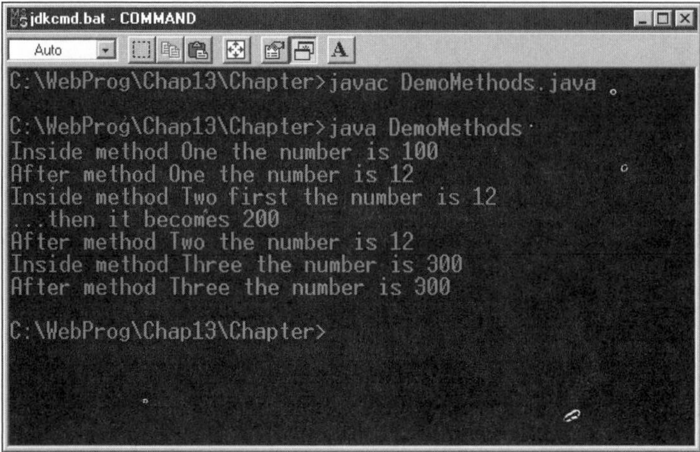

Figure 13-17 Output of `DemoMethods` program

8. Examine the output and confirm that the correct values are displayed in each case.
9. Experiment with the variable name within any method. For example, within `methodTwo()` change each of the four occurrences of `number` to any other identifier, such as `someValue`. When you save, compile, and run the program, the output is identical to the original version. Each method name is **local** to its method.
10. Close your text editor.

CREATING AND USING CLASSES AND OBJECTS

A **class** is a structure that contains both data and methods. A class describes the attributes and functionality of a category of objects. Once you have defined a class, you can create any number of objects that are specific instances of the class—just like your dog, my dog, and the dog next door are all specific instances of a class of creatures known as dogs. When you create an object, you use a special class method called a constructor. You learn about class attributes, methods, and constructors in the next sections.

Understanding Classes

Java supports two broad categories of classes: some classes contain only static methods such as the programs you have written so far; other classes, however, are intended to be prototypes for objects you create. Classes from which you can create objects provide definitions for the class's data fields and methods. When you create a Java class, first you must assign a name to the class, and then you must determine what data and methods are part of every object that is a member of the class.

Chapter 1 provides background on classes and objects.

Suppose you decide to create a class named `Employee`. One instance variable of `Employee` might be an employee number, and two necessary methods might be a method to set (or provide a value for) the employee number and another method to get (or retrieve) that employee number. To begin, you create a class header with three parts:

- An optional access modifier
- The keyword `class`
- Any legal identifier you choose for the name of your class

In the next steps, you create an `Employee` class.

To create an `Employee` class:

1. Open a new file in your text editor and type the following class header:

```
public class Employee
```

The keyword `public` is a class access modifier. Although you can use other modifiers, the `public` modifier is used most frequently.

2. After the class header `public class Employee`, you write the body of the `Employee` class, containing its data and methods, between a set of curly braces. Start a new line and type an opening curly brace. Then start a third line and type the closing curly brace for the class.

3. You place the instance variables, or fields, for the `Employee` class as statements within the curly braces. In this example, you declare an employee number that is stored as an integer. Programmers frequently include an access modifier for each of a class's fields, and the access modifier most frequently used is `private`. Type the following:

```
private int empNum;
```

Making data `private` is sometimes called **information hiding**, and is an important component of object-oriented programs. A class's private data can be changed or manipulated only by a class's own methods, and not by methods that belong to other classes. In contrast, most class methods are not usually `private`. The resulting `private` data/`public` method arrangement provides a means for you to control outside access to your data—only a class's nonprivate methods can be used to access a class's `private` data.

Besides data, classes contain methods. For example, one method you need for the `Employee` class that contains an `empNum` is the method to retrieve (or return) any `Employee`'s `empNum` for use by another class. Next, you add a method named `getEmpNum()` to the `Employee` class:

To add a method to the `Employee` class:

1. Within the `Employee` class, just after the declaration of the `empNum` field, insert a line and add the following method. The `getEmpNum()` method contains just one statement: the statement that accesses the value of the private `empNum` field.

```
public int getEmpNum()
{
   return empNum;
}
```

Notice that, unlike the class methods you created earlier in this chapter, the `getEmpNum()` method does not employ the `static` modifier. The keyword `static` is used for classwide methods, but not for methods that "belong" to objects. If you are creating a program with a `main()` method that you execute to perform some task, then many of your methods are `static`, so you can call them without creating an object. However, if you are creating a class from which objects are instantiated, most methods will probably be nonstatic, as you will be associating the methods with individual objects. Methods used with object instantiations are called **instance methods**.

When a class contains data fields, you want a means to assign values to the data fields. For an `Employee` class with an `empNum` field, you need a method with which to set the `empNum`. Next, you add an instance method to the `Employee` class to set the value of an `Employee`'s employee number. The method is a `void` method because there is no need to return any value to a calling program. The method receives an integer, locally called `emp`, to be assigned to `empNum`.

13

To add an instance method to the `Employee` class:

1. After the closing curly brace of the `getEmpNum()` method, insert the following `setEmpNum()` method:

```
public void setEmpNum(int emp)
{
   empNum = emp;
}
```

2. Save the file as **Employee.java**. Compile the class and correct any errors. You cannot execute this class because it does not contain a `main()` method. Instead, you must create another class that declares one or more `Employee` objects.

Declaring a class does not create any actual objects. A class is just an abstract description of what an object will be like if any objects are ever actually instantiated. Just as you might understand all the characteristics of an item you intend to manufacture long before the first item rolls off the assembly line, you can create a class with fields and methods long before you instantiate any objects that are members of that class.

A two-step process creates an object that is an instance of a class. First, you supply a type and an identifier, just as when you declare any variable, and then you allocate computer memory for that object. For example, you might define an integer as `int someValue;` and you might define an Employee as `Employee someEmployee;`, where `someEmployee` is an identifier you choose to represent an `Employee` object.

When you declare the `someEmployee` instance of the `Employee` class, you are notifying the compiler that you will use the identifier `someEmployee`. However, you are not yet setting aside computer memory in which the `Employee` named `someEmployee` might be stored—that is done only for primitive type variables. To allocate the needed memory you must use the **new operator**. You can define and reserve memory for `someEmployee` in one statement, as in `Employee someEmployee = new Employee();`. In this statement, `Employee` is the object's type (as well as its class), and `someEmployee` is the name of the object. The equal sign is the assignment operator, so a value is being assigned to `someEmployee`. The `new` operator is allocating a new, unused portion of computer memory for `someEmployee`. The value that is being assigned to `someEmployee` is a memory address where it is to be located.

The last portion of the statement, `Employee()` with its parentheses, looks suspiciously like a method name. In fact, it is the name of a method that constructs an `Employee` object. `Employee()` is a **constructor method**. You will write your own constructor methods as you learn more about Java, but when you don't write a constructor method for a class, Java writes one for you, and the name of the constructor method is always the same as the name of the class whose objects it constructs.

To write a program that instantiates an `Employee` object:

1. Open a new file in your text editor and enter the following program. It declares an `Employee` object and uses the `Employee` class `setEmpNum()` method to pass an integer to the private `Employee` class `empNum` field. The `main()` method then gets the `empNum` back out of the object and assigns it to an integer named `id`, which then is displayed.

```
public class EmployeeDemo
{
  public static void main(String[] args)
  {
    Employee someEmployee = new Employee();
    someEmployee.setEmpNum(1234);
    int id = someEmployee.getEmpNum();
    System.out.println("Number is " + id);
  }
}
```

2. Save the file as **EmployeeDemo.java**, and then compile it. If necessary, correct any errors, and save and compile again.

3. Execute the `EmployeeDemo` program. Figure 13-18 shows the output.

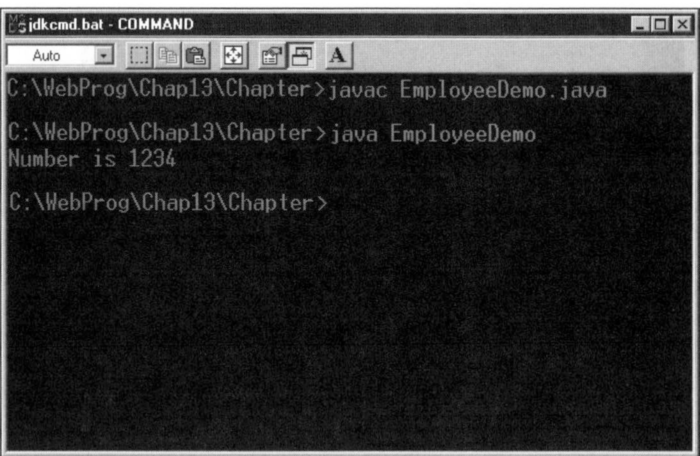

Figure 13-18 Output of `EmployeeDemo` program

Creating Constructors

When you create a class, such as `Employee`, and instantiate an object with a statement such as `Employee chauffeur = new Employee();`, you are actually calling a method named `Employee()` that is provided by the Java compiler. A **constructor method** is a method that establishes an object. The constructor method named `Employee()` establishes one `Employee` with the identifier `chauffeur`, and provides the following specific initial values to the Employee's data fields:

13

- Any numeric fields are set to 0 (zero).
- Any character fields are set to Unicode '\u0000'.
- Any `boolean` fields are set to `false`.
- Any object type fields are set to `null` (or empty).

If you do not want an `Employee`'s fields to hold these default values, or if you want to perform additional tasks when you create an `Employee`, then you can write your own constructor. Any constructor method you write must have the same name as the class it constructs, and constructor methods cannot have a return type. For example, if every `Employee` contains a `salary` field and has a starting salary of 8.65, then you could write the constructor method for the `Employee` class so the constructor initializes the `salary` field.

To add a constructor method to the `Employee` class:

1. Open the **Employee.java** file in your text editor.

2. On a new line below the declaration of the **empNum** field, add a declaration for salary as follows:

```
private double salary;
```

3. Below the method that gets the **Employee**'s ID number, include a **public** method to get the **private salary**:

```
public double getSalary()
{
   return salary;
}
```

4. Also include a constructor method. You can place the constructor method anywhere within the class, but because it is the first method that executes when you create a class object, many programmers place it as the first method after the field declarations.

```
public Employee()
{
   salary = 8.65;
}
```

5. Save the **Employee** file.

6. Open the **EmployeeDemo.java** file in your text editor. Change the class name to **EmployeeDemo2**, and save the file as **EmployeeDemo2.java**.

7. As the last two statements in the main() method, add statements that retrieve and print the Employee object's salary.

```
double sal = someEmployee.getSalary();
System.out.println("Salary is $" + sal);
```

8. Save the program, then compile and execute it. The output appears in Figure 13-19. Even though the EmployeeDemo2 class does nothing to explicitly set the Employee's salary, the salary is set because the class constructor is called automatically when the someEmployee object is instantiated.

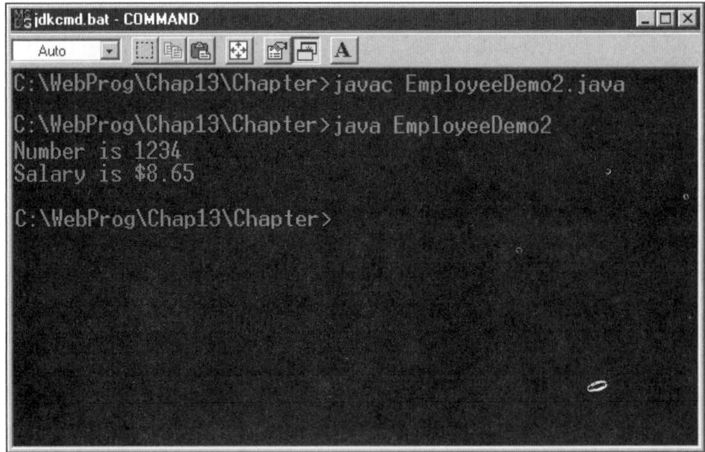

Figure 13-19 Output of `EmployeeDemo2` program

Chapter Summary

You could spend years studying all the aspects of the Java programming language. However, this chapter has provided you with an overview of how Java programs are constructed, including how they access methods, classes, and objects. In the next chapter, you learn how to create a specific type of Java object named `JApplet`. As you read the next chapter, keep the following points in mind:

- Java is an extremely popular language for writing programs as well as for learning about object-oriented programming principles that you can apply to other languages.
- Everything you write in a Java program is part of a class. Classes consist of a header and a body enclosed with curly braces. Class bodies contain data items, methods, and nonexecuting comments.
- To execute a Java program, you must compile the source code you wrote into bytecode and use the Java interpreter to translate the bytecode into executable statements. To compile your source code from the command line, you type `javac` followed by the name of the file that contains the source code. You can execute a program using the `java` command.
- The Java programming language provides for eight primitive types of data: `boolean`, `byte`, `char`, `double`, `float`, `int`, `long`, and `short`. A variable declaration includes a data type, an identifier, an optional assigned value, and an ending semicolon.

13

- You can use five basic arithmetic operators (+, -, *, /, and %) to manipulate values in your programs. Java provides you with a number of built-in objects that produce output. One of the easiest to use is `JOptionPane`. You can use the `showMessageDialog()` method to display text and the `showInputDialog()` method to receive user input.
- In Java, you can use the `if` or `if...else` statements to make decisions, and you can use a `while` statement to execute a body of statements continuously while some condition continues to be `true`.
- A method is a series of statements that carry out some task. Any class can contain an unlimited number of methods. A method you create must include the following elements: a declaration (or header or definition), an opening curly brace, a body, and a closing curly brace. The method declaration contains optional access modifiers, the return type for the method, the method name, an opening parenthesis, an optional list of method arguments, and a closing parenthesis.
- A class is a structure that contains both data and methods. A class defines a type from which you can create objects that contain the class's data fields and can use the class's methods. When you create a Java class, first you must assign a name to the class, and then you must determine what data and methods are part of the class. A constructor method is a method that establishes an object. Java automatically supplies a constructor if you do not create one; this default constructor provides an object's fields with default values.

Review Questions

1. Specific characteristics that have made the Java programming language so popular in recent years include ______________.
   a. its security features
   b. the fact that it is architecturally neutral
   c. both of these
   d. none of these
2. Which of the following is *not* a primitive data type in the Java programming language?
   a. boolean
   b. byte
   c. int
   d. sector

3. Which of the following elements is *not* required in a variable declaration?
   a. a type
   b. an identifier
   c. an assigned value
   d. a semicolon
4. The assignment operator in the Java programming language is ______________.
   a. =
   b. ==
   c. :=
   d. ::
5. A boolean variable can hold ______________.
   a. any character
   b. any whole number
   c. any decimal number
   d. the values `true` or `false`
6. The "equal to" comparison operator is ______________.
   a. =
   b. ==
   c. !=
   d. !!
7. The value 137.68 can be held by a variable of type ______________.
   a. int
   b. float
   c. double
   d. Two of the above are correct.
8. An escape sequence always begins with ______________.
   a. an 'e'
   b. a forward slash
   c. a backslash
   d. an equal sign

9. All Java applications must include a method named ________________.
   a. `main()`
   b. `start()`
   c. `java()`
   d. none of these
10. The `println()` method ________________.
   a. positions the cursor on a new line, then prints its argument
   b. prints its argument on the screen, and positions the cursor on the next line
   c. prints its argument on the screen, and positions the cursor at the beginning of the output line
   d. prints its argument on the screen, and positions the cursor at the end of the output line
11. `System` is a(n) ________________.
   a. method
   b. object
   c. parameter
   d. class
12. Java supports all the following comment types except ________________.
   a. line comments
   b. block comments
   c. javadoc comments
   d. return comments
13. The characters used in the Java programming language are represented in ________________.
   a. Unicode
   b. ASCII
   c. EBCDIC
   d. bytecode
14. `JOptionPane.showMessageDialog()` is a(n) ________________.
   a. application
   b. class
   c. method
   d. object

15. Determine the output of the following code:

```
int count = 0;
while (count < 4)
      {
              System.out.print(count + "  ");
              count = count + 1;
      }
```

a. 0 1 2

b. 0 1 2 3

c. 0 1 2 3 4

d. 4

HANDS-ON EXERCISES

As you create each of the following programs, save it in the Chap13\Exercises folder in your work folder.

Exercise 13-1

Write a Java program that displays your name and address on three lines on the screen. Name the program **PersonalInfo.java**.

Exercise 13-2

Write a Java program that declares variables to represent the length and width of a room in feet. Use `Room` as the class name. Assign appropriate values to the variables—for example, length = 15 and width = 25. Compute and display the floor space of the room in square feet (area = length * width). As output, do not display only a value; display explanatory text with the value, for example `The floor space is 375 square feet.`. Save the program as **Room.java**.

13

Exercise 13-3

Create a class named `Eggs`. Its `main()` method holds an integer variable named numberOfEggs to which you assign a value. Create a method to which you pass numberOfEggs. The method displays the eggs in dozens; for example, 50 eggs is four full dozen (and two left over). Save the program as **Eggs.java**.

Exercise 13-4

Create a class named `Monogram`. Its `main()` method holds three character variables that hold your first, middle, and last initials, respectively. Create a method to which you pass the three initials and which displays the initials twice—once in the order first, middle, last, and a second time in traditional monogram style (first, last, middle). Save the program as **Monogram.java**.

Exercise 13-5

Create a class named `Exponent`. Its `main()` method holds an integer value, and in turn passes the value to a method that squares the number and a method that cubes the number. The `main()` method prints the results. Create the two methods that respectively square and cube an integer that is passed to them, returning the calculated value. Save the program as **Exponent.java**.

Web Programming Projects

Save the programs that you create in these Projects in the Chap13\Projects folder in your work folder.

Project 13-1

1. Create a class named `Numbers` with a `main()` method that holds two integer variables. Assign values to the variables.
2. Create two additional methods, `sum()` and `difference()`, that compute the sum of and difference between the values of the two variables, respectively. Each method should perform the computation and display the results. In turn, call each of the two methods from `main()` that pass the values of the two integer variables. Save the program as **Numbers.java**.
3. Add a method named `product()` to the `Numbers` class. The `product()` method should compute the multiplication product of two integers, but not display the answer. Instead, it should return the answer to the calling `main()` program, which displays the answer.

Project 13-2

1. Create a class named `Student`. A `Student` has fields for an ID number, number of credit hours earned, and number of points earned. (For example, many schools compute grade point averages based on a scale of 4, so a three-credit-hour class in which a student earns an "A" is worth 12 points.) Include methods to assign values to all fields. A `Student` also has a field for grade point average. Include a method to compute the grade point average field by dividing points by credit hours earned. Write methods to display the values in each `Student` field. Save this class as **Student.java**.

2. Write a class named `ShowStudent` that instantiates a Student object from the class you created. Compute the `Student` grade point average, and then display all the values associated with the **Student**. Save the program as ShowStudent.java.
3. Create a constructor method for the `Student` class you created. The constructor should initialize each `Student`'s ID number to 9999 and his or her grade point average to 4.0. Write a program demonstrating that the constructor works by instantiating an object and displaying the initial values.

Project 13-3

1. Create a class named `Checkup` with fields that hold a patient number, two blood pressure figures (systolic and diastolic), and two cholesterol figures (LDL and HDL). Include methods to get and set each of the fields. Include a method named `computeRatio()` that divides LDL cholesterol by HDL cholesterol and displays the result. Include an additional method named `ExplainRatio()` that explains that the HDL is known as "good cholesterol" and that a ratio of 3.5 or lower is considered optimum. Save the class as **Checkup.java**.
2. Create a class named `TestCheckup` with a `main()` method that declares four `Checkup` objects. Provide values for each field for each patient. Then display the values. Blood pressure numbers are usually displayed with a slash between the systolic and diastolic values. (Typical numbers are such values as 110/78 or 130/90.) With the cholesterol figures, display the explanation of the cholesterol ratio calculation. (Typical numbers are such values as 100 and 40 or 180 and 70.) Save the program as **TestCheckup.java**.

CHAPTER

14

JAVA: PART II

In this chapter you will:

- Write Java applets
- Use a `JLabel`
- Change a `JLabel`'s Font
- Add `JTextFields` and `JButtons` to a `JApplet`
- Learn about event-driven programming
- Add output to a `JApplet`
- Understand the `JApplet` life cycle
- Create a complete, interactive `JApplet`
- Learn where to get help

In the last chapter you learned to write Java applications. You learned about Java syntax, data types, calling methods, and creating classes and objects. Applications are stand-alone programs. In contrast, **applets** are programs that are called from within another application. You run applets within a page on the Internet, or within another program called **appletviewer**, which comes with the Java Developer's Kit. In this chapter you will create Java applets. Java applets are popular among programmers, mostly because users can execute them using a Web browser on the Internet. A **Web browser** is a program that allows you to display HTML documents on your computer screen. Web documents often contain Java applets.

WRITING JAVA APPLETS

When you write a Java application, you:

- Write the application in the Java programming language, and then save it with a `.java` file extension.
- Compile the application into bytecode using the `javac` command. The bytecode is stored in a file with a `.class` file extension.
- Use the `java` command to interpret and execute the `.class` file.

Applications are stand-alone programs and always contain a `main()` method. An applet is not a stand-alone program—it must be called from within another program written in HTML, or Hypertext Markup Language. **HTML** is a simple language used to create Web pages for the Internet. When you create an applet, you:

- Write the applet in the Java programming language, and save it with a `.java` file extension, just as you do when you write an application.
- Compile the applet into bytecode using the `javac` command, just as you do when you write an application.
- Write an HTML document that includes a statement to call your compiled Java class.
- Load the HTML document into a Web browser (such as Netscape Navigator or Microsoft Internet Explorer), or run the Applet Viewer program, which in turn uses the HTML document.

HTML contains many commands that allow you to format text on a Web page, import graphic images, and link your page to other Web pages. Fortunately, to run a Java applet, you don't need to learn the entire HTML language; you only need to learn two pairs of HTML commands, called **tags**.

Unlike the Java programming language, HTML is not case sensitive, so you can use `<html>` in place of `<HTML>`, but using uppercase letters for HTML tags is conventional.

The tag that begins every HTML document is **`<HTML>`**. Like all tags, this tag is surrounded by angle brackets. `HTML` is an HTML keyword that means the code following the keyword is part of the HTML document that will execute. The tag that ends every HTML document is **`</HTML>`**. The insertion of the backslash before any tag indicates the tag is the ending half of a pair of tags. The simplest HTML document you can write is:

```
<HTML>
</HTML>
```

As with the Java programming language, HTML generally ignores white-space, so you can write the HTML document on one line as <HTML></HTML> if you want.

This simple program begins and ends and does nothing in the process; you can create an analogous situation in a Java method by typing an opening curly brace and following it immediately with the closing curly brace. Usually, of course, HTML documents contain more statements. For example, to run an applet from within an HTML document, you add an **<APPLET>** and **</APPLET>** tag pair. Usually, you place three attributes within the <APPLET> tag: **CODE**, **WIDTH**, and **HEIGHT**. For example:

```
<APPLET CODE = "SomeClass.class" WIDTH = 300 HEIGHT = 200>
```

The three parts of the APPLET tag are:

- `CODE =`, and the name of the compiled applet you are calling
- `WIDTH =`, and the width of the applet on the screen
- `HEIGHT =`, and the height of the applet on the screen

The name of the applet you call must be a compiled Java applet (with a `.class` file extension). The width and height of an applet are measured in pixels. **Pixels** are the **pic**ture **el**ements, or tiny dots of light, that make up the image on your video monitor. Many monitors display 640 pixels horizontally and 480 pixels vertically, so a statement such as `WIDTH = 300 HEIGHT = 200` creates an applet that occupies a little less than a quarter of most screens (half the height and half the width).

A VGA monitor displays 640 × 480 pixels. A Super VGA monitor displays up to 1280 × 1024 pixels. In general, the maximum size of your applets should be approximately 600 × 400 pixels to make sure that most people are able to see the entire applet. Keep in mind that the browser's menu bar and screen elements (such as the toolbar and the scroll bars) take up some of the screen viewing area for an applet.

14

Next, you create a simple HTML document that you use to display an applet you create in the next section. You will name the applet `Greet`, and it will occupy a screen area of 450 × 200 pixels.

To create a simple HTML document:

1. Open a new file in your text editor.
2. Type the opening HTML tag: **<HTML>**
3. On the next line, type the opening APPLET tag that contains the applet's name and dimensions:
   ```
   <APPLET CODE = "Greet.class" WIDTH = 450 HEIGHT = 200>
   ```

4. On the next line, type the applet's closing tag: **</APPLET>**
5. On the next line, type the closing HTML tag: **</HTML>**
6. Save the file as **testGreet.html** in the Chap14\Chapter folder in your work folder. Just like when you create a Java application, make sure that you save the file as text only. If you are using Notepad or another text editor, enclose the filename in quotation marks to save the `.html` file extension, as in "C:\WebProg\Chap14\Chapter\testGreet.html".

WRITING A SIMPLE JApplet USING A JLabel

Writing an applet involves learning only a few additions and changes to writing a Java application. To write an applet, you must:

- Add some import statements.
- Learn to use some Windows components and applet methods.
- Learn to use the keyword `extends`.

In Chapter 13, you used an `import` statement to access the javax.swing package within your application so you could use the `JOptionPane` class. Similarly, Java's creators developed a variety of classes to handle common applet needs. Most applets contain at least two import statements: `import javax.swing.*;` and `import java.awt.*;`. The javax.swing package contains a class named `JApplet`—every applet you create in this chapter is based on this class. (Java also supports an older class named `Applet`. However, most new applets are created using `JApplet`.) The javax.swing package also contains GUI component classes, such as `JOptionPane`, `JButton`, `JLabel`, and many others.

You easily can identify Swing components such as `JApplet` and `JButton` because they begin with an uppercase "J".

The java.awt package is the **Abstract Windows Toolkit**, or **AWT**. It contains classes that control the style of Windows components, such as their font and layout. You import both javax.swing and java.awt so you don't have to "reinvent the wheel" by creating these components yourself. For example, one of the simplest GUI components is a `JLabel`. **`JLabel`** is a built-in class that holds text you can display within a `JApplet`. The `JLabel` class also contains fields that indicate appearance information, such as font and alignment.

In the next steps you begin to create a JApplet that holds a JLabel.

To begin creating a JApplet:

1. Open a new file in your text editor and type the import statements you need for a JApplet:

```
import javax.swing.*;
import java.awt.*;
```

2. When you create an application, you follow any needed import statements with a class header such as public class AClass. Applets begin the same way as Java applications, but they also must include the words extends JApplet. The keyword **extends** indicates that your applet builds upon, or **inherits**, the traits of the JApplet class defined in the javax.swing package. Below the import statements, type the following class header:

```
public class Greet extends JApplet
```

3. As with other classes, the body of every JApplet class is contained between curly braces. Type the opening curly brace for the Greet class.

4. As with other objects, you can declare a JLabel without allocating memory, as in JLabel greeting;, and then later call the constructor with greeting = new JLabel();, or you can declare and call the JLabel constructor in one statement, as in JLabel greeting = new JLabel();. You can assign some text to the JLabel with the **setText() method**, as in greeting.setText("Hi there");. Alternatively, you can pass a String argument to the JLabel constructor when you declare greeting, as in JLabel greeting = new JLabel("Hi there");. Add a JLabel to your Greet JApplet as follows:

```
JLabel greeting = new JLabel("Hello. Who are you?");
```

5. Save the partially completed file as **Greet.java** in the Chap14\Chapter folder in your work folder.

The JApplet class provides a general outline used by any Web browser when it runs an applet. You already know that in a Java application the main() method is called automatically and it, in turn, calls other methods that you write. However, with an applet, the browser calls several methods automatically. Four methods that are included in every applet are:

- public void init()
- public void start()
- public void stop()
- public void destroy()

If you fail to write one or more of these methods, Java creates them for you. The methods Java creates have opening and closing curly braces only—in other words, they are empty. In order to create a Java program that does anything useful, you must code at least one of these methods.

The `init()` method is the first method called in any applet. You use it to perform initialization tasks, such as setting variables to initial values or placing applet components on the screen. You must code its header as `public void init()`.

To add an `init()` method to your Greet JApplet:

1. If it is not still open on your screen, open the **Greet.java** file in your text editor.
2. Add a header and an opening curly brace for the `JApplet`'s `init()` method.

   ```
   public void init()
   {
   ```

3. When you create a `JApplet`, you do not add components directly to the applet; instead you must provide a `Container` object to hold the `Swing` components you use. Add the following two statements to your applet. The first creates a `Container` object named `c` and uses the `getContentPane()` method to assign a value to `c`. The second statement adds the `JLabel greeting` to the content pane for the `JApplet`.

   ```
   Container c = getContentPane();
   c.add(greeting);
   ```

4. Add two closing curly braces—one for the `init()` method and another for the class.
5. Save the file as **Greet.java** in the Chap14\Chapter folder in your work folder.
6. Compile the program with the command `javac Greet.java`.
7. If necessary, correct any errors and then compile the program again.

To run the `Greet` applet, you can use your Web browser or the `appletviewer` command. In the following steps, you do both.

To run the applet using your Web browser:

1. Open any Web browser, such as Microsoft Internet Explorer or Netscape Navigator. You do not have to connect to the Internet; you will be using the browser locally.

You can start your Web browser by double-clicking the shortcut icon on the desktop, or by using the Start button. If you have problems starting your Web browser, ask your instructor or technical support person for help.

If you do not have a Web browser installed on your computer, skip to the end of Step 3.

2. Click **File** on the menu bar, and then click **Open** or **Open Page**. Then type **`C:\WebProg\Chap14\Chapter\testGreet.html`**, where "WebProg" is the name of your work folder and "C" is the name of the drive. Be sure to type the complete path for the HTML document that you created to access the Greet.class. The applet appears on your screen, as shown in Figure 14-1.

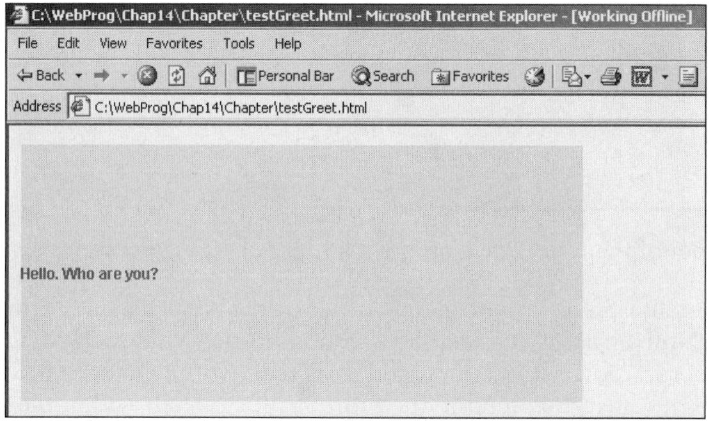

Figure 14-1 testGreet.html page in Web browser

3. Close your Web browser.

You also can view your applet using the `appletviewer` command, as you see next.

Some applets do not work correctly using your browser. Java was designed with a number of security features, so that when an applet displays on the Internet, the applet cannot perform malicious tasks, such as deleting a file from your hard drive. If an applet does nothing that might compromise security, then testing it using the Web browser or the `appletviewer` command will achieve the same results. For now, you can get your applets to perform better by using the Applet Viewer window.

To run the applet using the `appletviewer` command:

1. At the command line, type **`appletviewer testGreet.html`**. After a few moments, the Applet Viewer window opens and displays the applet, as shown in Figure 14-2.

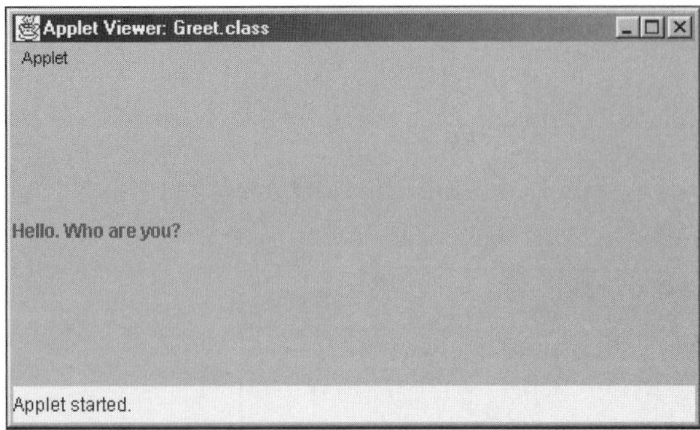

Figure 14-2 Output of the Greet2.java program in the Applet Viewer window

2. Use the mouse pointer to drag any corner of the Applet Viewer window to resize it. Notice that if you lengthen or shorten the window by dragging its bottom border down or up, the window is redrawn on the screen and the `JLabel` is automatically repositioned to remain centered within the window. If you narrow the window by dragging its right border to the left, the `JLabel` eventually becomes partially obscured when the window becomes too narrow for the display.
3. Close the Applet Viewer window.

Changing a Label's Font

If you use the Internet and a Web browser to visit Web sites, you probably are not very impressed with your `Greet` applet. You might think that the string "Hello. Who are you?" is pretty plain and lackluster. Fortunately, Java provides you with a `Font` object that holds typeface and size information. The **`setFont()` method** requires a `Font` object argument. To construct a `Font` object, you need three arguments: typeface, style, and point size.

The **typeface** is a `String` representing a font. Common fonts are Arial, Helvetica, Courier, and Times Roman. The typeface is only a request; the system on which your applet runs might not have access to the requested font and therefore might substitute a default font. The **style** applies an attribute to displayed text and is one of three arguments: `Font.PLAIN`, `Font.BOLD`, or `Font.ITALIC`. The **point size** is an integer that represents 1/72 of an inch. Normal printed text is usually about 12 points; a headline might be 30 points.

The typeface name is a `String`, so you must enclose it in double quotation marks when you use it to declare the `Font` object.

To give a `JLabel` object a new Font, you create the Font object, as in `Font headlineFont = new Font("Helvetica", Font.BOLD, 36);`, and then you use the `setFont()` method to assign the `Font` to a `JLabel`.

Next, you change the font of the text in your `Greet` applet.

To change the appearance of the greeting in the `Greet` applet:

1. Open the **Greet.java** file in your text editor. Change the class name to **`Greet2`**, and save the file as **Greet2.java**.
2. Position the cursor at the end of the line that declares the `greeting` label, and then press **Enter** to start a new line of text.
3. Declare a `Font` object named `bigFont` by typing:

   ```
   Font bigFont = new Font("TimesRoman", Font.ITALIC, 24);
   ```
4. Place the cursor to the right of the opening curly brace of the `init()` method, and then press **Enter** to start a new line.
5. Set the greeting `Font` to `bigFont` by typing:

   ```
   greeting.setFont(bigFont);
   ```
6. Save the file using the current filename (Greet2.java) and to the Chap14\Chapter folder in your work folder.
7. At the command line, compile the program with the command:

   ```
   javac Greet2.java
   ```
8. Open the testGreet.html file and change the class name from `Greet` to **`Greet2`**. Save the HTML file as **testGreet2.html**.
9. Run the applet using the HTML file by typing: **`appletviewer testGreet2.html`** at the command prompt. Figure 14-3 shows the output.
10. Close the Applet Viewer window.

14

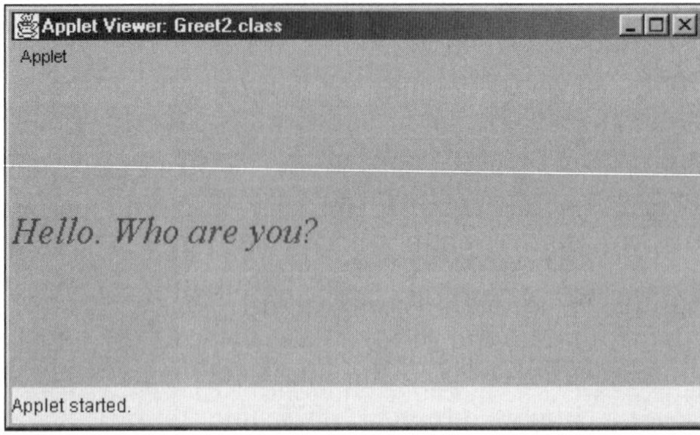

Figure 14-3 Output of the Greet2.java program using `bigFont`

ADDING JTEXTFIELD AND JBUTTON COMPONENTS TO A JAPPLET

In addition to `JLabel`s, applets often contain other window components such as `JTextField`s and `JButton`s. A **`JTextField`** is a Windows component into which a user can type a single line of text data. (Text data includes any characters you can enter from the keyboard, including numbers and punctuation.) Typically, a user types a line into a `JTextField` and then presses Enter on the keyboard or clicks a button with a mouse to enter the data. You can construct a `JTextField` object using one of several constructors:

- `public JTextField()`, which creates an empty `JTextField` with an unspecified length
- `public JTextField(int numColumns)`, in which `numColumns` specifies a width for the field
- `public JTextField(String initialText)`, in which `initialText` provides some initial text within the `JTextField`
- `public JTextField(String initialText, int numColumns)`, in which both initial text and width are specified

For example, to provide a `JTextField` for a user to answer the "Who are you?" question, you can code `JTextField answer = new JTextField(10);` to provide a `JTextField` that is empty and displays approximately 10 characters. To add the `JTextField` named `answer` to a `Container` named `c`, you write `c.add(answer);`.

To add a `JTextField` to the `Greet2` applet:

1. Open the `Greet2` applet in your text editor. Change the class name to **`Greet3`** and save the file as **Greet3.java**.

2. Position your cursor at the end of the line that declares the font, and press **Enter** to start a new line. Define a `JTextField` as follows:

   ```
   JTextField aTextField = new JTextField(10);
   ```

3. Add the `JTextField` to the `JApplet` container just below the statement that adds the `greeting` object to the `Container`.

   ```
   c.add(aTextField);
   ```

4. Save the file and compile it.

5. Open the testGreet2.html file, and change the reference to the class name from `Greet2` to **`Greet3`**. Save the file as **testGreet3.html**.

6. Run the applet using the HTML file by typing **`appletviewer testGreet3.html`** at the command prompt. When the `JApplet` runs, you see a viewing screen filled with a large text field that completely obscures the `JLabel` you added earlier. When you place multiple components within a `Container`, you must use a layout manager to control the position of the components. Close the applet. If it is not still open, open the **Greet3.java** file, position your insertion point at the end of the line that defines the `Container`, and press **Enter** to start a new line. Then set the layout manager for the `Container` named `c` using the following statement:

   ```
   c.setLayout(new FlowLayout());
   ```

7. Save the file and recompile it. Then use the **appletviewer testGreet3.html** command to run the `JApplet` again. This time, the components do not overlap, and the output looks like Figure 14-4. Close the applet.

14

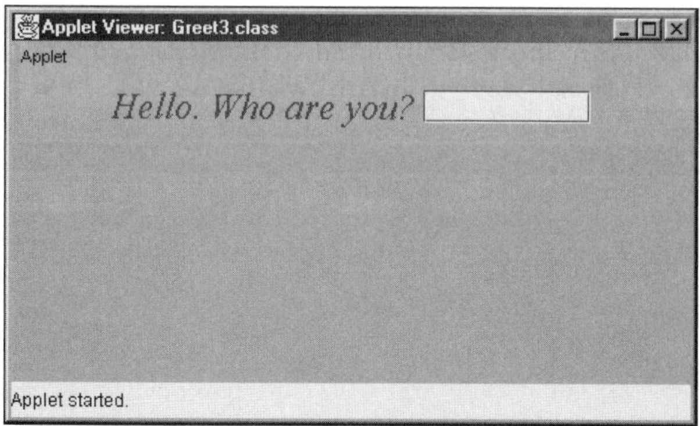

Figure 14-4 Output of the Greet3.java program using `FlowLayout` manager

The number of characters a `JTextField` actually can display depends on the font being used and the actual characters typed. For example, in most fonts, "w" is wider than "i", so a `JTextField` of size 10 using Arial font can display 24 "i" characters but only eight "w" characters.

Try to anticipate how many characters your users will enter when you create a `JTextField`. Even though the user can enter more characters than the number that display, the characters scroll out of view. It can be disconcerting to try to enter data into a field that is not large enough.

Several other methods are available for use with `JTextField`s. The **`setText()` method** allows you to change the text in a `JTextField` that already has been created, as in `answer.setText("Thank you");`. The **`getText()` method** allows you to retrieve the `String` of text in a `JTextField`, as in `String whatDidTheySay = answer.getText();`.

When a `JTextField` has the capability of accepting keystrokes, it is **editable**. If you do not want the user to be able to enter data in a `JTextField`, you can use the **`setEditable()` method** to change the editable status of a `JTextField`. For example, if you want to give a user only one chance to answer a question correctly, then you can prevent the user from replacing or editing the characters in the `JTextField` by using the code `answer.setEditable(false);`. If conditions change, and you want the user to be able to edit the `JTextField`, use the code `answer.setEditable(true);`.

A `JButton` is even easier to create than a `JTextField`. There are five `JButton` constructors. The two simplest are:

- `public JButton()`, which you use to create an unlabeled `JButton`
- `public JButton(String label)`, which you use to create a labeled `JButton`

For example, to create a `JButton` with the label "Press when ready," you write `JButton readyButton = new JButton("Press when ready");`. To add the `JButton` to an applet, you write `c.add(readyButton);`, where `c` is the content pane for the applet. You can change a `JButton`'s label with the **`setLabel()` method**, as in `readyButton.setLabel("Don't press me again!");`, or get the label and assign it to a `String` object with the **`getLabel()` method**, as in `String whatsOnButton = readyButton.getLabel();`.

Make sure that the label on your `JButton` describes its function for the user.

Next, you add a `JButton` to your applet.

To add a `JButton` to the `Greet` applet:

1. Open the **Greet3.java** text file in your text editor if it is not still open.
2. Position the cursor at the end of the line that defines the `Font bigFont` object, and then press **Enter** to start a new line of text.

3. Declare a `JButton` that says "Press here".

   ```
   JButton aButton = new JButton("Press here");
   ```

4. Position the cursor at the end of the `add()` statement that adds the greeting to the applet, and then press **Enter** to start a new line.
5. Add the `JButton` to the applet's content pane by typing:

   ```
   c.add(aButton);
   ```

6. Save the file and then compile it with the **`javac Greet3.java`** command.
7. Run the applet with the **`appletviewer testGreet3.html`** command. Your screen should look like Figure 14-5. Confirm that you can type characters into the `JTextField` and that you can click the `JButton` using the mouse. You haven't coded any action to take place as a result of a `JButton` click yet, but the components should be functional. Then close the Applet Viewer.

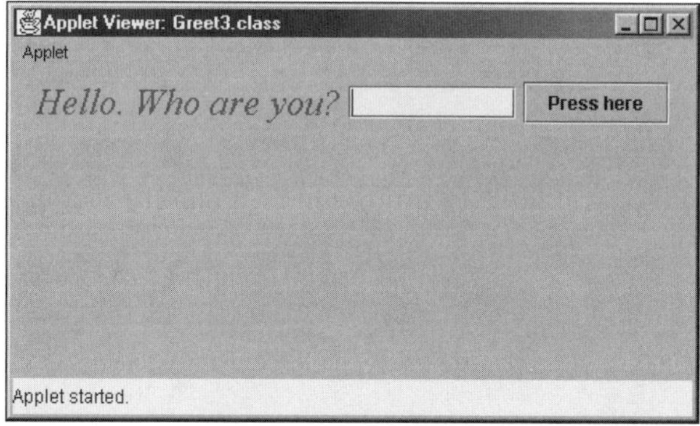

Figure 14-5 Output of the Greet3.java program containing a `JLabel`, `JTextField`, and `JButton`

14

EVENT-DRIVEN PROGRAMMING

An **event** occurs when someone using your applet takes action on a component, such as clicking the mouse on a `JButton` object. The Java applications you wrote in the last chapter were **procedural**—in other words, you dictated the order in which events occurred. You retrieved user input, wrote decisions and loops, and created output. When you retrieved user input, you had no control over how much time the user took to enter a response to a prompt, but you did control the fact that processing went no further until the input was completed. In contrast, with **event-driven programs**, the user might initiate any number of events in any order. For example, if you use a word-processing program, you have dozens of choices at your disposal at any moment in time. You can type words, select text with the mouse, click a button to change text to bold, click a button to change text to italics, choose a menu item, and so on. With each word-processing document you create, you choose options in any order that seems appropriate at the time. The word-processing program must be ready to respond to any event you initiate.

Within an event-driven program, a component on which an event is generated is the **source** of the event. A `JButton` that a user can click is an example of a source; a `JTextField` in which a user can enter text is another source. An object that is interested in an event is a **listener**. Not all objects can receive all events—you probably have used programs in which clicking on many areas of the screen has no effect at all. If you want an object, such as your applet, to be a listener for an event, you must register the object as a listener for the source.

Newspapers around the world register with news services, such as the Associated Press or United Press International. The news service maintains a list of subscribers, and sends each one a story when important national events occur. Similarly, a Java component source object (such as a `JButton`) maintains a list of registered listeners and notifies each one (such as an applet) when any event occurs, such as a mouse click. When the listener "receives the news," an event-handling method that is part of the listener object responds to the event.

A source object and a listener object could be the same object. For example, a `JButton` can change its label when a user clicks it.

To respond to user events within any applet you create, you must:

- Prepare your applet to accept event messages.
- Tell your applet to expect events to happen.
- Tell your applet how to respond to any events that happen.

Preparing Your Applet to Accept Event Messages

You prepare your applet to accept mouse events by importing the java.awt.event package into your program and adding the phrase `implements ActionListener` to the class header. The java.awt.event package includes event classes with such names as `ActionEvent`, `ComponentEvent`, and `TextEvent`. `ActionListener` is an **interface**, or a set of specifications for methods that you can use with `Events`. Implementing `ActionListener` provides you with standard event method specifications that allow your applet to work with `ActionEvents`, which are the types of events that occur when a user clicks a button.

You can identify interfaces such as `ActionListener` by the fact that they are "implemented," and not "imported" or "extended."

Telling Your Applet to Expect Events to Happen

You tell your applet to expect `ActionEvents` with the **`addActionListener()` method**. If you have declared a `JButton named aButton`, and you want to perform an action when a user clicks `aButton`, then `aButton` is the source of a message, and you can think of your applet as a **target** to which to send a message. The statement `aButton.addActionListener(this);` causes any `ActionEvent` messages (button clicks) that come from `aButton` to be sent to "this". In this context, "this" means "this applet." The keyword **`this`** is a Java term that means the current class.

Not all `Events` are `ActionEvents` with an `addActionListener()` method. For example, `TextEvents` have an `addTextListener()` method.

Telling Your `JApplet` How to Respond to Events

The `ActionListener` interface contains the **`actionPerformed(ActionEvent e)` method** specification. When an applet has registered as a listener with a `JButton`, and a user clicks the `JButton`, the `actionPerformed()` method automatically executes. You must write the `actionPerformed()` method, which contains a header and a body like all methods. You use the header `public void actionPerformed(ActionEvent e)`, where `e` is any name you choose for the `Event` (the button click) that initiated the notification of the `ActionListener` (the applet). The body of the method contains any statements you want to execute when the action occurs. You might want to perform some mathematical calculations, construct new objects, produce output, or execute any other operation. For example, Figure 14-6 shows an `actionPerformed()` method that produces a line of output at the operating system prompt.

```
public void actionPerformed(ActionEvent someEvent)
{
   System.out.println("I'm inside the actionPerformed() method!");
}
```

Figure 14-6 `actionPerformed()` method that produces a line of output

Next, you make your applet an event-driven program by adding functionality to the applet's `JButton`. When the user enters a name and clicks the `JButton`, the `JApplet` displays a greeting on the command line.

14

To make your applet an event-driven program:

1. If it is not still open, open the **Greet3.java** file in your text editor. Change the class name to `Greet4`, and save the file as **Greet4.java**.
2. As the third import statement in your program, add **`import java.awt.event.*;`**.
3. Position the cursor at the end of the class header (`public class Greet4 extends JApplet`), press the **spacebar**, and then type **`implements ActionListener`**.
4. Position the cursor at the end of the statement in the `init()` method that adds the `aButton` `JButton` to the applet, and then press **Enter**. Prepare your applet for button-source events by typing the statement `aButton.`**`addActionListener(this);`**.
5. You can request focus for a component when you want to direct the user's attention to it, or you want the user's first keystrokes to apply to that component. You can obtain focus for the `JTextField` by typing. (This is only a request—it might not be honored when you run your program.)

   ```
   aTextField.requestFocus();
   ```

6. Position the cursor to the right of the closing curly brace for the `init()` method, and press **Enter**. Next, you add the `actionPerformed()` method after the `init()` method but before the closing brace for the class. This method declares a `String` that holds the user's name, uses the `getText()` method on the answer `JTextField` to retrieve the `String`, and then displays a message to the user on the screen.

   ```
   public void actionPerformed(ActionEvent thisEvent)
   {
      String name = aTextField.getText();
      System.out.println("Hi there " + name);
   }
   ```

7. Save and compile the program.
8. Change the testGreet3.html document to execute the `Greet4` class and resave it as **testGreet4.html**. Execute the program using the **`appletviewer testGreet4.html`** command at the command prompt.
9. Type your name in the `JTextField`, and then click the **Press here** button. Examine your command prompt screen. The personalized message "Hi there" and your name appear on the command prompt. Figure 14-7 shows a typical execution of the program.

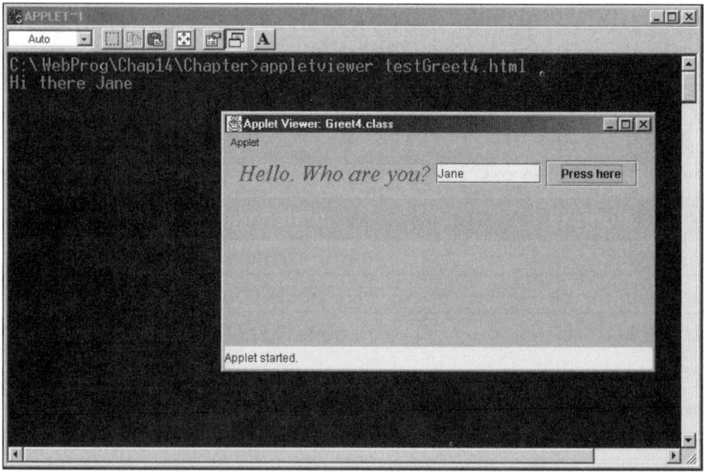

Figure 14-7 Execution of the `Greet4 JApplet`

You might need to drag the Applet Viewer window to a new position so you can see the output on the command line.

10. Use the mouse to highlight the name in the `JTextField` in the Applet Viewer window, and then type a new name. Click the **Press here** button. A new greeting appears on the command line.
11. Close the Applet Viewer window.

In most applets that contain a `JTextField`, there are two ways to get the applet to accept user input. Usually, you can enter text and click a button, or you can enter text and press Enter. If your applet needs to receive an event message from a `JTextField`, then you need to make your applet a registered `Event` listener with the `JTextField`.

14

To make your applet a registered `Event` listener:

1. In the Greet4.java text file, change the class name to **Greet5**, then save the file as **Greet5.java**.
2. Position the cursor at the end of the statement `aButton.addActionListener(this);` and then press **Enter**.
3. Make the answer field accept input by typing: **`aTextField.addActionListener(this);`**
4. Save and compile the program.

5. Change the testGreet4.html document to execute the Greet5 class and resave it as **testGreet5.html**. Execute the program using the **`appletviewer testGreet5.html`** command at the command prompt. Run the test.html file using the **`appletviewer testGreet5.html`** command at the command prompt. Confirm that you can enter a name in the **`JTextField`** either by clicking the **Press here** button or by pressing **Enter**.
6. Close the Applet Viewer window.

ADDING OUTPUT TO A JAPPLET

An applet that produces output on the command line is not very exciting. Naturally, you want to make changes within your applet as various events occur. For example, rather than using `System.out.println()` to send a greeting to the command line, it would be nice to add a greeting to the applet itself. One approach to this task would be to create a new `JLabel` that gets added to the applet's content pane with the `add()` method after the user enters a name. You can declare a new, empty `JLabel` with the statement `JLabel personalGreeting = new JLabel("");`. After the name is retrieved, you can use the `setText()` method to set the `JLabel` text for `personalGreeting` to `"Hi there " + name`.

To add a greeting to the applet itself:

1. Change the Greet5 class name to **Greet6** and save the file as **Greet6.java**.
2. Within the Greet6.java text file, remove the `System.out.println()` statement from the `actionPerformed()` method.
3. From the `init()` method, cut the line of code that declares the `Container` object (**`Container c = getContentPane();`**) and paste it just above the `init()` method header. You need to move this declaration because you will be using the `c` object within two methods, so its declaration cannot be only local within one of the methods.
4. Add the following statements to the `actionPerformed()` method to declare a new `JLabel` named `personalGreeting`, to set the text of the `personalGreeting`, and then to add the `personalGreeting` to the `JApplet`:

```
JLabel personalGreeting = new JLabel("");
personalGreeting.setText("Hi " + name);
c.add(personalGreeting);
```

5. Save and compile the program.

6. Change the testGreet5.html file to refer to **Greet6.class**, save the file as **testGreet6.html**, and then run the applet using the **appletviewer** command. Try typing a name in the JTextField, and then press **Enter** or click the **Press here** button. When you do, nothing happens.
7. Now use the mouse to resize the Applet Viewer window by dragging one of its borders, or by minimizing it and then restoring it. The personalGreeting appears.
8. Close the Applet Viewer window.

The personalGreeting does not appear in your applet after you enter a name because the personalGreeting is added to the applet too late. The init() method lays out all the applet components when the applet starts, and the c.add(personalGreeting); statement is not part of the init() method. The applet screen is drawn only when it is created or when the applet is out of date. When you minimize or resize an applet, it "knows" it must be redrawn to accommodate the new size. Similarly, if you open another application so all or part of your applet screen is hidden, when you close the window that appears on top, the underlying applet "knows" it must be redrawn. However, when you use add() to place a new component on the screen, the applet does not "realize" it is out of date.

You can cause the applet to know it is out of date by using the repaint() method to redraw the applet surface, an **invalidate() method**, which marks the window so it knows that it is not up to date with recent changes. Then, you can cause the changes to take effect by using the **validate() method**, which redraws any invalid window.

To add the invalidate() and validate() methods to the applet:

1. Within the actionPerformed() method of the Greet6.java file, position the cursor at the end of the c.add(personalGreeting); statement, and then press **Enter**. Then add the following statements:

```
c.repaint();
invalidate();
validate();
```

2. Save, compile, and run the applet. The greeting now displays immediately after you type a name and press Enter or click the "Press here" button. See Figure 14-8.
3. Close the Applet Viewer window.

14

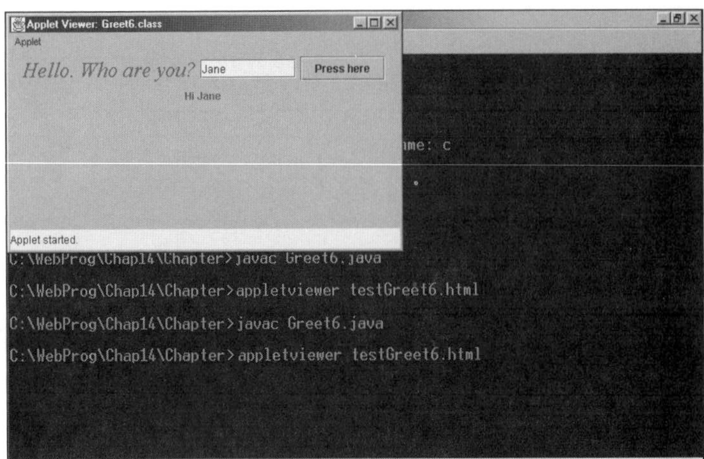

Figure 14-8 Execution of the `Greet6 JApplet`

If you can add components to an applet, you should also be able to remove them; you do so with the **`remove()` method**. For example, after a user enters a name into the `JTextField`, you might not want the user to use the `JTextField` or its `JButton` again, so you can remove them from the applet. You use the `remove()` method by placing the component's name within the parentheses. As with `add()`, the applet must be redrawn after `remove()` in order to see the effects.

To remove components from the applet:

1. Within the Greet6.java file, change the class name to **Greet7**, and then save the file as **Greet7.java**. Place the insertion point at the beginning of the `c.add(personalGreeting);` statement in the `actionPerformed()` method, and then press **Enter**. Then enter the following statements:

```
c.remove(greeting);
c.remove(aButton);
c.remove(aTextField);
```

2. Save and compile the applet. Open the **testGreet6.html** file, change it to refer to the Greet7 class, and save it as **testGreet7.html**.
3. Use the **`appletviewer`** command to execute the applet. When you enter a name and either press Enter or click the "Press here" button, the greeting is displayed and the `JTextField` and the `JButton` disappear from the screen.
4. Close the Applet Viewer window, and then close your text editor.

UNDERSTANDING THE JAPPLET LIFE CYCLE

Applets are popular because they are easy to use in a Web page. Because applets execute in a browser, the `JApplet` class contains methods that automatically are called by the browser—the names of four of these methods are `init()`, `start()`, `stop()`, and `destroy()`.

You already have written your own `init()` methods. When you write a method that has the same method header as an automatically provided method, you replace or **override** the original version. Every time a Web page containing an applet is loaded in the browser, or when you run the `appletviewer` command with an HTML document that calls an applet, if you have written an `init()` method for the applet, it executes; otherwise, the automatically provided `init()` method executes. You should write your own `init()` method when you have any initialization tasks to perform, such as setting up user interface components.

Overriding a method means creating your own version for Java to use instead of the automatically supplied version with the same name. It is not the same as *overloading* a method, which means writing several methods that have the same name but take different arguments.

The `start()` method executes after the `init()` method, and it executes again every time the applet becomes active after it has been inactive. For example, if you run an applet using the `appletviewer` command, then minimize the Applet Viewer window, the applet becomes inactive. When you restore the window, the applet becomes active again. On the Internet, users can leave a Web page, visit another page, and then return to the first site, causing the applet to become inactive and then active. You write your own `start()` method if there are any actions you want to take when a user revisits an applet; for example, you might want to resume some animation that you suspended when the user left the applet.

14

When a user leaves a Web page, perhaps by minimizing a window or traveling to a different Web page, the `stop()` method is invoked. You override the existing empty `stop()` method only if you want to take some action when an applet is no longer visible. You usually don't need to write your own `stop()` methods.

Advanced Java programmers override the `stop()` and `destroy()` methods when they want to add instructions to "suspend a thread," or stop a chain of events that have been started by an applet but not yet completed.

The `destroy()` method is called when the user closes the browser or Applet Viewer. Closing the browser or Applet Viewer releases any resources the applet might have allocated. As with `stop()`, you usually do not have to write your own destroy() methods.

In summary, every applet has the same life cycle outline, as shown in Figure 14-9. When any applet executes, the `init()` method runs, followed by `start()`. If the user leaves the applet's page, `stop()` executes. When the user returns, `start()` executes. The `stop()` and `start()` sequence might continue any number of times, until the user closes the browser (or Applet Viewer) and the `destroy()` method is invoked.

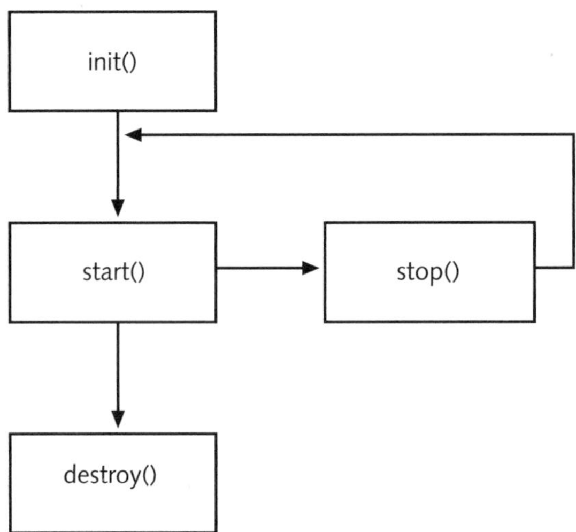

Figure 14-9 Applet life cycle outline

To demonstrate an applet's life cycle methods in action, you can write an applet that overrides all four methods, and count the number of times each method executes.

To demonstrate the life cycle of an applet:

1. Open a new text file in your text editor, and then type the following import statements that you need for the applet:

```
import javax.swing.*;
import java.awt.*;
import java.awt.event.*;
```

2. Type the following header for a `LifeCycle` applet. The applet includes a `JButton` that the user can press, so the `ActionListener` is implemented. (You can type the header all on one line, if you want. It is written on two lines here to fit on this page.)

```
public class LifeCycle
   extends JApplet implements ActionListener
```

3. Press **Enter**, type the opening curly brace for the class, and then press **Enter** again to start a new line.

4. Declare the following six Label objects that you use to display the names of each of the six methods that execute during the lifetime of the applet:

```
JLabel messageInit = new JLabel("init ");
JLabel messageStart = new JLabel("start ");
JLabel messageDisplay = new JLabel("display ");
JLabel messageAction = new JLabel("action ");
JLabel messageStop = new JLabel("stop ");
JLabel messageDestroy = new JLabel("destroy ");
```

5. Declare a JButton by typing:

```
JButton pressButton = new JButton("Press");
```

6. Declare six integers to hold the number of occurrences of each of the six methods. To declare the integers, type the following code on one line: **int countInit, countStart, countDisplay, countAction, countStop, countDestroy;**. Add a Container object to hold the JApplet's components:

```
Container c = getContentPane();
```

7. Add the following init() method, which sets a layout manager, adds one to countInit, places the components within the applet, and activates the JButton. Its final action is to call the display() method.

```
public void init()
{
   c.setLayout(new FlowLayout());
   ++countInit;
   c.add(messageInit);
   c.add(messageStart);
   c.add(messageDisplay);
   c.add(messageAction);
   c.add(messageStop);
   c.add(messageDestroy);
   c.add(pressButton);
   pressButton.addActionListener(this);
   display();
}
```

8. Add the following start() method, which adds one to countStart and calls display():

```
public void start()
{
   ++countStart;
   display();
}
```

9. Add the following `display()` method, which adds one to `countDisplay`, then displays the name of each of the six methods with the current count and indicates how many times the method has executed:

```
public void display()
{
   ++countDisplay;
   messageInit.setText("   init " + countInit);
   messageStart.setText("  start " + countStart);
   messageDisplay.setText("  display " + countDisplay);
   messageAction.setText("  action " + countAction);
   messageStop.setText("  stop " + countStop);
   messageDestroy.setText("  destroy " + countDestroy);
}
```

10. Add the following `stop()` and `destroy()` methods, which each add one to the appropriate counter and call `display()`:

```
public void stop()
{
   ++countStop;
   display();
}
public void destroy()
{
   ++countDestroy;
   display();
}
```

11. When the user clicks `pressButton`, the following `actionPerformed()` method executes; it adds one to `countAction` and displays it. Enter the method:

```
public void actionPerformed(ActionEvent e)
{
   ++countAction;
   display();
}
```

12. Add the closing curly brace for the class. Save the class as **LifeCycle.java** in the Chap14\Chapter folder in your work folder. Compile the file, correct any errors, if necessary, and compile again.

Take a moment to examine the code you created for LifeCycle.java. Each of the methods adds one to each of the six counters, but with the exception of `display()`, you never explicitly call any of the methods; each method is called automatically. Next, you create an HTML document to test LifeCycle.java.

To create an HTML document to test LifeCycle.java:

1. Open a new text file in your text editor.

2. Enter the following HTML document:

```
<HTML>
<APPLET CODE = "LifeCycle.class" WIDTH = 460
HEIGHT = 200>
</APPLET>
</HTML>
```

3. Save the file as **testLifeCycle.html** in the Chap14\Chapter folder in your work folder.

4. Run the HTML document using the command **appletviewer testLifeCycle.html**. Figure 14-10 shows the output. When the applet begins, the init() method is called, so one is added to countInit. The init() method calls display(), so one is added to countDisplay. Immediately after the init() method executes, the start() method is executed, and one is added to countStart. The start() method calls display(), so one more is added to countDisplay. The first time you see the applet, countInit is 1, countStart is 1, and countDisplay is 2. The methods actionPerformed(), stop(), and destroy() have not yet been executed.

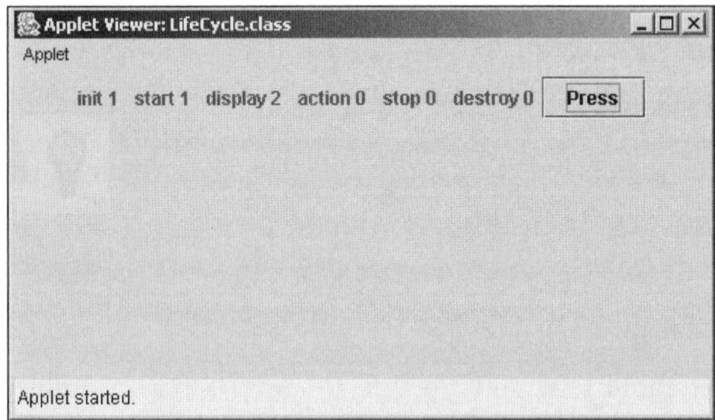

Figure 14-10 LifeCycle applet after startup

5. Minimize the Applet Viewer window, and then restore the window. The applet now looks like Figure 14-11. The init() method still has been called only once, but when you minimized the applet the stop() method executed, and when you restored it, the start() method executed. Therefore, countStop is now 1 and countStart has increased to 2. Additionally, both start() and stop() call display(), so countDisplay is increased by two, and it now holds the value 4.

14

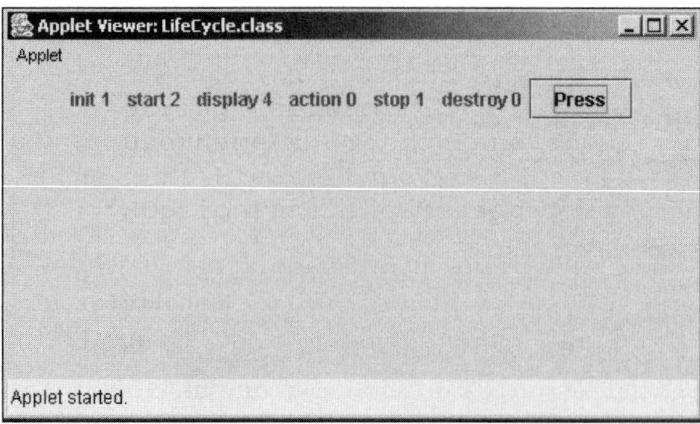

Figure 14-11 `LifeCycle` applet after being minimized and restored

Minimize and restore the AppletViewer window again. Now confirm that the `stop()` method has executed twice, the `start()` method has executed three times, and the `display()` method has executed a total of six times.

6. Click the **Press** button. The count for the `actionPerformed()` method now is 1, and `actionPerformed()` calls `display()`, so `countDisplay` is up to 7.
7. Continue to minimize, maximize, and press the button and note the changes that occur with each activity until you can correctly predict the outcome. Notice that no matter what you do, the `destroy()` method is not executed until you close the applet, and then it is too late to observe an increase in `countDestroy`.

Creating a Complete Interactive Applet

You now know quite a bit about Java, and are able to create a fairly complex application or applet. Next, you create an applet that contains several components, receives user input, makes decisions, uses arrays, produces output, and reacts to the applet life cycle.

The `PartyPlanner` applet lets its user estimate the cost of an event hosted by a party-planning service named Event Handlers Incorporated. Event Handlers uses a sliding fee scale so the per-guest cost decreases as the total number of invited guests increases. Table 14-1 shows the fee structure.

Table 14-1 Cost per guest for events

Number of guests	Cost per guest
1–24	$27
25–49	$25
50–99	$22
100–199	$19
200–499	$17
500–999	$14
1000 and over	$11

The applet lets the user enter the number of anticipated guests. The user can press Enter or click a `JButton` to perform the fee lookup and event cost calculation. Then the applet displays the cost per person as well as the total cost for the event. The user can continue to request fees for a different number of guests and view the results for any length of time before making another request or leaving the page. If the user leaves the page, however, you want to erase the last number of requested guests and make sure the next user starts fresh with zero guests.

To begin to create an interactive party planner applet:

1. Open a new text file in your text editor.
2. Type the following import statements, the `PartyPlanner` class header, and the opening curly brace for the class:

```
import javax.swing.*;
import java.awt.*;
import java.awt.event.*;
public class PartyPlanner
   extends JApplet implements ActionListener
{
```

3. You need several components: a `JLabel` for the company name, a `JButton` the user can click to perform a calculation, a prompt for the `JButton`, a `JTextField` in which the user can enter the number of invited guests, and two more `JLabels` to display output. Add the following code to implement these components:

```
JLabel companyName =
   new JLabel("Event Handlers Incorporated");
JButton calcButton = new JButton("Calculate");
JLabel prompt =
   new JLabel("Enter the number of guests at your event");
JTextField numGuests = new JTextField(5);
JLabel perPersonResult = new JLabel("Plan with us.");
JLabel totalResult = new JLabel("The more the merrier!");
```

4. Additionally, create a `Font` and a `Container` by typing:

```
Font bigFont = new Font("Helvetica", Font.ITALIC, 24);
Container c = getContentPane();
```

5. Use the `init()` method to set the layout manager, place components within the applet screen, and prepare the `JButton` and text entry field to receive action messages. Type the following code:

```
public void init()
{
   c.setLayout(new FlowLayout());
   companyName.setFont(bigFont);
   c.add(companyName);
   c.add(prompt);
   c.add(numGuests);
   c.add(calcButton);
   calcButton.addActionListener(this);
   numGuests.addActionListener(this);
   c.add(perPersonResult);
   c.add(totalResult);
}
```

6. Add the following `start()` method, which executes when the user leaves the applet and resets the resulting `JLabels` and the data entry `JTextField`:

```
public void start()
{
   perPersonResult.setText("Plan with us.");
   numGuests.setText("0");
   totalResult.setText("The more the merrier!");
   invalidate();
   validate();
}
```

7. Save the partially completed applet as **PartyPlanner.java** in the Chap14\Chapter folder in your work folder.

You finished the `init()` and `start()` methods for the `PartyPlanner` applet, placed each component in the applet, and reinitialized each component each time a user returns to the applet after leaving. At this point, the applet doesn't actually do anything; most of the applet's work is contained in the `actionPerformed()` method, which is the most complicated method in this applet. Next, you create the `actionPerformed()` method. You begin by declaring two parallel arrays—one array holds guest limits for each of seven event rates, and the other array holds the actual rates. One way you can declare an array in Java is by inserting square braces after the data type and providing a list of values between curly braces as shown in the following code. The array elements are then referred to using subscripts that have values ranging from zero through one less than the size of the array.

To complete the `PartyPlanner` applet:

1. Enter the following method header for `actionPerformed()` and declare two arrays for guest limits and rates:

   ```
   public void actionPerformed(ActionEvent e)
   {
      int[] guestLimit = { 0, 25, 50, 100, 200, 500, 1000};
      int[] ratePerGuest = {27, 25, 22, 19, 17, 14, 11};
   ```

2. Next, add the following variable to hold the number of guests. The user enters a text string into a `JTextField`, but you need an integer in order to perform calculations, so you can use the `parseInt()` method to convert the entered string into an integer.

   ```
   int guests = Integer.parseInt(numGuests.getText());
   ```

3. You need two variables: one to hold the individual, per-person fee for an event, and the other to hold the fee for the entire event. Enter the following variables:

   ```
   int individualFee = 0, eventFee = 0;
   ```

4. Enter the following variables to use as subscripts for the arrays: `int x = 0, a = 0;`.

5. Save the partially completed file as **PartyPlanner.java** in the Chap14\Chapter folder of your work folder.

There are a number of ways to search through the `guestLimit` array to discover the appropriate position of the per-person fee in the `ratePerGuest` array. One possibility is to use a `for` loop and vary a subscript from six down to zero. If the number of guests is greater than or equal to any value in the `guestLimit` array, then the corresponding per-person rate in the `ratePerGuest` array is the correct rate. Once the correct individual rate is found, the price for the entire event is determined by multiplying the individual rate by the number of guests. Once the appropriate individual fee has been found for a given event, you do not want to search through the `guestLimit` array any longer, so you set the subscript `x` equal to zero to force an early exit from the `for` loop.

Next, you continue the `PartyPlanner` applet by adding the code that searches for the correct fee based on the number of guests. Then you complete the applet.

To continue the applet:

1. Enter the following `for` loop:

   ```
   for(x = 6; x >= 0; --x)
      if(guests >= guestLimit[x])
      {
            individualFee = ratePerGuest[x];
            eventFee = guests * individualFee;
            x = 0;
   }
   ```

2. The only tasks that remain in the `actionPerformed()` method involve producing output for the user. Enter the following code to accomplish this processing:

```
perPersonResult.setText("$" + individualFee +
   " per person");
totalResult.setText("Event cost $" + eventFee);
```

3. Add two closing curly braces: one for the `actionPerformed()` method and one for the entire `PartyPlanner` applet.
4. Save the file, and then compile it at the command prompt.
5. Open a new text file in your text editor, and then create the following HTML document to test the applet:

```
<HTML>
<APPLET CODE = "PartyPlanner.class" WIDTH = 460
   HEIGHT = 200>
</APPLET>
</HTML>
```

6. Save the HTML document as **testPartyPlanner.html** in the Chap14\Chapter folder in your work folder. Then use the `appletviewer` command to execute the file. Your output should look like Figure 14-12. Test the applet with different guest numbers until you are sure that the per-person rates and event rates are correct. Minimize and restore the Applet Viewer window, and observe that any calculated fees are replaced with `start()` messages.

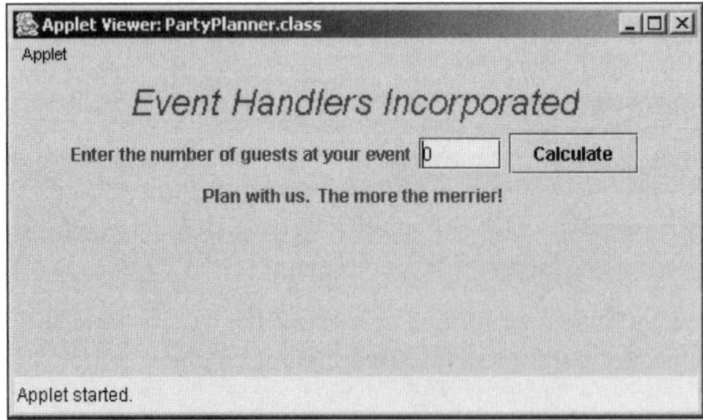

Figure 14-12 The `PartyPlanner` applet

7. Close the Applet Viewer window.

Getting Help

Now your Java programs are becoming more sophisticated—each program you write contains several methods and many individual statements. As you continue to learn about programming, many Java applications and applets you write easily could become 20 times larger than the ones you are writing now. There are hundreds of additional Java methods that you have not learned yet, and developers are constantly creating new objects for you to use. With all that programming code to write and all those methods to understand, it is easy to get lost. Fortunately, a few sources of help are available to you.

A wealth of material exists at the Sun Microsystems Web site, at *java.sun.com*. Of particular interest are the **FAQs (Frequently Asked Questions)** and the Help file, from which you can link to the java.sun home page.

Some Java newsgroups on the Web are listed in Figure 14-13. While you are still a novice programmer, it's a good idea to read the messages that are posted at these newsgroups. Refrain from adding comments of your own until you are sure you are not asking a question that has been asked dozens of times before.

comp.lang.java.advocacy	comp.lang.java.misc
comp.lang.java.announce	comp.lang.java.programmer
comp.lang.java.api	comp.lang.java.security
comp.lang.java.beans	comp.lang.java.setup
comp.lang.java.gui	comp.lang.java.softwaretools
comp.lang.java.help	comp.lang.java.tech

Figure 14-13 Java newsgroups

Chapter Summary

- Applets are programs that are called from within another application. You run applets within a Web page, or within another program called appletviewer, which comes with the Java Developer's Kit. An applet must be called from within another program written in an HTML (Hypertext Markup Language) document.
- HTML commands are called tags. Tags usually come in pairs. The tag that begins every HTML document is `<HTML>` and the tag that ends every HTML document is `</HTML>`.
- To run an applet from within an HTML document, you add the `<APPLET>` and `</APPLET>` tags to your HTML document. You can place three attributes within the `<APPLET>` tag: `CODE`, `WIDTH`, and `HEIGHT`.

- Most applets contain at least two import statements: `import javax.swing.*;` and `import java.awt.*;`. The java.awt package is the Abstract Windows Toolkit, or AWT.
- `JLabel` is a built-in class that holds text you can display within an applet. The `setText()` method assigns text to a `JLabel` or any other component. You use the `add()` method to add a component to a `JApplet`'s content pane.
- Four methods that are included in every applet are `public void init()`, `public void start()`, `public void stop()`, and `public void destroy()`. The `init()` method is the first method called in any applet. You use it to perform initialization tasks, such as setting variables to initial values or placing applet components on the screen.
- A `Font` object holds typeface and size information. To construct a `Font` object, you need three arguments: typeface, style, and point size. To give a `JLabel` object a new `Font`, you create the `Font`, then use the `setFont()` method to assign the `Font` to a `JLabel`.
- A `JTextField` is a Windows component into which a user can type a single line of text data. Typically, a user types a line into a `JTextField` and then presses Enter on the keyboard or clicks a `JButton` using the mouse to input the data.
- An event occurs when your applet's user takes action on a component, such as using the mouse to click a `JButton` object. Adding `implements ActionListener` to an applet's class header prepares an applet to receive event messages. You can cause the applet to know it is out of date by using the `invalidate()` method, which marks the window as not up to date with recent changes. Using the `validate()` method redraws any invalid window.
- When you are writing Java programs, you can get help from the Sun Microsystems Web site or from Java newsgroups.

REVIEW QUESTIONS

1. Applets are ______________.
   a. stand-alone programs
   b. Web pages
   c. called from within another application
   d. written in HTML
2. Which of the following is true about `appletviewer`?
   a. It is a method.
   b. You must code it yourself.
   c. It comes with the Java Developer's Kit.
   d. It must be called from within an HTML document.

3. When you write a Java applet, you save the code with the ________________ file extension.

   a. `.app`

   b. `.html`

   c. `.java`

   d. `.class`

4. Java applications and Java applets are similar because both ________________.

   a. are compiled using the `javac` command

   b. are executed using the `java` command

   c. are executed from within an HTML document

   d. have a `main()` method

5. A program that allows you to display HTML documents on your computer screen is a ________________.

   a. search engine

   b. compiler

   c. browser

   d. server

6. The name of any applet called using `CODE` within an HTML document must use the ________________ extension.

   a. `.exe`

   b. `.code`

   c. `.java`

   d. `.class`

7. `JLabel`s and `JButton`s are ________________.

   a. components

   b. containers

   c. applets

   d. constituents

8. The method that places a value within a previously constructed `JLabel` is ________________.

   a. `getValue()`

   b. `setText()`

   c. `fillLabel()`

   d. `setValue()`

9. The `add()` method ______________.
    a. adds two integers
    b. adds two numbers of any data type
    c. places a component within an Applet Viewer window
    d. places a text value within an applet component
10. Which of the following methods is *not* included in every applet?
    a. `init()`
    b. `add()`
    c. `stop()`
    d. `destroy()`
11. The first method called in any applet is ______________.
    a. `main()`
    b. `start()`
    c. `init()`
    d. whatever method appears first within the applet
12. A `Font` object contains all of the following arguments except ______________.
    a. language
    b. typeface
    c. style
    d. point size
13. A Windows component into which a user can type a single line of text data is a(n) ______________.
    a. `InputArea`
    b. `DataField`
    c. `JTextField`
    d. `JLabel`
14. `ActionListener` is an example of a(n) ______________.
    a. import
    b. applet
    c. interface
    d. component

15. If an applet is registered as a listener with a `JButton`, and a user clicks the `JButton`, the method that executes is ________________.
    a. `buttonPressed()`
    b. `addActionListener()`
    c. `start()`
    d. `actionPerformed()`

HANDS-ON EXERCISES

For the following exercises, save each program that you create in the Chap14\Exercises folder in your work folder. Create an HTML document for each exercise so that you can view and test the pages.

Exercise 14-1

Create an applet with a `JButton` labeled "Who's number one?". When the user clicks the button, display the name of your favorite sports team in a large font. Save this applet as **JNumberOne.java**.

Exercise 14-2

1. Create an applet that asks a user to enter a password into a `JTextField` and then to press Enter. Compare the password to "Rosebud"; if it matches, display "Access Granted". If not, display "Access Denied". Save the applet as **JPassword.java**.
2. Modify the password applet in the above exercise to compare the password to a list of five valid passwords: "Rosebud", "Redrum", "Jason", "Surrender", or "Dorothy". Save the applet as **JPassword2.java**.

14

Exercise 14-3

Create an applet with a `JButton`. Display your name in 8 pt font. Every time the user clicks the `JButton`, increase the font size for the displayed name by four points. Allow the font size to increase only as long as it remains less than or equal to 88 pt. Save the applet as **JIncreaseName.java**.

Exercise 14-4

Create an applet named **`JDialogDouble`** that displays a `JOptionPane` when the user clicks a `JButton`. Allow the user to enter an integer into the `JOptionPane`, then display double the value of the integer (multiplied by 2) in a `JTextField`.

Exercise 14-5

Create an applet named **`JSum`** that allows the user to enter two integers into two separate `JTextField`s. When the user clicks a `JButton`, the sum of the integers is displayed in a third `JTextField`.

Web Programming Projects

Save the programs that you create in these projects in the Chap14\Projects folder in your work folder.

Project 14-1

Create an applet named **`JCalculateBalance`** that allows the user to enter beginning balance, withdrawal, and deposit amounts in three separate labeled fields. The applet then calculates and displays the current balance.

Project 14-2

Kreative Kitchens sells a variety of kitchen appliances. Customers frequently ask for an estimate of the annual cost of running an appliance. Write an applet named **`JKilowatt`** that prompts the user for two values—the cost of a kilowatt hour of electricity and the estimated number of hours the appliance will run annually. Display the estimated annual cost.

Project 14-3

Create an applet named **`JPayroll`** for Handy Household Helpers, a service that needs a payroll applet to allow the user to enter two values for each of their employees—hours worked and hourly rate. When the user clicks a `JButton`, gross pay and net pay values are calculated. Gross pay is simply hours worked times rate. For the net pay value, federal withholding tax is subtracted from gross pay based on the following table:

Income	Withholding
0–99.99	10%
100.00–299.99	15%
300.00–599.99	21%
600.00 and up	28%

CHAPTER

15

JAVASERVER PAGES: PART I

In this chapter you will:

- Explore JavaServer Pages (JSP)
- Use JSP scripting elements
- Link to external files
- Understand declarations, expressions, and scriptlets
- Include JSP comments
- Process client requests

JavaServer Pages (JSP) is the Java-based technology for creating dynamic Web pages that run on any Web server, browser, or operating system. In a dynamic Web page, at least part of the content is generated when the user requests it. A dynamic Web page is interactive; it can accept information from the user, and retrieve and process information for the user.

If you are familiar with Active Server Pages (ASP), the Microsoft technology for creating interactive Web pages, JSP will also be familiar to you. Like ASP, JSP involves scripts you store and run on a Web server. However, JSP scripts use HTML and Java code instead of VBScript, and are ideal for Web servers such as Apache or Netscape that do not support ASP.

In this chapter, you create a simple JSP script and use the Apache Tomcat server to run the script. You will learn how to use page directives, include directives, action, scripting elements, and comments in your JSP pages. Then you will learn how to use request objects to process clients' requests.

EXPLORING JAVASERVER PAGES

JSP is a recently developed, server-based scripting language for creating dynamic HTML pages. Because you write a JSP script in Java, you can take advantage of the power of the Java programming language for networking and database access. You store a JSP script on a Web server; when a user's browser requests the script, the JSP code is executed on the Web server. The results are then included in the static part of that Web page that is sent to the browser. To execute the JSP page, the Web server must be able to run JSP code; it needs an engine to interpret JSP code. In this text, you will use Tomcat as both a stand-alone Web server and JSP engine. In order for the Web server to run JSP code, the Web page must be saved with the extension .jsp.

One characteristic that makes JSP easy and portable is that you can mix JSP code with HTML and XML tags. You identify the JSP code within your HTML code in one of two ways:

- Insert the <% ... %> server script delimiters before and after the JSP code.
- Use XML-based syntax.

This chapter focuses on the first method. Following is sample code that illustrates the syntax for using the server script delimiters:

```
<%
  out.println("Hello World!");
%>
```

When the Web server encounters the special tags <% and %>, it recognizes the statements within the tags as server-side script and executes instructions on the server.

In the following steps, you write a JSP script that displays the current date and time on the Web server.

To create a JSP script:

1. If necessary, use Windows Explorer to create a new folder in the Chap15 folder in your workfolder. Name this folder **Chapter**.
2. Open a new document in a text editor, such as Notepad, and type the following code:

```
<html><head><title>Date & time on the Web server</title>
</head>
<body>
The current date and time on the Web server are:
<%= new java.util.Date() %>
</body>
</html>
```

3. Save the file as **example1.jsp** in the Chap15\Chapter folder of your workfolder. Then close Notepad.

Before testing Web pages in Chapters 15 and 16, including examples, exercises, and projects, you need to start the Tomcat server. If the Tomcat server is not running, please start it now. See the *Read This Before You Begin* page at the beginning of this book for more information.

4. Start your browser and load the page using the following URL. Substitute the name of your workfolder where *workfolder* appears:

   http://localhost:8080/*workfolder*/Chap15/Chapter/example1.jsp

   The page shown in Figure 15-1 appears.

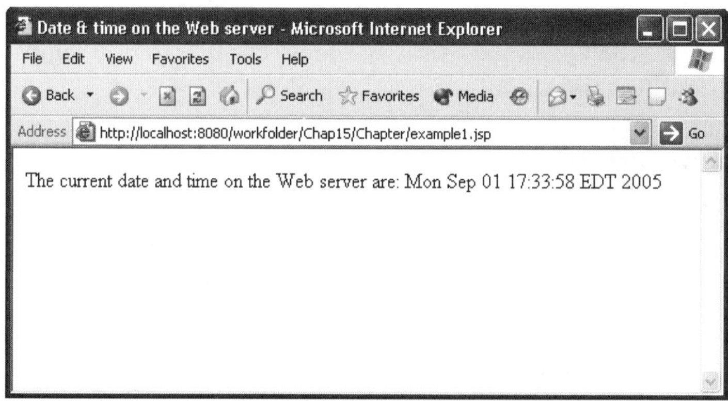

Figure 15-1 Current time on the Web server

The source code of the page as shown in your Web browser is as follows:

```
<html><head><title>Date & time on the Web server</title>
</head>
<body>
The current date and time on the Web server are:
Mon Sep 01 17:33:58 EDT 2005
</body>
</html>
```


This is nothing more than plain HTML. However, the highlighted line is generated dynamically when this page is requested. The rest of the page is hard-coded in advance. The JSP code `<%= new java.util.Date() %>` is executed on your Web server. The execution of the JSP code generates the content of the current time on the Web server; the server sends the newly generated content back to the client browser.

For a Web server to recognize the delimiter tags <% and %> and treat them as server-side script, you must save the file with a .jsp extension. Otherwise, the server sends the script code to the client without processing it on the server.

A JSP script consists of template data and JSP elements. The template data is HTML code, which the JSP processor passes on to the browser untouched. JSP elements are executed on the server and fall into four groups: directives, scripting elements, comments, and actions. Directives are messages to the JSP engine that apply to the entire page, and are organized into three categories that configure JSP parameters or extend the page's code: the page directive, include directive, and taglib directive. Scripting elements are subdivided into declarations, expressions, and code fragments, or scriptlets. Comments are used to document the code. The following section introduces JSP elements.

USING JSP SCRIPTING ELEMENTS

As mentioned earlier, JSP has three types of directives: page directives, include directives, and taglib directives. In the following sections, you learn about the first two directives. Among these directives, the page directive is the most complicated. It supports a wide range of attributes and functionalities.

Using JSP Page Directives

Page directive attributes apply to the entire JSP page; you use them to perform tasks such as setting the script language, importing Java classes, configuring the output buffer, and controlling the session. You can use the page directive anywhere in the JSP file, but it's good coding style to place it at the top of the file.

The basic syntax of the page directive is as follows:

<%@ page attribute1="value1" attribute2="value2" attribute3=... %>

Import Attribute

The **import** attribute describes the types (usually in Java class) that are available to the scripting environment. A Java **class** is a data type containing data members and methods. Java provides many prewritten classes, and lets you write your own classes. Classes enable the programmer to model objects that have **attributes** (represented as data members) and **behaviors** (represented as methods). You can use these data members or methods in your JSP code. For example, the class Date contains useful methods that deal with dates and times; you can declare an object of type Date from this class and use this object reference to handle dates and times. Once a class has been defined, the class name can be used to declare objects of the class. However, before you can use these prewritten classes or your own classes in your JSP code, you need to specify where these classes can be found. Java classes are grouped in a collection called a package. Such **packages** are referred to collectively as the Java class library or the **Java Applications Programming Interface (Java API)**.

Java contains hundreds of classes you can use in your JSP code. These classes are grouped into a number of packages. Packages are organized in a hierarchy, just as you have nested subdirectories on your hard disk. You can use the public classes in a package in two ways. The first is simply to give the full name of the package. For example, you can use

`<%= new java.util.Date() %>` to retrieve the time from your Web server. To use the class Date, you could include the entire path with the class name, although that approach is tedious. The simpler and more common approach is to use the import attribute of the page directive. When a Java class is imported to a JSP page, you can reference this class without explicitly specifying the class package names. Suppose that in your JSP code, you want to use the larger of two integer variables, such as var1 and var2. Without using any classes, you have to write code to compare the values of the two variables and then decide which of them is greater. For example, you could write the following code:

```
<% int theLargerOne = var1;
     if(var1 < var2){
        theLargerOne = var2;
     }
%>
```

A class named Math has a method called max that helps to decide which of the two numbers is greater. You can use this method to perform the same task as the previous code.

```
<% int theLargerOne = Math.max(var1, var2); %>
```

Notice that this code does not specify where to find the Math class. In fact, the following packages are imported automatically: java.lang.*, javax.servlet.*, javax.servlet.jsp.*, javax.servlet.http.*, and possibly some server-specific classes. A package name followed by the ".*" string means that all the public classes in this package are available to this JSP page. Because the class Math is in the java.lang.Math package, you do not need to import the Math class to use it in your JSP code.

Session Attribute

The HTTP protocol is a stateless protocol; that is, it maintains its state across multiple requests not supported within the protocol itself. What if you want to hold client information across multiple requests? For example, in an online shopping system, each item ordered must be added to a client's ongoing order. The order must maintain its state, and each order must be associated with a customer. JSP solves this problem by providing support for session management, a mechanism used to turn the HTTP stateless protocol into a stateful protocol. A **session** begins when any user requests a JSP page for the first time. The session attribute specifies how the page uses the predefined session object in JSP. If the attribute value is true, then the predefined (implicit object) session is bound to the existing session if one is running; otherwise, a new session is created and bound to the implicit session object. If the session attribute is not specified, the default setting is true. If the attribute value is false, then no session is created, and any attempt to access the Session object results in errors at the time the JSP is translated into a servlet. In the following steps, you learn how the session attribute works.

To work with session attributes:

1. Open a new document in a text editor, such as Notepad, and type the following code:

```
<%@ page import="java.util.*" session="true" %>
Is this a new session? <%= session.isNew() %><br>
Current time: <%= new Date() %> <br>
<% Date date = new Date(session.getCreationTime()); %>
The session created on: <%= date %><br>
```

2. Save the file as **example2.jsp** in the Chap15\Chapter folder of your workfolder. Then close Notepad.
3. If any browser windows are open, exit the browser.
4. Start your browser and load the page using the following URL. Substitute the name of your workfolder where *workfolder* appears:

   http://localhost:8080/*workfolder*/Chap15/Chapter/example2.jsp

   The page shown in Figure 15-2 appears.

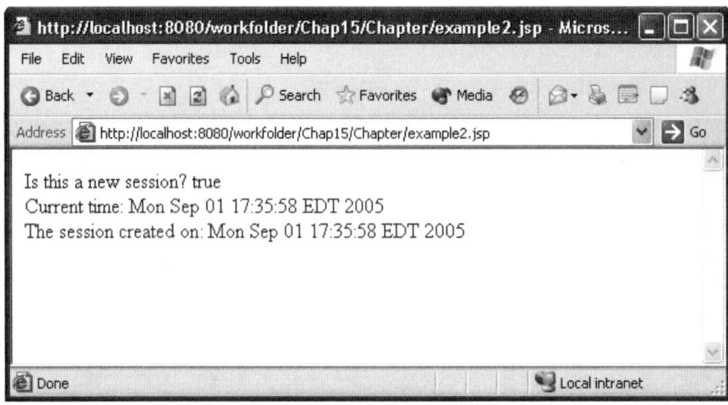

Figure 15-2 Session attribute example

To create a session, you must exit all browser windows and then open your browser and load a page. A session begins when a user requests any JSP page for the first time. Requesting an HTML page does not start a session. If you loaded a JSP page, then a session is already running (assuming it has not expired yet). Your page indicates that the session is not new, and lists when the session was created.

In example2.jsp, the session attribute is set to true. So the implicit Session object is created when a user requests any JSP file for the first time. If you request this page again (by clicking the Refresh button on the browser), a session is already running, so the page indicates that the session is not new. That is, the implicit Session object is bound to the existing session.

Buffer Attribute

The buffer attribute indicates that you manually control when the HTML output stream is sent back to the client browser. The buffer attribute specifies the size of the buffer used by the implicit out variable. Use of this attribute takes one of the two forms:

```
<%@ page buffer="sizekb" %>
<%@ page buffer="none" %>
```

If the value is none, there is no buffering and all output is written directly to clients. If a buffer is specified, output is buffered with a buffer size not less than the specified size. For example, `<%@ page buffer="16kb" %>` means that the document content should be buffered and not sent to the client until at least 16 kilobytes have been accumulated or the page is completed. The default buffer size is server specific, but must be at least 8 kilobytes.

The size of the buffer can only be specified in kilobytes, and the suffix "kb" is mandatory. In the following steps, you set the buffer attribute to see how the buffer attribute affects the output stream that is sent back to client.

To set a buffer attribute:

1. Open a new file in a text editor, such as Notepad, and type the following code:

```
<%@ page buffer="16kb" %>
The buffer attribute is set to "16kb"<br>
<hr align=left width=250 color=red>
Let's send some text to the HTML output stream<br>
The content is buffered.
<% out.clear(); %>
The buffered content is cleared from the buffer.<br>
```

2. Save this page as **example3.jsp** in the Chap15\Chapter folder of your workfolder. Then close Notepad.

3. Open your browser and load this page using the following URL. Substitute the name of your workfolder where *workfolder* appears:

   http://localhost:8080/*workfolder*/Chap15/Chapter/example3.jsp

   The page shown in Figure 15-3 appears.

15

In this example, the buffer size is set to 16 kilobytes. That means the output stream is sent back to the client until the buffered content reaches the buffer size or until this page is complete. The content in this page requires fewer kilobytes than the buffer size. Therefore, to test whether the content is buffered before it is sent to the client, you use the implicit variable out and call the clear method to clear the buffered content from the output stream. The method `out.clear()` clears whatever is buffered in the output stream. Therefore, the previous buffered content is not sent to the client. All buffered content before you call the `out.clear()` method is discarded.

Figure 15-3 Output stream and buffer attribute

Even if you set the buffer attribute to false, the JSP container, such as the Tomcat server you use in this text, may still do some buffering, so the content might not be sent immediately. You can force the buffered content to be sent immediately by calling the flush method of the implicit out variable.

IsThreadSafe Attribute

Suppose you are designing a Web page that assigns each visitor a user ID when the user visits your Web site for the first time. The following code segment assigns an ID to visitors:

```
<%! int idNumber = 0; %>
<%
    String userID = "Your user id is: " + idNumber;
    out.println(userID);
    idNumber++;
%>
```

The code `<%! int idNumber = 0; %>` declares the variable of idNumber with the initial value 0. The first visitor is assigned 0 and the value increments by 1, so the second visitor is assigned 1, and then the value increments by 1 and so on. Each request for a JSP page is processed through a thread. A **thread** is a process that handles client requests by executing the code sequentially. Each client request for this page generates a thread that requests access to this code segment. Assume the current value stored in the variable idNumber is 10. Joe requests this page and a thread called Thread A is generated to execute this code segment. Shortly after, Lynne visits this page and another thread called Thread B is generated. So two threads are executing the code segment simultaneously. Within Thread A, after Joe is assigned the ID number 10, the code `out.println(userID)` is executed. Before executing the next statement to increment the value stored in the idNumber variable, Thread B executes the code and assigns Lynne the value stored in the variable, which is still 10. Now Thread A updates the value of the variable, so the value of the variable is 11. Then Thread B updates the value also, so that after the two requests have been processed, the value stored in the variable idNumber is 12. Therefore the ID 11 is never assigned to a visitor. In such a scenario, the two visitors are assigned the same user ID. To prevent this from happening, you must not allow more than one visitor (one thread) to access this code segment at the same time. After a thread enters the block of code, no other thread can enter the same block until the first one exits (in other words, finishes the execution of the code block). Another term for exclusively accessing the code block is **synchronization**. JSP handles synchronization by using the isThreadSafe attribute.

As you know, your JSP page is ultimately compiled into a Java servlet class. The isThreadSafe attribute indicates whether the generated servlet is capable of responding to multiple simultaneous requests safely. Use of the isThreadSafe attribute takes one of the following forms:

```
<%@ page isThreadSafe= "true" %>
<%@ page isThreadSafe="false" %>
```

If the isThreadSafe attribute is set to true, you can assume that executing users' requests at the same time does not cause conflicts from an unexpected ordering of thread executions. If this attribute value is set to false, no more than one thread can execute the JSP code simultaneously. In this case, if a thread executes the code segment, the next thread must wait until the first one finishes execution. This means the system queues all requests and processes a single request at a time.

In some cases (such as page access counts), you may not care if two visitors are occasionally assigned the same ID value, but in other cases (such as user IDs), identical values can mean disaster. If you do not specify this attribute, the default value is set to true.

LINKING TO EXTERNAL FILES

When you design a Web application, you may want to provide the same navigation links and footer on each page. To do so, you could write the code for these elements on each page. However, this is tedious and prone to error. In JSP, you can avoid this scenario by placing the code containing the navigation links and footer in separate files. You can include other HTML or JSP files within a JSP file so that when you need to modify the link or footer, you modify only two files: the navigation links file and the footer file.

You can apply this technique when all pages in a Web application share common elements, such as headers, footers, and navigation bars. There are two ways to include files in a JSP page: static includes, via the JSP include directive; and dynamic includes, via the JSP include action.

Including Files at Page Translation Time

The JSP include directive has the following syntax:

<%@ include file=" relative URL " %>

When you use this method to include a file, the content of the specified page is read at translation time and merged with the original page when the page is requested for the first time.

The included file can contain only static content, such as HTML and plain text, or it can be a JSP file. Its contents are merged with the page that includes it, and the resulting page is converted into a servlet at translation time. In the following steps, you work with the include directive.

To use the include directive:

1. Open a new document in Notepad and type the following code:

```
<table border=1 cellspacing=0 cellpadding=2>
<tr><td bgcolor="#fffccc"><a href="#">Series</a></td>
    <td bgcolor="#fffccc"><a href="#">Student Download</a></td>
    <td bgcolor="#fffccc"><a href="#">Instructor Resources</a>
</td>
</tr>
<tr>
    <td bgcolor="#dddccc"><a href="#">Home</a></td>
    <td bgcolor="#dddccc"><a href="#">About Us</a></td>
    <td bgcolor="#dddccc"><a href="#">Contact</a></td>
    <td bgcolor="#dddccc"><a href="#">Find Your Rep</a></td>
</tr>
</table>
```

2. Save this page as **navigation.html** in the Chap15\Chapter folder of your workfolder. Then close the document.
3. Open a new document in Notepad and type the following code:

```
<%@ include file="navigation.html" %>
<hr color=red>
The navigation bar is merged from the included file
"<b>navigation.html</b>"
```

4. Save this file as **example4.jsp** in the Chap15\Chapter folder of your workfolder. Then close Notepad.
5. Open your browser and load **example4.jsp** using the following URL. Substitute the name of your workfolder where *workfolder* appears:

   http://localhost:8080/*workfolder*/Chap15/Chapter/example4.jsp

   The page shown in Figure 15-4 appears.

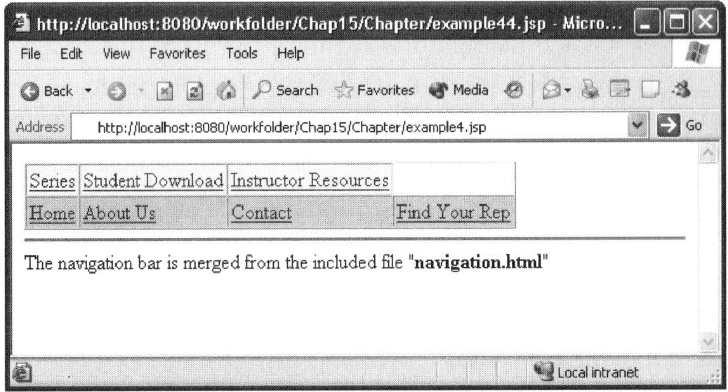

Figure 15-4 Include directive

As shown in Figure 15-4, the navigation links are merged into the original page. Now you can add more links to navigation.html.

To add links to navigation.html:

1. Open **navigation.html** in Notepad and add links as shown in the following bold text:

```
<table border=1 cellspacing=0 cellpadding=2>
<tr><td bgcolor="#fffccc"><a href="#">Series</a></td>
    <td bgcolor="#fffccc"><a href="#">Student Download</a></td>
    <td bgcolor="#fffccc"><a href="#">Instructor Resources</a>
</td>
    <td bgcolor="#fffccc"><a href="#">Bookstore</a></td>
    <td bgcolor="#fffccc"><a href="#">Support</a></td>
</tr>
<tr>
    <td bgcolor="#dddccc"><a href="#">Home</a></td>
    <td bgcolor="#dddccc"><a href="#">About Us</a></td>
    <td bgcolor="#dddccc"><a href="#">Contact</a></td>
    <td bgcolor="#dddccc"><a href="#">Find Your Rep</a></td>
    <td bgcolor="#dddccc"><a href="#">
       <input type=text size=10 name=rep></a></td>
    <td bgcolor="#dddccc"><a href="#">
       <input type=button value="search"></a></td>
</tr>
</table>
```

2. Save and close the navigation.html file. Reload **example4.jsp** in the browser.

Note that nothing changed. The newly added links are not displayed on the page. The content in the included file is merged into the appropriate page when the page is requested for the first time. That is, the content is merged when the page is translated into its corresponding servlet. The servlet converted from the JSP stays in memory until the JSP container removes it from memory, or until the server is down. Therefore, even though you modify the included content, when the original file (the file that contains the included page) is requested again, the servlet remains the same, so the content merged from the included file is not changed. That is why the include directive is called a static include.

You can indicate to the JSP container that the JSP page was modified by adding a space anywhere in the JSP. Then the JSP page is translated when it is next requested.

Including Files at Request Time

You can include files at request time by using the `<jsp: include>` action. It uses the following syntax:

<jsp:include page="Relative URL" flush="true" />

The included file can be a plain HTML page, a CGI script, a servlet, or another JSP page. The action does not merge the actual contents of the specified page at translation time. The page is included each time the JSP page is requested. That means whenever you modify the included file, the changes are reflected the next time the page is requested. You use the flush property to flush the output buffer of the current page before the new file is included. Currently, this must be set to true.

In contrast to the JSP include directive, the processing of the included file happens at the page request time. The output of the inserted file is inserted into the current page when the action tag is being processed at request time.

To include files at request time:

1. Open a new file in Notepad, and type the following code:

```
<HR>
Copyright &Copy 2005 CT.
```

2. Save this page as **footer.html** in the Chap15\Chapter folder of your work-folder. Then close the document.
3. Open a new document in Notepad and type the following code:

```
The footer is merged from the included file "<b>footer.html</b>"
<jsp:include page="footer.html" flush="true"/>
```

4. Save the file as **example5.jsp** in the Chap15\Chapter folder of your work-folder. Then close the document.

5. Open your browser and load **example5.jsp** using the following URL. Substitute the name of your workfolder where *workfolder* appears:

   http://localhost:8080/*workfolder*/Chap15/Chapter/example5.jsp

   The page shown in Figure 15-5 appears.

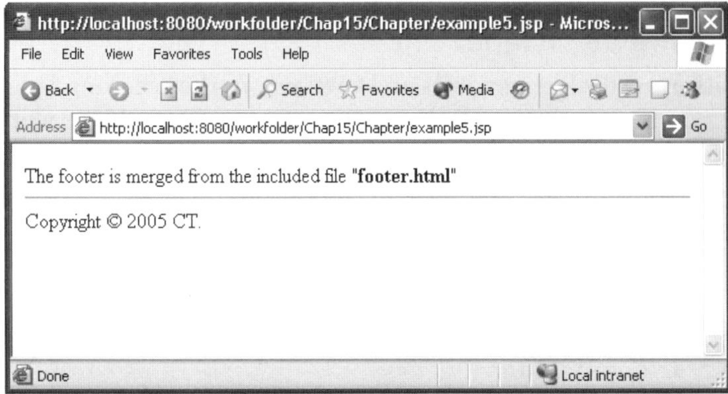

Figure 15-5 Include action

6. The footer is displayed on this page. Now modify footer.html by adding the text shown in bold:

```
<hr>
Copyright &Copy 2005 CT. All rights reserved.
```

7. Save and close footer.html. Close Notepad, open your browser and load **example5.jsp** using the following URL. Substitute the name of your workfolder where *workfolder* appears:

   http://localhost:8080/*workfolder*/Chap15/Chapter/example5.jsp

   The updated page with the new content is shown in Figure 15-6.

15

Figure 15-6 Include action updates the content of the included file

UNDERSTANDING DECLARATIONS, EXPRESSIONS, AND SCRIPTLETS

A JSP page needs scripting code (normally Java code) to make it a dynamic Web page. You need to use scripting elements to insert the Java code. There are three forms of scripting elements: declarations, expressions, and scriptlets.

JSP Declarations

You use a **declaration** to declare variables and methods in the scripting language used in a JSP page. The variables and methods declared are inserted into the servlet class generated when the JSP container translates the JSP page. A declaration has the following syntax:

<%! variable and method %>

For example, consider the page counter.jsp in the following code:

```
<%! private int count = 0;
    public int getCount(){
      return ++count;
    }
%>
```

The variable count in the previous example is initialized when the JSP page is initialized and is available to the getCount() method, which is declared after it.

Declarations do not produce any output to the output stream. If you try to output to the output stream, an exception occurs.

JSP Expressions

A JSP expression inserts the value of the expression directly into the output stream. It has the following syntax:

<%= expression(s) %>

Following is the counter.jsp page, modified so that the counter number is displayed:

```
<%! private int count = 0;
    public int getCount(){
      return ++count;
    }
%>
Welcome! This is the <%= getCount() %> time this page has
been visited!
```

When this page is accessed, the expression getCount() is evaluated, the value returned by the expression is an int value, (1, 2,...,) which is converted into a string and inserted into the output stream.

JSP Scriptlets

A scriptlet is a code fragment that is executed at request-processing time. Basically, you can embed any valid Java language code between the <% and %> tags. The basic syntax is as follows:

<% scriptlets %>

Below is the JSP script page to display a friendly greeting message.

To display a greeting message:

1. Open a new document in Notepad and type the following code:

```
<%@ page import="java.util.Calendar" %>
<%! private int count = 0;
    public int getCount(){
      return ++count;
    }
%>
<% Calendar calendar = Calendar.getInstance();
   int hourOfDay = calendar.get(Calendar.HOUR_OF_DAY);
   if(hourOfDay <= 12){
%>
   Good morning!
<% }
   else if(hourOfDay <= 18){
%>
   Good Afternoon!
<% }
     else{
%>
     Good Evening!
<%   } %>
The number of times this page has been visited is:
<%= getCount() %>
```

2. Save the file as **example6.jsp** in the Chap15\Chapter folder of your workfolder. Then close the document.

3. Open your browser and load **example6.jsp** using the following URL. Substitute the name of your workfolder where *workfolder* appears:

   http://localhost:8080/*workfolder*/Chap15/Chapter/example6.jsp

   The page shown in Figure 15-7 appears.

4. Reload this page several times; the page counter increases every time the page is reloaded.

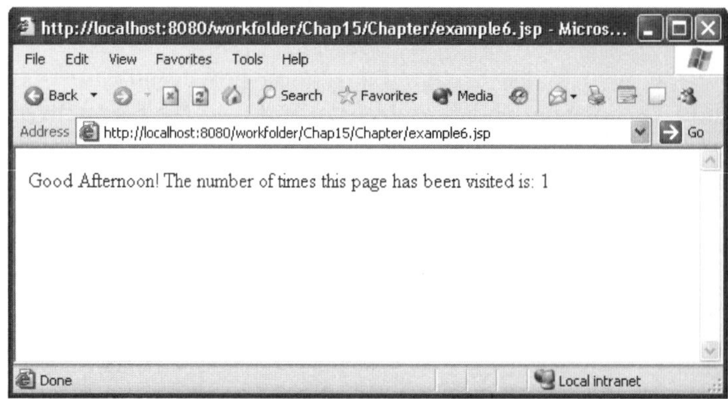

Figure 15-7 Greeting message with scriptlets

Note how the if-else structures are created by the multiple scriptlets.

Unlike JSP declarations, in which you can declare variables and methods only, you can include any JSP scripts in JSP scriptlets. You can declare variables, define methods, and send output to the output stream. But, the variables defined in JSP declarations and JSP scriptlets have different durations. The **duration** of a variable (also called its lifetime) is the period during which that variable exists in memory. Some variables exist briefly, some are repeatedly created and destroyed, and others exist for the entire execution of your Web application.

JSP has variables of **instance duration**. Variables of instance duration exist from the point at which the corresponding servlet that defines them is loaded into memory, usually when a JSP page is requested for the first time (when the JSP is converted to a servlet). JSP has other variables of **local duration**. Local variables are created when a program control reaches their declaration; they exist while the block in which they are declared is active, and they are destroyed when the block in which they are declared is exited. All variables declared in the JSP declaration have instance duration; all variables declared in scriptlets have local duration. In the following steps, you learn the difference between the variables declared in an JSP declaration and those declared in scriptlets.

To declare variables:

1. Open a new document in Notepad and type the following code:

```
<%! int count1 = 0; %>
<% int count2 = 0; %>
<% count1++; count2++; %>
Use the counter variable declared in JSP declaration<br>
<b>This page has been accessed
   <font size=6 color=red><%= count1 %> </font>
   <% if(count1 == 1) { %>
       time.
   <% }else{ %>
        times.
```

```
   <% } %>
   </b><br><br>
Use the counter variable declared in JSP scriptlet<br>
<b>This page has been accessed
   <font size=6 color=red><%= count2 %> </font>
   <% if(count2 == 1) { %>
       time.
   <% }else{ %>
        times.
   <% } %>
   </b><br><br>
<a href="example7.jsp">Reload this page</a>
```

2. Save the file as **example7.jsp** in the Chap15\Chapter folder of your work-folder. Then close the document.
3. Load this page using the following URL. Substitute the name of your work-folder where *workfolder* appears:

   http://localhost:8080/*workfolder*/Chap15/Chapter/example7.jsp

4. When this page is displayed, you see that both counter variables provide the correct information. Click the **Reload this page** link to reload the page several times. A page similar to Figure 15-8 is displayed.

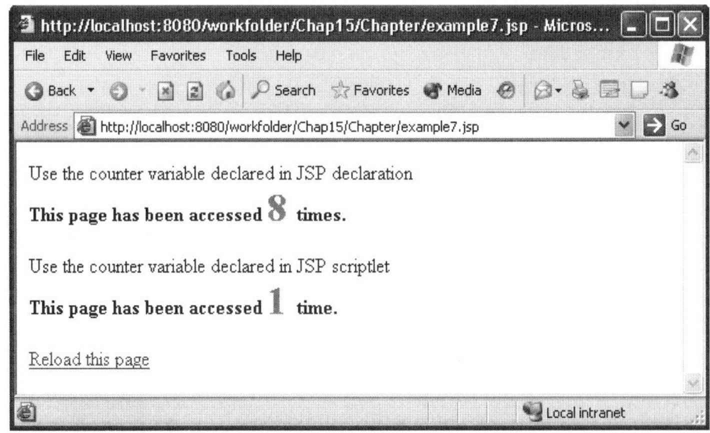

Figure 15-8 Variable duration

Each time the page is reloaded, the page counter variable declared in the JSP declaration increments by one, but the counter variable declared in the JSP scriptlet does not increment, as shown in Figure 15-8. Because the variable count1 declared in the JSP declaration has instance duration, this variable is loaded when you request this JSP page for the first time, and the variable stays in the memory. Subsequent requests for this page all use the same variable: count1, which exists in memory already. However, the variable count2 declared in the JSP scriptlet is created and initialized to 0 each time the page is requested.

15

INCLUDING COMMENTS

Comments improve your program's readability and are ignored when the program is translated. JSP has two types of comments: content comments and JSP comments. Content comments use the same syntax as in HTML:

<!-- *content comments* -->

Content comments are sent back to the client via the response output stream in the generated document. Because they are comments, they are not displayed on the browser, but can be viewed via the browser's View Source command. Content comments can have dynamic data by including the JSP expression inside the tag, as shown in the following example.

```
<!-- JSP Page = <%=
javax.servlet.http.HttpUtils.getRequestURL(request)%> -->
```

If you include this comment in your JSP page, the URL of the real page replaces the JSP expression when the page is requested. Then you can view it in the source code.

JSP comments usually document what the JSP page is doing or comment out portions of the codes that are not needed. Those comments, also called server-side comments, are not sent back to the client and can only be viewed in the original JSP page. When the JSP container processes the page, the JSP comments are ignored. Use of JSP comments takes one of the following three forms:

<%--
multiple line comments
-- %>
<%
    /* *Multiple line*
       comments */
%>
<% //*single line comment* %>

Every JSP page should begin with a comment describing the purpose of the page.

PROCESSING CLIENT REQUESTS

To process a client request, the Web server must execute the following steps:

1. Retrieve the data related to the request.
2. Process the data.
3. Send output to client.

When you use scripting elements in a JSP page, a number of objects are made available by the JSP container. These objects are called **implicit objects**, because you can use them without explicitly declaring them in your page. These objects are instances of classes defined by the servlet and JSP specifications. The available objects include request, response, out, session, application, and exception.

The terms variables and objects are used interchangeably in this chapter. If a variable has a type of class, it is called an object. You can imply that all objects are variables, but not all variables are objects.

In the following sections, you focus on how to use a request object to process clients' requests.

Each time you request a JSP page, the JSP container creates a new instance of the Request object. This object contains information about the request and the invoked page, including headers, client and server information, request URL, cookies, session information, and the input data.

You can use these implicit objects in JSP expressions or scriptlets, but not in a declaration.

Getting Header Information

HTTP requests can have a number of associated HTTP headers. These headers provide some extra information about the request. You can use the header information to customize the content you send to a client. There are dozens of possible headers; Table 15-1 lists several commonly used request headers.

Table 15-1 Common HTTP request headers

Header name	Description
Accept	Specify the media type, Multipurpose Internet Multimedia Extensions (MIME), the client prefers to accept. All media types are separated by commas. For example, the image format a browser prefers.
User-Agent	Gives information about the client software, including the browser name and version as well as information about the client computer. For example, Mozilla/4.0 (compatible; MSIE 6.0b; Windows NT 5.1) indicates it is Microsoft Internet Explorer running on Windows XP.
Referer	Gives the URL of the document that refers to the requested URL (that is, the document that contains the link the client followed to access this document)
Accept-Language	The default language setting on the client machine

To retrieve the value of a header, use the following syntax:

request.getHeader("*header name*");

This method returns a string containing information about that header passed as a parameter. For example, the code request.getHeader("Referer") returns the value of the header "Referer." Header names are not case sensitive, so, for example, request.getHeader("Referer") and request.getHeader("referer") are interchangeable. If a header name is not supported on a request, the getHeader method returns a null value.

The request object provides the method getHeaderNames, which returns an enumeration object containing all headers in the request. In the following steps, you use this method to get all header names and then use these header names to get corresponding header values.

To retrieve header names and values:

1. Open a new document in Notepad and type the following code:

```
<%@ page import="java.util.*" %>
<%
  String action = request.getParameter("action");
  if(action !=null && action.equals("getHeader")){
%>
<%
  Enumeration enu = request.getHeaderNames();
%>
<table border=1>
<tr>
  <th align=center colspan=2>Get Header Information Using
request object</th>
</tr>
<tr>
  <th align=center>Header Name</th>
  <th align=center>Header Value</th>
</tr>
<% while(enu.hasMoreElements()){
     String headerName = (String)enu.nextElement();
     Enumeration enum = request.getHeaders(headerName);
%>
     <tr>
        <td align=center> <%= headerName %> </td>
        <td align=center> <%= request.getHeader(headerName) %>
        </td>
     </tr>
<% } %>
</table>
<% } else{
%>
<a href="example8.jsp?action=getHeader">Request a page and
display headers</a>
<% } %>
```

2. Save this page as **example8.jsp** in the Chap15\Chapter folder of your work-folder. Then close Notepad.
3. Load this page using the following URL. Substitute the name of your work-folder where *workfolder* appears:

   http://localhost:8080/*workfolder*/Chap15/Chapter/example8.jsp

4. Click the link on this page. A page appears similar to the one shown in Figure 15-9.

Get Header Information Using request object

Header Name	Header Value
accept	image/gif, image/x-xbitmap, image/jpeg, image/pjpeg, application/vnd.ms-powerpoint, application/vnd.ms-excel, application/msword, */*
referer	http://localhost:8080/workfolder/Chap15/Chapter/example8.jsp
accept-language	en-us,zh;q=0.7,zh-cn;q=0.3
accept-encoding	gzip, deflate
user-agent	Mozilla/4.0 (compatible; MSIE 6.0; Windows NT 5.1; Q312461; .NET CLR 1.0.3705)
host	localhost:8080
connection	Keep-Alive
cookie	JSESSIONID=0332F3F03274837041D4699531578593

Figure 15-9 Header information

In this example, request.getHeaderNames() returns an enumeration of all header names on the current request. Two methods associated with an Enumeration object obtain all header names, and then the Request object method getHeader obtains the header values.

In some situations, you may want to send different content based on which browser a client uses. In this case, you must first determine the browser type. In the following steps, you identify the browser and send a different message based on the browser type.

To identify the browser and send a conditional message:

1. Open a new document in Notepad and type the following code:

```
<% String userAgent = request.getHeader("User-Agent"); %>
<% if(userAgent.indexOf("MSIE") != -1){ %>
    You are using Internet Explorer.
<% }else if(userAgent.indexOf("Netscape") != -1){ %>
```

```
        You are using Netscape Navigator.
    <% }else{ %>
        You are using a browser other than Netscape Navigator
     or Internet Explorer.
    <% } %>
```

2. Save the file as **example9.jsp** in the Chap15\Chapter folder of your workfolder. Then close Notepad.
3. Load this page using the following URL. Substitute the name of your workfolder where *workfolder* appears:

   http://localhost:8080/*workfolder*/Chap15/Chapter/example9.jsp

   If you use Internet Explorer, the page shown in Figure 15-10 appears.

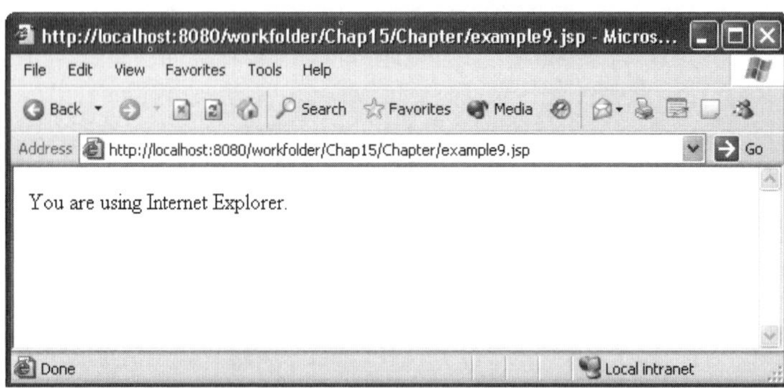

Figure 15-10 Detecting browser

Try to load this page in various browsers, if possible. This JSP code should detect the browser and display the appropriate message. In this example, the method of the request object getHeader("user-agent") returns a string that contains the client's browser and operating system information. If the client uses Microsoft Internet Explorer, the string should contain a substring "MSIE," so the method indexOf("MSIE") returns the index of the substring. If it returns –1, it means that the string does not contain "MSIE" and you continue testing for other browsers. If the client browser is Netscape Navigator, the string should contain a substring "Netscape." If the client is using Netscape Navigator, the method call indexOf("Netscape") should return the index of the substring other than –1.

Getting Client and Server Information

Companies like to know where the visitors to their Web sites come from. With this information, a company can develop marketing strategies to target various audiences. You can easily collect visitor information using a Request object. The Request object provides various methods you can use to retrieve client and server information, including the client computer name, client computer IP, Web server name, and Web server port. Every computer has an Internet Protocol (IP) address when the computer is connected to the Internet. The IP is an identifier for a computer or device on a TCP/IP network. Networks using the TCP/IP protocol route messages based on the IP address of the destination. An IP address can be randomly assigned to a computer or a computer might be assigned a static address. Regardless how it is assigned, the IP address must be unique. A computer may also have a name associated with its IP. You can get all this sort of client and server information as follows: the request.getRemoteAddr() returns the IP address of the client; the request.getRemoteHost() returns the name of the client computer (if the computer does not have a name, then the IP address is returned); the request.getServerName() returns the Web server name; the request.getServerPort returns the port number on which the Web server is running. In the following steps, you use these methods for getting the client and server information.

To retrieve client and server information:

1. Open a new document in Notepad and type the following code:

```
Client Information:<br>
<font face="Arial" size=1>
Your computer name: <%= request.getRemoteHost() %> <br>
Your computer IP address: <%= request.getRemoteAddr() %>
</font>
<br><br>
The Web server information:<br>
<font face="Arial" size=1>
The Web server name: <%= request.getServerName() %><br>
The running port number of Web server:
<%= request.getServerPort() %>
</font>
```

2. Save the file as **example10.jsp** in the Chap15\Chapter folder of your work-folder. Then close Notepad.

3. Load this page using the following URL. Substitute the name of your work-folder where *workfolder* appears:

   http://localhost:8080/*workfolder*/Chap15/Chapter/example10.jsp

   This page displays client and Web server information, as shown in Figure 15-11.

15

Form Collections

In the following sections, you learn to use other elements to build a form. These input elements include text, password, text area, hidden fields, select, check box, and radio button inputs.

Text, Password, Text Area, and Hidden Fields

The input elements in a form can hold data that is sent to the Web server for processing. For example, when you fill in the text boxes on a form and click the Submit button, all of the values you entered are sent to the Web server. The common input elements include text fields, password fields, hidden fields, and multiple lines of text, or text areas.

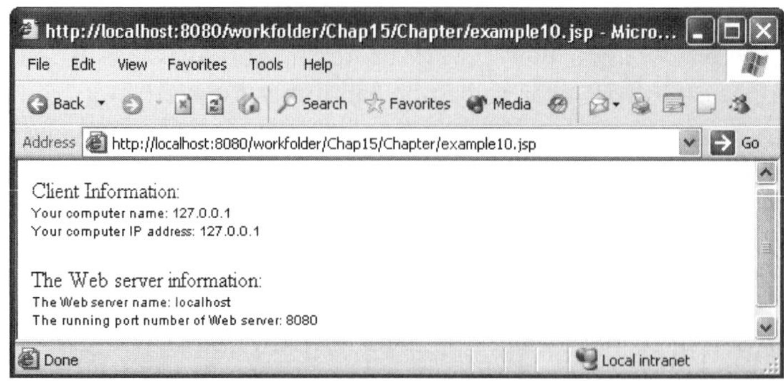

Figure 15-11 Client and Web server information

The **text fields** are used to accept single-line information, such as names, addresses, job titles, and telephone numbers. A text field is one of the most versatile input elements. There are three additional attributes that can be used with a text field:

- maxlength—Sets the maximum allowable length of the field, in characters
- size—Sets the width, in characters, of the input box that appears on the page
- value—Sets an initial value for the text field

The following sample code creates a field that handles state abbreviations, and includes a default value.

```
<input type="text" name="state" size="4" maxlength="2" value="VA">
```

Notice the difference in the values for maxlength and size attributes. The size attribute is larger, allowing for more display room, although the input is still limited to two characters by maxlength. This is done to compensate for the way some browsers handle the text. If size were only two characters, certain two-letter pairs wouldn't fit in the box for display.

The **password fields** are similar to the text fields, except that the characters typed into the text box by the user are converted to asterisks or bullet symbols for privacy. Use of password fields takes the following form:

<input type="password" name="*fieldname*">

All the attributes associated with text fields can be applied to password fields.

The **hidden fields** are another type of text field, but they are not displayed. A hidden field provides a way to send information that cannot be changed by the user to the server. Hidden fields are often used to pass information from one page to another. For example, if a user types a name or address on one form, the JSP script processes it and includes it on a second or follow-up form that retains the information in a hidden field. This makes it easier for the user because the user doesn't have to supply the information again. Use of hidden fields takes the following form:

<input type="hidden" name="*fieldname*" value="*hidden data*">

Even though the field is hidden from view on the browser, the user can still see it by viewing the HTML source code. Therefore, the hidden input field is not a good place to store private data.

The TextArea input type uses its own tag. It accepts multiple lines. A TextArea allows the user to enter larger amounts of information. The syntax for a TextArea is as follows:

<TextArea name="*fieldname*" rows="*numberOfRows*" cols="*numberOfColumns*">
</TextArea>

The rows and cols attributes are used to control the number of rows and columns displayed, respectively.

In the following steps, you use all of these inputs in a Web site that posts course materials. To access these materials, the client must set up an account first. The example Web site uses three pages; the first page asks a client to set up a user ID and a password; the second page collects the client's information; the third one displays all information collected from the first two pages.

To create Web pages with input elements:

1. Open a new document in Notepad and type the following code:

```
<form action="example11-2.jsp" method="POST">
<table align=center border=0>
<tr><td colspan=2>Get a CT ID and password for access to course
materials online!</td>
</tr>
<tr><td colspan=2><hr width=400></td>
</tr>
<tr><td align=right>User ID:</td>
    <td align=left><input type=text name="userID" size=15></td>
</tr>
<tr><td align=right>Password:</td>
    <td align=left><input type=password name="password" size=15>
</td>
</tr>
<tr><td colspan=2 align=center><input type=submit value="Submit">
</td>
</tr>
<tr><td colspan=2><hr width=400></td>
</tr></table>
</form>
```

2. Save the file as **example11-1.jsp** in the Chap15\Chapter folder of your workfolder. Then close the document.

3. Open a new document in Notepad and type the following code:

```
<form action="example11-3.jsp" method="POST">
<table align=center border=0>
<tr><td colspan=2>Please provide the following information</td>
```

15

```
</tr>
<tr><td colspan=2><hr width=400></td>
</tr>
<tr><td align=right>Name:</td>
    <td align=left><input type=text name="userName" size=25></td>
</tr>
<tr><td align=right>Address:</td>
    <td align=left><input type=text name=address size=25></td>
</tr>
<tr><td align=right>City:</td>
    <td align=left><input type=text name=city size=25></td>
</tr>
<tr><td align=right>State:</td>
    <td align=left>
      <input type=text name=state size=4 maxlength=2>
      Zip:<input type=text name=zip size=10 maxlength=5>
    </td>
</tr>
<tr><td colspan=2 align=center><input type=submit value="Submit">
</td>
</tr>
<tr><td colspan=2><hr width=400></td>
</tr></table>
<!-- use hidden fields to hold the information collected from
previous form-->
<input type=hidden name=userID value="<%=
request.getParameter("userID") %>">
<input type=hidden name=password value="<%=
request.getParameter("password") %>">
</form>
```

4. Save the file as **example11-2.jsp** in the Chap15\Chapter folder of your workfolder. Then close the document.

5. Open a new document in Notepad and type the following code:

```
Here is the information collected from two previous forms:
<hr width=350 align=left>
User ID: <%= request.getParameter("userID") %><br>
Password: <%= request.getParameter("password") %><br><br>
<%= request.getParameter("userName") %><br>
<%= request.getParameter("address") %><br>
<%= request.getParameter("city")%>
, <%= request.getParameter("state") %>
 <%= request.getParameter("zip") %>
<hr width=350 align=left>
```

6. Save the file as **example11-3.jsp** in the Chap15\Chapter folder of your workfolder. Then close Notepad.

7. Load the page **example11-1.jsp** using the following URL. Substitute the name of your workfolder where *workfolder* appears:

   http://localhost:8080/*workfolder*/Chap15/Chapter/example11-1.jsp

   The page is displayed, as shown in Figure 15-12.

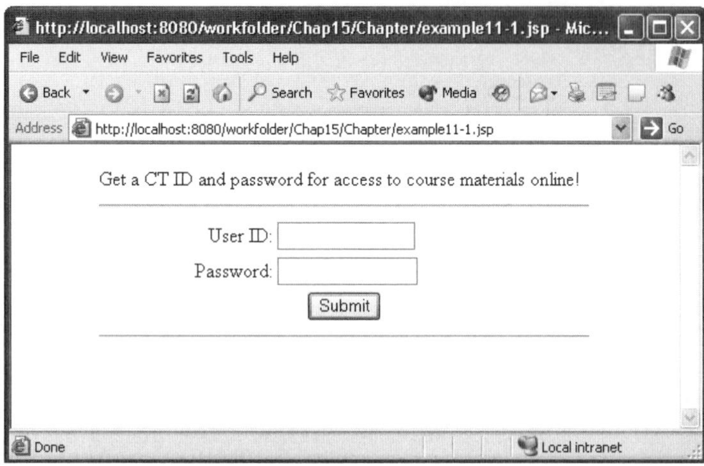

Figure 15-12 Example11-1.jsp

8. Type a **user id** and **password** in the appropriate text fields, and then click the **Submit** button. A new page is displayed, as shown in Figure 15-13. The user id and password information is retrieved and stored in hidden fields on the second form.

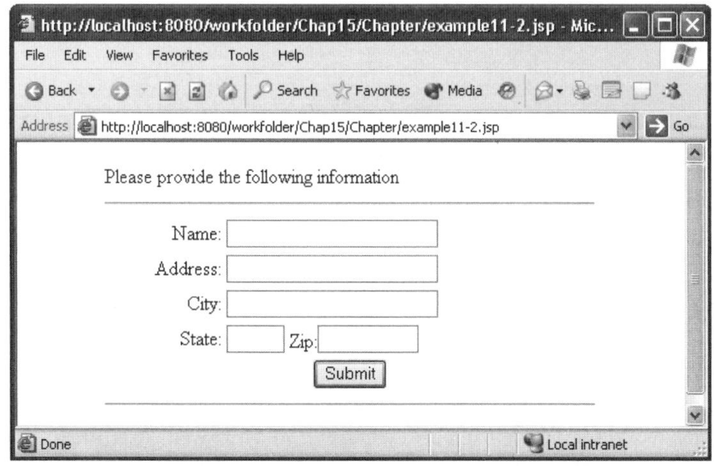

Figure 15-13 Example11-2.jsp

9. On the second form, the client provides a user name and address, and all the information is sent to the third page. The third page retrieves all the information collected on the first two forms and displays the information. The page displayed is similar to the one shown in Figure 15-14.

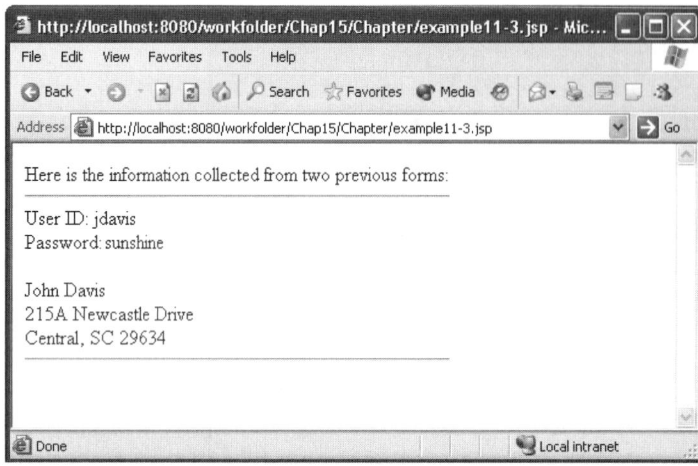

Figure 15-14 Example11-3.jsp

Select Fields

The select input field uses the <select> and </select> tags to provide a list of options from which the user may select. Your browser displays a <select> field as a drop-down list box. The use of the select input field takes the following syntax:

<select name="*fieldname*" size=*n multiple*>
<option value="*value*" selected>*Option1 text*
...additional options
</select>

The size attribute controls how many lines are visible at one time. If you don't specify a value, the size defaults to 1. If the number of options is greater than the size, a list box is displayed. The multiple attribute controls whether users may select multiple items from the list. If omitted, only one item can be selected.

To select multiple items from a scrolling list, hold down the Ctrl key and click the items you want to select.

The option tag is used to add items. It can contain two optional attributes: selected and value. The value attribute of the selected item is submitted as the value of the select field. The option text is the text that follows each option tag. The option text is displayed on the list. If a value attribute is not specified, the value of that option defaults to its option text.

To create a select field:

1. Open a new document in Notepad and type the following code:

```
<form action="example12.jsp" method=POST>
  <select name=state>
    <option value=MI>Michigan
    <option value=NC>North Carolina
    <option >South Carolina
    <option value=VA selected>Virginia
  </select>
  <input type=submit value="Submit">
</form>
```

2. Save the file as **example12.html** in the Chap15\Chapter folder of your workfolder. Then close the document.
3. Open a new document in Notepad and type the following code:

```
The state value you selected is:
<%= request.getParameter("state") %>
<br><br>
<a href="example12.html">Go back and try again</a>
```

4. Save the file as **example12.jsp** in the Chap15\Chapter folder of your work-folder. Then close Notepad.
5. Load **example12.html** using the following URL. Substitute the name of your workfolder where *workfolder* appears:

   http://localhost:8080/*workfolder*/Chap15/Chapter/example12.html

   This page is displayed, as shown in Figure 15-15.
6. Select a state from the list box, and then click the **Submit** button. The selected value is sent to example12.jsp, which processes the value.

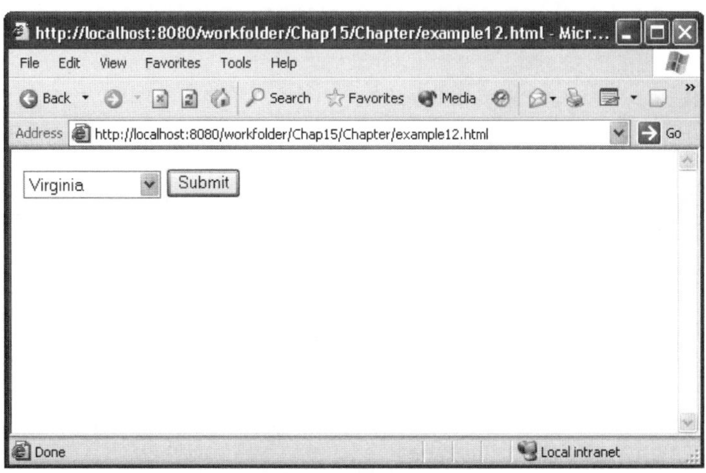

Figure 15-15 Working with a select field

In this example, the selected option defaults to "Virginia." You can select another state and submit the form. The selected option value is displayed. Because the value attribute for "South Carolina" is not set, if you select "South Carolina" from the list, the option text is displayed.

Check Boxes and Radio Buttons

The check box input element is a small box that the user clicks to place or remove a check mark. The use of a check box takes the following syntax:

<input type=*check box name="fieldname"* value="*a value*" CHECKED>*Descriptive text*

The value is what is sent to the Web server if a check box is checked. The checked attribute controls the initial status of the check box. Following a check box, descriptive text indicates what the user is selecting (or not selecting).

The descriptive text for a check box usually comes after the check box. But, it does not matter whether you put the descriptive text before or after its corresponding text.

Radio buttons (often called option buttons) are similar to check boxes, but they present a range of choices. Only one radio button in a group is selected at one time. The use of radio buttons takes the following syntax:

<input type=*radio name="fieldname"* value="*field value*" checked>*Descriptive text*

In the following steps, you use check boxes and radio buttons.

To create check boxes and radio buttons:

1. Open a new document in Notepad and type the following code:

```
<% String gender = request.getParameter("gender");
   String music = request.getParameter("music");
   if( gender !=null){
%>
    Gender: <%= gender %><br>
<% }
   if(music != null) {
%>
   Music types you listen to: <%= request.getParameter("music") %>
<% } %>
<hr width=250 align=left>
<form action="example13.jsp" method="POST">
  Gender: <input type=radio name=gender value="Female">Female
          <input type=radio name=gender value="Male">Male
  <br><br>
  What types of music do you listen to?<br>
  <input type=checkbox name=music value=Rock>Rock
  <input type=checkbox name=music value=Jazz>Jazz
```

```
    <input type=checkbox name=music value=Classical>Classical
    <input type=checkbox name=music value=Pop>Pop
    <br><br>
    <input type=submit value="Submit">
  </form>
  <hr width=250 align=left>
```

2. Save the file as **example13.jsp** in the Chap15\Chapter folder of your work-folder. Then close Notepad.
3. Load this page using the following URL. Substitute the name of your work-folder where *workfolder* appears:

   http://localhost:8080/*workfolder*/Chap15/Chapter/example13.jsp
4. Select a gender, click to check the music type(s) you listen to, and then click the **Submit** button. The information should be displayed on the top of the page, as shown in Figure 15-16.

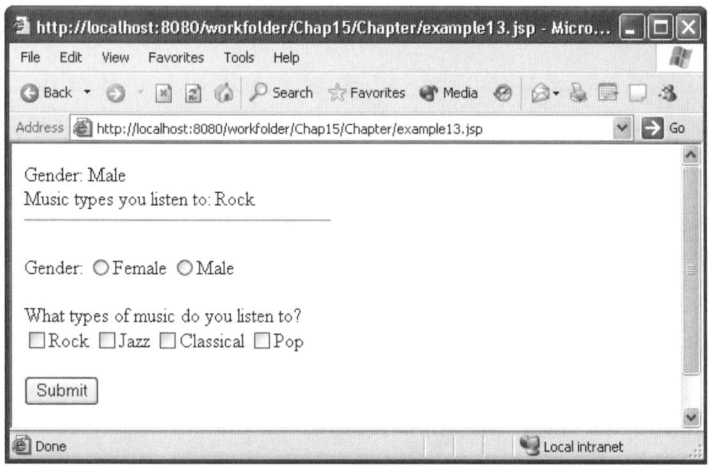

Figure 15-16 Check box and radio button

In the previous steps, if you check more than one music type, only the first checked music type is displayed. In the following section you learn how to handle multiple check box selections.

Working with Arrays

The JSP script you wrote in the previous example can't retrieve more than one selected music type.

To fix this problem, you can assign each check box a different name, but this is not the most efficient method.

In fact, this problem arises whenever multiple values are associated with a single object. Fortunately, the Request object provides another method that you can use to associate all the values with a single form element. The syntax is as follows:

request.getParameterValues("*elementName*");

This method returns a string array containing all the values associated with the element. (If the element name does not exist in the requesting form (that is, no check box or radio button has been selected), it returns null.) To access these values, you must use an array. For example, to get all the checked music types in the previous example, you can use the following code:

```
<% String music[] = request.getParameterValues("music");
   if(music != null && music.length != 0){
      out.println("Music types you listen to: <br>");
    for(int i=0; i<music.length; i++){
      out.println(music[i] + "<br>");
     }
   }
%>
```

In the following steps, you retrieve all the values associated with a select field.

To retrieve values associated with a select field:

1. Open a new document in Notepad and type the following code:

```
What are your favorite fruits?<br>
<form action="example14.jsp" method="POST">
  <select name="fruits" size=4 MULTIPLE>
    <option value="Apple">Apple
    <option value="Grape">Grape
    <option value="Banana">Banana
    <option value="Orange">Orange
    <option value="Peach">Peach
  </select>
  <br>
  <input type=submit value="Submit">
</form>
<hr width=200 align=left>
Your favorite fruits list:<br>
<%
  String fruit[] = request.getParameterValues("fruits");
  if(fruit != null && fruit.length != 0){
    for(int i=0; i<fruit.length; i++){
      out.println(fruit[i] + "<br>");
    }
  }
%>
```

2. Save the file as **example14.jsp** in the Chap15\Chapter folder of your work-folder. Then close Notepad.

3. Load this page using the following URL. Substitute the name of your workfolder where *workfolder* appears:

   http://localhost:8080/*workfolder*/Chap15/Chapter/example14.jsp

   This page is displayed as shown in Figure 15-17.

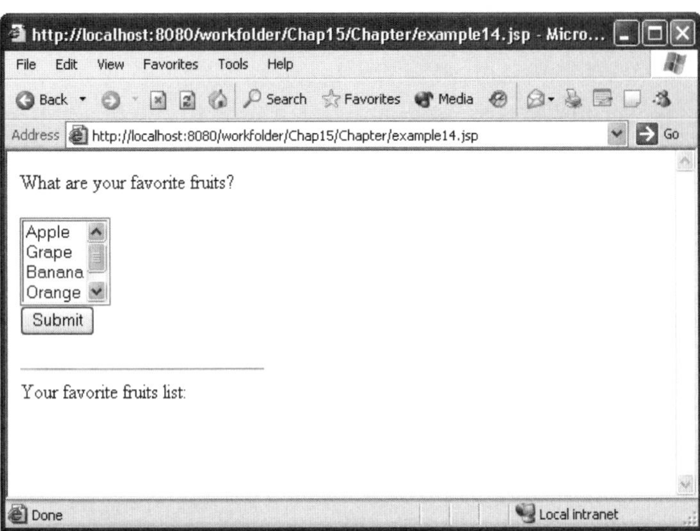

Figure 15-17 Working with arrays

4. Select more than one fruit type, and then submit the form. All the selected fruit types are displayed on your favorite list.

The code String fruit[] = request.getParameterValues("fruits") gets all selected values and assigns the returned values to an array. Then an if statement is used to test whether the value returned is null. If the returned value is not null, a for loop navigates all elements of the array, and then displays your list of favorite fruit types.

As for a select field, if the size is set to 1, or the size attribute is omitted (the default value is 1), the first item on the list is selected by default; if the size is set to other than 1, no item is selected by default.

You can use the getParameterValues method on all elements on a form. It returns an array containing values associated with the elements that have the same name attribute.

Before you process an array returned by the getParameterValues method, you must check if the array is null. If you try to access an array that is null, an exception occurs.

The names of Request object input fields are case sensitive. For example, "UserID" and "userID" are treated as two different parameters when used in the method getParameter.

Regarding the select field, if multiple selections are allowed, you also need to use the getParameterValues method to get all selected item values.

You learned that the getParameterValues method takes the name of input fields on a form as the parameter and returns all values associated with fields that have the same name attribute. The Request object also has a method getParameterNames. This method returns all the names of request parameters (the name attributes of all fields on a form). The returned value is an Enumeration object. This function is useful if the form is generated dynamically and the JSP page does not know in advance all the names of the fields in the form. Hands-on Exercise 15-5 shows you how to use this function.

CHAPTER SUMMARY

- A JSP directive affects the overall structure of the servlet that is created by the JSP page. There are three types of directives: page directives, include directives, and taglib directives.
- The page directive supports a wide range of attributes and functions. The attributes apply to the entire JSP page, and you use them to set the script language, to import Java classes, configure the output buffer, and control the session.
- The include directive allows you to insert a file into the servlet class at the time the JSP file is translated into a servlet. The include action allows you to add the include file in its response when the original JSP page is requested.
- A declaration is used to declare variables and methods in the scripting language used in a JSP page. The variables and methods declared are inserted into the servlet class generated when the JSP container translates the JSP page. Variables declared in a JSP declaration have instance duration.
- A JSP expression is used to insert the value of the expression directly into the output stream.
- A scriptlet is a code fragment that gets executed at request-processing time. Basically, you can embed any valid Java language code within a scriptlet. Variables declared in scriptlets have local duration.
- There are two types of comments you can use in a JSP file: content comments and JSP comments. Content comments are sent back to the client, and JSP comments are not.
- The Request object provides methods that allow you to retrieve header information as well as information about the client and server. The Request object also provides a method that allows you to access all values associated with the same field name on the form. This method returns all values as an array.
- You can use many input fields to collect information from clients. The information is sent to and processed on the Web server. The Request object provides methods to retrieve input field information.

Review Questions

1. Which of the following packages is/are imported to a JSP page automatically?
   a. java.util.*
   b. java.lang.*
   c. javax.servlet.*
   d. javax.servlet.jsp.*
   e. javax.servlet.http.*
2. Which of the following can be used to hold client information across multiple requests?
   a. a variable declared in a JSP declaration
   b. a variable declared in a scriptlet
   c. the implicit session variable
   d. the implicit out variable
3. When does a session begin?
   a. when an HTML page is requested
   b. when an HTML page is requested the first time
   c. when any user requests a JSP page the first time
   d. when a JSP page is requested the first time
4. Each browser window can have how many sessions at most?
   a. 0
   b. 1
   c. 2
   d. many
5. Which of the following statements sets the buffer size of the page directive to 16 kilobytes?
   a. <%@ page buffer="16" %>
   b. <%@ page buffer="16 kilobytes" %>
   c. <%@ page buffer="16kb" %>
   d. <%@ page buffer="16000" %>

6. Suppose the size of the content to be sent to a client is 20 kilobytes. If the buffer size is set to 8 kilobytes, then how many times is the buffer flushed? (Assume the Web server sends the content only when the buffered content reaches the buffer size or the page is complete.)
   a. 1
   b. 2
   c. 3
   d. 4
7. If the isThreadSafe attribute is set to false, how many threads can execute the JSP code simultaneously?
   a. 0
   b. 1
   c. 2
   d. many
8. Assume you set the page directive attributes as: <%@ page buffer="8kb" autoFlush="false" %>, and that the page sends 10 kilobytes of content to a client. When a client requests this JSP page, which of the following occurs?
   a. The content is sent to the client without any exception.
   b. An exception occurs, and the content is not sent to the client.
   c. No exception occurs, but the content is not sent to the client.
   d. The content is sent to the client, and an exception occurs.
9. If you want a page that uses an include file to reflect updated content of its included file, you should use:
   a. include directive
   b. include action
   c. no action
   d. no directive
10. You insert the following JSP code segment in a JSP page: <%! int aNum = 0; %> <% aNum++; %>. Assume this page has been requested 10 times by client A and 5 times by client B. The value stored in the variable aNum is:
    a. 10
    b. 15
    c. 5
    d. 0

11. You insert the following JSP code segment in a JSP page: <% int aNum = 0; aNum++; %>. Assume this page has been requested 10 times by client A and 5 times by client B. The value stored in the variable aNum is:
    a. 10
    b. 15
    c. 5
    d. 0
12. Which of the following statements is correct?
    a. Variables declared in scriptlets are created every time the JSP page is requested.
    b. Variables declared in scriptlets are created only the first time the JSP page is requested.
13. Which of the following statements is correct?
    a. Variables declared in a JSP declaration are created every time the JSP page is requested.
    b. Variables declared in a JSP declaration are created the first time the JSP page is requested.
14. Which of the following comments in a JSP page is sent to the client when the page is requested?
    a. <!--some comments -->
    b. <%-- some comments --%>
    c. <% /* some comments */ %>
    d. <% //some comments %>
15. Which of the following comment forms support(s) multiple-line comments in a JSP page? (Select all that apply.)
    a. <!--some comments -->
    b. <%-- some comments --%>
    c. <% /* some comments */ %>
    d. <% //some comments %>

HANDS-ON EXERCISES

If necessary, use Windows Explorer to create a new folder in the Chap15 folder in your workfolder. Name this folder **Exercises**. As you create each of the following programs, save the program in the Chap15\Exercises folder in your workfolder.

Exercise 15-1

In this exercise, you use the include directive to include a file in a JSP page.

To include a file in a JSP page:

1. Open a new document in Notepad and type the following code:

```
<HR width=250 align=left>
The temperature now in New York City is:
<font color ="blue"> 89</font>
<HR width=250 align=left>
```

2. Save it as **newyorktemperature.jsp** in the Chap15\Exercises folder of your workfolder. Then close the document.
3. Open a new document in Notepad and type the following code:

```
<%@ page import="java.util.Calendar" %>
<!-- This is a content comment. The name of this JSP page is
 <%= javax.servlet.http.HttpUtils.getRequestURL(request) %>
-->
<%-- get the time of the day for greetings --%>
<% Calendar calendar = Calendar.getInstance();
   int hourOfDay = calendar.get(Calendar.HOUR_OF_DAY);
   if(hourOfDay <=12){
%>
   Good morning!
<% } else if(hourOfDay <=18){ %>
   Good afternoon!
<% } else { %>
   Good evening!
<% } %>
<br>
<%@ include file="newyorktemperature.jsp" %>
```

4. Save this as **exercise1.jsp** in the Chap15\Exercises folder of your workfolder. Then close Notepad.
5. Load **exercise1.jsp** using the following URL. Substitute the name of your workfolder where *workfolder* appears:

   http://localhost:8080/*workfolder*/Chap15/Exercises/exercise1.jsp
6. This page displays the temperature in New York as 89. Now change the temperature to 95 in **newyorktemperature.jsp**, and reload this page by pressing F5, or by clicking the Refresh button on your browser. The temperature displayed is still 89. This is because you used the include directive to include a file. The included file has merged to the original JSP page when the original page was converted into a servlet, so the updated temperature is not updated in the servlet.

Exercise 15-2

In this exercise, you use the include action to include a file to another JSP page.

To include a file to another JSP page:

1. Open a new document in Notepad and type the following code:

```
<%@ page import="java.util.Calendar" %>
<!-- This is a content comment. The name of this JSP page is
 <%= javax.servlet.http.HttpUtils.getRequestURL(request) %>
-->
<%-- get the time of the day for greetings --%>
<% Calendar calendar = Calendar.getInstance();
   int hourOfDay = calendar.get(Calendar.HOUR_OF_DAY);
   if(hourOfDay <=12){
%>
   Good morning!
<% } else if(hourOfDay <=18){ %>
   Good afternoon!
<% } else { %>
   Good evening!
<% } %>
<br>
<jsp:include page="newyorktemperature.jsp" flush="true" />
```

2. Save the file as **exercise2.jsp** in the Chap15\Exercises folder of your workfolder. Then close Notepad.
3. Load this page using the following URL. Substitute the name of your workfolder where *workfolder* appears:

   http://localhost:8080/*workfolder*/Chap15/Exercises/exercise2.jsp
4. Change the temperature in New York to 93, and refresh this page by pressing F5. The new temperature is displayed.

Exercise 15-3

In this exercise, you design a guest book to allow a user to sign in. Users can view the list of user names in the guest book.

To create a guest book using a JSP declaration:

1. Open a new document in Notepad and type the following code:

```
<%@ page import="java.util.*" %>
<%! Vector userList = new Vector(10); %>
<% String action = request.getParameter("action"); %>
<% if(action == null){ %>
Please sign our <b>Guest Book</b><br>
<form action="exercise3.jsp?action=sign-in" method=POST>
  Name: <input type=text name=userName><br>
  <input type=submit value="Sign-in">
  <input type=reset>
</form>
<br>
<a href="exercise3.jsp?action=view">View User List</a>
```

```
<% }else {
        if(action.equals("sign-in")){
          String name = request.getParameter("userName");
          if(name != null && !name.equals(""))
            userList.addElement(name);
        }
        out.println("User List:");
        out.println("<hr width=150 align=left>");
        for(int i=0; i<userList.size(); i++){
          String tempS=(String)userList.elementAt(i);
          out.println(tempS + "<br>");
        }
        out.println("<hr width=150 align=left>");
        out.println("<a href=\"exercise3.jsp\">Sign-in</a>");
    }
%>
```

2. Save this file as **exercise3.jsp** in the Chap15\Exercises folder of your workfolder. Then close Notepad.
3. Load this page using the following URL. Substitute the name of your workfolder where *workfolder* appears:

   http://localhost:8080/*workfolder*/Chap15/Exercises/exercise3.jsp
4. You can sign the guest book or view the user names in the guestbook.

Exercise 15-4

In this project, you create news headlines using the include action. The news items are automatically updated on the main news page.

To view news headlines:

1. Use Notepad to create three news item files: **item1.html**, **item2.html**, and **item3.html**. Save them in the Chap15\Exercises folder of your workfolder, and add content as follows:

   Add the following content to item1.html:

   <B>News Item 1</B>

   Add the following content to item2.html:

   <B>News Item 2</B>

   Add the following content to item3.html:

   <B>News Item 3</B>
2. Open a new document in Notepad and type the following code:

```
Here are the news headlines for today:<br>
<OL>
  <LI><jsp:include page="item1.html" flush="true" />
```

```
    <LI><jsp:include page="item2.html" flush="true" />
    <LI><jsp:include page="item3.html" flush="true" />
  </OL>
```

3. Save the file as **exercise4.jsp** in the Chap15\Exercises folder of your workfolder. Then close Notepad.
4. Load this page using the following URL. Substitute the name of your workfolder where *workfolder* appears:

   http://localhost:8080/*workfolder*/Chap15/Exercises/exercise4.jsp

   This page is displayed as shown in Figure 15-18.

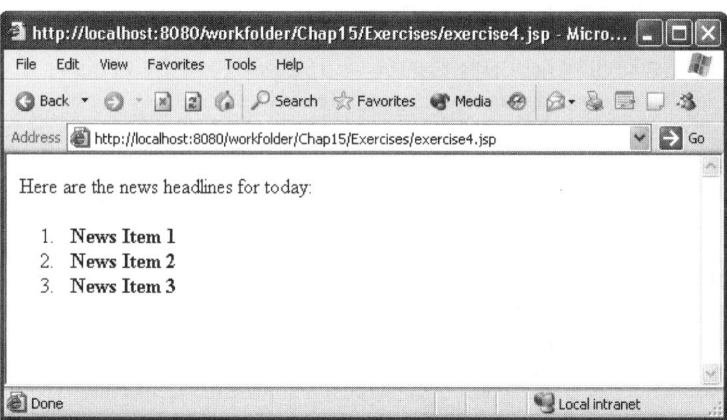

Figure 15-18

Exercise 15-5

Check boxes and multiple selections of select fields allow multiple values for a single field. The getParameterValues method is used to retrieve all the values associated with a single field. This method will return a string array. You must go through the array and extract each value. In this project, you design a virtual library search criteria Web page. This exercise contains two pages. The first page is used to collect search criteria; the second page is for retrieving information collected from the first page. There are two kinds of form elements, check box and select field. Note all check boxes have the same name "categories." You can use different names for each check box. The purpose of using the same name here is that you want to take advantage of the method getParameterValues. You can use the same name to get all the values the user selected. When you want to add more choices to the check boxes group, you don't need to change your JSP script. The select field lets the user choose multiple options from different topics.

15

The scriptlets that process the check box and select field are basically the same. The scriptlet first uses request.getParameterValues("categories") to get the values of the check box inputs. If a user has made a selection, the method returns a string array. Before you process the array, you must check whether the array is null. If the array has elements, you check the size of the array, send a message, and then you go through the array, fetching and displaying each string. Finally, if a user doesn't have any input, you also print a message.

To create check boxes and select fields:

1. Open a new document in Notepad and type the following code:

```
<Form action=exercise5.jsp method ="POST">
 Welcome to the virtual library.<br>
 Please select a category you want to browse:<br>
 <INPUT TYPE="checkbox" name="categories" value="Books">Books
 <INPUT TYPE="checkbox" name="categories" value=
 "Newspapers" checked>Newspapers
 <br>
 <INPUT TYPE="checkbox" name="categories" value=
 "Magazines">Magazines
 <INPUT TYPE="checkbox" name="categories" value=
 "LectureNotes">Lecture Notes
 <br><br>
 Please select a topic you are interested in:<br>
 <SELECT NAME="topic" size=4 MULTIPLE>
 <OPTION NAME="Accounting">Accounting
 <OPTION NAME="Art/Religion">Art/Religion
 <OPTION NAME="Computers">Computers
 <OPTION NAME="Management">Management
 <OPTION NAME="Engineering">Engineering
 <OPTION NAME="Financial">Financial
 </SELECT>
 <br><br>
 <INPUT TYPE="submit" name = "submit" value ="Search">
</FORM>
```

2. Save the file as **exercise5.html** in the Chap15\Exercises folder of your work-folder. Then close the document.

3. Open a new document in Notepad and type the following code:

```
<table>
<% String[] categories = request.getParameterValues
("categories");
   boolean noSearchCriteria = true;
   if(categories != null){
     noSearchCriteria = false;
%>
<tr> <td colspan=2 valign=center><hr></td> </tr>
<tr> <% if(categories.length ==1){ %>
 <td valign=top><b>The category for the search is:</b></td>
   <% } else { %>
     <td valign=top><b>The categories for the search are:
     </b></td>
   <% } %>
       <td><font face=Arial size=1 color=blue>
```

```
<%
    for(int i=0; i<categories.length; i++){
       out.println(categories[i]+"<br>");
     }
%>
</font> </td> </tr>
<% } %>
<% String[] topics = request.getParameterValues("topic");
   StringBuffer topicsb = new StringBuffer();
   if(topics != null){
      noSearchCriteria = false;
%>
<tr> <td colspan=2 valign=center><hr></td></tr>
<tr>
<% if(topics.length ==1){ %>
     <td valign=top><b>The topic for the search is:</b></td>
<% } else { %>
     <td valign=top><b>The topics for the search are:</b></td>
<% } %>
<td><font face=Arial size=1 color=blue>
<%
    for(int i=0; i<topics.length; i++){
       out.println(topics[i]+"<br>");
    }
%>
</font> </td> </tr>
<% } %>
</table>
<%= (noSearchCriteria)?"Sorry, but you didn't select any
search criteria!":"" %>
<br>
<a href="exercise5.html">Back to search page</a>
```

4. Save it as **exercise5.jsp** in the Chap15\Exercises folder of your workfolder. Then close the document.
5. Load **exercise5.html** using the following URL. Substitute the name of your workfolder where *workfolder* appears:

   http://localhost:8080/*workfolder*/Chap15/Exercises/exercise5.html
6. Specify your search criteria and submit the form. The specified search criteria are then displayed. Close your browser.

15

WEB PROGRAMMING PROJECTS

If necessary, use Windows Explorer to create a new folder in the Chap15 folder in your workfolder. Name this folder **Projects**. Save the files that you create in these projects in the Chap15\Projects folder in your workfolder.

Project 15-1

You are asked to create a guest book for a Web site. The guest book you have created in this chapter has a drawback: the guest data is lost if the server is down. Your manager asks you to save the registered guests' information permanently on your local file system. The guest book should meet the following requirements:

- When a user signs your guest book, the information is saved in the guest.data file.
- A user can view the names of guests who have already signed the book. The data is obtained from the file guest.data, where the guest data is stored.
- Prevent more than one user from writing information to the guest book file at the same time.

(*Hint*: You need to import java.io.* to perform any input/output operation on your local file system.)

Save the JSP file as **GuestBook.jsp** in the Chap15\Projects folder in your workfolder.

Project 15-2

CT-Online is a startup company made up of JSP enthusiasts who want to create a compelling, up-to-the-minute site for selling books online. The book list is always subject to change. Assume all book names are stored in the local file system in a file called books.txt, which is provided as a data file. You are asked to design a book index page that lists all the book names in that file. When the file books.txt is updated, the index page should always reflect the updated data.

Save the JSP file as **CTOnline.jsp** and the text file as **books.txt** in the Chap15\Projects folder.

Project 15-3

A small pizza place called Joe's Pizzeria is interested in reaching customers through the Internet. You are hired to develop a Web page that allows customers to place orders online. On this Web page, the customer is asked to specify the following information:

- Pizza size (small, medium, or large)
- Number of pizzas
- Preferred toppings
- Delivery (pickup or deliver)

After the customer provides all information and submits this form, the information collected from the form is displayed.

Save the JSP file as **Pizza.jsp** in the Chap15\Projects folder.

CHAPTER

16

JAVASERVER PAGES: PART II

In this chapter you will:

- Write JavaBeans
- Compile and install bean classes
- Use beans and set their properties
- Understand beans and forms
- Understand JavaBean scope
- Access a database from JSP
- Review a JDBC example

In the previous chapter, you learned basic concepts about JavaServer Pages (JSP). In this chapter, you learn how to create and use reusable components, which are called JavaBeans. A bean is an instance of a Java class, and lets you use object-oriented programming techniques to develop JSP scripts. You learn how to connect JavaBeans with forms to facilitate form processing. JavaBeans have scope, which determines where the bean can be referenced in JSP. You can define and use beans in four different scopes: page scope, request scope, session scope, and application scope. Finally, you learn how to access a database with JSP.

WRITING JAVABEANS

JavaBeans bring object-oriented programming technology to JSP scripts. Object-oriented programming languages dominate the modern software markets. Indeed, with object technology, most software is built by combining components. With JavaBeans, you can create platform-independent components that are reusable. The greatest virtue of JavaBeans, however, is that they are robust. **JavaBean** components are known as beans. Beans are Java objects that follow certain naming conventions. JavaBeans are commonly used in JSP scripts to facilitate form information processing and to implement business logic. Because beans are so important in automating business rules, you should be able to understand and use beans, although you may be not be required to write the beans yourself.

A bean is simply an instance of a Java class. A bean encapsulates its properties by declaring them private and provides public methods for reading and modifying its properties. In general, a bean provides two methods for each property: one to get the property and one to set the property. These **get** and **set** methods are also called **accessors** or getters/setters. However, to access a bean's properties with action tags in JSP, the method names should follow a few simple naming conventions. For example, for a property named foo, which is of type dataType, the get method is called getFoo and returns an element of dataType; the set method takes an argument of dataType and is called setFoo. In general, a bean is a Java class that has the following features:

- Public class
- Public constructor with no arguments
- Public set and get methods to simulate properties; the get method has no arguments

To create a simple bean with one property:

1. Open a new document in a text editor, such as Notepad, and type the following code:

```
package com.jspbook.chapter16;
public class SimpleBean{
  private String message;
  public SimpleBean(){
    message = "Hi there.";
  }
  public String getMessage(){ return message;}
  public void setMessage(String aMessage){ message = aMessage;}
}
```

2. Save the file as **SimpleBean.java** in the Chap16\Chapter folder of your work folder. Create these folders, if necessary, as you save the file. Then close Notepad.

Java classes are grouped in a collection called a **package**. In your application development, you may create many classes. These classes are grouped into a number of packages, which are folder structures used to organize classes. The first line of the preceding code defines a package named com.jspbook.chapter16. Later in this chapter, after this class is compiled, you will find a class named SimpleBean.class in the folder com\jspbook\chapter16.

The code `public class SimpleBean` starts a class definition. The class should be defined as public; otherwise, it can be accessed so that it can be used only by other classes in the same package. By convention, the class name should begin with a capitalized letter. If a name combines more than one word, the first letter of a word should also be capitalized. The code `private String message` defines a property or instance variable or data member of the class. Every Bean object contains one copy of each **instance variable**. A private property can only be accessed within the class definition. The code segment `public class SimpleBean(){ ... }` defines a public constructor with no argument. The constructor without an argument is also called the **default constructor**. To create and use a bean with action tags in JSP script, a default constructor must be provided. If no constructor is defined in your class, a default constructor is provided automatically. However, if any constructors are defined for a class, a default constructor is not created automatically; in this case, you must define a constructor with no argument in order to create a bean with action tags. You usually initialize instance variables within constructors. In the previous example, you assign an initial value to the instance variable `message`. A private property cannot be accessed outside of the class. To access it, you need to provide a public method. The `public getMessage` method is used to access the private property, and the `public setMessage` method is used to set the property with a new value.

Sun Microsystems specifies a convention for package naming. Every package name should start with your Internet domain name in reverse order. For example, if the domain is ebcity.com, you use the package name com.ebcity.

Finally, the bean class must be saved using the same name as the class name, and must have the extension of java. So, the class in the previous example must be saved as SimpleBean.java.

16

By convention, the first letter of a class name is capitalized; and the first letter of each following word is capitalized. For example, CalculateInterestRateBean is a class name. By contrast, the first letter of a method name is lowercase.

COMPILING AND INSTALLING BEAN CLASSES

To create objects from a class, the class must be available to the JSP engine. For example, to create a Date object, you must make the class package java.util.Date available. To be available, the class must be somewhere in the classpath. A **classpath** is a folder where the JSP engine looks for the required classes. How you reference the class package may vary among implementations, but most JSP containers provide standard folders where new bean classes can be installed.

To install bean classes in Tomcat, you install all the classes in the folder web-inf\classes under the root directory of your application. The source code can be saved anywhere. But for security reasons, you may want to store all your source files under the folder web-inf in a real application.

The class must be compiled and installed in the proper class path. When a class is compiled, the resulting class file (a file with the extension .class) is placed in the folder specified by the package statement. If the folder specified in the package does not exist, the compiler creates it. To compile a class in the Windows operating system, you use the following command:

```
javac -d classpath  classFile
```

To compile a class in a package, the option -d is passed to the compiler to specify where to create (or locate if these folders exist) all the folders in the package. The classpath is a folder where the JSP engine searches for the classes. The classpath is the folder c:\workfolder\web-inf\classes, and the classFile is the JavaBean file to be compiled. In the following steps you compile and install the SimpleBean.java in Windows.

In this text, the classpath is the folder c:\workfolder\web-inf\classes. Your drive and folder name might be different. Be sure to replace the drive name and "workfolder" to match the locations on your system. Note that from this point forward, you might need to replace the drive letter and "workfolder" with your work folder.

To compile and install a JavaBean file in Windows:

1. Open a DOS command window. Click **Start**, point to **Programs**, (point to **All Programs** in Windows XP), point to **Accessories**, and then click **Command Prompt**.
2. Type the following command, and then press **Enter** to change to the folder where the SimpleBean.java is located. Be sure to replace the drive name and "workfolder" to match the locations on your system.

   cd c:*workfolder*\Chap16\Chapter

3. Type the following command, and then press **Enter** to compile and install the bean class:

   javac -d c:*workfolder*\web-inf\classes SimpleBean.java

The folder c:\workfolder\web-inf\classes contains a folder called com; com contains a folder called jspbook; and jspbook contains a folder called chapter16. In the chapter16 folder, you should find the file SimpleBean.class.

USING BEANS AND SETTING THEIR PROPERTIES

To write Java classes, you must know the Java programming language. However, you do not need to know the Java programming language to use beans in your JSP scripts. By using action tags, you can use beans that are developed by other Java programmers. Most importantly, because beans are components, you can use beans in any JSP page when you need them.

JSP provides three basic tags for working with beans: one to bind a local variable to an existing bean or instantiate a new bean and make it available in the action tags and JSP script, one to get a property, and one to set one or more properties. Each tag is discussed in the following sections.

Instantiating Bean Object

The simplest way to make a bean available is to use the following code to load the bean.

```
<jsp:useBean id="bean_name" class="class_name" />
```

This action lets you create and load a JavaBean to be used in the JSP page. This usually means "instantiate an object of the class specified by class attribute, and bind it to a variable with the name specified by id attribute." In the preceding action tag, "bean_name" is the name that refers to the bean. The bean name must be a valid Java identifier (a combination of letters, numbers, and other characters, which cannot begin with digit), and it must be unique everywhere it is used. No two beans can have the same name in the same page. The bean name serves as a local variable reference to the bean object.

The "class_name" is the name of a Java class that defines the bean. You must specify the whole package name of the bean class. The execution of this action tag creates a new bean object and binds a local variable (the value of the ID attribute) to the object. The local variable is used to access the bean's properties.

Accessing Bean Properties

Once you have a bean, you can read existing properties via jsp:getProperty. The getProperty action tag takes the following syntax: 16

<jsp:getProperty name="*bean_name*" property="*property_name*" />

This tag retrieves the value of a bean property, converts it to a string, and inserts it into the output. The two required attributes are name and property. The "bean_name" is the same name specified in the ID attribute when the bean is created, and the "property_name" is the name of the property to get.

Setting Bean Properties

Once you have a bean, you can modify its properties using the jsp:setProperty statement. The setProperty action tag takes the following form:

<jsp:setProperty name="*bean_name*" property="*property_name*"
value="*a new property value*" />

This tag assigns a new value to the specified property. In this tag, the "value" attribute specifies the new value to be assigned to the bean property. In the following steps, you use this action tag to assign a new value to the bean property.

To assign a new value to the bean property:

1. Open a new document in a text editor, such as Notepad, and type the following code:

```
<HTML>
<HEAD><TITLE>Set and get bean property</TITLE></HEAD>
<BODY>
<H3>The original property value:</H3>
<jsp:useBean id="simpleBean" class="com.jspbook.chapter16.SimpleBean"/>
<H1>
<jsp:getProperty name="simpleBean" property="message"/>
</H1>
<H3>Set a new property value.</H3>
<jsp:setProperty name="simpleBean" property="message" value="Hello
World!"/>
<H3>The new property value is:</H3>
<H1>
<jsp:getProperty name="simpleBean" property="message"/>
</H1>
</BODY>
</HTML>
```

2. Save this as **example1.jsp** in the in Chap16\Chapter folder of your work folder. Then close Notepad.
3. Load this page using the following URL, replacing *workfolder* as necessary:

   http://localhost:8080/*workfolder*/Chap16/Chapter/example1.jsp

   This page is displayed as shown in Figure 16-1.

In the preceding example, the tag `<jsp:setProperty name="simpleBean" property="message" value="Hello World!"/>` sets the *message* property of the bean to the new value `"Hello World!"`, and then the getProperty tag is used to retrieve the new property value.

A property of a bean can be set as many times as you need. Each value of the property stays in effect until the next change. Each time you assign a new value to a property, the new value overwrites the old property value.

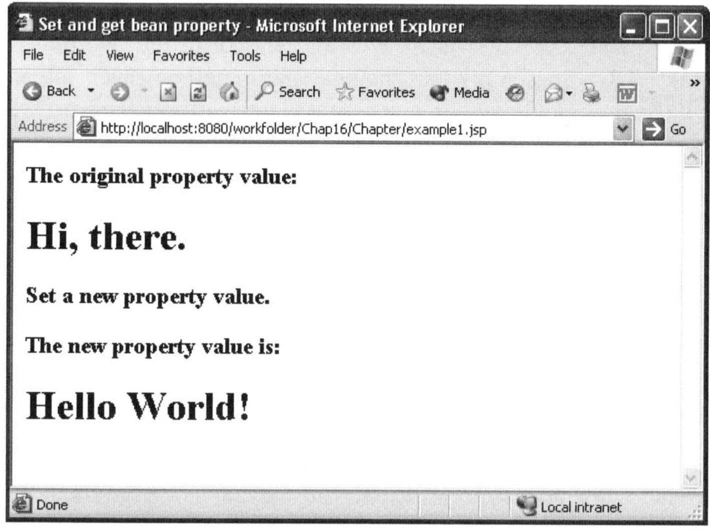

Figure 16-1 Set and get a bean's property

UNDERSTANDING BEANS AND FORMS

Dynamic Web pages are created in part with values that users provide via forms. Dynamic JSP pages often use these values to set the properties of JavaBeans. In the following sections, you will learn about the interaction between the properties of beans and the input parameters of forms.

Setting Properties with Form Input Parameters

There is a simpler way to assign an input parameter to a bean than the method you learned in the previous section. JSP provides a shortcut. If, for example, the form provides an input parameter called foo, and if the bean has a property that is also called foo, to set the foo property of the bean with the form's foo input parameter, you use the following code: 16

```
<jsp:setParameter name="bean_name" property="foo"/>
```

In this case, JSP assumes that the value assigned to the property comes from the form. This tag requires that the property name and the form's input parameter name match. Sometimes the name of the form parameter and the name of the property do not match. In this case, you use another attribute, `param`, to specify the form's input parameter, as follows:

```
<jsp:setProperty name="bean_name" property="propertyName""
param="inputFieldName"/>
```

This tag uses the form input field called "inputFieldName" to set the bean's property called "propertyName."

The action tag `<jsp:setProperty name="bean_name" property="bar"/>` does not mean that this bean has a property named "bar". But it does imply that the bean has a method called setBar.

There is one other version of the setProperty tag, which is the most powerful. This version looks through all the input fields provided by the form and all the methods provided by the bean, and links them together automatically. The tag takes the following form:

<jsp:setProperty name="*bean_name*" property="*"/>

If the form provides input field names called name1, name2, and so on, and the bean has methods called setName1, setName2, and so on, the field names and methods match perfectly, and the script calls all these methods automatically, as if you had written setProperty tags for all the properties. If a property (setter method) cannot find the match input field name on the form, it is ignored and no error occurs.

Bean properties can be of any data type, although most JavaScript pages deal with strings. The values you get from form input fields are always strings, and these strings are passed to the setter methods of the bean. If a setter method expects an integer and is passed a string, an exception occurs. In most cases, the JSP engine attempts to convert the string to an appropriate data type. For example, if a method expects an integer, the JSP engine calls Integer.parseInt to try to convert the passed string to an integer value. If this automatic conversion fails—perhaps because a user entered a nonnumerical value that cannot be converted into an integer—an exception occurs. Another, more robust approach, is to convert strings to appropriate data types in the setter methods.

Understanding Beans and Scriptlets

To use a bean, a Bean object must be created and bound to a variable. The execution of the tag `<jsp:useBean id="bean_name" class="class_Path"/>` locates or instantiates a Bean object from the class and binds the variable specified as "bean_name" to the Bean object. After the variable "bean_name" has been bound to the Bean object, you can use this variable as a reference to the Bean object in your JSP script. Because the variable is a reference to the Bean object, you can call all methods provided by the bean in your JSP scriptlets. In the following steps, you access a Bean object in scriptlets.

To access a Bean object in scriptlets:

1. Open a new document in a text editor, such as Notepad, and type the following code:

```
<HTML>
<HEAD><TITLE>Access Bean via Scriptlets</TITLE></HEAD>
<BODY>
<jsp:useBean id="simpleBean" class="com.jspbook.chapter16.SimpleBean"/>
<H3>The original property value:</H3>
<H1>
<%= simpleBean.getMessage()%>
```

```
</H1>
<H3>Set a new property value.<H3>
<% simpleBean.setMessage("Hello World!");%>
<H3>The new property value is:</H3>
<H1>
<%= simpleBean.getMessage()%>
</H1>
</BODY>
</HTML>
```

2. Save the file as **example2.jsp** in the in Chap16\Chapter folder of your work folder. Then close Notepad.
3. Load the page example2.html using the following URL, replacing *workfolder* as necessary:

   http://localhost:8080/*workfolder*/Chap16/Chapter/example2.jsp

   You should see the same page displayed as shown earlier in Figure 16-1.

UNDERSTANDING JAVABEAN SCOPE

You have learned how to instantiate a JavaBean object and how to use the Bean object in your JSP scripts. A Bean object can have one of the following scopes: page scope, request scope, session scope, and application scope. The bean scope determines where the bean can be referenced in JSP. The syntax for specifying the scope of a Bean object has the following form:

<jsp:useBean id="*bean_name*" class="*class_name*" scope="*bean_scope*"/>

Each scope specifies how long a bean exists in memory and where the bean object can be referenced. The four different scopes—page scope, request scope, session scope, and application scope—are discussed in the following sections.

Page Scope JavaBeans

16

Page scope is the default scope for JavaBeans, and is the scope used in all examples you have seen so far. Page scope Bean objects are available only to action tags or scriptlets within the page in which they are instantiated. These Bean objects disappear as soon as the current page is finished. To explicitly specify page scope, use the following syntax:

<jsp:useBean id="*bean_name*" class="*class_name*" scope="*page*"/>

A page scope Bean object can be modified as often as desired within the page, but all these changes are lost when the page is closed.

To illustrate the different scopes a bean can have, the following JavaBean class is used in the rest of the steps in this chapter. Please follow the steps to create, compile, and install the bean class in an appropriate classpath.

To create, compile, and install a bean class:

1. Open a new document in a text editor, such as Notepad, and type the following code:

   ```
   package com.jspbook.chapter16;
   public class Counter{
     private int counter=0;
     public int getCounter(){ return ++counter;}
   }
   ```

2. Save the file as **Counter.java** in the Chap16\Chapter folder of your work folder. Then close Notepad.

3. Open a DOS command window and change to the directory where the bean is saved by using the following command:

   cd c:*workfolder*\Chap16\Chapter

   Remember to substitute the appropriate name for your drive and work folder, if necessary, for this and any other step in this chapter.

4. Compile and install the bean class using the following command:

   javac -d c:*workfolder*\WEB-INF\classes Counter.java

The Counter bean has one property called counter, which is initialized to zero, and a getter method to get the counter property. Before the getter method returns the counter value, it increments the counter first. This simple bean is used to track the number of visits, or hits, to a Web page.

To test a page scope bean:

1. Open a new document in a text editor, such as Notepad, and type the following code:

   ```
   <HTML>
   <HEAD><TITLE>Page Scope</TITLE></HEAD>
   <BODY>
   The counter bean with page scope<br><br>
   <jsp:useBean id="counterBean"
     class="com.jspbook.chapter16.Counter" scope="page"/>
   This page has been accessed
   <b><jsp:getProperty name="counterBean" property="counter"/></b>
   time(s).
   <br><br>
   <a href="example3.jsp">Reload this page</a>
   </BODY>
   </HTML>
   ```

2. Save the file as **example3.jsp** in the Chap16\Chapter folder of your work folder. Then close Notepad.

3. Load this page using the following URL, replacing the *workfolder* as necessary:

   http://localhost:8080/*workfolder*/Chap16/Chapter/example3.jsp

4. Reload this page several times; the same counter value is displayed.

In this example, the bean is instantiated with page scope, and the getProperty action tag is used to modify the counter value and get the counter value after modification. However, because the bean has page scope, the Bean object disappears after the page is finished. So each time this page is requested, a new Bean object is created, and the bean is destroyed.

The page scope has the shortest lifetime among the four scopes. A page scope bean is repeatedly created upon request and destroyed after the execution of the page.

Request Scope JavaBeans

Request scope Bean objects have the same lifetime as the request object.This may seem no different from page scope, since presumably the request object lasts exactly as long as the page it requested. In most cases, when a client requests a JSP page, the server processes the page and provides it to the client. In this case, there is no difference between page and request scopes. However, you can separate requests using the JSP forward action.To forward a request to another page, use the following syntax:

<jsp:forward page="*relativeURL*"/>

This action tag lets you forward the request to another page. It has a single attribute, page, which consists of a relative URL.The forward action stops the processing of the current page and continues processing the same request on the new target page.The forward action passes the same request to the new target page.Therefore, the Bean object is also available to the target page. In the following steps, you create a request scope Bean object and use it from the pages involved in the same request scope.

To create a request scope Bean object:

1. Open a new document in a text editor, such as Notepad, and type the following code:

```
<HTML>
<HEAD><TITLE>Request Scope</TITLE></HEAD>
<BODY>
<jsp:useBean id="counterBean"
  class="com.jspbook.chapter16.Counter" scope="request"/>
<jsp:getProperty name="counterBean" property="counter"/>
<jsp:forward page="example4-2.jsp"/>
</BODY>
</HTML>
```

16

2. Save the file as **example4-1.jsp** in the Chap16\Chapter folder of your work folder.
3. Open a new document in your text editor and type the following code:

```
<HTML>
<HEAD><TITLE>Request Scope</TITLE></HEAD>
<BODY>
The counter request scope bean<br><br>
<jsp:useBean id="counterBean"
  class="com.jspbook.chapter16.Counter" scope="request"/>
This page has been accessed
<b><jsp:getProperty name="counterBean" property="counter"/></b>
time(s).
</BODY>
</HTML>
```

4. Save the file as **example4-2.jsp** in the Chap16\Chapter folder of your work folder. Then close Notepad.
5. Load the page example4-1.jsp using the following URL, replacing *workfolder* as necessary:

   http://localhost:8080/*workfolder*/Chap16/Chapter/example4-1.jsp

   This page is displayed, as shown in Figure 16-2.

When the page example4-1.jsp is initially requested, a request scope bean is created and its property is obtained via the getProperty action. However, the execution of the forward action forwards the request to example4-2.jsp, and the new target page continues processing the same request. Because the bean created in the old target page example4-1.jsp is a request scope bean, the Bean object is available within the same request. So the new target page does not create a new Bean object. Instead, the Bean object created in the old target page is used. The counter property increments by one in the original target page, so the getProperty action in the new target page returns 2. That is why you see the page displayed as shown in Figure 16-2. After processing the target page, the Bean object is out of scope and is destroyed. So reloading this page returns the same result.

Because the browser is not aware that more than one page is involved with forward action, the URL remains unchanged. Therefore, reloading the page by clicking the Refresh button reloads the original requested page.

The forward action stops the processing of the original target page, and forwards the request to the new target page. Any content buffered on the output stream is discarded when the request is forwarded to a new target page.

When you use the forward action, the target page processes the same request; therefore, all information encapsulated in the request is also available to the forwarded page.

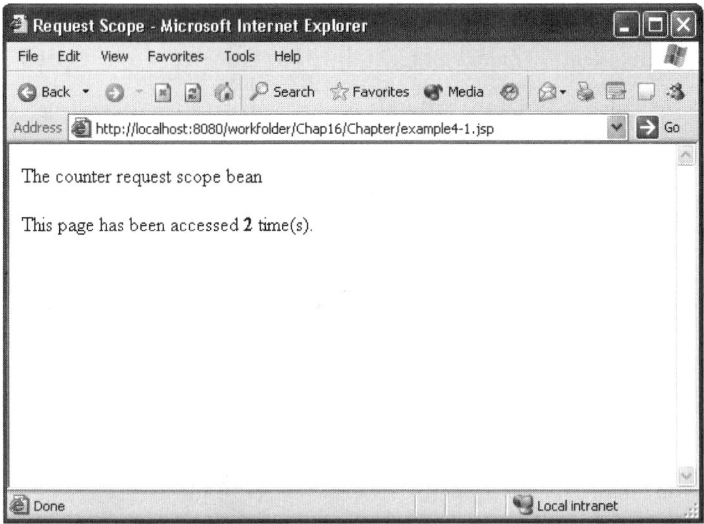

Figure 16-2 Forwarding request

Session Scope JavaBeans

Session scope Bean objects have the same lifetime as the session object. Like session scope variables, these beans can be referenced throughout the session in which they are created. In the following steps, you create a session scope bean and the same session Bean object is referenced throughout the current session.

To create a session scope bean:

1. Open a new document in a text editor, such as Notepad, and type the following code:

```
<HTML>
<HEAD><TITLE>Session Scope</TITLE></HEAD>
<BODY>
The counter session scope bean<br><br>
<jsp:useBean id="counterBean"
  class="com.jspbook.chapter16.Counter" scope="session"/>
This page has been accessed
<b><jsp:getProperty name="counterBean" property="counter"/></b>
time(s).
<br><br>
<a href="example5.jsp">Reload this page</a>
</BODY>
</HTML>
```

2. Save the file as **example5.jsp** in the Chap16\Chapter folder of your work folder. Then close Notepad.

16

3. Load this page using the following URL:

   http://localhost:8080/*workfolder*/Chap16/Chapter/example5.jsp

4. Click the **Reload this page link** to reload this page several times. This page should look similar to the one shown in Figure 16-3.

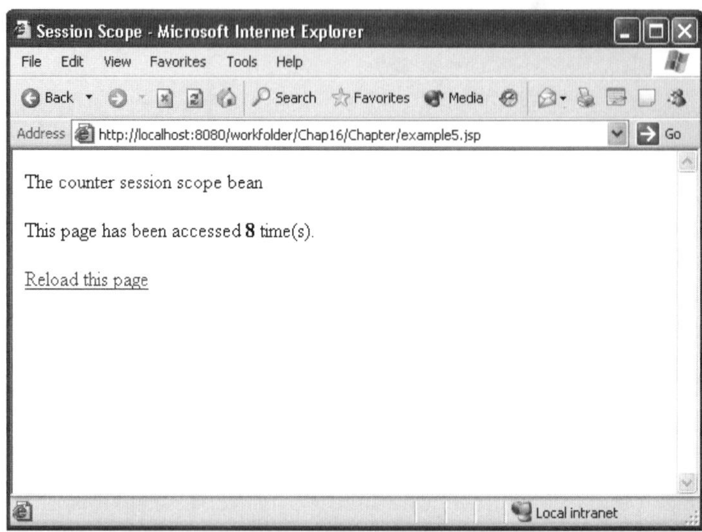

Figure 16-3 Session scope bean

A session scope bean is instantiated only once in a session. When a page having a session bean is requested, the JSP container determines whether the bean has been created in the current session. If a bean has been created, the existing bean is used. Therefore, a session scope bean is instantiated once and the bean can be referenced throughout the current session. In the preceding example, a session scope bean is instantiated when the page is requested for the first time. All subsequent requests for this page use the same bean as long as the current session is active. Unlike the page scope bean, the session scope bean can be referenced from any JSP page in the same session.

You use jsp:setProperty to give values to properties of beans that have been created earlier. You have done this outside of the jsp:useBean element as follows:

```
<jsp:useBean id="beanName" class="className" scope="beanScope"/>
...
<jsp:setProperty name="beanName" property="someProperty" />
```

In this case, the jsp:setProperty is executed regardless of whether a new bean is instantiated or an existing bean is found. In fact, the jsp:setProperty action tag can appear inside the body of a jsp:useBean element, as follows:

```
<jsp:useBean id="beanName" scope="beanScope">
  <jsp:setProperty name="myName" property="someProperty" />
</jsp:useBean>
```

Here, the jsp:setProperty is executed only if a new object is instantiated.

In the following steps, you design a shopping cart for an online bookstore. The shopping cart is implemented using a session bean. In these steps, you use a JavaBean class and three pages. You use the JavaBean class to create a shopping cart bean. An HTML page provides the list of items. Two JSP pages are for processing items on the shopping cart and checking out, respectively.

To design a shopping cart for an online bookstore:

1. If necessary, copy the file **ShopCart.java** from this book's CD to Chap16\Chapter folder of your work folder.
2. Open a DOS command window and change directories, if necessary, by typing the following command, and then pressing **Enter**:

   cd c:*workfolder*\Chap16\Chapter

   Remember to substitute the appropriate name for your drive and work folder, if necessary, for this and any other step in this chapter.
3. Compile and install the shopping cart JavaBean using the following command:

   javac -d c:*workfolder*\WEB-INF\classes ShopCart.java
4. If necessary, copy the files **example6.html**, **example6-1.jsp**, and **example6-2.jsp** from this book's CD to the Chap16\Chapter folder of your work folder.
5. Load the page example6.html using the following URL:

   http://localhost:8080/*workfolder*/Chap16/Chapter/example6.html
6. Check the items on the form, and then click the **Add** button to add them to the shopping cart.
7. You can add items to or remove items from the shopping cart before checking out. After checking out, a new session begins when you return to the shopping page.

16

Application Scope JavaBeans

A session scope bean can be referenced across multiple pages as long as the session where the bean was created is still active. Compared to page or request scope beans, session scope beans have longer lifetimes. Page scope, request scope, and session scope beans are associated with a single user, and cannot be shared across all users. The **application scope** bean, which persists across all users and all pages, is created once and exists throughout the execution of the Web application. The application scope bean is useful for handling data that needs to be available across users and pages. In the following steps, you create a page that tracks the number of visits all users make throughout the execution of the Web application.

To create a page that tracks the number of visits to a Web site:

1. Open a new document in a text editor, such as Notepad, and type the following code:

```
<HTML>
<HEAD><TITLE>Application Scope</TITLE></HEAD>
<BODY>
The counter application scope bean<br><br>
<jsp:useBean id="counterBean"
  class="com.jspbook.chapter16.Counter" scope="application"/>
This page has been accessed
<b><jsp:getProperty name="counterBean" property="counter"/></b>
time(s).
<br><br>
<a href="example7.jsp">Reload this page</a>
</BODY>
</HTML>
```

2. Save the file as **example7.jsp** in the Chap16\Chapter folder of your work folder.

3. Load this page using the following URL:

   http://localhost:8080/*workfolder*/Chap16/Chapter/example7.jsp

4. Reload this page several times, and then close the browser window, reopen the browser, and reload the page using the URL specified in Step 3. You should see the counter value number increase by one each time you access the page.

In the preceding example, the counter bean is created when a user requests the page for the first time. Because the bean has application scope, it stays in the memory and the same bean is used on successive requests from all users. So the counter bean reflects the total number of hits on this page by all users.

If the session scope bean has the same name as an application scope bean, then the application scope bean is hidden from the point where the session scope bean is referenced. To prevent an application scope bean from being hidden by a session scope bean, use different names for each bean.

ACCESSING A DATABASE FROM JSP

To develop a useful Web application, you need to add a database to your JSP pages. JSP can access a variety of relational databases. For most relational databases, you use the Java database package (java.sql.*) either through a JDBC (Java Database Connectivity) connection or through a JDBC to ODBC (Open Database Connectivity) bridge if the database requires an ODBC driver. ODBC is a technology developed by Microsoft to allow access to disparate database systems on the Windows platform. To access a database in JSP pages, you complete the following seven steps:

1. Load the JDBC driver.
2. Define the connection URL.
3. Establish the connection.
4. Create a statement object.
5. Execute a query or update the data.
6. Process results.
7. Close the connection.

These steps are discussed in detail in the following sections.

Loading the JDBC Driver

The first step in using JDBC is to obtain a JDBC driver for the specific database. The driver acts as the bridge between the JDBC classes (the classes used in JSP and JavaBean to access the database) and the database itself. The **driver** is a piece of software that knows how to talk to the database management system (DBMS). To load a driver, you only need to load the appropriate class. The syntax to load a driver takes the following form:

Class.forName("*fully qualified class name*");

Following are examples of statements that load a driver.

```
Class.forName("sun.jdbc.odbc.JdbcOdbcDriver");
Class.forName("oracle.jdbc.driver.OracleDriver");
Class.forName("org.mysql.Driver");
Class.forName("org.gjt.mm.mysql.Driver");
```

To load a driver, the driver class must be somewhere in the classpath. The JdbcOdbcDriver driver comes with the JDK. You must make other drivers available by putting them in the classpath. You can store these driver classes under the web-inf/classes.

The database driver must be loaded before the program can connect to the database. If the JSP cannot find the specified driver specified in the classpath, an `exception: ClassNotFoundException` occurs.

16

Many drivers for different databases can be loaded and made available at the same time, which allows JSP to use more than one database simultaneously.

Defining the Connection URL

Once a driver has been loaded, JSP can connect to a database. To make a connection, you need to specify the location of the database server. URLs referring to databases use the jdbc: protocol followed by a specific subprotocol and the name of the database. For some subprotocols, you may need to specify the database server host name and port number, user name and password, etc. The URLs are different in different databases.

For the jdbc:odbc bridge connection, the URL has the following syntax:

jdbc.odbc.data_*source_name*

The subprotocol odbc indicates that the connection will use jdbc to connect to a Microsoft ODBC data source. Recall that ODBC is a technology developed by Microsoft to allow access to disparate database systems on the Windows platform.

Establishing the Connection

To manipulate the data in a database, you must create a connection to the database server. To make the actual network connection, you need to pass the URL, the database user name, and the password to the getConnection method of the DriverManager class. The syntax of this method is as follows:

Connection conn = DriverManager.getConnection(*connURL,username, password*);

If the connection is successful, the getConnection method returns the connection. Then the connection makes a Statement object available, which queries the database.

Creating the Statement Object

A Statement object sends queries and commands to the database. The syntax to make a statement takes the following form:

Statement *stm* = *conn*.createStatement();

The following section shows how to use the Statement object to issue queries to the database.

Executing a Query or Command

Once you have a Statement object, you can use it to send SQL queries or commands to the database. The Statement object has two methods: the executeUpdate() method for updating a table, creating or modifying a table, and so on; the executeQuery() method is for retrieving data from a table. The executeUpdate() method returns an integer indicating how many rows were affected, and the executeQuery() method returns a ResultSet object containing the selected rows from a table in the database.

For example, to create a table by using the Statement object stm, you can issue a command to the database as follows:

```
stm.executeUpdate("CREATE TABLE product (productID char(5), name
varchar(15))";
```

This statement creates a table named product with two columns.

Processing ResultSets

The executeQuery method of a Statement object returns a ResultSet object. The ResultSet object contains the selected rows based on the query. This object provides methods to allow you to retrieve the data and use them in your JSP page. The simplest way to handle the results is to process them one row at a time using the resultSet's next method to move through the table a row at a time. The resultSet returned from the execution of a query maintains a cursor pointing to the position right before the first row (if there are any rows selected). When the next method is called, if there are more rows after the cursor position, the method call returns true and the cursor moves to the next row; if there are no more rows, it returns false. Within a row, resultSet provides various get*XXX* methods that take a column index or column name as an argument and return the results as a variety of different Java data types specified as *XXX* in the get*XXX* method. For example, if a field called ssn has the data type of integer in a table, you can use getInt("ssn"), and JSP returns the ssn as an integer in your JSP scripts. If the data type of a field named lastName, for example, is char or varchar in the database, you should use getString("lastName") to get the data. If you want to process all columns as strings in your JSP scripts, you can simply use the getString method for all columns, regardless of the actual column type. If you use the version that takes a column index, note that columns are indexed starting at 1, not at 0 as with arrays, vectors, and most other data structures in the Java programming language.

For example, suppose a table called employee has two columns: firstName and lastName. The following code segment illustrates how to process the resultSet:

```
String query = "select * from employee";
ResultSet rst = stm.executeQuery(query);
while(rst.next()){
      out.println(rst.getString("firstName") + "<br>" +
rst.getString("lastName");
}
```

Closing the Connection

You can explicitly close a connection to a database by calling the close method of a Connection object. Because you might have three objects when you access database through JSP, to close the connection, you should close the objects in the following order:

1. Close the resultSet.
2. Close the statement.
3. Close the connection.

Reviewing a JDBC Example

In this section, you use a JDBC-ODBC bridge to connect to a Microsoft Access database in your JSP page. First, you learn how to open a connection with your DBMS, and then, because what JDBC does is to send your SQL code to your database, you use the connection to create a table, insert data into the table, and then retrieve data from the table.

Registering the Database as an ODBC Data Source

This section shows you how to set up an ODBC data source in Microsoft Windows XP and Windows 2000. To connect to the database with the ODBC subprotocol, an ODBC data source must be registered with the system through the ODBC Data Source Administrator in the Windows Control Panel.

To set up an ODBC data source in Windows:

1. If necessary, copy the database **product.mdb** from this book's CD to the Chap16\Chapter folder of your work folder.
2. Open the Control Panel, and then double-click the **Administrative Tools** icon. (In Windows XP, make sure the Control Panel is in classic view.) Double click **Data Sources (ODBC)** to open the ODBC Data Source Administrator dialog box, shown in Figure 16-4. Click the **User DSN** tab if it is not selected.

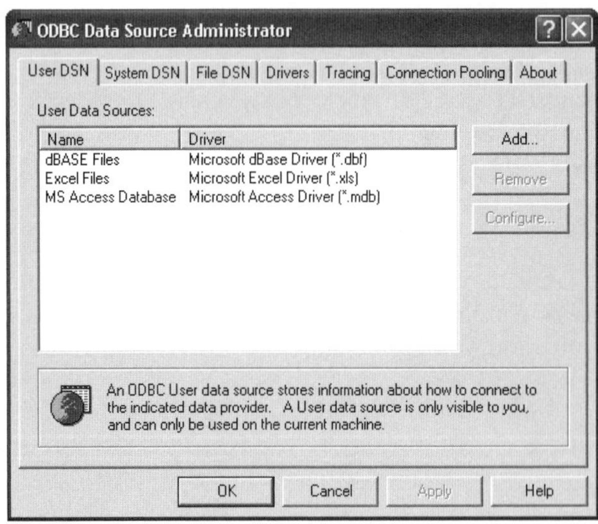

Figure 16-4 ODBC Data Source Administrator dialog box

3. Click the **Add** button. The Create New Data Source dialog window opens as shown in Figure 16-5. From the driver name list, click **Microsoft Access Driver (*.mdb)**, and then click **Finish**.

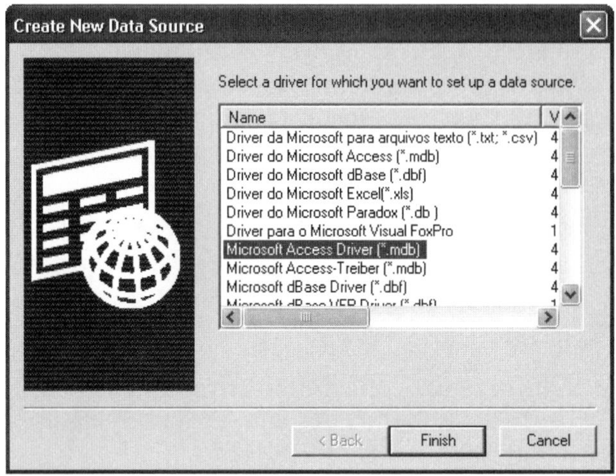

Figure 16-5 Create New Data Source dialog box

4. The ODBC Microsoft Access Setup dialog box opens, as shown in Figure 16-6. In the Data Source Name text box, type **productDSN**. Click the **Select** button to select the database. Locate **product.mdb** in the folder C:*workfolder*\Chap16\Chapter, select this database, and then click **OK** until you return to the ODBC Data Source Administrator dialog box. Click **OK** to close this dialog box. Close the Administrative Tools window.

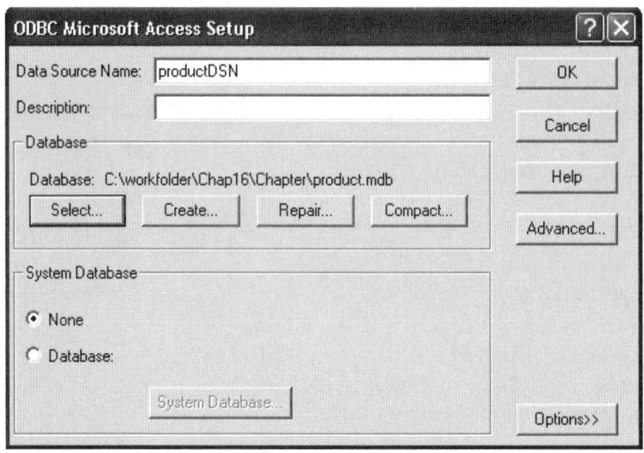

Figure 16-6 ODBC Microsoft Access Setup dialog box

The product.mdb database contains two tables: product and manufacturer. The product table contains the information about products sold in the online store; the manufacturer table contains information about manufacturers of these products. The product table includes the following fields: id for product id, name for product name, model, price, and manufacturerID. The manufacturer table includes the following fields: manufacturerID, name, address, city, state, zipCode, and phone. The product and manufacturer tables both contain the column manufacturerID, which means that you can use this field to link these tables and retrieve data based on the information in both tables. The id column is the primary key in the product table, and as such, it uniquely identifies each of the products sold in the online store. The manufacturerID is the primary key in the manufacturer table. The manufacturerID column in the product table is called a foreign key.

Now you have set the ODBC data source. You are ready to access the database from a JSP page.

Retrieving Data from Tables

In the following steps, you connect to the database and retrieve data from the product and manufacturer tables in the database. Specifically, you retrieve all the data from the product table and then display the data in an HTML table.

To retrieve data from the product.mdb database:

1. Open a new document in a text editor, such as Notepad, and type the following code:

```
<%@ page import="java.sql.*" %>
<%
 String url = "jdbc:odbc:productDSN";
 String username="";
 String password="";
 Connection  conn=null;
String classPath = "sun.jdbc.odbc.JdbcOdbcDriver";
 try{
    Class.forName(classPath);
    conn = DriverManager.getConnection(url,username,password);
  }catch(Exception exc){
    out.println(exc.toString());
  }
%>
<%
  Statement stm=null;
  ResultSet rst=null;
  stm= conn.createStatement();
  String query = "SELECT * FROM product";
  rst = stm.executeQuery(query);
%>
<table>
<tr>
<th>ID</th><th>Name</th><th>Model</th><th>Price</th>
<th>ManufacturerID</th>
</tr>
<% while(rst.next()){ %>
```

```
<tr>
    <td align=center><%= rst.getString("id")%></td>
    <td align=center><%= rst.getString("name")%></td>
    <td align=center><%= rst.getString("model") %></td>
    <td align=center>$<%= rst.getFloat("price") %></td>
    <td align=center><%= rst.getInt("manufacturerID") %></td>
</tr>
<%}%>
</table>
<%
  rst.close();
  stm.close();
  conn.close();
%>
```

2. Save the document as **example8.jsp** in the Chap16\Chapter folder of your work folder. Then close Notepad.
3. Load this page using the following URL:

   http://localhost:8080/*workfolder*/Chap16/Chapter/example8.jsp

   The page is displayed, as shown in Figure 16-7.

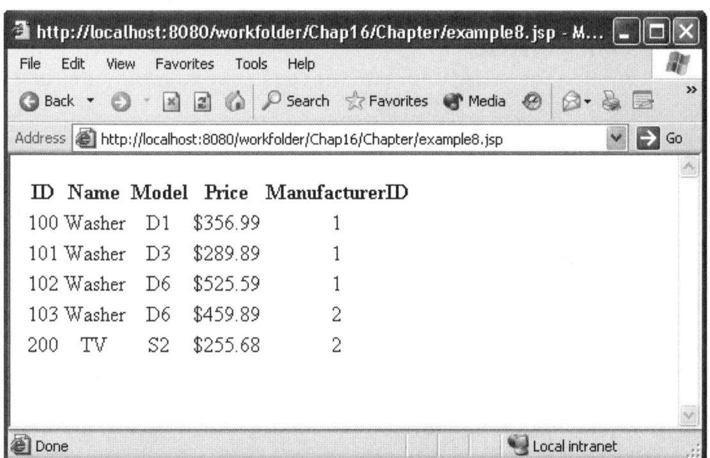

Figure 16-7 Retrieving data from the product table

The executeQuery statement retrieves all data from the product table and stores the retrieved data in the ResultSet object. The next method of the ResultSet object is used to get the selected rows one by one. For each row, the get*XXX* method is used to get the value for each column and the value is displayed in the HTML table. Then the next method of the ResultSet object returns false; it indicates all selected rows have been processed and the while loop ends.

In the data displayed in Figure 16-7, the last column is the manufacturer's ID. To provide more manufacturer information, you can display the manufacturer's name and contact phone number. Because you can retrieve data from both tables by linking the tables, you can write SQL statements to retrieve data from both the product and manufacturer tables as follows:

```
SELECT product.*, manufacturer.name, manufacturer.phone
FROM product, manufacturer
WHERE product.manufacturerID = manufacturer.manufacturerID
```

In the following steps, you retrieve data from more than one table on a JSP page.

To retrieve data from more than one table:

1. Open a new document in a text editor, such as Notepad, and type the following code:

```
<%@ page import="java.sql.*" %>
<%
 String url = "jdbc:odbc:productDSN";
 String username="";
 String password="";
 Connection  conn=null;
String classPath = "sun.jdbc.odbc.JdbcOdbcDriver";
 try{
    Class.forName(classPath);
    conn = DriverManager.getConnection(url,username,password);
  }catch(Exception exc){
    out.println(exc.toString());
  }
%>
<%
  Statement stm=null;
  ResultSet rst=null;
  stm= conn.createStatement();
  String query = "SELECT product.id, product.name,product.model, "+
      "product.price, manufacturer.name as mname,"+
     "manufacturer.phone FROM product, manufacturer " +
     "WHERE product.manufacturerID=manufacturer. manufacturerID";
  rst = stm.executeQuery(query);
%>
<table>
<tr>
 <th>ID</th><th>Name</th><th>Model</th><th>Price</th>
 <th>Manufacturer Name</th><th>Manufacturer Phone</th>
```

```
</tr>
<% while(rst.next()){ %>
<tr>
    <td align=center><%= rst.getString("id")%></td>
    <td align=center><%= rst.getString("name")%></td>
    <td align=center><%= rst.getString("model") %></td>
    <td align=center>$<%= rst.getFloat("price") %></td>
    <td align=center><%= rst.getString("mname") %></td>
    <td align=center><%= rst.getString("phone") %></td>
</tr>
<%}%>
</table>
<%
  rst.close();
  stm.close();
  conn.close();
%>
```

2. Save the document as **example9.jsp** in the Chap16\Chapter folder of your work folder. Then close Notepad.

3. Load this page using the following URL:

   http://localhost:8080/*workfolder*/Chap16/Chapter/example9.jsp

   The page is displayed, as shown in Figure 16-8.

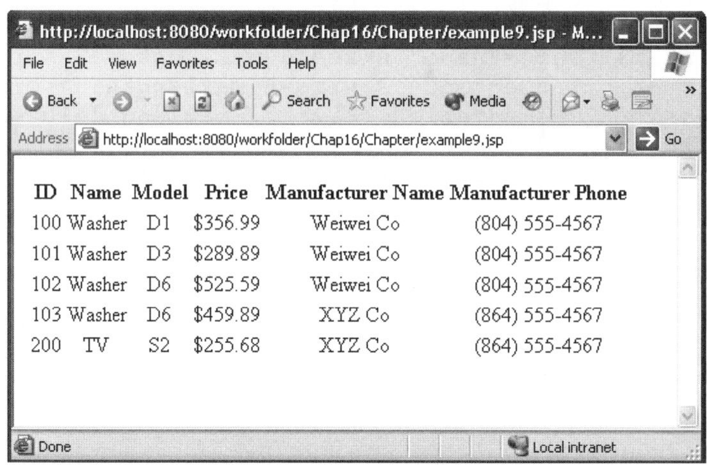

Figure 16-8 Retrieving data from both product and manufacturer tables

In the query, the columns include two names, one for the product name, and the other for the manufacturer name. If the same column name is selected from more than one table and you want to access the columns from all tables, you need to assign an alias to the column so that no two columns in the selected rows have the same column name. In this example, the name for the manufacturer table is assigned an alias name, mname, and the alias is used in the get*XXX* method.

Using Forms to Interact with a Database

You have learned how to access a database from a JSP page through JDBC. In this method, however, the SQL statements are hard-coded. In fact, to make your Web application dynamic, you need to provide a way for customers to interact with the database. For example, for an online banking system, the user IDs and passwords are stored in a table in the database, and a user provides their ID and password via a form. JSP looks up the ID and password in the table to see whether the table contains the ID and password. In this section, you design a form and a record, and then add the record to the product table through the form.

To use a form to add a record to the product table:

1. Open a document in a text editor, such as Notepad, and type the following code:

```
<HTML>
<HEAD><TITLE>Add data to database </TITLE></HEAD>
<BODY>
Please fill in the following fields and then click the <br>
Submit button to add data to the product table.<br><br>
Product Information:<br>
<form action="example10.jsp">
  ID:<input type=text name="id" size=5 maxlength=3><br>
  Name:<input name="name" size=16 maxlength=15><br>
  Model:<input name="model" size=6 maxlength=5><br>
  Price:<input name="price" size=13 maxlength=10><br>
  Manufacturer ID:<select name="mid">
                <option value="1">Weiwei Co.
                <option value="2">XYZ Co.
                </select><br><br>
  <input type=submit value="Submit"><br>
</form>
</BODY></HTML>
```

2. Save the document as **example10.html** in the Chap16\Chapter folder of your work folder.

3. Open a new document in the text editor and type the following code:

```
<%@ page import="java.sql.* " %>
<%
 String url = "jdbc:odbc:productDSN";
 String username="";
 String password="";
```

```
 Connection  conn=null;
String classPath = "sun.jdbc.odbc.JdbcOdbcDriver";
 try{
    Class.forName(classPath);
    conn = DriverManager.getConnection(url,username,password);
  }catch(Exception exc){
    out.println(exc.toString());
  }
  Statement stm=null;
  String id = request.getParameter("id");
  String name=request.getParameter("name");
  String model=request.getParameter("model");
  String prices=request.getParameter("price");
  String midS=request.getParameter("mid");
  float price=0;
  int mid=0;
  try{price = Float.parseFloat(prices);}catch(Exception exc){}
  try{mid = Integer.parseInt(midS);}catch(Exception exc){}
  stm= conn.createStatement();
  String query = "INSERT INTO product VALUES('"+id+"', '" +
   name +"', '"+ model + "', " + price +", "+ mid + ")";
  try{
    stm.executeUpdate(query);
    out.println("The data was added to the table successfully! ");
  }catch(Exception exc){
    out.println("Inserting data failed!");
  }
  stm.close();
  conn.close();
%>
<br><br><a href="example10.html">add more records</a>
```

4. Save the document as **example10.jsp** in the Chap16\Chapter folder of your work folder. Then close Notepad.
5. Load the page example10.html using the following URL:

   http://localhost:8080/*workfolder*/Chap16/Chapter/example10.html

   This page is displayed as shown in Figure 16-9.
6. Fill out the form and then click the **Submit** button. A record is added to the product table.

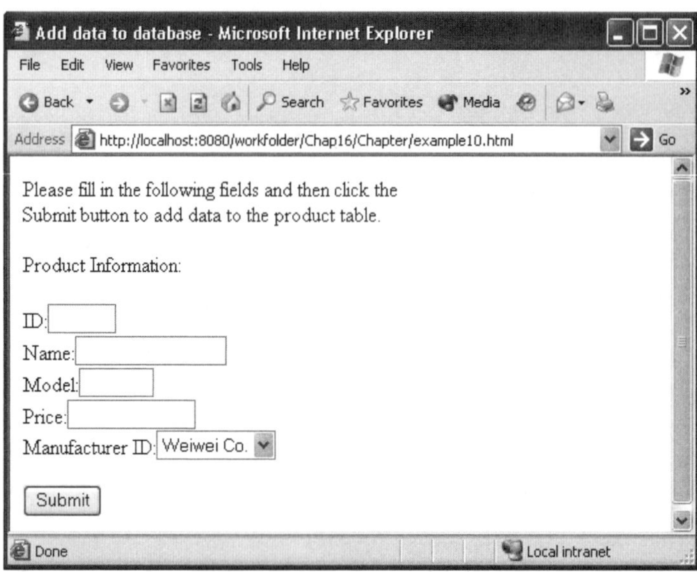

Figure 16-9 Adding a record to the product table

In this example, instead of directly entering the values to add to the product table, the values are collected from the form in the example10.html page. All product information collected from the form is retrieved by the example10.jsp page, which uses the data to construct a SQL command. Because the price column in the table has a data type of float, you can parse a string value to its corresponding float value. The manufacturer ID has an integer data type in the table, so the value is parsed into a corresponding integer value. The parsing is not required, as long as the data is not included in single quotations. For the char or varchar data type, however, the values must be included within single quotations. To verify the parsing issues, consider the following example:

```
String query1 = "INSERT INTO product VALUES('303', 'TV', 'S90', " +
                234.89 + ", " + 2 + ")";
String query2 = "INSERT INTO product VALUES('303', 'TV', 'S90', " +
                "234.89" + ", " + "2" + ")";
```

The values of query1 and query2 are identical. Although the price in query1 is provided as a float and the manufacturerID is an integer, in query2 they are all provided as Strings.

To add records to a table, the values for the columns having char or varchar data types must be included in single quotations.

Chapter Summary

- In general, a bean provides two methods for each property: one to get the property and one to set the property. To be able to get and set a bean's property, the getter and setter methods must following certain naming conventions.
- To instantiate a bean object from a class, the class must be available to the JSP engine. The class must be installed somewhere in the classpath, which is where the JSP engine searches for the classes it needs.
- JSP provides three basic action tags for working with beans: one to bind a local variable to an existing Bean object or instantiate a new Bean object, one to get a property, and one to set one or more properties.
- A JavaBean can be instantiated with one of the four possible scopes: page, request, session, and application scopes. Page scope beans have the shortest lifetime. They are created with the execution of the useBean action, and destroyed after execution of the page. Request scope beans have the same lifetime as the Request object. Session scope beans can be referenced throughout a session. They are destroyed when the session expires. Application scope beans have the longest lifetime. They are available across all users throughout the entire execution of the Web application.
- JDBC makes it possible to connect to a database from a JSP page and issue SQL commands to manipulate the database from a JSP page.
- You can create and modify tables, insert data into tables, update data in tables, delete data from tables, and get data from tables from a JSP page.

Review Questions

1. To access a bean's property named foo, the getter method name should be:
   a. getFoo
   b. getfoo
   c. foo
   d. Foo
2. To set a bean's property named foo, the setter method name should be:
   a. setFoo
   b. setfoo
   c. foo
   d. Foo

3. Which of the following scriptlets are equivalent to <jsp:getProperty name="aBean" property="foo"/>?
   a. <%= aBean.getFoo() %>
   b. <% out.print(aBean.getFoo()); %>
   c. <%= "foo" %>
   d. <%= aBean.foo %>
4. Which of the following scriptlets is/are equivalent to <jsp:setProperty name="aBean" property="foo"/>? (Select all that apply.)
   a. <% aBean.setFoo(); %>
   b. <% aBean.setFoo("foo"); %>
   c. <% aBean.setFoo(request.getParameter("foo")); %>
   d. <% aBean.setFoo(request.getParameterValues("foo")); %>
5. Which of the following scopes has the shortest lifetime?
   a. page scope
   b. request scope
   c. session scope
   d. application scope
6. Which of the following statements about the forward action tag is/are correct? (Select all that apply.)
   a. It causes the original request object to be forwarded to a new target page.
   b. It causes the contents buffered to the output stream in the original target page to be discarded.
   c. When it's called, none of the contents generated in the original target page are sent to the client.
7. The default scope in the useBean action tag is ______________.
   a. page scope
   b. request scope
   c. session scope
   d. application scope
8. If a request is not separated by the forward action, then the request scope bean in the page has the same scope as that in ______________.
   a. page scope
   b. session scope
   c. application scope

9. A session scope bean can be referenced ________________.
   a. by all users
   b. from all pages in the Web application
   c. from all pages in the same session
10. All changes made to a page scope bean are lost:
    a. when the page is opened
    b. when the page is closed
    c. only when the page is deleted
    d. when the page is updated
11. An application scope bean is instantiated how many times?
    a. 1
    b. 2
    c. 3
    d. more than three times
12. If a session scope bean and an application scope bean with the same name have been created, which of the following statements is/are correct? (Select all that apply.)
    a. The bean in the application can still be referenced.
    b. The application scope bean cannot be referenced.
    c. The session scope bean cannot be referenced.
    d. The session scope bean can be referenced.
13. An application scope bean is destroyed ________________. (Select all that apply.)
    a. when the Web server is shut down
    b. when the current session expires
    c. when the browser window is closed
    d. when a client computer is turned off
14. To connect to a database from JSP, which of the following must be done first?
    a. Create a statement object.
    b. Get a ResultSet object.
    c. Load the JDBC driver.
    d. Define the connection URL.
15. To close a connection to a database, which of the following orders is correct?
    a. first close resultSet, then close statement, and then close Connection
    b. first close connection, then close statement, and then close resultSet

Hands-on Exercises

If necessary, use Windows Explorer to create a new folder in the Chap16 folder in your work folder. Name this folder **Exercises**. As you create each of the following programs, save the program in the Chap16\Exercises folder in your work folder.

Exercise 16-1

In this exercise, you create a JavaBean that can be used to conduct an online poll.

To create a JavaBean to conduct an online poll:

1. If necessary, copy **PollBean.java** from this book's CD to the Chap16\Exercises folder of your work folder.
2. Open a DOS command window, and change directories by typing the following command and then pressing Enter: cd c:*workfolder*\Chap16\Exercises
3. Compile and install the bean class using the following command:

   javac -d c:*workfolder*\WEB-INF\classes PollBean.java

Exercise 16-2

In this exercise, you use the PollBean developed in Exercise 16-1 to conduct an online poll.

To conduct an online poll:

1. Open a new document in your text editor and type the following code:

```
<HTML>
<HEAD>
<TITLE>Using Poll Bean</TITLE>
</HEAD>
<BODY>
<b>Poll: </b>Do you believe in ghosts?<br><br>
<form action=exercise2.jsp method=post>
  <input type=radio name=answer value=yes>Yes    
  <input type=radio name=answer value=no>No<br><br>
  <input type=submit value="Submit">
</form>
<jsp:useBean id="pollBean" class="com.jspbook.chapter16.PollBean"
    scope="application"/>
<jsp:setProperty name="pollBean" property="answer"/>
<br>
<table align=left >
  <tr><th colspan=2 align=center>Poll Results</th></tr>
  <tr><td align=right><font size=1>Yes:</font> </td>
```

```
        <td align=center><font size=1><%=
  pollBean.getCountYes()%></font></td>
        <td width=100>
          <table>
            <tr>
              <td bgcolor=black align=center width=
                <%= pollBean.getWidthYes()%>>
                <font size=1 color=white>
                  <%= pollBean.getPercentYes()%></font></td>
            </tr>
          </table>
        </td>
    </tr>
    <tr><td align=right><font size=1>No:</font></td>
        <td align=center><font size=1 >
         <%= pollBean.getCountNo()%></font></td>
        <td width=100>
          <table>
            <tr>
              <td bgcolor=brown  align=center width=
                 <%= pollBean.getWidthNo()%>>
              <font size=1 color=white>
                <%= pollBean.getPercentNo()%></font></td>
            </tr>
          </table>
        </td>
    </tr>
    <tr><td align=right><font size=1>Total Votes:</font></td>
        <td align=center><font size=1>
            <%= pollBean.getTotal()%></font></td>
        <td><font size=1> </font></td>
    </tr>
  </table>
  </BODY>
  </HTML>
```

2. Save the file as **exercise2.jsp** in the Chap16\Exercises folder of your work folder. 16
3. Load this page using the following URL:

   http://localhost:8080/*workfolder*/Chap16/Exercises/exercise2.jsp
4. Read the poll question, and submit your answer.
5. Repeat Step 4 several times. The page shown in Figure 16-10 appears.

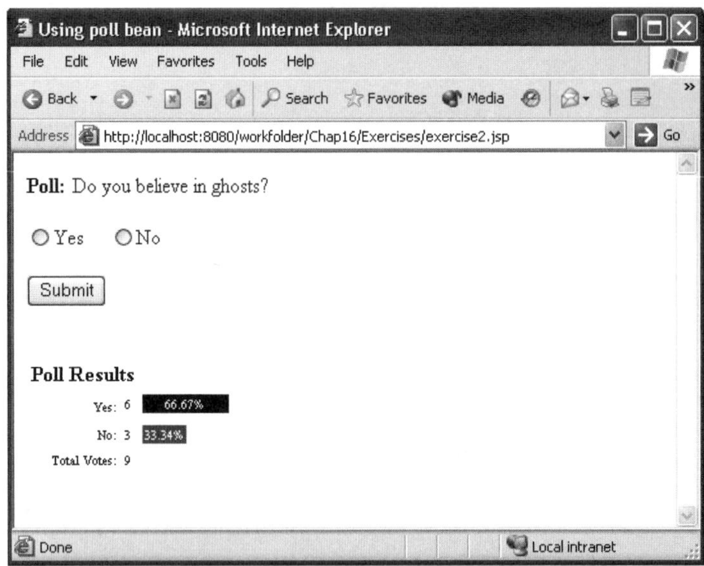

Figure 16-10

Exercise 16-3

In this exercise, you use a session scope bean to transfer data between forms on different pages. If a field on a form has been completed and the form submitted, then the field is automatically filled in when a user revisits the page.

To transfer data between forms:

1. If necessary, copy **DataBean.java** from this book's CD to the Chap16\Exercises folder of your work folder.
2. Compile and install the bean class properly.
3. If necessary, copy **exercise3-1.jsp** and **exercise3-2.jsp** from this book's CD to the Chap16\Exercises folder of your work folder.
4. Load the page exercise3-1.jsp using the following URL:

   http://localhost:8080/*workfolder*/Chap16/Exercises/exercise3-1.jsp
5. Fill in the form and click the **Next** button to submit the form; note that the page exercise3-2.jsp is displayed. Fill out the form and submit it. All the data you entered is displayed in your browser.
6. Click the link to return to either exercise3-1.jsp or exercise3-2.jsp. Notice that the form is filled in automatically with previously entered data. You can modify the data and resubmit the form.

Exercise 16-4

To use JDBC-ODBC to connect to a database, the database must be registered as an ODBC data source first. Given a Microsoft Access database, you will register it as an ODBC data source in this exercise.

To register a database as an ODBC data source:

1. If necessary, copy the Access database **customer.mdb** from this book's CD to the Chap16\Exercises folder of your work folder.
2. Open the Control Panel, and then open the Administrative Tools window. Double-click Data Sources (ODBC) to display the ODBC Data Source Administrator dialog box. Click the User DSN tab if it is not selected.
3. Click the Add button to open the Create New Data Source dialog box. In the driver name list, click Microsoft Access Driver (*.MDB), and then click Finish. The ODBC Microsoft Access Setup dialog box opens.
4. In the Data Source Name text box, type customerDSN. Click the Select button to select the database. Select customer.mdb in the Chap16\Exercises folder of your work folder. Click OK until you return to the ODBC Data Source Administrator dialog box. Click OK. Close the Administrative Tools window.

Now you have set the ODBC data source. You will use this data source name to access this database in the following exercise.

Exercise 16-5

In this exercise, you use JSP to access the customer database and display all customer information in an HTML table.

1. Open a new document in a text editor. Import the java.sql package and provide all connection information:

```
<%@ page import="java.sql.*" %>
<%
 String url = "jdbc:odbc:customerDSN";
 String username="";
 String password="";
 Connection  conn=null;
 String classPath = "sun.jdbc.odbc.JdbcOdbcDriver";
```

2. Add code to load the database driver based on the connection information (you are required to add this code segment).
3. Add the following code to create a Statement object and execute a query to get a resultSet:

```
<%  Statement stm= conn.createStatement();
    String query= "SELECT * FROM customer";
    ResultSet rst = stm.executeQuery(query);
%>
```

16

4. Add this code to process the resultSet and display the data in an HTML table. Then close the connection:

```
<table><tr><th>ID</th><th>Name</th><th>Address</th>
          <th>Zipcode</th><th>Phone</th></tr>
      <% while(rst.next()){%>
      <tr><td><%= rst.getString(1) %></td>
          <td><%= rst.getString(2) %></td>
          <td><%= rst.getString(3) %></td>
          <td><%= rst.getString(4) %></td>
          <td><%= rst.getString(5) %></td>
      </tr>
      <%}%>
</table>
<%
    rst.close();
    stm.close();
    conn.close();
%>
```

5. Save the document as **exercise5.jsp** in the Chap16\Exercises folder of your work folder.
6. Load this page in your browser. All the data in the customer table should be displayed in an HTML table.

WEB PROGRAMMING PROJECTS

If necessary, use Windows Explorer to create a new folder in the Chap16 folder in your work folder. Name this folder **Projects**. Save the files that you create in these projects in the Chap16\Projects folder in your work folder.

Project 16-1

EBCity provides various products for Web-based learning environments. The manager wants to add an online test system to the Web. You are hired to design this system. The requirements for the system are as follows:

- Five questions are displayed on each page. That means if there are 20 questions on a test, the questions appear over four pages.
- All answers are saved into a session bean before an examinee submits the test for grading.
- After the test is submitted, the bean is cleared either by expiring the current session or by deleting answers from the bean.
- Examinees can go back and modify their answers.

To complete this case project, you must develop a JavaBean class to carry answers from one page to another. To create the grading system, display all answers after an examinee submits answers for grading.

Project 16-2

You are required to design a shopping cart bean that can be customized as follows:

1. The bean can store the following information:
   - Item name
   - Price
   - Quantity
   - Subtotal for each item
   - Total for all items
   - Other features of items, such as color, size, weight, etc.
2. Item names can be determined within the JSP page instead of hard-coded.
3. The price for each item can be customized in a JSP page.
4. New features about products can be added dynamically.

Project 16-3

The XYZ Entertainment company hired you to develop a Web site to extend their business over the Internet. This company carries music CDs. You are asked to provide a page that allows clients to view all music that is currently available or to search for special music. All data is stored in a text file containing the composer's name and music title. Each record takes one line in the file, and the composer's name and music title are separated by a tab. Customers should also be able to search for music written by a particular composer.

CHAPTER

17

PHP: PART I

In this chapter you will:

- Prepare to use PHP
- Explore PHP for the first time
- Understand PHP basics
- Display PHP output
- Manage PHP program flow

This chapter introduces you to the PHP Hypertext Preprocessor scripting language, usually called Personal Home Page (PHP). PHP is among the most stable and efficient tools available for creating dynamic, interactive Web pages. In this chapter and the next, you will create an online, database-driven application that manages a small mailing list. During this process, you will examine most aspects of the PHP environment, including dynamic form creation, decision making in code, and database interaction with basic SQL commands. This chapter focuses on the PHP language itself, and Chapter 18 focuses on the interaction between PHP and MySQL.

Preparing to Use PHP

The PHP language was designed to help developers create dynamic and data-driven Web pages. It was created in 1994 by Rasmus Lerdorf as a simple macro language for building small, personal home pages, but quickly outgrew its original intended use and became one of the most popular Web development tools on the market. PHP is used on more than 1.5 million Web sites around the world, and the number continues to grow. It is now considered a tool of choice for all aspects of Web development, including creating dynamic Web content, business and e-commerce sites, and Web portals.

PHP interacts with one main external tool, the MySQL database management system, to access data stored in a database. MySQL must be installed on a functional Web server to interact with PHP, but this is a relatively easy step in setting up the PHP environment. See the "Read This Before You Begin" page in this book for more information.

PHP is a server-side scripting language that you can embed into HTML documents. You can also embed HTML in PHP scripts. One format can call external references to the other format as necessary. The approach in this chapter is to embed HTML tags into PHP files so you become acquainted with PHP scripts.

PHP scripts are parsed and interpreted on the server side of a Web application. Any resulting output from that action is then sent to the Web browser, which displays the page on the requesting client (the user).

PHP has a promising future because it is popular with Web developers and Web designers alike, and is powerful and easy to use. You often see PHP used in portal creations because it can handle larger projects as well as smaller personal home pages. As you work on the Web, note the links and addresses as they appear in the status bar or Address text box—many include the PHP extension. These pages are PHP scripts designed to provide interactivity.

Exploring the Open Source Phenomenon

You might know that some software companies develop software for profit and others create software because they enjoy it. PHP is open-source software, which means that it can be redistributed free of charge and its source code is available for development. The Linux operating system, for example, is also open-source software that is freely available and stable because it is maintained by a group of dedicated developers. More than one company can work on developing an open-source software product; such a product is typically developed by peers in the field, and can be reviewed and tested by thousands of people.

For a full discussion of open-source software, visit *www.opensource.org*. The site explains that certain rules must be followed for a product to be considered as having an open source. The site also publicizes many open-source products that might help you in future development projects.

Finding PHP Products

Because PHP is an open-source product, you can download it from the PHP Web site, *www.php.net*, which includes a product **FAQ** (frequently asked questions), a mailing list archive, and various articles on the PHP product line.

Before you download PHP you should also decide which Web server software you will use. The material in these two chapters uses the Apache Web server software, but you can use almost any other Web server (Microsoft Personal Web Server or IIS, for example) and produce the same results.

PHP has many built-in connections that allow you to interact with almost any back-end database, which is where a Web application stores data. Conversely, the front end of a Web application, also known as the Presentation layer, is what the user sees. MySQL is often used as a back-end database for Web content management because it is free (open source), supports multiple users and platforms, and has a powerful and reliable SQL interface. If necessary, you can obtain MySQL at *www.mysql.org*. If you are using a different database, PHP includes a generic open database connectivity (ODBC) set of protocols so you can manage your Web content.

As you can see, PHP is not necessarily a product that stands on its own. It usually needs database access to provide information for dynamic Web content. Because PHP travels over the Internet, it also requires a server to communicate between the client machine and the Internet server. Finally, it requires an HTML Presentation layer, which is supplied by browsers such as Netscape Navigator or Microsoft Internet Explorer.

Installing PHP

After obtaining the most recent version of PHP, you can install the software and start running it. If you need to install PHP on a Web server, let the server administrator do it for you. If you need instructions for installing PHP on a particular operating system, consult the user guide or the PHP Web site.

Exploring PHP for the First Time

To start working with PHP, you can create a script that contains HTML code. In the following steps, you create a PHP script that says hello to the world, as all programming languages encourage you to do. You can create the script using any text editor, such as Notepad in Windows or TextPad on the Macintosh. For a list of other PHP-friendly text editors, visit *www.itworks.demon.co.uk/phpeditors.htm*.

When you use an Apache Web server, you store HTML and other documents in a folder where the new Web service is located, usually in C:\Program Files\Apache Group\Apache\htdocs for an Apache installation. The following steps include instructions to save your files in the Chap17\Chapter folder in your work folder. Check with your instructor to see if you can create subfolders in the Apache\htdocs folder, such as Apache\htdocs\Chap17\Chapter, or whether the system administrator can redirect the Apache server to find the PHP files in the Chap17\Chapter folder in a different work folder.

To create a PHP script that displays "Hello, world!":

1. Open a new document in your text editor and type the following code:

```
<html>
<head>
     <title>Hello World Example</title>
</head>

<body>

<?

Echo "Hello, world!";

?>

</body>
</html>
```

2. Save the file as **helloworld.php** in the Chap17\Chapter folder in your work folder. Then close the text editor.
3. Start your browser. To open the file in the browser, type **http://localhost/Chap17/Chapter/helloworld.php** as the URL. The Web page appears, as shown in Figure 17-1.
4. Close your browser.

Remember that you are building a Web service, so you need to address your PHP files as if they are stored on a Web server even though they are stored on your local machine. When accessing a PHP file (or any Web-enabled file) that is being served from your local machine, always precede it with *http://localhost/*. This is why you referenced the helloworld.php file as *http://localhost/Chap17/Chapter/helloworld.php* in the previous steps.

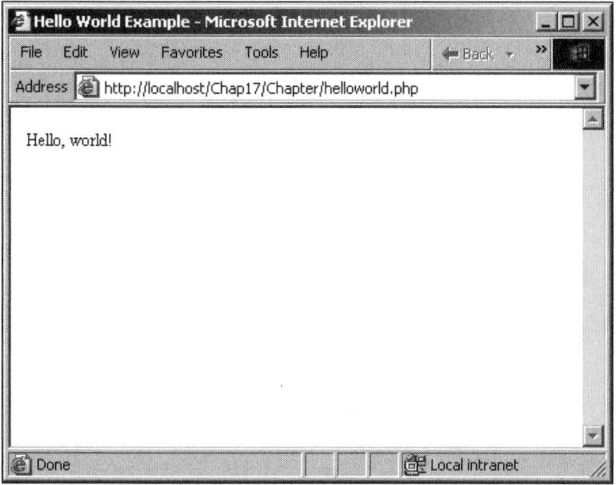

Figure 17-1 PHP Hello World example

In the previous steps, you embedded PHP code within HTML tags, yet the file is called a PHP file and has a .php file extension. Note that the PHP code is identified to the Apache server with the special HTML <? and ?> tag combination. These tags are all you need to tell the Web server to process PHP code in the file.

Including Files

When developing more than a single home page for the Internet, you probably want the pages to have a common look and feel. To make this possible, PHP has provided a method called **included files**. These files let you incorporate common artwork, contact information, and menu and link options into your Web pages with a minimum of code. (Included files have other advanced uses, but they are beyond the scope of this text.)

In the following steps, you examine some code first, and then focus on the included files.

To include files in a PHP script:

1. Open a new document in your text editor and type the following code:

```
<html>
<head>
      <title> Contents of Header.inc are here... </title>
</head>

<body>
<h1> This is a common header line </h1>
<h2> to be used across all my Web pages </h2>
```

2. Save the file as **header.inc** in the Chap17\Chapter folder in your work folder. Then close the file.

17

3. Open a new document in your text editor and enter the following code:

```
<? include("header.inc");  ?>

<br> <br>

<a href="secondpage.php"> Go to Second Page </a>

</body>
</html>
```

4. Save this file as **mainpage.php** in the Chap17\Chapter folder in your work folder. Then close the file.
5. Open a new document in your text editor and enter the following code:

```
<? include("header.inc");  ?>

<br> <br>

<a href="mainpage.php"> Return to Main Page </a>

</body>
</html>
```

6. Save the file as **secondpage.php** in the Chap17\Chapter folder in your work folder. Then close the text editor.

   The first file you created, header.inc, is simple HTML code that can be repeated on most Web pages. The file includes headers, signified by the <h1> and <h2> tag combinations. This include file is called in the two subsequent PHP files and included in these files by the Web server before being served to the client.

7. Start your browser and type **http://localhost/Chap17/Chapter/main page.php** (with no spaces) as the URL. The main page appears, as shown in Figure 17-2.

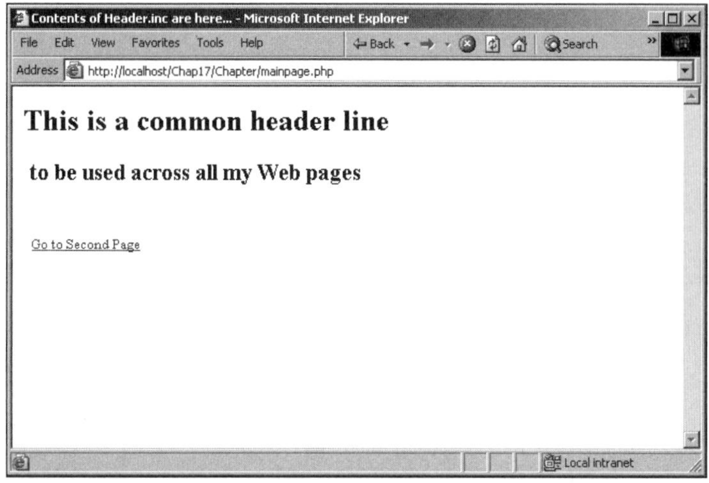

Figure 17-2 Main page with header.inc content included

8. Type **http://localhost/Chap17/Chapter/secondpage.php** as the URL. See Figure 17-3.

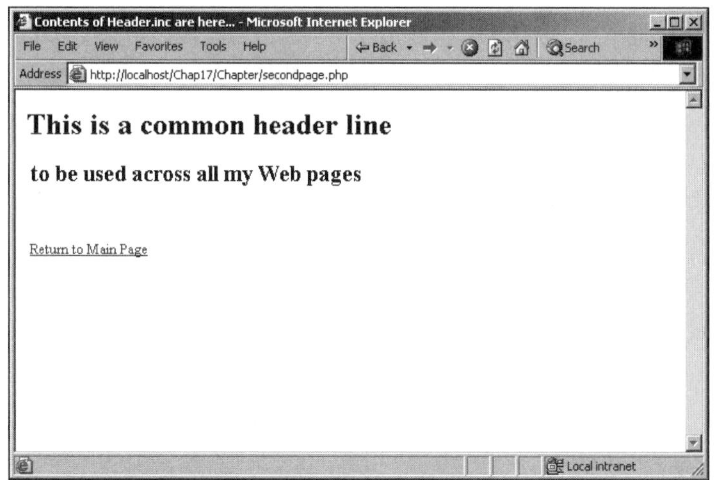

Figure 17-3 Second page with header.inc content also included

Note that the two pages have the same header and changing links.

UNDERSTANDING PHP BASICS

All statements in PHP are terminated with a semicolon (;). If you forget to end a statement with a semicolon, you see a parsing error such as this one:

```
Parse error: parse error in C:\Program Files\Apache
Group\Apache\htdocs\PHP_Site\template.php on line 10
```

When this error occurs, you should first look for a missing semicolon on the first or second line prior to the reported line. Parsing errors are often caused by missing semicolons.

Even though semicolons end all statements, they're only the beginning of what you need to know about PHP. The following sections provide more details to help you use the language.

Defining PHP Variables

You already know that in PHP, anything between the <? and ?> tags is interpreted as PHP code and converted into HTML on the server before being sent to the requesting client machine. All languages have variables and operators that act on the variables in this code. Variables in PHP are preceded with a dollar sign ($) and contain either letters or numbers. PHP is called a loosely typed programming language, meaning that you don't have to predefine your variables; you can define and use them as needed. However, you do have to follow certain rules for naming a variable:

- Precede the variable name with a dollar sign ($).
- Assign the variable a meaningful name that you can remember in the future.
- Name the variable with uppercase or lowercase letters, numbers, or the underscore (_) character.
- Do not allow the first character after the ($) sign to be a number.
- Variable names are case sensitive. For example, $UserName and $Username are considered different names.
- Assign the variable an initial value with a single equals (=) sign.

The code listing that follows includes examples of variables being defined. Each definition is followed with an inline comment (signified by the doubleslash characters: //) that explains why the definition is good, bad, or not advisable.

```
<? $Password = "bigdog";  // Good variable definition ?>
<? $1stName = "Peter"; // Bad: variable name starts with a number ?>
<? $variableOne = 1 ; // OK, but not advisable as the variable name is
vague ?>
<? $LastName == "MacIntyre"; // Bad: variable assignment is being done
with two equals signs ?>
```

Using Variable Scope

If a variable is defined at the start of a PHP file, it stays in memory until the end of that file. This is known as the variable's **scope**. If a variable is assigned a value of 5 in one PHP file, and that file calls another PHP file that has a variable of the same name, then the first variable is terminated and its value is lost. One major distinction that relates to a variable's scope involves the processing of Web-based forms. Any variables that are defined within a PHP/HTML form and sent to the server with the form's Post method are automatically sent with the called Post action and named in PHP by the same name used in the HTML form. Consider the following code excerpt:

```
<body><h1> Please enter amount and tax rate </h1>
<br><br>
<form action="taxcalc.php" method="post">
Amount  
<input type=text name="amount" size=15> <br><br>
Tax Rate:  
<Input type=text name="rate" size=15> % <br><br>
<Input type=submit name="submit" value="Submit form">
```

The form command in the previous example is calling a PHP file named taxcalc.php using the Post method. Two form variables (input types) are used on the form: amount and rate. When a user clicks the form's submit button, the PHP file is called (shown in the following code listing) and the variables in the form are sent (with their contents) to the PHP file and automatically named with the PHP variable-naming rules. You will see more of this approach in the rest of the chapter, as the HTML form will be frequently used.

```
<html>
<head>
   <title> Sales Tax Calculator </title>
</head>
<?
if ($SecondTime == "") {
   echo"
      <body><h1> Please enter amount and tax rate </h1>
      <br><br>
      <form action=\"taxcalc.php\" method=\"post\">
      <input type=\"hidden\" name=\"SecondTime\" Value=1>
      Amount  
      <input type=text name=\"amount\" size=15> <br><br>
      Tax Rate:  
      <Input type=text name=\"rate\" size=15> % <br><br>
      <Input type=submit name=\"submit\" value=\"Submit form\">  
      <Input type=reset name=\"reset\" value=\"Clear form\">
   ";
} else {
   $calc_tax = $amount + ($amount * ($rate / 100)) ;
   $amount = number_format($amount,2,'.','');
```

```
    $calc_tax = number_format($calc_tax,2,'.','');
    echo "
    <body><h1> The calculated tax rate is as follows : </h1>
    <table><tr><td> Entered Amount: </td>
    <td>$ $amount </td></tr>
    <tr><td> Entered Tax Rate: </td>
    <td>  $rate  % </td></tr>
    <tr><td> Calculated Tax  Amount: </td>
    <td>$  $calc_tax </td></tr>
    </table><br>
    <form action=\"taxcalc.php\" method=\"post\">
    <input type=\"hidden\" name=\"SecondTime\" Value=\"\">
    <Input type=submit name=\"submit\" value=\"Return to Calculator\">
    </form>
    ";
}
?>
</body>
</html>
```

When using the HTML form to define and send variables to a PHP file, think ahead to the PHP side of the equation and name the form variables in a way that allows the PHP interpreter to define them accurately.

Be sure to have Register Globals set to ON in your php.ini file in order for the form data to be sent with the POST method. Your Web server technical support staff or lab instructor may have to confirm this setting for you.

Understanding Variable Types

You can use a number of variables in PHP, but the two main categories are scalar (single value) and array (multivalue) variables. The types of scalar variables are shown in Table 17-1. Each variable belongs to a basic style of data normally known as a data type. Arrays will not be covered in depth in these PHP chapters, but be aware that you can use them when you have multiple values that relate to a single subject in your code.

Table 17-1 Scalar variable data types

Data type	Explanation
Integer	Nonfloating point numbers such as 1, 10, 200, and 50,000
Doubles	Floating-point numbers such as 1.1, 5.456, 10.03, and 2.4545
Boolean	Logical TRUE and FALSE values
String	Simple textual values such as "one" or "This is the day"

Keep in mind that these variables are assigned in PHP in a loose fashion. This means that simply assigning a variable a value also assigns it the data type of that value. Consider the following examples:

```
<? $Password = "bigdog";  // $Password is a string data type ?>
<? $Number = 192 ; // $number is an integer ?>
<? $Money = 10.03 ; // $Money is a Double ?>
```

Using Operators

Operators are symbols that are typically used to assign values, perform math functions, or determine a logical course of action. Table 17-2 describes the operators that PHP uses. Note that the rules and uses of the operators depend on their context.

Table 17-2 PHP operators

PHP operator	Description
Variable operators	
=	Value assignment operator: $user = "Peter";
+	Addition operator: $value = $one + $two;
-	Subtraction operator: $value = $one - $two;
*	Multiplication operator: $value = $one * $two;
/	Division operator: $value = $one / $two;
%	Modulus (remainder) operator: $value = $one % $two;
Comparison operators	
= =	Equality: $this == $that
===	Identical values (identical value and data type): $this === $that
!= (or) <>	Not equal: $this != $that
<	Less than: $this < $that
>	Greater than: $this > $that
<=	Less than or equal to: $this <= $that
>=	Greater than or equal to: $this >= $that
Logical operators	
!	NOT: ! $this => Returns TRUE if $this is False
&&	AND: $this && $that => Returns TRUE if both $this and $that are true
||	OR: $this || $that => Returns TRUE if either or both $this and $that are true

You can use parentheses to manage the order of execution of any PHP statement. For example, consider how the following calculations change when parentheses are used to control which calculation takes precedence:

```
total = 4 + 5 * 30 -15 ;   //  $total here is 139
// above code is equivalent to: 4 + (5 * 30) -15
$total = (4 + 5) * (30 -15) ;   //  $total here is 135
```

If math operations are not working as you expect, reexamine the code and see if a parentheses pair is missing or out of place.

Using Comments in Code

Like most computer languages, PHP allows you to add explanations to the code in the form of **comments**. These comments are ignored by the PHP parser, but are useful to you or anyone else who uses or maintains your code. Comments should be added whenever necessary to explain code that is hard to follow. If you have been paying attention to some of the code samples so far, you have seen the inline comments indicator (//) in action.

If used well, comments are a great asset to your code. To insert a comment in a single line of PHP code, you preface the comment with either a pound symbol (#) or two forward slashes (//). To comment multiple lines of code, use the '/*' and '*/' tags to enclose the comment. Review the examples in the following code and note some of the uses of comments.

```
<?
/*  ***********************************
Programmer: Peter Beck MacIntyre
Release Date: January 2005
Last Modified: February 2005
Code Use: To show the use of code comments
*********************************   */
$total = 4 + 5 * 30 -15 ;   //  $total here is 139
$total = (4 + 5) * (30 -15) ;   #  $total here is 135
// as you can see the above code will allow comments
// within the line of functioning code as well as here
// on lines by themselves
?>
```

Displaying PHP Output

To send results of your code to the users of your applications, you need a way to display information in your Web browser. PHP has two functions that allow this display: echo and print. You have already seen the echo command used earlier in this chapter with the "Hello, world!" example. The only difference between echo and print is that the print function returns a 1 or 0 integer (denoting success or failure, respectively), for the contents of the function being displayed. Because these functions are so similar, the code examples in these chapters use the echo command exclusively.

Note that Echo also has a shortcut syntax, in which you can immediately follow the opening tag with an equal sign, as in <?= $this ?>. This saves a few keystrokes.

For more advanced formatting of output, consider using the printf() and sprintf() printing functions. Printf() gives more power in the displaying of variables by changing integers to display as decimals at the same time as the variable is displayed, for example. Sprintf() works the same as printf() except that a string value is returned to PHP so that you can use it later in your code if so desired. Refer to PHP documentation for examples and further details.

The following syntax shows examples of how echo and print are used in PHP.

```
<? $var = "this is a string";
echo "Anything between these quotation marks will be displayed";
echo " in the browser, <br> including the contents of variables: <br>
$var ";
$good = print("  is being printed to the browser");
echo "<br> $good";    // places 1 on the browser if previous command
worked
?>
```

The output of the preceding code looks similar to Figure 17-4.

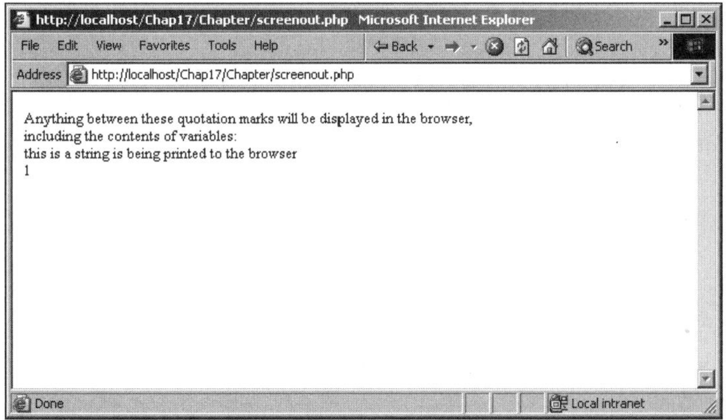

Figure 17-4 PHP code sending output to the Web browser

Also, be aware that if you want to send PHP reserved characters (such as double quotations) to the Web browser within the echo command, you must use the backslash character, as in the following example. (You will see this more clearly in the Hands-on Exercises at the end of this chapter.):

```
echo"<br> <form action=\"taxcalc.php\" method=\"post\"> ";
```

Managing PHP Program Flow

Now that you have seen how to make decisions in your code, you need to be able to react to the results of those decisions. You use the following four constructs to manage the flow of your PHP programs:

- If-then-else
- Switch-case
- For-next
- Do-while

The following sections cover the basic syntax for each of these constructs. Each section includes coding examples so you can see how the constructs work. As you become familiar with their uses, keep in mind that these constructs can be used in concert with each other. Be sure to avoid creating an endless loop, as they are hard to locate and debug.

Using the If-then-else Construct

The if-then-else logical flow construct is used in about 70 percent of flow control code. It tests a single or compound decision and then executes code based on the answer to the test. There are variations on this syntax, such as ignoring the else (FALSE) portion of the test or nesting more if-then-else tests within existing ones. The simple syntax for the construct is as follows:

```
If  (condition)
{
// code based on TRUE result of condition
} else {
// code based on FALSE result of condition
}
```

To see this construct in action, consider the following code:

```
<?
If  ($totalsales == 0)
{
echo "There were no sales recorded at this time ... ";
} else {
echo " <h2> Thank you for shopping at our online store ! </h2>";
echo "<h3> Please come by again soon... <br>";
echo "Your total purchase today was: $totalsales </h3>";
}
?>
```

As you can see in the previous code, a simple logical test is being performed on the value of $totalsales. If there are no sales ($totalsales == 0), then the first part of the echoed output is displayed in the browser. However, if the value of $totalsales is not 0, then the code assumes there is a sale (a positive value) and the customer is thanked for spending money at the store.

Notice that there is no test for the condition of a negative value, but you can change this by adjusting the previous code. Simply change the original condition to test for a less than or equal to state of the $totalsales variable. The changed line of code is in bold text in the following example.

```
<?
If  ($totalsales <= 0)
{
echo "There were no sales recorded at this time … ";
} else {
echo " <h2> Thank you for shopping at our online store ! </h2>";
echo "<h3> Please come by again soon… <br>";
echo "Your total purchase today was: $totalsales </h3>";
}
?>
```

You might want to thank someone who has bought over $1000 worth of merchandise from your store. You can alter the basic if-then construct to allow for that situation.

```
<?
If  ($totalsales <= 0)
{
echo "There were no sales recorded at this time … ";
} else {
if ($totalsales > 1000)
{
echo " <h2> Thank you for shopping at our online store ! </h2>";
echo "<h3> Please come by again soon… <br>";
echo "Because your total purchase today was: $totalsales </h3>";
echo " <h1> We want to give you a 10% discount on your next in-store
purchase with us ! </h1>";
echo " <h2> Please print this page for your records, and present it at
your next visit to our downtown location </h2>";
} else {
echo " <h2> Thank you for shopping at our online store ! </h2>";
echo "<h3> Please come by again soon… <br>";
echo "Your total purchase today was: $totalsales </h3>";
}
}
?>
```

17

The previous code is an example of **nesting** logical constructs within other logical constructs. This programming concept can be quite powerful and effective, but also confusing if overused. When you start to nest your code, you need to track the conditions and be sure that all the semicolons and curly braces are in the right place.

The if statement can also be written to execute on a single line of code, as in the following example: `if ($balance >= 5000) $Credit = 1;`

Using the Switch-case Construct

If you want to test for many values in the previous code example, you do not have to write continuous if-then conditions and nest them until you produce all the possibilities. Instead, you could use the switch-case construct. This construct lends itself to the solution of testing values for more than one situation. So, if a variable could hold any number between 1 and 10, and different code could be executed for each number value, then it would be quite cumbersome to have to write this code with a series of nested if statements. Instead, use the switch-case construct. The simple syntax for this construct is as follows:

```
Switch  ($value)
{
case 1 :
// code based on $value being equal to 1
[optional] break;
case 2 :
// code based on $value being equal to 2
[optional] break;
case 999 :
// code based on $value being equal to whatever number you want
[optional] break;
default :
// code based on $value being not already dealt with.
[optional] break;
}
```

In the previous example, note that the `break`; statement is shown as optional after each case condition. If this `break`; statement is not used, then the cases that follow it will also have their code executed. This can be useful if you want to program for those situations, but for now use the `break`; statement after each case condition. Also, the default condition at the end of the switch construct executes if none of the other conditions result in a TRUE state.

For the next example, suppose that you want to give different percentage discounts based on the amount of money that customers have spent. If they spend over $10,000, you will give them a 40 percent discount. In addition, customers will receive a 25 percent discount for purchases over $5000 and a 10 percent discount for purchases over $1000. Note that the case condition tests can only be performed with a simple equality test. In the following code example, you cannot test for the state of $totalsales being greater than 5000, but you can use simple, inline if decisions to determine a value from a variable's contents, and then execute the appropriate switch-case code.

```
<?
If  ($totalsales <= 0)
{
echo "There were no sales recorded at this time … ";
} else {
if ($totalsales >= 10000) $SwitchCase = 1;
if ($totalsales >= 1000 && $totalsales <= 9999) $SwitchCase = 2;
if ($totalsales >= 100 && $totalsales <= 999) $SwitchCase = 3;
if ($totalsales <= 100) $SwitchCase = 4;
switch ($SwitchCase)
{
Case 1:
echo " <h2> Thank you for shopping at our online store ! </h2>";
echo "<h3> Please come by again soon… <br>";
echo "Because your total purchase today was: $totalsales </h3>";
echo " <h1> We want to give you a 40% discount on your next in-store
purchase with us ! </h1>";
echo " <h2> Please print this page for your records, and present it at
your next visit to our downtown location </h2>";
break;
Case 2:
echo " <h2> Thank you for shopping at our online store ! </h2>";
echo "<h3> Please come by again soon… <br>";
echo "Because your total purchase today was: $totalsales </h3>";
echo " <h1> We want to give you a 25% discount on your next in-store
purchase with us ! </h1>";
echo " <h2> Please print this page for your records, and present it at
your next visit to our downtown location </h2>";
break;
Case 3:
echo " <h2> Thank you for shopping at our online store ! </h2>";
echo "<h3> Please come by again soon… <br>";
echo "Because your total purchase today was: $totalsales </h3>";
echo " <h1> We want to give you a 10% discount on your next in-store
purchase with us ! </h1>";
echo " <h2> Please print this page for your records, and present it at
your next visit to our downtown location </h2>";
break;
default:
echo " <h2> Thank you for shopping at our online store ! </h2>";
echo "<h3> Please come by again soon… <br>";
echo "Your total purchase today was: $totalsales </h3>";
break;
}
}
?>
```

Using the For-next Loop

Another kind of flow control construct is the for-next loop. This construct is best suited to repeating a set amount of code for a set amount of iterations. The syntax for this construct is as follows:

```
For (start condition; end condition; value adjustment)
{
// code to be executed...
}
```

For example, if you wanted to process a tax rate of 10 percent over a range of dollar values from $100 to $5000 in $100 increments, you would use the for-next construct. The following code provides an example:

```
<?
For ($money = 100; $money <=5000; $money = $money + 100)
{
//alternately you could write the increment equation as $money += 100
$total = $money + ($money * 0.10);
echo "The tax on $money at 10% is $total";
echo "<br>";
}
?>
```

The for-next construct is appropriate for repeating a process for a set number of times, but what happens when you don't know the ending point of a loop until run time? You can use the last item explained in this section, the do-while construct.

Using the Do-while Construct

Typically the do-while construct will perform indefinitely until a certain condition becomes TRUE. A variation of this construct is known as the do loop. The do portion of this construct always executes at least once, and continues executing until a condition is met. Because this kind of looping construct depends on a variable condition, that condition might never be reached (never become TRUE). Thus, you could create an endlessly running loop of code. The syntax of the do-while construct is as follows:

```
Do {
// code to be executed ...
}
while (condition);
```

An example of a do-while loop in action is shown in the following code:

```
<?
$number = 1;
Do {
echo " the current number is:  $number " ;
$number ++;
```

```
echo "<br>";
}
While ($number <= 50);
?>
```

This code runs as a counter until the variable $number equals 51. The $number ++; statement serves as the counter. The execution point then moves to the next line of executable code following the while portion of the loop.

Chapter Summary

- PHP is among the most stable and efficient tools available for creating dynamic, interactive Web pages. It started as a simple macro language for building small personal home pages, but quickly became one of the most popular Web development tools on the market.
- Because you are building a Web service when you use PHP, you need to address PHP files as if they are stored on a Web server, even though they are stored on your local machine. When accessing a PHP file that is being served from your local machine, always precede it with *http://localhost/*.
- All statements in PHP are terminated with a semicolon (;). Parsing errors are often caused by missing semicolons.
- To define variable names in PHP, you must precede them with a dollar sign ($) and use meaningful names that you can remember later. The first character after the ($) sign cannot be a number. Otherwise, you can use any combination of uppercase and lowercase letters, numbers, and the underscore (_) character. Variable names are case sensitive, and you must assign variables an initial value with a single equal (=) sign.
- To send the results of your code to the users of your applications, use the echo and print functions in PHP to display information in your Web browser.
- PHP handles its logical flow of programming with four basic constructs: if-then-else, switch-case, for-next, and do-while.

Review Questions

1. What does the acronym PHP stand for?
   a. Professional Home Page
   b. Personal Home Page
   c. Practical Hypertext Pages
   d. Professional Hypertext Product

2. Who created PHP, and in what year?
   a. Linus Torvalds, 1992
   b. Steven Wozniak, 1993
   c. Rasmus Lerdorf, 1994
   d. Klaus Mueller, 1995
3. PHP, like Linux and MySQL, is known as an ________________ product.
   a. open file
   b. open application
   c. open-source
   d. open door
4. Variable names must conform to which of the following rules? (Select all that apply.)
   a They must start with a ($) symbol.
   b. They cannot begin with a number (after the ($) symbol).
   c. They are not case sensitive.
   d. They must be capitalized.
5. Use the ________________ symbols to make inline code comments.
   a. /* and */
   b. # and //
   c. * and *\
   d. \\ and *
6. External files can be incorporated into the PHP file with the ________________ function.
   a. input (…)
   b. insert (…)
   c. include (…)
   d. import (…)
7. ________________ are the two main types of variables that PHP uses.
   a. Logical and array
   b. Scalar and logical
   c. Comparison and array
   d. Scalar and array

8. The ________________ command shows information on a Web browser from within PHP code and returns a value of 1 or 0 depending on success or failure.
   a. print (…)
   b. echo (…)
   c. array (…)
   d. post (…)
9. A construct that performs indefinitely until a certain condition becomes true is called ________________.
   a. if-then
   b. do-while
   c. switch-case
   d. for-next
10. The ________________ portion of the switch-case construct is used to do anything that the other case condition tests do not handle.
    a. otherwise ;
    b. default ;
    c. switch_else ;
    d. case_else ;
11. All statements in PHP are terminated with a(n) ________________.
    a. opening parenthesis (
    b. semicolon ;
    c. colon :
    d. period .
12. When accessing a PHP file (or any Web-enabled file) that is being served from your local machine, always precede it with ________________.
    a. *http://localhost/*
    b. *http://My documents*
    c. *http://home*
    d. *http://Webfiles*
13. Operators are symbols that are typically used to ________________.
    a. assign values
    b. perform math functions
    c. determine a course of action
    d. all of the above

14. The for-next loop has the following parts:
    a. for (start condition, value adjustment, end condition)
    b. for (value adjustment, start condition, end condition)
    c. for (start condition, end condition, value adjustment)
    d. for (end condition, start condition, value adjustment)
15. The do-while construct:
    a. can loop continuously until you run out of system resources
    b. can control the flow of programming code until a certain value changes
    c. can loop through a subset of programming code until a value is reached
    d. both a and c

HANDS-ON EXERCISES

If necessary, use Windows Explorer to create a new folder in the Chap17 folder in your work folder. Name this folder **Exercises**. As you create each of the following programs, save the program in the Chap17\Exercises folder in your work folder.

Recall that when you use an Apache Web server, you store HTML and other documents in a folder where the new Web service is located, usually in C:\Program Files\Apache Group\Apache\htdocs for an Apache installation. The following steps include instructions to save your files in the Chap17\Exercises folder in your work folder. Check with your instructor to see if you can create subfolders in the Apache\htdocs folder, such as Apache\htdocs\Chap17\Exercises, or whether the system administrator can redirect the Apache server to find the PHP files in the Chap17\Exercises folder in a different work folder.

Be sure to have Register Globals set to ON in your php.ini file in order for the form data to be sent with the POST method. Your Web server technical support staff or lab instructor may have to confirm this setting for you.

Exercise 17-1

Develop three Web pages with links among them all. Each page should have a common header that shows the company name (ACME Company), address, and phone number. Use include files so that the heading only needs to be created once.

To create three Web pages:

1. Open your text editor, and type the following code:

```
<html>
<head>
```

```
        <title>Common Header </title>
</head>
<body>
<h1> This is a common header line </h1>
<h2> for the ACME Company </h2>
<h3> located at 124 Any Street, Somewhere, MA
<br><br>
1-800-555-9876 </h3>
```

2. Save the file as **common.inc** in the Chap17\Exercises folder in your work folder, and then close the document.
3. Open a new document in your text editor, and type the following code:

```
<? include("common.inc");  ?>
<br> <br>
<a href="page2.php"> Go to Page 2 </a>
<br> <br>
<a href="page3.php"> Go to Page 3 </a>
</body>
</html>
```

4. Save the file as **page1.php** in the Chap17\Exercises folder in your work folder, and then close the document.
5. Open a new document in your text editor, and type the following code:

```
<? include("common.inc");  ?>
<br> <br>
<a href="page1.php"> Return to Page 1 </a>
<br> <br>
<a href="page3.php"> Go to Page 3 </a>
</body>
</html>
```

6. Save the file as **page2.php** in the Chap17\Exercises folder in your work folder, and then close the document.
7. Open a new document in your text editor, and type the following code:

```
<? include("common.inc");  ?>
<br> <br>
<a href="page1.php"> Go to Page 1 </a>
<br> <br>
<a href="page2.php"> Go to Page 2 </a>
</body>
</html>
```

8. Save the file as **page3.php** in the Chap17\Exercises folder in your work folder, and then close your text editor.
9. Start your browser, type http://localhost/Chap17/Exercises/page1.php in the Address text box, and press Enter.
10. Test the pages by clicking each link.

The pages should look like the following figures:

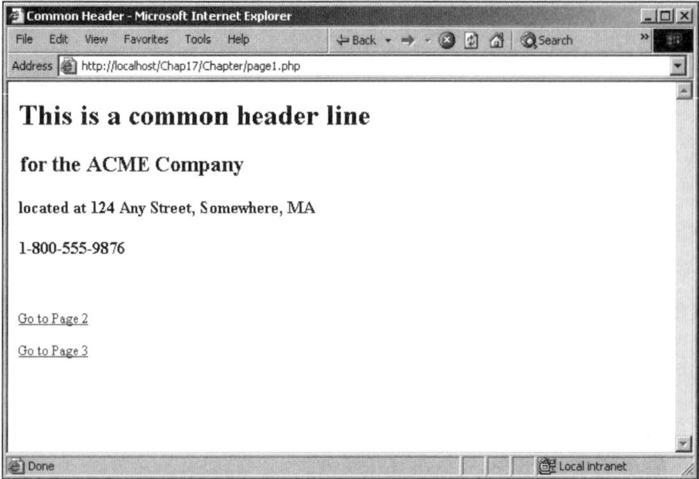

Figure 17-5

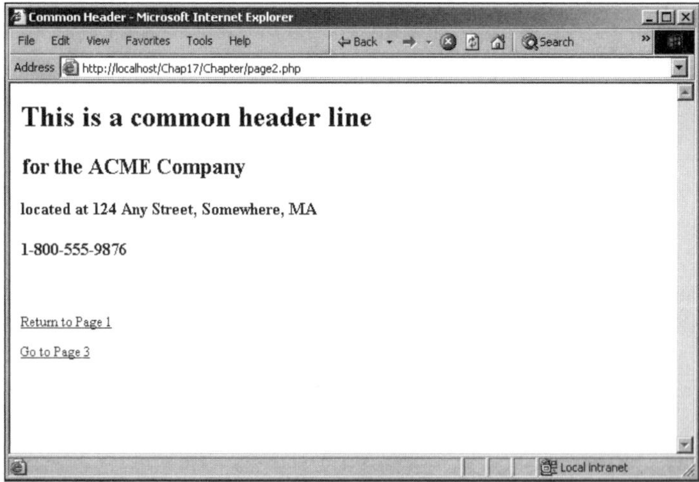

Figure 17-6

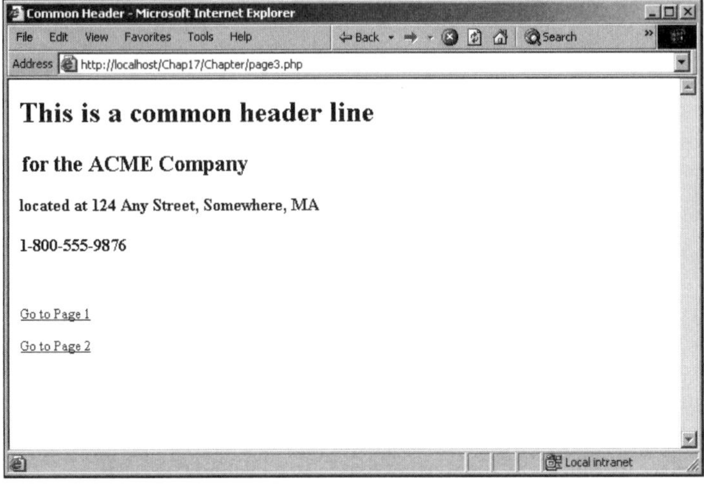

Figure 17-7

Exercise 17-2

Design a basic HTML form and use the Post method to redirect the form to another PHP page that displays the entered information in table format. Receive the following data fields: FirstName, LastName, address, city, and telephone number.

To design a basic HTML form:

1. Open a new document in your text editor, and type the following code:

```
<html>
<head>
      <title> Collecting Some Information </title>
</head>
<body>
<h1> Please provide the following information: </h1>
<br><br>
<form action="display.php" method="post">
First name:  
<Input type=text name="firstname" size=20> <br><br>
Last name:  
<Input type=text name="lastname" size=25> <br><br>
Address:  
<Input type=text name="address" size=25> <br><br>
City:  
<Input type=text name="city" size=15> <br><br>
Telephone Number:  
<Input type=text name="phone" size=15> <br><br>
<Input type=submit name="submit" value="Submit form">   
```

17

```
<Input type=reset name="reset" value="Clear form">
</form>
</body>
</html>
```

2. Save the file as **form_proj2.htm** in the Chap17\Exercises folder in your work folder, and then close the document.
3. Open a new document in your text editor, and type the following code:

```
<html>
<head>
      <title> Display the contents of a submitted form </title>
</head>
<body>
<h1> The following data was collected: </h1>
<table><tr><td> First Name: </td>
<td><? echo "$firstname"; ?></td></tr>
<tr><td> Last Name: </td>
<td><? echo "$lastname"; ?></td></tr>
<tr><td> Address: </td>
<td><? echo "$address"; ?></td></tr>
<tr><td> City: </td>
<td><? echo "$city"; ?></td></tr>
<tr><td> Telephone Number: </td>
<td><? echo "$phone"; ?></td></tr>
</table>
</body>
</html>
```

4. Save the file as **display.php** in the Chap17\Exercises folder in your work folder, and then close the document.
5. Start your browser, type http://localhost/Chap17/Exercises/form_proj2.htm in the Address text box, and press Enter.
6. Enter the information shown in Figure 17-8, and then click the Submit form button.

The form and resulting table should resemble Figures 17-8 and 17-9, respectively.

Collecting Some Information - Microsoft Internet Explorer

File Edit View Favorites Tools Help

Address http://localhost/Chap17/Chapter/form_proj2.htm

Please provide the following information:

First name: Dawn

Last name: Riley

Address: 31 Marjorie

City: Stratford

Telephone Number: 555-1234

Submit form Clear form

Done Local intranet

Figure 17-8

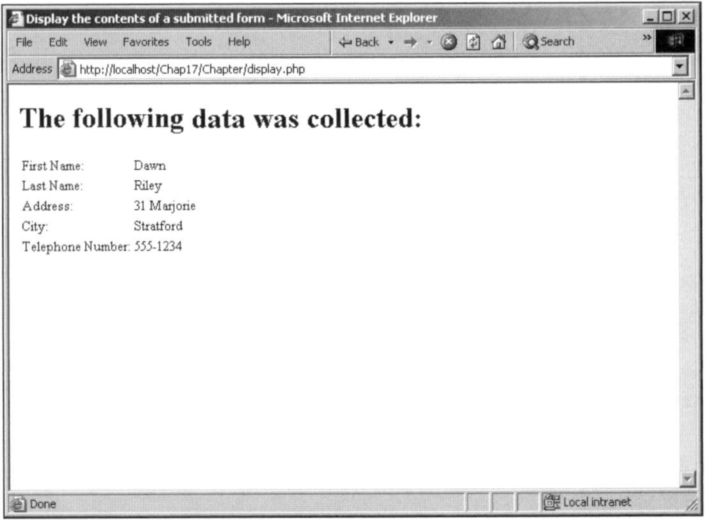

Figure 17-9

Exercise 17-3

Design a template form that calculates the sales tax on a dollar value. Allow the user to enter the tax percentage and the dollar amount of the purchase. Using logical program flow, create a single PHP file to collect the information, perform the calculations, and display the results.

To design a template form:

1. Open a new document in your text editor, and then type the following code:

```
<html>
<head>
      <title> Sales Tax Calculator </title>
</head>
<?
if ($SecondTime == "") {
     echo"
        <body><h1> Please enter amount and tax rate </h1>
        <br><br>
        <form action=\"taxcalc.php\" method=\"post\">
        <input type=\"hidden\" name=\"SecondTime\" Value=1>
        Amount  
        <input type=text name=\"amount\" size=15> <br><br>
        Tax Rate:  
        <Input type=text name=\"rate\" size=15> % <br><br>
       <Input type=submit name=\"submit\" value=\"Submit form\">
  
        <Input type=reset name=\"reset\" value=\"Clear form\">
     ";
} else {
     $calc_tax = $amount + ($amount * ($rate / 100)) ;
     $amount = number_format($amount,2,'.','');
     $calc_tax = number_format($calc_tax,2,'.','');
     echo "
     <body><h1> The calculated tax rate is as follows: </h1>
     <table><tr><td> Entered Amount: </td>
     <td>$ $amount </td></tr>
     <tr><td> Entered Tax Rate: </td>
     <td>  $rate  % </td></tr>
     <tr><td> Calculated Tax Amount: </td>
     <td>$  $calc_tax </td></tr>
     </table><br>
     <form action=\"taxcalc.php\" method=\"post\">
     <input type=\"hidden\" name=\"SecondTime\" Value=\"\">
     <Input type=submit name=\"submit\" value=\"Return to Calculator\">
     </form>
     ";
}
?>
</body>
</html>
```

2. Save the file as **taxcalc.php** in the Chap17\Exercises folder in your work folder, and then close the document.

3. Start your browser, type http://localhost/Chap17/Exercises/taxcalc.php in the Address text box, and press Enter.
4. Enter the information shown in Figure 17-10, and then click the Submit form button.

The form and result page should look like Figures 17-10 and 17-11, respectively.

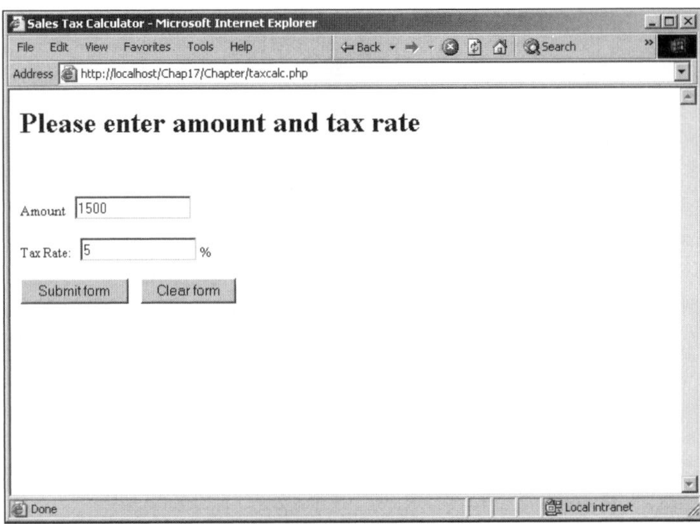

Figure 17-10

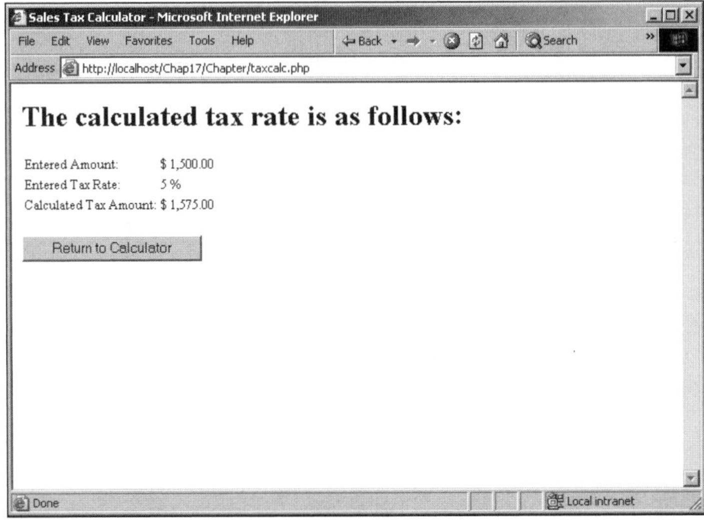

Figure 17-11

Exercise 17-4

Using programming flow control, determine a customer's status with a bank based on their credit rating or existing balance. Use Table 17-3 to determine the course of action, and then display the results in a table format.

Table 17-3

Status code	Balance amount	Status level
A	> $10,000	Preferred
B	> $1000	Regular
C	> $100	Caution
D	< $100	Avoid!

You can use a list box to allow for the entry of a credit code and a single-line entry box to enter a balance. Also, produce a printable form showing the results for an entered customer name, and provide a way to return to the main entry screen once the results are displayed.

To determine a customer's status:

1. Open a new document in your text editor and type the following code:

```
<html>
<head>
      <title> Customer Banking Status </title>
</head>
<body>
<h1> Please select a status code or enter a bank balance </h1>
<form method="post" action="creditstatus.php">
<table><tr><td>
Enter the customer's full name: </td><td></td>
<td><input type="text" name="fullname" size="25">
</td></tr>
<tr></tr>
<tr><td>
Select a status code</td>
<td></td>
<td>
<select name="statuscode" size="1">
<option value=0> No Status
<option value=1> A
<option value=2> B
<option value=3> C
<option value=4> D
</select></td></tr><tr></tr><tr><td>
or enter a bank balance </td><td>$</td>
<td><input type="text" name="balance" size="12"></td></tr>
```

```
<tr><td>(rounded to nearest dollar)</td></tr>
<tr></tr>
</table>
<br><br>
<input type="submit" value="Check Status">
</form>
</body>
</html>
```

2. Save the file as **enterstatus.html** in the Chap17\Exercises folder in your work folder, and then close the document.
3. Open a new document in your text editor, and type the following code:

```
<html>
<head>
     <title> Display the customer's bank status </title>
</head>
<body>
<h1> The customer information results in the following: </h1>
<table><tr><td>
<?
if ($statuscode > 0) {
 switch ($statuscode) {
       case 1:
?>
       For customer: <?= $fullname; ?> </td>
       <td></tr><tr><td>
       Selected status code was: A </td></tr>
       <tr><td>
       Therefore the credit status is: PREFERRED </td> </tr>
<?     break;
       case 2:  ?>
       For customer: <?= $fullname; ?> </td>
       <td></tr><tr><td>
       Selected status code was: B </td></tr>
       <tr><td>
       Therefore the credit status is: REGULAR </td> </tr>
<?     break;
       case 3:  ?>
       For customer: <?= $fullname; ?> </td>
       <td></tr><tr><td>
       Selected status code was: C </td></tr>
       <tr><td>
       Therefore the credit status is: CAUTION </td> </tr>
<?     break;
       case 4:  ?>
       For customer: <?= $fullname; ?> </td>
       <td></tr><tr><td>
       Selected status code was: D </td></tr>
```

```
            <tr><td>
            Therefore the credit status is: AVOID ! </td> </tr>
<?          break;
  }
} elseif ($balance > 0) {
          if ($balance >= 10000) $SwitchCase = 1;
          if ($balance >= 1000 && $balance <= 9999) $SwitchCase = 2;
          if ($balance >= 100 && $balance <= 999) $SwitchCase = 3;
          if ($balance <= 100) $SwitchCase = 4;
          switch ($SwitchCase) {
            case 1:
?>
            For customer: <?= $fullname; ?> </td>
            <td></tr><tr><td>
            Entered balance was:  $<?= $balance; ?> </td></tr>
            <tr><td>
            Therefore the credit status is: PREFERRED </td> </tr>
<?          break;
            case 2:  ?>
            For customer: <?= $fullname; ?> </td>
            <td></tr><tr><td>
            entered balance was:  $<?= $balance; ?> </td></tr>
            <tr><td>
            Therefore the credit status is: REGULAR </td> </tr>
<?          break;
            case 3:  ?>
            For customer: <?= $fullname; ?> </td>
            <td></tr><tr><td>
            entered balance was:  $<?= $balance; ?> </td></tr>
            <tr><td>
            Therefore the credit status is: CAUTION </td> </tr>
<?          break;
            case 4:  ?>
            For customer: <?= $fullname; ?> </td>
            <td></tr><tr><td>
            Entered balance was:  $<?= $balance; ?> </td></tr>
            <tr><td>
            Therefore the credit status is: AVOID ! </td> </tr>
<?
    }
}
?>
</body>
</html>
```

4. Save the file as **creditstatus.php** in the Chap17\Exercises folder in your work folder, and then close the document.
5. Start your browser, type http://localhost/Chap17/Exercises/enterstatus.html in the Address text box, and press Enter.

6. Enter the information shown in Figure 17-12, and then click the Check Status button.

The entry form should resemble Figure 17-12 and the results page should resemble Figure 17-13.

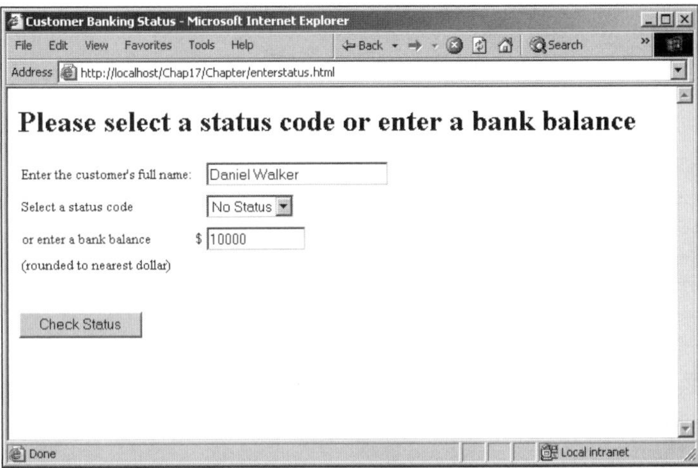

Figure 17-12

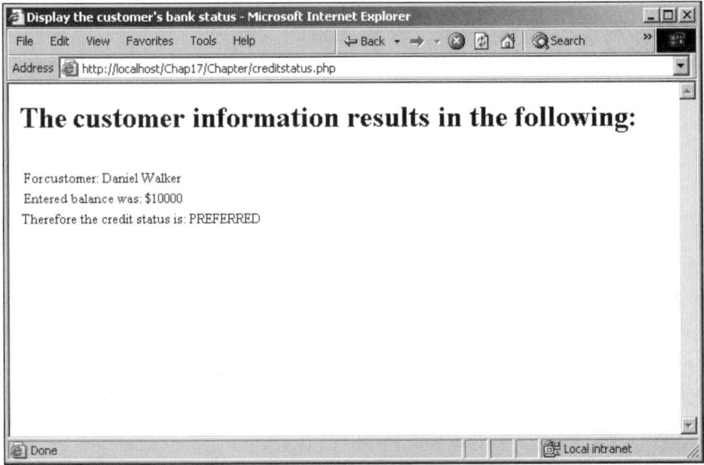

Figure 17-13

Exercise 17-5

Design a form to calculate the amount of money you have in a change drawer. Allow for the entry of pennies, nickels, dimes, quarters, 50-cent pieces, dollar coins, and two-dollar coins. Show the totals in both cents and dollars in a printable table. Also, provide a way to return to the coin entry page if necessary.

To design a form:

1. Open a new document in your text editor, and type the following code:

```
<html>
<head>
      <title> Change Cash Calculator </title>
</head>
<body>
<body><h1> Please enter your coin count and denomination </h1>
<br>
<form action="coincount.php" method="post">
Pennies:  
<input type=text name="pennies" size=6>    
Nickels:  
<input type=text name="nickels" size=6> <br>
Dimes:  
<input type=text name="dimes" size=6>    
Quarters:  
<input type=text name="quarters" size=6> <br>
50 Cent Coins:  
<input type=text name="fifty" size=6>    
1 Dollar Coins:  
<input type=text name="dollar" size=6> <br>
2 Dollar Coins:  
<input type=text name="twodollar" size=6> <br><br>
<Input type=submit name="submit" value="Calculate Coins">   
<Input type=reset name="reset" value="Clear form">
</body>
</html>
```

2. Save the file as **enterchange.html** in the Chap17\Exercises folder in your work folder, and then close the document.
3. Open a new document in your text editor, and type the following code:

```
<html>
<head>
      <title> Display the contents of a submitted form </title>
</head>
<body>
<h1> The following coins were counted and valued: </h1>
<?
$total_cents = $pennies + ($nickels * 5) + ($dimes * 10) + ($quarters *
25) + ($fifty * 50) + ($dollar * 100) + ($twodollar * 200);
$total_dollars = $total_cents / 100;
$total_cents_fmt = number_format($total_cents);
$total_fmt = number_format($total_dollars,2,'.','');
?>
<table><tr><td> Pennies: </td>
<td><? echo "$pennies"; ?></td>
```

```
<td> Nickels: </td>
<td><? echo "$nickels"; ?></td></tr>
<tr><td> Dimes: </td>
<td><? echo "$dimes"; ?></td>
<td> Quarters: </td>
<td><? echo "$quarters"; ?></td></tr>
<tr><td> 50-cent coins: </td>
<td><? echo "$fifty"; ?></td>
<td> 1-dollar coins: </td>
<td><? echo "$dollar"; ?></td></tr>
<tr><td> 2-dollar coins: </td>
<td><? echo "$twodollar"; ?></td></tr>
</table>
<h3> You therefore have: </h3>
<table><tr><td> Total in Cents: </td>
<td><? echo "$total_cents_fmt"; ?></td></tr><tr></tr><tr>
<td> Total Dollars: </td>
<td>$<? echo "$total_fmt"; ?></td></tr>
</table>
</body>
</html>
```

4. Save the file as **coincount.php** in the Chap17\Exercises folder in your work folder, and then close the document.
5. Start your browser, type http://localhost/Chap17/Exercises/enterchange.html in the Address text box, and press Enter.
6. Enter the information show in Figure 17-14, and then click the Calculate Coins button.

The entry form is shown in Figure 17-14 and the results page is shown in Figure 17-15.

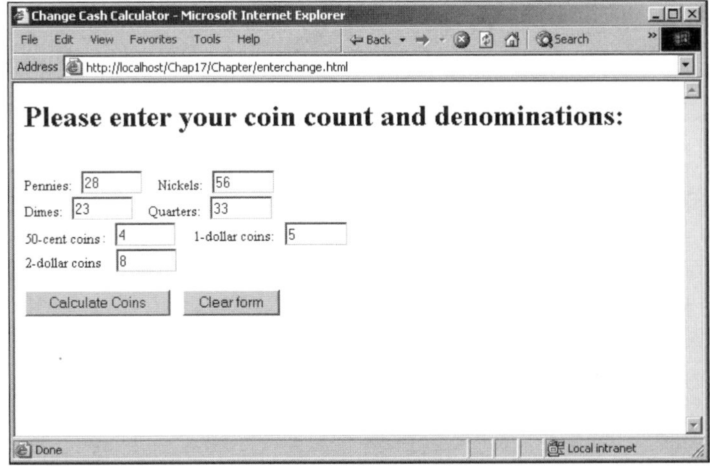

Figure 17-14

17

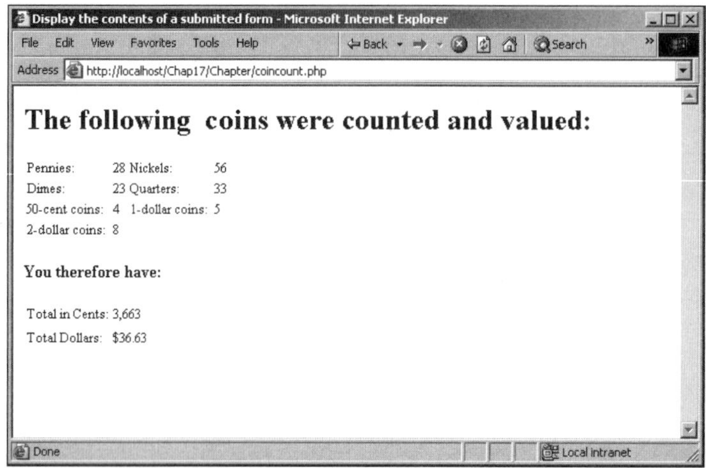

Figure 17-15

WEB PROGRAMMING PROJECTS

If necessary, use Windows Explorer to create a new folder in the Chap17 folder in your work folder. Name this folder **Projects**. Save the files that you create in these Projects in the Chap17\Projects folder in your work folder.

Project 17-1

Design a customer inquiry page for a car dealership. Think of all the information a dealership is interested in knowing about its potential customers. Besides basic contact data, this information includes a person's preference for new or preowned vehicles, compact or mid-size, 4-door or 2-door, and SUV or family van. Turn the submitted form into a printable table that only shows the details of the entered form data.

Project 17-2

A company from the Northeast wants to base its shipping costs on the area code of the location to where an item is shipped. Using the values in Table 17-4, provide a data entry form that accepts an area code, then displays the appropriate shipping charges based on the area code and weight of the item (in pounds) being shipped.

Table 17-4

Region name	Area code	Price for region
Boston and area	508, 617, 413	$2.50 per pound
Maine, New Hampshire, Vermont	207, 603, 802	$3.50 per pound
Selected Southeast cities	404, 706, 803, 910, 804, 813, 407	$5.00 per pound
Selected central state cities	614, 309, 314, 501, 515, 317, 606	$7.00 per pound
All other cities	All area codes not listed above	$11.00 per pound

Project 17-3

Design a form to compute a person's age based on an entered birth date. Allow the user to select the day and the month from list boxes, and to enter the year value as a single-line entry.

CHAPTER

18

PHP: PART II

In this chapter, you will:

- Examine the relationship between PHP and MySQL
- Plan a PHP Web application
- Create and use a logon window
- Manage system data
- Update a PHP Web application

This chapter explores using PHP to connect to and interact with a database. Although you can connect to many types of databases, such as ORACLE and DB2, this chapter uses MySQL, which is specially designed to work with PHP. Using PHP along with MySQL, you can maintain and update information such as user logon information, passwords, mailing lists, and product information. You can store this data in a database, which users can later access by entering a database field name on a Web form in their browser. The form can be sent to a Web server, where a PHP script waits to be executed. The script creates a query, retrieves data from the database, and sends records back to the browser, where it appears in a Web form. In this chapter, you examine the relationship between PHP and MySQL more closely, and then plan and build a Web application that connects to a database using PHP. You also create and use a logon window, manage system data, and set and test cookies.

Examining the Relationship Between PHP and MySQL

PHP is designed to work with MySQL to maintain and retrieve data stored in a MySQL database. MySQL is open-source software like PHP, and is therefore also powerful, flexible, and reliable. In this chapter, you develop a small application that interacts with a database and uses these PHP functions and statements to select and manipulate data from a MySQL database.

Before completing this chapter, make sure that MySQL is installed and running on your computer. You can download MySQL from *www.mysql.com*. Be sure to select the version of MySQL for the platform on which you will be running this product and to follow the installation instructions that the Web site provides.

To prepare for creating the mailing list Web application, you need to run the SQL code in the mailman.sql file to create your database within MySQL and establish the mailing list system's database structures.

To run the mailman.sql file:

1. Copy the **mailman.sql** file from the Chap18\Chapter folder in your data files to the Chap18\Chapter folder in your work folder. (Use Windows Explorer or My Computer to create these folders in your work folder, if necessary.)
2. Open a Command Prompt window by clicking the **Start** button, pointing to **All Programs**, pointing to **Accessories**, and then clicking **Command Prompt**. Change to the directory where MySQL is installed, which is c:\mysql\bin by default, by typing the following command, and then pressing **Enter**:

   cd c:\mysql\bin

   If MySQL is installed in a different directory, change to that directory.
3. To run the mailman.sql file, type the following command, and then press **Enter** (use the drive name and work folder name as appropriate for your system):

   mysql < C:*work folder*\Chap18\Chapter\mailman.sql

   The mysql command imports the mailman.sql file into the MySQL engine, and then creates the mailman database that you will work with throughout the rest of the chapter.
4. Close the Command Prompt window.

You can use any text editor to add to the SQL commands within this file, such as adding states to the prov table. The data files in the Chap18\Chapter folder also include a file named php_drop.sql. You can use this SQL file to delete the tables from mailman.sql, if you want to run mailman.sql more than once.

Planning a PHP Web Application

In this chapter, you develop an application called MailMan that performs basic mailing list tasks such as recording mailing addresses and printing out mailing labels, and shows what PHP can do when it interacts with databases. Before you start coding, plan the application. First consider the design of the MailMan system, which includes three major components: security logon, system maintenance, and mailing address management.

The security logon component is the gateway to the whole system. This component either grants or denies system access. A typical logon screen asks the user for a username and a password. The system then verifies that information against information stored in the database. If the user passes this security check, the other parts of the application become accessible.

The system maintenance part of the system keeps the applications that support the data in the database up to date. You typically need to add information, edit existing information, or delete information. Although users have already gained access to the system, you can help secure the data through the use of cookies. The data segments that users can change are lists of states and provinces and the user logon data itself. The MailMan application has two levels of system permissions that are verified each time a user logs on and tries to perform a specific task. Level 1 access is given to system administrators, which means that any user with this level of access can manage this system support data as well as the address information itself. A user with level 2 access is not allowed into this system maintenance area, but is allowed to access the address data.

The mailing address management component is the main portion of the system. Any user that gains access to the system is allowed to add, edit, or delete the data here.

The schematic diagram in Figure 18-1 shows the layout of the mailing list application.

Examining the Mailing List Data

The data in the mailing list database includes usernames, street addresses, states, and provinces. The following tables reflect the information in the mailing list database. Note that only one table includes mailing address information. The other tables support that table; one contains security access rights to the system and the other one lists the states and provinces for accuracy and ease of use in data entry of the mailing addresses. Table 18-1 includes the fields in the user table, including their data type and maximum size. Table 18-2 lists information about the fields in the address table, and Table 18-3 lists information about the fields in the state or prov table.

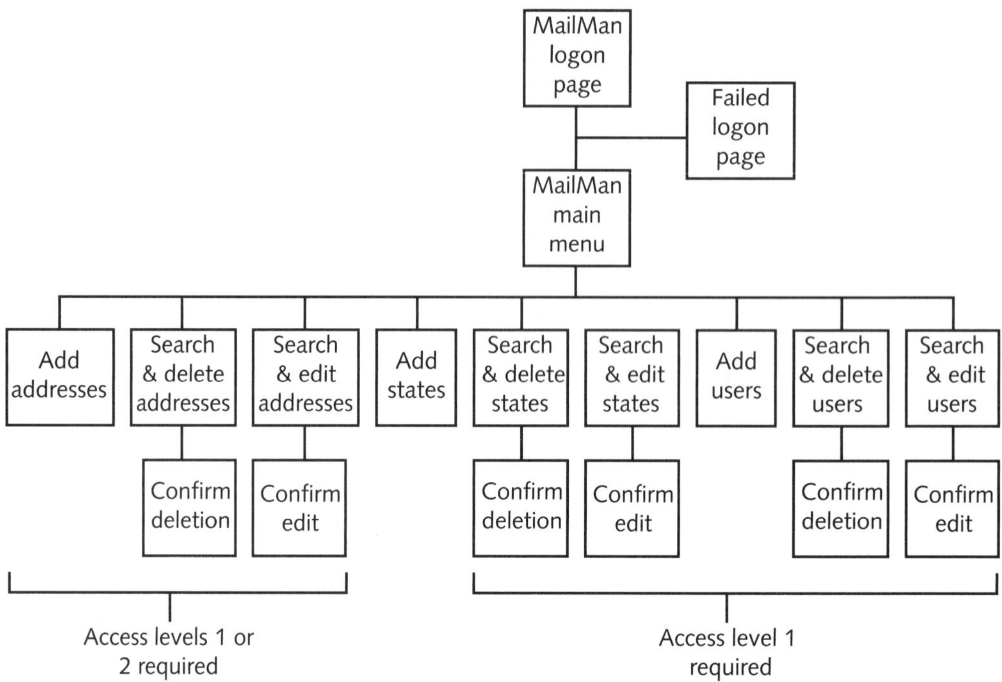

Figure 18-1 MailMan application schematic

Table 18-1 User table structure

Field name	Data type	Column size
userid	int	
firstname	varchar	25
lastname	varchar	30
username	varchar	15
password	varchar	10
accesslevel	int	
phone	varchar	14
email	varchar	35

Table 18-2 Address table structure

Field name	Data type	Column size
addressid	int	
firstname	varchar	25
lastname	varchar	30
address1	varchar	35
address2	varchar	35
city	varchar	25
prov	char	2
postal	varchar	12
phone	varchar	14
email	varchar	20

Table 18-3 Prov table structure

Fieldname	Datatype	Column size
provid	int	
provcode	char	2
provname	varchar	35

Setting Up Database Connections

To use PHP with the MySQL mailman database, you need to connect a PHP script to the database. When users attempt to log on, for example, you tell PHP to connect to the mailman database and check to see if the username and password the user entered matches data in the user table. To interact with a database, you must first tell PHP to connect to the database engine itself. If you are connecting to a MySQL database, you use the PHP mysql_connect function for this purpose. The syntax for this function is:

```
mysql_connect("localhost", "username", "password")
```

PHP allows you to connect to many other databases and connections that support PHP. See the PHP manual for details on these other database connection functions.

18

This connection function returns a value that holds the connection object so that you can use it again for other database actions. A **connection object** is a memory handle that PHP can use to communicate with the database in subsequent accesses. A complete syntax of this connection function follows. (Note that the username and password parameters are optional depending on how you set up the MySQL engine.)

```
<? $connection = mysql_connect("localhost", "username", "password");  ?>
```

For example, to connect to the MySQL database engine, you type `$connection = mysql_connect("localhost");` in a text editor.

After you gain access to a database engine using the PHP mysql_connect command to store the connection object's handle in the $connection variable, you need to establish a connection to a specific database. The database that you use in this chapter is called mailman. The PHP function to use for this step is called mysql_select_db and has the following syntax:

```
<? $db = "mailman" mysql_select_db($db, $connection) or Die("could not open $db);?>
```

Notice the use of the $db variable to take the name of the database. You could have used any valid PHP variable, but this one ($db) is easy to recognize as a database. Also, once the database name is stored in a variable, you can use this variable anywhere else in the code that requires the database name. If the database name changes, you only have to change your code in one place, and the rest of the code accesses the new name. The preceding code uses the $connection variable previously loaded with the database engine handle and the name of the database ($db).

The first command you examined (`mysql_connect("localhost", "username", "password"`) connects a PHP file to the MySQL database engine; the second command (`$connection = mysql_connect("localhost");`) connects to the mailman database. You will allow access to the database tables themselves in the next section as you build the logon window and test the user information. You will use the two commands you examined to begin creating a logon window.

Creating and Using a Logon Window

Figure 18-2 shows the user logon window that you will design for the MailMan application. The window allows space for entering the two parts of information that are required to gain access to this application: the username and password.

This page is based on a form that includes a call to a PHP file named trylogon.php. You can create the same form shown in Figure 18-2 by entering the following code.

Figure 18-2 User logon page

To create a logon form:

1. Open a text editor, such as Notepad, and type the following code:

```
<html>
<head>
      <title>MailMan Logon Window</title>
</head>
<body bgcolor="silver">
<TABLE cellSpacing=1 cellPadding=1 align=center>
<TR>
<TD>
      <P align=center>Welcome to the<BR> </P> </TD></TR>
<TR>
<TD>
      <H2 align=center>MailMan Mailing List </H2></TD>
</TR>
<TR>
<TD>
      <P align=center>Web Application</P> </TD>
</TR></TABLE>
<H4><center>
Please provide the requested information:</center></H4>
<FORM action=trylogon.php method=post>
<TABLE border=1 align=center cellSpacing=2 cellPadding=6>
<TR>
```

```
        <TD>Enter User Name:</TD>
        <TD><INPUT size=15 name=username></TD></TR>
    <TR>
        <TD>Enter Password:</TD>
        <TD><INPUT type=password size=15 name=password></TD></TR>
    <TR>
        <TD>
          <P align=center><INPUT type=submit value=Login
           name=submit></P></TD>
        <TD>
          <P
      align=center><INPUT type=reset value=Clear></P></TD>
    </TR></TABLE>
    </FORM>
    </body>
    </html>
```

2. Save the file as **mailman.html** in the Chap18\Chapter folder in your work folder.

Note that there is a reference to a file called trylogon.php within the mailman.html code you entered. Now you can create this file, which is pure PHP code, meaning it contains no embedded HTML code.

To create the trylogon.php file:

1. Open a new document in your text editor, and enter the following code:

```
<?
$connection = mysql_connect("localhost");
$db = "mailman";
mysql_select_db($db, $connection) or die( "Could not open $db");
$sql = "Select * from users where username = '$username' and
password = '$password'";
$result = mysql_query($sql, $connection) or die( "Could not execute
   sql: $sql");
$num_rows = mysql_num_rows($result);
if ( $num_rows > 0 ) {
      header( "Location: mailman_main.php" );
} else {
      header( "Location: failedlogon.html" );
}
?>
```

2. Save this file as **trylogon.php** in the Chap18\Chapter folder in your work folder.

3. Open your browser, such as Internet Explorer, type the following text in the Address text box, and then press **Enter** to display the mailman.html file as a Web page (replace *work folder* with the name of the work folder on your system):

http://localhost/*work folder*/Chap18/Chapter/mailman.html

The Web page should appear similar to the one shown earlier in Figure 18-2.

4. Log on to the MailMan Web application by typing **admin** in the User Name text box and typing **entry** in the Password text box. Then click the **Login** button.

When you click the Login button on the logon page, the page attempts to connect to the database, and the trylogon.php code attempts to log on to the application with the values it receives from the form (the mailman.html file). The $sql variable is given a string value of the SQL command that you want to pass to the MySQL engine once the valid connection is obtained. The trylogon.php file uses the mysql_query() function to execute that command from within PHP, and stores the result of that command (success or failure) in the variable called $result. The $result variable holds a result set of all the rows that were returned from the successful execution of the SQL command. If there are unique users in the database, $result should only have one row in it; upon failure, it should contain no values.

Note that although an SQL command sometimes returns no rows of data, the result of a mysql_query() function does not return an empty answer. The command of `$result = mysql_query($sql, $connection)` when tested as in `if ( ! $result )` always returns a TRUE value even when no rows are returned because $result simply stores the answer to the command. An empty result is still considered a result. Be sure to check the number of rows returned with the mysql_num_rows() function if you want to be sure that something of substance has been returned by the MySQL engine.

The next line of code (`$num_rows = mysql_num_rows($result);`) counts the number of rows that are returned from the MySQL engine based on the command that was sent to it, and stores that value in the variable called $num_rows. To gain access to the MailMan application main Web page, the number of rows should be greater than zero (0), meaning that there was a successful return of the SQL command. Otherwise, the user should be directed to the failed logon Web page. To redirect a user to a particular Web page, use the header() function, as in `header( "Location: mailman_main.php" );`. You can provide a link back to the main logon page for the user, or let them simply use the Back button on their browser's toolbar to return to the main page.

For now, you have successfully tested data that has been sent to a PHP file through a form by comparing the data to the contents of a database table, and have directed the user to an appropriate page depending on the result returned. Later, you will add statements to the code so that the access levels of the users who log on can be set and verified each time they navigate the application. You perform this task in the section on setting cookies.

MANAGING SYSTEM DATA

Refer back to the application schematic diagram in Figure 18-1 and note that three steps are performed with the data for system users and states or provinces. Users need to add information, edit information, and delete information. In the following section you add these steps for the system user information only. In the Hands-on Exercises at the end of the chapter, you perform similar steps to add province and state information and mailing address information.

In the following steps, you create a menu system for the MailMan application so that your users can select the task they want to perform. Then you add data to the system, and provide a way for your users to find the data that they want to edit or delete.

To create a simple menu system for the MailMan application:

1. Use a text editor to open the text file **mailmanmain_partial.htm** from the Chap18\Chapter folder in your student data files.
2. Type the HTML code shown in bold:

```
<html>
<head>
      <title>MailMan Main Window</title>
</head>
<body bgcolor="silver">
<TABLE cellSpacing=1 cellPadding=1 align=center >
<TR>
<TD>
      <H2 align=center>MailMan Mailing List </H2></TD>
</TR>
<TR>
<TD>
      <P align=center>Web Application</P> </TD>
</TR></TABLE>
<H4>
<CENTER>Please select the process that you want to perform<BR>
</CENTER>
<CENTER>
<TABLE border=1 align=center cellSpacing=2 cellPadding=6>
<TR>
    <TD>
      <H3>Address <BR>Information</H3>  </TD>
    <TD>
      <H3>System User <BR>Information</H3></TD>
    <TD>
      <H3>Provinces / States <BR>Management</H3></TD></TR>
```

```
<TR>
    <TD><A href="addaddress.php">
      <P align=left>Add Addresses</A></P> </TD>
    <TD><A href="adduser.php">
      <P align=left>Add System User</A></P></TD>
    <TD><A href="addprov.php">
      <P align=left>Add Province / State</A></P></TD></TR>
  <TR>
    <TD><A href="search_edit_address.php">
      <P align=center>Edit Addresses</A></P></TD>
    <TD><A href="search_edit_user.php">
      <P align=center>Edit System User</A></P></TD>
    <TD><A href="search_edit_prov.php">
      <P align=center>Edit Province / State</A></P></TD></TR>
<TR>
    <TD><A href="search_delete_address.php">
      <P align=center>Delete Addresses</A></P></TD>
    <TD><A href="search_delete_user.php">
      <P align=center>Delete System User</A></P></TD>
    <TD><A href="search_delete_prov.php">
      <P align=center>Delete Province / State</A></P></TD>
</TR>
</TABLE></CENTER></H4>
</body>
</html>
```

3. Save the file as **MailManMain.htm** in the Chap18\Chapter folder in your work folder.

The HTML code you added references the adduser.php file for adding new users to the Web application. In the adduser.php file, you collect the information from the system user, and then add that information to the database.

To open the MailManMain.htm page in a browser:

1. Open your browser, type the following text in the Address text box, and then press **Enter** to display the MailManMain.html file as a Web page (replace *work folder* with the name of the work folder on your system):

   http://localhost/*work folder*/Chap18/Chapter/MailManMain.htm

   The Web page should appear similar to the one shown in Figure 18-3.

18

In the following steps, you work with a PHP file called adduser.php to add the SQL commands within the PHP file that you need to collect user information and then insert that information into the mailman database. (Refer to Chapter 2 for more details on working with SQL commands.) The HTML code for adduser.php is the form that accepts the new user information and includes the common PHP header created for the MailMan application.

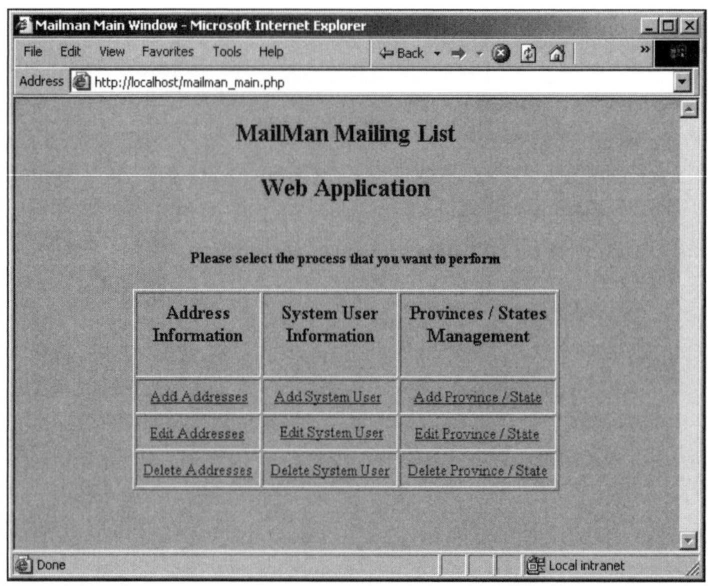

Figure 18-3 MailMan main page after logon was accepted

To add SQL commands for collecting and inserting user information:

1. Use a text editor to open the text file called **adduser_partial.php** from the Chap18\Chapter folder in your student data files.
2. Type the HTML code shown in bold:

```
<? include("mailman_header.inc");  ?>
<FORM action=saveuser.php method=post>
<TABLE cellSpacing=2 cellPadding=6 align=center border=1>
  <TR>
    <TD colSpan=4>
      <H3 align=center>Add System User Information</H3></TD></TR>
  <TR>
    <TD>First Name</TD>
    <TD><INPUT name=fname></TD>
    <TD>Last Name</TD>
    <TD><INPUT name=lname></TD></TR>
  <TR>
    <TD>User Name</TD>
    <TD><INPUT name=username></TD>
    <TD> Password</TD>
    <TD><INPUT name=password></TD></TR>
  <TR>
    <TD>Access Level</TD>
    <TD><SELECT name=accesslevel>
    <OPTION value=0 selected>select level
```

```
    <OPTION value=1>1
    <OPTION value=2>2
    <OPTION value=3>3
    </OPTION>
    </SELECT></TD>
    <TD>Phone #</TD>
    <TD><INPUT name=phone></TD></TR>
  <TR>
    <TD>E-mail</TD>
    <TD><INPUT name=email></TD>
    <TD><INPUT type=submit value=Save></TD>
    <TD><INPUT type=reset value=Reset></TD>
</TR>
  </TABLE>
</FORM>
</body>
</html>
```

3. Save the file as **adduser.php** in the Chap18\Chapter folder in your work folder.

The form's action statement calls the PHP code file saveuser.php. Now you will enter the PHP code that interacts with the database.

To create the PHP file that interacts with the database:

1. In a text editor, type the following code in a new document.

```
<?
$connection = mysql_connect("localhost");
$db = "mailman";
mysql_select_db($db, $connection) or die( "Could not open $db");

$sql = "SELECT Max(userid) AS currentid FROM users";
$result = mysql_query($sql, $connection) or die( "Could not execute
   sql:$sql");

$row = mysql_fetch_array($result);
$nextid = $row["currentid"] ;
$nextid++;

$sql = "INSERT INTO users  (userid, firstname, lastname, username,
   password, accesslevel, phone, email) ";
$sql = $sql . "VALUES ($nextid, '$fname', '$lname', '$username',
   '$password', $accesslevel,";
$sql = $sql . "'$phone', '$email')";

$res = mysql_query($sql, $connection) or die( "Could not execute sql:
   $nextid:  $sql");
```

18

```
if ( !$res ) {
      echo "problem adding to database";
} else {
      header( "Location: mailman_main.php" );
}
?>
```

2. Save the file as **saveuser.php** in the Chap18\Chapter folder in your work folder. Then close the document.

   The code in saveuser.php takes the values from the previous form, retrieves the highest userid value from the database, and increases that value by one. Then it inserts the new row into the database and returns the user to the main menu. You could display a thank you page or a confirmation page instead, but the simplest method here is to send them back to the start.

3. To see how the files you've created work together, open your browser, type the following text in the Address text box, and then press **Enter** to display the Web page (replace *work folder* with the name of the work folder on your system):

   http://localhost/*work folder*/Chap18/Chapter/adduser.php

   The Web page should appear similar to the one shown in Figure 18-4.

4. Add yourself as a new system user. Type your first name and last name in the appropriate text boxes. In the User Name text box, type a form of your name, such as your first and middle initials followed by your last name, as in **pbmacintyre**. In the Password text box, type **happy**. Click the **Access Level** list arrow and then click **1**. Type your phone number and e-mail address, and then click **Save**.

5. Close your browser.

The saveuser.php file uses the command called mysql_fetch_array(), which stores the answer of the command into a variable called $row. Arrays have rows and columns like a spreadsheet and they hold data in particular locations, as spreadsheets hold values in cells. In PHP, you can store the entire array in a single variable, as saveuser.php does with the $row variable. Then you can access the cells in an array by referencing the particular cells in the array. In the next section, you access data and list the rows that are returned from a SQL SELECT command.

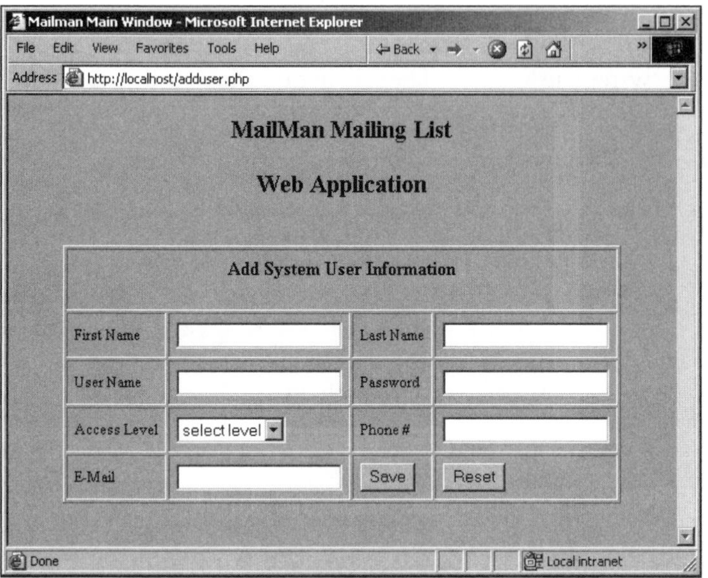

Figure 18-4 The Add System User Information page

Updating a PHP Web Application

In this section, you work on the other two main processes of data control—editing existing data and deleting old or unwanted data. With PHP and the nature of the Web, however, you need to pass data values between pages so that the application can maintain its control over the data that you want to affect. One way to accomplish this is to send data to another page through the transmission of an HTML form. You can also pass data between Web pages through Web links that use the question mark (?). Another way to pass data is to use cookies.

Passing Data Between Pages

You can use HTML to pass values embedded in links to other pages, but PHP can facilitate this process since you are using PHP to handle many other aspects of this Web application. Following is a typical hyperlink command with an embedded value.

```
<a href="transfer.html?amount=100"> Transfer Funds </a>
```

If this link is clicked, the transfer.html file is called and the value of 100 is passed to the called file contained in a variable named amount. If you are sending multiple values to the called page then you would separate the values and their variables with an ampersand character as in the following HTML code segment.

```
<a href="transfer.html?amount=100&userid=123"> Transfer Funds </a>
```

This code includes two variables, amount and userid, and two values, 100 and 123. In the following steps, you add statements to a PHP file to show the user all the values that are currently in the system user table. Then you can allow users to click one of the records to edit it.

To display values and let users select a record to edit:

1. Use a text editor to open the text file called **search_edit_user_partial.php** from the Chap18\Chapter folder in your student data files.
2. Add the following code shown in bold:

```
<?
include ("mailman_header.inc");
$connection = mysql_connect("localhost");
$db = "mailman";
mysql_select_db($db, $connection) or die( "Could not open $db");
$sql = "SELECT * FROM users";
$result = mysql_query($sql, $connection) or die( "Could not
   execute sql: $sql");
$num_result = mysql_num_rows($result);
?>
<TABLE cellSpacing=2 cellPadding=6 align=center border=1>
  <TR>
    <TD colspan=5>
      <H3 align=center>Click on the user
      record<BR> you want to edit</H3></TD></TR>
  <TR>
      <td> First Name </td>
      <td> Last Name </td>
      <td> User Name </td>
      <td> Phone # </td>
      <td> E-mail </td>
  </tr>
<?
for ($i=0; $i < $num_result; $i++) {
      $row = mysql_fetch_array($result);
      $id = $row["userid"];
      echo "<tr><td>";
      echo "<a href=\"edit_user.php?userid=$id\">";
      echo $row["firstname"];
      echo "</a></td><td>";
      echo $row["lastname"];
      echo "</td><td>";
      echo $row["username"];
      echo "</td><td>";
      echo $row["phone"];
      echo "</td><td>";
      echo $row["email"];
      echo "</td></tr>";
}
```

```
?>
</tr>
  </TABLE>
</body>
</html>
```

3. Save the file as **search_edit_user.php** in the Chap18\Chapter folder in your work folder.

In this code, the $sql variable is given to the SQL command to retrieve all the records from the user table. Then the result set is stored in a variable called $result. This result set uses a variable called $num_result to count the number of rows in the result set. This value is transferred into an array variable called $row within the for-next loop.

Notice that the anchor is set using the current rows value for the userid, even though it is not displayed on the Web page. Remember, if you want a literal special character to appear within an echo statement, precede it with a backslash (\ ) character. This userid is being used for uniquely identifying the selected record once a particular one is chosen.

Now that you have created the code for displaying user information in a table, you can create the code that lets you select a record from this table and then display detailed user information.

To create the code for finding the individual record and displaying it:

1. Use a text editor to open the text file called **edit_user_partial.php** from the Chap18\Chapter folder in your student data files.
2. Add the following code shown in bold:

```
<? include("mailman_header.inc");  ?>
<?
$connection = mysql_connect("localhost");
$db = "mailman";
mysql_select_db($db, $connection) or die( "Could not open $db");
$sql = "SELECT * FROM users WHERE userid=".$userid;
$result = mysql_query($sql, $connection) or die( "Could not execute
   sql: $sql");
$row = mysql_fetch_array($result);
?>
<FORM action=commit_edit_user.php method=post>
<input type=hidden name=userid value="<?= $userid ?>" >
<TABLE cellSpacing=2 cellPadding=6 align=center border=1>
  <TR>
    <TD colSpan=4>
      <H3 align=center>Update System User Information</H3></TD></TR>
  <TR>
    <TD>First Name</TD>
    <TD><INPUT name=fname value="<?= $row["firstname"] ?>" ></TD>
    <TD>Last Name</TD>
```

```
        <TD><INPUT name=lname value="<?= $row["lastname"] ?>"></TD></TR>
      <TR>
        <TD>User Name</TD>
        <TD><INPUT name=username value="<?= $row["username"] ?>"></TD>
        <TD> Password</TD>
        <TD><INPUT name=password value="<?= $row["password"] ?>"></TD></TR>
      <TR>
        <TD>Access Level</TD>
        <TD>
    <SELECT name=accesslevel>
    <? switch ($row["accesslevel"]) {
                case 1:  ?>
        <OPTION value=1 selected>1
        <OPTION value=2>2
        <OPTION value=3>3
        <?  break;
          case 2:  ?>
        <OPTION value=1>1
          <OPTION value=2 selected>2
        <OPTION value=3>3
        <?  break;
          case 3:  ?>
          <OPTION value=1>1
          <OPTION value=2>2
        <OPTION value=3 selected>3
    <? } ?>
        </OPTION>
        </SELECT></TD>
        <TD>Phone #</TD>
        <TD><INPUT name=phone value="<?= $row["phone"] ?>"></TD></TR>
      <TR>
        <TD>E-mail</TD>
        <TD><INPUT name=email value="<?= $row["email"] ?>"></TD>
        <TD><INPUT type=submit value=Save></TD>
        <TD><INPUT type=reset value=Reset></TD></TR>
      </TABLE>
    </FORM>
    </body>
    </html>
```

3. Save the file as **edit_user.php** in the Chap18\Chapter folder in your work folder.

The hidden variable userid is being set in the form so that when it is called by clicking the Submit button, the value for the userid is sent along with the form. Notice too, however, that the $userid variable that was sent to this code through the server from the previous PHP file via the (?) operator did not have to be established. The code knew that it was stored in memory and used it in both the forms hidden variable and the condition in the SQL command earlier in the code.

When the form is submitted, it calls the file named commit_edit_user.php, which takes the values from the form and commits them to the database. It then returns the user to the main MailMan Web page.

To create the commit_edit_user.php file:

1. Use a text editor to open a new document.
2. Type the following code:

```
<?
$connection = mysql_connect("localhost");
$db = "mailman";
mysql_select_db($db, $connection) or die( "Could not open $db");
$sql = "UPDATE users  SET firstname = '$fname', lastname = '$lname',
username = '$username', ";
$sql = $sql . "password = '$password', accesslevel = $accesslevel,
phone = '$phone', ";
$sql = $sql . "email = '$email' WHERE userid = $userid ";
$res = mysql_query($sql, $connection) or die( "Could not execute sql:
$nextid:  $sql");
if ( !$res ) {
      echo "problem updating database";
} else {
      header( "Location: mailman_main.php" );
}
?>
```

3. Save the file as **commit_edit_user.php** in the Chap18\Chapter folder in your work folder.

Now you can test the code you just entered.

To display the user records and select one:

1. Start your browser.
2. In the Address text box, type the following text, and then press **Enter** to display the Web page. Replace *work folder* with the name of your work folder.

   http://localhost/*work folder*/Chap18/Chapter/search_edit_user.php

   The code builds a table, shown in Figure 18-5. Your table will be different.

   The URL command in the status bar of this Web page shows the userid value set to 2. This is the URL command that will be passed if you click the second row.

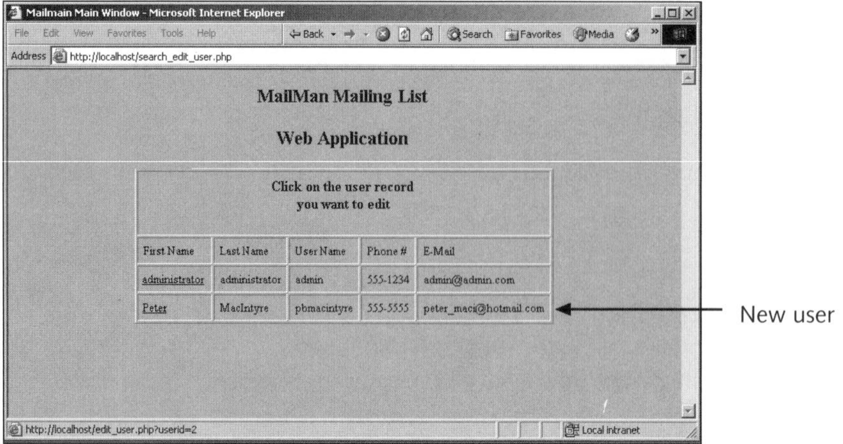

Figure 18-5 Table for editing records generated from the system user table

3. Click your first name, such as **Peter**. The user record you added in a previous set of steps appears. See Figure 18-6.

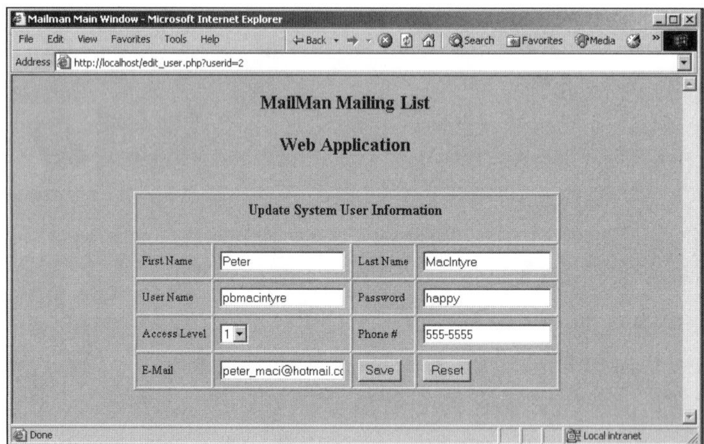

Figure 18-6 Record retrieved and displayed in the browser through PHP

You will perform the other tasks of deleting a system user and adding, editing, and deleting the mailing list data and the state or provinces table in the Hands-on Exercises at the end of the chapter. Now you can use cookies to protect the parts of the application that are restricted to certain access levels.

Setting and Testing Cookies

One way to establish security on a Web site is to set cookies and retrieve their values in other Web pages. This is similar to the task you just completed when you passed values to another Web page with the (?) character in the link to the page you want to access. With cookies, however, the values of the variables transferred to the Web page are not embedded in the link. Instead, they are established as memory variables that can be accessed from within the called Web page.

Using cookies is not a completely secure solution for Web access security—you should combine cookies with other forms of security to protect your data.

To use cookies for the MailMan application, you can adjust the code that you created for use in the logon process. The cookie is set only when the user has successfully passed the logon test. This means that you need to detect the access level of users once the program successfully locates them in the database. The program can do this at the same time that it tests the username and password against the user table.

To modify the trylogon.php code:

1. Use a text editor to open the text file **trylogon.php** from the Chap18\Chapter folder in your work folder.
2. Type the following code shown in bold:

```
<?
$connection = mysql_connect("localhost");
$db = "mailman";
mysql_select_db($db, $connection) or die( "Could not open $db");
$sql = "Select * from users where username = '$username' and
password = '$password'";
$result = mysql_query($sql, $connection) or die( "Could not execute sql:
   $sql");
$num_rows = mysql_num_rows($result);
if ( $num_rows > 0 ) {
      $row = mysql_fetch_array($result);
      $accesslevel = $row["accesslevel"] ;
      SetCookie("access",$accesslevel);
      header( "Location: mailman_main.php" );
} else {
      header( "Location: failedlogon.html" );
}
?>
```

3. Save the file as **trylogon2.php** in the Chap18\Chapter folder in your work folder.
4. Use a text editor to open **mailmain.html** in the Chap18\Chapter folder in your work folder. To change the appropriate reference call to trylogon2.php in mailman.html, change the following line of code:

```
<FORM action=trylogon.php method=post>
```

to this:

```
<FORM action=trylogon2.php method=post>
```

5. Save **mailmain.html** in the same location, and then close your text editor.

The code that you added means that once the program finds the username and password, it retrieves the user's access level from the table and stores it in the $accesslevel variable. Using the Setcookie( ) PHP function, the program sets a cookie that has the name of "access" and gives this cookie the retrieved value. Once the cookie is set in this code, it can be retrieved the same way an HTML form variable is—you reference it by preceding its name with a dollar sign ($) character.

There are other options to setting cookies in PHP, such as setting the expiration date, but in this program example, the cookie only exists in memory during the life of the Web browser's session. Once the browser is closed, the cookie also ceases to exist.

As is shown in this next portion of code, the retrieval of the cookie's value is straightforward. The result of this code is shown in Figure 18-7 following the code listing:

```
<?= "access level is:  " . $access ?>
```

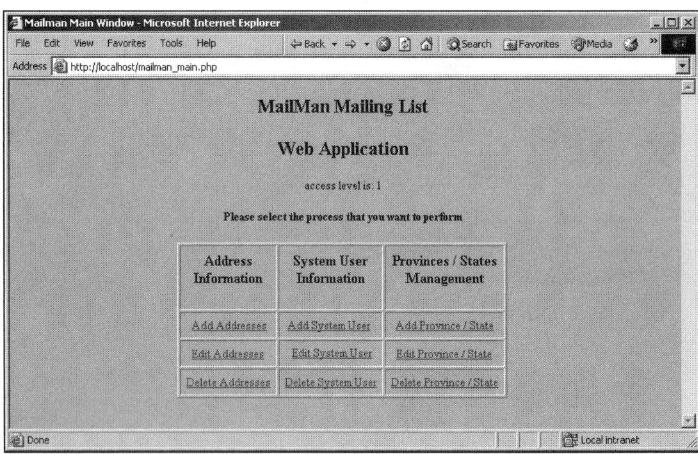

Figure 18-7 Result of cookie value being retrieved

Now that the access level is set for the particular session of using the MailMan application, you can check its value on every Web page within the application to ensure that the logged-on user has permission to go to certain pages. In this example, the access level of 1 is set to administration level (meaning access to anywhere within the application). An access level of 2 means that the user can access the mailing list data, but cannot change any of the user name or province/state data. You can test this value and direct the users accordingly by using an if statement.

To modify the adduser.php code:

1. Use a text editor to open the **adduser.php** from the Chap18\Chapter folder in your work folder.
2. Type the following code shown in bold:

```
<?
if ( $access != 1 ) header( "Location: unauthorized.html" );
?>
```

```
<? include("mailman_header.inc");  ?>
<FORM action=saveuser.php method=post>
<TABLE cellSpacing=2 cellPadding=6 align=center border=1>
  <TR>
    <TD colSpan=4>
      <H3 align=center>Add System User Information</H3></TD></TR>
  <TR>
    <TD>First Name</TD>
    <TD><INPUT name=fname></TD>
    <TD>Last Name</TD>
    <TD><INPUT name=lname></TD></TR>
  <TR>
    <TD>User Name</TD>
    <TD><INPUT name=username></TD>
    <TD> Password</TD>
    <TD><INPUT name=password></TD></TR>
  <TR>
    <TD>Access Level</TD>
    <TD><SELECT name=accesslevel>
    <OPTION value=0 selected>select level
    <OPTION value=1>1
    <OPTION value=2>2
    <OPTION value=3>3
    </OPTION>
    </SELECT></TD>
    <TD>Phone #</TD>
    <TD><INPUT name=phone></TD></TR>
  <TR>
    <TD>E-mail</TD>
    <TD><INPUT name=email></TD>
    <TD><INPUT type=submit value=Save></TD>
    <TD><INPUT type=reset value=Reset></TD></TR>
  </TABLE>
</FORM>
</body>
</html>
```

3. Save the file as **adduser2.php** in the Chap18\Chapter folder in your work folder.
4. Use a text editor to open **mailmain_main.php** in the Chap18\Chapter folder in your work folder. To change the appropriate reference call to adduser2.php in mailman_main.php, change the following line of code:

   ```
   <A href="adduser.php">
   ```

   to this:

   ```
   <A href="adduser2.php">
   ```

5. Save **mailmain_main.php** in the same location, and then close your text editor.
6. Start your browser. In the Address text box, type the following text, and then press **Enter** to display the Web page. Replace *work folder* with the name of your work folder.

18

http://localhost/*work folder*/Chap18/Chapter/mailman.html

The Welcome to the MailMan Mailing List page opens, shown earlier in Figure 18-2, where you can log on.

7. Type your username and password, and then click the **Login** button. The main MailMan page opens, shown earlier in Figure 18-7.
8. Click the **Add System User** link. The Add System User Information page, shown earlier in Figure 18-4.
9. Enter the following information to add a new user:

   First Name: **Sam** Access Level: **2**

   Last Name: **Yoshi** Phone #: **555-1234**

   User Name: **snyoshi** E-Mail: **snyoshi@email.com**

   Password: **pass**

   Note that users at access level 2 cannot add or edit users. Click the **Save** button.
10. Close the browser and then restart it to reset the cookie. Type the following text, and then press **Enter** to display the Web page. Replace *work folder* with the name of your work folder.

    http://localhost/*work folder*/Chap18/Chapter/mailman.html

    The Welcome to the MailMan Mailing List page opens so you can log on.
11. In the Enter User Name text box, type **snyoshi**. In the Enter Password text box, type **pass**. Then click the **Login** button. The main MailMan page opens.
12. Click the **Add System User** link. A message appears, as shown in Figure 18-8, because the access level of this user does not authorize him to edit system users.
13. Close your browser.

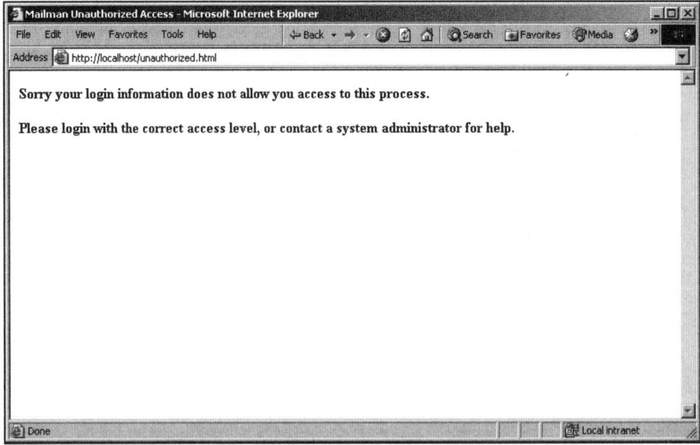

Figure 18-8 Unauthorized page shown to user

CHAPTER SUMMARY

- PHP is designed to work with MySQL to maintain and retrieve data stored in a MySQL database. MySQL is open-source software like PHP. You can create Web applications that interact with a MySQL database and use PHP functions and statements to select and manipulate data from the database.
- Plan a Web application to estimate your resource needs and the overall flow of how your application is expected to work.
- Use PHP to manage application data, such as editing existing data and deleting old or unwanted data. You can use a .php file to collect information from a user, for example, and then add that information to a database.
- You can include SELECT SQL statements in a .php file to access data in a database and list the rows that are returned.
- You can also use PHP to pass information between Web pages so that the application can maintain its control over the data that you want to affect. You can send data to another page through the transmission of an HTML form, pass data between Web pages through Web links that use the question mark (?), or use cookies.
- One way to establish security on a Web site is to set cookies and retrieve their values in other Web pages. With cookies, the values of the variables transferred to the Web page are established as memory variables that can be accessed from within the called Web page.

REVIEW QUESTIONS

1. PHP can only connect to the following database engines:
   a. Sybase System 11
   b. Microsoft Access
   c. ORACLE
   d. MySQL
   e. all of these
   f. none of these
2. MySQL can only execute SQL code from:
   a. outside the PHP environment
   b. within the PHP environment
   c. a special SQL script
   d. a Web server

3. You connect the PHP environment to the MySQL engine with the following function command:
   a. `mysql_connect()`
   b. `MysqlConnection()`
   c. `MySQL_Attach()`
   d. `mysql_join()`
4. Which of the following is the PHP function command used to execute SQL commands against a MySQL database table?
   a. `Execute()`
   b. `run_sql()`
   c. `mysql_query()`
   d. `MySQL_Execute()`
5. Which of the following is the PHP function command used to connect to a particular database with the MySQL database engine?
   a. `Mysql_database()`
   b. `mysql_select_db()`
   c. `database_conn()`
   d. `Connect_mysql()`
6. Which of the following is the PHP function command used for testing how many rows of data have come back from an executed MySQL command?
   a. `Mysql_rows_returned()`
   b. `mysql_num_rows()`
   c. `num_rows()`
   d. `rows_retrieved()`
7. You can redirect a Web user to another Web page with the PHP function command:
   a. `Link_to()`
   b. `redirect()`
   c. `header(…)`
   d. `goto_page()`
8. You can traverse a returned result set within PHP by using:
   a. `Walk_array()`
   b. `MySQL_fetch_array() function command`
   c. `Traverse()`
   d. `walk_results()`

9. You only use arrays in PHP for:
    a. managing SQL result sets
    b. managing groups of similar data
    c. managing groups of other arrays
    d. all of these
10. The way to increment a numeric variable in one line of PHP code is:
    a. `$counter++`
    b. `$counter = $counter . 1`
    c. `$counter+=`
    d. `++$counter`
11. The PHP character used to concatenate strings is the:
    a. plus (+)
    b. ampersand (&)
    c. period (.)
    d. question mark (?)
    e. none of these
12. The PHP character used to send data values through an HTML anchor link is the:
    a. question mark (?)
    b. slash (/)
    c. pound sign (#)
    d. ampersand (&)
    e. none of these
13. Which of the following is a way you can pass data between Web pages?
    a. form data
    b. cookies
    c. anchor links
    d. all of these
14. To use a variable in a pages script, which function command do you use to retrieve PHP variables in memory for a subsequent page?
    a. `retrieve()`
    b. `getvalue()`
    c. none, the variable can be directly accessed
    d. `GetCookie()`

15. Which of the following is true about cookies?
    a. Cookies can only be set to exist temporarily in memory.
    b. Cookies are a highly effective way to implement tight security on a Web page.
    c. Cookies are best consumed with a glass of warm milk.
    d. Cookies are a good way to invisibly hand data between Web pages.

HANDS-ON EXERCISES

Before you perform the following exercises, copy the folder named Exercises in the Chap18 folder in your data files to the Chap18 folder in your work folder.

Exercise 18-1

To create a Web form that allows customers to select car options:

1. Enter the following HTML into your text editor, and save it as **dealership.html** in the Chap18\Exercises folder in your work folder:

```
<html>
<head>
     <title> Collecting Auto Sales Information </title>
</head>

<body>
<H2>We are glad you have come to our discount virtual car lot </H2>
<H3><IMG height=80 alt=""
src="Carsym.jpg" width=120
border=0><BR>Please provide us with the following information so that
we can serve you better.</H3>
<form action="carpicks.php" method="post"><BR>Please tell us
about yourself:
<P>
<TABLE border=1>

  <TR>
    <TD>First name:</TD>
    <TD><INPUT name=firstname style="WIDTH: 178px; HEIGHT: 22px"
       size=22></TD>
    <TD>Last name: </TD>
    <TD><INPUT size=25 name=lastname></TD></TR>
  <TR>
    <TD>Address: </TD>
    <TD><INPUT size=25 name=address></TD>
    <TD>City:</TD>
    <TD><INPUT size=21 name=city style="WIDTH: 180px; HEIGHT:
       22px"></TD></TR>
```

```
  <TR>
     <TD>Telephone Number:  </TD>
    <TD><INPUT name=phone style="WIDTH: 174px; HEIGHT: 22px"
     ></TD>
    <TD>e-mail</TD>
    <TD><INPUT size=21 name=email
 style="WIDTH: 182px; HEIGHT: 22px"></TD></TR></TABLE><BR>Please also
    tell us about the kind of transportation you are interested in.</P
>
<P>
<TABLE border=1>

  <TR>
    <TD>Price Range</TD>
    <TD><SELECT name=pricerange >
      <option value=0 selected> Please select a value
      <option value=1 > Under $4,000
      <option value=2> Between $4,000 &amp; $6,000
      <option value=3> Between $6,000 &amp; $8,000
      <option value=4> Between $8,000 &amp; $10,000
      <option value=5> Between $10,000 &amp; $15,000
      <option value=6> Between $15,000 &amp; $20,000
      <option value=7> Between $20,000 &amp; $30,000
      <option value=8> Over $30,000</option>
      </SELECT></TD>
<TD>Color</TD>
<TD><SELECT name=color>
  <option value=0 selected> Please select a color
  <OPTION value=1 > Blue
  <OPTION value=2> Red
  <OPTION value=3> Green
  <OPTION value=4> White
  <OPTION value=5> Brown
  <OPTION value=6> Metallic Red
  <OPTION value=7> Metallic Blue
  <OPTION value=8> Black</OPTION>
  </SELECT></TD></TR>
<TR>
 <TD>Model Type</TD>
 <TD><SELECT name=modeltype>
   <option value=0 selected> Please select a model
   <OPTION value=1> 4-door sedan
   <OPTION value=2> 5-door hatchback
   <OPTION value=3> sport coupe
   <OPTION value=4> family van
   <OPTION value=5> 1/4 ton truck
   <OPTION value=6> 1/2 ton truck
   <OPTION value=7> 4-door luxury</OPTION>
   </SELECT></TD>
```

```
    <TD>Front wheel drive?</TD>
    <TD><INPUT type=checkbox name=frontwheel></TD></TR>
  <TR>
    <TD>Transmission</TD>
    <TD><SELECT name=transmission>
      <option value=0 selected> Please select a value
        <OPTION value=1>Manual 4 speed
        <OPTION value=2>Manual 5 speed
        <OPTION value=3>Automatic</OPTION>
        </SELECT></TD>
    <TD> Power Brakes?</TD>
    <TD><INPUT type=checkbox name=powerbrakes></TD></TR></TABLE>
</P>
<P>
<TABLE border=1>

  <TR>
    <TD colSpan=4>
      <P align=center>    Accessories:</P>
      </TD></TR>
  <TR>
    <TD>Tinted Glass?</TD>
    <TD><INPUT type=checkbox name=tinted></TD>
    <TD>Sun Roof?</TD>
    <TD><INPUT type=checkbox name=sunroof></TD></TR>
  <TR>
    <TD>CD Player?</TD>
    <TD><INPUT type=checkbox name=cdplayer></TD>
    <TD>Deluxe Cup Holder?</TD>
    <TD><INPUT type=checkbox name=cupholder></TD></TR>
  <TR>
    <TD>Cassette Player?</TD>
    <TD><INPUT type=checkbox name=cassette></TD>
    <TD>CD Changer?</TD>
    <TD><INPUT type=checkbox name=cdchanger></TD></TR>
  <TR>
    <TD>Leather interior?</TD>
    <TD><INPUT type=checkbox name=leather></TD>
    <TD>Engine Block Heater?</TD>
    <TD><INPUT type=checkbox name=blockheat>
      </TD></TR></TABLE>        
        <br><IMG height=80 alt=""
src="Carkeys.jpg" width=120
border=0><br>

<INPUT type=submit name="submit" value="Submit form">   
<INPUT type=reset name="reset" value="Clear form">
</P>
```

```
</form>

</body>
</html>
```

2. Enter the following code into your editor, and save it as **carpicks.php** in the Chap18\Exercises folder in your work folder:

```
<?
$connection = mysql_connect("localhost");
$db = "dealership";

mysql_select_db($db, $connection) or die( "Could not open $db");

$sql = "INSERT INTO requests (firstname, lastname, address, city,
   phone, email, pricerange, ";
$sql = $sql . "color, modeltype, frontwheel, transmission, powerbrakes,
   tinted, sunroof, ";
$sql = $sql . "cdplayer, cupholder, cassette, cdchanger, leather,
   blockheat) ";
$sql = $sql . "VALUES ('$firstname', '$lastname', '$address', '$city',
   '$phone', '$email', ";
$sql = $sql . "$pricerange, $color, $modeltype, '$frontwheel',
$transmission, ";
$sql = $sql . "'$powerbrakes', '$tinted', '$sunroof', ";
$sql = $sql . "'$cdplayer', '$cupholder', '$cassette', '$cdchanger',
   '$leather', '$blockheat') ";

$res = mysql_query($sql, $connection) or die( "Could not execute sql:
$nextid:  $sql");
 ?>

<html>
<head>
      <title> Customer's car selections </title>
</head>

<body>
<h2> Customer's car selections have been saved to the database </h2>

</body>
</html>
```

18

3. Enter the following SQL code into your text editor, and run it through the MySQL engine.

```
CREATE DATABASE dealership;
USE dealership;
CREATE TABLE requests (
  requestid int(11) NOT NULL auto_increment,
  firstname varchar(20) default NULL,
```

```
    lastname varchar(25) default NULL,
    address varchar(25) default NULL,
    city varchar(25) default NULL,
    phone varchar(14) default NULL,
    email varchar(45) default NULL,
    pricerange int(11) default NULL,
    color int(11) default NULL,
    modeltype int(11) default NULL,
    frontwheel int(11) default NULL,
    transmission int(11) default NULL,
    powerbrakes int(11) default NULL,
    tinted int(11) default NULL,
    sunroof int(11) default NULL,
    cdplayer int(11) default NULL,
    cupholder int(11) default NULL,
    cassette int(11) default NULL,
    cdchanger int(11) default NULL,
    leather int(11) default NULL,
    blockheat int(11) default NULL,
    PRIMARY KEY (requestid)
)
```

4. Save the file as **dealership.sql** in the Chap18\Exercises folder in your work folder, and then close your text editor.
5. Open a Command Prompt window (click the Start button, point to All Programs, point to Accessories, and then click Command Prompt). Change to the mysql\bin directory, and then type the following command at the DOS prompt to import the dealership.sql file into the MySQL engine. Then press Enter.

   mysql < C:*work folder*\Chap18\exercises\dealership.sql

   (If your work folder is stored on a drive other than C, use that drive letter instead of C.)
6. Launch your browser. Then test your code by typing http://localhost/*work folder*/Chap18/Exercises/dealership.html, replacing *work folder* with the name of your work folder.
7. Close your browser.

Exercise 18-2

Add the add processes to the MailMan application for the province/state module. The table in the mailman database is called prov. Be sure to test for the user's permission levels for these processes and direct users accordingly.

To add processes to the MailMan application:

1. Open a text editor, and then type the following code:

```
<?
if ( $access != 1 ) header( "Location: unauthorized.html" );
?>
```

```
<? include("mailman_header.inc");  ?>

<FORM action=save_prov.php method=post>

<TABLE cellSpacing=2 cellPadding=6 align=center border=1>
  <TR>
    <TD colSpan=4>
      <H3 align=center>Add Province / State Information</H3></TD>
</TR>
  <TR>
    <TD>Province / State Code</TD>
    <TD><INPUT name=provcode size=4></TD>
  </tr><tr>
    <TD>Province / State Name</TD>
    <TD><INPUT name=provname></TD></TR>
 <tr>
    <TD align=center><INPUT type=submit value=Save></TD>
    <TD align=center><INPUT type=reset value=Reset></TD></TR>

  </TABLE>
</FORM>

</body>
</html>
```

2. Save the file as **add_prov.php** in the Chap18\Exercises folder in your work folder.
3. Open a new document, and then type the following code:

```
<?
$connection = mysql_connect("localhost");

$db = "mailman";
mysql_select_db($db, $connection) or die( "Could not open $db");

$sql = "SELECT Max(provid) AS currentid FROM prov";
$result = mysql_query($sql, $connection) or die( "Could not
execute sql: $sql");

$row = mysql_fetch_array($result);
$nextid = $row["currentid"] ;
$nextid++;

$sql = "INSERT INTO prov (provid, provcode, provname) ";
$sql = $sql . "VALUES ($nextid, '$provcode', '$provname' )";

$res = mysql_query($sql, $connection) or die( "Could not execute sql:
$nextid:  $sql");
```

```
if ( !$res ) {
        echo "problem adding to database";
} else {
        header( "Location: mailman_main.php" );
}
?>
```

4. Save the file as **save_prov.php** in the Chap18\Exercises folder in your work folder.
5. Close the text editor, and start your browser.
6. Test your code by typing http://localhost/*work folder*/Chap18/Exercises/mailman.html, replacing *work folder* with the name of your work folder.
7. Close your browser.

Exercise 18-3

Add a report to the MailMan system that formats the addresses into a two-column mailing label format. Be aware here that you will be using two records of address information at a time in order to show the data side by side, so plan your use of variables carefully.

To add a report to the MailMan system:

1. Open a text editor, and enter the following code into a new document:

```
<? include("mailman_header.inc");
$connection = mysql_connect("localhost");
$db = "mailman";
mysql_select_db($db, $connection) or die( "Could not open $db");

$sql = "SELECT * FROM address";
$result = mysql_query($sql, $connection) or die( "Could not execute
   sql: $sql");
$num_result = mysql_num_rows($result);

?>

<TABLE cellSpacing=5 cellPadding=6 align=center border=1>

<?

for ($i=0; $i < $num_result; $i = $i + 2) {

      $row = mysql_fetch_array($result);

        echo "<tr><td>";
        echo $row["firstname"];
        echo " " . $row["lastname"];
        echo "<br>";
```

```
        echo $row["address1"];
        echo "<br>";
        echo $row["address2"];
        echo "<br>";
        echo $row["city"];
        echo ", " . $row["prov"];
        echo "<br>";
        echo $row["postal"];
        echo "</td>";

  $row = mysql_fetch_array($result);

  if ($row["addressid"] > 0) {

        echo "<td>";
        echo $row["firstname"];
        echo " " . $row["lastname"];
        echo "<br>";
        echo $row["address1"];
        echo "<br>";
        echo $row["address2"];
        echo "<br>";
        echo $row["city"];
        echo ", " . $row["prov"];
        echo "<br>";
        echo $row["postal"];
        echo "</td>";
  }
        echo "</tr>";
}
?>
</TABLE>

</body>
</html>
```

2. Save the file as **2up_label_report.php** in the Chap18\Exercises folder in your work folder.
3. Close the text editor, and start your browser.
4. Test your code by typing http://localhost/*work folder*/Chap18/Exercises/mailman.html, replacing *work folder* with the name of your work folder. Try to access the 2up_label_report report.
5. Close your browser.

18

Exercise 18-4

Create another access level (level 3) that has permission only to review the reports section of the MailMan Web application. Test for this new level of permission before granting access to the report section. You have to test for both this new level of permission and that of the administrator (level 1) by employing a combined logical OR condition or by nesting IF statements. If you need assistance, refer to Chapter 17 or the online help at the PHP home Web site.

To create another access level in the mailman system:

1. In a text editor, open the file **2up_label_report.php**, and enter the following code at the beginning of this file:

```
<? if ($access != 1)
{
        if ($access != 3)
        {
                header( "Location: unauthorized.php" );
        }
}
?>
```

2. Save the file with the same name in the Chap18\Exercises folder in your work folder.
3. Close the text editor, and start your browser.
4. Test your code by typing http://localhost/*work folder*/Chap18/Exercises/mailman.html, replacing *work folder* with the name of your work folder. Try to access the 2up_label_report report by logging onto the Web site as the administrator and creating new user accounts with level 2 and level 3 access permissions.
5. Close your browser and log onto the Web site with the two new accounts you created, and try to access the 2up_label_report page.
6. Close your browser.

Exercise 18-5

Review the existing code and find all the areas where the database connection code is repeated on each page. Combine this code into one file that can be called with the include function, and make the inclusion calls in each page that is affected.

To streamline your code:

1. Open a text editor, and enter the following code:

```
<?
$connection = mysql_connect("localhost");
$db = "mailman";
mysql_select_db($db, $connection) or die( "Could not open $db");
?>
```

2. Save the file as **mailman_dataconn.inc** in the Chap18\Exercises folder in your work folder.
3. Open the **save_prov.php** from the Chap18\Exercises folder in your work folder. This file already contains the connection code, which you can remove. Delete the code shown in Step 1. Then add the text shown in bold:

```
<? include("mailman_dataconn.inc"); ?>
<?
```

```
$sql = "SELECT Max(provid) AS currentid FROM prov";
$result = mysql_query($sql, $connection) or die( "Could not execute
   sql: $sql");

$row = mysql_fetch_array($result);
$nextid = $row["currentid"] ;
$nextid++;

$sql = "INSERT INTO prov (provid, provcode, provname) ";
$sql = $sql . "VALUES ($nextid, '$provcode', '$provname' )";

$res = mysql_query($sql, $connection) or die( "Could not execute sql:
$nextid:  $sql");

if ( !$res ) {
      echo "problem adding to database";
} else {
      header( "Location: mailman_main.php" );
}
?>
```

4. Save the file with the same name in the Chap18\Exercises folder in your work folder.
5. You could also change the following files in the same way:

2up_label_report.php	add_addr.php	commit_delete_addr.php
commit_delete_prov.php	commit_delete_user.php	commit_edit_addr.php
commit_edit_prov.php	commit_edit_user.php	delete_addr.php
delete_prov.php	delete_user.php	deleteuser.php
edit_addr.php	edit_prov.php	edit_user.php
save_addr.php	save_prov.php	saveuser.php
search_delete_addr.php	search_delete_prov.php	search_delete_user.php
search_edit_addr.php	search_edit_prov.php	search_edit_user.php
trylogon2.php		

6. Save all your changes, close the text editor, and start your browser.
7. Test your code by typing http://localhost/*work folder*/Chap18/Exercises/mailman.html, replacing *work folder* with the name of your work folder. Test the application.
8. Close your browser.

Web Programming Projects

Project 18-1

Add the edit and delete processes to the MailMan application for the province/state module. The table in the mailman database is prov. Be sure to test for the user's permission levels for these processes and direct users accordingly.

Project 18-2

Create the address management portion of the MailMan system. Allow for the add, edit, and deletion of mailing addresses. Be sure to populate the province or state selection list for entering data during the add and edit processes.

Project 18-3

Create a guest book application that allows the guests to your Web pages to enter comments to you about your Web site. The entries are to be stored in a database called guestbook and a table called visitors. The visitors table should have the structure shown in Table 18-4.

Table 18-4

Column name	Data Type	Particulars
guestid	Integer	Not null, autoincrement
fname	Varchar(20)	Null
lname	Varchar(25)	Null
visitdate	Timestamp	
city	Varchar(25)	Null
country	Varchar(25)	Null
comments	Text	Null
email	Varchar(45)	Null

Then create a simple report Web page that is password protected that asks you for a date range. Upon receiving the date range, display all the guest book entries that have arrived during that time frame.

CHAPTER

19

COLDFUSION MX: PART I

In this chapter you will:

- Learn the advantages of ColdFusion MX
- Use ColdFusion components
- Design a user interface that reuses code with ColdFusion
- Design HTML forms and ColdFusion form handlers
- Learn about program flow control in ColdFusion
- Use loops to perform repetitive tasks
- Redirect users to other Web pages

ColdFusion MX is a Web application server that lets developers design and deliver e-commerce and other Web-based applications. ColdFusion provides a set of tools that allows you to quickly create interactive, data-driven applications without using difficult and time-consuming programming languages. It allows you to create dynamic Web sites by using a tag-based, embedded language that is very similar to HTML.

ADVANTAGES OF COLDFUSION MX

The following list summarizes some of the advantages of using ColdFusion:

- You develop applications using a tag-based language that is embedded in documents, much like HTML. The ability to embed code allows you to create documents rapidly.
- You do not need to compile, link, or perform other labor-intensive activities associated with developing applications in traditional programming languages. ColdFusion applications are easy to build and test.
- ColdFusion supports numerous server-side tags, functions, and third-party components, providing most or all of the server-side processing you need to build sophisticated Web applications.
- Applications built using ColdFusion are easy to maintain because the scripts are embedded inside the documents.
- ColdFusion integrates with databases, e-mail servers, file systems, directories, and other enterprise systems, which allows you to develop enterprise-level, complex Web applications quickly and easily.
- ColdFusion is a scalable architecture that lets you combine many Web servers to handle heavy traffic from a large number of customer requests.
- ColdFusion is a cross-platform, Web application server that works on several different operating systems, including Windows 95/98, Windows NT, Windows 2000, Linux, Solaris, and HP-UX.

Given all of these advantages, thousands of companies around the world and several Fortune 500 companies use ColdFusion for building and maintaining their online businesses. Two such Web sites are *Autobytel.com* and *Crayola.com*. You can understand what ColdFusion can do for you by examining how these sites operate.

To examine a popular Web site that uses ColdFusion:

1. Start your Web browser, such as Internet Explorer.
2. Go to **www.autobytel.com**. Your Web browser displays the home page for *Autobytel.com*. Examine it briefly.
3. Click the hyperlink to **Buy a New or Used Vehicle**. See Figure 19-1. Your Web browser displays the main page for buying a car at Autobytel.com. Examine the URL and notice that the filename in it has an extension of .cfm.

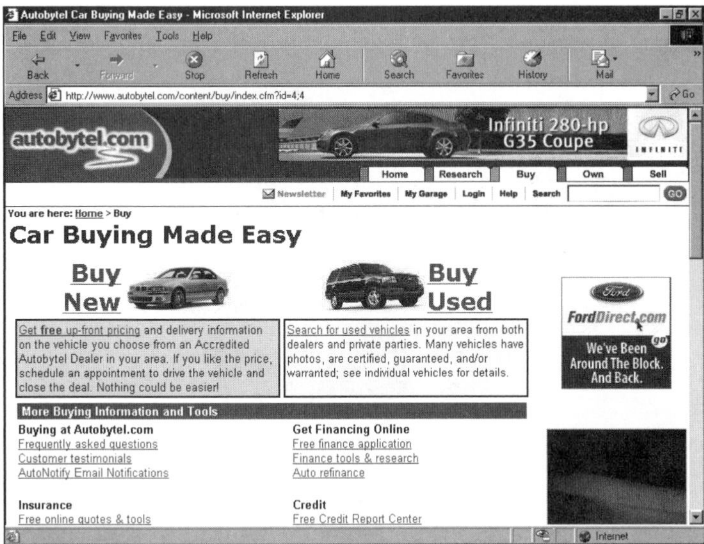

Figure 19-1 Buying a car at Autobytel.com

Founded in 1995, *Autobytel.com* was the first company to sell cars online. In 1999 it generated sales of over $13 billion. *Autobytel.com* uses ColdFusion to offer customers an interactive way to find information about cars, such as vehicle specifications, vehicle reviews, manufacturer's incentives, and dealer invoice prices. As shown in Figure 19-1, customers can find pricing and delivery information from accredited dealers and schedule appointments for test-driving cars. Customers can also use the Web site to apply for insurance, obtain financing and leasing information, and purchase certified preowned vehicles. Customers can register with the service section for personalized assistance, including service reminders sent by e-mail, appointment scheduling for vehicle maintenance, and recall information. People can sell their used cars through the classifieds section. Given its success in the United States, *Autobytel.com* has started operations in Canada, the United Kingdom, Sweden, and Japan.

To examine another popular Web site that uses ColdFusion:

1. Using your browser, go to **www.crayola.com**. Your Web browser displays the home page for *Crayola.com*. Examine it briefly. See Figure 19-2.

2. Move the mouse around on some of the hyperlinks. Examine the status bar and notice that most of the hyperlinks point to filenames with extensions of .cfm.

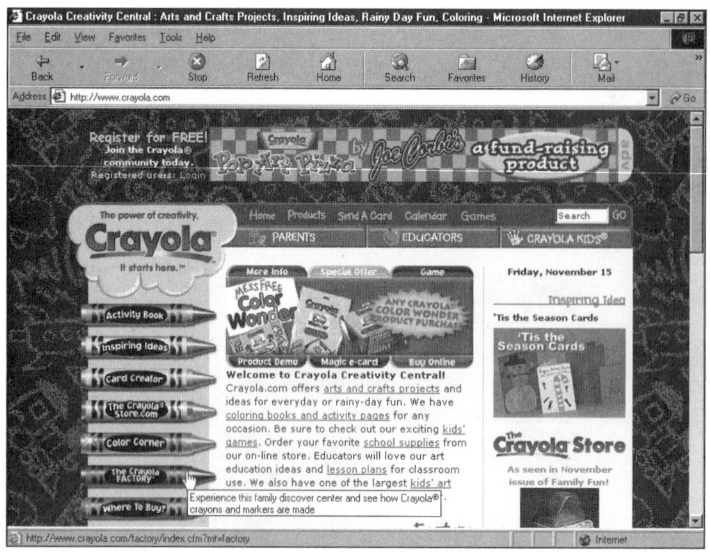

Figure 19-2 Crayola.com home page

Binney & Smith, the leading producer of children's art materials and the maker of Crayola products, selected ColdFusion to power *Crayola.com*. As shown in Figure 19-2, *Crayola.com* is a dynamic Web site that offers engaging and interactive arts and crafts projects for parents, educators, and children. Parents can find information about party ideas, travel tips, book reviews, and other related items by using simple menus. Users can create electronic greeting cards with personalized messages and send them for any occasion. Customers can purchase gifts after specifying a price range, the recipient's age, and product categories.

Web sites that use ColdFusion implement server-side processing to accomplish the following basic tasks:

- Manipulate numbers, strings, dates, and times and display them in several formats.
- Use conditional processing.
- Perform a task repeatedly.
- Handle data that users enter in HTML forms.
- Store and retrieve data in several different database systems that might be stored locally on the Web server or any other database server.
- Extract data from databases and create reports.
- Maintain data and process transactions.
- Validate data entered by users to ensure the integrity of the information.

- Manage cookies and keep track of a series of client interactions with a Web site.
- Interact with other services, such as e-mail and file systems.
- Upload user-supplied files.

Using ColdFusion Components

The real power of ColdFusion is its ability to enhance static HTML documents into Web pages that can process tasks. You may already be familiar with some similar methods such as Active Server Pages, PHP, and Java.

To develop dynamic Web applications using ColdFusion, you use three components: a text editor, the ColdFusion Server, and the ColdFusion Administrator.

- Use any text editor to create Web pages using HTML and **ColdFusion Markup Language (CFML)**. CFML is a server-side markup language you use with HTML to enable server-side processing by manipulating data, displaying output, and interacting with databases.
- **ColdFusion Server** runs the applications that you create in conjunction with a Web server. Adding the ColdFusion server to the process of sending requests from a client to a Web server provides the capability to perform additional processing before sending the results to the client.
- **ColdFusion Administrator** is a Web-based application that allows you to set up and maintain the ColdFusion server and its interfaces with other services, such as database and mail servers.

Using the Text Editor

In this chapter and the next, you can use the text editor of your choice to build information system applications. These applications can run on Microsoft IIS or another server your instructor specifies, as long as it has ColdFusion installed on it.

The ColdFusion chapters in this book use the TextPad text editor for some of its illustrations. TextPad is powerful shareware that is easy to use; you can download it from *www.textpad.com*, then use it for anything from replacing Notepad to editing text in a programmer's integrated development environment. With appropriate add-ons, TextPad can apply color codes to documents to help you easily identify regular text, HTML tags, HTML attributes, CFML tags, and other scripts.

Using ColdFusion Server

To understand how a ColdFusion server works with a Web server, you need to understand the interaction between client computers and servers. First, when you request an HTML document from a Web server, you might type the page's Uniform Resource Locator (URL) in your browser's address field, or you might click a hyperlink in an existing document. A Web server listens to client computers for requests, which are called Hypertext Transfer Protocol (HTTP) requests because they are usually formatted according to HTTP specifications. When a Web server receives an HTTP request for an HTML document from a client computer, the request includes the name of the requested document, the path to the document, the Internet Protocol (IP) address of the client computer making the request, and a few other details. Typically, the Web server logs some of these details in a log file or database, retrieves the document, and sends it back to the client computer based on its IP address. If the document is not found, an error message is sent back to the client.

When the client receives the HTML document, it uses the HTML tags to format the document according to the instructions contained in the tags. The client may make additional requests to the same server or other servers if any embedded graphics, background images, sound files, style sheets, or other files are required to complete the document. After all these files are received, the browser displays the entire formatted document. Web browsers may begin displaying the document before receiving all the files, and then update the page as they receive image files and other information. The client-server process is illustrated in Figure 19-3.

Now examine what happens when you request a ColdFusion document from a Web server that has ColdFusion Server installed. You request ColdFusion documents in the same way you request other Web resources—for example, by typing a URL or clicking a hyperlink. When you request a ColdFusion document, the client computer sends an HTTP request to the Web server. This HTTP request is formatted like a request for an HTML document, except that the document name has an extension of .cfm and is called a **ColdFusion template**. The Web server receives the HTTP request, recognizes the extension, and processes it accordingly as a request for a ColdFusion template. The Web server calls the ColdFusion server and passes all the information it received in the HTTP request to the ColdFusion server using Web server API.

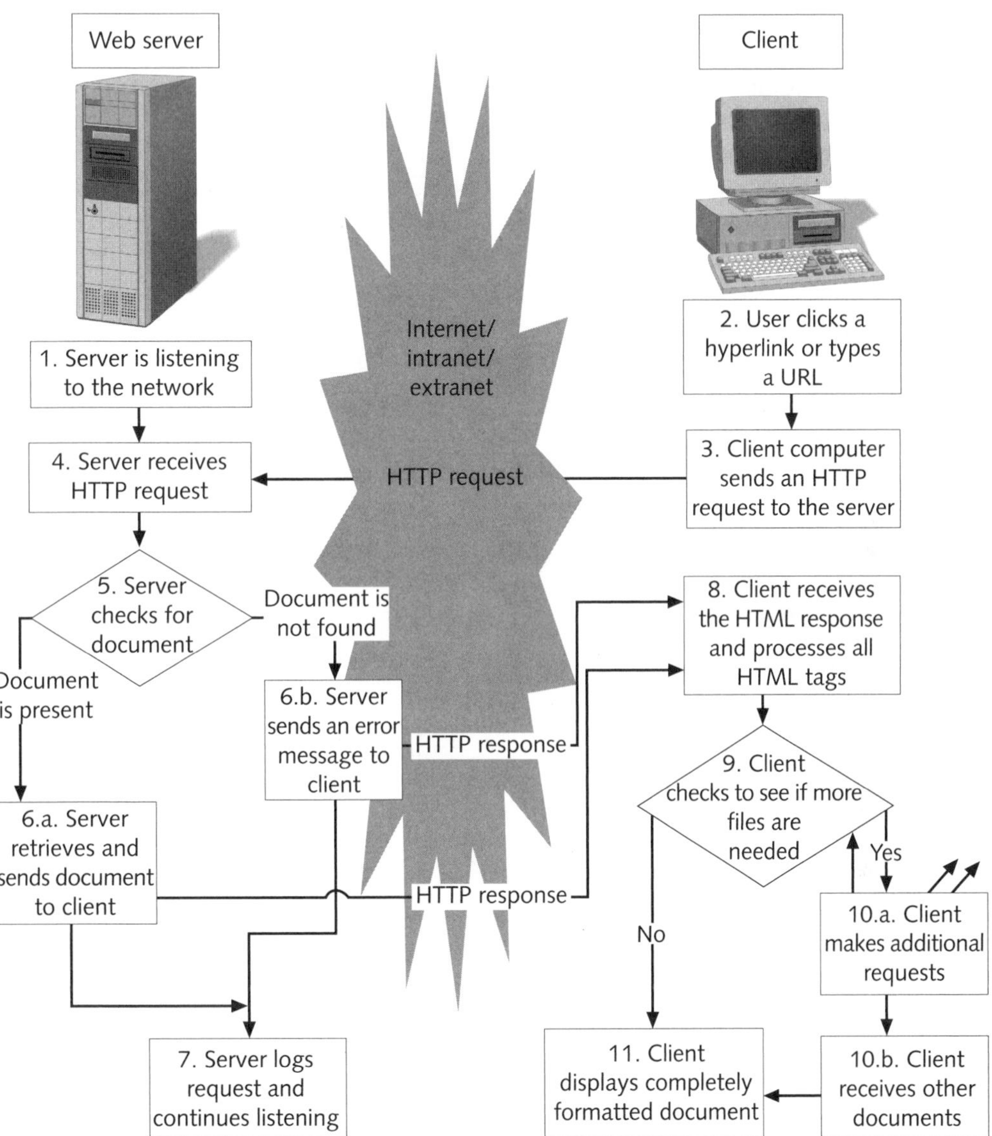

Figure 19-3 Client–server interaction for processing an HTML document request

The ColdFusion server takes over and retrieves the document from the disk, using the CFML tags to process the template according to the instructions contained in the tags. After the ColdFusion server processes the CFML, it returns a document to the Web server that contains only the HTML code and other text needed to display the Web page. The CFML in the document might instruct the ColdFusion server to manipulate data, perform calculations, access data from databases, work with files and folders, retrieve e-mail messages, or output data. The ColdFusion server sends this information to the Web server, which in turn sends it to the client as an HTTP response. Both the ColdFusion server and the Web server log these activities. The client computer receives the Web page, which now contains only HTML. It processes the HTML and sends other requests as needed. After the client receives all of the files, the browser formats and displays the complete Web page. This client-server process is shown in Figure 19-4.

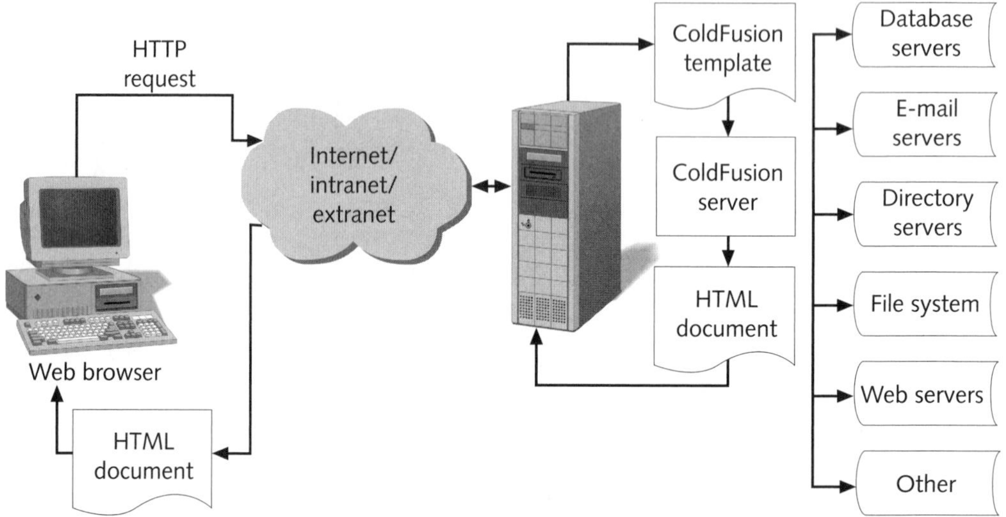

Figure 19-4 Client–server interaction for processing a ColdFusion template request

Using ColdFusion Administrator

ColdFusion Administrator is a secure, password-protected, Web-based application that allows you to configure ColdFusion Server and manage its performance. For example, you can set up ColdFusion Server to display a contact e-mail address when it encounters an error, or you can configure data sources for interacting with databases. You can turn on several levels of debugging information to assist you in development. For example, you can specify the mail server that ColdFusion uses to send e-mail messages. You can tell ColdFusion what files to use for logging and what information you want logged. You can restrict the execution of certain CFML tags that could harm your system when you allow remote development. The ColdFusion Administrator is entirely Web-based and provides a simple, intuitive interface for monitoring the server.

Depending on your server's configuration, you may not be able to access the ColdFusion Administrator.

DESIGNING A USER INTERFACE WITH COLDFUSION

To provide a realistic context for working with ColdFusion, this chapter uses a scenario involving a fictional real estate agency named CF Realtors. Cal and Fran Stevenson founded the CF Realtors Company in the early 1970s. CF Realtors specializes in residential sales, and is known for providing excellent service to its customers, both sellers and buyers. Cal and Fran believe that technology is a useful tool for increasing the effectiveness of their business. In the early 1980s, their company was one of the first in the Midwest to use local area networks to speed up the process of listing homes. Recently, they hired your company to launch a Web site for CF Realtors. They want the Web site to present information in a way that is appealing and easy to use.

After extensive interviews with company personnel and several rounds of design and modifications, you and your development team have determined the user interface for the site. Cal and Fran want a consistent look and feel for all pages on the Web site, similar to the one shown in Figure 19-5.

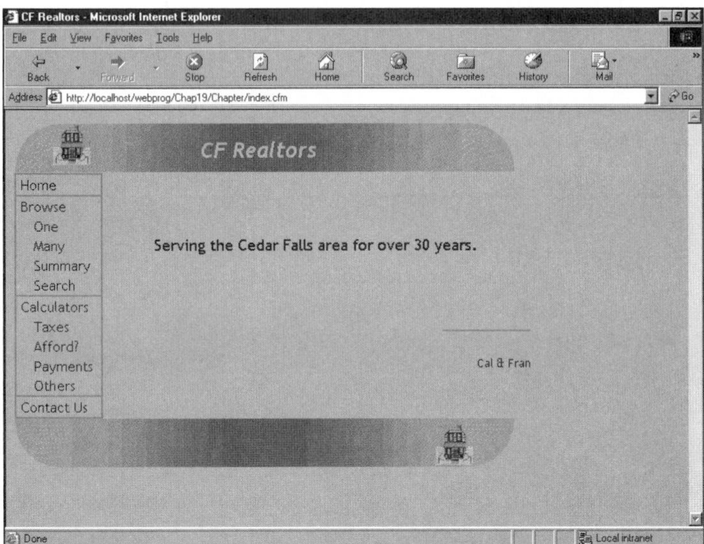

Figure 19-5 Planned user interface for CF Realtors

Because all the pages should have the same design, you might be able to use some of the same HTML and CFML code on each page. You ask one of your team members to investigate this possibility and see whether you can reuse common code.

19

Reusing Code

A simple way to reuse code in ColdFusion is to create a separate file for the common code. You use the CFINCLUDE tag to include the code in this file in other templates. The syntax for the CFINCLUDE tag is:

```
<cfinclude template="template_name">
```

When ColdFusion Server executes the CFINCLUDE tag, it searches for the template given by the TEMPLATE attribute and processes the code in the template, reading the HTML and CFML in the file you specify. The template treats the HTML and CFML referenced in the CFINCLUDE tag as if the code were copied and pasted into the template. The template_name could include a path relative to the current template in case the template to be included is located in another folder. CFML statements are generally known as tags because the statements are combined with HTML tags. The syntax, or programming rules, for writing these tags is similar to those for writing HTML tags. For example, most CFML statements have an opening and closing tag that are very similar to those in HTML.

Because the CFINCLUDE tag allows you to easily reuse code by including it in multiple templates, you decide to analyze the CF Realtors user interface to identify common elements in the design, as shown in Figure 19-6.

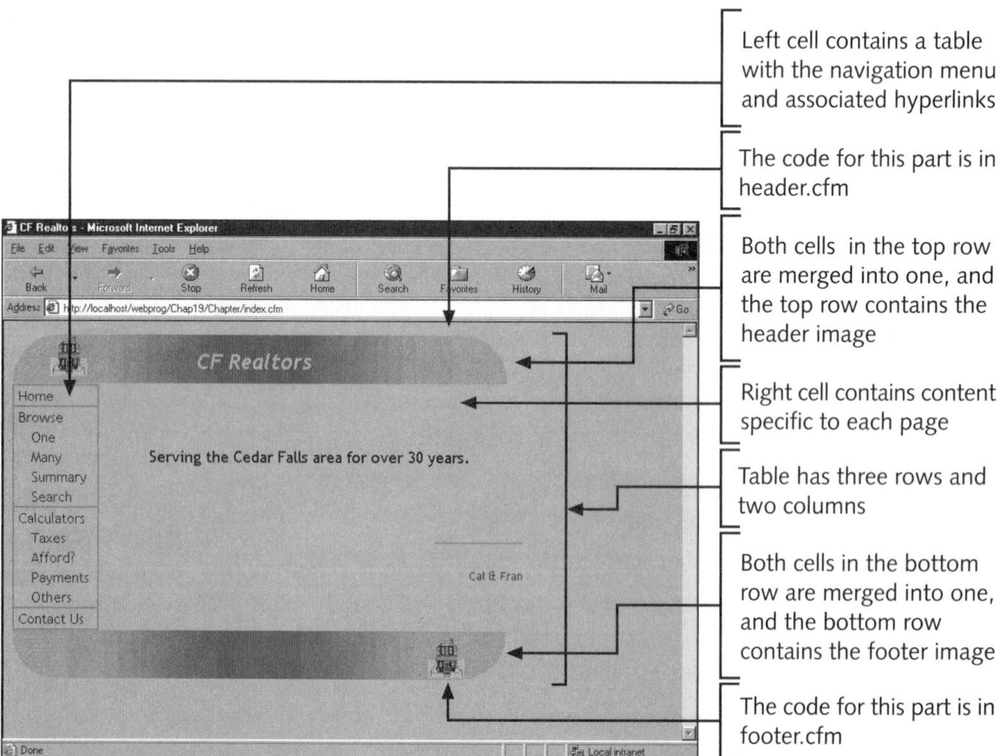

Figure 19-6 Common elements in the CF Realtors user interface

In the current design, a page consists of a table that has three rows and two columns. The top row of the table has two cells merged into one to contain the header image. Similarly, the bottom row of the table has two merged cells that contain the footer image. The middle row has two cells. The left cell contains another table with the navigation menu and associated hyperlinks. The second cell in the middle row contains the content specific to each page.

You decide to create a template named header.cfm to include all the code for starting the page with the document structure tags, the top row of the table along with the header image, and the navigation menu. You include this template at the top of all the other templates by using the CFINCLUDE tag. The code for header.cfm is shown in Figure 19-7.

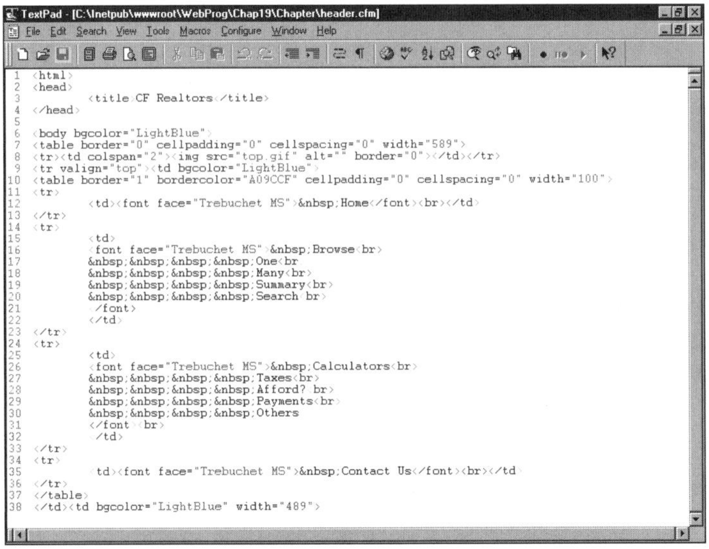

TextPad - [C:\Inetpub\wwwroot\WebProg\Chap19\Chapter\header.cfm]

```
1  <html>
2  <head>
3          <title>CF Realtors</title>
4  </head>
5
6  <body bgcolor="LightBlue">
7  <table border="0" cellpadding="0" cellspacing="0" width="589">
8  <tr><td colspan="2"><img src="top.gif" alt="" border="0"></td></tr>
9  <tr valign="top"><td bgcolor="LightBlue">
10 <table border="1" bordercolor="A09CCF" cellpadding="0" cellspacing="0" width="100">
11 <tr>
12         <td><font face="Trebuchet MS"> Home</font><br></td>
13 </tr>
14 <tr>
15         <td>
16         <font face="Trebuchet MS"> Browse<br>
17             One<br>
18             Many<br>
19             Summary<br>
20             Search<br>
21         </font>
22         </td>
23 </tr>
24 <tr>
25         <td>
26         <font face="Trebuchet MS"> Calculators<br>
27             Taxes<br>
28             Afford?<br>
29             Payments<br>
30             Others
31         </font><br>
32         </td>
33 </tr>
34 <tr>
35         <td><font face="Trebuchet MS"> Contact Us</font><br></td>
36 </tr>
37 </table>
38 </td><td bgcolor="LightBlue" width="489">
```

Figure 19-7 Text editor with the code in header.cfm

The code in lines 7 through 9 renders the large table. The table in the first cell of the second row contains the navigation links.

You use another template named footer.cfm for the bottom part of the page. The template includes the end tags for the second cell in the middle row, for the middle row itself, for the bottom row with the image, and for the document structure. You include this template in all the other templates by using the CFINCLUDE tag at the end of the template. The code for footer.cfm is shown in Figure 19-8.

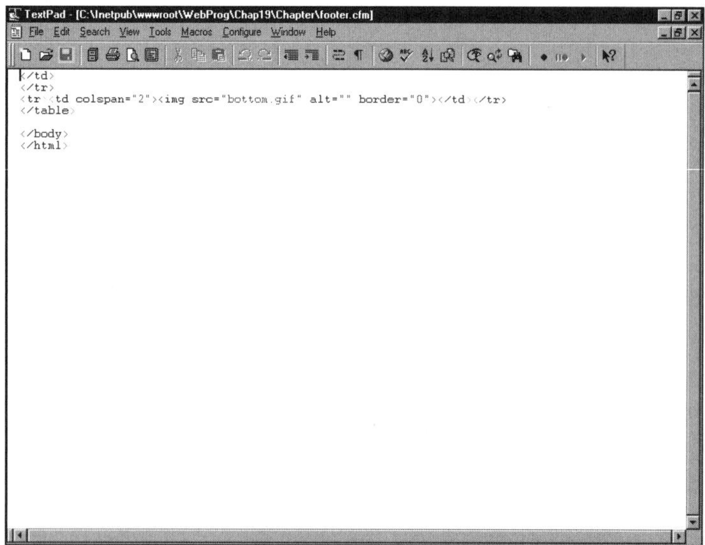

Figure 19-8 Text editor with the code in footer.cfm

The code in line 3 renders the third row in the table, and the code above it ends the second row. Any content between these two blocks of code is displayed in the second cell of the second row as the content specific to the particular template.

Considering this organization, the home page of the CF Realtors site is a set of CFINCLUDE tags with an appropriately formatted mission for the company between the tags. This template is named index.cfm, as shown in the following code:

```
<cfinclude template="header.cfm">
<font face="Trebuchet MS" size="+1"><br><br><br>
<p align="center">Serving the Cedar Falls area for over 30 years.</p>
</font>
<br><br><br>
<hr color="A09CCF" width="100" align="right">
<p align="right"><font face="Trebuchet MS" size="-1"> Cal &amp; Fran</font></p>
<br>
<cfinclude template="footer.cfm">
```

When you load the preceding template in your browser, you see the Web page shown in Figure 19-5.

When ColdFusion Server processes this code, it includes the code from header.cfm, and the content specific to the template. Then it includes the code from footer.cfm and creates HTML for the Web page. This HTML is shown in Figure 19-9. Notice that the entire HTML from the three templates is combined to create a complete Web page.

```
            Many<br>
            Summary<br>
            Search<br>
        </font>
        </td>
</tr>
<tr>
        <td>
        <font face="Trebuchet MS"> Calculators<br>
            Taxes<br>
            Afford?<br>
            Payments<br>
            Others
        </font><br>
        </td>
</tr>
<tr>
        <td><font face="Trebuchet MS"> Contact Us</font><br></td>
</tr>
</table>
</td><td bgcolor="LightBlue" width="489">
<font face="Trebuchet MS" size="+1"><br><br><br>
<p align="center">Serving the Cedar Falls area for over 30 years.</p>
</font>
<br><br><br>
<hr color="A09CCF" width="100" align="right">
<p align="right"><font face="Trebuchet MS" size="-1">Cal &amp; Fran</font></p>
<br>
</td>
</tr>
<tr><td colspan="2"><img src="bottom.gif" alt="" border="0"></td></tr>
</table>

</body>
</html>
```

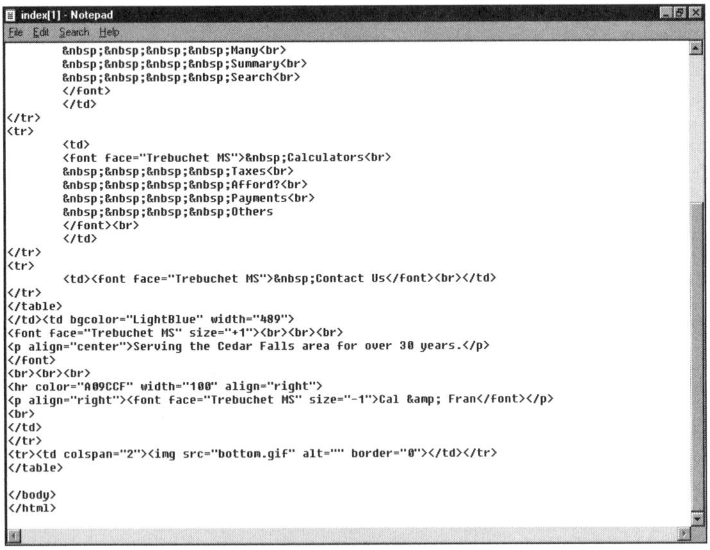

Figure 19-9 Source code for the home page

The CFINCLUDE tag is a simple and powerful tag. To illustrate this power, note that the format for all templates in the Web site can be simplified to the following code:

```
<cfinclude template="header.cfm">
HTML and CFML specific to the template.
<cfinclude template="footer.cfm">
```

This strategy ensures that the site has a consistent user interface and increases your productivity for implementing the Web site. Furthermore, if you or CF Realtors wants to change the site design, this strategy simplifies the recoding you have to do. For example, if CF Realtors wants to add rotating banner ads to the site after a few months, you simply include the rotating banner ad in the header.cfm file to display it on every Web page in the site.

Variables and the CFSET Tag

Most processing and data manipulation in computer programs is done by assigning values to variables, and ColdFusion is no exception. Variables and variable manipulation are fundamental to building ColdFusion templates. A **variable** is a named location in the computer's memory. Using appropriate programming statements, programmers can store values in variables or assign values to variables for manipulation.

19

The following example shows you how to create a ColdFusion template that includes variables and their associated values. These values and variables are preceded by **CFSET tags**. After you finish the example, you will learn more about CFSET tags and other aspects of ColdFusion code.

To create a ColdFusion template with variables:

1. Open a text editor, and then enter the following text.

```
<cfinclude template="header.cfm">
<hr color="A09CCF">
<h3 align="center">Taxes</h3>
<hr color="A09CCF">
<!-- Add Code to Initialize Variables -->
<cfset Price = 100000.00>
<cfset TaxRate = 0.02>
<!-- Add Code to Perform Computations -->
<cfset Tax = Price * TaxRate>
<!-- Add Code to output results -->
<cfoutput>
<table align="center" border="1" bordercolor="A09CCF" cellspacing="0">
<tr align="right"><td>Property value:</td><td>#DollarFormat(Price)#</td></tr>
<tr align="right"><td>Taxes:</td><td>#DollarFormat(Tax)#</td></tr>
</table>
</cfoutput>
<hr color="A09CCF">
<cfinclude template="footer.cfm">
```

2. Save the script as **taxesSol.cfm** in the Chap19\Chapter folder in your work folder. Recall that .cfm is the file extension for a ColdFusion template.
3. In your text editor, open **header.cfm** from your Chap 19\Chapter folder on the Data Disk.
4. Select **Taxes** in the Calculators section, and type **<a href= "taxesSol.cfm"> Taxes</a>** to create a hyperlink to taxesSol.cfm.
5. Save the **header.cfm** file with your changes in the Chap19\Chapter folder in your work folder.
6. Switch to your Web browser and go to http://localhost/*workfolder*/Chap19/Chapter/index.cfm and refresh the file.
7. Click **Taxes**. ColdFusion Server processes your request for taxesSol.cfm and displays the output shown in Figure 19-10.
8. Leave the browser open for the next set of steps.

Use the CFSET tag to define variables in ColdFusion and assign values to them. For example, consider the following statement (tag) from taxesSol.cfm:

```
<cfset Price = 100000.00>
```

When ColdFusion Server processes taxesSol.cfm and encounters this statement, the server recognizes this tag as part of CFML and executes it. A storage place in computer memory is given the name "Price" and a value of 100000.00 is stored in it. From this point on, you can use the Price variable anywhere else in the template. After the value is stored in memory, ColdFusion Server executes the next statement. Statements are executed sequentially, one after another, until the entire file has been processed. Any code that is not part of CFML is left as is.

Consider the next statement from taxesSol.cfm:

```
<cfset TaxRate = 0.02>
```

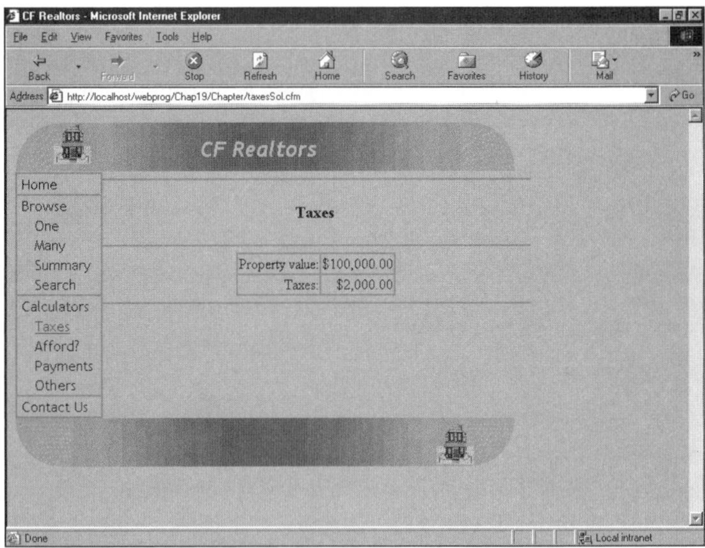

Figure 19-10 Web page displayed by taxesSol.cfm

When ColdFusion Server executes this statement, a variable named TaxRate is created and a value of 0.02 is assigned to it. The CFSET tag makes it easy to create variables and assign values to them.

Understanding Rules for Naming Variables

In the previous examples, you might have noticed the use of lowercase and uppercase letters in the variable names. Variables in ColdFusion are not case sensitive; in other words, TaxRate and taxrate are the same variable. However, it is always a good practice to use case consistently. Typically, you should use title case for variables, which means you should capitalize the first letter of every word.

ColdFusion has other rules for naming variables. For example, you cannot use spaces in variable names. As a general rule, ColdFusion variable names must begin with a letter; the remaining characters can be letters, numbers, or the underscore character (_). For example, Price, TaxRate, and Number_1 are valid variable names, but First Name, 2b_or_not2b, and divisible/2 are invalid. The use of a period in variable names carries special significance, which is discussed later in this chapter.

Creating Comments

As with other programming languages, you can use CFML tags to enclose comments. For example, the following comments appeared in the taxesSol.cfm file in the previous example:

```
<!-- Add Code to Initialize Variables -->
<!-- Add Code to Perform Computations -->
```

Like HTML comments, the opening tags of ColdFusion comments start with an opening bracket (<) and an exclamation point (!), followed by three dashes instead of just two. The tag that closes a ColdFusion comment consists of three dashes followed by a closing angle bracket (-->). When ColdFusion Server encounters the <!-- and --> tags, it ignores all of the text between the tags.

Comments are useful for documenting templates, such as describing its function, author, last modification date, and the template's logic and design. As with most programming languages, you should use comments to document essential information about your templates for your own benefit and that of other people who use your templates.

Processing Numbers

Originally, computers were designed to process numbers and perform computations with them. Even now, a lot of computer processing uses numbers. As demonstrated in the taxesSol.cfm example, ColdFusion lets you work with numbers such as 100000.00 and 0.02. ColdFusion can process **integers** (numbers without decimal or fractional parts) and **real numbers** (numbers with decimal parts). Developers can use both kinds of numbers as needed in a single template. ColdFusion supports the range of numbers from -10^{300} to 10^{300}, and most results are accurate to 12 decimal places. ColdFusion displays very small and very large numbers by using **scientific notation**, in which you express a value by using a number between 1 and 10, multiplied by a power of 10. For example, the value 16,000,000 in scientific notation is 1.6E7, and the value 0.00426 in scientific notation is 4.26E-3.

Using Arithmetic Expressions

You have already seen how to use a CFSET tag to assign values to variables. You can also use the CFSET tag to perform computations and assign the results to variables. Consider the following statement:

```
<cfset TaxRate = 0.02>
```

In this statement, the entry to the right of the equal sign is a value (0.02). You can also enter an expression to the right of the equal sign. A ColdFusion **expression** is similar to a mathematical expression; it can contain values, variables, and mathematical or arithmetic operators. For example, in the taxesSol.cfm file, ColdFusion Server processes and evaluates the statement <cfset Tax = Price * TaxRate> by assigning a value of 100000.00 to the Price variable and a value of 0.02 to the TaxRate variable, and then uses the multiplication operator (*) to multiply the variables. ColdFusion Server multiplies 100000.00 by 0.02, obtains a result of 2000.00, and then assigns the result to a new variable named Tax. In this statement, the current values assigned to the variables are used to perform calculations, and the result is stored to the left of the equal sign.

These types of expressions are called **arithmetic expressions**. They are formed by logically combining values, variables, and arithmetic operators. Table 19-1 lists ColdFusion arithmetic operators, their descriptions, and a few examples of their usage.

Table 19-1 ColdFusion arithmetic operators

Operator	Description	Restrictions	Examples
+	Addition	None	Price + TaxRate
-	Subtraction	None	CarCost - DownPayment
*	Multiplication	None	Price * TaxRate
/	Division	The right operand cannot be zero	InterestRate/12
^	Exponent	The left operand cannot be zero	Principal* (1 + InterestRate / 12) ^ 4
MOD	Gives the remainder (modulus) after a number is divided by a divisor; the result has the same sign as the divisor	The right operand cannot be zero	14/3 = 4 with a remainder of 2; therefore, 14 MOD 3 = 2, RowNumber MOD 2
\	Divides two integer values to result in an integer	The right operand cannot be zero	9\4 = 2, Number _of_Cols\7

Using the CFOUTPUT Tag, Pound (#) Signs, and Functions

When ColdFusion Server processes a ColdFusion template, the server sends HTML code to the Web server "as is" and executes actions specified in CFSET tags by assigning values to variables. When ColdFusion performs computations, it needs a mechanism to communicate the results with the browser. A **CFOUTPUT tag** displays the results generated by a CFSET statement. When ColdFusion encounters the <cfoutput> tag, it starts processing text by looking for variables enclosed in pound (#) signs, such as #Price#. When ColdFusion finds such a variable, it sends the variable's value to the server. This processing stops when ColdFusion encounters a closing </cfoutput> tag. The CFSET and CFOUTPUT tags appear as neatly formatted code in HTML.

For example, when ColdFusion Server finds the <cfoutput> tag in taxesSol.cfm, it looks for variables enclosed in pound signs. If you had #Price# in the template, it would display the value 100000.00. When #DollarFormat(Price)# is processed, the value 100000.00 is substituted for the variable named Price. The DollarFormat function formats the value with a dollar sign, commas, and a decimal.

A ColdFusion **function** is similar to a mathematical function—it processes one or more input values and returns a single output value. You can use functions to perform complex mathematical calculations, generate random numbers, control the display of data, and so on. For example, the DollarFormat function has the syntax DollarFormat(an_expression). The DollarFormat function processes a value, a variable, or an expression that forms its input (also known as an **argument**) and returns the value formatted with a dollar sign and two decimal places. When you want to format numbers with two decimal places and without dollar signs, you can use the DecimalFormat function. The DecimalFormat function has the syntax DecimalFormat(an_expression).

CFML tags are not case sensitive; the tags </CFOUTPUT> and </cfoutput> are the same. The code in the ColdFusion chapters of this book uses lowercase CFML tags.

You can see the HTML code that is generated by ColdFusion Server by opening taxesSol.cfm in a Web browser and examining the page's source code.

To view the HTML code for a ColdFusion template:

1. Click **View** on the Internet Explorer menu bar, and then click **Source**. Figure 19-11 shows the source code. Notice that the page doesn't contain any CFML tags; ColdFusion Server converted the entire page into HTML so a browser could interpret and display it. In addition, the CFOUTPUT statements show the values assigned to the variables, but not the CFOUTPUT statements themselves.

```
            Afford?<br>
            Payments<br>
            Others
        </font><br>
        </td>
</tr>
<tr>
        <td><font face="Trebuchet MS"> Contact Us</font><br></td>
</tr>
</table>
</td><td bgcolor="LightBlue" width="489">
<hr color="A09CCF">
<h3 align="center">Taxes</h3>
<hr color="A09CCF">





<table align="center" border="1" bordercolor="A09CCF" cellspacing="0">
<tr align="right"><td>Property value:</td><td>$100,000.00</td></tr>
<tr align="right"><td>Taxes:</td><td>$2,000.00</td></tr>
</table>

<hr color="A09CCF">
</td>
</tr>
<tr><td colspan="2"><img src="bottom.gif" alt="" border="0"></td></tr>
</table>

</body>
</html>
```

Figure 19-11 HTML source code for taxesSol.cfm

2. Click the **Close** button to close the source code window.

Understanding Operator Precedence

When evaluating expressions that contain more than one operator, ColdFusion uses a system of operator precedence. For example, when ColdFusion evaluates the expression 6 - 3 * 2, the multiplication is performed first, so 6 - (3 * 2) would be evaluated as 6 - 6, for a result of 0. If a system with no operator precedence were to evaluate this expression, it would result in (6 - 3) * 2 = 3 * 2 = 6. Table 19-2 shows the precedence for arithmetic operators in descending order. The second column identifies the precedence when similar operators exist in the same expression (such as 6 * 5 / 5 * 6).

Table 19-2 Arithmetic operator precedence (highest to lowest)

Operator	Multiple similar operators	Precedence
( )	Inner to outer, left to right	First
^	Right to left	Second
* and /	Left to right	Third
\	Left to right	Fourth
MOD	Left to right	Fifth
+ and -	Left to right	Sixth

As the table shows, you can use parentheses in an expression to make ColdFusion Server process the parenthetical expressions before any others.

Designing HTML Forms and ColdFusion Form Handlers

When a client requests an HTML document or a ColdFusion template that contains a form, the Web server retrieves the document and sends it to the client. The browser processes the embedded HTML tags and displays the document along with the form. The user enters data in the form and submits it. The Web server receives this data along with the name of the ColdFusion template that should process it.

The ColdFusion template that processes a form is called the form handler. A **form handler** contains CFML code to process the data received by the ColdFusion server. The Web server passes control to the ColdFusion server along with the data the user entered. The ColdFusion server uses the form handler to process the data and then outputs an HTML document to the Web server, which subsequently sends it to the client. Typically, the client receives a confirmation page to let users know the data was processed successfully. The browser then displays the document.

In your study of HTML, you may have learned that there are two stages for designing HTML forms. First, you create the form and the necessary controls to collect the data you need. Second, you design or specify a form handler to process the data collected by the form on the server. Designing and processing forms in ColdFusion works the same way, and requires two files. You design the form using HTML or CFML controls, and then you create a ColdFusion form handler to process the data entered into the form.

To create an HTML form to be processed by a ColdFusion template:

1. Switch to your text editor, and open a new file for editing.
2. Type the following text:

```
<cfinclude template="header.cfm">
<hr color="A09CCF">
<h3 align="center">Affordability Calculation</h3>
<hr color="A09CCF">
<form action="processAffordFormSol.cfm" method="post">
<table align="center" border="1" bordercolor="A09CCF" cellspacing="0">
<tr align="right">
<td>Enter your gross monthly income:</td>
<td><input type="text" name="grossIncome"></td>
</tr>
<tr align="center">
<td colspan="2"><input type="submit" value="Calculate..."></td>
</tr>
</table>
</form>
<hr color="A09CCF">
<cfinclude template="footer.cfm">
```

3. Save the file as **affordFormSol.cfm** in the Chap19\Chapter folder in your work folder.
4. Open **header.cfm** from the Chap19\Chapter folder and select **Afford?**.
5. Type **<a href=" affordFormSol.cfm">Afford?</a>** to create a hyperlink to the new file.
6. Save the **header.cfm** file after making the changes.
7. Switch to your Web browser, and open **Chap19/Chapter/index.cfm**. Reload the file if necessary.
8. Click the **Afford?** link. Your browser displays a Web page with a form similar to the one in Figure 19-12.

Handling Form Data

The Web page shown in Figure 19-12 contains a form with a text box control named grossIncome and a Submit button. Users can enter their gross monthly income and then click the Calculate button to submit the form to the server.

After users enter their income and click Calculate, the Web browser uses the POST attribute of the METHOD tag to send the form data as an attachment to the Web server. Using Web server API, the data is passed from the file to the ColdFusion server, which then executes the ColdFusion form handler specified in the ACTION attribute. The ColdFusion server creates variables in the FORM scope for the data it receives. This scope consists of a variable beginning with the word "FORM," then a period and the control name. For example, if you want to access the data entered in the text box with a NAME attribute value of "grossIncome," you use the variable FORM.grossIncome.

The ColdFusion server creates variables for every control and then assigns to these variables the data passed to the Web server by the browser.

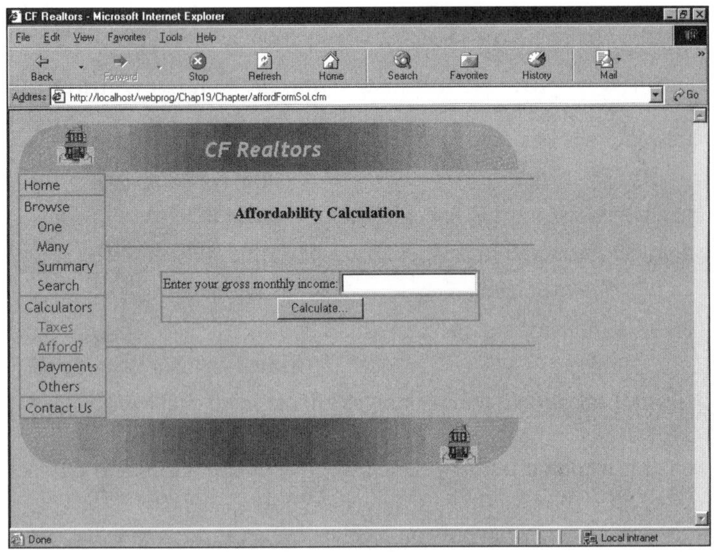

Figure 19-12 Web page displayed by affordFormSol.cfm

Next you will create a form handler that continues the previous example and calculates the maximum allowable monthly housing expense. Lenders in general consider the maximum as 26% to 28% of gross monthly income for conventional home loans.

To create a form handler named processAffordFormSol.cfm to calculate the maximum allowable monthly housing expense:

1. Switch to your text editor, and open a new file for editing.
2. Type the following text:

```
<cfset grossIncome = FORM.grossIncome>
<cfset maxHousePayment = grossIncome * 0.28>
<cfinclude template="header.cfm">
<hr color="A09CCF">
<h3 align="center">Affordability Calculation Results</h3>
<hr color="A09CCF">
<cfoutput>
<table align="center" border="1" bordercolor="A09CCF" cellspacing="0">
<tr align="right">
<td>Your gross monthly income:</td>
<td>#DollarFormat(grossIncome)#</td>
</tr>
<tr align="right">
<td>Maximum allowable monthly house payment:</td>
<td>#DollarFormat(maxHousePayment)#</td>
</tr>
</table>
```

```
</cfoutput>
<hr color="A09CCF">
<cfinclude template="footer.cfm">
```

3. Save the file as **processAffordFormSol.cfm** in the Chap19\Chapter folder in your work folder.
4. Switch to your Web browser, and load **Chap19/Chapter/index.cfm**.
5. Click the **Afford?** link, and type **5000** in the text box.
6. Click the **Calculate** button. Your browser displays a Web page similar to the one in Figure 19-13.

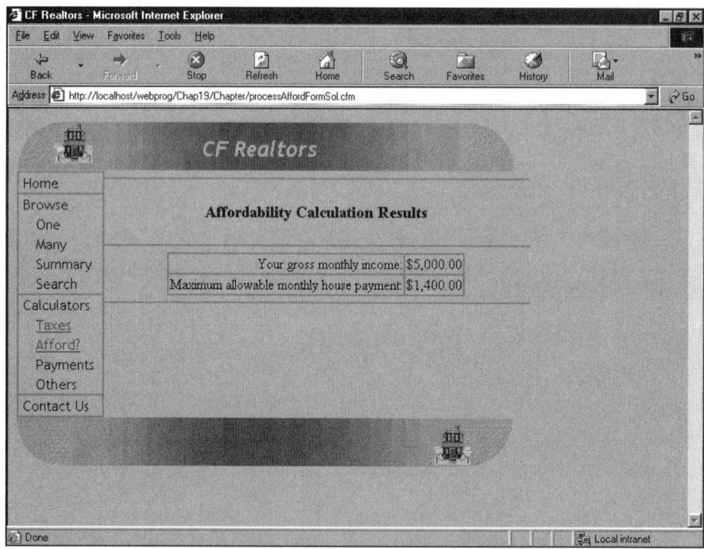

Figure 19-13 Web page displayed by processAffordFormSol.cfm with the maximum allowable monthly house payment

As described earlier, after the user clicks the Calculate button, ColdFusion Server ultimately creates a variable named FORM.grossIncome, assigns it a value of 5000, and starts executing the statements in the template. When the first CFSET statement is executed, the value of the variable FORM.grossIncome is assigned to another variable named grossIncome. When the second CFSET statement is executed, a variable named maxHousePayment is created and assigned a value of 5000 * 0.28 = 1400. Then, the form processes the CFOUTPUT statement and displays the values of the variables enclosed by pound signs in the HTML table.

Processing user-entered form data is simple using the ColdFusion Server. All you need are variables in the form handler that are identical to the names of the form controls, except with the prefix FORM. You can handle other controls in HTML forms like in a fashion similar to the way you handle option buttons, check boxes, and text boxes.

FLOW CONTROL IN COLDFUSION

In the previous sections you learned that a computer program can contain a series of statements that execute sequentially from beginning to end. ColdFusion Server processes ColdFusion statements in similar sequential fashion, although the HTML in a template is left as is. When ColdFusion Server encounters an output statement, it produces HTML and generates text in the appropriate places.

When a program's statements are executed one after another, the program has a **sequence flow-control structure**. Sometimes, however, you have to deviate from sequentially processing statements. For example, you might need to execute sets of statements repeatedly, or you may need to stop processing at a certain statement. When you must change the order in which statements are executed or choose which statements should be executed, use flow-control statements.

Using Selection to Control Program Flow

In computer programming, you often need to select a course of action depending on circumstances. **Selection** is a flow-control construct in which you instruct the computer to examine two or more alternatives, and then choose a course of action to solve a problem. For example, the decision to rent or buy a house could depend on how long a person is planning to stay in it.

To model situations like these that require selection, you use conditions. A **condition** is a comparison of two quantities; at a particular time, a condition is either true or false. You use relational operators to compare quantities in conditions. For example, you can determine whether a person is an adult by comparing the person's age to 21. If the age is greater than or equal to 21, then the person is an adult.

In the previous statement, "greater than or equal to" is a **relational operator**. This operator is represented by the letters GE in ColdFusion. For example, if the person's age is assigned to a variable named personsAge, the condition in ColdFusion that determines if a person is an adult is "personsAge GE 21." Depending on the value stored in the variable named personsAge, the personsAge GE 21 condition is evaluated as either true or false. If the value of the variable personsAge is 30, the condition is true and the person is an adult. If the value of the variable is 15, the condition is false and the person is not an adult.

Using CFIF Tags

When you need to select an action to perform based on the result of a condition, you can use a CFIF tag. A **CFIF tag** is a flow-control tag that you use to set up a selection construct in ColdFusion. A CFIF tag has the following syntax:

```
<CFIF condition>
      True action
<CFELSE>
      False action
</CFIF>
```

19

This syntax introduces three new tags: CFIF, CFELSE, and /CFIF. To set up a selection construct in ColdFusion, you start with the CFIF tag and follow it with the necessary code. Next you enter the CFELSE tag and follow it with more code, and finally you use the closing /CFIF tag. You must always use these three tags in the CFIF-CFELSE-/CFIF sequence.

When ColdFusion Server executes a CFIF tag, it evaluates the condition specified in the tag. If this **CFIF condition** evaluates to true, ColdFusion Server performs the true action, which includes all of the CFML and HTML between the CFIF and CFELSE statements. If the true action is executed, ColdFusion Server skips the false action and continues executing the statement below the closing /CFIF tag. If the CFIF condition evaluates to false, ColdFusion Server skips the true action and performs the false action. The false action includes all of the statements between the CFELSE tag and the closing /CFIF tag. After executing the false action, ColdFusion Server executes the statements below the closing /CFIF tag. As you can see, a CFIF tag allows you to perform an action when a condition is true and to perform a different action when a condition is false.

You can modify a CFIF tag by excluding the CFELSE tag. Essentially, the CFELSE part of a CFIF statement is optional. If you exclude the CFELSE tag, the CFIF tag executes an action if a condition is true; otherwise, it skips the action. The syntax for such a CFIF tag is:

:<CFIF condition>
    True action
</CFIF>

If the CFIF condition evaluates to true, the true action is performed. If the CFIF condition evaluates to false, it doesn't perform the true action.

Next you will use the CFIF tags in actual code. First you will create a form, and then you will create a form handler that uses a CFIF tag. The form is necessary because a CF Realtors agent has asked you to design a template that helps customers decide whether they should rent or buy a house. She says a simple rule of thumb for making this decision is to consider how long you will occupy a house. If you expect to live for five or more years in the house, buying is better than renting. The agent asked you to design a Web page that takes this logic into consideration, so you use a form with a control named occupationYears for providing input to the template.

To create an HTML form that helps users decide whether to rent or buy a house:

1. Switch to your text editor, and open a new file for editing.
2. Type the following text:

```
<cfinclude template="header.cfm">
<hr color="A09CCF">
<h3 align="center">Buy vs. Rent Calculation</h3>
<hr color="A09CCF">
<form action="processBuyVsRentSol.cfm" method="post">
<table align="center" border="1" bordercolor="A09CCF" cellspacing="0">
<tr align="right">
```

```
<td>Enter the number of years<br>you are planning to stay:</td>
<td><input type="text" name="occupationYears"></td>
</tr>
<tr align="center">
<td colspan="2"><input type="submit" value="Submit"></td>
</tr>
</table>
</form>
<hr color="A09CCF">
<cfinclude template="footer.cfm">
```

3. Save the file as **buyVsRentSol.cfm** in the Chap19\Chapter folder in your work folder.
4. Open **header.cfm** from the Chap19\Chapter folder, and select **Others**.
5. Type **<a href=" buyVsRentSol.cfm">Others</a>** to create a hyperlink to the new file.
6. Save the **header.cfm** file after making the changes.
7. Switch to your Web browser, and open **Chap19/Chapter/index.cfm**. Reload the file if necessary.
8. Click **Others**. Your browser displays a Web page with a form like the one in Figure 19-14.

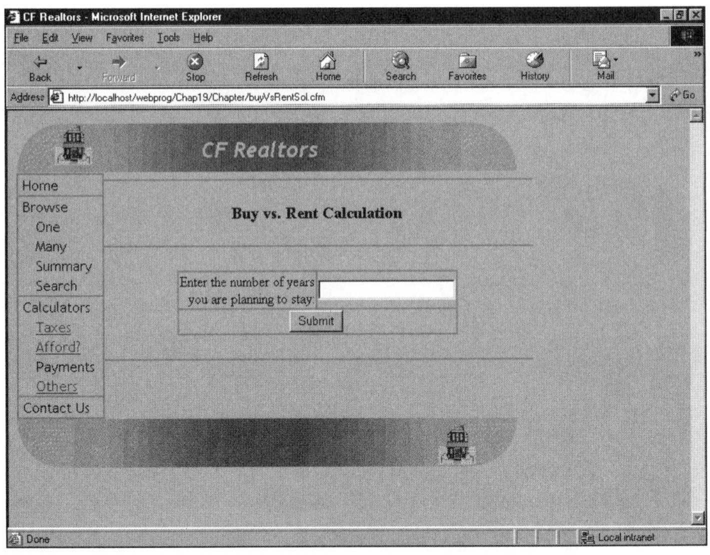

Figure 19-14 Web page displayed by buyVsRentSol.cfm

When the user submits this form, ColdFusion Server executes the processBuyVsRentSol.cfm template. Your next task is to design this template, which includes a CFIF tag.

To create a form handler named processBuyVsRentSol.cfm with a CFIF tag:

1. Switch to your text editor, and open a new file for editing.
2. Type the following text:

```
<cfset occupationYears = FORM.occupationYears>
<cfinclude template="header.cfm">
<hr color="A09CCF">
<h3 align="center">Buy vs. Rent Results</h3>
<hr color="A09CCF">
<br><br>
<cfif occupationYears GE 5>
It is better to buy because you are planning to live in the house for five or more years.
<cfelse>
It is better to rent because you are planning to live in the house for just
<cfoutput>#occupationYears#</cfoutput> years.
</cfif>
<br><br>
<hr color="A09CCF">
<cfinclude template="footer.cfm">
```

3. Save the file as **processBuyVsRentSol.cfm** in the Chap19\Chapter folder in your work folder.
4. Switch to your Web browser, and load **Chap19/Chapter/index.cfm**. Refresh your Web page.
5. Click **Others**, and type **6** in the text box.
6. Click **Submit**. Your browser displays a Web page like the one in Figure 19-15.

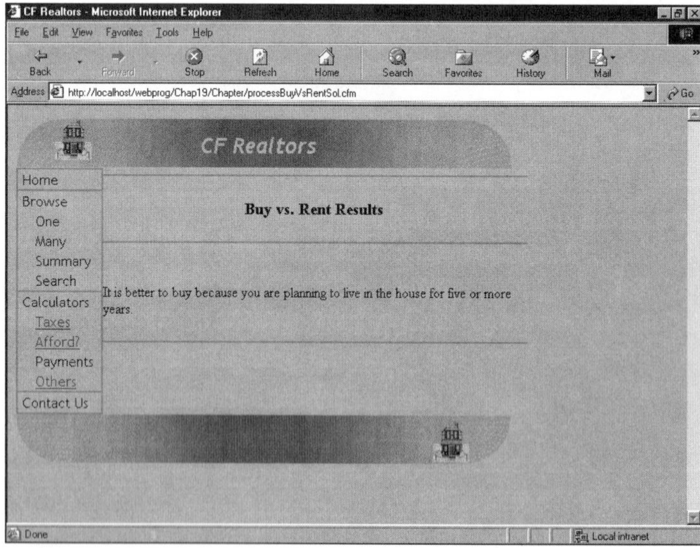

Figure 19-15 Web page displayed when a value of 6 is entered and the form is submitted

When ColdFusion Server executes this program, the variable occupationYears is assigned the value entered in the occupationYears text box, which is 6 in this case. When the server processes the CFIF tag, it evaluates the condition "occupationYears GE 5." Because the variable occupationYears has a value of 6, and 6 is clearly greater than or equal to 5, the condition evaluates to true. As a result, the ColdFusion Server performs the true action and displays the following text: "It is better to buy because you are planning to live in the house for five or more years."

You also need to see what happens when the condition is false.

To execute the false action statement in the CFIF tag:

1. In your Web browser, click the **Others** hyperlink.
2. Type **2** in the text box, and click **Submit**. Your browser displays a Web page like the one in Figure 19-16.

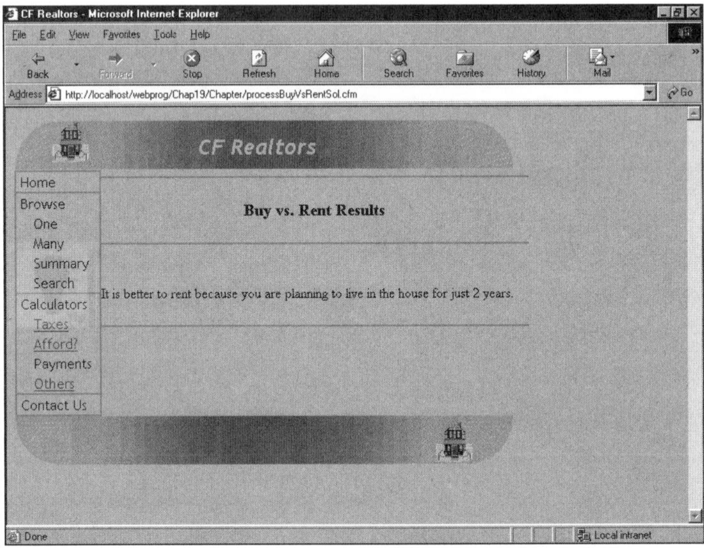

Figure 19-16 Web page displayed when a value of 2 is entered and the form is submitted

When ColdFusion Server executes this program, the variable occupationYears is assigned the value entered in the occupationYears text box, which is 2 in this case. When the server processes the CFIF tag, it evaluates the condition "occupationYears GE 5." Because the variable occupationYears has a value of 2, and 2 is not greater than or equal to 5, the condition evaluates to false. As a result, the ColdFusion Server performs the false action and displays the following text: "It is better to rent because you are planning to live in the house for just 2 years." Note that ColdFusion substituted 2 for <cfoutput>#occupationYears#</cfoutput>.

Working with Relational Operators

You used the GE relational operator in the previous template to perform the "greater than or equal to" comparison. This operator is one of six standard relational operators you can use in ColdFusion. Table 19-3 lists these operators and their descriptions.

Table 19-3 Standard relational operators in ColdFusion

Operator	Description
GE	Greater than or equal to
GT	Greater than
LE	Less than or equal to
LT	Less than
EQ	Equal to
NEQ	Not equal to

Using Loops to Perform Repetitive Tasks

Sometimes your programs need to perform the same task more than once, such as processing payroll for company employees. When you need to execute a set of statements in a program many times, you can use repetition flow-control statements. To create these statements in ColdFusion, you use a CFLOOP tag. The CFLOOP tag helps you implement FOR loops, LIST loops, WHILE loops, and QUERY loops.

- When you know exactly how many times a set of statements must be executed, you use FOR loops.
- Use a WHILE loop to execute a set of statements repeatedly as long as a certain condition is true.
- A LIST loop allows you to execute a set of statements repeatedly, such that for each execution, a variable takes a different value from a value list.

The following sections describe each of these loops. You will learn about QUERY loops in the next chapter.

Using FOR Loops

A **FOR loop** allows you to execute a set of statements a predefined number of times. A FOR loop in ColdFusion has four attributes—INDEX, FROM, TO, and STEP—and has the following syntax:

```
<CFLOOPƒINDEX= "for_variable"
FROM= "start_value" TO= "end_value"
STEP= "increment_value">
Statements containing HTML and CFML that are to be executed in the loop
</CFLOOP>
```

You must set the **INDEX attribute** to the name of a variable that controls the execution of the loop. This variable is called the **control variable**. You set the **FROM attribute** to a value or expression that provides the start value for the control variable. The **TO attribute** stores an end value for the control variable. The STEP attribute stores an increment value for the control variable. When ColdFusion Server executes a FOR loop like the one in the preceding syntax, the control variable (for_variable) is first assigned start_value, and all statements between the CFLOOP tags are executed. Then, increment_value is added to for_variable and the statements between the CFLOOP tags are executed again. This process is repeated as long as the value of for_variable is not more than the value in end_value. When the value in for_variable exceeds the value in end_value, repetition is terminated and processing continues by executing the statement below the closing CFLOOP tag.

To illustrate the value of FOR loops, consider the real estate axiom "Location is everything." If you ask any realtor the three most important factors for choosing a property, the clichéd response is "Location, location, location." In the following exercise you create a simple FOR loop for displaying this repetitive list.

To create a FOR loop:

1. Switch to your text editor, and create a file.
2. Type the following text:

```
<cfinclude template="header.cfm">
<ul>
<cfloop index="i" from="1" to="3">
<li><b>Location</b></li>
</cfloop>
</ul>
<cfinclude template="footer.cfm">
```

3. Save the document as **factorsSol.cfm** in the Chap19/Chapter folder on the server, and then view the results in a browser. See Figure 19-17.

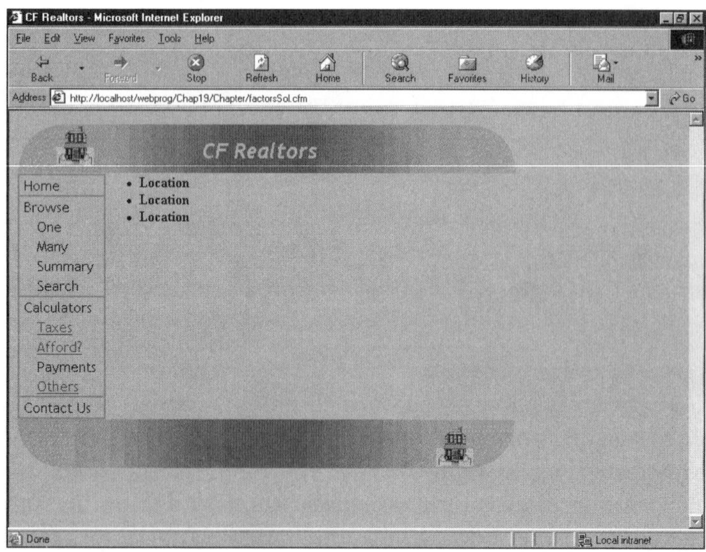

Figure 19-17 Web page displayed by factorsSol.cfm

4. In your Web browser, click **View** on the menu bar, and then click **Source**. Scroll down to the end. The source code for the FOR loop example page is shown in Figure 19-18.
5. Close your text editor.

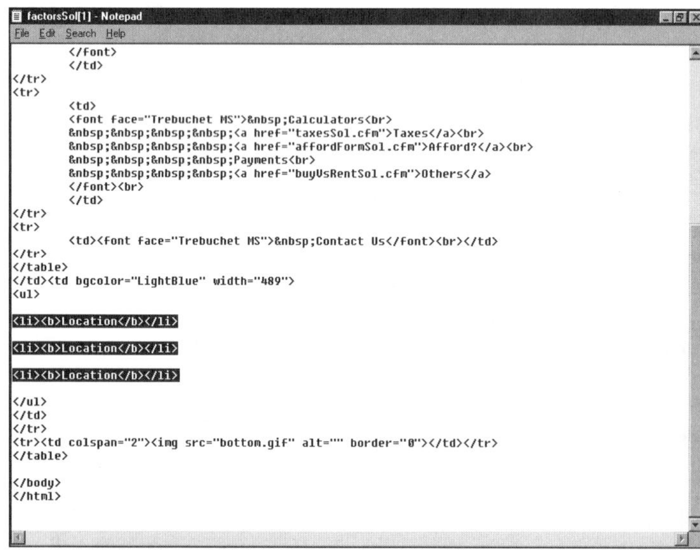


```
        </font>
        </td>
</tr>
<tr>
        <td>
        <font face="Trebuchet MS"> Calculators<br>
            <a href="taxesSol.cfm">Taxes</a><br>
            <a href="affordFormSol.cfm">Afford?</a><br>
            Payments<br>
            <a href="buyVsRentSol.cfm">Others</a>
        </font><br>
        </td>
</tr>
<tr>
        <td><font face="Trebuchet MS"> Contact Us</font><br></td>
</tr>
</table>
</td><td bgcolor="LightBlue" width="489">
<ul>

<li><b>Location</b></li>

<li><b>Location</b></li>

<li><b>Location</b></li>

</ul>
</td>
</tr>
<tr><td colspan="2"><img src="bottom.gif" alt="" border="0"></td></tr>
</table>

</body>
</html>
```

Figure 19-18 HTML source code for the Web page displayed by factorsSol.cfm

In the previous procedure, ColdFusion Server first includes the code from header.cfm. Then, when ColdFusion Server executes the statement <cfloop index="i" from="1" to="3">, it assigns a value of 1 to variable i and executes the statements between the CFLOOP tags. The statements between the CFLOOP tags are just HTML code (<li><b>Location</b></li>); this code is sent as is to the browser. After the first line is displayed, the FOR loop uses the default STEP value (1) to increment the variable i from 1 (the FROM value) to 2. Because the value 2 is still in the range of the FOR loop (from="1" to="3"), the loop continues and transmits the HTML code (<li><b>Location</b></li>) again to the browser. The loop is repeated until the value of the variable i is 4, which ends the loop; the HTML code below the closing CFLOOP tag is transmitted as is. This FOR loop displays the same output three times as a bulleted list.

Using LIST Loops

ColdFusion LIST loops allow you to implement a repetition construct in ColdFusion templates. Like FOR loops, LIST loops have a control variable. LIST loops allow you to list the values for the control variable, instead of mathematically computing them as in FOR loops.

LIST loops have two attributes. The first attribute, INDEX, must be set to the name of the control variable. The second attribute, LIST, must be set to a value list, which is a list of values separated by commas. The syntax for a LIST loop is:

<CFLOOP INDEX= "list_variable" LIST= "value_list">
Statements containing HTML and CFML that are to be executed repeatedly
</CFLOOP>

When ColdFusion Server executes a LIST loop, the list_variable is assigned the first value in the value_list, and the loop executes all statements between the CFLOOP tags. Then the second value in the value_list is assigned to list_variable and the statements between the CFLOOP tags are executed again. This process is repeated for every value in value_list. After the last value from value_list is assigned, statements are executed once and repetition is then terminated; processing continues by executing the statement below the closing CFLOOP tag.

To create a ColdFusion template with a LIST loop:

1. Start your text editor, and open a new file.
2. Type the following text:

```
<cfinclude template="header.cfm">
<hr color="A09CCF">
<h3 align="center">Links to Realtor Resources</h3>
<hr color="A09CCF">
<ul>
<cfloop index="company" list="RealEstateABC.com,HomeGain.com,
REALS.com,RealEstateAward.com,Realtors.com">
<cfoutput>
```

19

```
<li><a href="http://www.#company#">#company#</a></li>
</cfoutput>
</cfloop>
</ul>
<hr color="A09CCF">
<cfinclude template="footer.cfm">
```

3. Save the file as **realtorCompaniesSol.cfm** in the Chap19\Chapter folder in your work folder.
4. Switch to your Web browser, and open **Chap19/Chapter/realtorCompaniesSol.cfm**. Your browser displays a Web page with a bulleted list of hyperlinks similar to the one in Figure 19-19.
5. Click any of the hyperlinks in your Web browser.

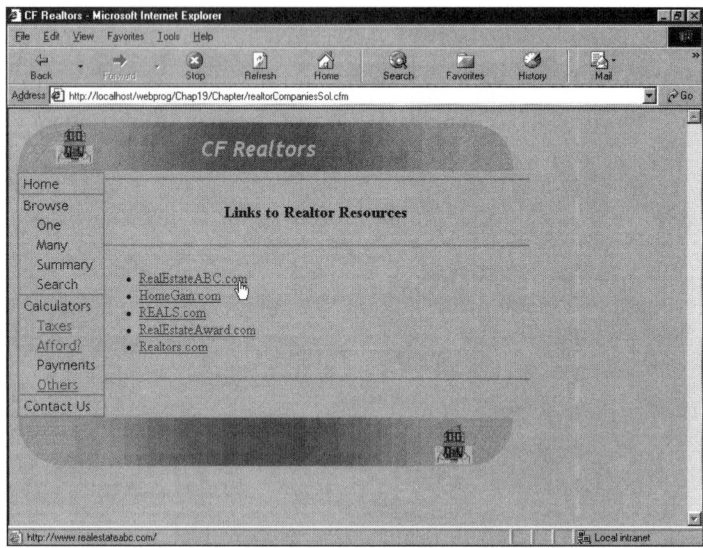

Figure 19-19 Web page displayed by realtorCompaniesSol.cfm

When the ColdFusion server executes realtorCompaniesSol.cfm, all the HTML code before the CFLOOP tag is sent as is to the Web browser. Then the server processes the CFLOOP tag. It creates a variable named company, assigns it *RealEstateABC.com*, and starts executing the statements inside the CFLOOP tags. It processes the CFOUTPUT tags next and substitutes *RealEstateABC.com* for #company# in the HREF attribute, as well as in the anchor tags, to produce the code for a list item with a hyperlink, as shown in Figure 19-19. When the server encounters the /CFLOOP tag, it assigns the next value in the value list (*HomeGain.com*) to the company variable. It executes the statements inside the loop again to produce another hyperlink. This process is repeated until the values in the value list are all used. Then the server outputs the code below the closing CFLOOP tag.

Using WHILE Loops

FOR loops and LIST loops execute a set of statements repeatedly for a certain number of times. By contrast, the number of times a set of statements is executed with a WHILE loop depends on the situation. A WHILE loop in ColdFusion has only one attribute, which is known as a while condition. The syntax for a ColdFusion WHILE loop is:

```
<CFLOOP CONDITION= "while condition">
Statements containing HTML and CFML that are to be executed repeatedly
</CFLOOP>
```

When ColdFusion Server executes a WHILE loop, the while condition is tested; if it is true, the server executes all statements between the CFLOOP tags. ColdFusion then tests the while condition again. If the while condition is true, the statements between the CFLOOP tags are executed again; otherwise, repetition ends and ColdFusion continues by executing the statement below the closing CFLOOP tag. Make sure that values of expressions being compared in a while condition change due to actions performed by inside statements so that the loop can terminate normally.

As an example of using WHILE loops, say that a client is interested in listing a property for sale with CF Realtors. A comparative study of recently sold properties suggests a list price of $125,000 for the client's property. However, the client wants to list the property at $160,000, and wants to reduce the price by 5% each month until it is sold. If the property is sold when the price is just below $125,000, he wants to know how long the property has been listed for sale. One of your project members has designed a ColdFusion template (timeTillSale.cfm) that accepts three URL parameters: listPrice (160000), expectedPrice (125000), and priceReduction (0.05). The template also displays the time the property is expected to be on the market. Your task is to experiment with the template and learn from it.

To use WHILE loops:

1. Start your text editor, if necessary.
2. Open **timeTillSale.cfm** from your Chap19\Chapter folder on the Data Disk. See Figure 19-20.
3. Start your Web browser, if necessary.

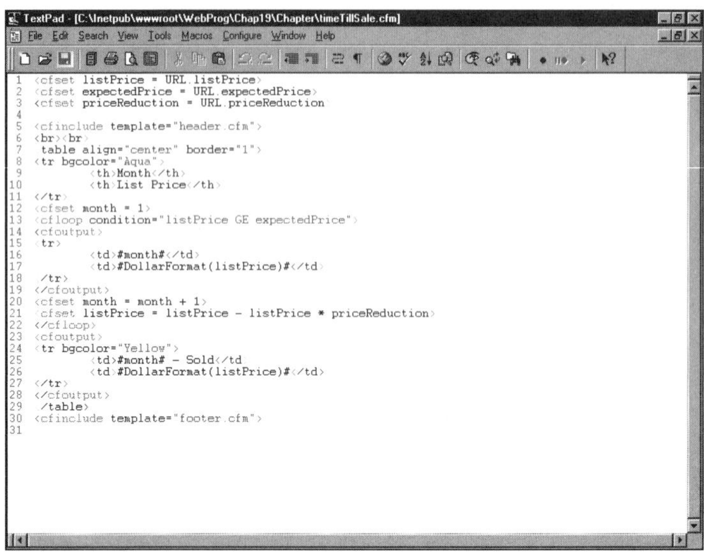

```
<cfset listPrice = URL.listPrice>
<cfset expectedPrice = URL.expectedPrice>
<cfset priceReduction = URL.priceReduction>

<cfinclude template="header.cfm">
<br><br>
<table align="center" border="1">
<tr bgcolor="Aqua">
        <th>Month</th>
        <th>List Price</th>
</tr>
<cfset month = 1>
<cfloop condition="listPrice GE expectedPrice">
<cfoutput>
<tr>
        <td>#month#</td>
        <td>#DollarFormat(listPrice)#</td>
</tr>
</cfoutput>
<cfset month = month + 1>
<cfset listPrice = listPrice - listPrice * priceReduction>
</cfloop>
<cfoutput>
<tr bgcolor="Yellow">
        <td>#month# - Sold</td>
        <td>#DollarFormat(listPrice)#</td>
</tr>
</cfoutput>
</table>
<cfinclude template="footer.cfm">
```

Figure 19-20 timeTillSale.cfm in text editor

4. In the address bar, type the following address and code:
   `http://`*`your_server_name/work folder`*`/Chap19/Chapter/timeTillSale.cfm?listPrice=160000&expectedPrice=125000&priceReduction=0.05`

   Substitute the name of your server and work folder as appropriate. When you finish, press **Enter**. Your Web browser displays the page shown in Figure 19-21.

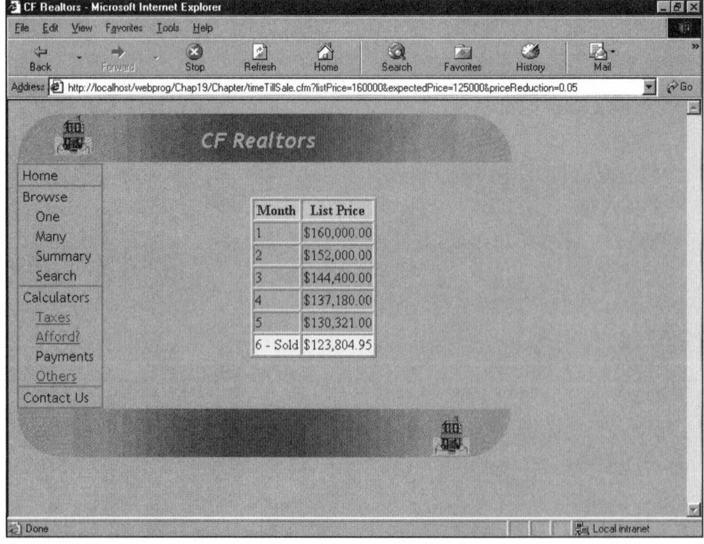

Figure 19-21 Web page displayed to calculate time until sale

5. Click **View** on the menu bar, and then click **Source**. The text editor opens with the HTML source code for the document. If necessary, scroll down a little as shown in Figure 19-22.

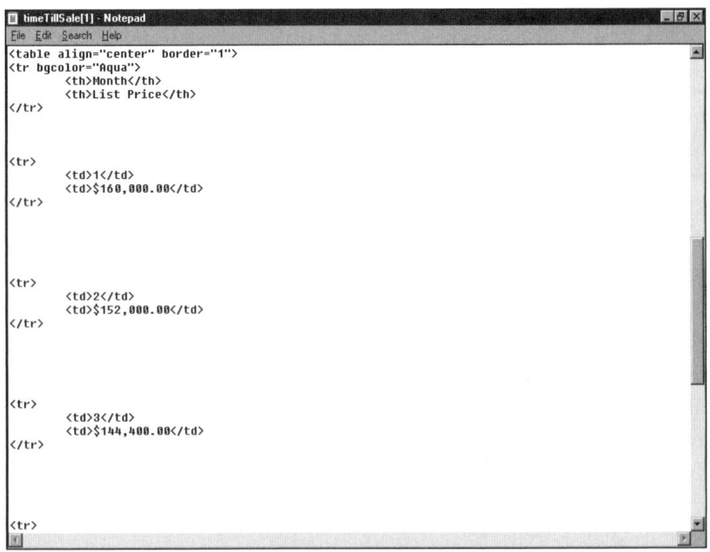

Figure 19-22 HTML code created by timeTillSale.cfm in Notepad

6. Compare Figures 19-20 and 19-22.

   When ColdFusion Server executes timeTillSale.cfm, it creates URL-scope variables, similar to the way that FORM-scope variables were created earlier in this chapter. The variables listPrice, expectedPrice, and priceReduction are created and assigned the appropriate values from the URL query string. The server sends the HTML for the header to the Web browser, then creates a variable named month and assigns it a value of 1. ColdFusion then evaluates the condition in the CFLOOP tag. The list price of $160,000 is greater than the expected price of $125,000, and the condition is true. Statements inside the loop are executed, the month is displayed, and the list price is formatted as currency in a table row. You are assuming that the property does not sell at this price. Next, the variable month is incremented by 1 to 2, and a new list price is computed by applying the proper reduction. The condition in the CFLOOP tag is evaluated with the new list price; it is still true, so statements inside the loop are executed and a table row is displayed. The month is incremented to 3 and a newer list price is computed. Processing occurs in this fashion until the condition is false—that is, when the list price is not greater than the expected price. When the condition is false, the processing of the statements inside the loop is terminated and the statements below the loop are executed. A final row of the table is output with the caption Sold. The rest of the code completes the code for the document.

7. Close your text editor.
8. Change the list price to **180000** in the address bar of your Web browser, and press **Enter**. It now takes nine months to sell the property.
9. Close all programs.

Redirecting Users to Other Web Pages

Just as you can use flow control within a template, you can also use flow control within a Web site. For example, most Web sites have hyperlinks that let users connect to other Web pages. Usually a user must click a hyperlink to open the hyperlink's target. Sometimes, however, Web site designers need a way to load a new page in the browser without requiring any interaction from the user. For example, when a user clicks a button to send the data entered into a form to a ColdFusion server, the server might process the data and then send a redirection instruction back to an application's home page with a URL parameter and a confirmation message. In such a case, you might see a "data processed successfully" message at the top of the browser window with the home page below it. This redirection is usually transparent to the user. **Redirection** is part of the HTTP protocol that allows designers to send an "object has moved" message to a Web browser with information for its new location. You can redirect users to other pages in ColdFusion by using the CFLOCATION tag. Its syntax is:

<CFLOCATION URL="aURL">

When the ColdFusion server processes this statement, all execution stops and the server sends a redirection instruction to the browser. This instruction includes an HTTP "object has moved" message that is sent back to the browser with a specified URL. The browser is tricked into thinking that this page is now at a new location, so it sends an appropriate Web server request. You can specify the parameter "aURL" as a **relative location** that does not include a complete path or as an **absolute location** that includes a complete path. To translate a relative location into an absolute location, append the path of the current page to it. When you use an absolute location, you can redirect a user to another Web site.

You should use relative locations as much as possible. It is much easier to maintain a Web site with relative links, especially when you need to move content and reorganize the site's folder structure, because the links are relative to the location of the files.

To create a template that redirects a user to another location:

1. Switch to your text editor, and open a new file.
2. Type **<cflocation url= "http://kaparthi.cba.uni.edu/ColdFusion">**.

3. Save the file as **goToColdFusionAuthorsSol.cfm** in the Chap19\Chapter folder in your work folder.
4. Switch to your Web browser, and open the template you created.
5. Close all programs.

The ColdFusion server executes the CFLOCATION tag and sends an "object has moved" HTTP response to the Web browser with the new location of the object. Your Web browser sends another request to this new location and automatically opens the author's home page. Unless you had been told about the redirection, you wouldn't have known it occurred.

You must have an Internet connection to open the author's Web site.

Chapter Summary

- ColdFusion is a complete Web application server that allows you to rapidly create and deliver dynamic, interactive, data-driven, Web-based applications.
- You use three components with ColdFusion: a text editor of your choice for creating and editing HTML documents and ColdFusion Markup Language (CFML) templates; ColdFusion Server, which communicates with the Web server and processes ColdFusion templates; and ColdFusion Administrator, a Web-based application that you use to set parameters for the ColdFusion Server.
- CFML is a server-side markup language used with HTML to enable server-side processing by manipulating data, displaying output, and interacting with databases.
- Forms are objects in HTML documents that help collect data from users. Forms contain data-entry controls such as text boxes and submit buttons. Use the INPUT tag to create these controls.
- Adding forms to a Web site is usually a two-step process. First you design the form, and then you design a form handler to process the data entered in the form. You specify the filename of the form handler in the ACTION attribute of a form. When the form is submitted, ColdFusion Server executes the ColdFusion form handler.
- You can use three constructs for controlling program flow in ColdFusion. In the sequence construct, statements in a program are executed one after another from beginning to end. You use a selection construct to model situations where statements are executed based on circumstances. When statements must execute repeatedly, you use the repetition construct.

- Use loops to perform repetitive tasks in ColdFusion. When you know exactly how many times a set of statements must be executed, you use FOR loops. Use a WHILE loop to execute a set of statements repeatedly as long as a certain condition is true. A LIST loop also executes a set of statements repeatedly; for each execution, a variable takes a different value from a value list.
- Use the CFLOCATION tag to redirect an HTTP request.

Review Questions

1. Which of the following is *not* an example of how the ColdFusion application server enhances the capabilities of a Web server?
   a. handles data that users enter in HTML forms
   b. extracts data from databases and create reports
   c. changes image colors when users move the cursor over them
   d. interacts with other services, such as e-mail and directory systems
2. Which tag is used to assign values to ColdFusion variables?
   a. CFLOOP
   b. CFSET
   c. CFOUTPUT
   d. CFINPUT
3. CFML is an abbreviation for ________________.
   a. ColdFusion Meta Links
   b. ColdFusion Modular Language
   c. ColdFusion Markup Language
   d. Calculations For Meta Layers
4. Comments in ColdFusion begin with which set of characters?
   a. `<!--`
   b. `<!---`
   c. `<!//`
   d. `<!-`
5. Which of the following is *not* an arithmetic operator in ColdFusion?
   a. /
   b. MOD
   c. ^
   d. ()

6. When ColdFusion encounters the <cfoutput> tag, it starts processing text by looking for variables enclosed in ________________ signs.

   a. #

   b. /

   c. \

   d. ^

7. Which of the following is an attribute of a FORM tag that contains the name of a ColdFusion template?

   a. Action

   b. Method

   c. Name

   d. Style

8. A ColdFusion form handler ________________.

   a. cannot contain CFML

   b. is executed when the user submits a form

   c. displays a form for a user to handle data

   d. has an extension of .cfform

9. Which of the following is not a flow-control construct in ColdFusion?

   a. sequence

   b. binary

   c. selection

   d. repetition

10. Which of the following ColdFusion statements allows you to implement a selection flow-control construct?

   a. CFSET

   b. CFLOOP

   c. CFOUTPUT

   d. CFIF

11. Which of the following is *not* a relational operator in ColdFusion?

   a. GT

   b. LT

   c. EQ

   d. NT

12. Which of the following ColdFusion statements allows you to implement a repetition flow-control construct?
    a. CFSET
    b. CFLOOP
    c. CFOUTPUT
    d. CFIF
13. Which of the following CFLOOP attributes is used in FOR loops, LIST loops, and WHILE loops?
    a. INDEX
    b. LIST
    c. CONDITION
    d. none of the above
14. If a FOR loop with an index running from 1 to 10 is enclosed in a LIST loop with 15 elements, how many times does the server execute the statements inside the inner loop?
    a. 10
    b. 15
    c. 25
    d. 150
15. Which of the following ColdFusion tags allows you to redirect users to another Web page?
    a. CFOUTPUT
    b. CFSET
    c. CFLOOP
    d. CFLOCATION

HANDS-ON EXERCISES

If necessary, create a folder named **Exercises** in the Chap19 folder in your work folder before performing the following exercises.

Exercise 19-1

In this exercise, you design an HTML form. The form contains text boxes and a Submit button that allow a bank teller to enter the number of pennies, nickels, dimes, and quarters in a customer's deposit.

To create a two-column form:

1. Create the HTML form shown in Figure 19-23. In your form, use a two-column table with right-aligned labels and left-aligned controls. Save this file as **Ex19-01.htm** in the Chap19\Exercises folder in your work folder.

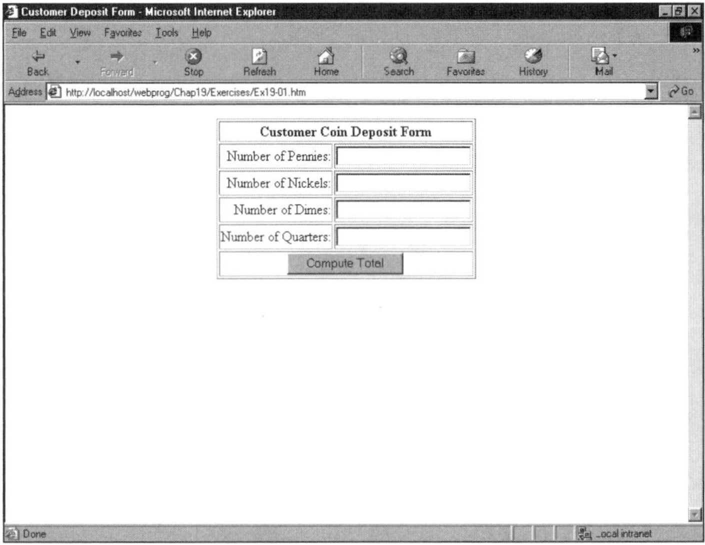

Figure 19-23

2. Create a form handler for the coin deposit form, which should display the total value of coins in cents and dollars as an HTML table. Use two CFSET statements to initialize a Total_In_Cents variable and a Total variable. The Total_In_Cents variable computes the total value of all pennies, nickels, dimes, and quarters. The Total variable divides the results of the Total_In_Cents variable by 100.
3. Enter the CFOUTPUT statements to display the resulting values in the second column. Format the Total output as currency.
4. When you finish, save the form handler as **Ex19-01.cfm** in the Chap19\Exercises folder in your work folder, and then open the form (/Chap19/Exercises/Ex19-01.htm) in your Web browser. To test your program, enter 23 for the Pennies value, 8 for Nickels, 34 for Dimes, and 12 for Quarters, then submit the form. The result should look like Figure 19-24.

19

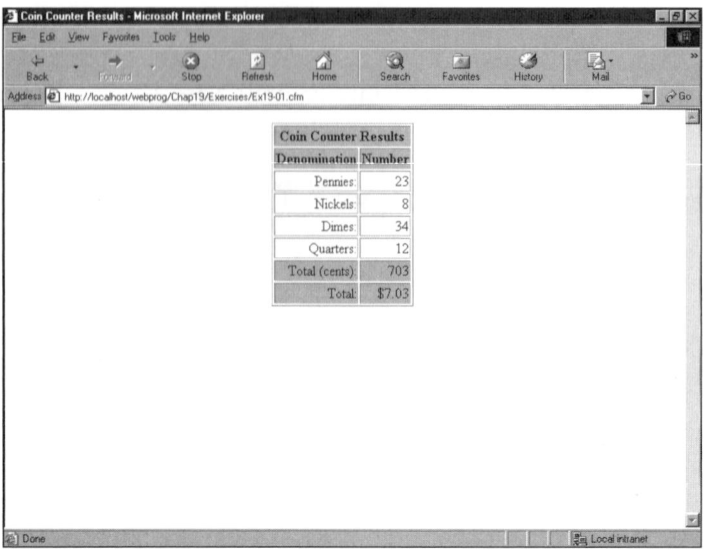

Figure 19-24

Exercise 19-2

A department store is having a red tag sale. Red-tagged items are marked down 75%. As part of its promotional efforts, the store wants you to set up a form on its Web site (Figure 19-25).

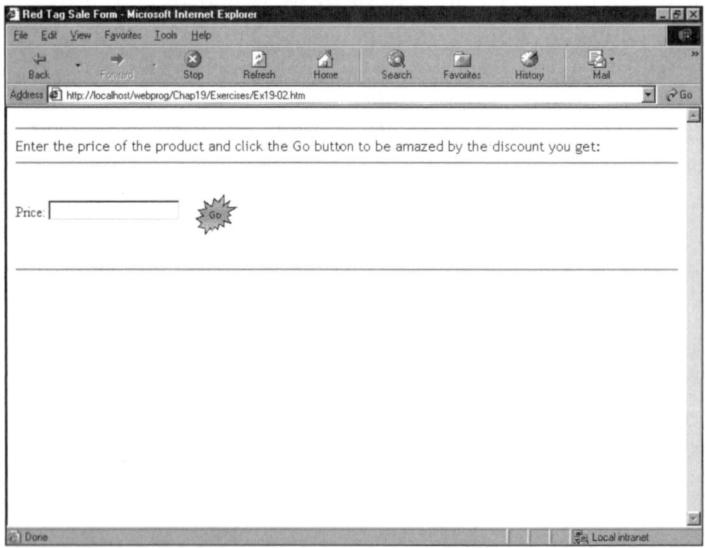

Figure 19-25

To create the form:

1. In a text editor, create a Web page named **Ex19-02.htm**. Save this file in the Chap19\Exercises folder in your work folder. The Ex19-02.htm page should contain a text box for entering the price of the product and a Submit button with a Go caption. Use **go.gif** from the data files for this chapter.
2. Design a ColdFusion form handler to show this product's price, discount, discounted price, sales tax, and total price.
3. Use CFSET tags to assign the user-entered value to the price variable, 0.75 to the DiscountRate variable, and 0.07 to the TaxRate variable.
4. Compute the Discount as Price times DiscountRate, DiscountedPrice as Price minus Discount, Tax as DiscountedPrice times TaxRate, and TotalPrice as DiscountedPrice plus Tax.
5. Format the template's output as an HTML table. Format dollar amounts as currency.
6. When you finish, save the file as **Ex19-02.cfm** in the Chap19\Exercises folder in your work folder, and then view the form in your Web browser. Test your program by entering a price of $50 and $100. See Figure 19-26.

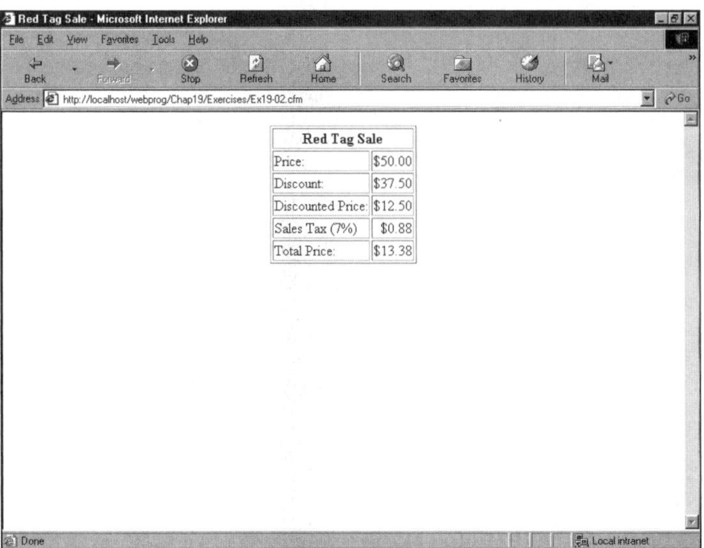

Figure 19-26

Exercise 19-3

A regional bank decides to offer a preferred status to its checking account customers if they have $5,000 or more on deposit in their account. Customers who have other accounts or less than $5,000 in checking accounts are given a regular status.

To design a ColdFusion template:

1. If the type of customer account is a URL parameter named accType and the amount on deposit is a URL parameter named balance, design a ColdFusion template to classify the customer into one of two categories: Preferred status or Regular status. Recall that you can access values of URL parameters by using URL-scoped variables such as URL.accType and URL.balance.
2. Use two CFIF statements to solve this problem. Use an outer CFIF statement to select an action based on whether a customer has a checking account or some other account with the bank. Design an inner CFIF statement to check the account balance and to assign the proper status to the account. Use a string variable named status and assign it a literal "Preferred" or "Regular" by using a CFSET statement such as <CFSET status = "Preferred">.
3. Use Figure 19-27 to design your template and its output. When you finish, save the template as **Ex19-03.cfm** in the Chap19\Exercises folder.
4. Test your template by opening Ex19-03.cfm?accType=Checking&balance=6000, Ex19-03.cfm?accType=Checking&balance=4000, and Ex19-03.cfm?accType=Savings&balance=6000.

Figure 19-27

Exercise 19-4

CF Realtors has asked you to design mortgage payment calculators on its Web site. Cal and Fran believe that such helpful aids will make their Web site more popular and increase their business.

To design a form that performs calculations:

1. Design a form with three text boxes and two submit buttons, as shown in Figure 19-28. Save this page as **Ex19-04.htm** in the Chap19\Exercises folder in your work folder. The captions and names for the controls are described in the following table and shown in Figure 19-28:

Label/Value	Control name	Type	Comment
Amount of loan:	p	Text	
Interest APR (%):	apr	Text	Users enter the annual percentage interest rate here; the monthly interest rate r would be apr/1200
Number of loan years:	y	Text	If y is the number of loan years, then the term in months n would be y * 12
Calculate Monthly Payment	buttonType	Submit	Monthly payment = p*r/(1-(1+r)^(-n))
Display Interest Rate Change Table	buttonType	Submit	Should display a table of monthly payments with interest rate from apr - 1 to apr + 1 in increments of 0.25

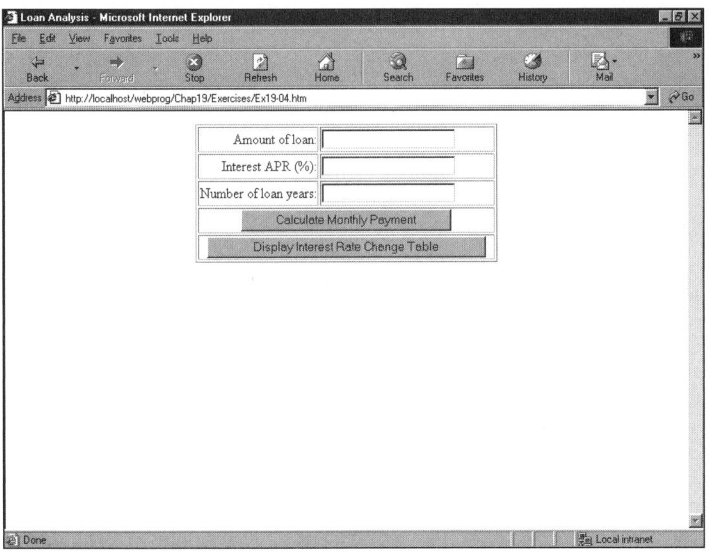

Figure 19-28

19

2. FORM.buttonType is assigned a value of "Calculate Monthly Payment" or "Display Interest Rate Change Table," depending on the button the user clicks. You can use a CFIF statement with the condition FORM.buttonType EQ "Calculate Monthly Payment" to check whether the user has clicked the first button or not.

3. Design a form handler named **Ex19-04.cfm** in the Chap19\Exercises folder in your work folder that computes and displays the monthly payment when the user clicks the Calculate Monthly Payment button. Using the formulas in the previous table, first compute the monthly interest rate (r), then the term in months (n), and then the payment.
4. Test your template by using the values 100000, 6, and 15 in the text boxes for the amount, interest rate, and term, respectively. Your results should look like Figure 19-29.

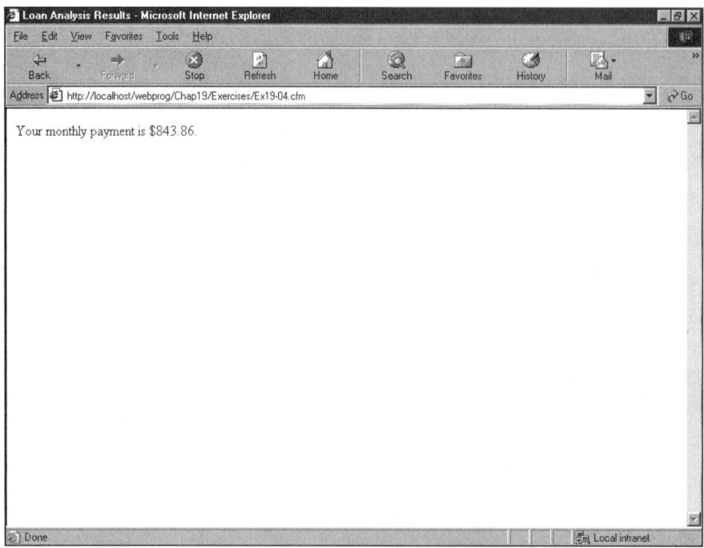

Figure 19-29

If the user clicks the Display Interest Rate Change Table button, then the result should be a table of monthly payments for all interest rates from apr - 1 to apr + 1, as shown in Figure 19-30.

5. To generate the table, use the following FOR loop:

```
<cfset lower_limit = FORM.apr - 1>
<cfset upper_limit = FORM.apr + 1>
<cfloop index="iAPR" from="#lower_limit#" to="upper_limit" step="0.25">
<cfset r = iAPR / 1200>
<cfset p = ...
Display table row...
</cfloop>
```

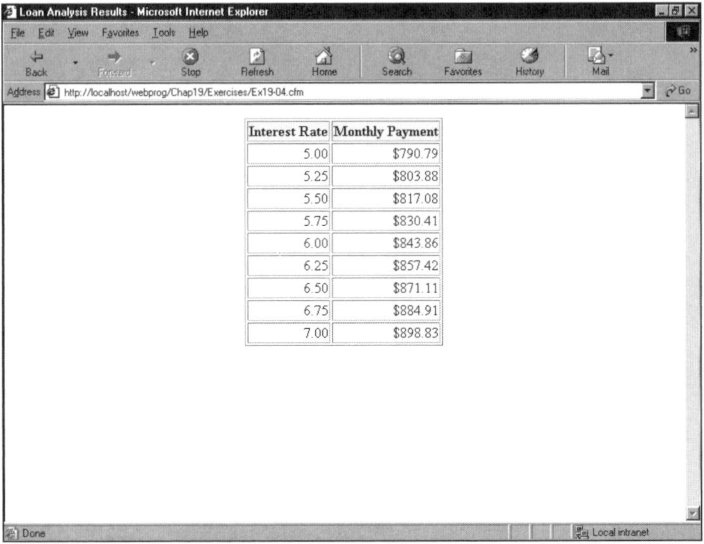

Interest Rate	Monthly Payment
5.00	$790.79
5.25	$803.88
5.50	$817.08
5.75	$830.41
6.00	$843.86
6.25	$857.42
6.50	$871.11
6.75	$884.91
7.00	$898.83

Figure 19-30

Exercise 19-5

Randomly generated passwords are easy to forget, and pose a security threat because users often write them down. A leading Internet portal assigns passwords to users by combining two words and a number so that they are easy to remember and hard to guess.

To design a template that assigns passwords:

1. Design a ColdFusion template that combines all words in the list "cold,static,dynamic" with all words in the list "asp,java,php,fusion" to produce a bulleted list of valid passwords. This template should process two URL parameters named list1 and list2. For simplicity, you are not required to add a number. See Figure 19-31.

Use two LIST loops nested within each other to produce all possible combinations of words.

2. When you finish, save your template as **Ex19-05.cfm** in the Chap19\Exercises folder in your work folder. Test your template by opening \Chap19\Ex19-5.cfm?list1=cold,static,dynamic&list2=asp,java,php,fusion.

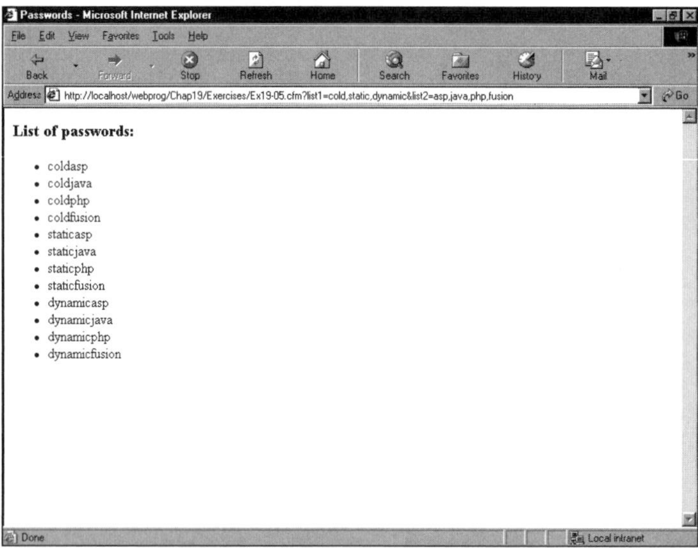

Figure 19-31

Web Programming Projects

Project 19-1

Research the case studies available at *www.macromedia.com* and write a one-page report that describes how companies are using ColdFusion.

Project 19-2

Design a check-out form for an e-commerce site. It should contain the following fields: Name, Address, City, State, Zip, Phone, E-mail address, ProductID, and Quantity. The form should also contain a Submit button with a Next caption. When the user submits the form, all the user-entered data should be displayed neatly in an HTML table, along with a button labeled "Above information is correct—place the order." No action has to be taken when the user clicks this button.

Project 19-3

A Midwestern company wants to analyze its customer data. The company wants to identify the states the customers live in based on their telephone area code, according to Table 19-5.

Table 19-5

Area code	State
319, 515, 712	Iowa
218, 320, 507	Minnesota
414, 608, 715, 920	Wisconsin
308, 402	Nebraska
314, 417, 636, 660, 816	Missouri
Other	Other

Design a ColdFusion template that uses a URL parameter named customersAreaCode and outputs the state where the customer lives. Experiment with different values for the customersAreaCode parameter.

CHAPTER

20

COLDFUSION MX: PART II

In this chapter you will:

- ♦ Design a database and folder structure for a Web application
- ♦ Learn about Open Database Connectivity (ODBC) standards
- ♦ Set up database connectivity with ColdFusion
- ♦ Generate columnar reports
- ♦ Display data from specific records as Web pages
- ♦ Create navigation options
- ♦ Generate tabular reports
- ♦ Generate group total reports
- ♦ Create templates for extracting data interactively

In other chapters, you learned about databases, data storage, and data retrieval. In this chapter, you will apply these concepts to extract data from databases using ColdFusion MX and then publish that data on a Web server. In Chapter 19, you worked through a scenario involving CF Realtors. In this chapter, Cal and Fran want every listed property of CF Realtors to be available through their Web site. To add this functionality, you must integrate the site with a database. The database must include information about the properties available for sale as well as the agents who work for CF Realtors. The properties (houses for sale, for example) and agents become the database entities that are stored in tables. You decide to use Microsoft Access to store the data about properties and agents.

DESIGNING A DATABASE AND FOLDER STRUCTURE

After analyzing the user requirements and the existing system, you determine that the CF Realtors database should have two tables: a table named Properties to store information related to properties that are currently listed for sale and a table named Agents to contain information related to agents. A Microsoft Access database named CFRealtors.mdb is in the Chap20\Chapter folder. The Properties table in it has a key field named PropertyID, a text field that contains a unique listing number for each property. Similarly, the Agents table has a primary key field named AgentID that contains an agent's initials or a unique three-character code. The two tables are related in the following fashion: a particular agent lists a property; to define this relationship, the Properties table also has a field named AgentID to store information about its listing agent. Table 20-1 shows the structure for the tables in the database with examples of data contained in the fields.

Table 20-1 Structure of database tables

Properties table structure			
Field name	**Data type**	**Size**	**Examples of data**
PropertyID	Text	7	CFR4568
TypeOfHouse	Text	50	two-story home
YearBuilt	Number	Integer	1990
NumBedrooms	Number	Integer	4
NumBathrooms	Number	Single	3, 3.5
Area	Number	Integer	3909
Rooms	Text	150	laundry room, master bathroom, master bedroom, workshop
OtherFeatures	Text	150	cathedral ceilings, hardwood floors, pantry, walk-in closet(s)
Price	Currency		$243,543.00
Location	Text	50	Cedar Rapids
ZipCode	Text	10	52401
ImageFilename	Text	50	MVC-867E.JPG
AgentID	Text	3	JPP
Agents table structure			
Field name	**Data type**	**Size**	**Examples of data**
AgentID	Text	3	RTH
FirstName	Text	50	Richard
MiddleInitial	Text	1	T
LastName	Text	50	Hadik
EmailAddress	Text	50	rhadik@cfrealtors.com
Address	Text	255	873 Main Street

Table 20-1 Structure of database tables (continued)

Agents table structure			
Field name	**Data type**	**Size**	**Examples of data**
City	Text	50	Cedar Rapids
State	Text	2	IA
ZipCode	Text	10	52402
WorkPhone	Text	30	(319) 555-2873

Planning the Folder Structure

After extensive discussion, your team has decided to design the folder structure for storing the templates and pictures as follows:

- The home page and all the other templates used by customers will be in the main folder or the root folder of the Web site (Chap20\Chapter).
- The database will be stored in the same folder.
- Property pictures will be stored in a subfolder named PropertyImages (Chap20\Chapter\PropertyImages).
- Graphics associated with the user interface will be in their respective folders.

For ColdFusion to access data stored in Microsoft Access databases or from database servers, you must first set up connections to the databases on the server.

Open Database Connectivity (ODBC) Standards

Open Database Connectivity (**ODBC**) is Microsoft's standard for connecting Windows applications to databases and database servers. ODBC provides an open, vendor-neutral way of accessing data stored in a variety of proprietary personal computer, minicomputer, and mainframe databases. An ODBC driver is systems software that runs on the Web server and provides the functionality for connecting databases to other applications. Figure 20-1 shows how an ODBC driver connects a client computer, a Web server, and a database.

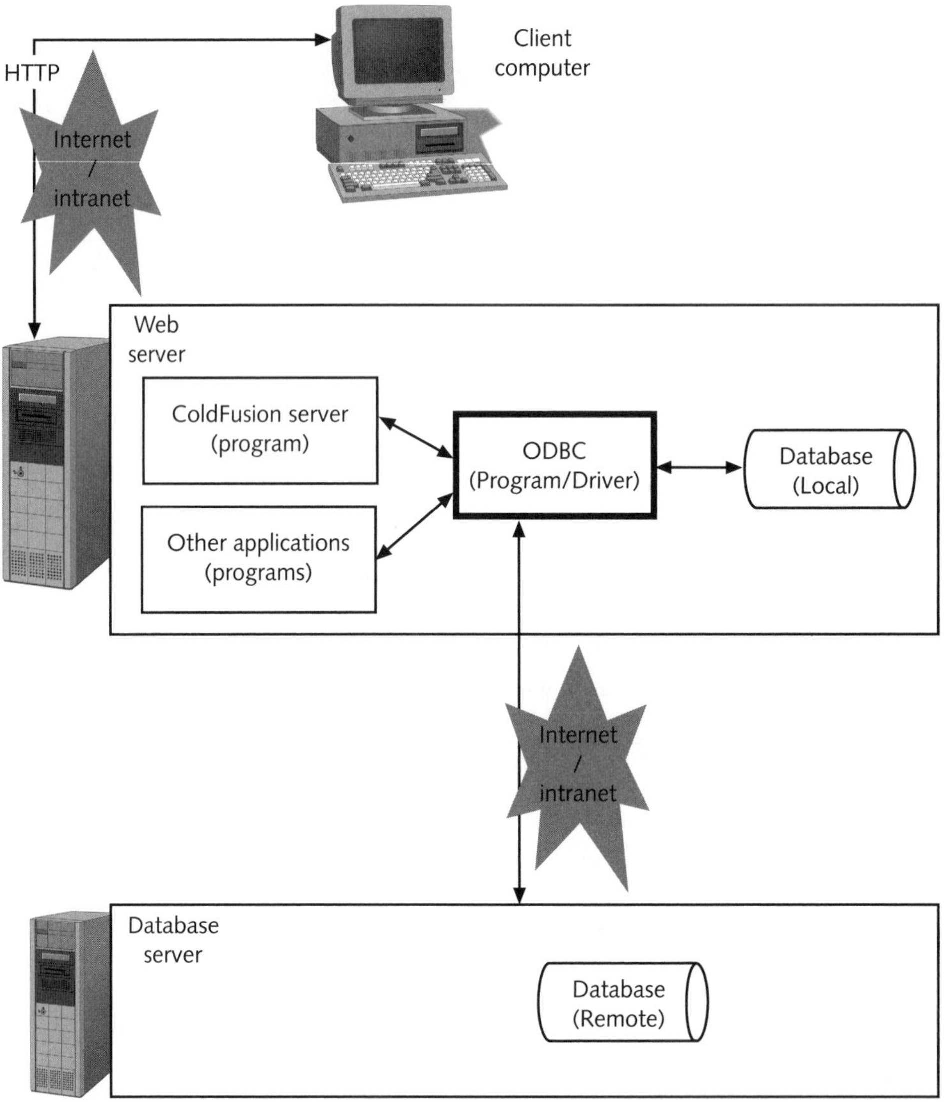

Figure 20-1 Role of the ODBC driver

To access data from a database in ColdFusion, you must first set up an ODBC connection to the database. The ODBC driver interacts with the database and the ColdFusion server interacts with the ODBC driver. Every ODBC connection has a **data source name** and this name is useful for accessing the data in its database. OBDC is based on the specification of the SQL Access Group, an industry standards group. With ODBC, you can use SQL, which lets you store data, create tables, update data, and complete other database tasks regardless of which database system contains the data. Once you have a ColdFusion application working, you can easily **upsize** the database that contains your data from Microsoft Access to an Oracle server or a SQL server by changing the ODBC connection. This change does not require any changes to the CFML. You use ColdFusion Administrator to set up or change ODBC connections.

To complete the CF Realtors Web site, you need to set up an ODBC connection to the CFRealtors.mdb database that is stored in the Chap20\Chapter folder. If necessary, create the Chap20\Chapter folders in the work folder on your system, and then copy the CFRealtors.mdb file from the student data files to the Chap20\Chapter folder before performing the following steps.

To set up an ODBC connection:

1. Click the **Start** button on the taskbar, point to **Programs** (point to **All Programs** in Windows XP), point to **Macromedia ColdFusion MX**, and then click **Administrator**. The ColdFusion MX Administrator Login page opens in a browser. See Figure 20-2.

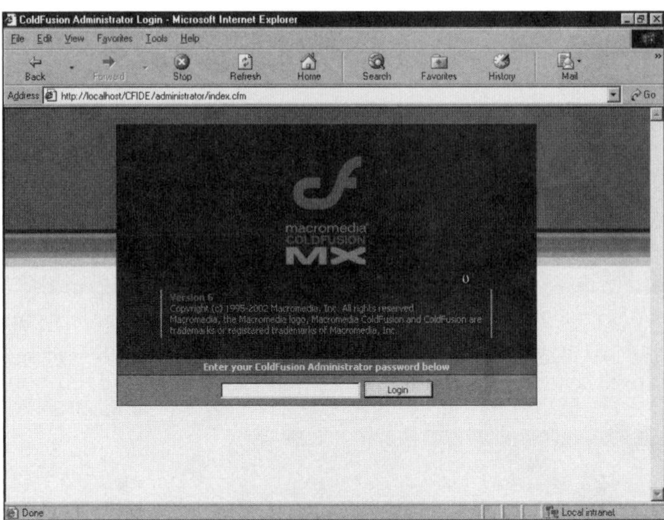

Figure 20-2 ColdFusion Administrator login page

Depending on the computer configuration you are using, your instructor may have already set up an ODBC connection for you. You must have an administrator's password to complete the following steps. Check with your instructor or technical support staff before completing these steps. If you cannot complete these steps at the computer, read them so you can learn how to set up an ODBC connection.

2. Enter the administrator password for your server, and then click the **Login** button. The ColdFusion Administrator page opens and displays the Web-based console for configuring the settings for ColdFusion Server and managing its resources. See Figure 20-3.

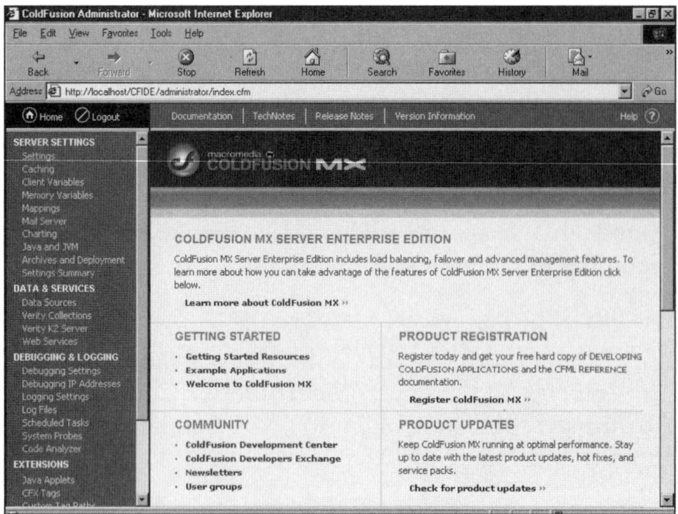

Figure 20-3 ColdFusion Administrator page

If this is the first time you are using the Administrator, a Welcome window appears before the ColdFusion Administrator page. Click **Web – ColdFusion Administrator** to get to the index page. If this option does not appear in the Welcome window, click the **Show this message on next visit** check box to remove the check mark, and then click the **Close** button to open the index page.

3. Click the **Data Sources** link in the data and services section on the left side of the page. The Web page shown in Figure 20-4 opens. This page lets you select the ODBC driver for the database that contains your data. It might also display a list of data sources available to ColdFusion that have already been configured.

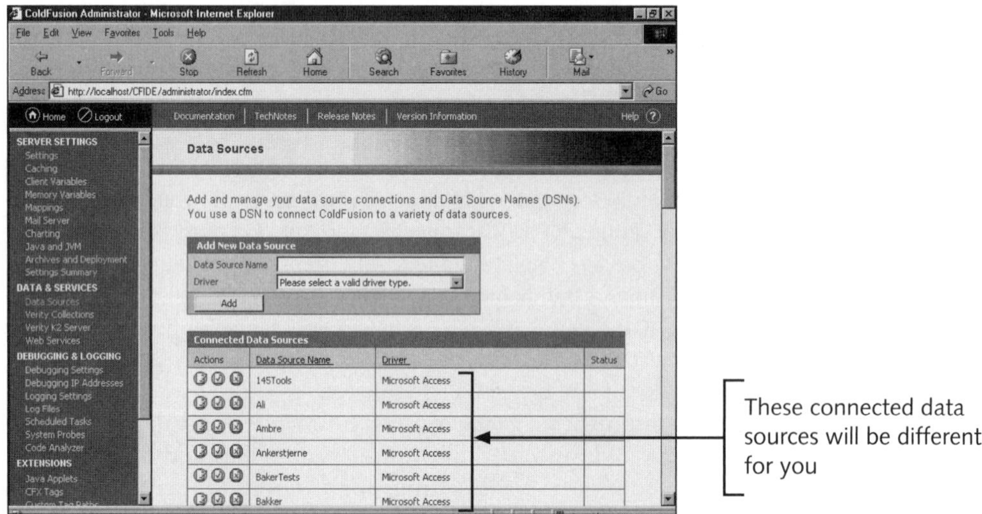

Figure 20-4 ODBC Data Sources page

4. Click the **Driver** list arrow to display a list of database drivers for database systems available on your computer.
5. Click **Microsoft Access** in the list.
6. Click in the **Data Source Name** text box, and then type **CFRealtors.** You use this data source name to identify the database connection in ColdFusion.
7. Click the **Add** button. The Microsoft Access Data Source page opens as shown in Figure 20-5.

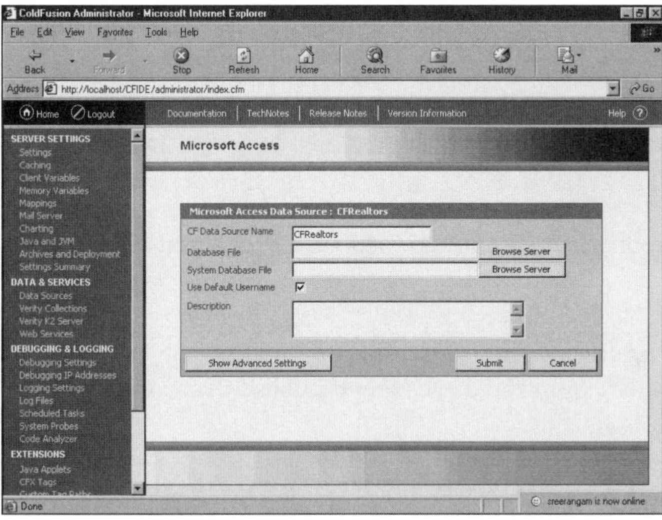

Figure 20-5 Microsoft Access Data Source page

8. Click in the **Database File** text box, and type the path to the database file on your disk, such as C:\InetPub\wwwroot\WebProg\Chap20\Chapter\CFRealtors.mdb. Note that you can also use the **Browse Server** button to search for the .mdb file.
9. Click the **Submit** button. An ODBC connection to the database is established and ColdFusion tests the database connection. Any error is reported with suggestions for troubleshooting. See Figure 20-6. You have successfully established an ODBC connection named CFRealtors to the CFRealtors.mdb database.

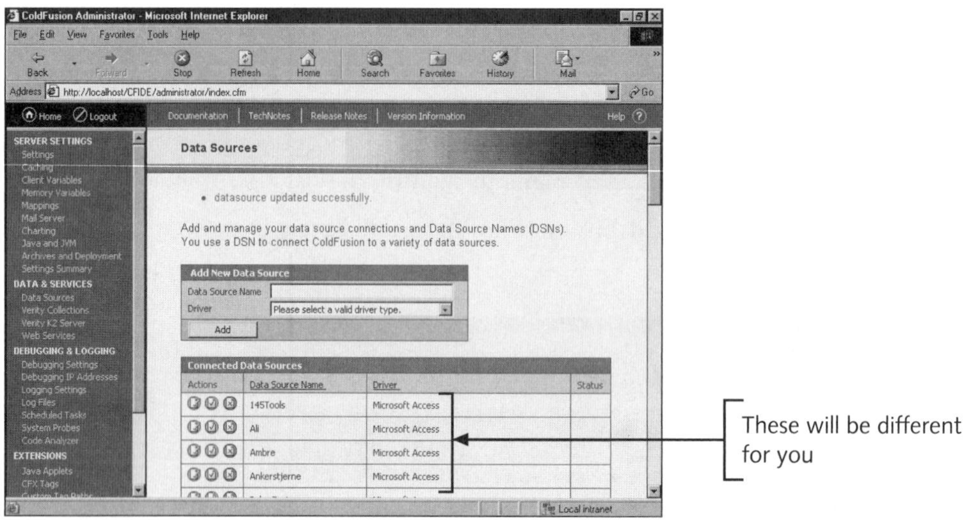

Figure 20-6 ODBC connection successfully made to CFRealtors.mdb

10. Close the browser to exit ColdFusion Administrator.

Now that you have established a connection to the database, you can design ColdFusion templates that extract data from the database and publish them on the server.

SETTING UP DATABASE CONNECTIVITY WITH COLDFUSION

Extracting data and publishing it on the Web with ColdFusion is a two-step process. The first step involves executing a SQL SELECT statement to extract the data from the database into the computer's memory. This data is called a Query object (or just a query) or a record set. The second step involves using a repetition flow-control structure to loop through the records in the record set and output the data.

Using the CFQUERY Tag

You use the CFQUERY tag to execute a SQL SELECT statement in a ColdFusion template. The syntax for the CFQUERY tag is as follows:

```
<cfquery datasource="datasource_name" name="query_name">
SQL SELECT statement
</cfquery>
```

The CFQUERY tag has two important attributes. The DATASOURCE attribute is the data source name of the ODBC connection. The second attribute is the NAME of the query. The guidelines for query names are the same as the ones for variable names. When ColdFusion Server processes a CFQUERY statement, it executes the SQL SELECT statement against the database specified in the ODBC connection named *datasource_name*. The result of the SQL SELECT statement is stored in the server's memory as a Query object. You use a QUERY loop flow-control structure to process the data in the Query object.

Using QUERY Loops

ColdFusion QUERY loops implement a repetition flow-control structure. For each repetition, you have access to the data in a particular record in the database Query object. QUERY loops have one important parameter—the name of the Query object. The syntax for a QUERY loop is as follows:

<cfloop query="query_name">
Statements containing HTML and CFML that are to be executed repeatedly with access to data from the query
</cfloop>

The flowchart for a QUERY loop appears in Figure 20-7.

To understand how a QUERY loop works, you can visualize the Query object in the computer's memory as the table shown in Figure 20-7. When ColdFusion Server executes the QUERY loop, the first record in the Query object is the current record. It is useful to picture an arrow pointing to the current record. ColdFusion Server creates variables in the computer's memory—one for each field in the query—using the field names. Each variable created in this manner is assigned the value of the field in the current record. Initially, because the first record is the current record, the values in the first record are assigned to these variables. Then ColdFusion Server executes all statements between the CFLOOP tags. The second row in the Query object becomes the current record, all the values in the second row are assigned to the variables that are named after the fields, and the statements between the CFLOOP tags are executed again. This process is repeated for every record in the Query object. After the last record is processed, statements are executed once, and then repetition is terminated and processing continues by executing the statement below the closing CFLOOP tag. The statement in the CFLOOP tags uses the variables that ColdFusion Server has created based on the fields in the query. You can output these values using CFOUTPUT tags and pound signs, use these variables in computations, or for any other purpose based on your application requirements.

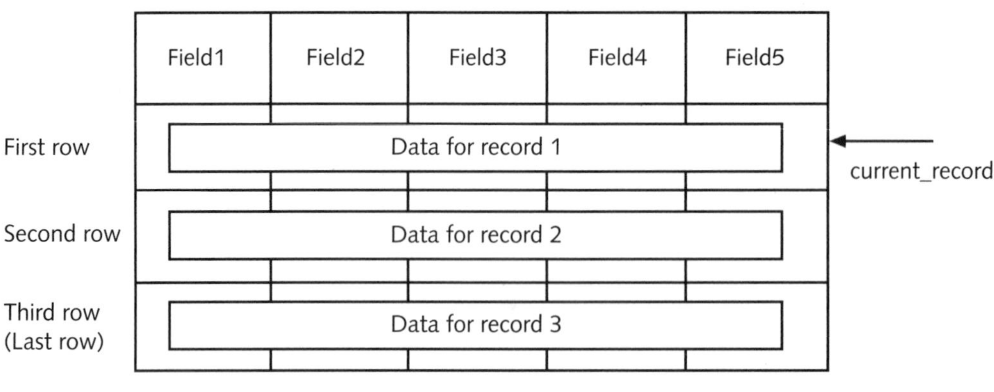

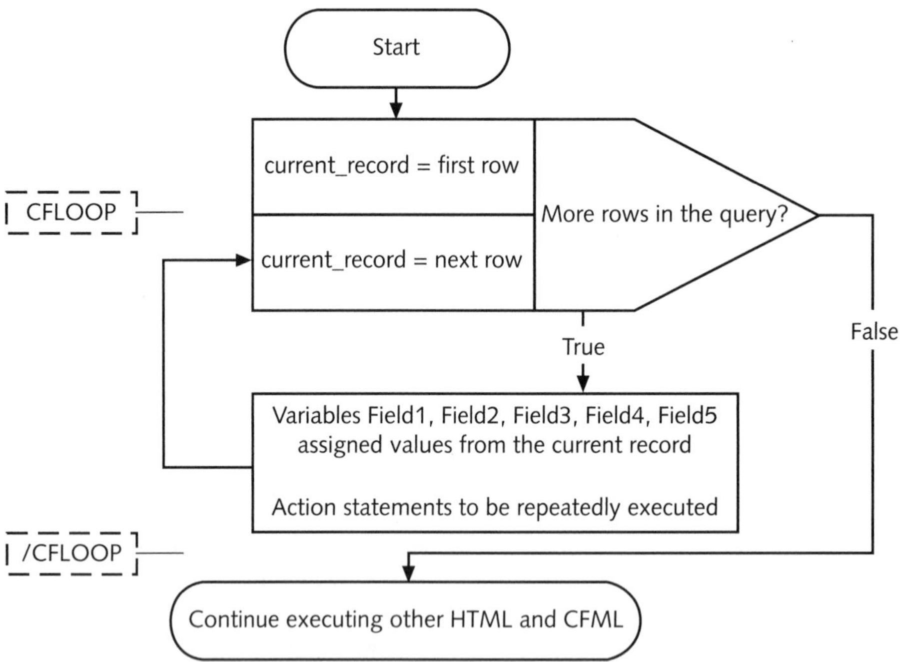

Figure 20-7 Flowchart for a QUERY loop

The following example (Example20-1.cfm) illustrates the data retrieval using the CFQUERY tag that is produced as output using a QUERY loop:

```
<cfquery datasource="cfrealtors" name="getLocations">
SELECT DISTINCT Location, ZipCode FROM Properties
</cfquery>
<html>
```

```
<head>
<title>Locations Example</title>
</head>
<body>
<h3> List of Zip Codes and Locations with Properties for Sale</h3>
<ul>
<cfloop query="getLocations">
<li> <cfoutput>#ZipCode#</cfoutput> - <cfoutput>#Location#</cfoutput>
</cfloop>
</ul>
</body>
</html>
```

The preceding code produces the output shown in Figure 20-8.

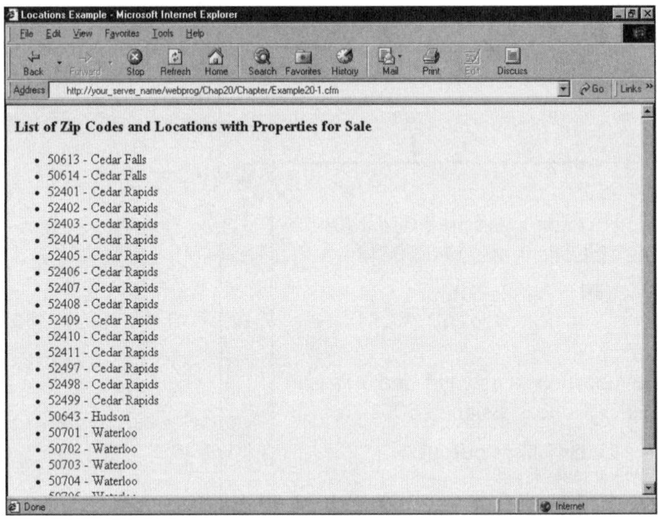

Figure 20-8 Web page displayed by Example20-1.cfm

When ColdFusion Server executes the template, the SQL SELECT statement is executed against the ODBC data source named CFRealtors. The ODBC data source points to the CFRealtors.mdb database file. The SQL SELECT statement selects data from the Properties table and the CFOUTPUT tags output it. See Figure 20-9.

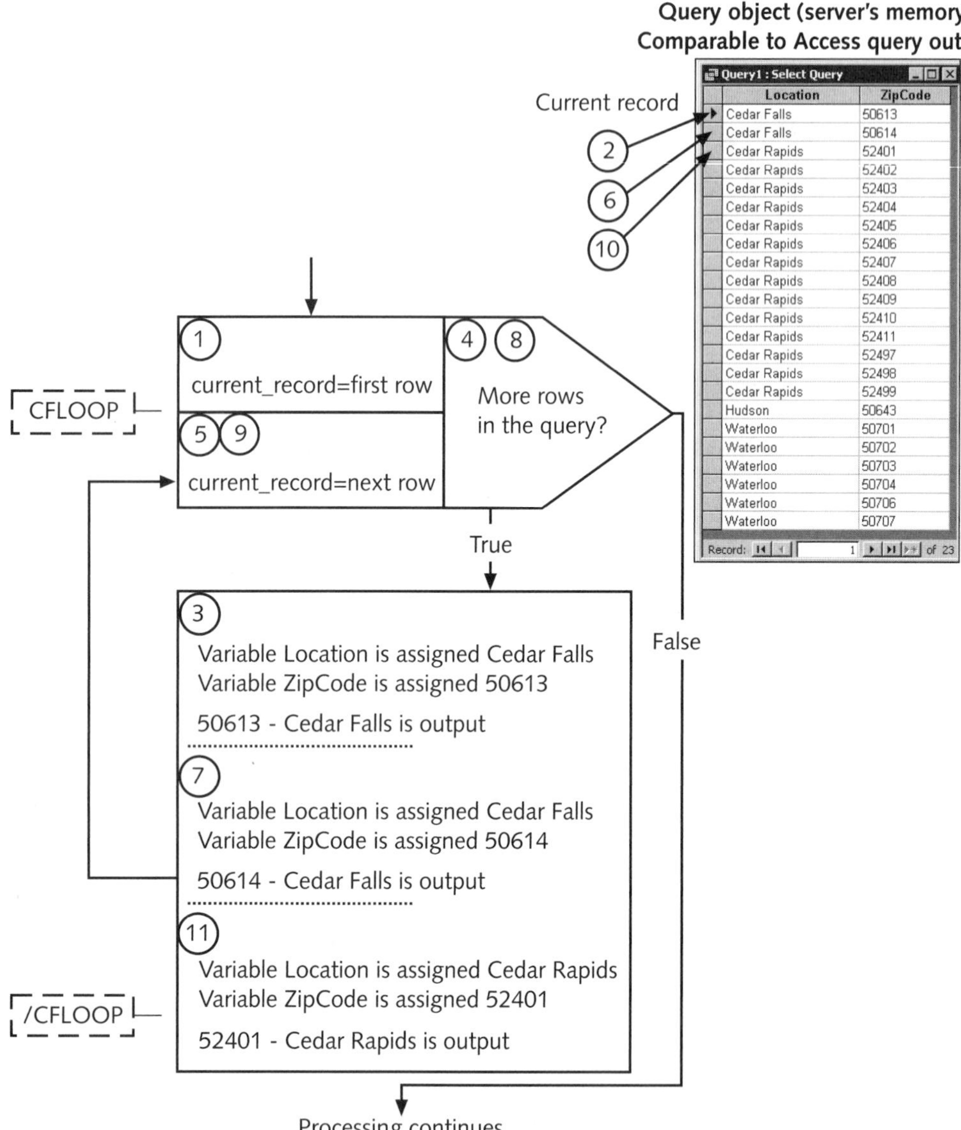

Location	ZipCode
Cedar Falls	50613
Cedar Falls	50614
Cedar Rapids	52401
Cedar Rapids	52402
Cedar Rapids	52403
Cedar Rapids	52404
Cedar Rapids	52405
Cedar Rapids	52406
Cedar Rapids	52407
Cedar Rapids	52408
Cedar Rapids	52409
Cedar Rapids	52410
Cedar Rapids	52411
Cedar Rapids	52497
Cedar Rapids	52498
Cedar Rapids	52499
Hudson	50643
Waterloo	50701
Waterloo	50702
Waterloo	50703
Waterloo	50704
Waterloo	50706
Waterloo	50707

Figure 20-9 Flowchart for Example20-1.cfm

Next, this Query object is associated with the name getLocations. Then the rest of the template code is processed. The HTML is output as is and the CFML is processed. When ColdFusion Server executes the CFLOOP statement, the Query object with the name getLocations (the one previously created) is used to execute the statement. The numbers in the following discussion correspond to the circled numbers in Figure 20-9.

1. The first row is activated as the current record. You can compare the Query object in the server's memory with the output produced in Microsoft Access by using a similar SQL statement as shown in Figure 20-9. (Access does not have to be installed on the server computer. This comparison is only for the purposes of learning how data retrieval works.)
2. The current record pointer points to the first row of the Query object in the server's memory.
3. Variables corresponding to the field names Location and ZipCode are created. The variable Location is assigned the value Cedar Falls, and the variable ZipCode is assigned the value 50613. The statements inside the CFLOOP tags are executed next. The CFOUTPUT tags are processed and the values of the variables Location and ZipCode are output as – Cedar Falls and 50613 in the Web page.
4. The ColdFusion Server checks for more records.
5. The next record is activated as the current record.
6. The current record pointer moves to the second record.
7. The variable Location is assigned the value Cedar Falls and the variable ZipCode is assigned the value 50614 and Cedar Falls and 50614 is output in the Web page.
8. ColdFusion Server checks for more records.
9. The next record is activated as the current record.
10. The current record pointer moves to the third record.
11. The variable Location is assigned the value Cedar Rapids, and the variable ZipCode is assigned the value 52401 and Cedar Rapids and 52401 is output.
12. Processing continues in a similar manner until all records are processed. Once all the records are processed, processing continues below the /CFLOOP tag.
13. The rest of the document is produced as output. The results appear in a list because of the embedded HTML tags <ul>, <li>, and </ul>.

Using a CFLOOP to Process a Subset of Records

Optionally, a QUERY loop can have two additional attributes named STARTROW and ENDROW with values startrow_value and endrow_value. All the records in the Query object are numbered sequentially starting from 1 at the top. Processing starts with the record numbered startrow_value and continues until the record numbered endrow_value is processed. This allows you to restrict the output to a certain number of records in the record set or the Query object. For example, you can use these attributes to display records in multiple pages consisting of ten records each.

The syntax for a QUERY loop with these additional attributes is as follows:

<cfloop query="query_name" startrow="startrow_value" endrow="endrow_value">
Statements containing HTML and CFML that are to be executed repeatedly with access to data from the query
</cfloop>

The following example (Example20-2.cfm) illustrates processing of a subset of data using a QUERY loop with the STARTROW and ENDROW attributes, which are highlighted in the following code, and causes the restriction in the displayed records.

```
<cfquery datasource="cfrealtors" name="getLocations">
SELECT DISTINCT Location, ZipCode FROM Properties
</cfquery>
<html>
<head>
<title>Locations Example 2</title>
</head>
<body>
<h3> List of Zip Codes and Locations with Properties for Sale</h3>
<ul>
<cfloop query="getLocations" startrow="16" endrow="18">
<li> <cfoutput>#ZipCode#</cfoutput> - <cfoutput>#Location#</cfoutput>
</cfloop>
</ul>
</body>
</html>
```

The preceding code produces the output shown in Figure 20-10.

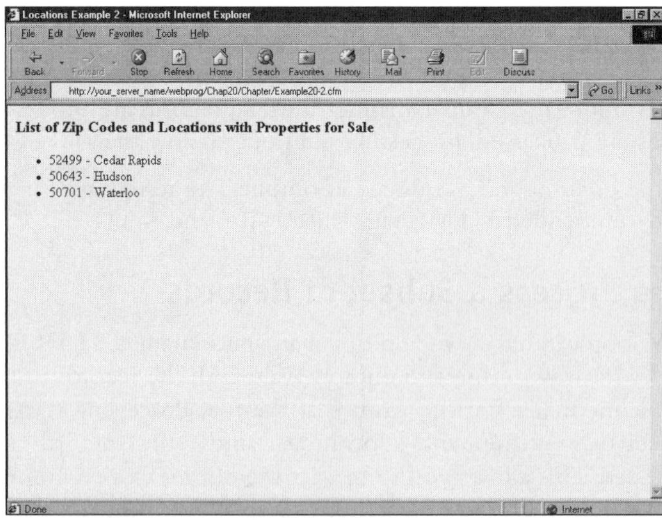

Figure 20-10 Web page displayed by Example20-2.cfm

ColdFusion Server creates a Query object similar to the previous example. This Query object is associated with the name getLocations. Then the rest of the template code is processed. The HTML is output as is and the CFML is processed. When ColdFusion Server executes the CFLOOP statement, the Query object with the name getLocations (the one previously created) is used to execute the statement. The numbers in the discussion below correspond to the circled numbers in Figure 20-11.

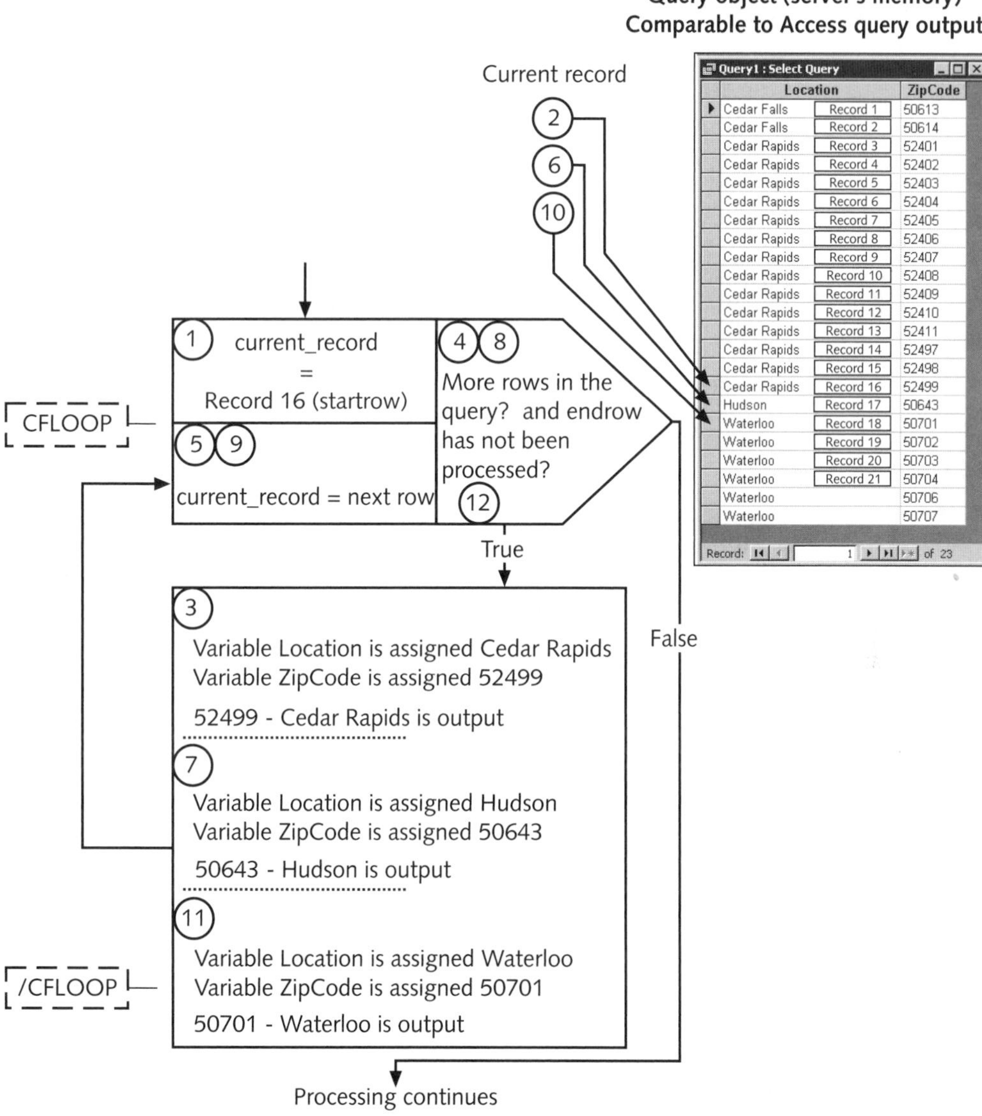

Figure 20-11 Processing a subset of records in a Query object

1. The row numbered startrow is activated as the current record. (The 16th row is activated as the current record because the value of the attribute STARTROW is 16.)
2. The current record pointer points to the 16th row of the Query object in the server's memory.
3. Variables corresponding to the field names Location and ZipCode are created. The variable Location is assigned the value Cedar Rapids, and variable ZipCode is assigned the value 52499. The statements inside the CFLOOP tags are executed next. The CFOUTPUT tags are processed and the values of variables ZipCode and Location are output as 52499 – Cedar Rapids.
4. ColdFusion Server checks for more records. It also checks to determine if the endrow (row 18) has been processed.
5. The next record (record 17) is activated as the current record.
6. The current record pointer moves to the 17th record.
7. The variable Location is assigned the value Hudson and the variable ZipCode is assigned the value 50643, and 50643 – Hudson is displayed.
8. The endrow has not been processed yet, so processing in the loop continues.
9. The next record (record 18) is activated as the current record.
10. The current record pointer moves to the 18th record.
11. The variable Location is assigned the value Waterloo, and the variable ZipCode is assigned the value 50701, and 50701 – Waterloo is displayed.
12. ColdFusion Server checks for more records. It also checks to determine if the endrow (record 18) has been processed. There are more records in the Query object, but the endrow (record 18) has been processed. Therefore, execution of the statements inside the loop is stopped, and control is transferred to the statement below the closing CFLOOP tag.
13. The rest of the document is produced as output. Similar to the first code example, the results appear as a list because of the embedded HTML tags <ul>, <li>, and </ul>.

When the STARTROW and ENDROW are the same value, only one record is processed. This technique of setting the STARTROW and the ENDROW value the same is useful for extracting a single record from a query record set and is the basis for the following section on columnar report generation.

Generating Columnar Reports

When you extract data from a database table one row at a time, typically you extract data from all the fields (columns) and generate a report containing information from them. This process of extracting and displaying data is called **columnar report generation**.

Cal and Fran want you to design ColdFusion templates that allow potential clients to browse through the properties available for sale one at a time. They want you to display a picture of the property along with its price and location. Further, they want you to display the rest of the information as sketched in Figure 20-12.

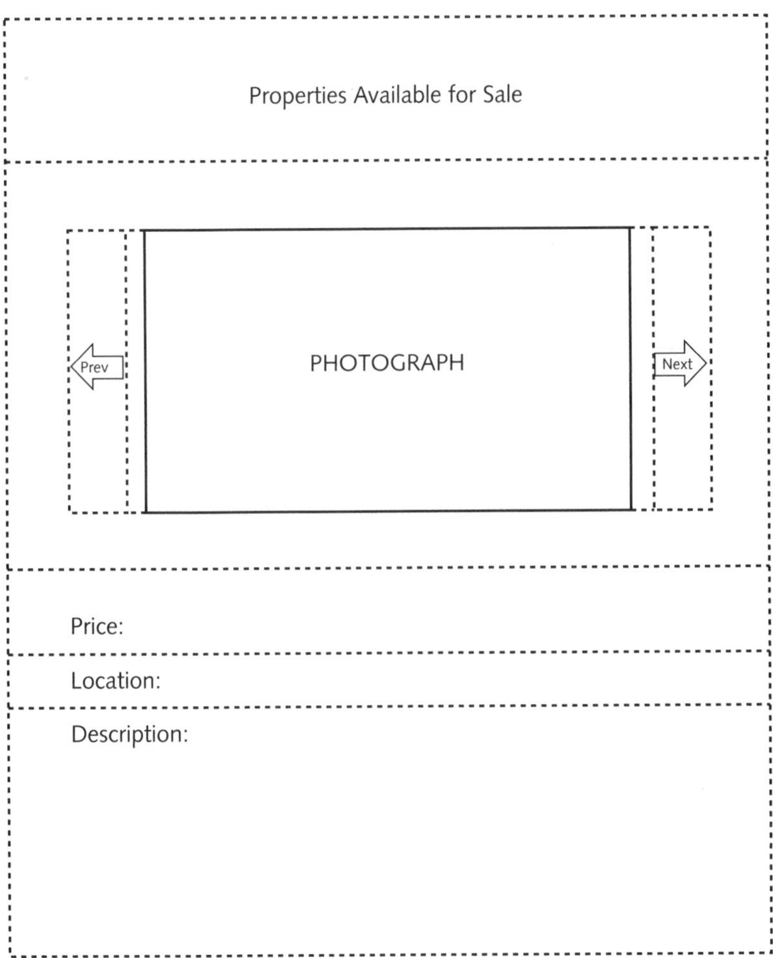

Figure 20-12 Sketch of Web page to list properties

To extract data from a table and display it one record at a time:

1. Start a text editor, such as Notepad or TextPad, and then open **detail.cfm** from the Chap20\Chapter folder in your student data files.
2. Start your Web browser, and open **http://*your_server_name/work folder/*Chap20/Chapter/detail.cfm** to preview the Web page. Carefully study the Web page layout.
3. Switch to your editor, and then examine the code that created this page.

Your first task is to extract data from the Properties table and display the first record in the format shown in Figure 20-12. You will modify this template to display other properties later on in the chapter. To display the data, you use a CFQUERY tag and a SELECT statement.

To prepare to use a CFQUERY tag to retrieve data:

1. With the insertion point on the very beginning of line 1, press **Enter**, press the **Up Arrow** key to move to the new line, type **<cfquery datasource="cfrealtors" name="getData">**, and then press **Enter**.
2. Type **SELECT * FROM Properties** to extract all the fields and all the records from the Properties table. Although you are planning to display only one record from the table, you are selecting all the records. The display will be restricted to one record in the CFLOOP tag later.
3. Press **Enter**, and then type **</cfquery>**. The CFQUERY now contains the SQL statement to select all records from the Properties table. You add a CFLOOP to select only the first record.
4. Click at the end of the line containing <cfinclude template="header.cfm">, and then press **Enter**. Type **<cfloop query="getData" startrow="1" endrow="1">**. See Figure 20-13.

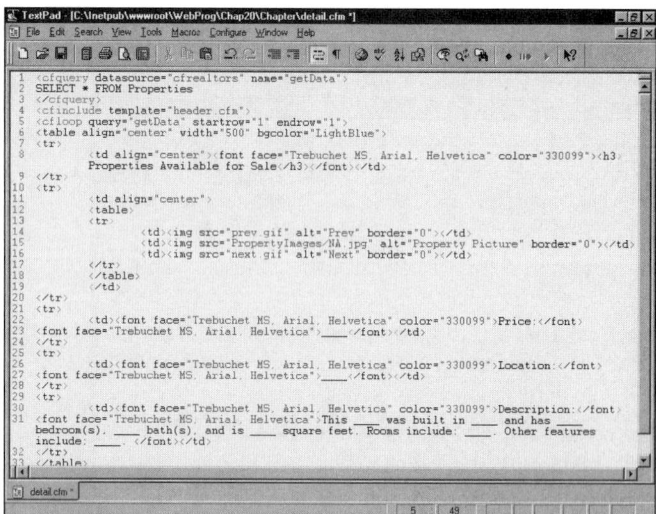

Figure 20-13 Editing detail.cfm in a text editor

This statement designs the QUERY loop for extracting data from the Query object created by the CFQUERY tag. Notice that the values for the STARTROW and the ENDROW attributes are both equal to 1, indicating that the loop processes only the first record, or the first property. When ColdFusion Server executes this statement, it creates variables corresponding to the fields selected in the SELECT statement. As all the fields in the properties table are selected in the SELECT statement, it creates variables named PropertyID, TypeOfHouse, YearBuilt, NumBedrooms, NumBathrooms, Area, Rooms, OtherFeatures, Price, Location, ZipCode, ImageFilename, and AgentID. Then it assigns values from the fields in the first record of the Properties table to variables with the same names as the fields. It assigns the value of the PropertyID field in the first record (CFR4567) to variable PropertyID, the value of the TypeOfHouse field (Home) to variable TypeOfHouse, and so on. All the variables that are created and the values assigned to them are shown in Table 20-2.

Table 20-2 Data extracted from the first record

Variable	Value
PropertyID	CFR4567
TypeOfHouse	Home
YearBuilt	1953
NumBedrooms	3
NumBathrooms	1
Area	1300
Rooms	eat-in kitchen, great room, laundry room
OtherFeatures	hardwood floors, walk-in closet(s), wet bar
Price	$132,456.00
Location	Cedar Rapids
ZipCode	52498
ImageFileName	MVC-005E.JPG
AgentID	DCL

To use a CFQUERY tag to retrieve data:

1. Click at the end of the line containing </table> at the bottom of the template, press **Enter**, and then type **</cfloop>** to close the QUERY loop. Notice that the entire table is enclosed in the QUERY loop. You generate the values extracted from the database table in the appropriate locations next.
2. Approximately in the middle of the document, select **NA.jpg**, and replace it with the following text: **<cfoutput>#ImageFilename#</cfoutput>**. This statement produces the property image filename for the property. Notice that you are using the appropriate path to the PropertyImages folder that contains these graphics on the data disk. Also, the value of this variable is the data in the field named ImageFilename. This CFOUTPUT statement produces the filename of the picture for the record selected by the query. For example, for the first record, the partial HTML code generated would be <img src="PropertyImages/ MVC-005E.JPG" alt="Property Picture" border="0">. The browser makes an additional request to the Web server to serve the image file when it processes the IMG tag, and then it displays it after it receives the file.

20

3. In the Price cell, select ________________, and type **<cfoutput># DollarFormat(Price)#</cfoutput>**. When ColdFusion Server executes this statement, it formats the value in the variable named Price for the current record as currency and outputs it. Recall that the first record is the current record as the values of attributes STARTROW and ENDROW are both equal to 1.
4. In the Price cell, select ________________, and type **<cfoutput>#Location# – #ZipCode#</cfoutput>**. This statement produces the value in the Location variable, a space, a hyphen, a space, and then the value in the ZipCode variable for the current record.
5. Edit the text in the Description cell by producing the values of the appropriate variables as follows: **<cfoutput>**This **#TypeOfHouse#** was built in **#YearBuilt#** and has **#NumBedrooms#** bedroom(s), **#NumBathrooms#** bath(s), and is **#Area#** square feet. Rooms include: **#Rooms#**. Other features include: **#OtherFeatures#.</cfoutput>**.
6. Save the file, and then view it in your Web browser by opening **http://*your_server_name*/*work folder*/Chap20/Chapter/detail.cfm**. (Be sure to substitute the name of your server and work folder as appropriate.) See Figure 20-14.

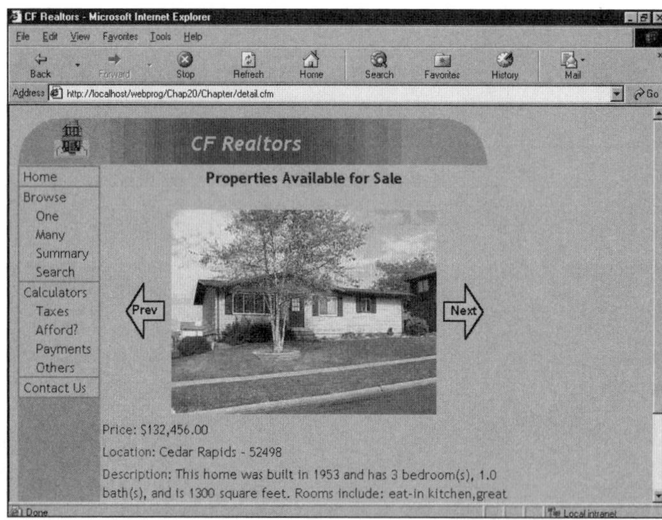

Figure 20-14 Web page displayed by detail.cfm

The template correctly selected the first record from the Properties table and displayed information from it using the CFOUTPUT tags. The Prev and Next arrows will eventually let the user browse other records selected by the query. You add this functionality later in the chapter.

Notice that the Rooms and OtherFeatures fields contain lists with comma-separated values with no spaces after the commas. To make the output grammatically correct you need spaces after the commas. You can use the REPLACE string function to replace all occurrences of commas in those fields with a comma and a space.

To modify detail.cfm by using the REPLACE function:

1. Switch to your text editor.
2. Select **#Rooms#** in the Description section, and type **#Replace(Rooms,”,”,”,** and then a space followed by **“,”ALL”)#**. When ColdFusion Server processes this function, it replaces *all* occurrences of commas in the value of variable Rooms with commas followed by spaces and displays the result.
3. Similarly, select **#OtherFeatures#** and type **#Replace(OtherFeatures,“,”,“,** and then a space followed by **”,“ALL”)#**. When ColdFusion Server processes this function, it replaces *all* occurrences of commas in the value of variable OtherFeatures with commas followed by spaces and displays the result.
4. Save the file with the same name and in the same location.
5. Switch to your Web browser and refresh the document. Notice that there are now spaces after the commas in the list of rooms and other features.

Now that you have output the first property successfully, you modify the template to display other specific properties.

DISPLAYING SPECIFIC RECORDS

You can use the startrow and endrow values to select specific records from a table, as you will see next.

To change the rows selected by the template:

1. Switch to your text editor, and then in the tag <cfloop query=“getData” startrow=“1” endrow=“1”>, change the value for the endrow attribute from 1 to **3**.
2. Save the file with the same name and in the same location, and then view the document in your Web browser and refresh the page. Scroll down the page. Three property listings appear because the QUERY loop is executed three times and displays records 1, 2, and 3 on this single Web page. Three records are selected because the start row is 1 and the end row is 3.
3. Switch to your text editor, and change the value of the startrow attribute from 1 to **3**.

4. Save the file, and then refresh the document in your Web browser. Notice that only the third property in the table is displayed this time and the values of both the startrow and endrow attributes are equal to 3.

Essentially these steps reinforce the importance of the startrow and endrow attributes. To summarize, if you use the same value for the startrow and endrow attributes, only one record is displayed from the Properties table and the position of this record corresponds to the value of these attributes. If you want a simple way to control which property is displayed, you can use a variable (for example, displayRecordNumber) to set the value of the startrow and endrow attributes. Next, you modify the template to use a variable for controlling the display.

To add a variable to control which property is displayed:

1. Switch to your text editor, click at the very beginning of line 1, press **Enter**, and then press the **Up Arrow** key to move to the new line.
2. Type **<cfset displayRecordNumber = 233>**. When ColdFusion Server executes this statement, it creates a variable named displayRecordNumber and assigns a value of 233 to it. This statement displays record number 233 in the Properties table.
3. In the CFLOOP tag, select the value **3** for the startrow attribute, and then type **#displayRecordNumber#**. When ColdFusion Server executes this statement, it uses the current value of the displayRecordNumber variable (233) as the value for the startrow attribute.
4. On the same line, replace the value 3 for the endrow attribute with **#displayRecordNumber#**. Similar to the startrow attribute, when ColdFusion Server executes this statement, it uses the current value of the displayRecordNumber variable (233) as the value for the endrow attribute. Because the startrow and endrow attributes are both set to 233, the server displays the 233rd record.
5. Save the file and refresh it in your Web browser. You are now displaying the 233rd property in the Properties table. See Figure 20-15.

If necessary, click your browser's Refresh or Reload button to load the current page.

You can display any property that you want without changing the CFML in the document by using a URL parameter. Therefore, it makes more sense to use a parameter on the URL to control which property is displayed rather than hard-coding the record number of the property to be displayed. In the following steps, you modify the detail.cfm template to use a URL parameter.

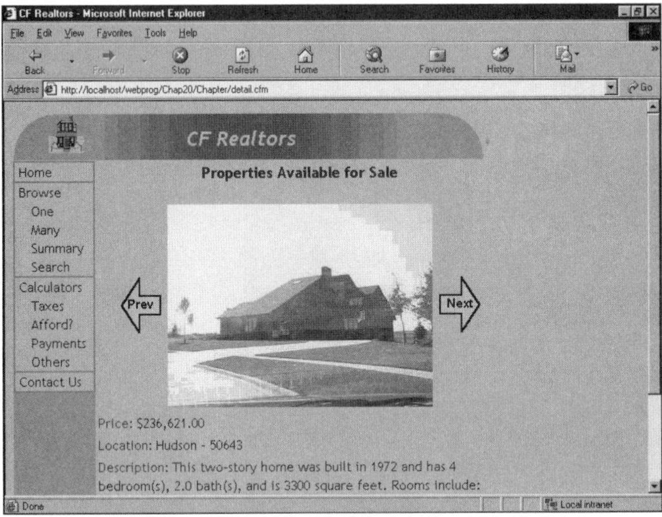

Figure 20-15 Displaying property number 233

To add processing of URL parameters to the template:

1. Switch to your text editor, click at the very beginning of line 1, press **Enter**, and then press the **Up Arrow** key to move to the new line.
2. Type **<cfparam name="URL.recNo" default="1">**. When ColdFusion Server executes this statement, it checks to see whether there is a parameter on the URL named recNo. If there is a parameter with that name, no action is taken. If there is no parameter on the URL with that name, the server creates a variable and assigns a value of 1 to it.

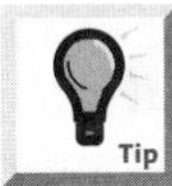

The CFPARAM tag can be used for assigning default values to URL parameters. When this document is opened in the browser without any URL parameter, the CFPARAM tag creates a variable name URL.recNo and assigns it a value of 1. Opening this document without a URL parameter is the same as opening the document with ?recNo=1 appended to the document's URL.

3. On the next line, select **233**, and then type **URL.recNo**. When ColdFusion Server executes this statement, it assigns the value of the URL parameter to the variable named displayRecordNumber. Remember that this variable sets the value of the startrow and endrow attributes in the QUERY loop to control which property is displayed.
4. Save the file, switch to your browser, select the URL in the Address bar, type **http://*your_server_name*/*work folder*/Chap20/Chapter/detail.cfm?recNo=125**, and then press **Enter**. (Be sure to substitute the name of your server and work folder as appropriate.) See Figure 20-16. You are viewing property number 125 in the Properties table. This record was selected by the parameter you added to the URL.

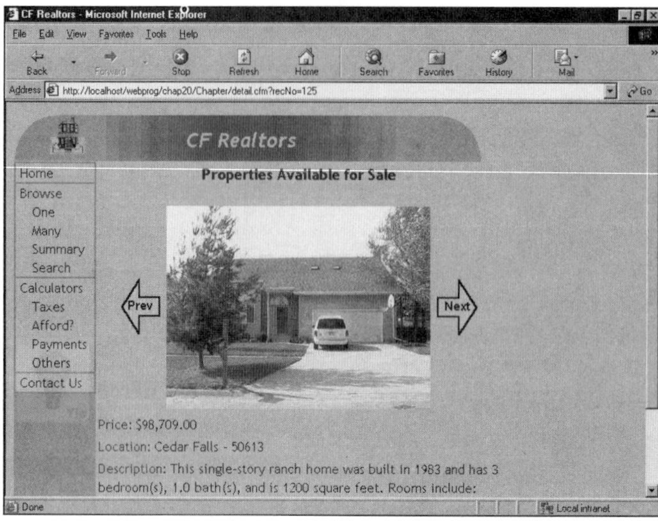

Figure 20-16 Displaying property number 125 using a URL parameter

CREATING NAVIGATION OPTIONS

The detail.cfm template contains two pictures that produce the Prev and Next arrow buttons. When this page is completed, a user can click the Prev button to return to a previous property listing selected by the query. Clicking the Next button shows the next property listing selected by the query. You need to activate these buttons to provide them with the functionality to scroll through the records selected by the query. As you are passing the record number of the property to be displayed using the recNo URL parameter, all you need are links to the same document with appropriate record numbers for the next property and the previous property. In general, if you are viewing the displayRecordNumber property, the next property is displayRecordNumber + 1 and the previous property is displayRecordNumber – 1. For example, if you are viewing the 125th property, the next property is record number 126 and the previous property is record number 124.

To activate the navigation buttons:

1. Switch to your text editor. If necessary, click at the end of the line containing <cfset displayRecordNumber = URL.recNo>, and then press **Enter** to insert a new line.
2. Type **<cfset nextProperty = displayRecordNumber + 1>**, and then press **Enter**.
3. Type **<cfset previousProperty = displayRecordNumber – 1>**.
4. Select the entire IMG tag (**<img src="prev.gif" alt="Prev" border="0">**) as shown in Figure 20-17.

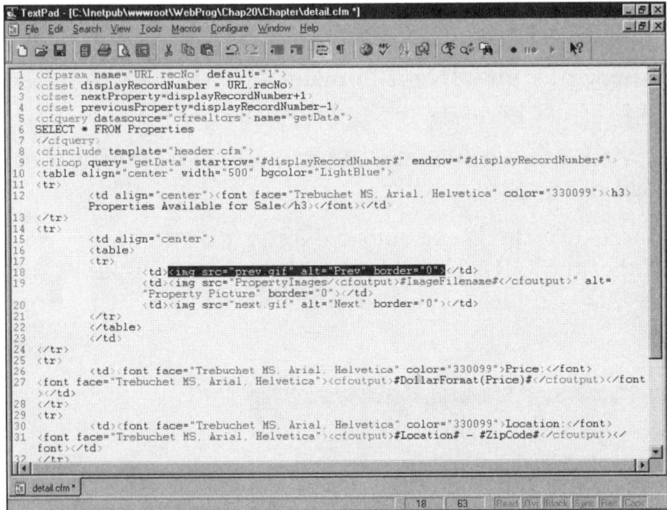

Figure 20-17 Adding navigation capabilities to detail.cfm

5. Type **<a href="detail.cfm?recNo=<cfoutput>#previousProperty# </cfoutput>"><img src="prev.gif" alt="Prev" border="0"></a>**. See Figure 20-18. You have created a hyperlink to the previous property in the Properties table.

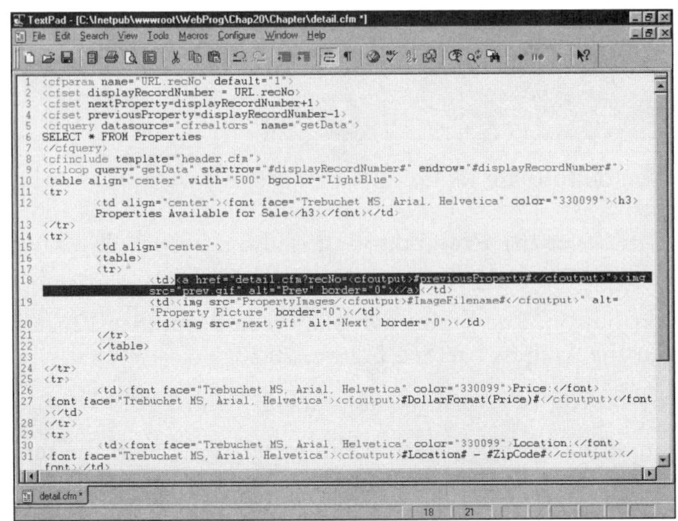

Figure 20-18 Anchor tags inserted around the Prev button image

20

6. Scroll down, similarly select the entire IMG tag for the Next button, and type **<a href="detail.cfm?recNo=<cfoutput>#nextProperty#</cfoutput>"> <img src="next.gif" alt="Next" border="0"></a>**. You have created a hyperlink to the next property in the Properties table.
7. Save the file, switch to your browser, and then click the **Refresh** or **Reload** button to reload the page.
8. Move the pointer over the **Next** button. Notice that the image is now a hyperlink and that the URL in the browser's status bar displays ...recNo=126. The hyperlink that you created now uses the next record as its target. See Figure 20-19.

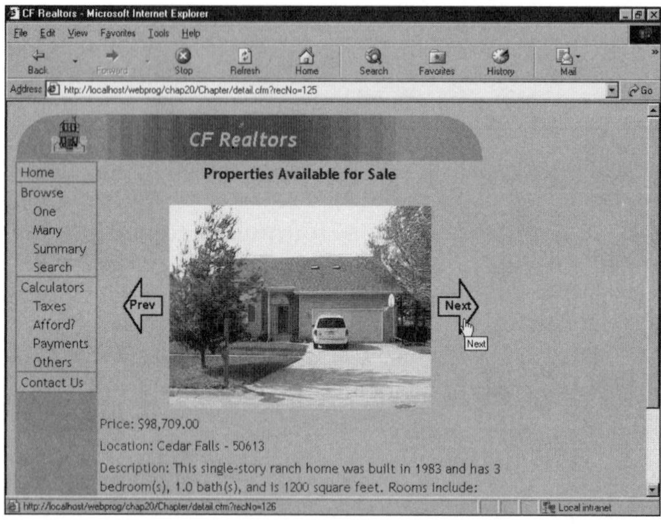

Figure 20-19 Navigation buttons are set up

9. Move the pointer over the **Prev** button. It is also a hyperlink, and the URL in the browser's status bar displays ...recNo=124.
10. Click the **Next** button. The browser displays record number 126, as indicated by the URL in the Address bar. See Figure 20-20.
11. Click the **Prev** button to return to the previous record (125).
12. Navigate through the list of properties and experiment with the template.

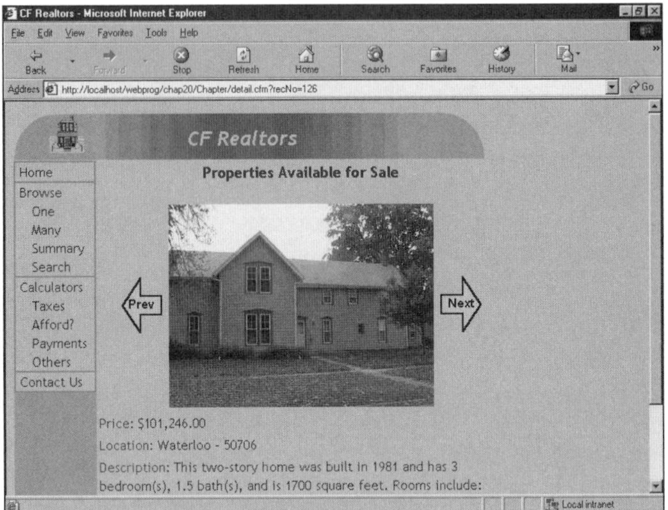

Figure 20-20 Record number 126 is displayed

Finally, consider what would happen if the first property is displayed and a user clicks the Prev button. If the first property is displayed, the previous property's record number is computed as displayRecordNumber – 1, and the result would be zero. The server would be requesting a document with URL ...display.cfm?recNo=0. ColdFusion Server would generate an error because the startrow attribute of the QUERY loop would be zero, which isn't a valid request. To design the template to prevent this error, you have to use a CFIF statement and display the previous image only when the variable named previousProperty has a value greater than zero (GT 0).

Similarly, consider what would happen if the last property is currently displayed and a user clicks the Next button. The startrow attribute would be greater than the number of records in the Query object and the statements in the QUERY loop could not be executed, resulting in the display of a blank page. To fix this potential problem, you have to use a CFIF statement and display the Next button only when the value of the variable named nextProperty is less than the number of records in the query's record set (LE to the number of records in the record set). Obviously, the next question is how do you determine the number of records in a Query object. When ColdFusion Server executes the CFQUERY tag with the name query_name, it creates a variable named query_name.recordcount and sets its value to the number of records in the Query object. You can use this variable in the CFIF statement for the Next button.

To selectively display the navigation buttons:

1. Switch to your text editor, and then click between the opening TD and A tags on the line that creates the Prev button (...<td>|<a href="detail.cfm?recNo=<cfoutput>#previousProperty#</cfoutput>">...).

2. Type **<cfif previousProperty GT 0>**.

3. Click between the closing A and TD tags on the same line, and then type **</cfif>**. See Figure 20-21. When ColdFusion Server executes this CFIF statement, it displays the Prev button only if the value of the previousProperty variable is greater than zero.

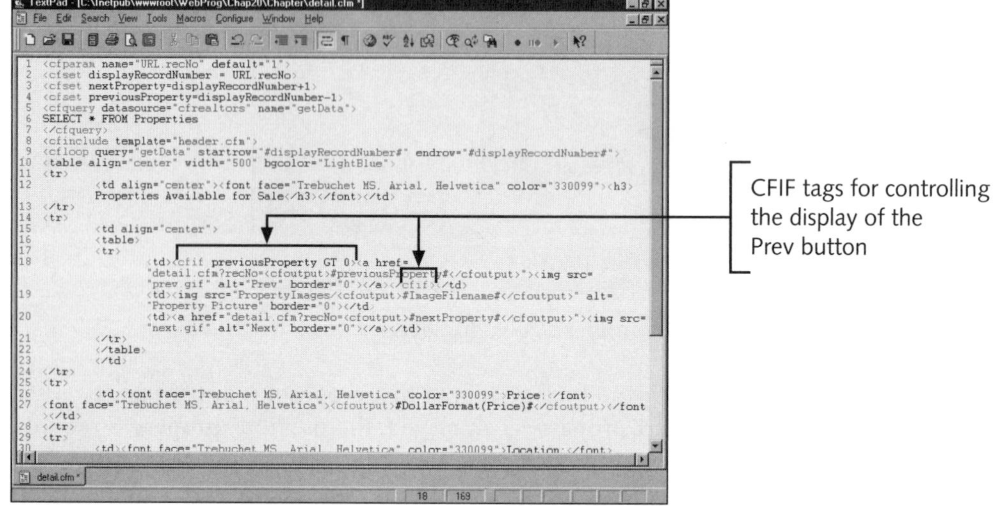

Figure 20-21 Controlling the display of the Prev button

4. Click between the opening TD and A tags on the line that outputs the Next button, and then type **<cfif nextProperty LE getData.recordcount>**.

5. Click between the closing A and TD tags on the same line, and then type **</cfif>**. See Figure 20-22. When ColdFusion Server executes this CFIF statement, it displays the Next button only if the value of the nextProperty variable is less than or equal to the number of records in the record set.

6. Save the file, switch to your browser, edit the URL in the Address bar to **http://*your_server_name*/*work folder*/Chap20/Chapter/detail.cfm?recNo=1**, and then press **Enter**. (Be sure to substitute the name of your server and work folder as appropriate.) See Figure 20-23. The browser displays the first record. Notice that the Prev button is not displayed.

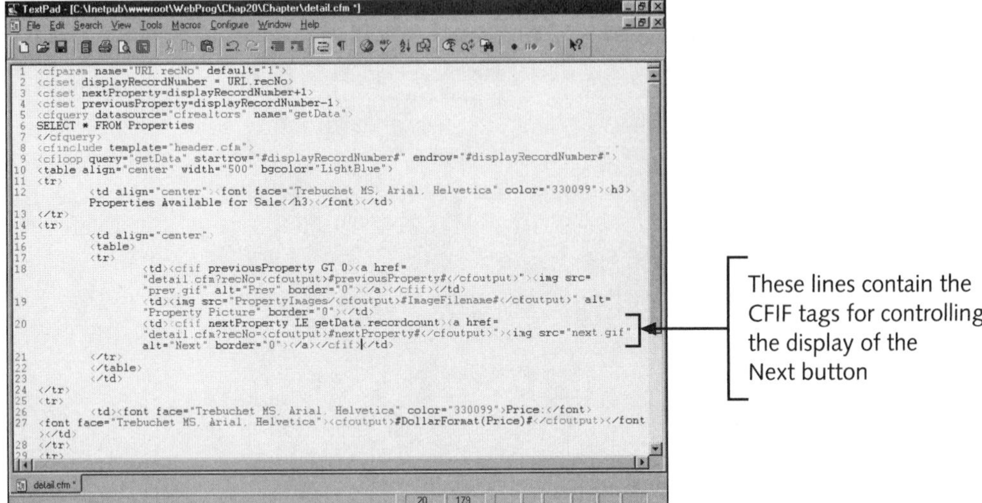

Figure 20-22 Controlling the display of the Next button

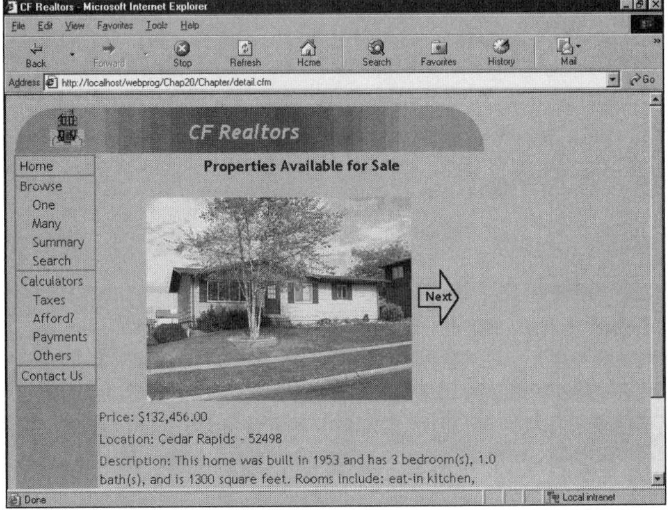

Figure 20-23 Record number 1 displayed in the browser

7. Click the **Next** button. See Figure 20-24. Notice that both buttons are displayed now.

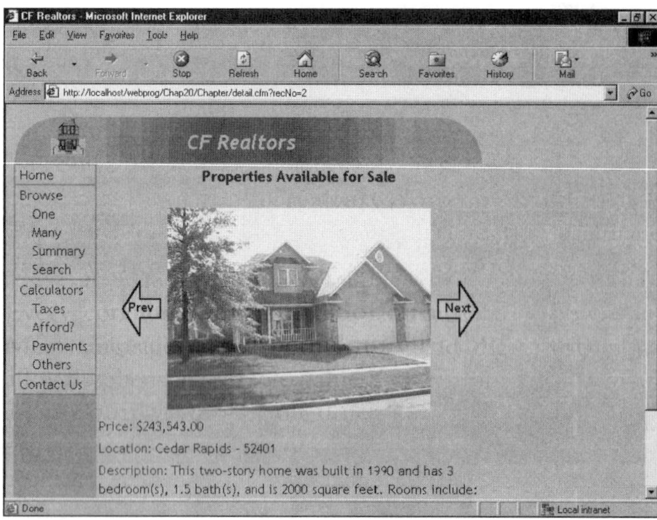

Figure 20-24 Record number 2 displayed in the browser

8. Edit the URL in the Address bar so it reads **http://*your_server_name*/*work folder*/Chap20/Chapter/detail.cfm?recNo=310**, and then press **Enter**. (Be sure to substitute the name of your server and work folder as appropriate.) See Figure 20-25. Notice that the Next button is not displayed. This is the last property in the table and the value of variable nextProperty is 311, which is not less than or equal to the value of the variable getData.recordcount (310, or the number of records in the table).
9. Close all programs.

Your template now displays one property at a time (one record at a time). Later, you will add a hyperlink to detail.cfm in header.cfm so that it is available in the menu. You extracted all the fields from one record and displayed them using an attractive layout, and also provided buttons to navigate through the record set. In other words, you generated a columnar report; all columns from a particular record are displayed. In the next section, you learn about tabular report generation.

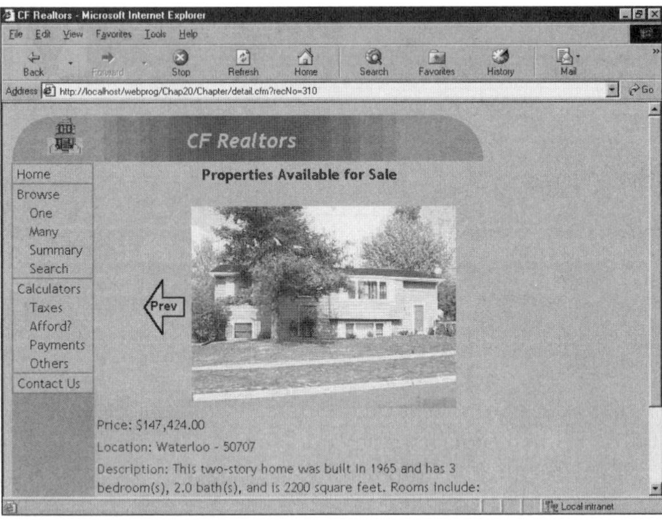

Figure 20-25 Record number 310 displayed in the browser

GENERATING TABULAR REPORTS

When multiple rows (records) are extracted from database tables and displayed in the form of a table on one page, you are generating a tabular report. Typically, you have navigation buttons to advance to the next set of records or return to the previous set of records.

Fran is pleased with the detail.cfm ColdFusion template that allows potential clients to browse through the properties available for sale one at a time. However, she is concerned about clients having to spend a lot of time viewing all of the properties in the Properties table. She now wants you to design a template that displays four records at a time in the form of a table with just the price, location, and a thumbnail of the property (smaller version of the picture). The template should also allow potential clients to view a page with more property details if they want. She has sketched her requirements, which appear in Figure 20-26. Your task now is to create this template.

To extract data from a table and display it as a tabular report:

1. Start your text editor, and then open **tabular.cfm** from the Chap20\Chapter folder in your student data files.

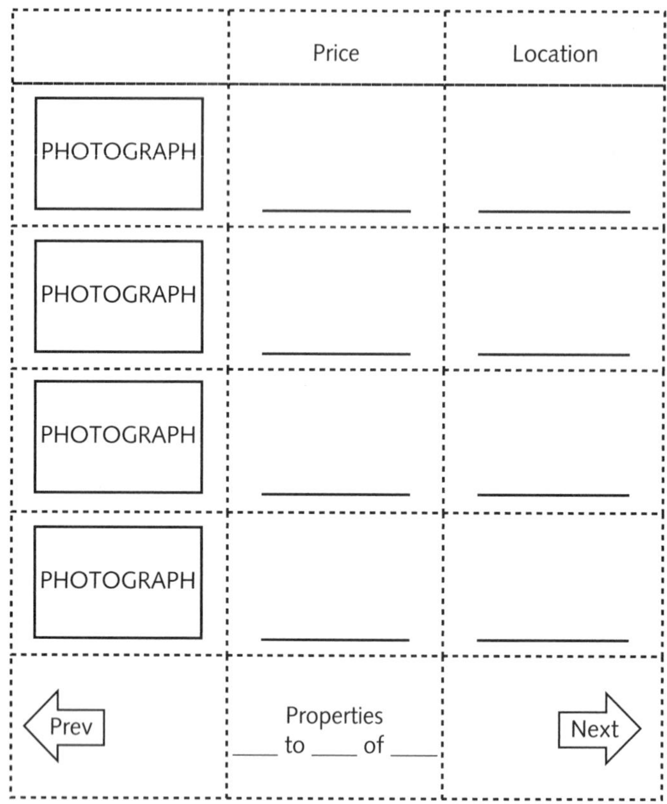

Figure 20-26 Sketch of the tabular report

2. Study the HTML code, and then view the document in your Web browser by typing **http://*your_server_name*/*work folder*/Chap20/Chapter/tabular.cfm** in its Address bar. (Be sure to substitute the name of your server and work folder as appropriate.) See Figure 20-27. Compare this with the requirements sketched in Figure 20-26, noting that this table has only one row instead of four. Your task is to enclose the row of the table inside the QUERY loop that loops four times to display four rows in the table, and at the same time display each property's information in a single row.
3. Switch to your text editor, click at the very beginning of line 1, press **Enter**, and then press the **Up Arrow** key to move to the new line.

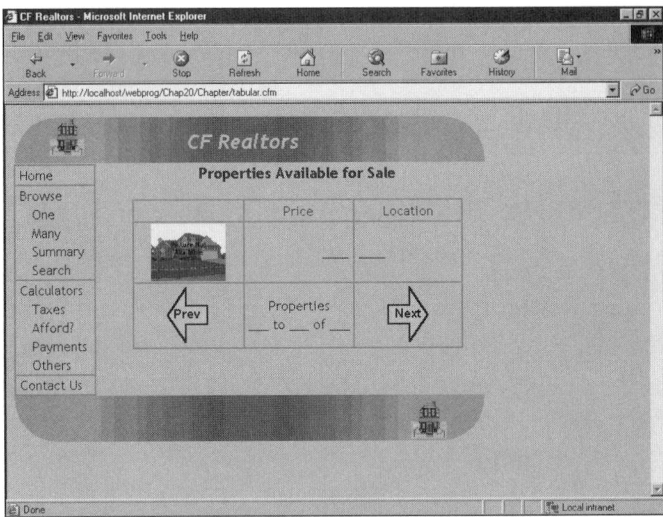

Figure 20-27 Web page displayed by the initial tabular.cfm

4. Type **<cfparam name="URL.recNo" default="1">**, and then press **Enter**. When ColdFusion Server executes this statement, it checks to see if there is a parameter named recNo on the URL. If there is one, no action is taken. If there is no parameter on the URL, it creates a variable named URL.recNo and assigns it a value of 1. In other words, if you type in the URL for this template without a parameter, it is the same as typing the URL with the parameter recNo=1.

5. Type **<cfset startrow = URL.recNo>**, and then press **Enter**. The record number that is passed on the URL is the number of the property that is displayed first. When ColdFusion Server executes this statement, it assigns the value of the URL parameter recNo to a newly created variable named startrow. You want to display a total of four properties at a time, so the end row is startrow+3.

6. Type **<cfset endrow = startrow + 3>**, and then press **Enter**. When the server executes this statement, it creates a variable named endrow and assigns it a value that is equal to the sum of the value of the startrow and the number 3.

   Your next task is to compute variables used for navigating from one set of records to another set. If records startrow to endrow are being displayed, the first record in the next set of records is startrow+4.

7. Type **<cfset nextProperty = startrow + 4>**, and then press **Enter**. The first record of the previous set of records is startrow-4.

8. Type **<cfset previousProperty = startrow – 4>**, and then press **Enter**. Finally, you need to execute the SQL SELECT query to select all the records in the properties table.
9. Type **<cfquery datasource="CFRealtors" name="getData">**, and then press **Enter**.
10. Type **SELECT * FROM Properties**, and then press **Enter**.
11. Type **</cfquery>** to close the QUERY loop.
12. Save the file and refresh it in your Web browser. Notice that the output is still the same. Fix any errors that appear.

You have initialized some variables and executed a CFQUERY tag. The output remains the same because you have not used any output statements. In the next set of steps you add the QUERY loop flow-control statement and output the values of fields at the appropriate points.

To output the values extracted using a CFQUERY and display them:

1. Switch to your text editor, and carefully study the table. Notice that there are three rows in the table. The top row is the header row. The middle row displays the image of the property with its data, and the bottom row displays the navigation buttons and the record number. The middle row should be repeatedly executed in the QUERY loop.
2. Click in the blank line between the top row and the middle row, and type **<cfloop query="getData" startrow="#startrow#" endrow="#endrow#">**.
3. Click in the blank line between the middle row and the bottom row, and type **</cfloop>**.

   When ColdFusion Server executes these tags, it displays the data from the Query object starting with the startrow record and ending with the endrow record. Four rows are displayed: startrow, startrow+1, startrow+2, and startrow+3. The variable endrow has a value equal to startrow+3.
4. In the middle row of the table, select **NA.jpg**, and then type **<cfoutput>#ImageFilename#</cfoutput>**.
5. Select ________________ in the second column, and type **<cfoutput>#DollarFormat(Price)#</cfoutput>**.
6. Select ________________ in the third column and type **<cfoutput>#Location#</cfoutput>**.
7. Scroll down if necessary and in the third row of the table, select ________________ **to** ________________ **of** ________________, and then type **<cfoutput>#startrow# to #endrow# of #getData.recordcount#</cfoutput>**. See Figure 20-28.

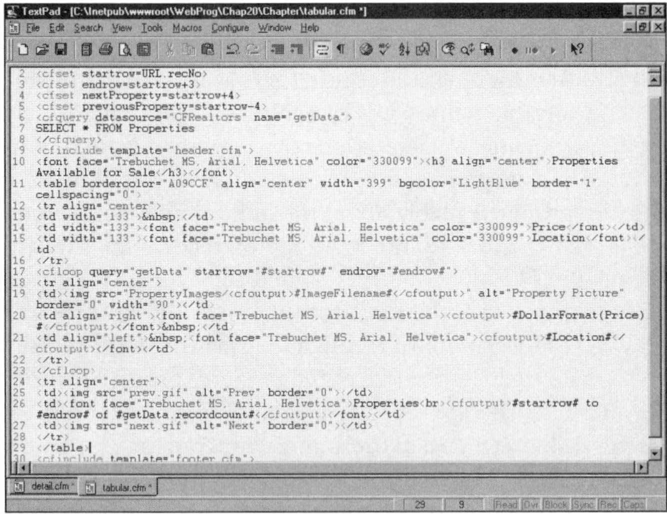

Figure 20-28 Edited tabular.cfm

8. Save the document.
9. Switch to your Web browser, and refresh **http://*your_server_name/work folder/*Chap20/Chapter/tabular.cfm**. (Be sure to substitute the name of your server and work folder as appropriate.) See Figure 20-29.

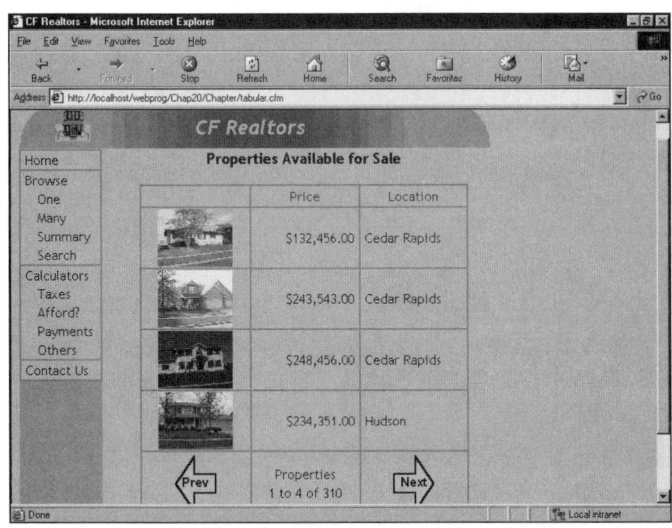

Figure 20-29 Web page displayed by tabular.cfm showing properties 1 to 4

10. Switch to your text editor, and study the code.

The Web browser sends a request to the Web server for tabular.cfm. The Web server recognizes that it is a ColdFusion document and transfers control to the ColdFusion server. ColdFusion Server executes the document. Because there is no parameter on the URL, ColdFusion Server creates a variable named URL.recNo and assigns it a value of 1 when it processes the CFPARAM tag. Variables startrow, endrow, nextProperty, and previousProperty are created and assigned appropriate values. The CFQUERY is executed and all the records from the properties table are extracted. Variable getData.recordcount is created and assigned a value equal to the number of records in the query. Then, ColdFusion Server outputs the HTML code as is. When the QUERY loop is executed, the table row is output four times with the data from the first four records in the Query object. Notice that the WIDTH attribute of the IMG tag has been set to 90. When the Web browser processes this tag, it reduces the size of the property image. The price, location, and other variables are output at the appropriate locations to render the Web page as a tabular report. Your next task is to make the navigation buttons operational. Also, similar to what you did in the columnar report, you have to hide the Prev button at the beginning of the records in the table and hide the Next button at the end of records in the table.

To activate the navigation buttons:

1. In the third row of the table, click to the left of the IMG tag for the Prev image.
2. Type **<cfif previousProperty GT 0><a href="tabular.cfm?recNo=<cfoutput>#previousProperty#</cfoutput>">**.
3. Click to the right of the IMG tag, and type **</a></cfif>**.
4. In the third row of the table, click to the left of the IMG tag for the Next image.
5. Type **<cfif nextProperty LE getData.recordcount><a href="tabular.cfm?recNo=<cfoutput>#nextProperty#</cfoutput>">**.
6. Click to the right of the IMG tag, and type **</a></cfif>**. See Figure 20-30.
7. Save the file with the same name and in the same location, switch to your Web browser, and then refresh tabular.cfm.
8. Navigate the record set by clicking the **Next** and **Prev** buttons. Notice that the record number in the URL changes in increments of four, because you are viewing four records at a time.

To decrease the download times for the images, typically you need two graphics for each property. One would be a regular picture such as the ones on the student data disk, and others would be smaller versions of these files, or thumbnail graphics. To accommodate this, you need another field in the Properties table named thumbnailFilename.

Your final task here is to make each of these smaller graphics a hyperlink so that clients can open a page with more details about the selected properties by clicking the picture.

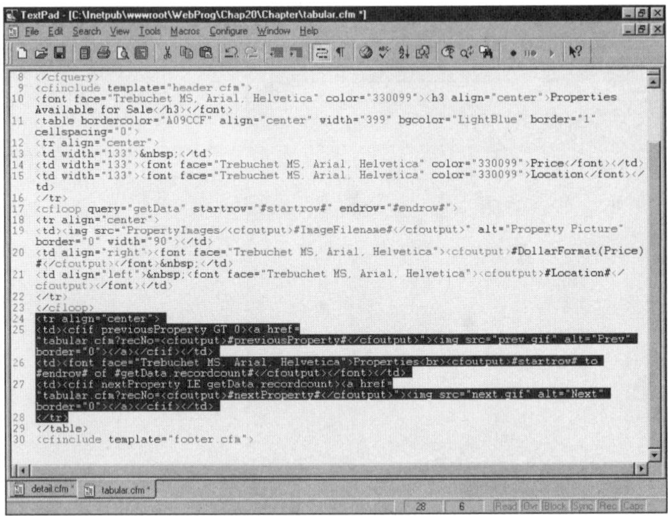

Figure 20-30 tabular.cfm with activated naviation buttons

To create picture hyperlinks:

1. Switch to your text editor, and in the second row of the table, click to the left of the IMG tag for the property picture. Similar to the recordcount property of a query, the currentrow property of query has a value equal to the position of the current record in the query object. You link this image to the detail.cfm template with an appropriate value for the URL parameter. Remember that you created detail.cfm earlier in the chapter.

2. Type **<a href="detail.cfm?recNo=<cfoutput>#getData.currentrow# </cfoutput>">**.

3. Click to the right of the IMG tag, and type **</a>**.

4. Save the file with the same name and in the same location.

5. Switch to your Web browser, and refresh **tabular.cfm**. Point to the second picture. Notice that the pointer changes to the hyperlink pointer, indicating that this picture is a hyperlink. See Figure 20-31.

6. Click the second **picture**. The detailed Web page for that property opens.

You have successfully extracted multiple records from a database table and displayed them in an HTML table. You have provided buttons to navigate from one set of records to another set. Further, each property picture is a hyperlink to a Web page that displays detailed information about that property. Such a capability in which a user can look up detailed information from a summary is known as a **data drill-down** capability.

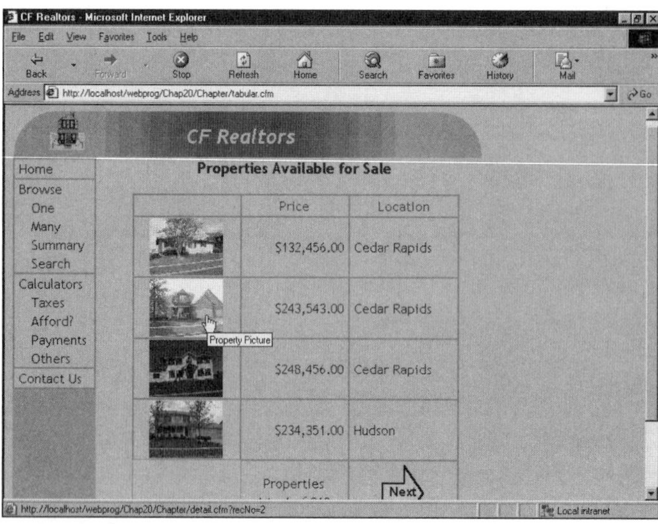

Figure 20-31 Tabular report with hyperlinks

GENERATING GROUP TOTALS REPORTS

In the previous two sections, you learned how to extract data from database tables and display one record at a time and how to display multiple records in a tabular format. In this section, you will display records in a tabular format and also compute statistics about groups of records to summarize data. This kind of reporting is useful for designing information systems that allow business managers to monitor organizational performance.

Fran wants you to design a few templates to help her better understand business trends so she can effectively manage her organization. She wants you to design a template that displays the total of all property prices, the average property price, the number of listed properties in a single location, and the properties with the maximum and minimum prices in each location where CF Realtors is currently listing properties for sale. To provide Fran with this information, you need to create a group totals report. Earlier, one of your project members created a template to display the required statistics for the properties listed in Hudson. You need to change the template to dynamically create reports for all locations.

To create a group totals report:

1. Switch to your text editor, and close all open files.
2. Open the file **statistics.cfm** from the Chap20\Chapter folder.
3. Switch to your Web browser, open **statistics.cfm**, and preview the page. Notice that the page lists the number of properties currently for sale in Hudson, along with the sum, average, maximum, and minimum price for all properties listed in Hudson.

4. Switch to your text editor, and then carefully study the code that created this template. This template extracts data from the Properties table and displays it in an HTML table. The SQL SELECT statement uses a WHERE clause to select only those properties from the city of Hudson. The QUERY loop outputs the information in an HTML table. Notice that you are using only one set of CFOUTPUT tags for enclosing all the variables. Your task now is to display summary information for all the locations. Because locations may be added or deleted from the CF Realtors sales area, and subsequently from the Properties table, you need to query the database for all locations with properties listed.
5. Click at the very beginning of line 1, press **Enter**, and then press the **Up Arrow** key to move the insertion point to the new line.
6. Type **<cfquery datasource="cfrealtors" name="getLocations">**, and then press **Enter**.
7. Type **SELECT DISTINCT Location FROM Properties**, and then press **Enter**.
8. Type **</cfquery>** to close the query tag.
9. Click at the end of the CFINCLUDE tag on the next line, and press **Enter**.
10. Type **<cfloop query="getLocations">**. You are designing a template with nested query loops. The outer loop loops over all the locations, and the inner loop displays summary information for each location. Note that the inner loop loops only once for each outer loop because there is only one record in the Query object.
11. Click at the end of the line containing the closing CFLOOP tag for the inner loop at the bottom of the template, press **Enter**, and then type **</cfloop>** to close the outer query loop.

The next step is to use the variable named Location (in the inner loop), which is created when ColdFusion Server executes the outer loop.

To output the Location in the outer loop, and to use it in the inner query:

1. Select the word **Hudson** in the H3 header tags, and then type **<cfoutput> #Location#</cfoutput>**. When ColdFusion Server executes this statement, it displays the value of the Location field in the current record as a heading for the table.

   Now you have to change the SQL in the inner loop to display summary information from the location in the current record.

2. In the inner CFQUERY tag, select the word **Hudson** in the WHERE clause, and then type **#Location#**. See Figure 20-32.

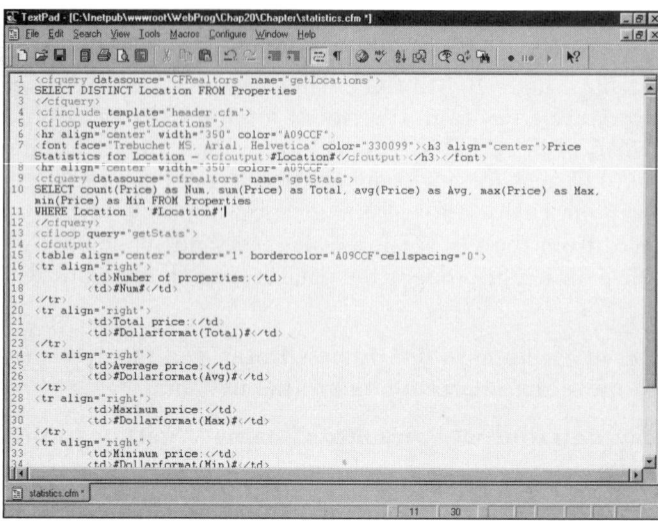

Figure 20-32 Editing statistics.cfm in your text editor

3. Save the file, and refresh your Web browser. See Figure 20-33.

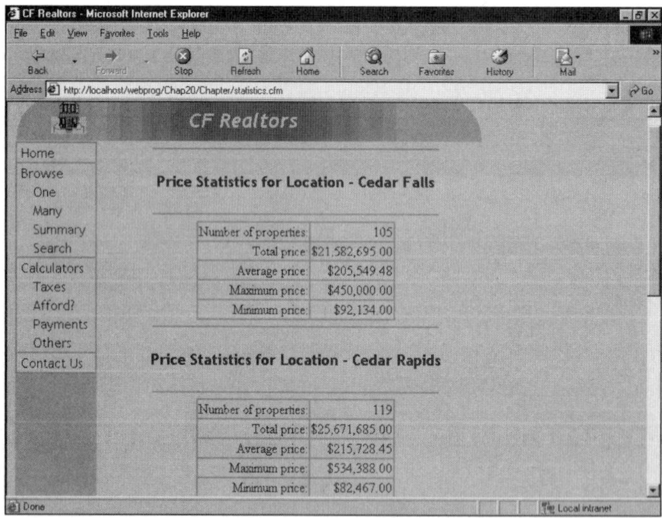

Figure 20-33 Web page displayed by the completed statistics.cfm template

The statistics.cfm template contains the following SQL statement:

```
SELECT count(Price) as Num, sum(Price) as Total, avg(Price) as Avg, max(Price)
as Max, min(Price) as Min FROM Properties
WHERE Location = '#Location#'
```

When ColdFusion Server executes this statement, the server substitutes the value of the variable Location for #Location#, and then it executes the SQL statement. This is a very powerful technique that allows you to create dynamic SQL statements. You are changing the SQL statement that is executed each time the outer QUERY loop is executed. This technique is also useful for building the capability of interactive data extraction into the design of a Web page.

Creating Templates for Extracting Data Interactively

By using variables enclosed in pound signs in CFQUERY tags, you can dynamically change the SQL SELECT statements being executed. This allows you to extract data from databases based on user requests.

Based on the feedback received from some of CF Realtors' clients, Cal and Fran have requested you to design a form that narrows the number of properties displayed in the detail.cfm template. Clients have indicated that price, location, and number of bedrooms are very important criteria when they search for a new house. You have to design both the form as well as the form handler for this application.

To design the search criteria form by dynamically populating a select box:

1. Switch to your text editor, and close all open documents.
2. Open **searchForm.cfm** from the Chap20\Chapter folder.
3. Switch to your Web browser and preview the page. This page lets a user enter a maximum amount for their home purchase and a minimum number of bedrooms. You add the information to collect data about the desired location next.
4. Switch back to your text editor, and then carefully examine the code that created this template. This template contains a form with the ACTION attribute set to a form handler named processSearch.cfm, which you will create later. There are two text boxes with input controls named maxPrice and minBedrooms, which collect the maximum price and the number of bedrooms desired by the client. The form also contains a submit button with the caption "Find Properties." Because you want to limit the locations to only those available in the Properties table, you extract data from the database and populate a select box with all possible locations that are stored in the database.
5. Click at the very beginning of line 1, and create a blank line, type **<cfquery datasource="cfrealtors" name="getLocations">** in the new line, and then press **Enter**.
6. Type **SELECT DISTINCT Location FROM Properties**, and then press **Enter**.
7. Type **</cfquery>**. See Figure 20-34.
8. Click at the end of the line containing <td align="right"> below the cell containing Location:, press **Enter**, type **<select name="Location"> <cfloop query="getLocations"><cfoutput>**, and then press **Enter**.
9. Type **<option value="#Location#">#Location#**, and then press **Enter**.

20

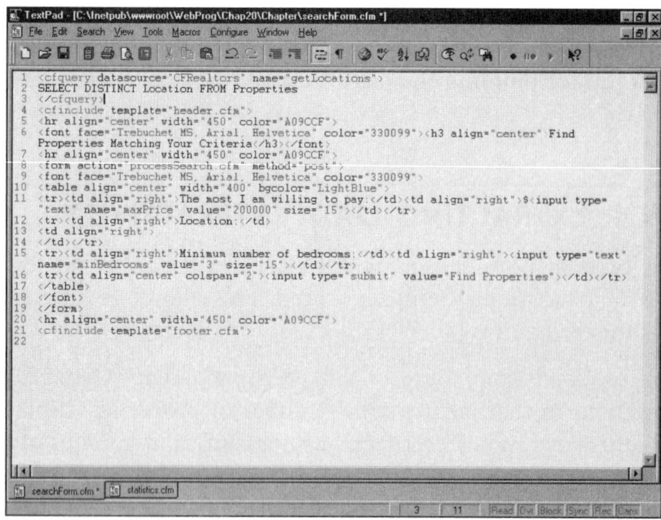

Figure 20-34 Editing searchForm.cfm in your text editor

10. Type **</cfoutput></cfloop></select>**.
11. Save the file and open it in your Web browser.
12. Click the **Location** list arrow. See Figure 20-35. You have extracted data from a database table and populated a select box. The SELECT statement uses the DISTINCT operator and the Location field. The query loop outputs options in the select box—one for each record in the Query object. You can't submit the form yet, however, because there is no form handler.

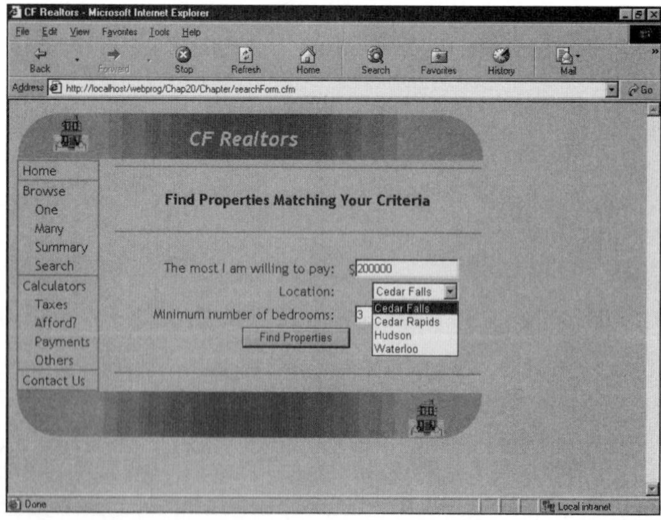

Figure 20-35 Web page displayed by searchForm.cfm

The next task is to design the form handler for this data. The form handler for this form is going to be very similar to the detail.cfm application. You need to add a WHERE clause to the SQL SELECT statement that utilizes the data the user enters in the form. You need properties with prices lower than the value entered and located in the requested location with the minimum number of bedrooms specified. The WHERE clause for this situation is WHERE Price<=#maxPrice# AND Location='#Location#' AND NumBedrooms>=#minBedrooms#. You also have to keep in mind that there are navigation buttons for looking at the next property and the previous property, and you need to make the template extract data matching these criteria even when those buttons are clicked. You have to design the template to handle data posted by the form as well as be able to process data passed as URL parameters.

To design the form handler for dynamic extraction of data:

1. Switch to your text editor, open the file **detail.cfm**, and then save it as **processSearch.cfm** in the Chap20\Chapter folder.
2. Click at the end of the line containing the SELECT statement (SELECT * FROM Properties), press the **spacebar**, and then type **WHERE Price<=#maxPrice# AND Location='#Location#' AND NumBedrooms>=#minBedrooms#**. See Figure 20-36. Notice that you did not type the "FORM." prefix for the form variables. Even though you have been using FORM.control_name as the format for accessing the data entered in form controls, the FORM. prefix is optional. Whenever a variable is used, ColdFusion Server checks to see if there are any regular variables of that name. If there aren't any, it checks to see if there are any FORM variables or URL parameters of that name and uses them if found. Similarly, the prefix URL. for accessing URL parameters is also optional. You have to use the prefixes whenever possible to avoid confusion for anybody reading your code. Here you are not using the prefixes because you are going to use form variables once in the SELECT statement, and later you want to use URL parameters when the user clicks the navigation buttons. When ColdFusion Server executes this statement, it substitutes the values entered by the user in the WHERE clause, and then the SQL SELECT statement extracts only those properties that match the criteria specified by the user.
3. Save the **processSearch.cfm** file.
4. Switch to your Web browser. Do not change the price or the number of bedrooms, select **Hudson** as the location, and then click the **Find Properties** button. See Figure 20-37. Notice that the first property is located in Hudson. Notice that the URL in the Address bar of your Web browser shows the name of the form handler, processSearch.cfm. Move the pointer over the Next button and notice that it is still linked to the detail.cfm file. If you click the Next button, the next property in the Properties table is selected, instead of the next property located in Hudson. You need to change the links so that they point to the processSearch.cfm template and pass the user-entered criteria as URL parameters.

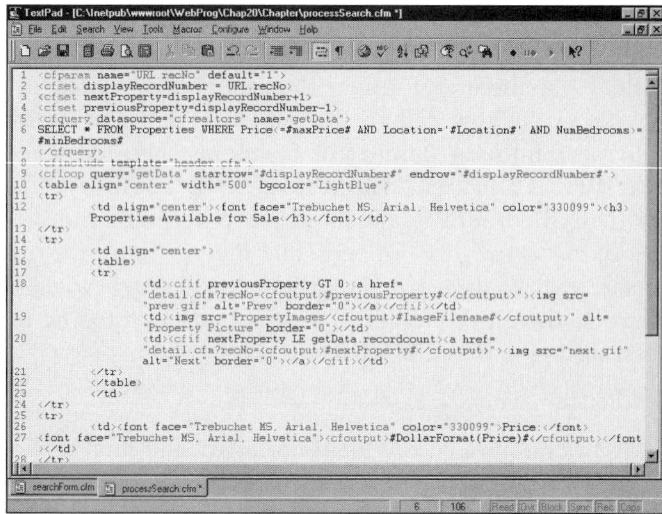

Figure 20-36 Revising the SELECT statement

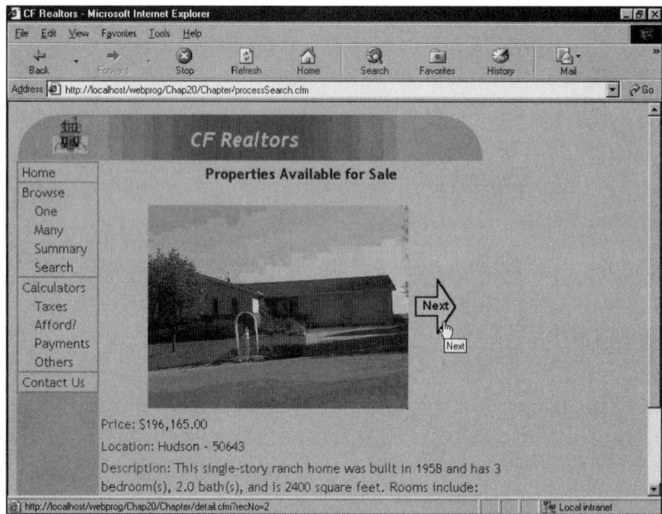

Figure 20-37 Output for properties in Hudson

5. Switch to your text editor, and in the anchor tag for the previous property, change the value of the HREF attribute to **processSearch.cfm?recNo=<cfoutput>#previousProperty#&maxPrice=#maxPrice#&Location=#URLEncodedFormat(Location)#&minBedrooms=#minBedrooms#</cfoutput>**.

   This template needs the criteria that the user entered when the user clicked the Next button. You are passing the values entered as URL parameters. The second time this template is executed, the SQL SELECT statement processes the variables that have been passed as parameters on the URL. This is the reason you did not use the URL. prefix or FORM. prefix for these variables. The first time they are the data the user enters directly in the form, and the second time around it is the data passed on the URL. Notice that you are using the URLEncodedFormat function for the location variable, which allows for the possibility that there could be spaces in the Location. Next you encode it to do so. It is a good practice to enclose all parameters passed on URLs in this fashion. You can save some typing by not using this function on parameters that are numbers.

6. In the anchor tag for the next property, change the value of the HREF attribute to **processSearch.cfm?recNo=<cfoutput> #nextProperty#&maxPrice=#maxPrice#&Location=#URLEncodedFormat(Location)#&minBedrooms=#minBedrooms#</cfoutput>**.
7. Save the **processSearch.cfm** file, and browse the **searchForm.cfm** file again. Select **Hudson** as the location, do not change the price and bedroom default values, and then click the **Find Properties** button. Click the **Next** button until you see all seven properties that match your criteria. Notice the URL when navigating among the properties. You can also experiment by changing the price and number of bedroom values, and then clicking the **Find Properties** button.

   Finally, you have to create links to all the files you created in this chapter in the header.cfm file under the Browse section.

8. Open **header.cfm** in your text editor and create a hyperlink to **detail.cfm** for the option **One**, to **tabular.cfm** for option **Many**, to **statistics.cfm** for option **Summary**, and to **seachForm.cfm** for option **Search**.
9. Refresh your Web page, and click each link.
10. Close your browser and your text editor.

This chapter demonstrates powerful features of ColdFusion Server. You extracted data from databases and published it in the form of Web pages. You created columnar reports, tabular reports, and group total reports. Further, you built interactive Web sites that respond to user requests and extract data.

Chapter Summary

- Open Database Connectivity (ODBC) is a Microsoft standard for connecting applications to databases. You use ColdFusion Administrator to set up ODBC data sources, which you can then access using ColdFusion.
- Extracting data from databases and publishing it on the Web is a two-part process. The CFQUERY tag is used for executing SQL SELECT statements to create record sets with data extracted from databases. A QUERY loop created using the CFLOOP tag is used for implementing a repetition flow-control structure to access and display data from all the records in the record set.

- When you present complete information (all or most fields) about an entity one record at a time, you are generating a columnar report. This report is useful for presenting all the details about a particular entity. Typically, navigation buttons are provided to navigate from one record to another.
- When you present partial information or all information about multiple records in the form of a table, you are generating a tabular report. Typically, navigation buttons are provided to navigate from one set of records to another.
- Group total reports are useful for designing management information systems. Tabular reports are presented along with summaries of critical data items.
- ColdFusion allows you to use variables enclosed in pound signs in CFQUERY tags with included SQL statements. This feature allows you to build interactive data extraction features in Web sites.

Review Questions

1. What is ODBC?
   a. Optimal Data Broadcasting Criteria
   b. Open Database Connectivity
   c. Other Data Blocking Constraints
   d. none of these
2. The two-step process for extracting data from databases and publishing it on a Web site is:
   a. Create an ODBC connection, and write the CFML for publishing the data.
   b. Use a CFQUERY tag to extract data and a QUERY loop to publish it.
   c. Design the database, and then create an ODBC connection.
   d. Enter data and then extract it.
3. Where is the data stored after it is extracted with CFML?
   a. in the database
   b. in the client computer
   c. in a cookie
   d. in computer memory
4. What CFLOOP attributes are required to design a QUERY loop?
   a. QUERY
   b. DATASOURCE and NAME
   c. QUERY, STARTROW, and ENDROW
   d. DEFAULT and NAME

5. How do you display the total number of records in a Query object named query_name?
   a. <cfoutput>#query_name.recNo#</cfoutput>
   b. <cfoutput>#query_name#</cfoutput>
   c. <cfoutput>#query_name.currentrow#</cfoutput>
   d. <cfoutput>#query_name.recordcount#</cfoutput>
6. What is a columnar report?
   a. a report that displays data from one record at a time
   b. a report that displays data in the form of columns
   c. a report that displays all the fieldnames (column names) from a database table
   d. a report that displays data in a table
7. How do you design a navigation mechanism for a columnar report?
   a. You use CFIF statements.
   b. You use the STARTROW and the ENDROW attributes of the CFLOOP tag.
   c. You use a URL parameter.
   d. all of these
8. When you restrict navigation past the end of the records in a table, what is the name of the query variable needed to accomplish this?
   a. currentrow
   b. displayRecordNo
   c. number_of_records
   d. recordcount
9. What is a tabular report?
   a. a report that displays data from one record at a time
   b. a report that displays multiple records in a table
   c. a report that displays all the fieldnames (column names) from a database table
   d. none of these
10. What is the difference between the navigation design for tabular reports and columnar reports?
   a. both are the same
   b. In columnar reports the next record number and the previous record number differ by two, and in tabular reports they differ by twice the number of rows in the table.
   c. In columnar reports you use only the STARTROW attribute, and in tabular reports you use both the STARTROW and the ENDROW attributes.
   d. You don't need a CFLOOP in columnar reports because you are displaying only one record at a time.

11. What is the name of the variable created prior to each execution of the statements inside a QUERY loop that identifies the number of the record being processed?
    a. currentrow
    b. thisrecord
    c. thisrow
    d. recordcount
12. What is a data drill-down capability in information systems design?
    a. to navigate from one Web site to another using hyperlinks
    b. to navigate from one record to another record in a database
    c. to navigate from the summary to a detailed description
    d. to navigate from a report displaying data from one table to one displaying data from another table
13. What is a group totals report?
    a. a report with aggregate summary data
    b. a report that displays a group of records
    c. a report that typically uses two QUERY loops
    d. a and c
14. How do you build a capability for interactively extracting data from databases using ColdFusion?
    a. Use a dynamic SQL statement with variables in #s.
    b. Use a form for the user to enter data.
    c. Use a QUERY loop to create a select box.
    d. a and b
15. A query named getBanks extracts columns BankID and BankName from a database table. Give the code for the QUERY loop to dynamically populate a select box named Bank. Use the BankName for the description and the BankID as the value for the options.
    a. <select name=“Bank”><cfloop query=“getBanks”><cfoutput>
<option value=“#BankID#”>#BankName#
</cfoutput></cfloop></select>
    b. <select name=“BankName”><cfloop query=“getBanks”><cfoutput>
<option>#Bank#
</cfoutput></cfloop></select>

c. <select name="Bank"><cfloop query="getBanks"><cfoutput>
<option value="#BankName#">#BankID#
</cfoutput></cfloop></select>

d. <select name="BankName"><cfloop query="#BankName#"><cfoutput>
<option>#BankID#
</cfoutput></cfloop></select>

Hands-on Exercises

Exercise 20-1

Cal and Fran have requested your organization to design an intranet application for displaying all details of agents as shown in Figure 20-38. Your Graphics Department has designed a document named agentDetail.cfm using data for one of the agents. It is available on the student data disk in the Chap20\Exercises folder.

To convert it into a database-driven Web page:

1. Examine the Agents table in the CF Realtors database in Microsoft Access, and then design a CFQUERY tag for extracting information from it in your text editor.
2. Design a columnar report and display information from the database at the appropriate locations in the HTML table.
3. Build a navigation capability by hyperlinking the navigation buttons appropriately.
4. Prevent navigation beyond the data records by using appropriate CFIF statements for controlling the display of the navigation buttons.
5. Save the file using the same name (**agentDetail.cfm**), and test your application.

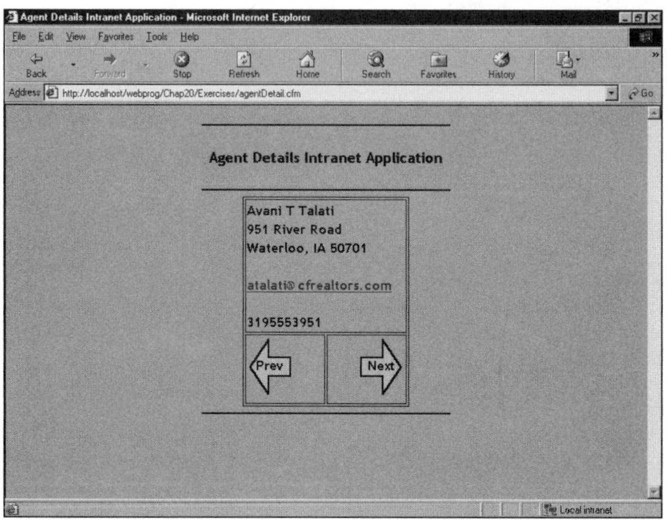

Figure 20-38

Exercise 20-2

CF Realtors' agents are very excited with the Agent Details Intranet Application that you created in Exercise 20-1. They find it a convenient way for sending e-mail to each other. They request your organization to simplify the process of finding an agent by designing a Web page that lists all the agents' names as shown in Figure 20-39.

To design a tabular report:

1. Create a new template named **agentTabular.cfm**, and save it in the Chap20\Exercises folder on the server.
2. Design CFQUERY tags to extract agent names from the Agents table.
3. Design a QUERY loop to output the data as shown in Figure 20-39.
4. Implement a data drill-down capability. Display the drill-down.gif graphic for each agent and hyperlink it to the detailed information obtained by agentDetail.cfm for the particular agent.
5. Save the file with the changes you made, and test your application.

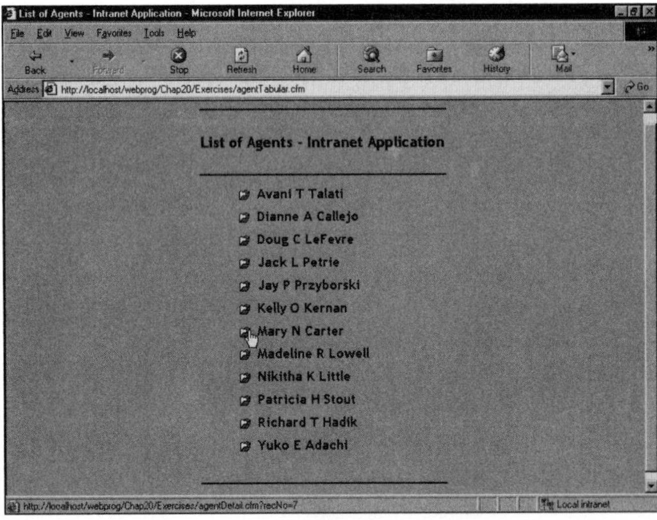

Figure 20-39

Exercise 20-3

To create a group totals report:

1. Create a group totals report as shown in Figure 20-40. Cal and Fran want to use this report to monitor the performance of their agents. Notice that the table's title has the full name of each agent in the Agents table of the CF Realtors database. The data in the table includes summary information such as the number of properties listed by each agent, the total dollar amount

of all listed properties, and the average, maximum, and minimum price of all listed properties for each agent below the heading that contains their name.

2. When you are finished, save the template as **agentStatistics.cfm** in the Chap20\Exercises folder on the server. Remember that you need two nested QUERY loops to design a group totals report. The outer QUERY loop loops over all the records in the Agents table, and the inner QUERY and its loop displays summary information from the Properties table.

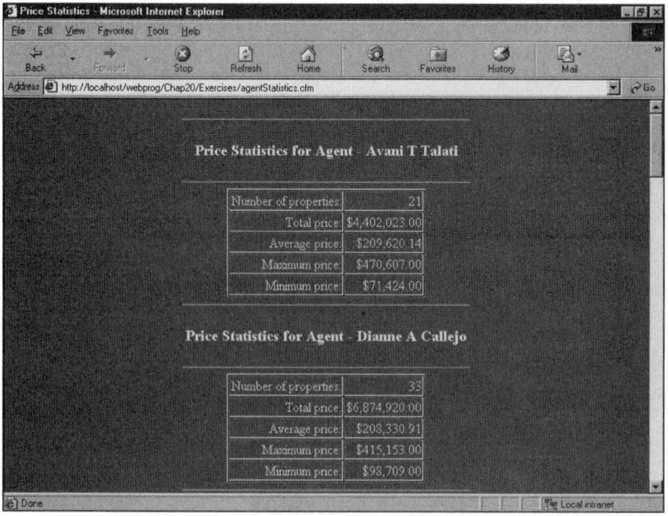

Figure 20-40

Exercise 20-4

To display the listing agent information with property information:

1. Copy the **header.cfm** and **footer.cfm** files from the Chap20\Chapter folder of your Data Files to the Chap20\Exercises folder in the work folder on your hard disk. Open **detail.cfm** from Chap20\Chapter folder in your text editor, and save it as **Ex20-04.cfm** in the Chap20\Exercises folder.

2. Click Search, and then Replace to replace all occurrences of detail.cfm in the template with Ex20-04.cfm. Replace PropertyImages with ../Chapter/PropertyImages.

3. Add CFML to display the name of the agent along with an appropriate caption at the bottom of the property description as shown in Figure 20-41. First you need an appropriate query to extract the data, and then you need another QUERY loop to display the data.

4. Hyperlink the name of the agent to Ex20-04b.cfm with a URL parameter named AgentID and an appropriate value for it. Open agentDetail.cfm in your text editor. Save it as **Ex20-04b.cfm**.

5. Modify the template so that the agent's detailed information is displayed to the customer when he or she clicks the agent name hyperlink as shown in Figure 20-42. (*Hint*: You have to use the value of the URL in the SQL SELECT statement to extract the listing agent's information.)

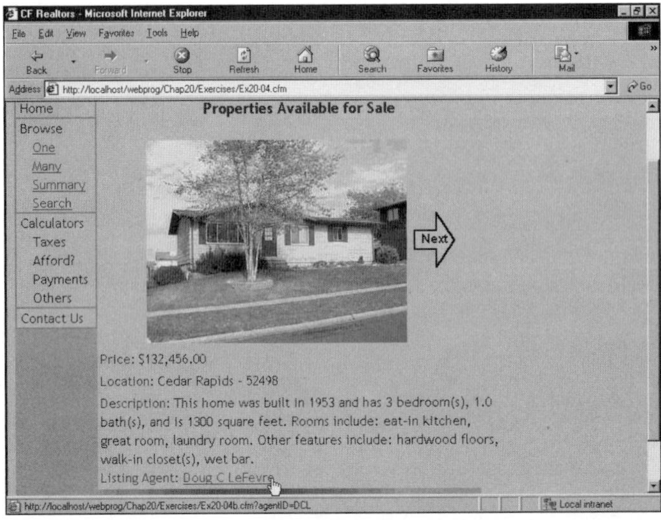

Figure 20-41

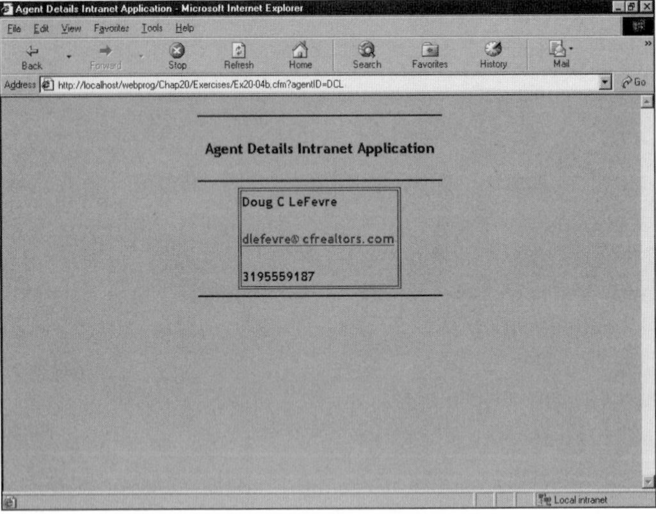

Figure 20-42

Exercise 20-5

To add search criteria:

1. Open **\Chap20\Chapter\searchForm.cfm** using your text editor. Save it as **\Chap20\Exercises\searchForm.cfm** in the work folder on your system.
2. Open **\Chap20\Chapter\processSearch.cfm** and save it as **\Chap20\Exercises\processSearch.cfm** in the work folder on your system.
3. Add other search criteria to the form in searchForm.cfm: Minimum price (text box named minPrice) and maximum age (text box named minYearBuilt) of the house as shown in Figure 20-43.
4. Modify **processSearch.cfm** so that it takes into account these additional criteria and displays the properties found.
5. Modify the hyperlinks in the navigation buttons to incorporate these additional criteria.

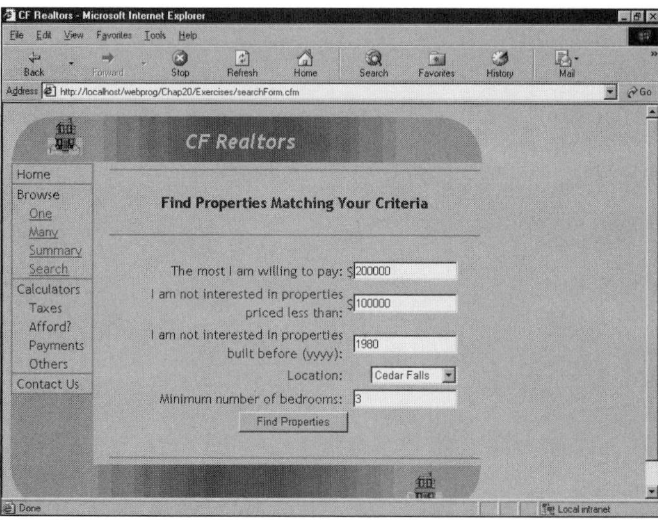

Figure 20-43

Web Programming Projects

Project 20-1

Create an ODBC connection to HardwareStore.mdb on your data disk named hardware_store. Examine the database in Microsoft Access. Your task is to design a data drill-down storefront application to this database. Design a template named displayCategories.cfm that displays a bulleted list of all the product categories from the Categories table. When the user clicks any category, all the products in that category are displayed as a bulleted list.

20

Project 20-2

Design a columnar report (productDetail.cfm) to display information about all products in the hardware store. Provide navigation buttons. Design a tabular report (productTabular.cfm) displaying 10 products at a time, and provide links to detailed descriptions in the columnar report.

Project 20-3

Design an intranet application for the hardware store. The management wants you to create a list of all the customer names and the total amount of all their product selections next to the customer names. The amount for each product is its price times the quantity. The total amount is the sum of the amounts for all the products selected by the customer.

Glossary

.NET Framework — A software component required to run any application created in Visual Studio .NET. The .NET Framework has two parts: the Common Language Specification and the .NET Framework class library.

.NET Framework class library — In Visual Studio .NET, a collection of all of the types, or classes, defined by the .NET Framework.

Abstract Windows Toolkit (AWT) — The part of a programming language that contains classes that control the style of Windows components used such as their font and layout format. In Java, java.awt is the AWT package.

access modifier — Programming code that defines the circumstances under which a class can be accessed.

ActiveX Data Objects (ADO.NET) — The classes in the System.Data namespace that VB .NET uses to provide database access.

ADO.NET — *See* ActiveX Data Objects.

algorithm — A list of steps for solving a logical or mathematical problem.

applet — A program that is called from within another application.

appletviewer — A program you use to run applets within a Web page or within another program.

application scope — Objects that persist across all users and pages, is created once, and exists throughout the execution of the Web application.

architecturally neutral — Describes a programming language that lets you write programs that run on any platform.

argument — Represents information that is needed by a method in order to perform its task. *See also* method.

arithmetic expression — An expression that logically combines values, variables, and arithmetic operators to perform a calculation, and stores the result to the left of an equal sign. *See also* expression.

ASP.NET server control — A reusable ASP.NET component that can perform the same work as traditional HTML controls. You can access ASP.NET controls through a .NET programming language using server-side code.

assignment operator — The equal sign (=); any value to the right of the equal sign is assigned to the variable on the left of the equal sign.

attribute — In a database, a single piece of information for an entity. When you work with classes, a data field is called an attribute. In XML, a parameter that you use to configure elements.

attribute declaration — In XML, a statement that declares all of the attributes that are allowed or required for a particular element.

AWT — *See* Abstract Windows Toolkit.

bean — An instance of a Java class.

binary operators — Operators that manipulate values in programs and use two arguments—one value to the left of the operator and another value to the right.

binary selection — *See* dual-alternative selection.

Boolean data — Data that holds only one of two values—true or false.

Boolean expression — A statement that represents only one of two states, usually expressed as true or false.

bytecode — A program written in the Java programming language is compiled into bytecode, or Java Virtual Machine Code. The compiled bytecode is subsequently interpreted on the machine where the program is executed. Any compiled program will run on any machine that has a Java programming language interpreter.

cardinality — The numeric relationships between related entities.

CDATA attribute type — In XML, an attribute that can accept any combination of character data, with the exception of tags and elements.

central processing unit (CPU) — The computer hardware that processes data items by organizing them, checking them for accuracy, or performing mathematical operations on them.

CGI — *See* Common Gateway Interface.

CGI script — A script that follows the standards specified by the CGI protocol. CGI scripts send their output—typically HTML—to the Web server. The Web server transmits the HTML to your Web browser, which renders the Web page.

char — A C# data type that holds a single character.

class — In object-oriented programming, a descriptive category that contains a group of objects. In a program, a class defines a set of attributes that characterize any member (object) of the class.

classpath — In JavaServer Pages, a folder where the JSP engine looks for the required classes.

CLR — *See* Common Language Runtime.

CLS — *See* Common Language Specification.

code — Instructions to the computer to perform a task.

code behind the form — Statements that execute as the user clicks the buttons and interacts with other control instances on an electronic form.

columnar report generation — Extracting and displaying data from a database table by extracting data from all the fields (columns) and then generating a report containing information from the fields.

comment — A nonexecuting statement that you place in programming code to document the program. A comment can contain various types of remarks, such as the purpose of the code, your name and the date you wrote the code, or instructions to future designers and developers who may need to modify your work.

comment out — To turn a programming statement into a comment so that the compiler will not execute its command. This helps you pinpoint the location of errant statements in malfunctioning programs.

Common Gateway Interface (CGI) — The protocol that allows a Web server to communicate with CGI scripts. *See also* CGI script.

Common Language Runtime (CLR) — A component in Visual Studio .NET that keeps track of allocated memory, and returns that memory to the managed heap when the object is no longer used. *See also* managed heap.

Common Language Specification (CLS) — Part of the .NET Framework that defines a set of standards allowing Visual Studio .NET languages and the applications written using those languages to seamlessly operate with each other. *See also* .NET Framework.

comparison operator — An operator that compares two items and results in a true or false, or Boolean, value.

compiler — The software that translates programming code into instructions the computer can understand. Also called an interpreter.

conditional statement — A programming statement that executes one group of statements when a condition is true and optionally another group of statements when the condition is false. Also called decision-making statement.

connection object — A memory handle that PHP can use to communicate with a database and continue accessing the database.

constant — A data item that cannot vary.

constructor method — In Java, a method that constructs an object.

content — In XML, the information contained within an element's opening and closing tags.

Content-type header — An HTTP header line that a CGI script uses to perform its first task.

control — A visual element such as text boxes and buttons, that usually appear on a form or dialog box in which a user enters or selects data.

CPU — *See* central processing unit.

culture — In Visual Studio .NET, a set of rules that determines how culturally dependent values such as money and dates are displayed.

data hiding — *See* encapsulation.

data source — A repository for data, such as a database, text file, or spreadsheet.

data type — The format and size of a piece of data.

database — A collection of data that is organized and stored in electronic format and accessible by a computer.

decision-making statement — *See* conditional statement.

declaration — A simple statement that tells the computer which type of data to expect in a program. In XML, the line in an XML document that specifies the version of XML being used.

default constructor — A constructor without an argument.

default namespace — The namespace applied to all of the elements and nested elements beneath the element that declares the namespace.

descendant class — A class that can inherit all of the attributes of the original class (or parent class). Also called child class.

document type declaration — In XML, a tag that defines the structure of a DTD.

Document Type Definition (DTD) — In XML and other languages based on SGML, defines the elements and attributes that can be used in a document.

DTD — *See* Document Type Definition.

dual-alternative decision — A decision with two possible outcomes.

dual-alternative selection — Logic with two possible outcomes: depending on the answer to the question, the logical flow proceeds either to one outcome or the other. The choices are mutually exclusive; that is, the logic can flow only to one of the two alternatives, never both. *See also* conditional statement.

duration — The period during which a variable exists in memory. Also called lifetime.

dynamic Web page — An interactive Web document, such as an online form, that can accept information from the user and also retrieve information for the user.

editable field — A field that can accept keystrokes.

element — In XML, a tag pair and the information it contains.

element declaration — In XML, defines an element's name and the content it can contain.

empty element — In XML, an element that does not require an ending tag.

encapsulation — Declaring variables locally within program modules. The data or variables in a program are completely contained within, and accessible only to, the module in which they are declared. In other words, the data and variables are "hidden from" the other program modules.

entity — A person, place, or thing for which you store information.

enumeration — List of values.

escape sequence — In Java, a way to store any character, including nonprinting characters such as a backspace or tab, in a char variable. An escape sequence always begins with a backslash.

event — When someone using your program takes action on a component, such as clicking the mouse on a button.

event handler — A method called as a result of specific events.

event-driven program — A style of program where the user might initiate any number of events in any order, such as typing words, selecting text with the mouse, or clicking a button to change text to bold. *See also* procedural.

explicit namespace — In XML, a namespace assigned to individual elements in an XML document.

expression — A statement that can contain values, variables, and mathematical or arithmetic operators.

Extensible Markup Language (XML) — A markup language used for creating Web pages and for defining and transmitting data between applications.

external storage — Permanent computer storage outside the main memory of the machine on some device such as a floppy disk, hard disk, magnetic tape, or CD. In other words, external storage is outside the main memory, not necessarily outside the computer. *See also* internal storage.

floating-point — A fractional numeric variable that contains a decimal point.

flowchart — A pictorial representation of the logical steps it takes to solve a problem.

focus — To make a window or other screen element active.

for loop — A loop that allows you to execute a set of statements a predefined number of times.

form handler — In ColdFusion, a template that processes a form. A form handler contains ColdFusion Markup Language (CFML) code to process the data received by the ColdFusion Server.

format specifier — In C#, one of nine built-in format characters that define the most common numeric format types.

format string — A string of characters that contains one or more placeholders for variable values.

function — A programming procedure that processes one or more input values and returns a single output value. You can use functions to perform complex mathematical calculations, generate random numbers, and control the display of data.

garbage collection — The process of returning memory to the managed heap. *See also* managed heap.

GET method — In Perl, the default value for the METHOD property that appends data to the end of the URL specified in the ACTION property, and is similar to sending the data using a hyperlink. The server retrieves the data from the URL and stores it in a text string for processing by the CGI script. In Java, one of two methods for a property that reads the property. *See also* SET method.

global variable — A variable within a program that is known to the entire program and is available to every module in a program. That is, every module has access to a global variable, can use its value, and can change its value.

high-level language — A language such as Java or Visual Basic .NET available for programmers to use because someone has written a translator program (a compiler or interpreter) that changes the English-like language in which the programmer writes into the low-level machine language that the computer understands. *See also* compiler.

HTML — *See* Hypertext Markup Language.

Hypertext Markup Language (HTML) — A simple language used to create Web pages.

IDE — *See* Integrated Development Environment.

if-then — A form of the if-then-else structure, or dual-alternative selection, where no "else" action is necessary. *See also* dual-alternative selection.

if-then-else — *See* dual-alternative selection.

IL — *See* intermediate language.

implicit object — An object you can use in a program without explicitly declaring the object.

import — In JavaServer Pages, an attribute that describes the types (usually in Java class) that are available to a scripting environment.

information hiding — *See* encapsulation.

inherit — To build upon the traits of a class.

inheritance — The process of acquiring the traits of one's predecessors.

initialization — An assignment made when a variable is declared.

instance — An object from a class.

instance method — A method used with object instantiations, where you associate a method with an individual object.

instantiate — To create a class object with a statement that includes the type of object and an identifying name.

integer variable — A whole-number numeric variable; programming languages such as C# and Java distinguish between integer variables and other types of numeric variables.

Integrated Development Environment (IDE) — A program that allows you to create, test, debug, and deploy programs.

intermediate language (IL) — The compiled form of a program.

internal storage — Computer storage within the machine, also called memory, main memory, or primary memory.

interpolation — The process of replacing a variable's name with the variable's contents.

interpreter — A special program that translates a program for the host machine. *See also* compiler.

JavaBean — A Java object that can be used in JSP scripts to create reusable, platform-independent, robust components.

javadoc — Block comments in Java that can be used to generate documentation with a program named javadoc.

just in time (JIT) — In Visual Studio .NET, the compiler that translates intermediate code into executable statements. *See also* intermediate language.

listener — An object that is interested in an event. *See also* event.

literal constant — A constant whose value is taken literally at each use. *See also* constant.

literal string — A series of characters that will appear exactly as entered when a program is run.

local variable — A variable whose name and value are known only to its own module. A local variable is declared within a module and ceases to exist when the module ends.

logic — The organization of program instructions so that they work properly—they are organized in a specific sequence, with no instructions left out, and with no extraneous instructions.

logical comparison operators — Comparison symbols that express Boolean tests. For example, many languages use the equal sign (=) to express testing for equivalency. *See also* Boolean expression.

loop — A programming instruction that repeats actions while a condition continues.

loop body — In a programming loop, the block of statements that are executed during each cycle of the loop.

loop control variable — In a programming loop, the variable that changes each time it passes through the loop and determines whether the loop will continue.

low-level machine language — *See* machine language.

machine language — The software a programming language uses to translate its instructions into the computer's on-off circuitry language.

main loop — A basic set of instructions that are repeated for every record in a program.

managed heap — In Visual Studio .NET, an area of memory managed by the Common Language Runtime. *See also* Common Language Runtime.

method — A series of statements that carry out a task.

method overloading — A condition that occurs when different methods exist with the same name but different argument lists.

Microsoft Intermediate Language (MSIL) — A machine-independent language into which Visual Studio .NET applications are compiled.

mixed content element — In XML, an element that contains character data and other elements.

modal dialog box — A window that appears when a program runs and stops program execution until the user takes action.

module — A collection of prewritten code stored in a file.

module-level variable — A variable that can be used by all of the event handlers on a form or in a class. *See also* event handler.

MSIL — *See* Microsoft Intermediate Language.

namespace — A scheme that provides a way to group similar classes. In Visual Studio .NET, the primary logical building block in the .NET Framework object hierarchy. In XML, a separate collection of the elements and attributes of an XML document.

new operator — In Java, the operator that allocates a new, unused portion of computer memory for a variable.

numeric character reference — A special character that refers to its numeric position in the Unicode character set. *See also* Unicode.

numeric constant — A specific numeric value that does not change.

object — A specific item that belongs to a class.

object-oriented programming — A style of programming that focuses on an application's data and the methods that manipulate that data.

object-oriented programming language — A programming language where you work with reusable components to create programs.

ODBC — *See* Open Database Connectivity.

Open Database Connectivity (ODBC) — The Microsoft standard for connecting Windows applications to databases and database servers.

operator precedence — The order in which parts of a mathematical expression are evaluated. Multiplication, division, and modulus always take place prior to addition or subtraction in an expression.

override — To replace the original version of a method with a method that you write.

package — A group of Java classes. Packages are referred to collectively as the Java class library or the Java Applications Programming Interface (Java API).

page scope — Objects that are available only to parts of a JSP page in which they are instantiated. These bean objects disappear as soon as the current page is finished.

parameter — Represents information that is needed by a method in order to perform its task. *See also* method.

parser — A program that checks whether an XML document is well formed. A non-validating parser simply checks whether an XML document is well formed. A validating parser checks whether an XML document is well formed and also whether the document conforms to an associated DTD.

Perl — *See* Practical Extraction and Report Language.

pixel — A picture element, or tiny dot of light, that combines with other pixels to create a visual image.

polymorphism — An object-oriented programming feature that allows the same operation to be carried out differently depending on the context.

Practical Extraction and Report Language (Perl) — The most widely used language for creating CGI scripts.

pragma — A special type of Perl module that pauses the execution of a script to allow users to enter information from the keyboard.

precision specifier — A code that controls the number of significant digits or zeros to the right of the decimal point.

predefined character entity — One of five special symbols used to display content instead of the code that structures an XML document.

primary key — The field in a database table that uniquely identifies each record stored in the table.

private — Data that cannot be accessed by any method that is not part of the class.

procedural — A style of program that dictates the order in which events occur, such as first retrieving user input, then executing decisions and loops, and then creating output. *See also* event-driven program.

programming language — An organized system for writing computer instructions.

pseudocode — An English-like representation of programming code. Pseudo is a prefix that means "false," and to code a program means to put it in a programming language; therefore pseudocode simply means "false code," or sentences that appear to have been written in a computer programming language but don't necessarily follow all the syntax rules of any specific language.

public access — Methods that other programs and methods can use that control access to private data.

redirection — The part of the HTTP protocol that allows designers to send an "object has moved" message to a Web browser with information for its new location.

reference type — Data that stores a memory address in a variable rather than data.

request scope — Objects that have the same lifetime as the related request object in JavaServer Pages.

root element — An XML element that contains other elements on a page.

scalar variable — A variable that can store precisely one value—typically a number or a string.

scientific notation — A numeric format that expresses a value by using a number between 1 and 10, multiplied by a power of 10. For example, the value 16,000,000 in scientific notation is 1.6E7, and the value 0.00426 in scientific notation is 4.26E-3.

scope — Part of a variable that indicates which procedures can use the variable, and when memory is allocated for the variable.

script — A set of instructions written in a scripting language that tells a computer how to perform a task. A script associated with a dynamic Web page, for example, tells the computer how to process the data submitted by or retrieved for the user.

selection — A programming construct in which you instruct the computer to examine two or more alternatives, and then choose a course of action to solve a problem.

self-describing — Tags associated with an XML document that are defined within the document itself instead of a separate DTD.

sentinel value — A limit or ending value that stops a loop when it matches the loop control value. *See also* loop.

sequence flow-control structure — A program organized so that its statements execute one after another.

server control — An element of ASP.NET Web pages that you can access with code on the Web server.

session — The time when a program is running and accepts input and processes information. In JavaServer Pages, a session begins when any user requests a JSP page for the first time.

session scope — Objects that have the same lifetime as the related session object in JavaServer Pages.

SGML — *See* Standard Generalized Markup Language.

significant digits — The mathematical accuracy of a value.

single-alternative selection — Logic that requires action for only one outcome of the question. *See also* dual-alternative selection.

solution — In Visual Basic .NET, several folders containing the files necessary to test, compile, execute, and distribute an application to other computers.

source — Within an event-driven program, a component on which an event is generated.

source code — An uncompiled program written in a programming language.

Standard Generalized Markup Language (SGML) — A markup language that separates the actual content of a document from the way the content is displayed and formatted. XML is based on SGML.

standard numeric format string — Characters expressed within double quotes that indicate a format for output.

statement — An instruction that can be executed by a program.

static Web page — An HTML document whose content is established at the time the page is created and does not change.

string — A specific character value or values, such as "Chris".

synchronization — Exclusively accessing a block of code; in JavaServer Pages, after a thread enters the block of code, no other thread can enter the same block until the first one exits (in other words, finishes the execution of the code block).

syntax — The rules governing the structure and content of programming.

tag — In markup languages such as HTML, a pair of commands.

terminal statement — The final statement in a segment of pseudocode that signals the pseudocode is finished.

thread — A process that handles client requests by executing the code sequentially.

unary selection — *See* single-alternative selection.

Unicode — A standardized character set of numeric representations capable of displaying characters from all the world's languages.

Uniform Resource Identifier (URI) — Generic term for identifying namespaces and addresses on the World Wide Web.

Uniform Resource Locator (URL) — A unique address that identifies a Web page; also called a Web address.

URI — *See* Uniform Resource Identifier.

URL — *See* Uniform Resource Locator.

user agent — A device that can retrieve and process documents created in XML and other markup languages such as HTML and XHTML. A user agent can be a traditional Web browser, a mobile phone, or a personal digital assistant (PDA).

user interface — Represents what users see when they run a program.

validating parser — In XML, a program that checks to see whether an XML document is well formed and compares the document to a DTD to ensure that it adheres to the DTD's rules.

value type — Data stored directly in the memory allocated to a variable.

variable — A named location in computer memory that can hold different values at different times.

variable declaration — The statement in a program that declares all variables the program will use.

ViewState — Technology that ASP.NET uses to manage the content of the controls.

W3C — *See* World Wide Web Consortium.

Web browser — A program that allows you to display HTML documents on your computer screen.

Web form — A Web page in which a user can enter or select data.

Web server — A computer that provides services, such as locating a requested file and sending it back to clients on the Internet or a local intranet. A Web server can accept and process requests for Web pages, images, executable programs, and other files.

Web service — On the Web, the process that receives requests from clients, and then responds to those requests.

well formed — An XML document that adheres to XML syntax rules.

World Wide Web Consortium (W3C) — An organization that oversees the development of Web technology standards.

XML — *See* Extensible Markup Language.

xmlns — An XML attribute that assigns a namespace to an element; to this attribute you assign the URI that you want to use as a namespace.

Index

B

C

D

F

G

H

J

K

L

T

U

Y

Z